"Phantom of Fear"

ALSO BY ROBERT LYNN FULLER

The Origins of the French Nationalist Movement, 1886–1914 (McFarland, 2012)

"PHANTOM OF FEAR"

The Banking Panic of 1933

Robert Lynn Fuller

McFarland & Company, Inc., Publishers
Jefferson, North Carolina, and London

Much of this work previously appeared in *Drifting Toward Mayhem: The Bank Crisis in the United States, 1930–1933* (lulu.com, 2009).

LIBRARY OF CONGRESS CATALOGUING-IN-PUBLICATION DATA

Fuller, Robert Lynn, 1953–
Phantom of fear : the banking panic of 1933 /
Robert Lynn Fuller.
p.   cm.
Includes bibliographical references and index.

ISBN 978-0-7864-6510-1
softcover : acid free paper ∞

1. Banks and banking — United States — History — 20th century.
2. United States — Economic conditions — 1918–1945.
3. United States — Politics and government — 1933–1945.
4. United States — Politics and government — 1929–1933.
5. Roosevelt, Franklin D. (Franklin Delano), 1882–1945.
I. Title.
HG2481.F847 2012   330.973'0917—dc23   2011043173

BRITISH LIBRARY CATALOGUING DATA ARE AVAILABLE

Front cover image: Crowd at New York's American Union Bank
during a bank run early in the Great Depression

Manufactured in the United States of America

*McFarland & Company, Inc., Publishers
Box 611, Jefferson, North Carolina 28640
www.mcfarlandpub.com*

To my wife,
Lynda Fuller Clendenning

"It needs no prophet to tell you that when the people find that they can get their money — that they can get it when they want it for all legitimate purposes — the phantom of fear will soon be laid." — Franklin Delano Roosevelt, first fireside chat, March 12, 1933

Contents

depression that had gripped the country for more than three years? Or should they use this opportunity to institute a wide range of reforms, which they all agreed were badly needed and long overdue? They decided to do both. They proved more successful at instituting reforms than in prodding economic recovery. But the first act of the New Deal administration, addressing the banking crisis—the focus of this book—was unambiguously intended to prod recovery and to a limited extent it did. Nevertheless, President Roosevelt was presented right away with a clear opportunity to initiate reform by introducing a federal guarantee of bank deposits, which he declined to do. In fact, he vigorously opposed the suggestion and only reluctantly agreed to sign deposit guarantee legislation before the hundred days were over.[2]

The Emergency Bank Act of March 9, 1933, was just that: a temporary fix intended to address a very immediate crisis. And yet, it contained a revolutionary clause with profound long-term consequences. It suspended the link between the dollar and gold, which was intended to bring immediate relief to the Federal Reserve Bank—fast losing gold to Europe—and give the administration greater flexibility in crafting monetary policy. President Roosevelt's monetary policies over the next few years were intended to end the Great Depression, but failed to do so. Nevertheless, initially suspending the gold standard and ultimately devaluing the dollar put an end to the crushing monetary deflation that had plagued the nation for years and kept the country in the grip of the terrible business slump. Ending price deflation did not end the Depression, but it stopped it from getting worse and helped reverse the downward spiral.[3]

Like the toppling of the gold standard, the federal bank holiday bore a significance that transcended its intentions. The federal usurpation of states' rights to control their own banks demonstrated the vast reach of a president willing to extend his authority into untouched realms when no one else was able or willing to act, and few objected. Such presidential boldness in peacetime was unprecedented and previously unthinkable. It was not even clear that the president had legal authority to shutter national banks, which answered to the comptroller of the currency within the Treasury Department. There were clearly defined rules for the comptroller to close national banks, and national emergency was not one of them. Nevertheless, the federal bank holiday was gladly accepted by almost all Americans as a vigorous response to a desperate situation when almost all agreed action was needed.

After the comparatively anemic responses of President Herbert Hoover to the Depression, most Americans were happy that, finally, the United States had a president who would take vigorous action to set things right. A Republican senator from Michigan, Arthur Vandenberg, told an assembly in Grand Rapids in June 1933, "I pay my sincere and unequivocal tribute to the courage of a President who would dare dream of such colossal concentrations of responsibility. I wish him well. I pray that new impulse of life now starting in our economic veins may well throb with sustained vitality. Meanwhile I drop a flower upon the constitution's grave—implicitly believing, however, in the resurrection." This sentiment was shared even by many Democrats who had backed Roosevelt in his 1932 electoral bid, such as Pierre du Pont, who lamented in September 1933 that "much of what has been done [in Washington] seems to have been necessary under the circumstances, but one cannot but regret the powers that are being placed in the hands of the President and his advisors, quite contrary to the Constitution and on the pretext that the country is virtually at war. But the big 'job' is being done and it is now not right nor fair to find fault. Certainly it is better to be doing something rather than sitting back and doing nothing."[4]

The Great Depression was in its fourth year, already long by recent American standards. The American people and its business class in particular were used to economic ups and downs. Workers were laid off from work with great regularity in most industries, which operated on a rush and bust basis. But four years was extraordinary, and these had been extraordinarily bad years. One of the factors that particularly tried peoples' faith in America's economic and political traditions was that economic activity had seemed to pick up on more than one occasion. People had gotten used to hearing that better days were just around the corner. By March 1933, Americans had heard that a lot, and yet, people were still willing to believe it was true. And by then people were ready for drastic action. The bank crisis had finally prodded intransigent businessmen, formerly skeptical or hostile to reform, into demanding reforms. Business leaders like Winthrop Aldrich, president of the Chase National Bank, Walter Teagle of Standard Oil, Edward Stettinius, Jr., of U.S. Steel, and Melvin Traylor of the First National Bank of Chicago, all demanded the federal government lead the way to a better, more rational economy, and that Congress pass legislation to reorder the entire system. Such legislation would have stood little chance of serious consideration had the economy not come close to total collapse in March 1933 because of the frailties of banks and the waves of, first, failures and, then, holidays they provoked. Congress, bankers, businessmen, and state-level politicians had argued in circles for years, even decades, about necessary financial reforms, government-supported pensions, federally regulated utilities, support for farmers, help for the unemployed and destitute, and more. Now, finally, in the closing days of the winter of 1932–1933, the United States had an inspiring and vigorous president — despite debilitating polio— to lead America into a new era of plenty, order, and personal security.

Progressives had urged reforms for years, even decades. Now America was about to undertake those reforms because Congress was controlled by a majority that could be roused to enact them. That the 73rd Congress would vote sweeping legislation to overhaul the American economic system could not have been predicted during the 1932 electoral campaigns. Very few politicians running for office, aside from a few progressives and the odd socialist, called for sweeping reforms. Even Franklin Roosevelt called for a cautious approach to handling the economy that would not upset the apple cart. He suggested a few reforms and hinted that dramatic alterations might lie ahead, but offered no specifics about really dramatic actions. He had vied against the electrical utilities industry for years and promised to do something about high-cost electricity. He also pledged to restore forests and take poor farmland out of production. Congress implemented both of these proposals in FDR's first hundred days and put hundreds of thousands of men and women to work to accomplish them. However, in 1932 FDR proposed little else beyond vague promises of bromides to fix whatever was wrong with the country. Nevertheless, he inspired confidence, which Herbert Hoover no longer did. The American people rejected Hoover as much as they put their faith in Governor Roosevelt of New York.

The banking crisis and the attendant holidays changed everything. The banking panic of March 1933 made the New Deal revolutionary, rather than simply a new Democratic administration with a few pet projects, such as soil conservation and utility regulation, to implement. The banking crisis changed peoples' thinking about the American way of doing things. The Depression dampened much talk about "rugged individualism," and further promoted cooperation and government coordination of the economy. People who had boosted the "new era" of the 1920s could not utter the words in 1933 without a sneer; even Republicans denounced the 1920s as "an era of excess." That system had to go and it did.

Faith in capitalism as it was understood and practiced in the 1920s had survived the doldrums of 1930, the vicissitudes of 1931, the false promises of recovery of 1932, but the opening months of 1933 proved to be its final undoing.

During the summer of 1932 things appeared to be getting better. Factories were hiring, people were buying more cars, tax revenues were up, and paychecks were more reliable, if smaller. People were relieved of a great anxiety. But then things slowed again in the late summer and fall as the presidential campaign heated up. Factory orders were canceled, and people were thrown back onto the streets. Nervous about the future, shoppers stopped buying. Plans postponed since 1929, which had been dusted off in 1932, were put back on the shelf. People waited nervously for the new administration to take office.

People wanted to know what the new president was going to do. Rumors circulated: He was going to go off the gold standard. He was going to reintroduce silver-backed dollars. He was going to print money freely. Prices were going to rise. Both consumers and businessmen asked, if that were true, would it not be better to buy now, before the price hikes? But what if we bought now and prices continued to fall? We would be stuck with high priced goods we might not be able to sell later. If we bought on credit, could we pay it off later? Businessmen did not want to be stuck with unwanted inventory that they could not unload if things got worse. People beseeched the president-elect to make a statement about what he intended to do. He said nothing. President Hoover urged Roosevelt both publicly and privately to tell the American people what his policies were going to be. He remained silent. Even friendly Democrats and Roosevelt's advisors urged the president-elect to make a public statement to let the people have some idea of his intentions. He gave no hints. People continued to wait. Everything was on hold. Buying was put off. Selling was postponed. The economy shrank as everybody waited. And as the economy continued to spiral downward, banks collapsed at a greater rate: 95 in November, 153 in December, 237 in January 1933, 148 in February. The closings in January were accompanied by some widely publicized bank runs by anxious depositors.

Banks that provisioned the economy with credit lay at the heart of the early years of the Depression. American banks had been in trouble for some time before 1929. The bank crisis was caused by price deflation, which in the 1920s was greatest in the farm sector of the economy. The agricultural depression of the 1920s caused thousands of banks, mostly small and in rural areas, to fail. When deflation spread from farming to manufacturing and the rest of the economy in 1929, banks in towns and cities failed at a greater rate. Once the banking crisis left the farm and came to town, it was only a matter of time before some really big banks failed. A few large banks indeed failed in 1930, but not many, and none that were crucial to the economy. In 1931 that changed, when some very large banks failed, taking the savings of hundreds of thousands of small depositors and freezing the accounts of thousands of businesses. Still, the closed banks were not big players in the economic life of the country, so the nation could survive their loss and did. In 1932, that was no longer true. Some really big and important banks were in trouble and threatening to collapse unless the federal government intervened. The Reconstruction Finance Corporation (RFC) saved several and postponed the day of reckoning for others.

When the Depression practically closed down the auto industry, and with it Detroit, a chain reaction was unleashed that radiated from Detroit to the rest of the country until it hit New York City, the banking capital of the world. Bankers and public officials feared banks would fall like dominoes until they threatened the biggest dominoes of all in New York. And to prevent that from happening, first state governors and then President Roosevelt declared a banking moratorium for the entire country. Public authorities feared a popular reaction that could force thousands of banks to close permanently. However, the anticipated wave of panic never mounted. The moratorium froze the crisis and supposedly stopped a cascade of bank runs and subsequent bank failures. But the populace remained calm, and the holiday did not fix the banks nor, by itself, revive the economy. Going off the gold standard fixed the banks by reversing the business-killing deflation, allowing prices to rise and increasing business revenues, which made it easier to repay bank loans. Higher prices prodded the economy back from the depths, even if it remained sluggish for the next eight years. Nevertheless, banks continued to write off billions of dollars in bad assets and remained wary of granting new loans into the 1940s.

Bank reform, so much debated before 1933 and finally rushed through Congress in spring 1933, had little impact on the health of banks. The Glass-Steagall Act of 1933 had practically no effect on the American economy and very little on the well-being of banks. The provision of the act that created the Federal Deposit Insurance Corporation (FDIC) had a lasting importance but failed to achieve what it was supposed to: restore confidence in banks. It took the United States Congress until the 1980s to begin to dismantle the banking regime put into place by the Glass-Steagall Act and to allow commercial and savings banks to offer services previously forbidden. The FDIC lives on. The well intended act was finally repealed in 1996. It probably did no real harm while it was in force.

The impact of the banking crisis was largely psychological. It changed Americans' thinking about the economy, allowing deep structural reforms to be enacted by Congress, which would not have been possible without the shock of looming financial collapse. The banking crisis convinced many officials high in the hierarchy of American finance that maintaining the gold standard was not worth the price, and leaving it would open up avenues to recovery otherwise closed. Some very unorthodox ideas about unbalanced budgets, government insurance, federal regulation, and taxation were openly debated, and in some cases put into action, that minus the bank crisis would never have received serious consideration. This is the story of that crisis.

This is not the first work to address the panic of 1933. In 1973, Susan Estabrook Kennedy published *The Banking Crisis of 1933*, which remains the only monographic study of the 1933 crisis. Kennedy concentrates on high politics and the formation of government and Federal Reserve policy from the late 1920s until the onset of the panic in late February 1933. She does a credible job of presenting a thoughtful and informed narrative of events, but almost entirely leaves banks and the American public out of the story. This poses a problem because at the time bankers and public officials blamed the crisis on the panicky American citizenry. That explanation of the panic was widely accepted at the time and has been repeated ever since. She also believes that the banking crisis was brought about by a flawed banking system established by ill-considered laws rather than by the intractable economic depression that wrecked havoc upon the banking system. According to Kennedy and most historians (and importantly, politicians) that flawed system was fixed by the Glass-Steagall Act of 1933 that gave the United States a rational and strong banking system subsequently impervious to such panics. This, too, represents orthodoxy that has permeated histories of the Great Depression.[5]

The standard conception of the banking panic of 1933 is well represented by David M. Kennedy's 1999 work *Freedom from Fear*, which claims, "Americans reacted this time [February 1933] with hair-trigger haste and last-ditch desperation. By the thousands in every village and metropolis, they scurried to their banks, queued up with bags and satchels, and carted away their deposits in currency or gold." That did not happen. This mythical version of events is further boosted in a recent popular history of President Roosevelt's first hundred days in office, *The Defining Moment*, by Jonathan Alter, which repeats this version of the 1933 panic as the result of panicky depositors sucking banks dry through coast-to-coast bank runs, thus threatening the very foundation of our economic order. This is the mistaken understanding of the panic that this book seeks to overturn.[6]

In their seminal work, *A Monetary History of the United States, 1867–1960,* published in 1963, Milton Friedman and Anna Jacobson Schwartz argued that the banking panic resulted from inept Federal Reserve policy compounded by national and international fears—inspired by rumors—of impending monetary inflation by the incoming Roosevelt administration. For Friedman and Schwartz, the drain of gold out of banks into private hands within the United States in early 1933 clearly reveals public distrust not of banks but of the future value of the currency. Friedman and Schwartz's explanation was widely influential among some economists but resisted by most historians, who clung to the orthodox version of the panic as a product of public distrust of banks. In 1987, Barrie A. Wigmore published an insightful article in the *Journal of Economic History*, "Was the Bank Holiday of 1933 Caused by a Run on the Dollar?," which echoed the Friedman and Schwartz interpretation and argued that the national holiday declared by President Roosevelt was in response to the drain of gold out of New York flowing to London in anticipation of a devalued dollar under the new president. Wigmore rightfully argued that big bankers and Federal Reserve officials in New York and Chicago were more worried about the flight of gold than about any shortage of currency to meet anticipated public demands. He presented a version of the panic in which the big bankers and Federal Reserve officials who shaped public policy were distracted by the fate of the dollar and not overly troubled about the condition of the American banking system. In 1996, Elmus Wicker published *The Banking Panics of the Great Depression*, which also presented conclusions at dramatic variance from the accepted wisdom. He maintained that the panic was provoked not by nervous depositors demanding their monies, but by anxious public officials worried that banks in their state or Federal Reserve district would be undermined by jumpy governors in *other* states closing *their* banks and increasing pressures on the banks that remained open. Wicker and Wigmore's interpretation of the crisis has been widely accepted by economists but, as evidenced by the versions presented by David Kennedy and Jonathan Alter, has little influenced historians or journalists. I hope to promote the version accepted by Wigmore, Wicker, and most economists by bringing to bear a broader array of evidence commonly used by historians and by presenting a traditional historical narrative that proffers a more elaborate discussion of the events surrounding the panic. Such a discussion and explanation would seem to be more urgently needed now because of the wave of misunderstanding and misinformation about 1933 and the role of banks in the Great Depression that has been broadcast since the financial excitement of 2008. The works of Friedman, Wigmore, and Wicker do not appear to have made much of a dent in the orthodoxy established about the crisis under the Roosevelt regime.[7]

CHAPTER ONE

Boom, Crash, and Slump

In 1910 Vincent Bendix invented a drive unit for an electric starter for automobiles, which Chevrolet began installing in its cars in 1914, ensuring Bendix's place in the quickly expanding auto industry. In 1923 he expanded his stake in the auto industry when he began manufacturing auto brakes in South Bend, Indiana. The American Midwest bred thousands of businessmen like Bendix who saw opportunities and took chances, many of which paid off handsomely, in the booming 1920s. In 1924, seeking to profit from the bullish stock market, he did what so many other prospering businessmen did: he offered stock to the public. Bendix prospered and his optimism was so expansive that in 1928 he bought the enormous Potter Palmer Mansion on Lake Shore Drive in Chicago and announced his intention to spend $25 million to erect "the world's largest hotel" on the site. The following year he founded Bendix Aviation to establish his niche in the revolution of the future: air travel. The Depression that took hold of the country and then the world in 1929 put a stop to many of Bendix's plans. Not a brick of his Lake Shore Drive hotel was ever laid, and he was eventually forced to give up the site to creditors. By 1936, as striking workers occupied his South Bend plant, he saw no way to pay off his $14 million in debts and declared bankruptcy. That was the 1920s and 1930s for Vincent Bendix and many other Americans like him.

The 1920s offered the promise of prosperity, comfort, speed, and advancement to many who grasped the opportunities available. The 1930s changed all that because the Depression settled slowly on the nation in 1929. It had actually come to the American South earlier when prices and business slackened in 1928. By early 1929 it hit the Midwest and quickly spread to the rest of the nation, except New York and Detroit. The battle of the titans waged between Ford, with his new Model A, and General Motors, which struggled to keep Chevrolet as the best selling passenger car in America, kept Detroit and much of the Great Lakes Basin humming until midsummer. But even the auto giants could not ignore falling sales and overproduction for long, and in August they called off the contest and cut back production. By fall, only New York City was still booming and even there the pace of business was slowing.

The causes of the Great Depression remain a subject of dispute. As the American economy slowed in the early 1930s, many people blamed the high levels of debts incurred during the rapid economic expansion of the 1920s. As long as the country prospered during the boom decade, few worried too much about domestic debts, and, indeed, had the expansion continued the debts could have been paid off without great difficulty. But when the economy contracted sharply after the Crash of 1929, paying off those debts became more urgent and more burdensome. An irony noted by many later in the 1930s, especially John Maynard Keynes, was that as debtors paid off their obligations incurred when times were good, the economy shrank even more. Expanding credit provided the principal means for an economy to grow and when it contracted, so did the economy, provoking a downward cycle of layoffs, shrinking sales, and deflation. The speed of this downward spiral increased in 1931 and 1932 when prices for commodities, manufactured goods, real estate, securities, and labor dropped precipitously. As deflation increased, banks, which had loaned tens of billions of dollars during the 1920s, faced bleak prospects of successfully collecting those loans and staying in business. Many loans went bad and banks began to fail in increased numbers.

As early as December 1929, some Americans began to assert that the descending Depression was the inevitable ending to the wild party of the 1920s. Within a few years even many boosters of big business began to repeat this line of reasoning, which eventually became accepted orthodoxy about both the 1920s and the 1930s: the 1930s were the inevitable (and deserved) reckoning. That was nonsense then and remains so today. It was, however, the way things turned out. America's top bankers believed that prosperity and stability had been assured by the creation of the Federal Reserve Banks in 1915, which was supposed to guide the country's bewildering assortment of credit-granting institutions and keep commerce and industry furnished with an adequate and reliable money supply. American banks had survived crashes and panics before. The system of national banks created by President Abraham Lincoln and the Republicans in 1863 and 1864 weathered the Panic of 1893 remarkably well, even though the country fell into a severe depression. The unhappy travails of the mid–1890s convinced many businessmen that to avoid the drearily recurring panics and depressions, the country needed a stable national currency, rather than the chaotic system of notes issued by 3,800 different national banks. To make matters worse, this anarchic array of notes was backed entirely by bonds issued by the U.S. Treasury Department, linking the money supply to federal debt rather than to commercial needs. Many bankers and businessmen were convinced this monetary system made no sense and ill-served the country. Calls for a national currency backed by short-term commercial debt (bankers' acceptances and commercial paper) mounted after 1893 until the next panic gripped the country in 1907. The experience so scared the country's bankers that they mounted a successful campaign to found a central bank to issue currency backed by commercial rather than government debt. The Federal Reserve Bank was created by Congress in 1914 to do just that.[1]

To avoid a central bank dominated by either Washington, D.C., or Wall Street, Congress authorized a decentralized bank with twelve district branches (and numerous sub-branches), each governed by a board elected by the banks that contributed to the system. The Federal Reserve Bank was owned by its members ("member banks"), each of which was required to subscribe to bank stock and to keep reserves on deposit at the district banks. Member banks could borrow money from the Reserve Bank to make up any shortfall in reserves, allowing them to make more efficient use of their resources. The Federal Reserve's promoters argued the bank would strengthen banks and provide greater stability to the nation's commerce because all member banks could draw on the central bank to meet sudden demands for cash and resources could be easily shifted from one Reserve Bank district to another to satisfy unusual regional demands for funds. To make sure the system worked, Congress required all national banks to join. State-chartered institutions were invited and encouraged to join, but few did. The new bank proved its worth during the First World War when it coordinated with the Treasury Department to fund the massively expensive war effort and keep what remained of the civilian economy operating more-or-less smoothly.[2]

The expansion provoked by the war in Europe, starting in 1914, lifted all sectors of the American economy to heights of unprecedented production and sales. European demand for the products of America's mines, factories, banks, and farms was nearly insatiable.

Exports of goods and capital to Europe jumped enormously: Americans shipped $1.5 billion in goods to Europe in 1914 and $4.1 billion in 1917. The U.S. declaration of war on April 6, 1917, allowed Congress to vote nearly unlimited credit to the government to finance the hostilities. The federal budget expanded from $734 million in 1916 to $12.7 billion in 1918, pumping huge sums into the already heated economy.[3]

American participation in the First World War produced long-lasting effects on the economy. Government debt ballooned to figures not seen since the Civil War. All the money and manpower that poured into shipbuilding, munitions, armaments, and other supplies gobbled up by the military had to come from somewhere. To pay for the war the government issued billions of dollars worth of Liberty Bonds, which stuffed the investment portfolios of banks, insurance companies, trust-company accounts, Federal Reserve Banks, and average citizens. Industrial activity of all sorts boomed, but so did prices. Production in some sectors slackened considerably: new housing construction was postponed, as was much public investment in roads, water projects, and the like. Industrial plants expanded to meet demand, but the demand was mostly for war-related goods. Only a small decrease in the production of consumer products was sufficient to push prices up dramatically.

To prevent the economy from dashing itself on the shoals of unchecked inflation, the government created the War Industries Board in May 1917 to keep prices in check and encouraged the populace to invest their bulging purses of spare cash in Liberty Bonds. Despite the best efforts of the government to prevent it, the country suffered price inflation anyway. The wholesale price index nearly doubled from 1914 to 1917 and increased half again by 1920. Farm commodity prices rose along with all others, but not especially in advance of other products. To choke off that inflation after the war, the Federal Reserve Bank raised interest rates to 4 percent in October 1919, to 6 percent in January 1920, and then to 7 percent in June. This had the desired effect: credit contracted and prices started falling by late spring. However, by summer 1920 the economy was stalled and a deep depression gripped the country. Unemployment shot up as orders were canceled and factories turned off their machines and the lights. The Federal Reserve Bank had proven that it could influence prices by setting interest rates, and had also shown that it could force the economy into depression by charging a high price for credit.[4]

By December 1921, Federal Reserve interest rates had dropped to 4.5 percent. Treasury Secretary Andrew Mellon, appointed by Republican President Warren Harding in 1921, worked assiduously to lower the high income tax rates imposed during the war and succeeded in convincing Congress to lower rates in 1922 and again in 1924. Flush with cash from the rising economy, Americans went on a spending spree. A tremendous thirst for consumer goods of all kinds had built up during the war years, and with credit more freely available in 1922, that thirst could be satisfied. This desire for goods was not limited by any means to automobiles but extended to housing, clothes, new electric-powered conveniences, such as washing machines and refrigerators, and a whole range of goods that had been in short supply during the war years. Americans also clamored to be entertained and bought radios by the millions; they spent millions of hours watching movies in new palaces built to bring them the latest adventures or comedies from Hollywood. They paid $720 million to watch movies in 1929 alone. American businesses were eager to feed the public's appetite for more.[5]

Demand for automobiles during the 1920s was nearly insatiable, and the auto industry expanded and innovated to meet it. Henry Ford ordered the construction of the largest integrated industrial plant in the world at River Rouge, Michigan, just south of the Detroit

city limits. Other auto companies— Packard, Chrysler, General Motors, Auburn, Studebaker, Hudson, Nash, and more — joined in to roll millions of vehicles off American assembly lines: 2.2 million in 1920, 3.7 million in 1924, and 5.6 million in 1929, the peak year of
American auto production.[6]

The popular enthusiasm for automobiles provoked an explosion in investment in ancil-
lary products: tires, gasoline, filling stations, and the like. Between 1920 and 1925 American
consumption of gasoline more than doubled, and by 1929 it would increase by another 60
percent. Autos stoked a nationwide demand for roads and bridges built with public money.
States, counties, and towns spent unprecedented sums to build and pave roads as hundreds
of thousands of miles of dirt roads were covered in macadam to accommodate cars and
trucks. The public invested $358 million in roads in 1920, which increased steadily to $1.1
billion in 1929 when spending peaked. During the decade American federal, state, and
county governments spent $6.9 billion to build 1.5 million miles of roads, and that does
not include roads built by municipalities. Much of this was financed by bonds, that is, with
borrowed money. By 1930, state governments alone owed $1.6 billion on road-construction
bonds.[7]

The country witnessed an unprecedented construction boom during the 1920s as new
buildings of all sorts went up around the United States. New buildings proved to be America's largest investment of the decade as new construction rose steadily to peak at $12 billion
in 1926. Houses, hotels, office buildings, apartment buildings, schools, public buildings,
movie theaters, stores, gas stations, bus stations, and factories went up by the hundreds of
thousands. Contractors built hundreds of thousands of new houses in towns and cities
across the country, accounting for a third to half of this boom. Construction of new office
buildings and stores peaked in 1927 at $1.1 billion worth of new facilities. All of this was
done with borrowed money that had to be paid off over time. Some of it was financed by
companies through new stock issues, but in most cases banks and insurance companies put
the money up front, with expectation of repayment over a period of five to 20 years. Big
banks and trust companies in New York and Chicago packaged mortgages for big office
buildings, hotels, and apartment towers into mortgage bonds that they resold as investments
to their customers, other banks, and insurance companies. Between 1919 and 1930, banks
created such bonds with a face value of around $4.5 billion.[8]

Trust companies, savings banks, commercial banks, building and loan associations,
and insurance companies funneled tens of billions of dollars into construction projects
large and small. Thousands of neighborhood savings and loans arranged mortgages for
houses and handled payments for house buyers, who bought on credit. A bungalow in a
new subdivision in Chicago could be bought for $2,500, with half financed by a five-year
renewable mortgage arranged by a real-estate broker and most often provided by a local
savings and loan. Fifteen- and even 20-year mortgages that did not require renewal became
available and more common during the decade. Trust companies, insurance companies,
and state banks supplied a ready secondary market for mortgages. Metropolitan Life Insurance, which had $9 million invested in single-unit residential first mortgages in 1919, owned
$477 million of such mortgages in 1929. It bought another $334 million in mortgages on
apartment buildings and small multi-family dwellings. Prudential Life Insurance Company,
the largest mortgage owner in the United States, invested $873 million in residential mort-
gages by 1929. The Mutual Benefit Life Insurance Company of Newark owned $228 million
in mortgages in 1931, representing 40 percent of its investment portfolio. After 1927 Congress
allowed national banks to invest more money in mortgages, and they increasingly bought

mortgages as well, assuring a steady flow of money into new homes. But new sources of credit for home buyers opened up just when the cost of money was going up, so few home-owners actually benefitted.[9]

In early 1928, the Federal Reserve Bank raised interest rates three times in four months to curb a steady drain of gold to Europe and to restrain the mounting flow of funds into stock exchanges. Because the building craze was financed on credit, the Federal Reserve Bank's rate increase powerfully influenced its pace. The tightening credit did not noticeably restrain new building right away. Issues of building permits hit an all-time record for the first nine months of 1928, when almost one billion dollars worth were approved. However, the construction fever soon leveled off. Building had peaked in New England in 1925 and then slowly declined. In most states housing construction peaked in 1926, and activity after-ward shifted to commercial buildings, stores, hotels, factories, utilities, and the like. Even after the Fed's rate hike, new construction by utilities, railroads, and industry continued to climb because companies in these sectors could use retained earnings or investment funds raised in the stock or bond markets and did not rely on bank loans. Railroad and electrical utility construction did not peak until 1930, which probably testifies to how long such projects took from drawing board to completion.[10]

The economic ride through the 1920s was not fast and smooth, but bumpy and marked by sudden accelerations and braking. American banks went through as much turmoil and heady giddiness during the 1920s as other sectors of the economy. Many banks prospered with their clients. Others suffered with them and went through the same uneven growth and sudden decline as sectors of the economy expanded and contracted. Federal Reserve bankers were still learning how to use the tools at their disposal to help the economy along. While most economists since then have argued they were learning slowly and badly, most officials of the Fed did not believe it was their job to help boost the economy. As far as they were concerned, the Federal Reserve Bank was given the responsibility to ensure the economy had enough money to meet its needs, and if the economy contracted it was the Fed's job to reduce the money supply and not increase it.[11]

During the 1920s, state banks and national banks engaged in risky competition for business, each trying to gain an advantage over the other. Bank reform continued to be a quest for some, but disunity and bitter disagreements over how best to alter the system kept any serious reform from advancing. Nevertheless, changed rules about branch banking did have a clear impact on the system: the ability to *acquire* branches spurred national banks into a drive to take over or merge with other banks. Ultimately, this caused the total number of banks to fall as a host of small and medium-sized banks disappeared into the ledgers of larger banks. But the most urgent banking phenomenon of the decade resulted from one of the most notorious conditions in the American economy: thousands of small country banks disappeared across the country as American farms suffered one of their worst decades since the drought of the 1880s.

Trouble on the Farm

Henry Ford dreamed of placing a Ford tractor on every American farm — and a good many overseas as well. During the good years, 229,332 American farmers acquired tractors; as farm prices fell more farmers turned to mechanization to boost their yields. In 1923, Mr. Ford's new River Rouge industrial complex churned out 102,000 tractors, and by 1925,

473,848 farmers owned at least one. Farmers invested heavily in machines, tractors, combines, and trucks to reduce their costs and to make farming more efficient, borrowing money which they gambled could be recouped from crop sales. Yet as farm output mounted, prices continued to decline, so that only the most modern and efficient farmers prospered. By 1930, when prices had plummeted to historic lows, farm mechanization had reached impressive proportions: 851,457 farmers owned 920,021 tractors. Almost as many farms had trucks as had tractors: 845,335 farms boasted a truck in 1930. As farm prices kept falling, farmers either acquired the latest farm machinery or chanced losing their land. Stubbornly low prices for almost all agricultural goods kept farmers in a perpetual state of debt and anxiety.[12]

The farm crisis of 1920s especially afflicted the West and Midwest. The downward spiral of prices had wreaked havoc upon the big farm states of the north-central United States that grew most of America's wheat — the Dakotas, Montana, and Minnesota. When farmers suffered, so did their banks, which failed by the hundreds each year with depressing regularity until 1928, especially in the north-central states. Iowa led the nation in bank failures from 1921 through 1929 with 529 out of a national total of 5,714. Minnesota and the Dakotas were not far behind: 419 banks closed in Minnesota, 427 in North Dakota, and 396 in South Dakota. These four wheat-growing states accounted for 31 percent of all bank failures in the United States during the 1920s. Montana, which had prospered with the wheat boom of the war years, went through a depressing wringer afterward as prices dropped: 68 banks failed in 1921, 53 in 1922, 121 in 1923, 84 in 1924, 41 in 1925, and 25 in 1926 when, having significantly thinned the ranks, the reaper seems to have largely finished cutting down Montana banks.[13]

States dominated by farming, such as Minnesota and the Dakotas, were often governed by legislatures and laws shaped by agrarian populism and its attendant anti–big-business mentality. Such laws kept banks small, local, and weak. When farms and businesses dependent upon them started wilting, so did the banks that serviced them. Rural banks failed in record numbers across the farm belt despite the creation of the Federal Reserve System, which was disinclined to intervene. From 1921 through 1925, 2,911 banks suspended operation. After 1925, the stability of banks only declined: from 1926 through 1929, another 2,803 went under. The vast majority of those banks were small, located in western or southern agrarian states, and served farmers. Because the collapsing banks were small, and the amounts of money lost were relatively minor, almost no action was taken in Washington, D.C., or in state capitals to shore up banking in general. State banks that did not belong to the Federal Reserve System and followed state laws were left to fend for themselves. What the fragility of rural banks showed to those who paid attention — and many did — was the repercussion of price deflation on banks. The rural banking crisis provoked a good deal of discussion in financial and political circles about what to do, if anything. The debate grew louder and more urgent once price deflation became general and the banking crisis spilled out of rural America and into cities big and small, but still almost nothing was done to address the problem until 1932, by which time the problem had turned into catastrophe.[14]

The Securities Markets in the 1920s

Many businesses had learned the disadvantages of bank debt during the harrowing downturn of 1921–22 and had vowed to avoid it in the future. As more Americans trusted their savings to stock markets and developed a taste for corporate investment, more corporations chose to raise funds by issuing stocks. The popularity of relying on stock sales to raise money grew during the decade so that by 1928 and 1929 most medium-sized and even many small companies chose to finance their businesses by issuing new securities. As the growing popularity of stocks overshadowed commercial loans from banks, most bankers were persuaded of the wisdom and utility of operating securities-selling affiliates.[15]

The movement by large corporations toward using securities to raise money, the growth of consumer credit, and mortgages for building shifted the country's credit market in a dramatic way. Before the 1920s boom, bank credit went mostly to businesses. In 1922, 47 percent of bank loans went to commercial borrowers, only 12 percent of loans accepted securities as collateral, and another 9 percent went into household mortgages. By the end of the decade, business consumed only 33 percent of all loans, securities-backed loans accounted for 20 percent, and mortgages had grown to 18 percent. More corporations financed their operations using their own revenues or raised capital on the securities markets, reducing their reliance upon banks. The companies that continued to rely on bank loans were worrisomely frail. In 1922, 43 percent of commercial loans could be used as collateral for Federal Reserve loans. By 1929, only 38 percent were so eligible. The quality of business loans remaining with banks by the end of the decade had deteriorated. And the loans backed by securities and real estate, which had replaced business loans as bank assets, relied on collateral that had ballooned in value during the decade. Banks accepted them as collateral on the assumption that they would retain their value. They did not.[16]

Some states allowed banks to buy and own stock as investments (surprisingly, conservative New York was one), but they rarely did so after the collapse of the canal boom in the 1840s destroyed so many banks. All banks that joined the Federal Reserve System, for example, were required to buy and hold stock of the Federal Reserve Bank, which paid dividends reliably every year. Banks sometimes bought and held stock in other banks in states where it was permitted. But investments in corporate stock never amounted to a significant share of bank investments. Corporate stock amounted to less than 4 percent of securities held as investments, and three-quarters of those were held by state banks — mostly trust companies.[17]

Most banks — except some state-regulated savings banks in the Northeast — accepted stocks and bonds as security for loans. In 1925 and 1926 about one-third of loans from member banks were secured by securities; more than 90 percent of those loans used corporate stocks and bonds as collateral. This practice was as common among country member banks as it was among New York City banks. Later in the decade, when the stock markets were roaring, borrowers arranged loans secured by stocks for the purpose of buying more stocks. The practice of securing loans with stocks and bonds was already common and widespread before the stock market boom of the late 1920s: such loans constituted 27.4 percent of all bank loans in 1915. By 1929 securities backed 35 percent of all bank loans in the United States. Fed economist Emanual Goldenweiser claimed by fall 1929, securities backed 60 percent of bank loans.[18]

There was also nothing new about the common practice of banks loaning money directly to stockbrokers, who used the loans to buy stocks for clients. Since early in the nineteenth century when banks held surplus funds and had no other use for their deposits, they funneled money to the big banks in the financial centers, where it was reloaned at profitable rates to brokers who used it to finance sales of stocks and commodities. In the 1920s the practice grew in popularity with banks looking for ways to earn top dollar on their deposits and with security brokers who could offer stocks for sale to the man on the street "on margin." For these "call loans" the buyer put up as little as 20 percent of the price of a security and the brokers' loans financed the rest with the security serving as collateral for the loan. In October 1929 brokers' loans amounted to $9.2 billion — nearly 10 percent of the G.N.P. Almost $8.6 billion of this amount was lent to brokers in New York City to finance purchases on the New York Stock Exchange. However, only about 30 percent of that amount was provided by banks, as many people and corporations with money to spare had discovered the profitability of such loans. It has become commonplace to exclaim that brokers' loan rates had risen to 20 percent in 1929, but they hit that rate only once on a single day — the morning of March 26 — during a scare when cornered investors desperately needed money to pay margin calls. Nevertheless, throughout 1929 interest rates paid on brokers' loans remained higher than available elsewhere to those with money to lend.[19]

By March 1929 all banks had loaned brokers $1,875 million while non-banks had dumped $4,950 million into the loans. By October 4, just as the market was developing tremors, bank loans to brokers had increased by only $10 million while non-banks had extended another $1,690 million. That is, the vast majority of funds on loan to brokers that propped up securities prices did not come from banks at all; thus, the Federal Reserve was ill-positioned to influence either the amount of credit available to the markets or its price. The Fed was regrettably aware of the situation.[20]

The growing volume of money diverted to brokers' loans provoked a good deal of hand wringing in 1928, when many people in positions of responsibility wanted to stop or at least slow the practice. Directors of the Federal Reserve Bank were appalled when brokers' loans absorbed $5.5 billion by the fall of 1928. The influential head of the Cleveland Trust Company, Colonel Leonard Ayers, told the American Bankers Association (ABA) conference in October that brokers' loans were responsible for pushing stock prices to dangerously unrealistic heights and ought to be brought back to earth. He blamed the stock markets for soaking up money that otherwise would have financed corporate bonds used to build new office buildings and plants, and to buy the equipment to work them. Not everyone was so dour. Charles Mitchell of the National City Bank in New York observed that brokers' loans constituted only slightly more than ten percent of the value of stocks listed on the exchanges, which was a manageable and not risky amount. The chief economist for the Chase National Bank, Benjamin Anderson, thought the amount in such loans in 1928 was perhaps a bit too high, but he was confident that market forces would soon bring a correction and the amount would return to normal. Progressive Senators Smith Wildman Brookhart of Iowa and Robert La Follette from Wisconsin were outraged and demanded that Congress take charge of such matters and ban or at least curb brokers' loans. Senator Brookhart boomed on the Senate floor that stock speculators borrowing money from banks drained money from farmers in his state who could not get loans they needed. He proposed a bill that would require banks to keep 100 percent reserves. An inveterate foe of the Federal Reserve Bank, the senator also wanted to take the power to set interest rates away from the Federal Reserve Bank and give it to Congress. At Senate hearings held by La Follette in 1928 about stock market speculating and call loans, Oliver M. Sprague was the only economist who testified that overproduction of crops caused farm distress and that banks went bust in the Great Plains because they were too small and too numerous. Sprague additionally defended branch banking and argued that call loans were much safer investments for banks than loans secured by farms or agricultural goods. He must have felt lonely, indeed.[21]

The Federal Reserve Bank proved reluctant to interfere with the workings of the system.

If the banking system caused misery for some, that was for politicians to address, not the Federal Reserve Bank. The Federal Reserve Board ignored the problem of collapsing banks in the West as beyond its purview. Besides, board members argued, banks that went bust deserved to because they were poorly managed. Federal Reserve Governor Roy Young told the gathered members of the ABA at their 1928 convention that no one could expect the Federal Reserve System to act as a general policeman for banking in America. It was intended to see that the banking system was supplied with adequate seasonal and emergency funds, and that was all it was supposed to do. Jacob Seibert, editor of the *Commercial and Financial Chronicle*, responded in an editorial that if Young's observation were true, it was past time for the Fed to withdraw some of that $1.5 billion in credit then available, as there was no need for it beyond speculating on the stock market. Wayne Putnam of the Detroit Union Trust Company disagreed. He blamed the Federal Reserve Bank for raising interest rates so high that it made bonds prohibitively expensive and deflated the bond markets. The Federal Reserve charged 3.5 percent interest on loans at the beginning of 1928. It raised rates to four in February, to 4.5 in May, and again to five in July. In August 1929, in an effort to cool the rampant speculation on the stock exchanges, the Federal Reserve Bank raised rates again, to 6 percent. This was not universally seen as wise among Federal Reserve officials. Given the slowing economy and falling prices, board member Charles Hamlin thought the rates were moving in exactly the wrong direction. It is not difficult to conclude that too much money was streaming into the stock exchanges. During the first eight months of 1929, investment trusts that sold stock in order to raise capital to buy other companies' stocks sold almost $1.5 billion in shares. In September 1929 they sold another $525 million worth, or 41.6 percent of all stock sold on the floors of America's exchanges that month. By fall money was being raised in the stock market simply to take advantage of the stock-market craze.[22]

Banks benefited from the rising economy of the 1920s as the booming economy drew billions of dollars into growing banks. The total number of banks declined through failures and mergers, while the amount of money entrusted to them ballooned. New rules for both national and state banks allowed them greater leeway to handle this growing heap of funds, but for the most part banks continued to invest as they had been doing for decades. The Federal Reserve Bank gave the nation a powerful tool to influence the economy if its directors cared to use it, which they were generally reluctant to do. The rise of enormous banks in the money centers, especially New York and Chicago, may have raised eyebrows and alarms among some progressives, but overall it was a healthy development that strengthened the banking system. The rise of bank holding companies, on the other hand, worried many. It need not have led to dangers any more than the creation of such holding companies as General Motors, General Electric, or AT&T did in earlier decades. But the enormous debts piled up by bank holding companies to buy up banks presented a clear danger if the economy unraveled and the debts could not be paid off. And that is what happened after 1929.[23]

The tale of the Crash of the New York Stock Exchange in October 1929 has been retold often enough that it does not require repeating here. The Crash did not cause the Great Depression, but its contribution to it is still the subject of controversy among economists. The buoyant stock market kept the economy chugging along in 1929 when, otherwise, it would have already stalled. Money unemployed elsewhere in the United States had for decades found its way to New York City banks, which loaned it to Wall Street brokers, who found uses for it. By summer 1929, when the economy was slowing in the rest of the nation, the country was burdened by a large supply of money without much demand, which found its way to Wall Street. When the market crashed, the downturn that already afflicted much of the nation hit New York City. When business in New York slowed, the decline in the rest of the country became worse because demand by New York for steel, glass, concrete, bricks, limestone, and plaster to put up the fantastic art-deco skyscrapers that were quickly remaking New York's skyline suddenly stopped. The overheated commercial real-estate market in New York quickly cooled after the Crash and its chill radiated out just as quickly. Auto production had been the one other bright spot in the U.S. economy in 1929, but as consumer spending pulled back in face of the evidence of the economic slowdown, auto sales plunged. Auto sales normally slackened in the fall, but in November 1929 demand for cars almost collapsed, shifting production into very low gear. After the Crash and the recession in New York, and the auto industry hit the brakes, the Northeast and Great Lakes Basin slid into the Depression that had started to slowly take hold of the rest of the country the previous summer. From Maryland to Louisiana, much of the South had been struggling since the summer of 1928. The West had slumped into torpor in the spring, but looked like it might be awakening in the fall of 1929, only to have the Crash send it back into a lull.[24]

Besides scaring the daylights out of a lot of bankers, the impact of the Crash upon American banks was not so great as might be imagined. As business slowed, bank clearings, deposits, and debits all slid downward nationwide. Bank loans were curtailed by $1,364 million between December 1929 and June 1930. While this pulled a lot of money from the economy, contributing to the slump, it did not really hurt banks. Along with a lot of other joint-stock ventures, bank stocks lost a great deal of value, but vast sums of bank money did not go up in smoke. In fact, the vast majority of money loaned by banks against securities was repaid, and banks suffered little immediate adverse fallout from the Crash. New York banks took pride in their ability to bail out brokerage houses that suddenly needed hundreds of millions of dollars. Brokers' loans in New York dropped from $8.5 billion to $6.1 billion during the course of October 1929. Banks outside of New York and non-bank sources of brokers' loans called in their monies as quickly as they could; in two weeks, out-of-town creditors withdrew $2,237 million that had been loaned to brokers to underwrite securities sales. As non-banks scrambled to pull money out of the market, big New York banks stepped into the breach, loaning $974 million to brokerage firms to keep them solvent. This strategy worked remarkably well and the firms were able to pay back the loans quickly without loss to the banks. New York banks loaned another $260 million directly to firms that owed money to brokerage houses. Thus, the proportion of loans to brokerage houses owned by banks actually grew after the Crash. By the end of 1929, brokers' loans had fallen to $4,110 million; $1,660 million of that amount was provided by banks. This was a liquidation of debt unprecedented in U.S. history.[25]

The Depression and the Banks

Initially, the economic slowdown did not hit banks too roughly. Bank failures were a bit more frequent in late 1929 and early 1930 than they had been earlier in 1929, but the country had gotten used to bank failures and no one was unduly alarmed at first. The same sort of banks collapsed that had been failing for years: small, rural, and underutilized. However, that changed as the economy continued to slow and the Depression took hold of business and the banks.[26]

The first serious wave of bank failures struck the upper South in November 1930 when a chain of banks and affiliated companies owned by Rogers Caldwell of Nashville collapsed. Starting in 1917, Caldwell had gathered together numerous companies and a sizable chain of banks into his holding company, Caldwell and Company. This included banks (his flagship bank, the Bank of Tennessee), insurance companies, securities-underwriting operations, and industrial companies that all began to falter even before the Crash. Desperate to raise capital, Caldwell formed alliances with other less-than-scrupulous businessmen also looking for salvation. He formed a partnership with a former U.S. senator, newspaper publisher, speculator, and political operator in Nashville, Colonel Luke Lea, who believed that banks would provide him with the wherewithal to broaden his operations. Caldwell also formed an alliance with an equally flailing and ethically supple Louisville banker, newspaper publisher, and political operator, James Brown, who ran (very badly) the renowned National Bank of Kentucky and had no idea of Caldwell's difficulties. Brown had created his own holding company in 1929, the Bancokentucky, which then borrowed tens of millions of dollars from the hapless Bank of Kentucky to finance an ill-considered bank-buying spree. Caldwell bought a small stake in another chain of banks owned by an apparently up-right Arkansas banker, Aleysius B. Banks, who was also swimming against the economic tide. Lashed together to the mast, Caldwell, Lea, Brown, and A.B. Banks went down with their leaking financial ships taking scores of banks with them.[27]

The Bank of Tennessee failed first and went into federal receivership on November 7, 1930, provoking a frightening series of bank runs in Nashville and Knoxville. When the Bank of Kentucky fell into federal receivership ten days later, freezing $41 million in deposits in the bank, eight correspondent banks in Louisville did not bother to open in the morning. The city of Louisville was subjected to a general bank run, and six more banks closed during the course of the day. The sudden collapse of Caldwell and Company unleashed a frightening series of bank runs in Nashville, Louisville, Knoxville, Asheville, Memphis, Little Rock, and small towns in between, which forced scores of banks to close freezing the deposits of hundreds of thousands southerners.[28]

In just two weeks, more than 110 banks in the South or nearby closed or suspended operations. Most of those failures were caused directly or indirectly by the calamity unleashed by the failure of the Bank of Tennessee: 55 in Arkansas, 15 in Kentucky, 9 in North Carolina, 7 in Missouri, 7 in Indiana, 6 in Illinois, and 2 in Iowa. Many of those banks survived to reopen. Arkansas banks started reopening after five to ten days (some had to close again) and North Carolina authorities reported deposits flowing back into Asheville banks by the end of November. Mergers were quickly arranged for many of the weaker banks and North Carolina depositors recovered all of their money. A new bank was chartered to take over the affairs of the three banks in Hendersonville, North Carolina — all of which were declared solvent by state bank examiners. But the ripples from the crash continued for several weeks: small rural banks with their funds frozen in the Bank of Kentucky or the American Exchange Trust Company in Little Rock, and without access to Federal Reserve loans, had no recourse but to close — many of them for good. Banks in Paoli and Orleans in southern Indiana that did correspondent banking in Louisville, without access to other funds, closed in late November.[29]

Until November, 114 banks in the St. Louis Federal Reserve district which included Louisville, Little Rock, and Memphis, had suspended operations in 1930, freezing $30.5 million. Then came November, when the district registered a record number of bank failures: 141, tying up $133 million in deposits. The numbers were similar for the other affected districts. In the Richmond district, which encompassed western North Carolina, three failures in September and two in October became sixteen in November, freezing $27 million in deposits. The Atlanta district, which included central and eastern Tennessee, saw two bank failures in September and one in October. Then came sixteen failures in November, freezing $30.6 million in deposits. The Caldwell disaster froze over $190 million in deposits and caused the collapse of scores of banks—some of them the biggest in town—in seven states. The failure of many of these banks could be blamed on Rogers Caldwell only indirectly, for dozens of the smaller banks affected by the contagion were overloaded with non-paying mortgages, and needed only a slight nudge to push them into insolvency. In Asheville, many of those mortgages belonged to new homeowners in western North Carolina towns who could not make their payments, and the state bank examiner blamed the disaster on the collapse of real-estate prices. In Arkansas, banks held thousands of mortgages incurred by farmers who, by harvest time 1930, could no longer make ends meet. In any event, the collapse of housing and farm-land prices had rendered millions of mortgages across the country of doubtful value and worthless as security for loans from larger banks. Thus, many of these shuttered banks teetered on the edge of failure and needed only a slight nudge, provided by Caldwell and Company, to send them over the precipice. Nevertheless, when federal receivers found that the Caldwell-owned Holston-Union National Bank in Knoxville carried on its books more than $9.2 million in worthless or questionable loans out of a total of $14.6 million, they blamed its collapse on incompetent management and not on unfavorable economic conditions. They made the same judgement of the Bank of Kentucky, which carried $17.7 million in bad or dubious loans out of slightly more than $37 million on its books.[30]

Bank holding companies proved to be especially vulnerable to the economic contraction. In the course of the 1920s small and medium-sized banks became big banks through mergers and acquisitions often undertaken with borrowed money. Bankers just as often created holding companies to buy banks and other financial service companies, and those bankers frequently created holding companies with money borrowed from their own banks. That is, bankers granted themselves and close associates loans, which they then used to buy stock in holding companies. The holding companies then often borrowed more money in order to buy more banks. Some bankers, and (later) many politicians, saw this entirely legal maneuver as somehow unethical and shady, while most bankers at the time saw it as normal operating procedure. In fact it was quite normal so long as the loans were properly evaluated by bank staff and handled as a regular loan, like any other. Unfortunately, that was not always the case. Very risky loans were granted by bankers to themselves and friends with insufficient collateral, jeopardizing the solvency of their own banks. Buying healthy banks ought not to have been risky and therein lay the problem: in 1930 many banks were in ill health and posed risky investments. And this was not always obvious to the bankers who bought rickety banks, believing they were making sound investments. When bankers borrowed money from their own banks to purchase other banks that were close to insolvency, they jeopardized the solvency of their own institutions. This happened too many times after the Crash, and the practice brought the banking system in some states to the edge of collapse.

The collapse of Caldwell's financial empire in the South was soon followed by a colossal breakdown in New York City, where the Bank of United States foundered in December. The men who ran the affairs of the Bank of United States, Bernard Marcus and Saul Singer, were not so colorful and probably not so ethically compromised as Caldwell, Lea, and Brown, but they took big risks and played fast and loose with hundreds of millions of dollars entrusted to them by modest New Yorkers, and came close to losing much of it. The Bank of United States was founded by Bernard Marcus's father, Joseph, in Manhattan's lower east side in 1913. During the 1920s the bank prospered with the city and its immigrant inhabitants. It expanded through mergers and established new branches and service subsidiaries that sold securities and backed real-estate development companies stacking new buildings throughout Manhattan. By fall 1929, the Bank of United States boasted 57 branches, resources of $315 million, and deposits of $220 million in 440,000 accounts.[31]

After the Crash, the bank's fortunes changed abruptly. The bank had expanded too quickly in 1928 and 1929, and its principal owners had taken on too much debt to finance expensive mergers. In order to maintain the price of the bank's stock, which was slipping in fall 1929, Marcus and Singer devised a plan to sell shares to the bank's depositors with oral (not written) agreements to buy back the shares at face value upon demand. In October 1929 the bank sold $6 million worth of bank stock to 30,000 depositors. Still nervous about the bank's frail financial condition Marcus cast about for merger partners, encouraged by New York State Superintendent of Banking Joseph Broderick,. Just weeks before the Crash, a big New York investment house, J.W. Seligman, pulled out of talks to acquire a major portion of the bank. Marcus claimed the savvy Wall Street bankers had premonitions of the impending Crash, while financial journalist Morris R. Werner believed someone provided the Wall Street firm a copy of a scathing bank examiner's report on the Bank of United States. In two months, bank assets dropped to $277 million, including $49 million in cash in its vaults. It still held $226 million in deposits in December 1929. But the bank's heavy investments in New-York real-estate mortgages, which began to lose value as the recession of 1929 deepened into the depression of 1930, caused the assets listed on its books to depreciate quickly. Mortgage payments slowed and bank loans to builders, developers, and real estate companies had to be written down or off. Bank real-estate affiliates which had borrowed millions of dollars from the bank, could not repay their loans. On 1 April 1930 Saul Singer, wrote to his stockholders, "the Bankus Corporation has naturally felt the result of the slowing down of activities generally prevailing in its field of operation. While we feel that this condition is only temporary, our board, nevertheless, felt it to be part of conservatism to reduce the rate of our dividend [to fifty cents per share]."[32] Despite the slow down, Bernard Marcus pursued new clients and opened new branches. In the first three months of 1930, the bank added 55,457 new accounts and expanded to 58 branches. The bank also counted 20,411 stockholders. But the bank slowly leached deposits. By June 1930 it had lost only a few million dollars, but the bank's fortunes ebbed as the year dragged on. By December it had only $161 million left in deposits and too many of its $90 million in mortgages were not paying.[33]

On Wednesday, December 10, a small merchant from the Bronx went to his local branch and asked to sell back his bank stock that bank salesmen had promised could be resold to the bank at any time at the original price. When the manager tried to talk him out of it, he went outside and told others the bank refused to buy back the stock. As word spread, crowds gathered at other branches in the Bronx and in Brooklyn. Armored cars brought extra cash to branches under siege and everyone was paid. One man stood in line for two hours to withdraw the two dollars in his savings account. By evening mounted police had to be called to handle crowds of 20,000 to 25,000 who besieged the branches. Many withdrew their funds until the bank closed at 8 P.M., its regular hour, yet crowds estimated at 5,000 still lingered outside the bank. A bank vice president told the press that 2,500 to 3,000 depositors withdrew $2 million in one day at a single branch.[34]

On Wednesday evening, December 10, when Superintendent Broderick gathered lead-ing Wall Street bankers, New York politicians, and businessmen at the Federal Reserve Bank to devise a rescue plan for the bank, the assembled financial leaders were reluctant to involve their institutions with the Bank of United States. The bank had expanded too quickly and absorbed too many real estate loans, which now were not paying. Bankers such as Morgan partner Thomas Lamont and Charles Sabin of the Guaranty Trust Company had no interest in thrift accounts, and, they said, knew nothing about them. As Owen Young, president of General Electric and a director of the Federal Reserve Bank, conferred with Federal Reserve Governor George Harrison, Charles Mitchell of National City Bank, Albert Wiggin of Chase National, and others at the Federal Reserve Bank, the anxious Broderick was largely kept out of the discussions. When admitted, he implored the bankers to save the bank, warning that its collapse would produce dire consequences. The titans of finance were not convinced. The Morgan Bank had played a famous part in ending the banking panic of 1907, but as the Bank of United States was a state-chartered bank, held no correspondent banking accounts, and was not even a member of the New York Clearing House Association, the gathered did not worry that its failure would precipitate a general banking crisis. Its poor financial con-dition resulted from bad management more than bad business conditions, so why not let it fail?[35]

Broderick and the grandees met at the Fed until 4 A.M., when they decided there was no recourse to closing the bank. They all agreed the bank would never withstand the run that would surely hit on Thursday morning if its doors opened. At 9 A.M. Broderick announced to the press that a syndicate of banks would immediately honor 50 percent holdings of anyone with a Bank of United States passbook, and within a reasonable amount of time, certificates of deposit (CDs) would be issued to all depositors for their remaining funds. How much of those funds depositors would realize in the future depended on the fortunes of the receivers who would sell off bank assets over time. Bank officials told the press they were confident that all depositors would get back 100 percent of their money. When liquidation was finally completed in May 1944, receivers recovered 84 percent of the bank's 1930 assets.[36]

Although the collapse of the Bank of United States did not spill over into other cities, similar failures with analogous problems rocked other towns. A week after the 1930 collapse of the Bank of United States in New York, Bankers Trust Company, with 19 branches and $34 million deposited in 135,000 accounts, closed its doors in Philadelphia. Only ten weeks earlier the bank held $42.5 million in deposits. The bank, owned by a prominent Philadel-phia real-estate tycoon, Albert Greenfield, was heavily invested in mortgages in the city, which by the fall of 1930 were faltering. Since July the bank had lost $17 million in deposits, and had been forced to sell its best assets to raise cash. As rumors circulated that the trust company's remaining assets were hopelessly frozen in defaulted mortgages and bad loans, the flight of money accelerated. In the last three days of its existence as a functioning bank, Bankers Trust saw that trickle turn into a torrent, and the directors asked the state secretary of banking to assume control of the institution.[37]

The foundering of Bankers Trust provoked a frightening run on the Franklin Trust Company in Philadelphia the same day. The bank's officers assured customers there was plenty of cash and allowed them to withdraw as much as they wanted. Armored trucks arrived with more money from the Philadelphia Federal Reserve Bank as police and bank guards kept order in the lobby and outside the bank. As of Monday night the bank had assets of $50 million, and Joseph Wayne, president of the Philadelphia National Bank, assured the public that the Franklin Trust Company was sound and the Clearing House Association stood behind it. Nevertheless, 20,000 of the bank's 150,000 depositors made withdrawals before the day was out. Most of those withdrawals were reportedly by small savers and not by companies, which probably saved the bank. When corporate clients lost faith in a bank, its fate was frequently sealed.[38]

The most influential bankers in Philadelphia acted swiftly to save the Franklin Trust Company, unlike their compatriots in New York, who did little to head off the collapse of the Bank of United States. The bankers of New York treated the distress of the Bank of United States as nature taking its course in the financial market. By fall 1930, the market was turning brutal and nature was unforgiving. All too often assets sold by anxious banks in 1930 had been good in 1929, but were less attractive a year later, and had to be sold at a loss on a very sluggish market. With banks nation-wide trying to raise cash, it fell to the Federal Reserve Banks to supply it. They did not: bill discounting fell to historic lows throughout most of 1930, and bills bought from member banks rose only slightly from the already low amounts of 1929. Milton Friedman and Anna Schwartz have argued that Federal Reserve member banks were largely unaffected by the general collapse, which confined itself mostly to small vulnerable banks — the same type which had been collapsing for the past decade. Some of the larger banks, such as Chemical Bank of New York, did lend a helping hand to calm the situation in Tennessee and Kentucky. The Federal Reserve Banks discounting of eligible commercial paper rose only slightly from November to December from $221 million to $338 million, which still paled compared to the monthly billion-dollar discounting the bank had routinely undertaken during 1929. Serious trouble developed in the South only when member banks ran out of eligible paper to discount. The Fed stepped up buying paper on the open market somewhat and the money supply expanded only modestly — as it almost always did from November to December. Friedman and Schwartz seem to be justified in viewing Fed action as too little and too late.[39]

While missteps by the Fed failed to ease the crisis for banks, it is hard to conclude the Fed caused the bank crisis. The deep-seated cause was the disastrous economic slump, as illustrated by the case of Arkansas. No state was more severely struck by bank failures in 1930 than Arkansas, where 135 banks suspended operations. Thirty-four of those banks reopened before the year was out, and another 36 reopened by June 30, 1931 (by which time another 12 had failed.) When seeking to explain the bank failures in Arkansas in 1930 and 1931 Robert E. Wait of the Arkansas Bankers Association put "too many banks" at the top of his list, followed by "improved roads." He subscribed to the thesis that the dying off of banks was simply the result of changes in the bank market brought about by improved transportation. Thus, little rural crossroads banks, with few assets to sell and small capital to call upon, met their timely death when conditions turned unfavorable and their customers literally drove away. In 1930 and 1931 conditions for such banks in Arkansas were very unfavorable and the likelihood of their continued existence extremely remote. However, Mr. Wait also added to his list too rapid an expansion of credit and too much "wild-cat investing" in the 1920s. Perhaps he had Rogers Caldwell in mind. He added bad management, too many insider loans, too many criminals working in banks, too many bad decisions by bankers, drastic wage cuts and layoffs, overproduction of crops, and fear and hysteria among depositors. In other words, there were many reasons why banks failed, and the circumstances in Arkansas in 1930 were propitious for failures. Certainly the collapse in the price of crops and value of farm land in 1930 and 1931 (an astounding 23 percent) would have severely restricted the ability of farmers in Arkansas to raise loans and conduct business as usual with their local banks. Banks in Arkansas would have been extremely hard pressed to loan money to lumber mills, when demand for southern pine had tumbled, or for cotton, with prices heading ever lower. Management at many small rural banks may have been amateurish, but it is difficult to see how professional management could have saved most of these small banks destined for receivership. And when a small solvent bank had its money frozen in a larger correspondent bank, which happened to many banks in Kentucky, Tennessee, Arkansas, and Illinois in the fall of 1930, the most professional management could not save it in the short run. Fortunately, many such banks survived in the long run.[40]

Many interested parties argued at the time that bad management and injudicious investments caused banks to collapse. This was the natural mechanism of the free-market system and ought to be allowed to operate. Bad bankers and weak banks were weeded in periods of stress. To a certain extent this was true. Rogers Caldwell, Colonel Lea, James Brown, Bernard Marcus, and Saul Singer had repeatedly shown themselves to be bad stewards of other people's money and the entire system was better off without them. Caldwell and Company serves as an illustration of what could and did go wrong when weak companies fell into the maw of the Depression. That Caldwell and Brown escaped prison was perhaps a damning indictment of the legal systems of Tennessee and Kentucky, but the failures of their banks and investment houses were financial justice in action. Marcus and Singer were not so lucky: both ended up in Sing-Sing Prison. Colonel Lea and his son both ended up behind bars in North Carolina. The banking collapse of 1930 was not the failure of the system, but its vindication, the argument went. Among those who advanced this argument was the governor of New York, Franklin Delano Roosevelt.[41]

Governor Roosevelt viewed the events with the same sangfroid as the Morgan partners. Roosevelt's father had been a banker, as was his uncle, Frederic Delano, who was a director of the Federal Reserve Bank of New York. Prodded by a scandal revealed after the collapse of the City Trust Company in early 1929, Roosevelt appointed Robert Moses to head a board of inquiry into banking practices in New York State and to make recommendations. Despite a highly critical report and recommendation for numerous reforms in the state's banking laws, Governor Roosevelt endorsed only minor tinkering with the laws. Another bank collapse in Brooklyn in July 1929 brought renewed calls for further reforms, and again the laws were subjected to minor adjustments—mostly strengthening the office of the state's banking superintendent. On the day of the closing of the Bank of United States, Governor Roosevelt returned from his vacation in Warm Springs, Georgia, and held a brief meeting with Lieutenant Governor Lehman at Roosevelt's east-side town house. They issued no public statement. After the collapse of the bank, Roosevelt discovered his concern for depositors in New York and his animus against bankers. Finally, in March 1931, Roosevelt asked the legislature in New York to apply the laws that governed savings accounts in savings banks to thrift accounts in commercial banks as well, and he denounced the legislature's recent kowtowing to bankers when they failed to pass laws to protect depositors. Then he denounced bankers.[42]

Many Americans shared Governor Roosevelt's growing skepticism about bankers. The wide publicity given to the spectacular banking flops and the attendant attention devoted to trials of crooked bankers encouraged many people to believe that banks failed because they had fallen into the clutches of criminals. Ambitious prosecutors saw clearly the electoral profits to be reaped from vigorous pursuit of malfeasant bankers. Even Superintendent Broderick became the subject — twice — of New York prosecutors looking for big fish to fry. While some bankers—such as Marcus, Singer, Caldwell, Lea, and Brown—clearly earned the enmity of both citizens and juries, too many among the public drew the wrong conclusions. Malfeasance was not the principal reason why banks failed; the shrinking economy was, and prosecutors pursuing unlucky bankers contributed nothing to end the slump and probably helped to push it just a bit deeper. As the economy continued to sag, even banks with competent management fell victim to the times. It became difficult for many Americans to distinguish good bankers from bad bankers, and many made no effort to separate the two.

Economists Milton Friedman and Anna Schwartz assert that the collapses in the South and New York initiated a slow leaching of deposits from banks across the United States as people lost faith in their banks. The dramatic wave of failures in the South petered out and produced no immediate echo elsewhere, but the news traveled all across the land and made an impression upon anxious Americans watching factories lay off more workers and building projects halt unfinished. The collapse of the Caldwell chain was closely followed by the *Atlanta Constitution* and the *St. Louis Post-Dispatch*, just as the closing of the Bank of United States was reported in detail in the *Boston Globe*. The *Globe* reported without much substantiation, "many of its big depositors had invested heavily in stocks. When the stock market broke in 1929 a number of its loans were impaired by too thin collateral." Loans on stock had, indeed, gotten the bank into trouble, but loans to stock speculators in 1929 had little to do with the bank's failure. Its collapse merited mention in a tiny article on New York banks' stocks buried in the *Denver Post*. Yet, overall, news about banks was bad and people received it anxiously. One Kentucky businessman brooded to Democratic National Executive Committee Chairman Jouett Shouse the collapse of the Bank of Kentucky "is the most awful thing. To the Mohammedan, the Koran was not more sacred than was the Bank of Kentucky to the average man and women hereabouts." Shouse replied, "a vast number of people, particularly poorer people, have entirely lost faith in the solidity and security of the banks. I happen to know of numerous instances here in Washington of the withdrawal of deposits by working men." The "hoarding" process, where small depositors trusted tin cans in their kitchens more than local banks, had begun.[43]

Deposits in American banks, which had peaked in December 1928 at $56.8 billion, had fallen to $53.2 billion by March 1930; by the end of the year they stood at just $53 billion — a decline of $1.74 billion. In the judgment of the Federal Reserve Bank, most of that decline could be attributed to hoarding. In the last six months of 1930, depositors had withdrawn $236 million from banks, forcing banks to liquidate assets in order to come up with currency. This liquidation of assets hurt businesses dependent upon bank credit, especially those whose loans were recalled prematurely or renewals refused. The sudden tightening of credit rippled throught the economy as banks restricted new loans. Banks had loaned $41.7 billion in December 1929; by June 1930 loans had dropped to $40.5 billion and to $38 billion by December 1930. Bank credit had shrunk by $3.6 billion, or fifteen times the amount of money that fled the banking system through cash withdrawals since June. About half of the reduction in loans could be attributed directly to the liquidation of assets in response to currency withdrawals. The other half can be attributed to businesses using deposits to pay off loans as they fled from debt. As both banks and businesses removed deposits from their books in order to satisfy loans, that money simply disappeared from the banking system and, thus, from the economy. While banks replaced loans by bonds to some extent, total bank assests still shrank by $2.2 bilion. Banks had weathered a bad year, but early in 1931 a long descent in balances started to steepen.[44]

The Crisis of 1931

The nation suffered through 1930 by trimming, cutting back, and belt tightening all around. Ironically, such financial husbandry helped make matters worse, and the slowdown got only slower. The nationwide decline in investment especially troubled the Midwest, the center of America's heavy industry. When orders dwindled for the country's iron and steel firms, the problems of manufacturing and mining only piled upon the trials already faced by agriculture. Thus, the financial center of the Midwest, Chicago, was more severely struck than any other important national banking hub. Trouble for industry in the Midwest meant trouble for banks in Chicago.

As bad as conditions were in 1930, they were not yet calamitous. Even though 900 companies reported cutting wages, auto companies still sold 2,785,000 vehicles in 1930 compared to 4,587,000 in 1929. While business was off $14.6 billion (the total decline in bank debits), bank deposits fell only $2.3 billion — from $55.3 million in December 1929 to $53 billion a year later — not a dramatic drop compared to seasonal fluctuations throughout the 1920s. Deposits actually increased in the second quarter of the year in some of the most important Federal Reserve districts — New York, Boston, Philadelphia, and San Francisco. Savings in thrift accounts grew by $267 million during the year. Life insurance companies sold an additional 4.8 million policies, and premiums collected increased by $125 million. In the early months of 1931 there was widespread expectation of a business revival. President Litchfield of Goodyear Tires said that the trough had been reached and business would improve in 1931: Goodyear would increase tire production by 50 percent in January. In December 1930, the president of AT&T, William Sherman Gifford, predicted the Depression would end early in 1931. When steel orders grew late in 1930 and prices advanced in response, many thought the economy had turned the corner and the *San Francisco Chronicle* ran the headline "Production Gains Likely Early in '31." Showers Brothers Furniture in Indiana ordered 2.5 million board feet of southern-gum lumber in December 1930 in anticipation of imminent economic revival. Securities prices rose with the growing optimism.[45]

Yet, despite such expectations and rosy predictions by President Hoover, calamity indeed loomed. The Depression deepened in 1931; hardship spread and worsened. Members of the Federal Reserve Board remained optimistic until prices receded again in March. Disappointing corporate quarterly reports in April dashed many hopeful expectations. Commodity prices stubbornly refused to rise, guaranteeing that whole sectors of the world economy would remain mired in the doldrums. Prices for farm produce, which had fallen 25 percent during 1930, slid another 20 percent in 1931. Factory employment that had fallen 20 percent in 1930, fell another 21 percent in 1931. Sawmill payrolls dropped to nearly one-third of their mid–1920s levels. In heavy industries such as iron and steel fabrication, payrolls in 1931 were almost half their 1929 levels. Production of steel, which had fallen by more than half in 1930, fell by almost half again from March to October 1931. Auto production, which was widely expected to revive in the spring of 1931, fell to levels last seen in the depression year 1921. Auto companies that turned out 232,000 vehicles per month in 1930, produced only 164,000 per month in 1931. In November 1931 the industry hit a postwar low: 49,000 vehicles. The usual autumn expansion in business and production did not occur in 1931. By November bank debits and clearings had dwindled to levels not seen since the war. In the center of American business, New York City, volumes of transactions had fallen to about half of the previous December. Midwestern financial centers witnessed a similar commercial funk: debits and clearings in Cleveland, Chicago, and Kansas City were off by about 40 percent from the previous December. Unemployment lines grew longer, as did soup lines.[46]

The spreading stagnation, unemployment, and canceled orders made 1931 the worst year for bank failures in American history. Before the year was over, 2,803 banks disappeared. Eight hundred and twelve of those banks were absorbed through mergers, but the remainder shut their doors and were forced to turn their books over to government regulators for liquidation. The failed banks were backed by an accumulated capital of $208 million and held deposits worth $1.7 billion, which all became frozen at least temporarily. While banks suffered from problems unique to banks, they were also dragged down by the generally depressed conditions of the economy, which grew worse as 1931 progressed. As the year progressed deposits steadily declined everywhere except in New York and Boston, where they mounted in the spring. But then deposits slumped even in the Northeast as business stalled in the summer. Customers began drawing down their savings accounts, forcing banks to draw down their reserves and liquidate assets to come up with cash. Most American banks sold their assets in New York City and, having little better to do with the proceeds after satisfying withdrawal slips presented at their counters, banks left their money on deposit in big New York City banks where it could be called upon on short notice. Normally such lingering reserves had been invested by the New York banks as broker loans, but by the beginning of 1931, new issues of securities of all kinds were running at only one-third the rate of the market high of 1929. By summer the stock market was becalmed with little trading. New issues had dropped by half; by the end of the year, they fell by half again to only $278 million for the last quarter. Brokers owed banks $587 million in December 1931, about 7 percent of the amount they owed in October 1929. Thus, money languished in New York vaults unwanted and unused, even when offered at 1.5 percent.[47]

Economists and historians differ on the reasons for the steep decline of 1931, but they agree that severe blows to international finance initiated by the American debacle greatly aggravated the situation in Europe, and troubles in Europe found their way back to the United States. With the unwinding of the American economy, banks cut back loans to Europe. As credit dried up, European banks—especially those in Germany and Austria — scrambled to find new money to pay off previous loans. When in spring 1931 the largest bank in Austria, the Rothschild's Credit-Anstalt in Vienna, took on the sizable debts of a weak Austrian bank, the Boden-Credit-Anstalt, it took on a burden greater than it could carry. Loaded down with bad debts, the Credit-Anstalt was forced to close in May 1931 setting off a chain of events that reverberated through Germany, France, and ultimately Great Britain. Though hardly noticed in the United States at the time, the Austrian crisis unleashed a run on banks in Austria, Germany, and Hungary that provoked a flight of capital and gold. The Hungarians responded by declaring a three-day bank moratorium that closed all banks and stopped gold and currency from exiting the country. The Germans followed the Hungarian example and shuttered all banks, good and bad, indefinitely until the excitement had passed. When banks reopened, clients were permitted to withdraw only a fraction of their accounts. British banks tried to buttress the weakened institutions in Central Europe, until they, too, ran out of credit. When word spread that Britain had reached the limits of its credit, gold, which had just fled Germany, now fled England — mostly heading toward Paris. With gold fleeing the vaults in London, the Bank of England suspended convertibility of the pound. On September 21, 1931, Britain went off the gold standard. Other countries quickly followed: Denmark, Sweden, and Norway immediately embargoed gold exports. The British departure from gold sent shockwaves across the Atlantic which pushed nervous investors at the New York Stock

Exchange into a frenzy of selling. Stocks listed on the exchange lost nearly half their value; bonds lost nearly a quarter. The second stock market crash in 18 months sent shudders through the American economy, and hopes for recovery were dashed.[48]

The European crisis aggravated an already bad situation. In an effort to help dampen the European crisis, President Hoover called for a moratorium on payment of international debts incurred during the war. Not wanting to let Germany suspend reparation payments, the French hesitated, but eventually went along. The war-debt predicament that had plagued trans–Atlantic relations since 1920 was at least postponed. By late summer, the American economy hesitated and tottered, not seeming to know which way to head, up or down. Market indicators all pointed down, but the normal autumn uptick in business and pro-duction occurred hesitantly as optimists had predicted. Payrolls increased and workers were called back to work. It looked as if conditions might turn around, even if the men who worked the markets did not show much confidence. But then the European storm hit the United States. American loans to fund imports stopped, causing imports to plummet. Exports soon followed. New York City, the heart of American international trade, business, and finance, turned unmistakably sullen.[49]

At the end of the summer, the big New York banks were flush with unwanted cash, which banks throughout America left lingering in correspondent accounts where they earned at least meager interest. And the big New York banks sat on their own excess reserves. When the financial troubles in Europe induced Europeans to develop a sudden appetite for gold, and lots of it, they looked to the United States to find it. As Europeans bought gold, $725 million left New York banks, which suddenly found themselves not so flush with cash. In order to raise cash, big New York banks did what smaller banks nationwide had been doing all year: they sold securities to improve their cash position. This had a disastrous effect upon the securities markets that now had plenty of sellers and few buyers. Prices plummeted ever lower. End-of-summer hesitancy about the future was displaced by decided discouragement. For the rest of 1931, all economic indicators headed down, and the eddy became a maelstrom.[50]

Most bank failures of 1930 and early 1931 resembled the failures of previous years. They tended to occur west of the Appalachian Mountains, and the majority of failed banks were still small, state-chartered institutions. Except for the few big banks already discussed, most of the institutions that succumbed to the deteriorating economy were supported by a small capital base; served tiny, usually rural, regions; and were not members of the Federal Reserve System. Most failed banks were those that most observers expected to disappear sooner or later anyway. The full fury of the tempest hit the United States when the European financial storm reached North America and banks failed at twice the rate of the previous year. In June 1931, 167 banks, holding $196 million in deposits suspended operations. After a relatively quiet July (93 bank failures), 158 banks closed in August, with $186 million in deposits. In September another 305 banks, holding $237 million in clients' money, closed their doors. But October proved the worst month for banks in American history: 522 banks, with $494 million in deposits, failed.[51]

Alarmed by the flood of gold leaving their New York vaults, the hectic dumping of assets by American banks, and the frantic demand for currency emanating from the nation's interior, the Federal Reserve Bank raised its discount rate sharply on October 9, 1931 from 1.5 percent to 2.5 percent, and again on October 16 to 3.5 percent. At the same time the New York Fed raised its discount charge for eligible paper bought on the open market by the same percentages. That is, it offered less money in exchange for paper it was offering to buy. This mostly touched foreign central banks—primarily the Bank of France—which had been dumping hundred of millions of dollars of American commercial paper onto the New York market since summer and buying gold. In response, the New York Federal Reserve Bank bought eligible paper on the open market: $600 million from July to October. The supply of Federal Reserve notes pumped into circulation increased accordingly, from $1.95 billion in August to $2.5 billion by November. This raised the amount of money in circulation to levels not seen since 1920: $5.25 billion. Even so, this was not enough to satisfy the frantic scramble for cash by Americans, and hence their banks. The big banks in New York did not help matters when they simultaneously raised their rates for short-term loans to other banks from 2 percent to 3. On 24 October they raised them again to 4 percent. To defuse any notions of a Wall Street conspiracy against the rest of America, big banks in other major cities raised their rates even higher. Banks in the South and west of the Appalachians wanted 4.85 percent for bank loans in mid–October, which they raised to 5.18 percent in late October. Actions by the Fed and the big banks did not dampen the crisis; banks, unable to convert assets quickly enough to meet their depositors' demands for cash, failed by scores all over the country from New Jersey to Nebraska and Texas.[52]

Economists and bankers at the time were convinced that people withdrew their money from banks and hoarded it at home out of fear for the security of banks. In the fall of 1931, President Hoover confided to journalists the dangers posed by hoarding but was loath to say too much about it lest the jittery public pull even more money out of banks. He finally made a public appeal in February 1932 for Americans to leave their money in banks and not hoard it in cookie jars. The Federal Reserve Bank noted a decrease in bank deposits in the fall of 1930 and a steady increase in demand for 50 and 100 dollar bills, which had little practical use at the time. By the end of 1931 the number of large denomination bills in public hands had doubled, and Federal Reserve officials assumed the extra $700 million in large bills was demanded by hoarders. In response, Treasury Secretary Ogden Mills offered the public one-year bonds at 2 percent interest in small denominations ($50, $100, and $500) as a device to put hoarded money back to use.[53]

The diminution of deposits — both time and demand — closely paralleled the drop-off in business activity throughout the country. Bank debits and clearings fell off by billions of dollars from spring to the fall of 1930, and again from spring to the fall of 1931. Bank debits in the New York Federal Reserve district alone plunged from $41.7 billion in March 1930 to $23.2 billion in November. Sales were terrible for businesses of all kinds. Commercial bank loans declined by nearly $4 billion from June to December as companies grew increasingly wary of being in debt, or banks refused to renew loans as they searched for greater liquidity. Nervous individuals withdrew savings from banks to hide in suitcases and tin cans, accounting for about half of the drop in bank depositis in late 1930. As the postal saving accounts suggest, people sought safer havens, but the postal accounts grew by only $330 million during the course of 1931, an amount dwarfed by the total drop in deposits in U.S. banks from $51.4 billion in March 1931 to $46.26 billion in December. In nine months $5.17 billion left the banking system, a decline of 11 percent. Industrial production dropped in those same nine months from an index (1923–1925 average = 100) of 87 to 73; manufacturing payrolls fell from 75 to 56; and prices of all kinds were falling. But did deposits and bank loans decline because business slowed, or did they decline because bank credit shriveled as banks called in loans to satisfy demands for currency by hoarders? Probably both forces were at work, yet it seems undeniable that banks cut off credit in order to satisfy demands for cash, as argued by Milton Friedman and Anna Schwartz.[54]

The Crisis in the Midwest

The Great Depression was, more than anything else, a collapse of investment in building and manufacturing throughout the United States. Because the Great Lakes Basin was the center of American heavy industry, the collapse in demand for capital goods caused serious hardships in the smoky cities that had churned out the metal products demanded by growing towns and industries. When the building boom collapsed, the Midwest felt the thud almost as profoundly as the South, which provided much of America's building materials. Factories in Illinois, Wisconsin, and Michigan turned out tractors, combines, and other farm machines throughout the 1920s regardless of the slump in commodity prices. When the Depression resulted in a devastating collapse of farm prices, demand for tractors and other machines evaporated. During the 1920s Midwestern factories also poured forth automobiles and trucks at breakneck pace, and when America's insatiable appetite for autos slackened in 1929, demand for steel, tires, glass, metal alloys, leather, and other components of autos, produced mostly in the Midwest, dwindled as well. When the economy cooled, and then froze, the freeze in the Midwest was the hardest. Because Chicago was a leading center of the enormous midwestern economic boom of the 1920s, when the bubble burst, the bang there was the loudest. And because Chicago's banks provided much of the money that fueled the boom, those banks suffered the most when the boom ended.

By June 1931, the depressed real-estate market and a heavy spate of foreclosures caused many Chicago banks to groan under the weight of bad mortgages. Small banks in outlying districts were particularly hard hit and relied on good relations with big banks in the Loop to remain solvent. When some of the big Loop banks merged in June, rumors raced through the city that banks all over were in trouble, and Chicagoans by the tens of thousands ran to their banks to secure their monies. Mayor Anton Cermak pleaded with Chicagoans to trust their banks, but dozens of weakened banks could not survive the onslaught; by July, 45 banks had disappeared from Cook County. Most of those banks were small neighborhood banks, but the mighty Foreman State National Bank, with $220 million in assets, also vanished into a forced merger.[55]

Towns and cities along the shores of the Great Lakes suffered badly in 1931. Bank clearings in the Cleveland Federal Reserve District began a steady downward slide in February 1931 that hit bottom in March 1933. Northern Ohio and western Pennsylvania felt the downturn as demand for steel, glass, coal, auto parts, machine tools, and tires diminished. Banks in Toledo suffered through a dramatic falloff in business, thinning their ranks from 46 state-chartered banks to five after rumors fed a citywide bank run in June 1931. By summer 1931, steel production in the United States was running at about one-third of capacity, and steel companies were retiring obsolete plants and equipment — about 5 percent of total capacity. The slump in demand for coal and iron, and the subsequent layoffs and wage cuts, sapped the vitality of the region and slowly drained the banks until they could survive no more. No fewer than 13 national banks failed in the coal-mining region south of Pittsburgh in the first six months of 1931. The slack demand for coal and steel, and the cost-cutting response exacted a toll on Pittsburgh banks. On September 21, 1931, the oldest bank in Pittsburgh shut its doors unleashing a wave of failures that fed upon itself as banks shed deposits and assets, and people lost confidence in their banks. When the Bank of Pittsburgh, N.A., closed, it dragged down with it Highland National Bank and the Franklin Savings and Trust Company. In the week that followed eight more Pittsburgh banks closed their doors. The shock waves emanated out from Pittsburgh over the next several weeks, taking a score of banks down in western Pennsylvania, West Virginia, and eastern Ohio. Before the year was out, 137 Pennsylvania banks, capitalized at $31.74 million and holding deposits worth $271 million, suspended operations.[56]

The Crisis in the East

The kind of troubles that nearly crippled Chicago was soon familiar all over. The Depression did not literally move east like the 20th Century Limited, speeding from Chicago toward New York City, but the economic slowdown markedly afflicted the Midwest first and then blighted the East. When building and manufacturing slowed, consumers kept on consuming, so that medium-sized cities in the East that turned out products bought at retail felt only a slight chill at first. They weathered 1930 and early 1931 without great suffering even while profits nearly disappeared and most businesses cut back. As the Depression ground on, spending slouched and business conditions in light industries deteriorated as well, visiting layoffs, bankruptcy, and bank failures to towns and cities to the east of Chicago. When light manufacturing slumped, New England felt the chill, and its financial center, Boston, experienced its own hard times. As international trade dwindled areas such as the South which produced commodities for export and northeast financial centers—especially New York—that provided funds and services that promoted trade, were likewise visited by hardship. The kind of troubles that nearly crippled Chicago was soon familiar all over.[57]

Towns and cities in Ohio that manufactured consumer goods such as Cincinnati, which turned out soap, chemicals, petroleum products, leather goods, and processed food, while not untouched, were less severely afflicted by the downturn. Likewise, Philadelphia, Boston, and New York were less dependent than Chicago and Cleveland on heavy industry and were thus less severely touched by the economic slowdown. Northeastern towns and cities had diverse economic bases that catered more to consumers than to businesses, and consumer spending though it slowed in 1930 and 1931, did not stall like business investment did. Only in the second half of 1931 did department-store and chain-store sales in the United States fall more than 10 percent from their mid–1920s average. Banks suffered proportionally along with the businesses that depended upon them.[58]

The economic slump had become unmistakably national as incomes fell in every state. Bank runs became general on the New Jersey shore in early October 1931 after national bank examiners took over the First National Bank of Ocean City. Its president, Hiram Mowrer, who had worked at the bank for 33 years, took a dive off the peer and drowned himself when the troubles of the bank became overwhelming. As the news spread, every bank in Ocean City was deluged by depositors seeking to withdraw funds, and the panic quickly spread to neighboring towns and counties. As the national economy slowed, it hit the financial center of the country, New York City. The economy in New York had shuffled through 1930 and early 1931, but turned sour in the summer and started a long steady descent though the fall and into the winter. Bank clearings for New York City slid from $30 billion in January 1931 to $22.6 billion in July, and then to $14.9 billion in November. In 11 months they had been cut in half! The decline in deposits in the Federal Reserve district from March to December was more modest: $710 million. Because the biggest banks in New York City served the nation, and not just the city, the national slowdown was clearly reflected in the condition of New York's mightiest banks. As business declined and international trade ebbed, the big banks and trust companies in New York that served and relied upon that business cut back loans, shed deposits, and bulked up on other investments, which consisted mostly of United States government bonds. New York City member banks increased their holdings of United States securities by nearly $500 million during the course of 1931.[59]

Those quarters that had enjoyed the greatest prosperity in the boom years, such as New York City, now had to pay a price. It became commonplace in the 1930s to say that Americans were reaping the penalty for their overindulgence in the 1920s. Whether Americans overbought, overbuilt, and overinvested in the 1920s is subject to dispute. But it was sadly true that all of the debts incurred to do all that building and buying had to be repaid as business slackened and incomes fell, honoring those obligations became harder. As the city's economy shrank, it became at first difficult, and then impossible, to pay off obligations undertaken earlier. From January to October 1931 mortgages worth $375 million were foreclosed in New York City. This included $125 million in Manhattan alone, with seizures of 133 of the new apartment buildings that had gone up in the 1920s. The 28-story El Dorado went under the auctioneer's hammer in November. The 29-story Majestic Apartment Building on Central Park West at 72nd Street cost $9.4 million — a fantastic amount in its day — to build, and the building's management could not meet a $987,000 payment that was due on December 1, 1931. The mighty Majestic followed the path of the San Remo, the Beresford, and El Dorado— all sumptuous towers within a short stroll along Central Park West, finished in 1930 or 1931, and bankrupt by late 1931.[60]

By December 1931 New York City sidewalks were trod by tens of thousands of unemployed. Despite this evidence of the arrival of hard times in New York City and the erosion of assets and deposits in the city's banks, banks in the city remained sound. A few banks failed in Queens, and a national bank in Manhattan with $2 million in deposits folded up in August, but overall, the economic slump did not bring devastation to New York banks as in Pittsburgh and Toledo.

The economic slowdown in Massachusetts hit its banks harder. Deposits in Boston banks had declined just as loans had dwindled since the heady days of 1929. New England's largest bank, the First National Bank of Boston, bulged with deposits of $469 million at the end of 1929 and had outstanding loans of $354 million. By December 1931 its deposits had slipped to $416 million and its loans had been scaled back to $257 million. Boston's other banks experienced similar reverses. The fall of 1931 brought a wave of bank failures to Massachusetts. The Medford Trust Company went under in October, freezing $5.3 million in 18,000 accounts, including the deposits of 3,000 business clients, and instilling justifiable fear in the community. Within a week the Highland Trust Company in neighboring Somerville succumbed. It held $5.4 million in deposits, four-fifths of which were in savings rather than business accounts. The same day the smaller Revere Trust Company failed to open and tension grew in the Boston area.[61]

The explosion came in mid–December when the Federal National Bank in Boston was taken over by federal examiners causing a string of banks and trust companies in Lawrence, Lowell, Lynn, Brockton, Worcester, Salem, Gloucester, and Cambridge to collapse, freezing $60.5 million in deposits. The Boston bank catastrophe of December 1931 shared a common trait with those suffered in other states: the Massachusetts banks and trust companies were dragged down by a holding company of recent organization. The Federal National Bank had merged with various banks and trust companies during the 1920s to become a sizable institution in Boston, but it had only recently acquired other banks through purchase by a holding company, the Federal National Investment Trust, organized by Daniel Mulloney in

1929. It acquired banks while business was slack: the Bancroft Trust Company (deposits of $6 million) in 1929, the Brockton Trust Company (deposits of $1.5 million) in December 1930, and the Lawrence Trust Company in June 1931. Bank President Mulloney, like James Brown, Rogers Caldwell, and A.B. Banks, went on a shopping spree and acquired good assets and bad. As in Kentucky and Tennessee, the failure of the weak parent institution wrought havoc on affiliates, rather than weak subsidiaries dragging down a strong parent bank. Similarly and contemporaneously, the overextension of the Peoples Investment Company, the largest bank-holding company in South Carolina, brought down the whole chain of banks.[62]

The Depression caught up with the banks. Brash bankers played for high stakes and had taken on debts to expand while the winnings could be had cheaply. They had bet that the economy would turn around before their hands were called. Neither holding companies nor branch banking caused banks to fail. While we can conclude that lax state oversight helped sink 96 banks in Ohio in 1931, 19 national banks—supervised more rigorously by federal examiners—also failed in Ohio (freezing $26 million in deposits). The real cause of bank failures in Ohio was the same as in Illinois, South Carolina, Pennsylvania, or Massachusetts: terrible business conditions caused a dramatic contraction in bank loans, which, in turn, forced deposits to shrink. Nervousness about the immediate future convinced bankers to increase reserves by liquidating assets. They sold their best assets first, leaving banks with weaker assets, in many cases mortgages and commercial loans that proved difficult to collect. As the conditions of bank assets weakened, banks risked having their books seized by vigilant examiners, who were just doing their jobs. If weakened banks happened to be so unlucky as to be subjected to a bank run by their customers, they could easily be so drained of cash that they could not survive. Strong banks could and did survive ferocious runs, which perhaps served a Darwinian purpose by hurrying the extinction of weak banks. One can conclude, as many did at the time, that bad management killed banks. This was probably true in 1930 before the Depression had become "Great," but by 1931—and especially late 1931—even well-managed banks succumbed to the relentless strain of the economic slump. Even the comptroller of the currency offered no criticism of the management of 117 of the 311 national banks that had failed by October 31, 1931, and assumed that it was poor economic conditions that had ruined them.[63]

By late fall 1931 the entire country was in desperate straits. The federal government had done little to attack the problems that beset the economy. Until then, many Americans had agreed with Treasury Secretary Andrew Mellon that the best help the government could render was to stay out of the way and allow the economy to cure itself. Dour President Herbert Hoover had tried his best to cheer up the country with no noticeable impact on the economy. After the British suspended convertibility of the pound in September 1931, the U.S. economy and the nation's banks sank to such depths that much of the public decided the time for government intervention had arrived. Even many bankers came to that conclusion.

CHAPTER TWO

President Hoover Hesitates

When the stock market started its precipitous decline in October 1929, President Herbert Hoover thought his most useful contribution to calming the nerves of investors would be to remain quiet, which is what he did. However, when reporters clamored for some kind of statement from the president, Hoover finally said on October 25, "The fundamental business of the country, that is production and distribution, is on a sound and prosperous basis." The president, no doubt, believed that to be true, however, he also believed that business in the United States was divided into three fundamental parts—not two—and that the third, finance, was far from sound. Although he again refrained from comment when urged by editorial writers in November to join in the chorus of businessmen promoting the good sense of buying stocks while they were still a bargain, he recognized deflationary dangers to the economy. Thus, he urged his cabinet and the states' governors to speed up spending on public projects. He sought to calm the agitated waters by bringing together leading industrialists and financiers at the White House to determine the best course of action through sober discussion. White House conferences with Henry Ford, Walter Teagle of Standard Oil, Owen Young of General Electric, Pierre du Pont, Alfred Sloan of General Motors, Julius Rosenwald of Sears, and railroad, manufacturing, and insurance executives by the dozen produced promises to maintain current spending but no noticeable effect upon the condition of business.[1]

Herbert Hoover proved to be the wrong man to have in the White House during the economic collapse. Although this sentiment was soundly reinforced by the election results of 1932, evidence of Hoover's limitations abounded even before the Crash. Because he had never held an elected office before he occupied the White House, he was ill prepared to treat with politicians, especially hostile opponents out to discredit everything for which he stood. Although he had had to work with congressmen as secretary of commerce from 1921 to 1929, he had always done so as a presidential appointee, responsible to the president and not to Congress. Moreover, he saw himself more as a nonpartisan technocrat than as a Republican and did his best to promote that image. He was not without certain negotiating skills—as evidenced by his success in getting southwestern states to agree upon a water-sharing formula for the Colorado River—but he ultimately failed to understand that politicians had to be handled differently from businessmen, with whom he dealt more easily, and so stumbled badly on numerous occasions. He made public announcements at variance with private agreements previously forged with politicians; for example, after promising not to support a bill, he announced his approval to the press. He failed to recognize who his friends were in Congress and to make small concessions to them in order to bag bigger game. He vetoed minor bills backed by his Republican allies that he should have signed. In short, he did not know how to forge and keep alliances that could deliver compromise programs that he could live with even if they did not meet his ideal.[2]

In the few months he was in office before the Crash, Hoover managed to annoy and disappoint both Democrats and Republicans who could have been his friends and allies. Hoover became bogged down in endless wrangling over the tariff question and lost much goodwill in Congress through inept dealings to force a bill to his satisfaction. He also became entangled in sticky questions about the federal regulation of electric utilities. Hoover wanted to refurbish the Federal Power Commission—created under Wilson in 1920 to license power-generating dams on navigable interstate waterways— to supervise electrical utilities much as the Interstate Commerce Commission regulated railroads. But this proposal offered too little for progressives such as Nebraska Senator George Norris, who wanted federal generation and distribution of power, and too much for conservative Republicans such as Senate President Pro Tem George Moses of New Hampshire, who wanted to leave all such questions to the states. Hoover ultimately won a little more authority for the Federal Power Commission at the cost of strained relations with Congress.[3]

When Hoover needed congressional support in the dire circumstances that evolved after October 1929, he found it difficult to gain. To make matters worse, Hoover faced the fractured and bitterly divided 71st Congress, which would have been difficult for any president to tame. Fourteen rebellious Republican progressives, including George Norris, Hiram Johnson of California, James Couzens of Michigan, William Borah of Idaho, and Robert La Follette from Wisconsin—collectively dubbed "the sons of the wild jackass" by conservative Senator Moses—viewed Hoover as an errand boy for Wall Street. They offered no cooperation and proved impossible to appease on the rare occasions when Hoover tried. Hoover did not have much better rapport with conservative Republicans who controlled the levers of congressional machinery. Senate Majority Leader James E. Watson of Indiana; Republican Whip Simeon Fess of Ohio; and President Pro Tem Moses all judged Hoover little better than a socialist. This left Hoover only a minority group of Republican and Democratic moderates with whom he could reasonably expect to work, and he rarely proved adept at handling even them. Hoover had little more success with the press, whom he collectively irritated early in his presidency through his highhandedness and barely concealed contempt for journalists. Charles Michelson, a paid publicist for the Democratic National Committee and, hence, a professional propagandist, almost lamented that Hoover made his job too easy and was astounded how quickly Hoover alienated even staunchly Republican newsmen.[4]

During the congressional election campaigns of 1930, Republicans, and President Hoover in particular, tried to palliate the severity and longevity of the Depression. Hoover tried to reassure voters that the worst was behind the country and prosperity would soon return. He told the American Bankers Association in October 1930 that the origins of the Depression lay outside of the United States and doggedly stuck to this argument for the rest of his life. Democratic politicians, on the other hand, emphasized the economic troubles on election hustings and blamed it entirely on the Republicans, President Hoover in particular. Democratic National Chairman John Raskob; his friend and DNC executive committee chairman, Jouett Shouse; their publicist, Charley Michelson; and Dayton publisher and one-time Democratic presidential candidate, James Cox, hammered away at the Republicans' and Hoover's responsibility for the Smoot-Hawley Tariff, which they blamed for strangling trade and deepening the Depression. In fact, Hoover did not favor the tariff, and his reaction during the Senate debate was remarkably similar to that of Democrats: he mostly kept quiet and did nothing to help its passage. Once passed, his unenthusiastic announcement accepting the bill in June 1930 resembled an apology more than a celebration.[5]

While most voters did not blame Hoover for high unemployment, they did blame him for his constant cajoling to look on the bright side and his Pollyannaish assertions about the imminent return of prosperity. Democrats ceaselessly paraded Republican optimism and fecklessness before the voters, blaming the worsening situation squarely on Hoover and his party's policies. Claude Bowers, publisher of the Democratic-friendly *New York World*, charged on CBS radio that the Hoover administration was the union of "corrupt business with corrupt politics." Despite much bluster, the election was actually more a referendum on Prohibition than on the tariff question, and "drys" lost heavily to "wets." Republicans lost seats to Democrats although they retained control of both houses by a few seats. Nevertheless, Republican progressives generally fared better in the elections than moderate would-be allies of Hoover did, and, as a consequence, President Hoover was loath to call an uncooperative Congress into special session to address pressing problems. Hoover hoped the economy would right itself of its own accord before the feisty and rancorous 72nd Congress met in December 1931. Instead, conditions worsened.[6]

In his opening message to Congress in December 1929, Hoover asked Congress to look into bank reforms. True to his associative spirit he recommended that Congress join with bankers to recommend ways to strengthen the system. Otherwise, the president did not express great concern about the banking situation in the country. With bank troubles intensifying in 1931, discussion of bank reform grew more urgent. The leading Democrat on the Senate Banking and Currency Committee, Carter Glass of Virginia, had been agitating for some means to curb call loans for stock speculation, and saw this as a prime opportunity to promote a bill to rein in Wall Street. As the spiritual father of the Federal Reserve Bank, Glass naturally saw the bank as a powerful tool to guide bankers' actions and believed it the best device to stop call loans. Glass had also become persuaded that security-dealing affiliates of banks and trust companies encouraged banks to loan money for speculation, and he wanted such affiliates completely separated from banks and trust companies entrusted with depositors' monies as a means to curb loans for stock speculation. He also believed strongly that legalizing branch banking for national banks would greatly strengthen the whole system. In June 1930, Senator Glass had introduced a bill to correct these problems for consideration by the Senate Committee on Banking and Currency. Senator William King, Democrat from Utah, went even further and called for a thorough investigation of the whole banking system. Although King's resolution was passed, the Senate committee failed to report a bill before the 1930 elections intervened to forestall any serious reform of the system.[7]

In January the Senate Banking and Currency Committee began hearings into comprehensive bank reform. By then, Senator Glass had become alarmed at the scale of bank failures and decided to incorporate ideas into his bill to help stop them. He called for larger minimum capital requirements for members of the Federal Reserve System (then set at $25,000) and larger mandatory cash reserves to be maintained by banks. Most importantly, he decided that branch banking offered the sturdiest mechanism to keep deposits safe. He urged the creation of a federal "Liquidation Corporation" to take over the assets of banks that had already failed in order to quickly restore depositors' money and not flood the weak market with undervalued securities. With Congress out of session and not scheduled to meet until December, such legislation would not be considered by the full Senate for many months yet.[8]

Reforms favored by members of Hoover's administration went even further than the conservative senator from Virginia. Undersecretary of the Treasury Ogden Mills questioned the wisdom of the "dual system" of state-chartered and national-chartered banks and added his voice to others' calls for a separation of investment and commercial banking. In his first annual report to President Hoover, and again before Congressional hearings, Comptroller of the Currency John Pole called for legislation allowing regional branch-banking privileges to be extended to national banks. He was certain that once the wisdom of the device was demonstrated by national banks, state banking laws would be altered for state-chartered banks as well. In February 1930, he pointed out that the failure of 5,600 banks in nine years tied up nearly two billion dollars worth of deposits of over seven million customers, feeding calls for a major overhaul of the system. He noted that state borders did not provide rational boundaries for bank operations and recommended that national banks be allowed to operate in more than one state. This proposal was seconded by Undersecretary Mills. Governor of the Federal Reserve Board Eugene Meyer joined the chorus for reform and recommended ending the dual system and placing all banks under national supervision.[9]

For its part, the American Bankers Association stuck to its position of favoring unit banking and states' rights. The ABA had long been dominated by small bankers— always fearful of being dictated to by the largest of big-city banks— and usually reflected their views and interests. In 1929 the ABA softened somewhat on the question of branch banking and charged a committee, headed by Rudolph S. Hecht of the Hibernia Bank of New Orleans, to look into the question and make recommendations. The committee reported in 1930 that the ABA should endorse county-wide branch banking in rural areas and metropolitan area branch banking for cities. However, it stuck to its previous devotion to states' rights and called for such reforms to be implemented on a state-by-state basis, not imposed by the federal government. The ABA, after rebuffing branch-banking motions for years at their annual conventions, endorsed Hecht's proposal. However, in 1931 the ABA, on the recommendation of Hecht's committee, again rejected any federal hand in reforming the banking system in the United States. They insisted that the principal cause of bank failures remained poor management and foolish bankers and that it would be foolhardy for government at any level to save such bankers from their folly. Bankers must look to bankers for the solutions to their own problems, and to that end Hecht recommended better education for bankers and state regulators and more cooperation among bankers. That was the extent of bank reform endorsed by the ABA in 1931 and would remain so until Franklin D. Roosevelt took office in 1933.[10]

With his philosophical distaste for government-imposed remedies, Hoover was apprehensive about the looming meeting of a hostile House of Representatives in December. Congress had not met since March 1931, when the Republican-controlled 71st Congress disbanded. November 1930 polling actually left control of the next Congress in the hands of Republicans by a slim margin, but in the long interim between the elections and the convocation of the legislature, numerous by-elections and appointments delivered control of the House to the Democrats. Although Republicans still controlled the Senate, they held it by a one-vote margin (47–48), and the 14 Republican progressives— George Norris, William Borah, James Couzens, and Hiram Johnson, among others—called for new government programs to steer the economy. In order to forestall congressional action to buttress the banking sector, Hoover called for voluntary action by bankers themselves.[11]

The Credit Paradox

Business conducted by banks had clearly dwindled over time. Loans by banks slowly ebbed from December 1929. At first the decline was not dramatic, but in early 1931 credit offered by banks shrank alarmingly. Between December 1929 and December 1931 credit shrank by 25 percent. Credit withered most severely in the Chicago and Atlanta Federal Reserve Districts, where the decline was close to 37 percent. The Saint Louis and Kansas City districts were not far behind, with credit contracting by 35 percent. As loans offered by banks dwindled, business stalled and the economy slowed even more.[12]

Many businessmen, officials, and even bankers assumed that the decline in credit contributed heavily to the enormity of the Depression. However, they disagreed on the reasons for the decline in bank lending to businesses. Did banks refuse to loan money? Or did businesses refuse to borrow? Even George Anderson, the ABA representative in Washington, D.C., was not sure, and called this question, "the credit paradox." Magnus Alexander of the National Industrial Conference Board spoke for many when he asserted that during the course of 1930 and 1931 bankers became nervous and refused to lend money to any but their most reliable clients. Thus, reserves of cash built up in bank vaults and did nothing to fuel the economy in the spring of 1932. William Wallace Atterbury, president of the Pennsylvania Railroad, similarly argued that there was little difference between a bank vault and a mattress: money in either place did the economy no good. The dearth of loans to businesses greatly frustrated Federal Reserve Board Governor Eugene Meyer, who had pleaded and browbeaten Federal Reserve governors to increase the money supply through open-market purchases of securities, only to have the extra money sit in bank vaults as excess reserves. President Hoover believed that bankers mulishly sat on piles of cash that could be helping business. Even the chief economist at the Chase National Bank, Benjamin Anderson, lamented that banks outside New York City withheld credit from reliable customers in order to preserve high levels of liquidity. This complaint was widely echoed in farm states where farmers and small businessmen protested that banks would not accept their collateral for loans because the bigger banks, on which the small banks depended, would not approve the security. G.A. Middleton, a cotton merchant in Charleston, complained that banks would no longer accept his warehoused cotton as collateral for loans because they were too nervous to part with the cash in their vaults. A bank president in North Carolina affirmed to Carter Glass that was specifically the case at his bank.[13]

The uncertain value of collateral weighed upon the system. Michigan Senator Arthur Vandenberg—a banker from Grand Rapids—suggested to Federal Reserve Governor Eugene Meyer that American banks be allowed to adopt the system of "Lombard loans" common in much of Europe, where individual bankers are allowed to accept any collateral they judged worthy. This would address the problem of insufficient security for loans that plagued businesses and banks in the Midwest. Meyer responded that United States banks held collateral worth 30 times as much as all money borrowed from the Federal Reserve System in 1930. From Meyer's perspective, there was little the Fed could do to shake money loose from the bankers' tight grip. As banks all over tightened their loan standards and viewed applications more critically, the Federal Reserve Bank of New York concluded, "To an increasing number of borrowers credit became difficult to obtain at any price." It is difficult to fault banks that refused a loan to a Kentucky concrete processor without enough business to offer any accounts receivable as collateral. All he had to offer for security was his machinery, which banks refused to consider.[14]

Another school of thought argued that worried businessmen avoided borrowing. Lehigh University economist Frederick Bradford argued that since 1929 companies had struggled to get out of debt and in 1931 wanted to stay out of debt. Rather than borrowing from banks, companies operated on their revenues and did not distribute earnings as dividends, preferring to keep them as working capital. Indeed, business borrowing by the leading 310 industrial companies was down by 26 percent from 1929 (from $1.3 billion in 1929 to $993 million in 1931.) George Edwards, chair of the Economics Department at C.C.N.Y., echoed Professor Bradford. He pointed out that banks were eager to loan money to companies with the highest credit rating because their paper was the easiest to sell to raise cash and there was always a willing market for such investments, but those very corporations had reduced borrowing and instead chose to operate on their revenues.[15]

It seems reasonable to conclude that businesses did not want to borrow and banks did not want to lend. When the National Industrial Conference Board undertook a survey in 1932 to determine if bank credit was being withheld from American business, it concluded that banks had indeed tightened credit starting in the fall of 1931. As banks searched for liquidity, they refused new loans to old customers, declined to renew loans when previous practice had been to renew, and, less frequently, called in loans before they were due. Although banks were reluctant to recall loans, some banks had little choice when faced with the need to replace diminished reserves. On the other hand, the Conference Board's survey of 3,438 manufacturing concerns revealed that almost half had had no difficulty obtaining credit since 1929. Among those firms without credit problems the Conference Board found that many had not requested any loans since 1929. Almost 39 percent of the surveyed firms did not avail themselves of bank loans even before 1929. Thus, about 60 percent of manufacturing firms — the concern of the Conference Board — depended on banks in any event. Only 466 (13.5 percent of firms surveyed) reported they had been denied credit since 1929. Not surprisingly, half of those firms had fewer than 250 employees, and 31 percent had fewer than 100. Only one in five firms seeking credit was denied, and one in three of very small firms. The largest firms were the least likely to seek credit and the least likely to be refused. Half of refused firms had "high" or "good" credit ratings, according to R.G. Dunn and Company, contributing to a sense of grievance against bankers among two-thirds of those businessmen refused credit. The report pointedly noted that a large measure of resentment by businessmen against bankers — even among businessmen who had no credit problems — was directed against New York City banks, which many assumed exercised too much influence over all other banks.[16]

In fact, loans had declined from 77 percent of deposits in June 1929 to 68 percent in June 1931. There were certainly factors that discouraged banks from offering loans. Small-business bankruptcies and mortgage defaults were rising at frightening rates. The ABA noted with great alarm that the federal court in Philadelphia had ruled that banks could not sell notes and securities held as collateral for loans to companies that had declared bankruptcy, except by permission of the court. This froze bank-held collateral while bankruptcy proceedings ground on and on in federal courts. In 1930, 24,000 banks held $11.5 billion of such collateral, and many companies tread perilously close to bankruptcy, inducing justifiable hesitancy among bankers. At the same time bankers complained that in the summer of 1931 commercial paper sold for only 1¾ percent, and New York banks had large reserves of cash they could not find customers to borrow. Indeed, dealing in bankers' acceptances — the most fungible of commercial paper and the easiest and most efficient way for banks and reputable companies to finance trade — declined dramatically in the fall of 1931. Outstanding acceptances (60-to-90-day loans that financed inventories) had fallen from a high of $1.7 billion in December 1929 to $974 million by December 1931. A Cleveland banker complained to Ohio Senator Robert Bulkley that New York banks had stopped buying his paper and, thus, his bank had stopped offering such loans to its clients. Federal Reserve Banks actually increased their purchases of acceptances two- and threefold until by November 1931 they held over three-quarters of outstanding acceptances. It would be difficult to pin this particular problem on the Fed.[17]

Economists and bankers at the time were convinced that people withdrew their money from banks and hoarded it at home out of fear for the security of banks. In the fall of 1931, President Hoover confided to journalists the dangers posed by hoarding, but was loath to say too much about it lest the jittery public pull even more money out of banks. He finally made a public appeal in February 1932 for Americans to leave their money in banks and not hoard it in cookie jars. The Federal Reserve Bank noted a decrease in bank deposits in the fall of 1930 and a steady increase in demand for $50 and $100 bills, which had little practical use at the time. By the end of 1931, the number of large denomination bills in public hands had doubled, and Federal Reserve officials assumed the extra $700 million in large bills was demanded by hoarders. In response, Treasury Secretary Ogden Mills offered the public one-year bonds at 2 percent interest in small denominations ($50, $100, and $500) as a device to put hoarded money back to use.[18]

The diminution of deposits—both time and demand—closely paralleled the drop-off in business activity throughout the country. Bank debits and clearings fell by billions of dollars from spring to fall in 1930, and again from spring to fall in 1931. Sales were terrible for businesses of all kinds, and businesses paid off bank loans, which were not renewed either because companies grew increasingly wary of being in debt, or because banks refused to renew loans as they searched for greater liquidity. Nervous individuals increasingly withdrew savings from banks to hide it in suitcases and tin cans: currency held outside of banks increased by $819 million from June 1931 to December. As business velocity slowed, bank loans and deposits declined, and as payrolls shrank and people reluctantly relied on their savings, time deposits slowly ebbed.[19]

Greatly worried by slowing economy, President Hoover called 24 Federal Reserve bankers and Treasury officials to a meeting at the White House to discuss the national situation in September 1931. He hoped he could count on voluntary cooperation among America's bankers to steady the financial situation. Hoover philosophically favored private initiative, perhaps guided by advice from government experts, but he believed voluntary action undertaken in a spirit of public-spirited cooperation would inevitably lead to the most desirable ends, both public and private. Hoover proposed that the largest banks subscribe to a $500 million fund to make loans to banks that would not qualify for Federal Reserve loans, either because they were not members of the system or because the quality of their securities was too weak. If half a billion dollars proved insufficient, he suggested the new agency be authorized to borrow an additional one billion dollars from cooperating banks. Hoover further suggested that bankers organize committees in each Federal Reserve district to review loans to worthy banks. To hammer out the details of the proposal, a private meeting of 40 financial figures was quietly arranged at Treasury Secretary Andrew Mellon's house in Washington, D.C., early in October. Hoover suggested to the bankers and insurance company heads that instead of calling in weak loans, it would be better to make new loans to banks weighed down by too many under-performing loans, in order to buy time for everyone involved. Federal Reserve Governor Meyer, although skeptical that the voluntary association would be enough, promised Federal Reserve assistance to such an organization, should it be formed. Melvin Traylor of the First National Bank of Chicago and Walter Lichtenstein, chief economist at the Federal Reserve Bank of Chicago, were also deeply skeptical of the proposal. Other bankers showed little enthusiasm for the project, but agreed at least to discuss it with fellow bankers in their home states.[20]

The next day the dejected president forced himself to attend a World Series baseball game in Philadelphia to be seen acting casually in public. He was met by chants of "we want beer!" That evening, the bankers agreed to form the proposed agency and call it the National Credit Corporation (NCC). Feeling that the bankers were uninterested in loaning money to save farm mortgages, Hoover met with the chairman of the Federal Farm Loan Board, Paul Bestor, to discuss setting up a separate government program to loan an additional billion dollars to institutions making farm loans. The next day he met with 32 congressional leaders from both houses to discuss his proposals. He told them that fear prompted people to withdraw money from banks and hoard it, making it unavailable for normal credit use. He argued that the nation needed action to restore public confidence in the banks and that his proposed agencies would do just that. The New York Clearing House Association had already agreed to make available $150 million, or 2 percent of their deposits, to fund the NCC. He asked the assembled congressmen to consider legislation liberalizing the rules to allow the Federal Reserve Bank to issue greater amounts of currency to increase liquidity in the country. As Hoover had predicted, some members backed a rescue agency set up and funded by the government, while others recoiled at such government intrusion into the free market. Carter Glass, always intensely interested in protecting the mission and integrity of the Federal Reserve Bank, objected to liberalizing the backing for Reserve notes and loans. After sometimes heated discussion, Hoover agreed that if his proposed voluntary agency did not work, he would ask Congress to form a government agency, similar to the War Finance Corporation, to serve the same purpose.[21]

Sections of the NCC were set up in each of the 12 Federal Reserve districts and subsidiaries established in each state as National Credit Associations (NCA). Only banks that joined the NCA by buying stock were eligible to seek loans from the NCC. However, New York bankers knew from the beginning they would have to put up most of the capital for the new organization and acted quickly to protect their interests. To spread the responsibility, a board was chosen that included prominent bankers from Chicago, St. Louis, and Boston. The board quickly agreed upon rules for granting loans, accepting collateral, and establishing regional review to assess the quality of applications. The American Bankers Association greeted the creation of the NCC with muted enthusiasm. ABA Vice President Frank Sisson, of the Guaranty Trust Company of New York, asked members to support the project, which they generally did. The ABA joined President Hoover in crediting news about the NCC with injecting renewed optimism into the economy in October and November 1931. Hoarding and bank runs slowed, and, indeed, a small uptick in activity followed its implementation. Bank clearings, which had fallen dramatically in July and August, picked up in October. The number of bank failures, which had risen alarmingly from August through October to 522, dipped in November to 169.[22]

The plan was greeted with genuine relief in much of the country, where bankers believed the NCC would provide them with much needed help. Alfred Sloan, of General Motors, and William Atterbury, of the Pennsylvania Railroad, hailed the creation of the NCC as a great deed by President Hoover. The clearing house associations of Hartford, Cleveland, Pittsburgh, and Chicago expressed confidence in the worthiness of the project and promised to help it. The National Association of Mutual Savings Banks joined in praising the new organization. The Michigan Association of the NCC quickly got under way after hundreds of bankers met in Detroit and greeted the plan with enthusiasm. The Peoples Wayne County Bank joined and claimed to have helped 50 Michigan banks in only a few months. Bankers meeting in Indianapolis thought the NCC might help restore confidence among the public, but had little confidence themselves that the money offered by the new organization would do much to restore frozen accounts. On November 7, Goodwin Rhett, president of the Peoples State Bank of Charleston, South Carolina, with 49 branches, informed South Carolina NCA Secretary Henry Johnson that unless his bank obtained a $500,000 loan immediately, it could not open on Monday morning. Johnson quickly convoked a meeting of the state NCA, which approved the loan, pending delivery of acceptable security. The Peoples Bank had been hemorrhaging deposits for months, and the NCA loan bought the bank some time. But before December was out Rhett was back seeking another $200,000, which he received. Two days later Rhett delivered his bank into the hands of the state bank examiner. The NCA brought his bank momentary relief, but not salvation. In its fleeting existence the South Carolina NCA loaned $1.9 million to eight troubled banks. Four of them, which together borrowed $1,425,000, closed their doors before the end of 1933. One of those banks, the Central Union Bank of Columbia, held $10 million in assets in 1931 and was headed by the chairman of the state NCA. All NCA loans in South Carolina were eventually repaid.[23]

The NCC provided a momentary psychological boost to bankers and at least temporarily ameliorated the banking crisis. The seepage that had been leaching money from banks by the millions every week had temporarily slowed. The stock markets rallied and stopped their dismal slide and exports slowed dramatically. But money already withdrawn from banks did not return, and soon the heavy withdrawals began again. A string of high-profile foreclosures on hotels and big new apartment buildings in cities dampened the sense of hopefulness among citizens, businessmen, and bankers alike. Seizures of property for nonpayment of taxes continued apace in November, and faced with declining prices, businesses continued to shed employees in an effort to cut costs. By mid–December 1931 the apparent soothing effect had worn off. The modest $1 million transferred by the NCC to the Exchange Trust Company in Boston, to be parceled out to area banks as needed during the December crisis, had no noticeable impact on the events. Bank failures nationwide jumped to 353 in December, tying up $319.3 million in deposits. Public confidence in banks remained shaky and even longtime public officials, such as the former senator from Utah Frank Cannon, privately expressed doubts about the viability of the entire system. Postal savings accounts, backed by the federal government, grew from a modest $165 million in January 1930 to $245 million in December as people transferred their savings from banks to a government entity. With each passing month in 1931, the amounts in postal accounts grew by millions until by December 1931 they held $605 million. This was dwarfed by the $19.1 billion accrued in life-insurance policies and by the $10 billion still held in mutual savings banks. But the trend was unmistakable and noticed by many: despite actions by the government, bank customers were withdrawing their savings and looking for safer havens. It was going to take more than the NCC to restore the economy.[24]

The NCC was crippled at birth, however. In the event that a bank obligated to the NCC banks failed, the NCC contributing banks would have to stand in line along with everybody else to reclaim what they could from the bank's assets. Moreover, the Michigan State Supreme Court ruled shortly after the formation of the NCC that public depositors, such as county governments, had priority claims on the salvageable assets of failed banks. Thus, NCC member bank depositors and shareholders would be subsidizing local governments by helping to rescue their deposits in failed banks, with little hope of reclaiming their own investments. Although welcoming the NCC, Michigan Senator Arthur Vandenberg saw it as a stopgap measure. Something more powerful was still needed. The chairman of the First National Bank of Detroit, Wilson Mills, agreed and wrote to President Hoover urging him to convene Congress as soon as possible to set up a new body with greater power, backed by the federal government, to shore up the banks. It had become obvious to many that the NCC was insufficient tonic for the illness that beset America's banks.[25]

In any event, the NCC was seen by the men who ran it as a temporary measure, and the bankers who contributed to it were justifiably leery of losing their investment. When Congress met, Democrats immediately criticized the organization for its reluctance to grant loans. They did so with good reason: by early December the board in New York had approved only $10 million in loans. By the time it went out of business, it had loaned only $144 million of its $500 million capital to 644 banks. When they agreed to form the group, the bankers had expected that the federal government, backed by the Treasury, would step in to make loans directly to banks. Bankers who had contributed to the NCC, moreover, expected the federal government to assume their loans, if a successor organization should be created. One was created, it did not take over the loans, and the NCC ended as a money-losing proposition for the banks that had agreed to cooperate in its formation.[26]

While the NCC was being organized in October, President Hoover suggested another bromide to soothe the troubled banks. Because the number of defaulted mortgages posed enormous problems for the banks, he, like many others, believed if foreclosures could be postponed or avoided altogether, everybody would be better off. As secretary of commerce, Hoover had mooted setting up a system of regional mortgage banks similar to the Federal Reserve System, which did not accept mortgages as security at its discount windows. Hoover revived the idea of the Federal Home Loan Board (FHLB) in October 1931. He hoped that, supplied with $600 million in government money, the system would buy mortgages from financial institutions and resell them as debentures (bonds) to banks and insurance companies. Building societies and savings and loans generally liked the idea. President of the of U.S. League of Building and Loan Associations, William E. Best, told Congress that the FHLB "will lead the way to a recovery for American business." Wilson Mills claimed that every banker he talked to "gives the heartiest public approval to the president's plan. Many of our prominent citizens are likewise doing so." Because worries about defaulting on a mortgage weighed so heavily on the minds of so many, newspapers generally greeted the proposal favorably. The *Detroit Free Press* announced the plan with banner headlines.[27]

Not everyone was so enthusiastic. Indiana Senator James Watson, who backed the bill, surveyed real-estate and mortgage-handling opinion nationwide and found it to be divided roughly evenly between proponents and opponents. The institutions that were expected to buy the instruments greeted the proposed FHLB with cool reserve. The ABA generally distrusted government programs to loosen credit and considered this to be another such scheme. The Merchants Association suggested the scheme might be helpful in the short run, but federal intrusion in the market was never a good thing in the long run.[28]

President Hoover's proposals to address the crisis also met resistance from within his own administration. By fall 1931, Treasury Secretary Andrew Mellon had fallen seriously out of step with Hoover. Mellon, who had amassed a vast fortune as an industrialist and banker in Pittsburgh, was very much a product of the 19th century and firmly committed to a laissez-faire economy. He believed that the best way to end the Depression was to allow it to run its course and let prices find their natural level. If that forced thousands of companies into bankruptcy, and millions of workers into temporary unemployment, so be it. That approach to the economy had lost most adherents by late 1931, when Hoover began taking more advice from Undersecretary Ogden Mills, and Mellon became an object of public scorn and ridicule in the press. Mellon considerably aggravated his own problems when, in September 1931, a banking panic hit his hometown, Pittsburgh, where he owned large interests in numerous banks and trust companies. When local bankers gathered to save what they could, Mellon adopted a most unhelpful attitude: poorly managed banks ought to be allowed to fail. Mellon also stood to gain considerable financial advantage from the distress of one of his largest competitors, the Bank of Pittsburgh, N.A. He offered to help save the bank with a small loan in exchange for a majority interest in the bank's stock. This extraordinary proposal from a high government official was certainly not the financial statesmanship people expected. President Hoover, as well as the hometown press, were gravely disappointed in his secretary of the Treasury, as were the thousands of Pittsburghers and city businesses who had deposited $44 million in the Bank of Pittsburgh, N.A., before it went into receivership, freezing their accounts.[29]

Hoover had other problems aside from sharp divisions with his secretary of the Treasury: in December he would have to work with an irascible Congress controlled by coalition Democrats and progressive Republicans. He had demonstrated little skill in dealing with the Republican-dominated Congress and now he would have to negotiate with the Democrats to find a path out of the morass. The inevitable convocation of the 72nd Congress came on December 7, 1931, and Democrats controlled the House under Speaker John Nance "Jack" Garner from Texas, who proved to be a tricky partner for the president. Although a loyal and partisan Democrat, Garner was also moderately conservative with orthodox economic views and not overly prone to populist enthusiasms. The world views of the two leaders were not notably different. While neither of the two called himself a progressive, both believed that active government could improve the quality of peoples' lives, and looked favorably upon many progressive innovations of the prewar era. Their personalities, however, were worlds apart, and Garner was not endowed with the necessary surfeit of patience to deal with Hoover.[30]

Having both Secretary Mellon and Speaker Garner wielding power in the capital proved to be a prescription for dysfunction. After spending 21 years as an obscure representative from Uvalde, Texas, Garner came to national attention in 1921 as the leading opponent of Treasury Secretary Andrew Mellon's proposed tax cuts. In an effort to boost investment during the severe slump of 1921, Mellon recommended that the steep income-tax rates imposed during the war be reduced from 65 percent to 25 percent. Only the richest Americans paid the highest rate and Mellon did not suggest that the 4-to-8 percent rate paid by average Americans be reduced, because he did not look to them for business investment. In any event, Treasury reports showed that those who paid the highest rates were channeling their incomes into tax-free government securities to the detriment of commercial securities. Mellon had hoped that lowering the tax rate on these richest Americans would coax them to reinvest in commercial projects. But Garner had no interest in any of this. His interest was in electing a Democratic Congress in 1922 and a Democratic president in 1924. Supported by progressive Republicans, Garner was able to defeat Mellon's tax proposal in 1921 and keep the highest rate at 50 percent. When Mellon resubmitted his plan in 1923, Garner again led a coalition of Democrats and Republican insurgents to derail the proposal and kept the latest reduction of the highest tax rate to 40 percent. In the fight Garner attacked Mellon and the Republicans as the servants of the trusts, who sought to shift their burden onto the backs of the poorest Americans. Garner certainly knew that the poorest Americans paid no income taxes, and only 18 percent of working people made enough money to even be required to file a tax return at all. Unquestionably Garner was the more astute politician, and Mellon proved himself to be vote-deaf by resubmitting the same proposal in 1923 that had been defeated by Garner's demagoguery in 1921, without even adding a sweetener to lower the income-tax rates on the most modest tax payers.[31]

A friendlier Congress elected in the Republican landslide year of 1924 gave Secretary Mellon the tax cuts he sought in 1926 and freed all Americans who earned less than $4,000 a year from any taxes at all on their incomes. Modest workers got their tax break as did the rich. However, Garner's enmity for Mellon lived on, and Mellon attracted another inveterate opponent in Michigan Senator James Couzens, who first sat on and then chaired a committee investigating Internal Revenue Service favoritism toward Mellon interests (among others) during Mellon's tenure. The hearings dragged on for more than a year without turning up anything incriminating, but Mellon greatly resented the attacks upon his integrity and repaid the favor by opening an IRS investigation into Senator Couzens's tax returns. The IRS case against Couzens also dragged on (for three years) and similarly found no cause for reproach against the senator. It certainly did produce another permanent nemesis for Secretary Mellon, with ultimately important political consequences for the Hoover administration when it needed the cooperation of Senator Couzens. Jack Garner launched another attack upon Mellon late in 1928 when he charged that the IRS gave undue tax leniency to companies associated with Secretary Mellon and his family. Another congressional investigation of Mellon interests found nothing remiss, but the inflamed mutual hostility between Garner and Mellon made their future cooperation unlikely. Although a Republican, Couzens was already a confirmed foe of Hoover and most everything he stood for, and his unshakable hostility toward Hoover and bankers ultimately proved tragic for the nation when Couzens stood at the center of the 1933 Michigan bank crisis that inaugurated the nationwide shutdown of the banking system.[32]

James J. Couzens, was born in 1872 in Chatham, Ontario, and at 18 moved to Detroit where he took a job as a railroad car checker for the Michigan Central Railroad. He rose through the ranks to coal clerk, where his dogged perfectionism and diligence so impressed one railroad client, coal dealer Alex Malcomson, that Malcomson hired him to work for his company. Always on the lookout for new business deals that offered the possibility for profits, Malcomson entered into a partnership with young Henry Ford to build motor cars. Malcomson installed the eagle-eyed and upright Couzens in the fledgling firm to keep an eye on the books and protect his interests. Couzens quickly proved himself indispensable to both Ford and Malcomson by seeing to it that the Ford Motor Company made money rather than lose it and by overseeing the establishment of a vast network of Ford dealerships to sell the cars. Couzens proved crucial to the phenomenal success of Ford and his company. When, in 1906, Henry Ford reorganized the company and jettisoned some of his original investors, who had proven themselves obstacles to Ford's willful plans for the company, Ford received 59 percent of the Ford Motor Company's stock and Couzens 11 percent. Malcomson was one of the obstacles disposed of.[33]

By 1915 James Couzens was vice president and treasurer of the Ford Motor Company. But the usually fraught relations between Couzens and Ford became more tense yet: with war raging in Europe, Couzens's sympathies leaned toward the British, while Henry Ford was resolutely antiwar. When Ford wrote an editorial in the company newspaper stridently opposing loans to England and insulting to Lord Balfour — then in Washington negotiating for them — Couzens objected that the company newspaper was an inappropriate venue for such opinions. When Ford forcefully disagreed, Couzens resigned. Upon his resignation Couzens became president of the Bank of Detroit and a director of the Detroit Trust Company. He had already broadened his interests by entering local politics in 1913 when he became commissioner of street railways and an ardent proponent of public ownership of city transit. His long and dogged campaign to place the city streetcars under public control pitted him against many of the city's most powerful businessmen, who either sat on the board of the Detroit Union Railways or took its side. The city finally took over streetcars in 1922. In 1916 Couzens took on crime and police corruption by becoming commissioner of police, and profited from the associated publicity to catapult himself into the mayor's chair in 1919. As mayor of Detroit, his righteousness, inflexibility, and hot-headedness alienated more of the population who had until then remained outside the aura of Couzens's impatience and bad temper.[34]

When Michigan Senator Truman Newberry became entangled in scandal and resigned in 1922, Michigan's progressive governor, Alex Groesbeck, appointed Couzens to fill his remaining term. Couzens found the new position so much to his liking that he ran for it in 1924 and won, and still sat as a Republican senator from Michigan when Congress debated its course in 1932. Couzens was also an extremely wealthy man. When Ford bought out all the other shareholders in the Ford Motor Company in 1919, Couzens held out for $13,444 per share, or a total of $29,308,858. By the time he sold out to Henry Ford, Couzens had already reaped an additional $10 million in dividends. Couzens's millions from Ford aroused the interest of Secretary Mellon and the IRS at a most providential time for all involved, but relegated a sad legacy when broad cooperation was needed to solve the nation's economic crisis.[35]

In an effort to coordinate his policies with the Congress, Hoover asked Republican leaders Indiana Senator Watson and New York Representative Bertrand H. Snell to find out what the Democrats intended to propose for the upcoming term. They both reported that the Democrats were determined to take no responsibility for any program and to pin the blame for conditions on the Republican administration in order to win the presidency in 1932. This was not just the resentful ranting of frustrated Republicans. When discussing Democratic plans for the up-coming Congress, South Carolina Senator James Byrnes wrote to his friend, Arkansas Senator and Minority Leader Joe Robinson:

> In my opinion it would be unwise for the Democrats to prepare a definite legislative pro-
> gram. The responsibility for legislation rests with the party in power. The people should be
> constantly advised that they are responsible. Should we prepare a legislative program, we
> would of course, be unable to enact legislation carrying it into effect and would only suc-
> ceed in diverting attention from the responsibility of the Republican administration.... Of
> course, if the Democrats organize the House, the situation will be different so far as that
> body is concerned. However, we will still lack the power to legislate as long as we have a
> Republican president and I think we should, if possible, let the responsibility rest where it
> belongs, with the Republican administration.[36]

Byrnes and the Democratic leadership in the Senate acted on Senator Byrnes's advice and started the new Congress by lobbing attacks against Hoover and the Republicans, who still supposedly controlled the upper house. Byrnes went on to become an early backer of presidential contender Franklin Delano Roosevelt and a close advisor to Roosevelt on legislative matters after the Democratic electoral triumph of 1932. Byrnes's attitude toward cooperation and pinning responsibility for catastrophe on the political opposition did not change after November 1932, when, as we shall see, it became the policy of the president-elect.[37]

When the House organized in December 1931, the Democrats held 220 seats and the

Republicans 214, giving new Speaker of the House, Jack Garner, a slender majority. When President Hoover asked the new Congress to take a number of steps to address the Depression, including the creation of a temporary new body modeled upon the War Finance Corporation (WFC) and a federal office to buy mortgages, the reaction was predictably partisan. Nevertheless, bills to create the new offices were introduced in both houses directly, on December 9, and Speaker Garner promised the president he would move it through the House with dispatch. After much loud and divisive debate the Reconstruction Finance Corporation (RFC) was created in January 1932 to loan money to otherwise sound financial institutions that needed time to get their affairs in order. Such loans to banks, savings and loans, mortgage companies, insurance companies, utilities, and railroads had to be fully secured with collateral, but the collateral did not need to meet the stringent requirements of the Federal Reserve Bank. President Hoover promised that the new organization would be run as a responsible business and not waste the taxpayers' initial $500 million investment on lost causes. The RFC was authorized at the outset to borrow another $1.5 billion from the Treasury if necessary.[38]

Democrats generally favored the proposal and, after some bitter sniping, accepted the RFC as a good idea. Since numerous senators, including Republican Arthur Vandenberg from Michigan and Democrat Robert Bulkley of Ohio, had asked Hoover to revive the War Finance Board, strong backing in the Senate was assured. Hoover's greatest obstacles proved to be Republican progressives, including Michigan Senator James Couzens, who denounced the bill as a gift to railroads; Republican Representative Fiorello La Guardia of New York, who proclaimed the bill "a millionaire's dole"; and Wisconsin's Senator John Blaine, who delayed the bill's passage by weeks by refusing to accept the House version as the Senate's. Nebraska Senator George Norris said of the bill, "You are using the taxpayers' money and giving to the very bankers, some of them international bankers, who are largely responsible for the condition in which the country now finds itself." California Republican progressive Hiram Johnson went a step further when he wrote to his sons,

> Congress has passed a great Act for giving bankers a dole.... The Israelites who control us by controlling our money, on both sides of the political fence, were united in favor of the measure. On the Republican side we had the Morgan House, Otto Kahn, and Hoover's financial advisor, Eugene Meyer. On the Democratic side were Barney Baruch and his co-workers in the Wilson vineyard.... I am mighty suspicious of a scheme which had its genesis as this one did, and which was pushed to success by such doubtful individuals.[39]

Banking opinion was cautiously optimistic, thinking the proposal could not hurt, but those favoring fundamental banking reform feared it might take the place of more useful legislation. Businessmen represented in the United States Chamber of Commerce, railroad and insurance executives, and many important bankers, such as Melvin Traylor of Chicago, testified before Congress on the worthiness of the project. Newspaper response to the RFC was likewise generally favorable. The *Chicago Tribune* editors thought it would be helpful but worried that it could not be kept free from the corruption of political pressure and favoritism. The *New York Times* castigated the progressives for blocking the bill's passage and called it the right "tonic for the patient." The *Baltimore Evening Sun* thought it would greatly reduce bank failures.[40]

To help smooth passage of the bill, Hoover agreed to pick directors acceptable to Congress and allow Speaker Garner and Minority Leader Robinson to pick two of the seven. Garner, seconded by Carter Glass, picked Texas businessman Jesse Jones. Neither Garner nor Glass knew Jones well, but both liked him and were well acquainted with his reputation for hard work, dynamism, and integrity. Senator Robinson picked Harvey C. Couch, a loyal Democratic railroad and utility tycoon from his home state of Arkansas who knew banks and finance well and held typically orthodox economic views. Hoover appointed Federal Reserve Board Governor Eugene Meyer chairman of the new organization, hoping his knowledge and prestige would convince bankers and the Federal Reserve to cooperate in the venture. To represent the West and small banks Hoover chose Wilson McCarthy, a Republican banker from Utah. New Treasury Secretary Ogden Mills and Farm Board Chairman Paul Bestor — both New Yorkers well-connected on Wall Street — rounded out the board of directors of the RFC.[41]

To counterbalance Mills and Bestor, Hoover tapped Chicago banker and former vice president of the United States, Charles Dawes, then serving as the American ambassador to Great Britain, to act as president of the RFC. As a midwesterner leery of Wall-Street dominance over the nation's business, Dawes appealed to most Democrats; however, the volatile Dawes proved to be of questionable suitability, which became apparent only after his resignation six months later. Dawes had trained as a lawyer and invested his earnings, first in Nebraska real estate and then in banking. In the 1890s he developed an interest in gas utilities and made a fortune buying up small gas companies. After a failed bid in 1902 to become senator from Illinois, he founded the Central Trust Company of Illinois in Chicago with prominent backers. Moving in the highest circles of business and politics, Dawes amassed a tidy fortune and a vast web of friends and connections, which ultimately placed him in the vice presidency of the United States under Calvin Coolidge and at the Court of St. James under Hoover.[42]

By 1929 the "Dawes Bank"[43] had absorbed the business of many other Chicago trust companies, banks, and savings and loans to become one of the premier financial institutions of Chicago, capitalized at $12 million. While Dawes negotiated loans for Germany and did his part to slow a worldwide naval armaments race, his bank in Chicago merged with others and grew to gargantuan proportions. In 1929 the Dawes Bank created the Central Illinois Company to serve as a holding company for banks in Iowa, Ohio, Michigan, Missouri, Kentucky, Minnesota, Wisconsin, Nebraska, Pennsylvania, New York, California, Oregon, and Washington. The ambitions of the Dawes Bank were not modest. When the panic hit Chicago in 1931 the bank played a prominent part in trying to save as much as possible. And in July 1931 it merged with the National Bank of the Republic and the Chicago Trust Company to form the Central Republic Bank and Trust Company, becoming one of the largest financial institutions in America.[44]

The RFC set up shop in the old Commerce Building and was able to start processing loans within weeks because it quickly staffed its positions with personnel with prior experience of considering emergency loans. Federal Reserve Governor Eugene Meyer, chairman of the RFC Board, had previously been a director of the War Finance Corporation, which had formally gone out of business only a few years before. Most of the responsibilities and much of the professional staff of the WFC had been absorbed by various farm-relief agencies established by the federal government during the 1920s. Thus, Meyer called back to work as many of the old WFC staff as could be rounded up quickly in Washington. Meyer also guaranteed the close cooperation of the Federal Reserve Bank and its 12 district offices. The RFC set up regional offices immediately in all Federal Reserve districts by relying on the bank's personnel, facilities, and vast network of contacts among local bankers and businessmen. Committees were quickly cobbled together in every state to receive and assess loan requests submitted to RFC regional offices. The regional offices also benefited by recruiting staff from the old WFC and government farm-relief agencies in the states. Thus, the precedent of the WFC and farm-relief programs proved vital in getting the RFC up and running with exceptional speed. Journalist Willard M. Kiplinger, who visited the RFC headquarters at midnight in March, described it as humming with activity, just as it was again at 9 A.M. the next morning.[45]

Dawes and the other directors of the new RFC decided to turn their attention to banks before taking on the thorny problem of the nation's ailing railroads. The first loan, for $15 million, went to A.P. Giannini's Bank of America on February 8. The operation of the RFC loan program bore immediate results. The fall of 1931 had been catastrophic: 305 banks closed in September; in October, 522 banks had failed; in November, another 169; and in December, 353 more banks suspended operations. The RFC began dispensing money in February, when it loaned $45 million to banks and trust companies, and another $25 million to railroads. Loan approvals increased rapidly in March when another $115 million was allocated to banks, $60 million to railroads, and $18 million to savings and loans, insurance companies, and other financial organizations. In two months, 974 applications had been approved. The effort appeared to be having an impact: in January 1932, 334 banks failed; in February, another 115 closed; in March, 45 banks suspended operations; and in April, 68 banks closed. It remains unclear whether the number of bank failures fell because RFC loans provided endangered banks with the cushion of cash that they needed, or because the hoopla surrounding the program restored sufficient public confidence to slow the leaching of deposits and the public hoarding of cash. Most likely, a combination of the two worked for a time to stabilize the banking situation.[46]

Freshman Representative Wright Patman from Texas had his own idea of how to fix the economy: impeach Treasury Secretary Mellon. Seconded by Representative La Guardia, Patman had no trouble finding enough votes to establish a committee to investigate the actions of the unpopular secretary. When hearings commenced in mid–January, President Hoover dreaded the damage they would do to his administration. When Mellon failed to endorse the RFC, President Hoover decided that Mellon's service no longer served the nation's best interests, and he preferred to have Ogden Mills as his treasury secretary in any event. Mellon had to go. As Charles Dawes had recently left the Court of St. James, the post of ambassador to Great Britain was available, and the anglophile Mellon — whose son Paul had just graduated from Cambridge University — seemed the perfect choice. When he accepted the post and left for London, Congressman Patman charged that he had fled the country to escape prosecution.[47]

President Hoover remained convinced that public hoarding was the principal cause of bank weakness, and asked Frank Knox, publisher of the *Chicago Daily News*, to lead a public relations program to combat hoarding and convince people to either spend their money or put it back into the banks. Hoover hoped to use patriotic appeals and public relations to shore up the banks, much as public hoopla had sold Liberty Bonds to the public during the war. He gathered at the White House an extraordinary crowd of businessmen, union leaders, newspaper publishers, and fraternal, patriotic, social, and civic organization heads and urged them to get their members and followers in line to spend money or return it to the banks. G.E. President Owen Young formed a committee of industrialists and the nation's biggest banks to urge people to buy commercial bonds to keep money usefully employed and ensure a steady flow of funds to industries in trouble. Secretary Mills publicized on the radio small-denomination Treasury bonds available to the public as a means to coax cash out of sugar bowls and from underneath the floorboards. He promised the government would deposit the proceeds in banks of all sizes all across the country to make it available for those who needed it.[48]

Meanwhile, congressmen had ideas of their own about how to fix the financial problems of the United States. Members rushed to submit bills to buttress banks, and one of the most popular palliatives was to promise federal guarantee for deposits. Three bills to guarantee deposits were submitted on the opening day of Congress by representatives from Oklahoma, Nebraska, and Illinois. The following day, a representative from South Carolina offered a bill requiring the Federal Reserve to guarantee member-banks' deposits. Before the end of January 1932, Representative La Guardia from New York and two representatives from Ohio added three more deposit-guarantee bills for consideration. Henry Steagall, chairman of the House Banking and Currency Committee, did not submit his bill for deposit guarantees until March 7, by which time five more bills demanding federally sponsored deposit insurance of some kind had already been submitted.[49]

Proposals to inflate the currency proved almost as popular. Senator Wheeler Burton of Montana submitted a bill in January reestablishing a bimetal basis for the currency, forcing the Treasury to issue notes backed by silver as well as gold. Maryland Representative Thomas Goldsborough revived his 1922 proposal for a "commodity dollar" and offered an amendment to the National Bank Act that demanded the Federal Reserve Bank issue new currency notes until commodity prices had reached the levels achieved in 1926. In May the House actually passed the Goldsborough Amendment, which then went to the Senate, where — roundly denounced by economists and the financially orthodox — Senator Glass saw to it that it sat bottled up in his Banking and Finance Committee for the rest of the year. New York Senator Robert Wagner urged the Senate to fund $1 billion for a massive public works program to put men back to work and get money flowing again within the economy, hoping to reverse the downward spiral. He insisted the program be funded through federal borrowing, rather than by raising taxes, as any tax increase would hurt both business and consumers, and borrowing would employ not just idle men, but idle money. New York and Illinois congressmen tried mightily to authorize the RFC to loan money to states and municipalities, but lost the battle in the Senate.[50]

On January 22, Senator Glass submitted his comprehensive bank reform bill to the Senate. It proposed to separate commercial and investment banking, to mandate branch banking in all states, and to enlarge membership of the Federal Reserve System. But the bill went further, hoping to institute sweeping changes to the nation's banking laws and address every ill of the banking system. His bill called for an increase in reserve requirements for all national banks; an end to loans from Federal Reserve member-banks for the purpose of buying stocks or making loans that accepted stocks as collateral; an end to banks underwriting stock flotations or authorizing loans to companies where bank officers served as directors of the company; an end to loans by bankers to themselves, relatives, or other bank officers; and an end to banks paying interest on demand deposits (checking accounts). The bill additionally sought to allow federal regulation of bank holding companies; to mandate branch banking for national banks in states that allowed state-chartered banks to operate branches; and to create a federally chartered Liquidation Corporation to assume control of closed banks. Glass also called for minor changes in the works of the Federal Reserve Bank and a major change in the way it issued currency: he proposed that the Federal Reserve Bank be authorized to issue notes backed by Treasury bonds as well as commercial bonds. This reflected a dramatic change in his view of the money supply and harkened back to the days when national-bank notes used to circulate backed by Treasury bonds locked in national banks' vaults. Nevertheless, it was supposed to allow the Federal Reserve to have a more flexible money policy. Not surprisingly, such a sweeping bill immediately encountered opposition from senators who jealously guarded their states' prerogatives. Under a storm of heavy criticism, Senator Glass withdrew his bill and sent it back to committee.[51]

The committee tinkered with the bill, adjusting it to satisfy objections from representatives of the Federal Reserve System, and reintroduced it in March, minus the Liquidation Corporation, only to meet another barrage of criticism from senators bitterly divided about how to proceed. Glass again withdrew the bill. The committee redrafted the bill and reintroduced it a third time in April, when it again encountered withering criticism. Faced with the summer recess and the impending political campaign season, Glass consented in June to have the bill retired from the Senate calendar without being withdrawn. Evidently, the banking crisis of the fall of 1931 was bad enough to prod Congress into creating the RFC, but not dire enough to provoke sweeping reform of the nation's bank laws. Bank reform was becalmed for the time being.[52]

Just as Senator Glass was offering his preferred fix to the country's banking woes to the Senate, Alabama Representative Henry Steagall, chair of the House Banking and Finance Committee, offered his own bill to the House. His bill proposed the federal government offer insurance to guarantee bank time deposits (savings accounts) up to a modest amount for any bank that belonged to the Federal Reserve System. He wanted a federal insurance agency to pay depositors in failed banks 50 percent of their accounts up to one thousand dollars and the balance of their accounts up to $2,500 within 18 months. All of this Carter Glass — and most bankers — thought the height of folly. Bank guarantee programs had an unhappy history in the United States. A number of states had enacted deposit guarantee laws, but all of them ultimately failed because state legislatures proved unwilling to allocate sufficient funds to make them effective. New York State first guaranteed deposits in 1827, but the reimbursement fund was empty by 1829 and the law was abolished in 1842. Other attempts were made: Oklahoma enacted a deposit guarantee law in 1908; Kansas, Texas, and Nebraska followed in 1909; Mississippi, the Dakotas, and Washington State all passed such laws in the next three years. Oklahoma abandoned the effort in 1923, Texas followed in 1927, and by 1929 only Nebraska and Mississippi retained their programs. In 1930, Nebraska allowed the state fund to run dry, and Mississippi struggled unsuccessfully to maintain their fund through bond sales. By the time Representative Steagall submitted his bill, there were no operating deposit-guarantee programs in the United States.[53]

The gulf that separated Senator Glass from Representative Steagall guaranteed that no banking reform would pass both houses in 1932. The House passed Steagall's bill in May 1932 and forwarded it along to the Senate. There, Glass's hostility to Steagall's bill kept it dormant for the rest of the year. Roosevelt's hostility to federal guarantee of bank accounts was widely known to insiders (but not by the public), and Jesse Jones claims Steagall's proposal was tabled in Congress during the summer of 1932 because of it. Carter Glass, who believed federal bank insurance was a bad idea, received scores of letters from bankers and assorted businessmen urging him to support Steagall's proposal. Others objected that it would either force banks to join the Federal Reserve System or face a lethal drain on deposits as customers withdrew funds in order to deposit them into insured accounts. Operators of small banks and businesses generally favored the deposit guarantee proposal, while those at the largest banks and businesses more often opposed it.[54]

The bills proposed by Glass and Steagall met with strong, yet divided, reactions from business interests, especially bankers. Small bank interests tended to oppose the Glass reforms because they feared its provisions would prove too onerous for banks with few resources and small staffs. On the other hand, the same bankers tended to favor Steagall's deposit insurance scheme that was almost universally opposed by large banks, which claimed it would subsidize small and poorly run banks that ought to go out of business. Businessmen of all sorts expressed opinions about the bills, and generally approved of them, even if they expressed reservations about some aspects. The chief economic advisor to the Federal Reserve Bank of Chicago, Walter Lichtenstein, objected that despite weaknesses in the banking system, reform would only make matters worse by undermining confidence in the system and by imposing greater financial burdens on banks already tottering on the edge. The Banking Committee of the U.S. Chamber of Commerce substantially agreed with him. But the clear and strong divisions of opinion about the bills and the wide gulf between them kept either one from being adopted as the nation's law. The Steagall bill passed the House in May — unlike Glass's bill, which faded away in the Senate because of lack of consensus — but in the upper house it progressed no further than Senator Glass's committee. Glass's strong opposition to the deposit insurance proposal, the stringent criticism it aroused in some banking circles, and the opposition of the Democratic candidate for the presidency, Franklin Delano Roosevelt, kept Steagall's bill stalled in the Senate.[55]

Despite the difficulties Glass and Steagall encountered in passing a bank reform bill, 1932 did witness the passage of a Glass-Steagall Act, but of a different kind. On February 11, Carter Glass received an urgent summons to the White House, where the president explained that since the end of 1931 the nation's financial situation had become increasingly precarious. Partly to feed the constant public demand for more cash to put in their pockets — or mattresses — the Federal Reserve Bank had been buying eligible commercial paper and trade acceptances at a high rate, pumping the system full of Federal Reserve notes. At the same time, commercial activity was slowing, so that eligible paper to discount was becoming scarce. In February 1931, $315 million of these 60-to-90-day notes were outstanding, along with $1.52 billion in bankers' acceptances, which financed international trade and usually originated and stayed in New York. By February 1932, these amounts had dropped to $103 million and $919 million, respectively. The Federal Reserve Bank was established to provide credit and currency to feed business as it expanded or slowed by issuing currency backed by commercial paper (60 percent maximum) and gold (40 percent minimum). While available commercial paper dwindled, gold had been flowing freely out of Federal Reserve vaults toward Europe because nervous Europeans — especially the French — wanted their gold close by. Thus, the gold stock and commercial paper that backed Federal Reserve notes were both diminishing dangerously close to their legal limits. Thus, the Fed would either have to start recalling money by selling commercial paper for which there was little market or find new backing for its notes. Government officials justifiably feared that recalling currency would be highly deflationary and put the American economy in a terrible bind. Banks might run out of cash, possibly provoking a general crash of the banking system.[56]

On February 7, 1932, Secretary Mills warned the president that crisis loomed for the dollar and something needed to be done right away. Several Federal Reserve District Banks had to sell so much gold in January that they held only the legal minimum and were forced to buy more gold from other Federal Reserve Banks. New York, which was busy shipping gold to Europe, was in no position to sell more to Philadelphia or Boston. Hoover convened a meeting of high-level Treasury, Federal Reserve, and RFC officials who agreed that the best way to avert the crisis was to liberalize backing for Federal Reserve notes. Treasury bonds were abundantly available, easily traded, and would serve best to back Federal Reserve notes. But the law would have to be changed to allow it. To that end, Hoover called Glass, Steagall, and Republican congressional leaders to the White House to explain the problem and to urge them to act quickly in view of the pressing need. They agreed to allow the measure as a temporary expedient, and Carter Glass reluctantly acquiesced to lend his name to a bill to be submitted in the Senate as soon as possible. Thus, the note-liberalization component of the bank-reform bill was detached and submitted separately in both houses on an emergency basis. The Glass-Steagall Act of 1932 passed both houses without debate and was signed into law by the president on February 27.[57]

News of the Glass-Steagall Act had an immediate effect on markets, which rallied at the news. Bankers who had worried about running out of money now worried less. Senator Glass wrote to the *American Bank Association Journal*, minimizing the crisis, explaining that the purpose of the bill was to restore confidence. For his part, Glass was confident that the Fed would not have to use the authority the bill gave it and had been assured by Governor Eugene Meyer it would not be needed. In fact, the bill was used by the Fed to increase the money supply in May, and by the end of 1932, the Fed increased its holding of U.S. government securities by over $1 billion, giving it ample reserve to keep on increasing the money supply should it choose to do so. Russell Leffingwell of Morgan and Company saw this move as dangerously deflationary. It encouraged banks to dump commercial loans in exchange for government securities because they were more easily converted into cash on short notice. Commercial credit, already in short supply, would become even harder to find, forcing the economy to contract further.[58]

Nineteen-thirty-two was the year the Depression was supposed to end. A survey of 135 business editors conducted by the *New York Times* in December 1931 concluded that the worst days were behind the country and the economy should pick up. Prices hit lows not seen since before the wartime inflation. Overall prices had dropped by one-third since the mid–1920s, and many assumed they had hit bottom. Federal Reserve Governor Meyer and his staff believed a natural price floor had been achieved and smarter Fed policy combined with the ameliorative effects of the RFC would now produce a slow but steady recovery. With confidence boosted by the Glass-Steagall Act and the smooth workings of the RFC, Fed staff believed they could at last "break the back of the Depression." Economists predicted that with prices so low, spending would pick up and, as shoppers again consumed in larger quantities, business would revive. Business journalists believed housing construction would increase in view of low costs and built-up demand that had gone unmet for the past several years. Many argued that fierce competition to survive during the Depression had driven unfit firms out of business, leaving only the strongest and most resourceful to lead their respective fields, and that meager sales had led to tremendous innovation that lowered costs and created demand for new and improved products. The Depression had actually prodded research and stimulated many new ideas and much original thinking. Some assumed this would act as a catapult to hurl the economy forward to an even greater height than witnessed in the 1920s. The country evidently had seen the worst of the banking crisis, which supposedly peaked in 1931 when nationwide bank failures reached the frightening tally of 2,295, after the nation had suffered 1,352 failures in 1930. The pace of suspensions slowed in early 1932.[59]

The economy responded to the optimism that greeted the RFC and the Glass-Steagall Act only fleetingly. After a momentary upswing in March, economic indicators began to sputter. The auto industry was still anemic. Monthly auto production increased by nearly

20,000 vehicles from January to April, but it usually increased during that season, and in the 1920s the expansion was usually by 100,000 to 150,000 units. Seasonally adjusted employment, which had been falling continuously since 1929, increased from January to February, but then fell again, as did payrolls. Banks failed in relatively limited numbers in early 1932. But the economy did not respond as expected and, as it continued to sputter and cough, optimism turned to disappointment and dark political clouds gathered.[60]

CHAPTER THREE

Political Clouds Darken

When the economy failed to respond to the rush of palliative legislation passed by the 72nd Congress the national mood darkened. The two houses of Congress turned into a battleground between factions, which failed to agree on what to do about the stalled economy. Bank reform stalled as Senator Glass's bill languished in Representative Steagall's House committee and Steagall's bill similarly lay dormant in the Senate committee. With bank reform safely shelved for the time being, Congress took up cutting the budget and raising taxes, and the real political fireworks began. As the presidential campaign gathered momentum and attention, it divided the country into warring camps. As the debates grew heated, bitter, and then deadlocked, the economy unraveled. The good done by the Glass-Steagall Act and the RFC was soon undone by division and discord. President Hoover later charged that Democrats deliberately choked the economic recovery in order to take over the government in the 1932 elections. Business optimism, briefly revived in the spring, faded in summer and unemployment rolls added new names. The municipalities that administered those rolls often had no more money to pay out. In this gloomy atmosphere more Americans developed harsh opinions about business and businessmen in general, and attitudes within the halls of Congress hardened and soured. Americans organized and agitated for their own projects to revive the economy or just to better their own condition. In this atmosphere, World War I veterans launched a march on Washington, D.C., to demand the early payment of their bonus.[1]

Public agitation for inflation prodded Congress to consider proposals that frightened and depressed bankers, businessmen, and their allies. Economists and bankers testified against the Bonus Bill, claiming the bill was inflationary and would undermine confidence in the currency and federal credit. Businessmen showered Congress with letters urging a restoration of business confidence as the first priority. Nevertheless, in April the House passed the Goldsborough Bill, which required the Federal Reserve to raise commodity prices by issuing more notes whenever prices fell. The Federal Reserve reacted by pumping hundreds of millions of dollars into circulation every week in an effort to render the mechanisms of the Goldsborough Bill moot. Consequently, Americans and foreigners became increasingly nervous about inflation, and gold started to flee the United States for safe havens in Europe, especially France and the Netherlands. Chase National Bank's chief economist, Benjamin Anderson, called the Goldsborough Bill "absurd," and Morgan and Company's Russell Leffingwell thought it "stupefying." Princeton economist Edwin W. Kemmerer worried that fears of inflation undermined business confidence, and "the most important consideration in the United States today is to inspire confidence." Hearings in Congress that dragged bankers and financial leaders, such as Winthrop Aldrich of the Chase National Bank and Otto Kahn of Kuhn Loeb, to explain why their institutions had sold dubious foreign bonds to the public, helped sink the bond markets ever lower. California progressive Hiram Johnson crowed to his sons that the fruits of his exposure of "international bankers" had been splashed across the front pages of "every metropolitan paper in the country—I except none.... [Even] the papers in the east that were owned by the international bankers that hated me with a fierceness impossible to describe, nevertheless were compelled to publish the facts and there never was anything with which I was connected that had so much publicity." Business slowed and bank clearings fell dramatically as April turned to May.[2]

The economy and politics were both caught in a downward spiral: the more the economy deteriorated the more politicians bickered; the more politicians thundered and threatened, the more the economy slowed. As business confidence waned, decisions were postponed. Investors and business managers responded to the political agitation and uncertainty by doing nothing. Securities markets remained in the doldrums. The *Commercial and Financial Chronicle* claimed that prolonged discussion of pending tax bills, looming budget deficits, and the agitation for a veterans' bonus kept the financial markets in "a highly disturbed state." As politicians in the state capitals and Washington debated what to do, businessmen became ever more hesitant to commit themselves and their enterprises to new ventures. While businessmen exercised greater caution, demagogues, such as the Detroit-based "radio priest" Father Coughlin, became more strident and brazen. During the debate on the Bonus Bill, Father Coughlin turned up the volume of his broadcast vitriol against railroads and bankers, whom he regularly flayed as "banksters" and little better than Al Capone's goons. Coughlin quickly spawned imitators: an evangelical preacher in St. Petersburg, Florida, urged his congregants to go to their banks and withdraw all of their money in gold.[3]

The bitter jousting over the RFC bill did not die after the program started functioning, and progressives continued to assail it as the economy failed to revive. Although the RFC was operating smoothly in the spring of 1932, reviewing loans and dishing out money by the hundreds of millions of dollars, it was an object of controversy almost from the start. Part of the RFC mandate was to loan money to railroads that had run into difficulties because they had less freight to move. Congress was not concerned about the health of the railroads themselves, nor about the welfare of their stockholders, but about the large place the roads occupied within the national financial structure. Railroads relied heavily on bond sales for cash flow. In good times railroad bonds had been considered as good as gold—the so-called "high-grade bonds" approved by state regulators as sound investments for insurance companies and savings banks. In early 1932 savings and loans across the country held $2.4 billion in railroad bonds, commercial banks and trust companies held another $1.15 billion, while insurance companies owned $3.26 billion. By February 1932 many railroads were in serious danger of defaulting on $400 million of those bonds. RFC loans to railroads were intended to prevent the catastrophic results of defaults from rippling through the economy until they hit "widows and orphans."[4]

The urgent need for help from the RFC ran up against the American people's long tradition of blaming most problems on the railroads. The secretary of the Virginia State Horticultural Society spoke for many when he said, "If worst comes to worst, let the railroads go to the devil, but save the homes of these farmers." When the RFC was created by Congress, Senator Couzens—chairman of the Senate Interstate Commerce Committee—insisted that the Interstate Commerce Commission (ICC), which regulated railroads, be given a voice in approving RFC loans to railroads. The ICC was never known for its sympathy for railroad companies and balked at approving a $12.8 million loan to the Missouri-Pacific

Railroad on the grounds that the money would immediately be turned over to J.P. Morgan and Company, Kuhn-Loeb, and the Guaranty Trust Company of New York, which owned the railroad's debts. Morgan and the others had agreed to pay $1.5 million in interest on Missouri-Pacific bonds due in January on condition that the railroad reimburse them with money borrowed from the RFC in February. On February 1, the railroads won a hard-fought concession from railroad workers to cut pay by 10 percent. The leaders of the ICC could see little reason why Wall Street should get their money while workers had to give up theirs. Many in Congress shared that view, among them Senators Couzens, Robert La Follette, Jr., and William Borah, who denounced the loan application and the entire mission of the RFC to bail out banks, which was their real objection. Ogden Mills and Charles Dawes defended the loans, reasoning that railroads were eligible for loans in the first place only because their bonds were so widely owned by financial institutions and that granting loans to railroad companies was not intended to save the roads, but to save the bondholders. RFC director Jones advanced the pragmatic, if Machiavellian, position that the loan would hurt the RFC in the eyes of Congress and so it should not be granted. Besides, Jones and the ICC commissioner leading the charge against the Missouri-Pacific loan did not believe that Morgan would allow the railroad to default and thus go into bankruptcy.[5]

When the Missouri-Pacific debate broke out in Congress, some recent unpopular actions by big bankers had tainted their reputations among the public. New York bankers had attracted much unwanted publicity when they rejected several pleas from big cities, such as Detroit, Chicago, and New York, for big loans. Bankers had attached conditions to any prospective loans, which proved highly irritating to the public and progressive politicians who passed judgment on RFC actions that favored banks. When Detroit begged for another $5 million loan to pay city employees, New York and Chicago bankers countered that the city had to trim another $6 million from its budget first. When the mayor asked the city school board to find another $2 million in cuts, an outraged city councilman suggested the city pay salaries with money set aside to pay off previous bank loans. Instead, faced with a $60 million deficit, Detroit cut its museum budget by $300,000, laid off 840 employees, stopped all public improvement projects, cut relief and welfare funds by $10 million, and eliminated the city recreation budget. Predictably, these measures did not meet popular approval. When New York bankers offered a loan to New York City on condition the city double the subway fare from five cents to a dime, New York Democratic Senator Royal Copeland denounced the bankers' demands as "outrageous and inexcusable ... playing politics with human misery." That none of the RFC loans went to the big New York banks— National City, Chase National, Bankers Trust, or Guaranty Trust— made little difference because in the minds of many, all the money ultimately ended up in their vaults anyway. Even some businessmen, such as President Nelson of United States Sugar, echoed this charge.[6]

By June 1932, the billion dollar loans granted by the RFC had produced no noticeable improvement in the economy. From June 1931 to June 1932, loans and investments by American banks fell from $55 billion to $46 billion. Bank loans had contracted by $8 billion while deposits had shrunk from $52 billion to $42 billion. Perhaps more worrisome, banks in New York had refused to accept new deposits from out-of-town banks because they could not usefully employ the money. The Federal Reserve received similar reports about banks outside of New York. To its detractors, the RFC was a miserable failure that did nothing but give cash to bankers who stashed it in their vaults. More ominously for the RFC, its supporters were beginning to have doubts as well. Bankers started to complain that RFC terms for loans were too stringent, that it demanded too much collateral, its interest rates were too high, and the loans had to be paid back too quickly. Even prominent members of the Federal Reserve Bank, such as Owen Young and New York Fed Governor George Harrison, thought the RFC had too much power and was usurping the role of the Fed. Many bankers, businessmen, and Federal Reserve members observed that, even worse, most banks paid off their obligations with RFC loans but did not then resume commercial loans to businesses. Perhaps RFC loans saved some banks from collapse, but they did nothing to revive business, which was their ultimate purpose. RFC Chairman Eugene Meyer fretted that because the RFC had become the lender of last resort, it treated the hardest cases, many of which had waited too long to apply for help. Because many of these hard cases had already pledged their best assets for loans, all they had left to offer as collateral were assets of doubtful value, causing RFC examiners to appear exceptionally miserly. Perhaps Meyer was right, but from its inception the RFC evaluated collateral for loans at market value rather than face value — a practice at variance from national bank examiners who reported to the comptroller of the currency.[7]

When the economy failed to revive in the summer of 1932, as Meyer had promised Hoover it would, Fed bankers blamed the RFC, and Hoover listened to them seriously. Hoover had not yet lost faith in the RFC, but he began to lose faith in Meyer. Meyer had acted as a lighting rod for progressive attacks since his appointment as an ex-officio director of the RFC. New York congressman Fiorello La Guardia had attempted to block his appointment during House debate on the bill, calling Meyer, "a caddie for the four big banks [of New York]."[8] When he attacked Meyer's record as head of the War Industries Board, Democrats and Republicans alike sprang to Meyer's defense and drowned out La Guardia. But Meyer developed the bad habit of making appointments without consulting the other directors, which irritated his relations with them, and word of discontent among the directors naturally made its way back to the White House. RFC Chairman Meyer had never really gotten along with RFC President Charles Dawes, and their mutual coolness turned frigid during the debate over the Missouri-Pacific loan, when Dawes sided with the ICC. Although a Republican, Dawes often sided with the Democratic appointees on the RFC board. He resented the financial dominance of Wall Street — he called the New York Stock Exchange "that peanut stand on Wall Street" — and complained that the big Wall Street firms ought to show a willingness to sacrifice along with everybody else. As the pressures of the office wore on him, Dawes came to resent and dislike Meyer, so when Meyer pushed through the Missouri-Pacific loan against the majority opinion of the board, Dawes was furious. By June, Dawes had had enough and announced his intention to resign as president of the RFC. Hoover then saw his opportunity to revamp the directors and perhaps rehabilitate the image of the agency in the eyes of its growing ranks of detractors.[9]

When the bloom had faded from the RFC, other proposals to revive the economy regained life. Wright Patman's Bonus Bill was the subject of well-publicized hearings in which Patman attempted to sell his bill not as a "pump-priming" device that would put money into the pockets of men who would spend it, injecting much needed fuel into the empty tank of American business, but as an overtly inflationary bill. Patman revived populist arguments from the 1890s that the extra billions would raise prices, helping to ease the lot of debtors and farmers. Father Charles Coughlin latched on to the argument and gave it a nationwide audience on his radio program. If the primary ill in America was deflation — constantly falling prices — that bankrupted businessmen and farmers, and caused banks to collapse, so the reasoning went, why not inflate prices to reverse the catastrophe and end it? The Republican and Democratic leaders who stood in a position to change policy, in contrast, retained orthodox ideas about "sound money" and the evils of inflation. In their view, the nation had only to look at the sad European experiences with inflation during the 1920s, particularly the hyperinflation in Germany in 1923-24, to find strong arguments against inflating the U.S. currency. Arguments for inflation failed to move the men who led Congress. Democratic Senators Robinson and Glass, House Majority Leader Henry T. Rainey, and Speaker Garner, and especially Republican Senators Watson, Moses, and Fess, and House Minority Leader Bertrand Snell all stood their ground as defenders of "sound money."[10]

Nevertheless, the Bonus Bill proved too seductive for the House to turn down. Capitol Hill was flooded with 20,000 veterans carrying petitions and lobbying their congressmen to support the $500 bonus for veterans. The bill barely passed in the House. When the inflationist senator Elmer Thomas of Oklahoma moved to have it immediately considered in the Senate, he was voted down and the bill was referred to committee, emerging to be overwhelmingly rejected by the Senate in a final rush to conclude business before the summer recess. Most veterans encamped in Washington accepted Congress's offer of train tickets to return home and left town, leaving only a remnant of bitter-enders who were removed from their camps by army troops, when local police proved insufficient for the job. Images of army troops rousting the remaining veterans and supporters from their shantytown encampment provided forceful propaganda against Hoover during the election campaign, much to the enduring delight of Democrats. When Roosevelt saw photos in the newspapers of troops burning the marchers' pathetic camps, he knew he had won the election.[11]

To bring the federal budget closer to balance — all admitted a balanced budget was now out of the question — Hoover asked for cuts in some expenditures and increases in taxes to raise revenues. Congress cooperated in making cuts, but the House seriously differed with the president on the best way to raise revenues. Hoover proposed a national 2.5 percent sales tax on business, which was passed by the Senate in March but met determined resistance from progressives in the House, again led by La Guardia. Garner and the Ways and Means Committee initially supported the sales tax, as well as increases in income, inheritance, and corporate taxes. Garner promised Hoover that he would see the new tax through the House. But when 50 Democrats and 15 Republicans demanded a 65 percent tax on incomes over $5 million — to "soak the rich" in La Guardia's words — and Garner attracted the condemnation of veteran Democrats Josephus Daniels and John Dewey for being too cooperative with Ogden Mills, and the disapproval of New York Governor Roosevelt, he thought twice about the sales tax and joined the opposition. Garner was initially puzzled by Roosevelt's antagonism to the national sales tax because Garner had discussed the idea with him before agreeing to support it in the House and left New York with the distinct understanding that the governor favored the proposal. Many people would have that experience with Roosevelt over the next decade. Nevertheless, in a party caucus Garner conceded that party unity was more important than the sales tax, and pledged not to oppose the tax, but not support it either. The sales tax was then rejected by the House, and relations between Republicans and Democrats within Congress soured. Nevertheless, both parties agreed to rescind the tax cuts of 1926 and impose taxes on bank checks, gasoline, fur coats, as well as raise income, estate, corporate, and various "nuisance taxes."[12]

As soon as Garner was selected as Speaker of the House his friends in Uvalde, Texas, organized a "Garner for president" club, which the Speaker found gratifying, but did not take too seriously. Even when similar clubs sprang up around Texas, Garner assumed he was being posed as a favorite-son candidate to give him extra leverage at the June Democratic convention. But in January 1932, William Randolph Hearst started agitating for Garner's nomination because he found the other likely Democratic candidates too internationalist. Hearst liked Garner's conservative economic stance, coupled with a skeptical attitude toward eastern capital. Garner also had a strong appeal to rural Democrats nationwide who found the field of presumed candidates — Roosevelt, Al Smith, Owen Young, Maryland Governor Albert Ritchie, and Newton Baker — too urban, too eastern, and too predisposed to forgive European debts. While Garner occupied himself with a full schedule of legislation in the House, Hearst pursued his campaign of boosting Garner and slighting Roosevelt as the Tammany candidate — a charge without any merit. When Garner won the California Democratic primary on May 3 — with much assistance from Hearst — suddenly everything changed. Garner really was a serious contender for the presidency, or at least a kingmaker.[13]

Under pressure from progressives, sensing a change in the political winds, and now a serious presidential contender, Garner's stance toward his Republican rival, Herbert Hoover, and his programs altered dramatically. Although Garner had supported the RFC, he was becoming impatient to see RFC loans granted to railroads, insurance companies, and banks trickle down to help the unemployed. He, too, joined the ranks of its critics and demanded legislation be amended to allow RFC loans directly to towns and states, as well as to businesses and even individuals, if the RFC judged the loans would put the unemployed to work. Garner, who had previously opposed public-works bills as too expensive, now supported one to build post offices and federal courthouses around the country. Garner got behind New York Senator Robert Wagner's proposal for a massive works program, funded by $2.3 billion in RFC loans. As the *Chicago Tribune* pointed out, in January only radicals would have supported such a proposal, but by May even conservative New York Representative Bertrand Snell supported it.[14]

Indeed the political temper of the country had changed since the winter; by late spring Americans were growing increasingly disappointed with the failure of government programs to revive the economy. Walter Lippmann had stopped believing that minor tinkering with interest rates would turn the economy around and had come to think that massive public-works projects were needed. Even business opinion was lining up behind Garner and Wagner's program of public works. Paul Shoup, president of the Southern Pacific Railroad, argued that years of neglect by railroads had led to a massive backlog of maintenance and repair. Now, when money and labor were cheap, was the time for the RFC to loan huge amounts to the roads to undertake the work. He also praised big public projects, such as the Queens-Midtown Tunnel in New York, which soaked up millions of investment dollars, provided a needed service, and would be self-liquidating and not burdensome to taxpayers. William Randolph Hearst put the considerable weight of his newspaper chain behind Wagner's proposal, which, in Hearst's view, was too modest: only $5 billion would do. Even Federal Reserve Governor Meyer thought there was merit to proposals to use public funds to redevelop the Lower East Side of Manhattan.[15]

Debate over the public-works bill provoked a sharp break between President Hoover and the progressives in Congress. Hoover denounced Garner's bill as "a gigantic pork barrel ... raid on the public treasury" intended to buy votes, which provoked caustic responses from the Speaker. Hoover's intemperate reaction to the public-works bill provided the *casus belli* for the battle between them which then erupted. Garner said he did not expect any measures from Hoover that would benefit the middle classes nor any "real cooperation." Relations between President Hoover and Speaker Garner frayed more severely as the Speaker developed ambitions to sit in the White House himself and each jockeyed for advantage. Garner charged that every time the president opened his mouth public confidence froze just a bit more.[16]

The front-runner for the Democratic nomination, New York Governor Franklin D. Roosevelt, faced a crowded field in a party divided between "wets" and "drys" on the Prohibition question, and between internationalists and isolationists on questions of foreign relations, war debts, and tariffs. As his campaign began in earnest in January 1932, Roosevelt adopted a cautious stance calculated to offend as few Democrats as possible, hedging his bets with vague platitudinous speeches calculated to offend no party faction. He offered no specific program to end the Depression, yet adopted a position of unstinting hostility toward the Hoover administration, one political position not likely to offend many Democrats. In a radio speech broadcast in April, he severely criticized the way the Hoover administration was handling the Depression by giving massive loans to big business: "The two billion dollar fund which President Hoover and the Congress have put at the disposal of the big banks, the railroads and the corporations of the nation is not for him [the forgotten man]." Roosevelt charged that government loans to small banks intended to save farms and homes ended up in the vaults of distant big banks and did nothing to help the "forgotten man." The "forgotten man" speech provoked a furious response from Roosevelt's one-time mentor and now primary opponent, Al Smith, who denounced any effort to pit "class against class," and appeal to radicalism. The Democratic Party was still run by a team put into place by Al Smith and widely viewed as friendly toward business: National Committee Chairman John J. Raskob, lately of General Motors and then a vice president of the DuPont Corporation, and Executive Committee Chairman Jouett Shouse, a prominent Kansas City lawyer and newsman. But Raskob, Smith, and Shouse had no influence over Roosevelt, who steadily maneuvered to oust Shouse and Raskob from party leadership. Roosevelt tilted ever closer toward the progressives and with him went much of the party.[17]

The increased hostility of Democrats toward business produced a noticeable chill within industry. Instead of being optimistic about the months ahead, many businessmen and economists turned increasingly gloomy. Edwin Kemmerer testified before Congress days after Roosevelt's speech that attacks upon the RFC by the New York governor greatly undermined everything the RFC was trying to do. America's capitalists, who directed much of the nation's business investment, viewed events in Washington with increased alarm. When House Democrats and Republican progressives pushed through an income tax bill that raised the maximum tax to 65 percent on incomes over $5 million, Irénée du Pont complained to Delaware Senator Townsend, "Of course I am worried by the recent action of the House of Representatives in the matter of taxation. The slogan 'soak the rich' is bad enough when it comes from socialists and Bolsheviks, but coming from our representatives, and at a time when public confidence is at a low ebb, it is to say the least unfortunate." Paul Warburg denounced the veterans' bonus as "stark madness" that "involves the gravest danger for our domestic and foreign situation," sentiments echoed by Charles Dawes in testimony before Congress. Dawes thundered that the bonus payment would ruin government credit and destroy the optimism that was just returning to markets. Bernard Baruch announced publicly that high taxes, uncertainty over the budget, and the potential for monetary inflation induced by unwise government policies kept stalling the recovery. Benjamin Anderson of the Chase National Bank told a conference of manufacturers in Chicago that business had legitimate concerns in the summer of 1931, but those fears became much worse than justified by fundamental economic conditions, and from that summer to the summer of

1932 "security prices and the volume of business were contracted unduly under the influence of false fears." Anderson insisted that business opinion exaggerated the danger to the gold standard, and its fears that Congress would wreck U.S. credit, or that Germany would collapse were uncalled for. He said that "there were vague, indefinite fears of the general collapse of the capitalistic system," which were completely unjustified. Justified or not, investors still did not invest, and managers at all levels trimmed their sails for rough weather, perhaps causing the storm to worsen.[18]

Business leaders, however, were sharply divided about the best course of action for the country. General Motors President Alfred P. Sloan was so distressed by what he heard emanating from Washington, D.C., that he suggested to Pierre du Pont that executives of the 25 biggest American industrial corporations ought to band together to draw up a political program for the country. Democratic Party Chairman John Raskob went even further in circulating a plan to establish a super government of "experts," such as Owen Young, Bernard Baruch, and Charles Dawes, to be given complete budgetary autonomy to implement programs they thought helpful while Congress recessed to get out of their way. The New York Conference of General Contractors called for a massive increase in federal spending on public works, while the General Contractors Association of Delaware and the Wilmington Chamber of Commerce demanded reduced federal taxes and spending, and a balanced budget. As the economy spiraled downward, so did the national mood. And as the American spirit sagged, so did the economy in a self-perpetuating downward cycle.[19]

Chicago: The Center of the Storm

Since 1929 the economy had deteriorated the furthest in the industrial Midwest. As the economy slumped ever lower in 1932, the hardest blows hit Chicago, where both parties met to select their presidential candidates. In 1932, 170,000 Chicago families received some form of charity, and suburban towns ran out of funds to pay their employees. By June 1932, Chicago payrolls languished at just one-third of their 1929 high. Average weekly pay for workers who still had jobs in manufacturing had fallen from $31.60 to $20.20. The population of Chicago actually declined as people gave up hope of finding work and left town. Over one-quarter of Loop office space begged for renters, and between 20 and 25 percent of Chicago renters had fallen behind in their rent. The situation was worst in the working-class districts and particularly severe in the African American quarters where most renters were months behind in rent. In 1931, 20 percent of the 9,500 apartments managed by the Chicago Title and Trust Company were empty. Foreclosures continued until almost one billion dollars worth of mortgages in Chicago had been canceled by the summer of 1932. In the first six months of 1931, 3,099 foreclosures were filed in Cook County, for $125 million. In 1932 the situation deteriorated and Chicago courts ordered 15,201 foreclosures, worth $574.6 million. By the end of the year, holders of trust deeds had asked for foreclosure on two billion dollars worth of mortgages.[20]

In 1932 the economy in Chicago was becalmed. Building activity fell further from the already low levels of 1931. In the first six months of 1932, building contracts declined 57 percent from the year before; housing construction was down 73 percent. The Drake and the Blackstone Hotels—two of the grandest in Chicago—went into receivership. In 1928, the Drake had a mortgage for an astounding $5 million. Fewer workers in Chicago and its region worked even fewer hours as payrolls continued to shrink. In the Chicago Federal

Reserve District 2,232 companies cut their payrolls 7 percent from May to June. Auto sales were off nearly 60 percent from 1931, and from May to June auto manufacturing payrolls declined 10 percent. As people throughout the United States ate less meat, work in slaughterhouses in Illinois dropped to meager levels. This provided one bright spot in the midwestern economy: as Americans ate less meat they ate more cheese.[21]

In December 1931, Samuel Insull, founder of Insull Utilities Holding Company and Corporations Securities Company, informed his bankers he could not meet yet another margin call. He owed Chicago banks $150 million, all of it secured by Insull stocks. By April 1932 several Insull utilities were in receivership and his holding company defaulted on its loans. Thousands of Chicagoans had invested sums small and large in Insull stocks, and when they read the news of Insull's insolvency in their newspapers they knew they, too, were in big trouble. Samuel Insull had assembled the third largest collection of utility companies in the United States. He created holding companies to control holding companies, which held utility stocks. The largest of five such firms was the Middle West Utilities Company that controlled more than a billion dollars worth of stock in more than 100 companies that generated or distributed electricity or natural gas. In 1930 the various companies in the Insull fold were worth over $2.5 billion, served 4.5 million customers, and generated one-eighth of the electricity sold in the United States. But in order to increase control over these far-flung utility companies, Samuel Insull and his brother, Martin, created a series of holding companies to buy stock in the holding companies. All together, they created 95 companies that owned stock in utility companies, or companies that owned utility companies and sold stocks in their various holding companies to the public. When the Insull companies began collapsing in 1932, because they could not pay their debts, most of that stock became worthless, enraging much of the public and sending a chill throughout Chicago and beyond.[22]

As business slowed and unemployment increased in Chicago, the tax revenues that fueled the city dwindled. The city of Chicago had no money to pay its teachers in spring of 1931, so it paid them nothing. Then, in the summer, instead of paying them back wages, the city gave them IOUs in the form of scrip. Some teachers sold their scrip for 63 percent of face value. In September a federal judge ruled that the city had no right to print money and ordered it to stop. In response the city paid its teachers in "tax anticipation warrants," which traded for 81 percent of face value if a teacher could talk anyone into accepting them. In 1932, teachers, police, firemen, and other city workers were paid nothing for three months. In the spring, Mayor Anton Cermak begged Chicago banks to loan the city another $40 million so he could pay the municipal employees, or at least $8 million so he could meet the city's obligation to bondholders due on July 1. Cermak pointed out to the bankers that Senator Wagner had just proposed an amendment to a bill that would appropriate $50 million to distressed cities so they could pay their teachers and police. A citizens' committee pleaded with the banks for $10 million in anticipation of an imminent RFC loan to the city. On June 22, Wagner's amendment was overwhelmingly rejected by the Senate. The bankers did not lend Chicago the money. In August, Chicago offered $8 million in bonds, and when it found no takers, it tried to sell the bonds itself at retail with little success. But if the city were in trouble then all of its bondholders were in trouble. Many of those bondholders were local banks.[23]

Other jurisdictions suffered the same troubles as Chicago, and across the country cities paid their creditors only with difficulty. When bankers discovered just how shaky the finances of New York City were, the city was forced to promise to cut expenses and raise bond interest rates first from 1⅜ to 4.5 percent on one-year bonds; by December 1932 New York rates rose to 5.5 percent. In 1932, 697 separate municipal bond offerings, seeking $260 million, found no bidders. Cleveland offered $5,332,000 in bonds at 6 percent and raised only $1,372,000. Kearny, New Jersey, offered $2,333,000 in bonds at 6 percent and found no takers at all. The state of Montana offered to sell bonds worth $1.5 million at 5 percent and likewise found no buyers. Philadelphia, like Chicago, resorted to selling $20 million in bonds over the counter when banks showed no interest in buying them. Mississippi was able to sell only one-half of a $12.5 million bond offering. Louisiana could not sell a bond all year.[24]

The RFC was authorized to buy bonds but, despite the best efforts of Senator Wagner, only for self-liquidating projects and not for struggling towns, counties, or states. The RFC bought $62 million worth of bonds at 5 percent interest from the California toll-bridge authority to finance a bridge from San Francisco to Oakland, but this was a pet project of President Hoover, who personally lobbied the RFC to make the loan. That projects pushed by President Hoover, in his home state of California, obtained large RFC loans during a presidential campaign attracted predictable attention from Democrats with worthy projects of their own. Democrats, in particular, criticized the California loans while cash-starved cities, such as Chicago, laid off more teachers, firemen, and police.[25]

The sagging economy of Chicago and the subsequent financial woes of its government invariably dragged banks down with it. Deposits in Chicago banks shrank by another $200 million in the first half of 1932 and outstanding loans declined by $300 million. Banks could not withstand the steady drain of deposits, the delinquency of their loans, and the falling value of their collateral. As usual, the weakest banks fell first. Among the victims of the shrinking monetary environment was African American businessman Anthony Overton and his Douglass National Bank, which closed its doors on May 20, 1932. Since December 1929 the Douglass Bank had lost most of its deposits, which dwindled from $1.5 million to under $600,000 by December 1931. Business for the bank had almost disappeared: it had extended almost $1 million in loans in 1929 but only $279,000 by the end of 1931. Overton's real difficulty arose from his Victory Life Insurance Company, which sold policies not only to black Chicagoans, but to clients as far away as New York and New Jersey. When the Illinois State Insurance Examiner declared the company insolvent, New Jersey and New York likewise voided its license to sell insurance, and the company's investors in New York demanded that Overton step down as president, which he did. When news of Overton's distress became known in Chicago, the last black-owned bank in the city could not weather both the sour economy and bad publicity. Deposits drained away to $420,000, and when the bank was liquidated over two-thirds of its assets were judged doubtful and its remaining depositors received only 12 cents on the dollar.[26]

Misfeasance or Malfeasance?

Political tensions inspired by the downturn had been brewing since late 1930. Public anxiety over the slump and the rising tide of bank failures encouraged elected officials to search for culprits who could be blamed for everyone's troubles. Bankers made perfect targets, and as the volume of obloquy directed against them in Chicago grew, public trust in banks correspondingly deflated. By June 1932, with Democratic delegates streaming into Chicago for their nominating convention, the campaign against bankers provoked horrific bank runs and subsequent stunning founderings, with political reverberations of their own. With the first uptick in Illinois bank failures in the spring of 1931, the Republican State's Attorney John A. Swanson created a special office to investigate closed banks, or more accurately, failed bankers. Assistant State Attorney Henry Ayers convened a grand jury and summoned crowds of failed Chicago bankers to appear before it. By July 1931 Ayers had investigated 14 closed banks and issued seven indictments. He then handed out 12 indictments to officers and employees of the City State Bank, including one to bank vice president Seymour Stedman, an attorney who in 1920 ran for vice president of the United States on the Socialist Party ticket with Eugene Debs. The City State Bank was owned by the Cooperative Society of America, which still owed the bank more than a million dollars when the society folded in 1929. Stedman served on the board of directors and as a vice president of the bank only because a federal judge appointed him to the position as a trustee in 1924, when the bank went through an earlier period of troubles. Stedman was better known as a dogged defender of socialists, who were dragged into courts on various charges of treason, incitement to riot, or fomenting revolution, than as a banker, no less an embezzler.[27]

In November 1931, State's Attorney Swanson declared that he would use the grand juries to find out what happened to peoples' deposited money. He promised to drag bank customers who had defaulted on loans before the grand jury to find out if they had any assets that could be seized by the state, sold, and the proceeds turned over to depositors who had lost money. Swanson intended to prosecute every and any failed banker he could lay hands on, and by hook or by crook, see that they saw the inside of a barred cell. *The Chicago Tribune* reported, he "has decided to use extralegal means if necessary to help out the depositors." In two weeks prosecutors issued arrest warrants for 14 bankers. The bank cases became so pressing that Swanson put Ayers in charge of a special bureau with eight auditors, a clerk, and a stenographer to dispose of them. They poured through the records of every closed bank in Cook County and by November had indicted 57 bankers. Swanson declared that unless bankers made good on lost deposits they would be hauled before a grand jury for conspiracy to defraud depositors.[28]

One such case was that of Jesse Binga, who was indicted in March 1931 for embezzling $250,000 from the Binga Bank in Chicago's Southside, which closed in July 1930. Assistant State's Attorney Ayers claimed Binga took out inadequately secured personal loans in order to speculate in Chicago real estate. The charges did not stick. So he was charged with embezzlement for depositing in his personal account $39,000 he had accepted in 1929 as an investment in a new bank he intended to charter. At his trial Binga claimed to have accepted the money "in trust" for the bank, which never opened. Some members of the jury believed his assertion and refused to find him guilty, resulting in a hung jury. But the state prosecutor was determined to see the 67-year-old Binga behind bars and in 1933 successfully prosecuted him for "criminal mismanagement."[29]

At least one Berwyn Heights banker, Francis Karel, president of the First America National Bank and Trust Company, fell victim to Chicago's shady ways of practicing politics. After his bank took over several distressed local banks, he agreed to sell one of the bank buildings to the local government for $100,000 and accepted a $10,000 "commission" for the sale. He claimed that he never got the commission — or the $100,000 for the bank building — but turned it over to the city commissioners who authorized the purchase. In court the number of alderman caught up in the scheme grew to 13 and the "commission" had transformed into "campaign contributions." The judge was dubious and sent Karel and six of the aldermen to prison. Perhaps some bankers were outright thieves, but many appear to have been guilty of little more than carrying assets on their books at face value rather than deflated market value. Almost all were charged with making loans to themselves, family, or friends—which was not illegal in 1931 and a common practice nationwide—and then having fallen upon the same hard times as everybody else in Chicago, including the city, and been unable to pay back the loans. Seventy-two-year-old Edward McCabe, former president of the Lake View State Bank was arraigned in his bed, seriously ill with heart disease, for having made false statements to a bank examiner. Carl Mueller, president of the Laramie State Bank, charged with embezzling, seems to have been guilty primarily of having once been a plumber, which Ayers mentioned repeatedly to the press. The charges did not stick in court. Ayers similarly stressed that Lavergne Lindgren, head cashier of the Maywood State Bank and charged with embezzlement, was formerly a telephone operator. Any banker who, in an effort to save his struggling bank, signed an examiner's report claiming that securities held as collateral for loans were worth their face value rather than market price was potentially guilty of making false statements to a state official. Bank officers who could not repay their loans—and many could not—were charged with embezzlement. Occasionally these charges held up in court and even survived appeals, but not often.[30]

The officers of the City State Bank, including socialist Seymour Stedman, were charged with accepting deposits when they knew the bank was about to fail. Eight of the 12 accused actually faced a judge in a courtroom, and five were convicted. Two, including Stedman, were sentenced to prison, however they remained free pending appeal. When the appeal was heard in 1935 by three judges in the Court of Appeals, they unanimously ruled that Stedman and the other officer were innocent and the case never should have proceeded to trial in the first place. Jesse Binga was not so successful. His appeal was denied and, despite a petition signed by Clarence Darrow and 10,000 Chicagoans, the governor refused to release the 71-year-old Binga from Joliet State Prison. In 1938 he was paroled and survived by doing odd jobs for Saint Anselm's Catholic Church in Chicago. In 1941 the governor issued a full pardon to Binga, who at 77 still worked for the church.[31]

In June 1932, Chicagoans read in their papers the testimony streaming out of the trial of real estate and bank promoter John Bain, a Scottish immigrant who had started as a plumber, began building houses, and with partners become a major real-estate promoter in Chicago. The prosecutor charged that Bain had conspired with family members to swindle $13 million from his banks. When closed, his banks held only $14 million in deposits and claimed assets worth $21 million, which included all the loans to himself and his family. Newspapers revealed that he had borrowed money from his own banks, using worthless stocks as security, to provide capital to found new banks, and had borrowed another $1.75 million to finance his real estate developments. Bain countered that his collateral had been solid when pledged, but lost value after the onset of the Depression. Unhappily, Bain, a Chicago commissioner, had further advanced loans to fellow politicians unsecured by any collateral at all. Unsecured "character loans" always smelled a bit fishy when issued to politicians. Worse for Bain, he was accused of looting his bank on its way down. Knowing the weak condition of his banks, he took out additional loans of $500,000 within two months of their closures and credited himself for a $90,000 loan just eight days before the state auditor took over his banks.[32]

The city was already on edge from the Bain trial when prosecutors announced the arrest of Vice President Clemens Shapiro and two employees of the Division Street State Bank for plotting to swindle the bank; depositors besieged the bank and money flowed out of it until it closed its doors on June 15, 1932. Troubles grew at other Chicago banks for the rest of the week as more depositors demanded their money from their banks. On June 20, when banks in Chicago were failing at an alarming rate because of runs by nervous depositors and the city already on edge, State's Attorney Swanson announced, "More indictments are expected shortly," including charges against unnamed bankers, who conspired to defraud depositors of $1 million at an unnamed bank. The following day, Chicago was immersed in a general bank run that hit banks in outlying regions of the city and big banks in the Loop without distinction as crowds of anxious depositors swarmed to get their money out of banks as soon as possible. Five state banks and a national bank in the Chicago area closed their doors and turned over their affairs to receivers.[33]

Thirty Chicago banks had failed in the first five months of 1932. In three weeks in June, 25 more banks in Chicago and outlying areas closed their doors because of the irresistible and unfulfillable demands of their depositors. Zealous prosecutors, such as Swanson, righteously condemning bankers as crooks and damning them as thieves in the eyes of the public who had entrusted their savings to local banks, had a deplorable impact on the small neighborhood banks of Chicago. Such accusations were limited to neither Illinois nor bankers. Banking Superintendent Joseph Broderick was prosecuted in New York for "neglect of duty" because he had allowed the Bank of United States to fail on his watch. His first trial in February 1932 ended in a mistrial after Governor Roosevelt personally vouched for the integrity of his superintendent. But New York prosecutors were not to be deterred, so they hauled him into court again in May. State attorneys argued that Broderick should have closed the Bank of United States long before its collapse, but jurors were unconvinced and released Broderick, who returned to his job as superintendent of banking. Bernard Marcus and Saul Singer of the Bank of United States were not so lucky; both were convicted of "misapplication of bank funds" in June 1931 and hauled off to Sing Sing Prison when they lost their appeal shortly after Roosevelt's inauguration in 1933.[34]

Notorious cases of embezzlement received nationwide publicity, such as the case of Gilbert Bessemyer, president of the Guaranty Building and Loan Association in Los Angeles. He admitted bilking his association and several allied companies of $8 million over nine years trying to make good a $2 million investment in a flopped oil venture. When he was arrested in December 1930, his Bank of Hollywood closed immediately. But how common was "defalcation," the term for embezzlement preferred by bank examiners? In Washington state 16 bank officers were convicted of embezzlement from 1925 to 1932, with ten banks forced to close as a result. In 1931, Washington state had 303 banks, savings and loans, and trust companies, of which 92 were national banks. Five employees of three Washington national banks were convicted of defalcation from October 1930 to October 1931, in addition to the 16 cases involving state-charter institutions. Thus, the number of bank employees in Washington guilty of malfeasance of some sort was not great, but not insignificant either.[35]

During the same period from 1930 to 1931, 261 officers and employees of national banks were convicted nationwide of criminal violations of federal banking laws. About two-thirds were convicted for embezzling. In October 1930 there were 7,243 national banks in the United States. If all the convicted employees worked for different banks—and they did not, many worked in pairs—3.6 percent of all national banks would have been known victims of employee scams. Four of those convicted were bank employees in Chicago, and none of the three banks they worked in closed. All of those convicted in Chicago were low-level employees and none officers of a bank. Of the 261 bank employees convicted in federal court nationwide, 57 were officers of a bank: presidents, vice presidents, cashiers, one auditor, and two court-appointed receivers. About one-third were convicted of embezzlement and the rest most commonly were convicted of "false entry" or "misapplication of funds." Those charges could have been leveled to cover a variety of malfeasances, but had the officers gained personally from the misdeeds they surely would have been charged with embezzlement. They also would not likely have received suspended sentences and probation — the most common sentence meted out for "false entry" and "misapplication of funds." Criminal malfeasance in Chicago on the scale assumed by State's Attorney Swanson is inconceivable, even assuming that Chicago was plagued by more dishonest bankers than the average town, which might very well have been the case. In fact, two of the national banks that failed in the June panic in Chicago were under investigation by the Justice Department for bank fraud. The president of the South Ashland National Bank and the vice president of the Standard National Bank were both suspected of self-serving deals that weakened their banks. In both cases mismanagement helped push the banks into failure.[36]

A lot of the prosecution of bankers by public servants like Swanson was undoubtedly playing to the crowd. People were angry about lost or frozen deposits and wanted "justice," whether anyone was guilty of wrongdoing or not. After the collapse of the remnant of the second Bank of the United States, Philadelphia prosecutors dragged Nicholas Biddle into court in 1842 on charges of conspiracy and fraud. Biddle's lawyers had the charges thrown out by the judge, but it is far from certain that he would have survived a jury trial, given the degree of public animosity whipped up against Biddle. In Chicago in 1932, public outrage over bank failures prodded Swanson to meet public demands for justice, and public opinion about bankers was turning overtly hostile. No doubt many would have agreed with an unemployed machinist from Connecticut who declared to Charles Dawes, "Bankers of this country ... are the damnedest, rottenest, and most despicable lot of liars, thieves, cheats, and shysters in existence."[37]

The relentless onslaught by Swanson and Ayers, and the nonstop bad publicity for banks finally caught up with Chicago while the Democrats were in town for their convention to nominate their presidential candidate. On Wednesday, June 22, panic descended upon the Loop. Nervous crowds waited in long lines to withdraw their savings from even the largest banks in Chicago. On Thursday, a chain of banks in the outer regions of Chicago assembled by John Carrol closed their doors under the strain of the throngs. On Friday, eight more banks closed. All day Friday weary tellers in Loop banks counted and handed out tens of millions of dollars to Chicagoans trying to save what they could from what appeared to be looming financial doom brought on by crooked bankers. When banks opened on Saturday morning long lines had already formed of people who had been unable to reach a teller's window on the preceding days.[38]

The scene of panic among Chicago's skyscrapers was witnessed by RFC Director Jesse Jones, who had arrived in Chicago that Saturday as a delegate to the Democratic Convention. "From my hotel, that ominous Saturday morning, I walked through the Loop and watched the tail end of the week's terrible runs on the big downtown banks. Thousands of frantic, rumor-spreading depositors were still milling about every bank entrance on LaSalle, Clark, and Dearborn Streets. Bank lobbies swarmed with nervous customers." Another observer, insurance executive Henri Couteron, wandered around the Loop on Thursday and Friday and was shaken to the core by what he saw. He told Charles Dawes that he had never witnessed such hysteria and that if it continued the country was doomed. One Loop bank, the Chicago Bank of Commerce, had already called it quits after the excitement of the week and did not bother opening on Saturday morning as crowds besieged other Loop banks. The state-chartered bank that was not a member of the Federal Reserve System had lost

$4.5 million in deposits since 1931, and continued to lose $500,000 a day in the prior week. Three smaller suburban banks also threw in the towel that morning.[39]

The drain on resources at the one-year-old Central Republic Bank and Trust Company had been severe. Since its formation in 1931 with $240 million in deposits, the "Dawes Bank" had leached money and the past week had been brutal, after which the bank had about $130 million left in deposits. The deteriorating condition of the bank was widely known in banking circles, and rumors circulated in New York and Washington that Dawes was about to use the RFC to bail out his own bank. By June 1932, Charles Dawes faced the future gloomily. On June 6, he suddenly resigned as president of the RFC. The pressures of the job were enormous and his relationship with RFC Chairman Eugene Meyer had deteriorated to the breaking point. When word of difficulties at his bank in Chicago reached him in Washington, he decided it was time to leave the capital. He told a meeting of startled RFC directors that he was resigning immediately and intended to take charge of his bank in Chicago. He announced nonchalantly to the press that he intended to take a "vacation of a month or two" with Mrs. Dawes before resuming his position as chairman of the board of his Chicago bank. He had no such intention. The day before he resigned Chicago was hit by the worst run on banks in its history. On the day of Dawes's resignation, 25 Chicago banks failed to open.[40]

On Saturday morning, more than ten thousand customers waited to get into the First National Bank, which had already paid out $50 million in four days. Melvin Traylor's bank had tremendous resources and could afford to honor the demands of his customers, but even the First National had its limits. As noon approached on Saturday, Traylor feared that perhaps that limit was fast approaching. At 11 o'clock, as crowds still jammed the lobby waiting to get onto the main floor of the bank, Traylor squeezed his way into the center of the savings department and climbed upon a pedestal of a marble pillar to address the crowd. He yelled, "Ladies and gentlemen, my name is Traylor, the chief executive of this bank ... naturally I am delighted to see so many of our customers here." He thanked them for their business and told them if they wanted their money, they were entitled to it and would get it. He assured them the bank was sound, and every one of them would get every penny they had entrusted to his bank. "I want to ask your cooperation to the end that we may work as easily as possible. We want you to have your money and then you can feel that we are a good safe bank, and you can bring it back again and we will keep it for you until you want it again." He made another speech in the banking department on the second floor a few minutes later. His speeches had the intended effect: the crowd applauded and some began to drift away. The hesitant ebbing of the throng soon became a mass departure as the crowded lobby emptied back onto LaSalle Street. As the crowds dispersed from Traylor's bank, customers followed from other Loop banks soon after and calm returned. The bank run ran out of breath. By the end of the week, only five Chicago banks remained open. One of them was Dawes's Central Republic Bank, which went through the same travails on Saturday, June 25, as Traylor's First National.[41]

In one week Loop banks paid out $100 million in cash to nervous depositors, and tens of millions more fled to correspondent banks outside of Chicago and Illinois. Dawes believed that even the big Loop banks would founder in this storm. From his experience as comptroller of the currency, when he had ordered banks in similar straits closed, he reckoned his own bank too exhausted to survive. In six months it had lost $42 million in deposits — mostly from commercial accounts — which weighed heavily on Dawes's mind. On Saturday night he decided to close the Central Republic Bank, and for the first time since he had returned to Chicago the previous week, he had a night of untroubled sleep. On Sunday morning, June 26, he called Chicago's other leading bankers and asked them to meet him at his offices that morning to discuss the previous week's events and what to do. At the Sunday morning meeting he announced the closing of the Dawes Bank to the assembled bankers. Melvin Traylor argued with Dawes that such a move would reignite the events of the past week and soon force all banks in Chicago to close. Traylor seemed confident that help from Chicago banks and a modest loan from the RFC would tide the Dawes Bank over the troubles, but Dawes refused to be swayed. He argued that only a federal guarantee of deposits could save banks in America. Dawes refused to ask for RFC help, believing that in the long run all banks were doomed. Nevertheless, Traylor was sure if the Dawes Bank closed, the rest of Chicago's banks could not survive the ensuing storm. Thus, he called President Hoover at his Virginia mountain retreat and urged him to intervene and save the Dawes Bank at all cost. Impressed by Traylor's urgency, Hoover spent hours that Saturday on the telephone with Treasury officials and members of the Federal Reserve Banks urging them to work out a plan to save Chicago's banks. He asked the head federal bank examiner in Chicago to get in touch with Jesse Jones at his Chicago hotel.[42]

Traylor met other Chicago bankers in his office at the First National later Sunday morning and called Jesse Jones. Traylor asked Jones to accompany him to another meeting at Dawes's bank at noon, where Dawes repeated his determination to close his bank on Monday morning. He told the assembled bankers it was not fair to trusting customers to give all of the bank's money to distrusting depositors demanding their cash, even though the bank was sound. It would be better to close the bank and see everybody got their fair share. In any event, Dawes was sure when banks reopened correspondent banks in the countryside would withdraw all of their money, leaving city depositors stranded. In an attempt to thwart Jones's proffered help, Dawes demanded that if his bank took an RFC loan it would have to be big enough to cover every remaining deposit in the bank: $90 million. This was an absurd demand and former president of the RFC Dawes knew it, which is why he assumed it would be rebuffed.[43]

Jesse Jones called President Hoover at his rural Virginia retreat and insisted that the Central Republic Bank was too important to lose. Jones went back to the bank and began to examine the bank's books right away, and after a few hours called Hoover again to recommend an RFC loan of $90 million to the Dawes Bank. Jones believed the bank fundamentally sound and endowed with ample solid assets. Hoover talked to Ogden Mills and called Jones back, saying the Central Republic Bank had to be saved. RFC examiners arrived that night and began poring through its books. Fed Governor Eugene Meyer was notified on Sunday morning at his farm in Mount Kisco, New York, and was equally upset by the news. He convened an emergency meeting of bankers at the Federal Reserve Bank of New York, where Morgan partners Thomas Lamont and Parker Gilbert joined New York Fed Governor George Harrison and others that evening. The New York bankers also recommended that the bank be saved, lest it start a wave of collapses that could not be stopped, and offered to put up $10 million. Dawes did not believe the loan could be arranged by opening hour on Monday, so rejected any deal that involved out-of-town banks. Besides, his trust in New York bankers was such that he wanted the accord in writing. He continued to insist that the bank could be liquidated and all of its liabilities paid off at 100 percent, which would be preferable to a $90 million loan. By 4 A.M. examiners had inspected the books and declared the collateral worth $90 million, and Jones authorized a loan for $80 million. Other Chicago banks put up $10 million and New York banks agreed to loan the Dawes bank $5 million, which Dawes did not want, but it was a condition of the RFC loan.[44]

Dawes accepted the loan at the urging of Hoover and promised Meyer and others that he would draw upon the loan only as needed and assured them that its purpose was not to help the bank through liquidation. But by the end of the week, the bank lost another $15 million in deposits and within five weeks the Central Republic Bank was liquidated anyway. Its place was taken by the City National Bank and Trust Company, with Dawes as chairman of the board. As a stockholder with 52 shares of the Central Republic Bank, Dawes paid his $5,200 assessment; Dawes Brothers, Inc., paid more than a million dollars in 1936. Central Republic stock also fared poorly upon release of the news about the RFC loan: the preceding week it had traded at $50 per share; after the loan was announced, it was offered at six, but takers would buy only at four. At one point its value dropped to a single dollar. However, the poor showing of Dawes Bank stock was not the most painful legacy of the Dawes loan.[45]

Charles Dawes was famous throughout the country for having been vice president under Calvin Coolidge, an important diplomat, and being a well-connected Republican banker. That the former president of the RFC left his office in the Treasury Building, took a train to Chicago, and speedily received the largest loan ever granted by the new government agency smelled more than a little foul to many Americans. It smelled especially fishy to Democrats, who used the stink as an effective weapon in the 1932 election campaign. The Dawes loan became a burdensome political liability for President Hoover, who had personally intervened to see the loan approved, and the Republicans generally in the 1932 election contest. The bank was saved only temporarily and Dawes's reputation was permanently stained. Within days of the loan, Dawes received an impressive volume of hate mail that often vilified all bankers along with Dawes. John Carroll, whose chain of banks in outer Chicago had been allowed to collapse without the benefit of an RFC loan, publicly charged that the RFC had conspired with the big Chicago banks to wreck the city's smaller banks, making it easier for the Loop banks to take over all banking in the city. The accusations were contradicted by the consistent efforts of Loop banks to save as many smaller banks as possible. In the first half of 1932, the RFC loaned $113 million to 63 Chicago banks (including $80 million to the Dawes Bank). Five of those banks failed anyway.[46]

The remaining Chicago banks, including the Central Republic, opened normally to a relatively quiet Monday morning. In a single week in June 26, banks in Chicago failed and the city's institutions lost $74 million in demand deposits and another $29 million in time deposits. Some of that money was immediately redeposited into U.S. Post Office savings accounts. The central post office in Chicago, which normally operated between 25 and 30 windows to serve savings customers, had to use 100 windows each day of the panic week to receive between two and three million dollars in new deposits per day, when on a normal day the post office received around $200,000 in new deposits. The Federal Reserve Bank had pumped $117 million in cash into the Chicago banks through rediscounting and open market operations. All of the failed banks had suffered severely in the Depression that weighed more heavily upon Chicago than most American cities. The mostly neighborhood banks were loaded down with nonperforming mortgages, bad loans, and defaulted bonds, and were losing deposits fast. Chicago had passed through a crisis, yet the system seemed to have worked as intended to solve it. Most of the credit for saving Chicago's banks should have gone to the Chicago Federal Reserve Bank, the Clearing House Association, and the big Loop bankers who banded together to save those banks that were salvageable.[47]

The Democratic Convention in Chicago

The Democratic Party convention meeting in Chicago may have contributed in a small way to the pandemonium unleashed within the city. With Melvin Traylor up for nomination by the Illinois delegation as a favorite-son candidate at the convention, rumors circulated on the streets that Traylor's First National Bank — Chicago's largest — was in deep trouble and about to close. These rumors circulated with a lot of help from someone, for leaflets to that effect were disseminated on the city sidewalks, and people reported receiving anonymous phone calls warning of the bank's imminent collapse. Herbert Hoover and Charles Dawes asserted that communists were responsible for the rumor mongering (but Hoover also claimed it was directed against the Dawes Bank, rather than the First National). In fact, the communist press in most American cities had been advising its readers not to entrust their money to banks since the Bank of United States debacle in December 1930, though it seems doubtful that campaign inflicted much damage on banks. Cyril James suggests the rumors were payback in an effort to sabotage any possible attempt to draft Traylor for the Democratic presidential nomination, as unlikely as that event may have been. Al Smith, Jouett Shouse, and John Raskob had been promoting Traylor as an alternative to Roosevelt since the previous fall. He had gained the backing of Chicago Mayor Anton Cermak and many moneyed Chicago Democrats, especially those connected to utility companies who justifiably feared a Roosevelt candidacy. There is little likelihood that Roosevelt forces inspired the run on Traylor's bank. A more plausible explanation is that it was the work of resentful political operatives associated with Chicago's former mayor "Big Bill" Thompson or former governor Len Small, both of whom were Republicans ousted from office in April 1931 with help from the Democrat Traylor. Such a scare campaign would have been prosaic for Al Capone's political accomplice, "Big Bill."[48]

The nomination of Speaker Jack Garner for the presidential slot was more likely but, nevertheless, only a remote possibility in the event the delegates in Chicago deadlocked. He was the favored candidate of many southern delegates sworn to various favorite sons of the South, and other delegates from around the country who brought only lukewarm pledges to support Roosevelt. More importantly, Garner's primary victories in California and Texas handed him control of 90 delegates whose votes would be needed by any successful nominee. Garner earnestly wanted to avoid a convention deadlock as happened in 1924, which made certain the Democrats would not win back the White House. Garner assumed that Roosevelt was not only the most likely Democratic nominee, but also the most likely to beat Hoover, so he contemplated throwing his delegates behind Roosevelt at the most opportune moment. However, the Texas delegation would agree to swing their votes to Roosevelt only if Garner were also on the ticket. Meanwhile, in Washington, D.C., Senators Key Pittman of Nevada and Harry Hawes of Missouri obtained Roosevelt's consent to work for a Roosevelt-Garner ticket. Thus, Garner instructed his Texas and California delegates to vote for Roosevelt just as the New York governor's bandwagon was losing momentum, clinching the presidential nomination for Roosevelt and the vice-presidential slot for Garner.[49]

With Roosevelt and Garner carrying the flag for the party, the Democrats faced the very likely prospect of victory in November. The Chicago convention produced an orthodox platform dedicated to "to preserve a sound currency at all hazards, and to favor an international monetary conference," balanced budgets, repeal of the Prohibition Amendment, federal credit to states to provide unemployment relief, federal programs for useful public works to fight unemployment, and "to favor unemployment and old age insurance under state laws, [and] ... better financing" for farm mortgages. Much of the platform was taken up with demands for federal intervention in the securities markets and bank involvement in investments intended to prevent a repeat of the 1928-29 bubble and crash: federal regulation of securities and commodity trading; more information to the public about firms offering securities for sale, federal regulation of holding companies, more rigid supervision of national banks, better means to deliver funds to depositors in suspended banks, no use of bank deposits for loans to stock brokers, separation of security sales from commercial banking, and more forceful employment of the Federal Reserve Bank to restrict loans for speculation.[50]

Much of this represented the thinking of Carter Glass, embodied in his stalled bank-reform bill, about how to untangle banks from securities markets. Whether any of these proposals would prevent another bubble and crash should have been open to lively debate, but few people in either party openly challenged Glass's wisdom on the question. Indeed, the editors of the *ABAJ* routinely heaped praise on the perspicacity of the former secretary of the Treasury and current Virginia senator, even while rejecting many of his proposals. But even bankers' objections to Glass's proposals — and there were many objections — always took issue with the ill effects they might have upon banking, and rarely questioned whether the reforms would actually prevent banks from collapsing. Few bankers denied their share of responsibility in the stock-market bubble and crash. That banks were somehow responsible and the Crash, which somehow led to the waves of collapsing banks, had become accepted wisdom by the summer of 1932.[51]

Even though the editors of the *Commercial and Financial Chronicle* were among those who suspected that careless bankers and imprudent businessmen provoked the nation's troubles, they were troubled by the Democratic platform. They dismissed its attacks upon the Republican Party and the blame it saddled on Republicans for the country's economic woes as the usual partisan bluster to be expected in such documents. But the editors wondered what the Democrats meant when they blamed the Republicans for "fostering the merger of competitive businesses into monopolies and encourageing [*sic*] the indefensible expansion and contraction of credit for private profit at the expense of the public," and what such statements portended? When the Democrats called for a "drastic change in economic and governmental policies," what did they propose? The editors were puzzled that the Democrats blamed the Depression entirely on misguided Republican policies, but proposed no policies much different from those already endorsed by the Republicans. They feared the Democrats intended a return to the populist high jinks of William Jennings Bryan, which would bring nothing but chaos to the country, according to the editors. The platform contained no specifics to provoke alarm. Indeed it brimmed with suggestions catering to economic orthodoxies, but it projected a menacing tone that imbedded doubts in the minds of the editors, and no doubt many who thought as they did.[52]

While the Democratic platform and the candidacy of Jack Garner pleased economic conservatives, they were less sanguine about the prospects of a Roosevelt presidency. Roosevelt's long-standing animosity toward electrical utilities in New York State was well known and widely shared by the American public. Numerous prominent politicians, especially Republican Senator George Norris, who had doggedly campaigned for federal generation and distribution of electricity produced at the dams at Muscle Shoals, Alabama, held views even more antagonistic toward utility companies than those of Governor Roosevelt. The governor had espoused few ideas about bank reform, aside from advocating greater protection for thrift accounts. Little otherwise was known about Governor Roosevelt's attitudes toward business, except that revealed in his acceptance speech.[53]

In his acceptance speech delivered before the weary delegates in Chicago, Roosevelt attacked the failed leadership of the Republicans, not just in combating the Depression, but in having led the United States into the crisis through their policies throughout the 1920s. Low wages and skimpy dividends had kept the fruits of prosperity out of the hands of the people and kept them in corporate coffers, which loaned them to speculators on Wall Street. This view of the 1920s was actually endorsed by a surprising array of business leaders and would not have alarmed many as an overly radical view of events. He advocated greater supervision of securities markets and mandatory provision of reliable information to purchasers of securities—"publicity is the enemy of crookedness"—planks contained in the platform and already endorsed by the directors of the New York Stock Exchange and many Wall Street leaders. These suggestions were neither radical nor feared by business leaders. But he also claimed, "We must lay hold of the fact that economic laws are not made by nature. They are made by human beings." This was not likely to reassure skeptics. He also said at the end, "Throughout the nation, men and women, forgotten in the political philosophy of the government of the last years look to us here for guidance and for a more equitable opportunity to share in the distribution of national wealth." This standard progressive rhetoric, too, was not likely to comfort conservatives in either party. It could be interpreted many different ways, and there lay the rub: how did the Democratic nominee intend to apply this line of thinking? Those concerned that it might portend a radical departure would have to listen closely for further explanation and elaboration. Many did not like what they heard. Others did not like what they did not hear.[54]

With Hoover running for a second term, and Garner now officially part of the opposition ticket, there was little remaining likelihood of cooperation between the Speaker and the president. With prospects for united governmental action against the Depression dimmed, the likelihood of any government remedy for the economic situation faded. Instead, with Congress locked into combat against the president, and the two presidential candidates enmeshed in the full fury of partisan battle, politics and the actions, inaction, and malefactions of a bitterly divided government posed more of a threat to American welfare than proffered salvation.

CHAPTER FOUR

Indecision in 1932

In the latter half of 1932, bitter political discord cast its shadow over the United States and its economy. As political rhetoric heated up, the economy cooled down. Predictions of a fall revival in production, prices, and jobs came to naught as business slowed even more. Governor Roosevelt's electoral triumph in November did not allay political uncertainty, which in fact increased as the president-elect and Congress, dominated by Republican progressives and Democrats, issued mixed signals about what they intended to do in the future. The denouement of the November elections provided no relief because Roosevelt said very little about his plans. It was evident to most observers that Roosevelt had little intention of sticking to his campaign promises of cutting government expenses and balancing the budget. Rather than adding to inventories of unsold goods, businesses waited to see what the future held for their prospects. Investment slowed even more — if that were possible — and circulation of money slowed with it. Even as investment stalled, the consumption Depression was now clearly as grave as the investment Depression, as Americans stopped shopping and sales at retail stores slumped. People not only bought fewer cars, they burned less gasoline. Bank failures increased in the fall, but not in the horrific numbers seen in 1930 and 1931. The banking shocks of June 1932 really were the worst for the year; nevertheless, bankers, state officials, and politicians across the country remained very nervous about the levels of debt and Americans' ability to pay it off. The government programs instituted by the 72nd Congress seemed to have had some salutary effect upon the national credit structure, yet elected officials still cast about for remedies. All eyes focused on the president-elect, trying to discern what he might propose as a fix, but beheld little.

When Congress reconvened after the party conventions in Chicago, members rushed to pass a pile of legislation awaiting their attention. They hurried to push through a list of favorite projects and appropriations before the first session adjourned in mid–July for the beginning of the election campaign season. Many of the favored projects addressed complaints about legislation passed earlier in the session, such as the funding goals and limitations of the RFC. In June the House had authorized loans from the RFC directly to states and towns. Now the Senate considered the proposal. The House had already approved Garner's massive billion-dollar public-works bill, which in June awaited action in the Senate as New York Senator Wagner's equally ambitious public building program.

Under Speaker Garner's leadership the House passed several bills intended to increase economic activity, stimulate employment, and raise prices. The House passed the Goldsborough Bill in June that aimed to increase the currency supply until commodity prices moved upward. The Garner public works bill sought to create jobs, paychecks, and increased consumption through a $2.3 billion public works program. The Patman "fiat-money" bill to pay bonuses of $2.4 billion to veterans was intended to inflate prices and hopefully the economy. All of these bills demanded huge monetary outlays by the federal government that sank any possibility of a balanced budget. Not surprisingly, they were all forcefully opposed by purveyors of "sound money" and "sound credit," including Senator Moses and President Hoover. When considered in the Senate, Patman's bill was roundly defeated 62 to 18. However, Senator Wagner's public works bill was received with greater sympathy and passed by a slim margin only to be vetoed by President Hoover. It was subsequently reworked to exclude Garner's provision offering loans to individuals who promised to create jobs and scaled down to allot $330 million through the RFC. Additionally, the Senate voted to raise taxes, shed 50,000 federal employees, and cut the salaries of those remaining by 8¼ percent. With Democrats voting overwhelmingly for government expenses that paid no heed to balancing the federal budget, it became increasingly difficult to take seriously promises by the Democratic presidential candidate Roosevelt to deliver a balanced budget in 1933.[1]

Among bills awaiting decisions was a favorite of President Hoover's that sought to resurrect the prostrate home-mortgage market. Hoover had asked Congress in December 1931 to establish a Federal Home Loan Bank (FHLB), and they had been studying and debating the proposal since. Senator Watson of Indiana reported after surveying real-estate agents, investment bankers, and other interested parties that opponents and proponents of the proposed federal involvement in the home-mortgage market were about evenly divided. Despite a lengthy speech by Senator Couzens denouncing Hoover's suggestion, the Senate finally approved the creation of the FHLB and voted $125 million to buy mortgages from savings and loans, banks, and insurance companies. This was intended to slow down the pace of foreclosures, which had been picking up since the preceding fall, by allowing eligible homeowners to refinance their homes at lower rates for longer terms. Whether or not the FHLB reduced foreclosures by relieving some pressure on mortgage-granting institutions, it certainly allowed some financial institutions overly invested in mortgages to sell them and replace them with cash or assets acceptable as collateral to Federal Reserve member banks. In August the comptroller of the currency announced a 60-day moratorium on home mortgage foreclosures at the just-established FHLB to give clerks a chance to catch up on foreclosures. That Congress expressly excluded banks, trust companies, and insurance companies from receiving federal loans testified to the growing chill toward commercial banks among politicians.[2]

The Senate Banking and Finance Committee failed to report out the Steagall bank-deposit guarantee bill before the end of the session, so the issue was dead at least until December, when Congress would meet again. Senator Glass's bank reform proposals were similarly becalmed in the Senate. There would be no bank reform in 1932. The American Bankers Association could hardly make up its mind if this were good or bad. Despite mighty public boosting for Senator Glass's bill by important bankers, the *ABAJ* editorialized that the uncertainty of not knowing the future rules for banking was worse than any dire predictions of doom by opponents of the bill. Bankers meeting at the ABA convention in October were so divided on reform they issued no resolution on the question beyond opposition to federal guarantee of deposits.[3]

The RFC, which had been authorized in January to make loans only for six months, had to be reauthorized in July. In the process, its goals and purpose were modified in response to political difficulties that had arisen since its inception. The RFC had started out with great fanfare and received with a rush of enthusiasm. When the economy failed to respond to its injections of cash into tottering banks, railroads, and insurance companies, it started to attract more critics. When General Dawes resigned in June to return to Chicago on the brink, President Hoover used the opportunity to reorganize the leadership of the RFC. Both Fed Governor Meyer and Secretary Mills found its demands too onerous when they had other worries to occupy them. They both asked to leave and Hoover accepted their resignations. He was sorry to see Mills leave the RFC, but relieved at Meyer's departure from the board. To replace them and Dawes, Hoover tapped former senator Atlee Pomerene, a Democrat from Ohio acceptable to both conservatives and progressives, who then served as a legal counsel to the RFC in Ohio. Hoover hoped that putting the RFC in the hands of Democrats would make the Congress more cooperative and subject the new organization to less suspicion and attacks from Democrats in Congress. A Republican banker from Utica, Charles A. Miller, was placed in charge of management as president, because he was widely connected in New York, got along well with Democrats, and, like Dawes, was skeptical about Wall Street.[4]

By summer congressional leaders decided to use the RFC as the general cure-all agency to flush the country with government-sponsored money. The mission of the RFC was revised in Congress at the insistence of Speaker Garner to include loans directly to any corporation or individual likely to use the loan to create jobs. Garner was pushing this ball downhill, as the Republican Party had just included the same demand in their 1932 party platform. However, Hoover and the Senate objected to Garner's provision to allow loans to businesses and individuals. But Hoover compromised and transferred the authority to the Federal Reserve Bank instead, allowing it, for the first time, to make loans directly to business, rather than just to member banks. In response to the plights of big cities in distress, the House authorized the RFC to loan $300 million to municipalities and another $800 million to states and counties. It was also authorized to loan $1.5 billion to divers government authorities for self-liquidating projects, such as the Golden Gate Bridge, which intended to retire the loan through tolls collection.[5]

However, since the RFC's inception many congressmen and RFC officers had feared seeing the body turned into a political pork barrel, and insisted that the public projects considered for funding be carefully planned, worthwhile, and able to generate enough fees to pay off the loans in ten years. In order not to compete with the commercial credit market, the RFC also set the interest on its loans above market rates at 5.5 percent. Thus, the provision for public works, which was intended to generate jobs and inject money into the economy, was guaranteed to create work in the short run only for a handful of accountants, lawyers, and engineers involved in the complex and time-consuming process of designing and assessing big public-work projects. Under this program no jobs for bricklayers, ironworkers, cement finishers, and other working men would be created for many months, if not years, thus defeating the purpose of the bill and appropriation. In fact, not a dime was allocated before the November election and only tiny sums before the end of the year. The bulk of the appropriated money would be spent during the Roosevelt administration as plans for projects were finished and approved. By then the public-works program had been transferred from the RFC and placed under the Federal Emergency Relief Administration, run by Harry Hopkins. When Hopkins dispensed $300 million in May 1933 for public works, every cent had been appropriated in 1932 for projects initiated under the Hoover administration. The first shovel of dirt for the San Gabriel Dam in California — the initial phase of the $400 million in water projects planned for California — was turned on March 4, 1933, the day Herbert Hoover turned the White House over to Franklin Roosevelt.[6]

The program to loan money directly to states, counties, and cities for relief fared even worse than the public works program. The amount proposed by Garner and Wagner was cut by the Senate to $300 million — not enough to relieve the plight of desperate cities, such as Detroit, Chicago, and Philadelphia. By August, 13 states had applied for $200 million, and it was clear the fund would quickly be exhausted by the earliest applicants. This ensured a public hue and cry by those jurisdictions that had failed to get any relief money because they did not submit an application quickly enough. To allocate the money fairly the RFC drew up a complicated formula for distribution that promised to spread the money around geographically to towns big and small that needed it the most. When the money dribbled out slowly in small amounts, Chairman Pomerene defended the formula against critics who quickly complained of the slow-moving process.[7]

The snail's pace of disbursement angered Pennsylvania Governor Gifford Pinchot, who desperately wanted $45 million for his state's 1.5 million unemployed. On August 3, the RFC board replied to Pinchot that Pennsylvania needed to do more on its own to come up with money as other states had done. Illinois had doubled its income tax, so the RFC advised Pennsylvania to raise its gas tax, divert highway funds, and raise occupational taxes. This response that echoed the miserly demands of New York bankers upon strapped cities the previous spring angered Pinchot, who wrote an open protest letter to Chairman Pomerene denouncing the RFC as a dole for the wealthy. Senator Wagner and many who sympathized with the plight of the unemployed all across America publicly backed Governor Pinchot, who appealed directly to President Hoover in September. A few days later the RFC approved a $2.5 million loan for Pennsylvania. Pinchot exploded against this insult in another public letter to Pomerene accusing the RFC of caring only for "great banks, great railroads, and great corporations," and not at all for "the little fellow." Just days before the November polling, the RFC approved a loan to Pennsylvania for $5.5 million, which did nothing to burnish the image of the RFC or President Hoover. By December, RFC disbursements to Pennsylvania and its jurisdictions had doubled to $11 million, and by March 1933, RFC loans amounted to $26.7 million. The RFC process of allocating and disbursing the relief funds was so cumbersome and opaque that it generated only negative news stories, weighing down the Hoover administration with yet another albatross when polling day arrived in November. In the end, the arcane process for allocating funds did not shield the agency from accusations of political favoritism. United Mine Workers officials charged that the RFC had withheld funds from Pennsylvania and given them to Illinois before the election in a desperate effort to swing Illinois behind President Hoover. The charge was without merit. Hoover lost Illinois by 450,000 votes, while Pennsylvania was one of only six states to align behind the Republican candidate in 1932.[8]

While the mission of the RFC changed, the original objects of the RFC's concern — banks, railroads, and insurance companies — became the subjects of public distrust, or out-and-out political scorn. Just as the news of the RFC's rejection of Mayor Cermak's plea for $70 million to pay Chicago's teachers and firemen hit front pages, news of the $90 million RFC loan to the Dawes Bank hit as well. Curiosity expanded about where RFC money was going. Complaints about RFC monies flowing into Morgan coffers became broader, and publicists and politicians viewed the RFC loans with renewed skepticism. In 1932 the RFC approved $950 million in loans to banks, $330 million of which went to just 26 large banks in big cities. Of course, this is what the RFC was established to do, but most progressives and populists never approved of the RFC's mission in the first place, and news of big loans to big banks just poured fuel on populist fires. New York Representative La Guardia — never a friend of the RFC — charged that the RFC had spent $2 billion of public money and "no visible or tangible benefit to unemployment or agriculture had been produced. To the contrary, the loans have been directed to sources that in part are responsible for the financial chaos and have been used to entrench their wicked positions." In response to the shocking news of the Dawes Bank loan, Garner attached a section to the RFC reauthorization bill that forbade loans to any corporation that had officers who had served as officers of the RFC in the past six months.[9]

On July 16, 1932, the final day of the summer session of Congress before it retired from Washington for the campaign hustings, Speaker Garner — now the Democratic vice-presidential candidate — reattached to the conference version of the emergency relief bill an amendment that mandated the publication of information about all subsequent RFC loans. The provision had already been rejected by the Senate when offered as a clause of its RFC reauthorization bill. Garner had pushed for the amendment in the House that would have revealed details of all loans granted since February 1932, and insisted on an amendment in the House-Senate conference committee that would have publicized all new loans. In the wake of the Dawes loan, Garner claimed that Hoover ran the RFC for a "select clientele" rather than for "the people," and he hoped to show that the RFC loans were being distributed mostly to big banks and other friends of the president. Garner said after the bill passed, "I notice by the morning papers that he says he will study it in a few days and probably will sign it. He means he wants to have a few days in which to find out what Wall Street and J.P. Morgan think he should do about it."[10]

When his proposal encountered a barrage of opposition telegrams and letters from bankers to their congressmen, the proposal was reduced to the RFC providing a list of future loans and their terms to Congress, which would at least be better informed about how public funds were being spent. The directors of the RFC, President Hoover, and the majority of the Senate all opposed publicizing RFC loans, fearing that news of the loans would be perceived as adverse publicity for the banks that had taken them. Arousing public fears about the conditions of the banks that had sought and accepted loans would work against the purpose of the loans by undermining public confidence in the soundness of the institutions. Hoover had already vetoed the first version of the bill that arrived at his desk as too expensive and too expansive, but urgently wanted the RFC reauthorized. Minority Leader Robinson, who opposed the publicity clause, urged Hoover to accept it in the conference bill by promising that publicity about RFC loans would not be released by Congress during the recess, giving Hoover time to renegotiate the clause before the December session. Reassured the information would not be made public and the clause could still be removed, the president signed the bill. But House Majority Leader Rainey assured the public the lists would, indeed, be made public, and when Speaker Garner left Washington, D.C., for the summer recess, he instructed the House clerk to release the list to the press upon its arrival from the RFC.[11]

Business breathed a sigh of relief when Congress adjourned. The spree of allocations by Congress pushed through by Democrats and helpful progressive Republicans cast into doubt the commitment of either party to the principles of a balanced budget so recently enunciated at both parties' conventions. New York Representative Bertrand Snell said that business had improved ever since Speaker Garner went fishing in Texas, interrupting his campaign to "turn Congress into a pawn shop." The reaction to the congressional initiative of George Anderson, Washington correspondent of the *ABAJ*, was typical of many businessmen — "The country cannot squander itself into prosperity" — and in any event, the modest amounts injected into the economy by the federal projects were woefully insufficient if they were intended to spark the economy back into life. Benjamin Anderson of the Chase National Bank mused that the legislation that came out of Congress was not as bad as many of the outrageous and dangerous proposals that were discussed, delivering reassurance to America's businesses. In December the *ABAJ* reported that the performance of 30 high-grade bonds during 1932 directly mirrored political events. Good news provoked sudden rises in bond prices and sales, while bad news produced sharp drops. The bond-market prices peaked in March before the battle over taxes erupted in Congress and then remained depressed until Congress adjourned in July, when prices rallied once again. The noticeable improvement in securities markets in August actually spooked some Democrats, who had become convinced that Roosevelt's election was a sure thing. With the economy showing signs of renewed life, they became less certain of Democratic victory. Roosevelt's advisors Max Lowenthal, Adolf Berle, and Felix Frankfurter — and perhaps Roosevelt himself — believed Secretary Mills and Chairman Meyer had engineered a brief economic boom through inflationary policies to revive Hoover's electoral fortunes. Indeed, Roosevelt's friend Vincent Astor sourly reported a renewed optimism among Republican businessmen he encountered vacationing in Newport, Rhode Island.[12]

Many important businessmen and journalists predicted the return of prosperity once fall arrived. The London *Economist* announced the Depression in the United States was over. During the idle summer, businessmen practically held their breath waiting to see in which direction commodity prices would head in the fall. The economy did brighten slightly until early October, when the much celebrated improvement ran out of steam. Commodity prices declined, and third-quarter reports by railroads and corporations were melancholy indeed. The news was received unhappily by American business and consumers: the calm of the summer was followed by a drop in production in the fall when manufacturing normally lurched forward. In 1932 it advanced by a single step only at the very end of the year, and that was provided almost entirely by the auto industry, which hoped to capture popular imagination — and boost sales — through radically innovative new designs for the new-car fall season. Even low-cost "family" cars were being offered with the latest technology and sleek styling formally reserved for luxury models popularly associated with movie stars and gangsters. The auto companies gambled large sums on their new products — and lost most of their wagers. In the winter of 1931-32, auto companies rehired large numbers of workers to turn out cars for which there was little demand, but which the companies hoped against hope would find customers anyway. They did not, and by October 1932, the auto industry turned out paltry numbers of vehicles not seen since the war years: 35,107 passenger cars. G.M. lost $17.6 million in the third quarter; Chrysler lost $5.3 million; U.S. Steel lost $21 million. Aside from the textile industry — the only bright spot in the economy in the fall of 1932 — the fall brought cutbacks in hours and employment, and reductions in prices and wages. All signs of improvement in mid–1932 were confined to consumer industries, which boosted production of new-and-improved products in an ardent campaign to beat the competition. The locus of stagnation — heavy industry and construction — stirred not at all.[13]

The drastic decline of investment that had plagued the United States since 1929 only worsened. New issues of all kinds of securities sank to low numbers also not seen since before the war. Many states, counties, and towns, having exhausted their credit, gave up trying to sell bonds. State and municipal bond sales for the third quarter of 1932 reached a paltry $122 million, a number not seen since before the war. Railroads had likewise come to the end of their credit and could raise money neither by selling stocks or bonds, nor by pleading with banks. Railroads had issued $140 million in long-term bonds — beloved of savings banks and insurance companies—in June 1930. In June 1931 they issued $6 million. In June 1932 they issued $9,327,000, every penny of which was devoted to paying off old bonds. Even the RFC, created specifically to save the credit market for railroads, could do little to help by the summer of 1932 when railroad applications for loans subsided and amounts approved dwindled correspondingly. Until July 21 the RFC had authorized loans of $223.4 million to 38 railroads. In September it offered another $21.3 million to keep them going, but by December loans had fallen to $8,910,000. RFC loans dwindled at a time when railroads, having forgone dividends for the first time in the history of several lines, had little access to the bond market to raise money. Railroads sold only $61 million in bonds during 1932. The industry ended the year in the red by $122 million, and 13 roads fell into federal receivership.[14]

Utility companies, which had invested billions of dollars in new construction during the 1920s and reduced expenditures less and later than most private businesses after 1929, finally retrenched in 1932. Railroads, power companies, and phone companies all cut back expenses, especially on new construction. The $2 billion normally spent by railroads to buy new equipment and maintain tracks and cars was pared by the companies to $100 million. The American Locomotive Company delivered only 24 locomotives to railroads in 1932. Every one of them had been ordered in 1931; there were no orders at all in 1932. The railroads, which had in years past been a reliable and steady source of scrap metal for steel plants, stopped selling scrap both because they stopped replacing rails, bridges, and equipment, and because steel mills had little use for scrap anyway. AT&T reported a net loss of 268,000 phones in July; 201,000 in August; 90,000 more in September; and another 207,000 in October and November as people could no longer afford to pay for service. AT&T disconnected 766,000 phones in four months and lost money for the first time in its history. Electrical utilities, which continued to make profits, laid off more than 10 percent of their work force as energy consumption fell and the capacity to generate electricity exceeded demand. Even while they still made money and paid dividends, stock prices for utilities slumped to 55 percent of book value, making it almost impossible for utilities to raise money by issuing stock. Pacific Gas and Electric already had $20 million in the bank that was budgeted for an expansion program the company canceled in spring 1932 because of fears they would not be able to recoup the investment in the dim, unknown future. When the Insull midwestern utility empire vanished in a whirl of lawsuits, criminal prosecutions, and a mountain of bad publicity, utilities became even larger political targets. Electrical utilities, especially holding companies, which had served as juicy bait for progressives—especially Franklin D. Roosevelt—seeking state control of generation and distribution systems during the 1920s, now proved especially vulnerable to political harangues and became big slow-moving targets for firebrands.[15]

This decline in the bond markets seriously threatened banks that depended on income from bonds to pay their expenses and relied on them as assets to serve as collateral for loans from other banks, the Federal Reserve, or in the worst case, the RFC. The comptroller of the currency had instructed his examiners to accept bonds of dubious value at face value, but institutions were loath to accept them at face value as collateral for loans. When banks needed to raise money they sold their best assets first, and if bonds depreciated—and in 1932 many were depreciating rapidly—they could only be sold at a loss, and many were. To make matters worse, the state bank commissioner of Connecticut released lists of bonds acceptable as investments for savings banks. If a company's bonds fell off this list—and starting in 1931 many did—banks had to shed those bonds even at a loss. This influential list was closely watched by bank superintendents around the country, so a poor grade could spell ruin for companies issuing bonds and banks holding them alike. Holding depreciated bonds threatened the solvency of banks. The Somerville National Bank in Massachusetts was just one of many that became insolvent when bonds on its books depreciated badly.[16]

To combat this crisis in the bond market, two Morgan partners, Thomas Lamont and George Whitney, and a consortium of New York bankers, formed the American Securities Investing Corporation to prop up the sagging market. But they gathered a war chest of only $100 million to purchase bonds in search of buyers. Despite its seemingly gargantuan resources — it was money enough to buy every new corporate bond issued in the third quarter of 1932 — the amount devoted to its task was far from enough. Although backed by Felix Warburg, Charles Mitchell, Albert Wiggins, and other financial barons, it proffered insufficient aid to make any fundamental difference to shaky banks divesting their assets to increase their cash on hand. The corporation probably prevented the bond market from deteriorating any more, and allowed banks selling their assets to recoup somewhat higher prices, but it did not turn the financial situation of the country around any more than Owen Young's stable of committees trying to cheer up America's businessmen and get them investing again. Many bonds from weaker municipalities still could not find buyers, and bonds held by investors continue to lose value.[17]

Bank loans continued their steep decline that had started in 1930. In December 1931, all American banks held loans worth $31.4 billion. By the following June — the trough of economic activity — loans had fallen $3.5 billion to $27.9 billion. Bond holdings by banks, which had risen in the past to partially compensate for the fall in loans, had actually declined from December to June by $229 million. Thus, $3.74 billion had actually disappeared from the economy as business investment continued its long slide downward. The amount of currency held outside of banks also continued to climb: in June 1931, $3.65 billion lingered outside of banks; it increased to $4.47 billion by December in reaction to the deep troubles of late 1931. Instead of finding its way back into banks as conditions settled in the spring and as the various federal palliatives took effect, the amount hoarded mounted. By June 1932, $4.62 billion remained outside banks. From June 1931 to June 1932, nearly one billion dollars had fled the banking system, forcing banks to liquidate nearly $5.8 billion in assets because of the deposit multiplier working in reverse. And as markets remained dull, the book value of those assets was almost certainly greater than the amount received in compensation, forcing banks to sell investments at a loss. This dissolution of credit had a sorry impact not just on banks, but on the entire economy, which hit a new low in mid–1932.[18]

Added to the burden of finding money to pay hoarders, banks additionally were forced to write off bad investments. From June 1930 to June 1931, national banks alone wrote off $187 million in loans as hopeless. Over the next year banks added another $260 million to that heap of bad loans. As municipalities, counties, utilities, and others defaulted on bond payments, by June 1931 national banks wrote off another $119 million in bonds held as assets. By the following June they wrote off another $202 million. In two years, national banks alone wrote off $969.3 million in bad investments. A figure for looses by state banks is not available, but if their losses were comparable, they would have charged off an additional $877.2 million in loans and $522.2 million in securities. In two years the nation's banks probably wrote off around $2.37 billion in bad loans and defaulted securities.[19]

Trouble on the Farm

By 1932 the distress on America's farms had turned to disaster. Having suffered through the agricultural depression of the 1920s, the depth and length of the Depression that started in 1929, and the free fall of prices for farm products proved the final straw for hundreds of thousands of America's farmers. Western and midwestern farmers burned their corn for fuel rather than sell it at a loss. As early as the winter of 1930-31, residents of Idaho filled their coal bins with wheat because it was cheaper than coal. By 1932 wheat descended to a price not seen for 400 years. Farmers fed 25-cent wheat to their cattle rather then sell it at the silos, but the price of beef was so low many refused to sell their cattle either. Thousands of small truck and dairy farms in New England and the mid–Atlantic states were forsaken as struggling farmers put aside their tools, judging the toil not worth it. Marginal farmland all over the United States, but especially in the Northeast, was abandoned as less fertile land was allowed to go fallow.[20]

Farmers who had striven to improve their efficiency and productivity by buying farm machinery in the 1920s and had strained to make it pay, by 1932 had given up the battle. In 1931 International Harvester lost $15.4 million. Joseph S. Cullinan, a well-connected Houston business man, judged the condition of Texas farms as extremely fragile in 1932. Texas counties were experiencing severe difficulties collecting taxes owed by farmers, and Cullinan wrote Democratic Party Chairman John Raskob that if the state took legal action to wring the payments out of farmers, the government would find itself saddled with half the land in Texas and no one to buy it. In 1931 cotton prices fell to 5.9 cents per pound — a price never before seen in the United States — and South Carolina counties were owed $14.4 million in unpaid taxes by 150,000 farmers unable to pay. The situation only worsened in 1932 when South Carolina farmers reaped their scantiest harvest in decades: the total crop brought in only $52 million, less than half the 1930 total, a third of the 1929 figure, and one-fifth the bounty of 1923. Cotton earned South Carolina farmers a mere $26 million. Things were almost as bad on the Great Plains, where by 1932 in South Dakota 1.3 million acres of farm land had been seized in lieu of taxes. By summer of 1932, one-third of farm mortgages in the United States were behind payment or in full default.[21]

The Agricultural Bond and Credit Corporation, formed in the early 1920s to finance machinery for farmers, had loaned $38 million to midwestern farmers by 1930. They were able to collect $29 million of those loans in the course of the 1920s, but by summer 1932 they were unable to squeeze another dime out of their farm clients. By summer many midwestern farmers were tired of being squeezed. An insurance executive in Omaha complained, "The attitude around here these days is if a fellow can't pay the landlord, that's just too bad for the landlord. If a fellow can't pay his bills, then the creditor will just have to wait." Thousands of Iowa farmers had joined the populist Iowa Farmers' Union in the 1920s, seeking to find a political solution to their many problems. At the end of the 1920s, the 10,000-strong organization was promoting a "cost of production" scheme to gain government relief for hard-pressed farmers. In February 1932 the union sent a delegation to Washington to press for assistance, but they left discouraged about any prospect of real help from Congress or the Hoover administration. Thus, veteran militant Milo Reno dominated a meeting of 2,000 members of the Farmers' Union in Des Moines in May, and convinced them to form the Farm Holiday Association, to organize a nationwide farmers' strike to drive up prices and force politicians to take their demands seriously. Iowa farmers revealed new militancy that summer when they resisted with arms state agents seeking to test Iowa cows for bovine tuberculosis. The Holiday Association vowed to use whatever means necessary to enforce a nationwide farm strike to stop the production of food.[22]

When the president of the Agricultural Bond and Credit Corporation (ABC Corp.) toured the Midwest in the summer of 1932, seeing what could be done to salvage the company's investment, he was alarmed by what he saw. He was moved by the predicament both of Dakota farmers who could no longer pay for their machines and of the implement dealers who tried to repossess the machines. Dealers encountered resistance from the farmers and resorted to sneaking the machines out of farms after midnight. Often dealers found sheriffs had already seized the machines in lieu of back taxes, and the sheriffs refused to relinquish the machines despite the title to the machinery still held by the dealers. When dealers tried to get hold of farmers' wheat in silos, pledged as security against the loans, they discovered many farmers had not bothered taking their wheat to silos because of the low prices — 50 to 55 cents per bushel — offered by grain dealers. Some farmers held their wheat on their farms, waiting for the prices to rise, or fed it to their cows. Others did not even trouble themselves to harvest it. The ABC president reported seeing around Minot, North Dakota, where farmers were in open rebellion, fields full of wheat that should have been harvested. "In some areas the farm strike has taken a militant turn and pickets are patrolling the roads, urging farmers not to sell their products. The Governors of Montana, North Dakota, and Minnesota have expressed approval of a 'dollar wheat' strike movement and promised their cooperation." But local and state authorities refused to condone armed action by farmers. When farmers attacked railroad cars bringing milk and farm produce to Sioux City, county deputies, protected by mounted machine guns, responded with tear gas and mass arrests. With 55 of their brethren in custody, thousands of farmers then marched on the jail demanding their release. Rather than turn machine guns on the farmers, the sheriff obliged and let the arrested farmers go free.[23]

Striking farmers formed blockades to stop trucks from delivering produce. Milk on trucks that fell into the hands of strikers was dumped onto the road. The governor of Iowa deputized citizens outraged by the lawlessness, who attempted to escort convoys of milk trucks through the strikers outside Sioux City. One such convoy outside James, Iowa, came to a standoff between the armed escorts of 30 trucks and armed strikers determined not to let the trucks through to market. The striking pickets were well supplied with "Irish confetti" — bricks — to discourage truck drivers. Neither side wanted to open fire, and in the end the convoy turned around and did not reach the market. The governor had attracted a great deal of bad publicity when he had called out the state militia the previous summer during "the cow serum war," and was loathe to repeat the experience. Striking farmers in meetings from Sioux City to Omaha, Nebraska, denounced "eastern banking interests" and "international bankers," and demanded a debt moratorium and a temporary halt to evictions while a solution to their problems could be worked out.[24]

The farm strike gained a great deal of publicity for irate farmers of the Great Plains, but accomplished little else. After a good deal of commotion by state and national politicians, gravely concerned by such a ruckus on the farms in an election year, the strike largely petered out. The strikers succeeded in diverting milk and meat on the hoof from the Sioux City market to others — mostly Chicago, where prices continued to fall. Perhaps the most poignant result of the farmers' strike was the failure and bankruptcy of local small businessmen, such as truckers, who could not survive the fall harvest period without business. Some truckers lost their vehicles to repossessors.[25]

This agrarian turmoil seethed in the full glare of the national press, who devoted much coverage to the agitation. The number of farmers involved was in fact rather small; nevertheless, state and national politicians paid close attention and took the discontent very seriously. Claims that revolution simmered in the countryside were overblown then and in later accounts of the nation's distress. It had been many years since farmers had prospered, and many people were angry, some resorted to violence, and some called for radical solutions, but it is difficult to conclude that populist agitation was likely to lead to revolution — on the farm or elsewhere. Regardless, many people were fed up with conditions and would sanction radical measures to see things put right again. Politicians running for office in 1932, including the presidency, took notice and heed of the agitation and realized that the country not only would tolerate some radical experimentation, it might demand it.

The Election of 1932

The fall was deeply disappointing to all who expected an economic recovery to follow the summer doldrums. Ironically, Comptroller of the Currency John Pole, who had wanted to retire for some time but felt duty bound to stay in office so long as the situation looked dire, felt that the economic condition had calmed sufficiently by September for him to finally step aside. Prices and activity did indeed pick up a bit in September, as was usual in most years, but when prices slid in October, so did business. Americans went to the polls in November dejected that the fall "recovery" not only failed to arrive, but more jobs were slashed, orders canceled, and business was even slower than it had been during the very torpid summer of 1932. From September to October, bank clearings failed to rise by more than a few million dollars in most Federal Reserve districts, and actually fell in two: San Francisco and Boston. From October to November, they fell in every district, and in most districts by more than 10 percent. New York City banks negotiated the smallest dollar amount in checks in November 1932 since the Federal Reserve began keeping records. This was a national catastrophe almost as bad as November 1931.[26]

The presidential campaign of the summer heated up in the fall. After he left office, Herbert Hoover was obsessed by the corrosive character of the 1932 presidential campaign and devoted 119 pages of his memoirs to its rancor and his perception of its dastardly nature. The Democrats unleashed a broadside against not just Hoover and his administration, but against the entire Republican regime of the 1920s. In an August speech in Columbus, Ohio, Governor Roosevelt lambasted the "new economy" of the 1920s as a topsy-turvy world more familiar to Alice and the Mad Hatter than to the Americans who lived through it. He ridiculed the innovations of the 1920s as a "looking glass world" of "stock jobbery, salesmen, publicity, overseas loans, phony paper profits," increasing unemployment and overproduction, foolish investment in unneeded new plants that turned out too many goods that no one could afford to buy, all overseen by the Mad Hatter, Hoover.[27]

Roosevelt was no socialist, nor was he anti-business. "Wall Street Wizard" Bernard Baruch, who contributed $200,000 to the Roosevelt campaign, condemned accusations that Roosevelt was a radical as ridiculous, and pronounced his views "sound." Like all progressives Roosevelt was anti–*big* business, and especially hostile to "finance," personified by J.P. Morgan. His animus against finance was also fueled by personal resentments, of which he harbored many against the other rich boys he had met and endured at Groton and Harvard, and who had never fully accepted him. Roosevelt knew Treasury Secretary Ogden Mills, scion of a wealthy New York banking family, from Harvard, New York society, and as a neighbor in the Hudson River Valley estate country, and belittled him as "little Oggie" behind his back. Mills, according to Raymond Moley, was one Republican who genuinely gave Roosevelt pause because of his seriousness and profound understanding of public finance, so he dismissed him with mockery rather than confront his ideas directly. Whatever the source of his animus against America's wealthy, it was shared by a growing portion of the American public, most of whom had never heard of Groton, and Roosevelt amply exploited that prejudice in the 1932 campaign and years after.[28]

Yet, Roosevelt's campaign was badly received by many concerned by the plight of business. A prominent Delaware attorney who approved of Roosevelt's promise to repeal the Prohibition Amendment, nevertheless intended to vote for Hoover — without enthusiasm.

> I suppose that Governor Roosevelt has in mind the kick-the-chair protest vote which the Republicans captured in 1896.... The Democrats may reasonably expect to get that vote in 1932, but Gov. Roosevelt is going after it in such reckless manner, and by means of such wildly impractical promises, that I can hardly credit him even with sincerity; and that being so, I doubt his sincerity even on the prohibition issue. If he should succeed in saturating a considerable portion of the American public with some of the ideas which he has lately been advancing, it will not be long before a man who calls the attention of the people to some cold facts, such as the fact that the law of supply and demand cannot be changed by governmental action, and the fact that high wages cannot be paid unless there is a demand for the goods produced by the wage-earners, and the fact that it is not a proper function of government to make happy homes or to guarantee a job for every citizen, may be in danger of assassination.[29]

Of course, not all businessmen agreed. Texas Democrat Joseph Cullinan thought Roosevelt would bring long overdue reforms to business regulation that could only strengthen American business. A former Republican congressman from Butler, Pennsylvania, invested in the oil and gas business, Thomas Phillips, advised Jouett Shouse that only fear of Roosevelt and the Democrats assured the unpopular Hoover of any votes at all in Pennsylvania: "The fear seems to be somewhat general that the Democratic candidate, if elected, would mess things up worse if possible than they are now." Irénée du Pont, a "wet" Republican, was very leery of Roosevelt's campaign: "Mr. Roosevelt's utterances have shocked me. His assent to the maldistribution of wealth seems to me demagogic propaganda, appealing to such envy and greed as there are in the masses when at a time, above all others, discord and uncertainty should be eliminated. Aside from this I am fearful of his associates." His brother, Pierre du Pont, a Democrat who was close to Roosevelt rival Al Smith, hesitated to commit himself to the party nominee, and expressed the same reserve about those surrounding the Democratic nominee. "I feel that it would be a mistake for me to make a public statement supporting Mr. Roosevelt's candidacy at the present time.... I wish it were possible for him to make some announcement of his preferences.... My real fear in the situation is that Mr. Roosevelt may not be surrounded by those best qualified to assist in the administration of government affairs." Despite such hesitation, du Pont contributed $27,732 to the Democratic campaign and voted for Roosevelt in November.[30]

The people that Roosevelt had surrounded himself with as advisors in his "Brains Trust" did not attract universal approval. Thirty years later, Raymond Moley maintained that he had always been pro-business, however he took a dim view of Wall Street and had a low opinion of "the banking community." Upon Moley's recommendation, Roosevelt took on Rexford Tugwell, a Columbia University economist, as an advisor on economic questions. Tugwell was well known as a convinced proponent of national economic planning by the federal government. In 1931 before the American Economic Association, he called not only for the abolition of profits and business, but for scrapping the constitution and all outdated and obsolete laws and statutes from the 18th and 19th centuries. He stated unequivocally that "business will logically be required to disappear. This is not meant as an overstatement for the sake of emphasis; it is literally meant," and "no one [will be] exempt from compulsion to serve a planned public interest." In case any doubts lingered in listeners' minds about what he proposed, he added, "The future is becoming visible in Russia." Tugwell had not changed his thinking much by the time he was enrolled in Roosevelt's "Brains Trust," where he argued for the nationalization of credit, a proposal that Roosevelt never seriously entertained.[31]

Roosevelt himself was hardly reassuring in many of his public comments. Many of his sharp attacks were not against the Hoover administration or even the Republican leadership of the past 12 years, they were directed against American business and the prosperity of the 1920s. At Oglethorpe University he lamented the chaos of American industry and its woeful lack of "social planning," as opposed to planning by "special interests ... [whose] interests do not coincide with the interests of the Nation as a whole.... We cannot allow our economic life to be controlled by that small group of men whose chief outlook upon the social welfare is tinctured by the fact that they can make huge profits from the lending of money and the marketing of securities— an outlook which deserves the adjective 'selfish' and 'opportunist.'" According to Roosevelt, this selfishness should be countered by "controlling by adequate planning the creation and distribution of those products which our vast economic machine is capable of yielding." Private investment of capital had produced waste and maldistribution of goods and income, and rewards to labor would have to be greater while "rewards to capital, especially capital which is speculative, will have to be less." To achieve this Roosevelt promised "bold, persistent experimentation ... to correct, by drastic means if necessary, the faults in our economic system from which we now suffer." Roosevelt repeated much of this contention in a speech in September before the Commonwealth Club in San Francisco, where he again argued that "titans of finance" and "princes of property" could not be allowed to control the economic life of the country. Most Americans could agree with much of this, but it could mean many things, and the governor failed to clarify just what he meant. And that was what troubled American businessmen. They did not trust the progressive New York governor to make "drastic changes" that would allow the free enterprise system, as they understood it, to continue. State Department advisor and Roosevelt enthusiast Herbert Feis wrote a friend shortly before election day, "I am glad of his enthusiasm and buoyancy but I cannot escape the sense that he really does not understand the full meaning of his own recitations. I await confirmation that he realizes where the work is, what is going on, and what should be done."[32]

Throughout the campaign Roosevelt bashed the Hoover administration for incompetence and dithering. Roosevelt and Democrats continued to blame much of the Depression on the Smoot-Hawley Tariff. In speeches in Seattle and San Francisco, Roosevelt blamed the tariff for American inability to export, charging that Canada had enacted retaliatory tariffs against U.S. farm products, such as fruit, further depressing demand and prices. He went on to recommend barter as a solution to the trade slump. Roosevelt additionally mocked Hoover's program to help farmers as suggested by his secretary of agriculture, Arthur Hyde: "to plow up every third row and shoot every tenth cow." This, of course, was to be the New Deal program to manage agricultural surpluses proposed by his secretary of agriculture, Henry A. Wallace. A few days before the balloting, the respected and conservative senator Carter Glass took to the national airwaves in a surprising attack upon President Hoover and Treasury Secretary Mills. Glass charged that the United States was never close to going off the gold standard last February, as Hoover had asserted in a speech in Des Moines on October 4, and if it had been, then it was a dastardly act of the federal government to offer gold-backed bonds to the public knowing full well the government might not be able to pay off those bonds in gold. Until his November radio address, Senator Glass had largely stood aside from the contest because of ill health and discomfort about the Democratic candidate. However, after several attacks upon the Democrats in Congress by Hoover and other Republicans stumping for the president, Glass jumped in to reassure the public of the Democratic candidate's steadfast devotion to the gold standard and sound money. His anti–Hoover philippic shocked Hoover and Mills, and helped calm voter worries about Roosevelt's trustworthiness, even if the Virginia senator's own doubts about the Democratic candidate remained very much alive.[33]

Newspapers at the time failed to notice that the decision to have Glass rather than Roosevelt answer Hoover allowed Roosevelt to avoid making any definitive comment on the gold standard. Roosevelt stated to his advisors explicitly, "I do not want to be committed to the gold standard. I haven't the faintest idea whether we will be on the gold standard on March 4th or not; nobody can foresee where we shall be." In fairness to Roosevelt, he was right: no one knew if the United States would be on the gold standard come March, and he did not want to say anything that might hasten a separation from gold — an eventuality that Roosevelt evidently did not favor. But Roosevelt was open to "creative thinking" on currency and economic questions. In fact, he demanded it and excluded Newton Baker and John Davis— Democratic candidate for president in 1924 and lawyer to J.P. Morgan and Company—from his campaign because he considered their ideas on economic questions "timid."[34]

Of course, Republicans churned stormy waters by predicting dire consequences if Roosevelt were elected. Just before election day, Hoover warned 21,000 voters in New York's Madison Square Garden, and another 40,000 outside, that the radical Roosevelt would ram through revolutionary changes and destroy the fundamental basis of American government. If Democrats were allowed to experiment with the economy, he warned, "Grass will grow in the streets of a hundred cities, a thousand towns [and] ... weeds will overrun the fields of a million farms." President Hoover personally launched few attacks upon Roosevelt, but encouraged other Republicans to take the gloves off in the campaign. Republicans repeatedly warned voters that a Democratic victory in November would usher in an era of unprecedented danger posed by wild men let loose by Roosevelt and Democrats upon American business and traditions.[35]

Governor Roosevelt countered in a speech in Boston that Republicans "crack the whip of fear over the backs of American voters." And that "5,000 men in effect control American industry. These men, possessed of such great power, carry likewise a great responsibility. It is their duty to use every precaution to see that this power is never used to destroy or limit the sound public policy of the free and untrammeled exercise of the power of the ballot.... In violation of this duty some of these 5,000 men are invading the sacred political rights of those over whom they have economic power. They are joining in the chorus of fear initiated by the president, the secretary of the Treasury, and the Republican National Committee. They are telling their employees that if they fail to support the administration of President Hoover such jobs as they have will be in danger."[36]

The *Commercial and Financial Chronicle* editorialized, "It would be idle to deny that the presidential campaign is exerting a repressing effect upon business for the time being.... Each party intones that ruin and doom awaits us if the other wins." Even Democratic businessmen who backed Roosevelt believed that businesses were awaiting the election results before committing themselves to new expenditures. New York anti-prohibitionist crusader Jesse Ricks believed that business would improve no matter who won, but only if the winner committed himself to a balanced budget. This judgment was backed up by the observations of an Indiana entrepreneur, Edward A. Rumely, trying to drum up interest in prefabricated housing, who added:

> I find it impossible to get any business man to make a decision regarding the investment of money, in even small amounts, at the present time. As a result of my various contacts during the past six weeks, I felt that I was confronted with a stone wall. However, on checking up with others, I find that this is a general condition. Many firms have taken their traveling men off the road entirely and are holding them under salary but keeping them at home to save their traveling expenses because of their finding that it is futile to make effort at the present time.

Rumely, a Borah-progressive Republican, was among those who believed Roosevelt's election would lead to a restoration of confidence among consumers and producers.[37]

Franklin Roosevelt was elected president in a crushing victory over Herbert Hoover: 22,808,638 to 15,758,901. Hoover carried only six states, all in the Northeast. After the polling, conditions failed to improve as many, especially Democrats, had hoped and predicted. After the polling the *Commercial and Financial Chronicle* noted again, "There seems to be some hesitancy as before about embarking upon anything except routine transactions—the same reluctance to engage in new ventures that involve anything except the most ordinary risks." Federal Reserve Governor Eugene Meyer was among those who believed that Roosevelt's election and fears about his unknown program pushed the recovering economy into another slump. He noted that a wave of cancellations of orders already placed by businesses started on November 10. The lingering problem of the inter-allied war debts also hung over the heads of finance and business. Chase National Bank economist Benjamin Anderson told a conference of manufacturers in Chicago that business would not improve so long as the war debt question remained unresolved and kept international trade depressed. "Business is disappointed that the Hoover–Roosevelt conference on inter-allied debt was inconclusive to say the least, and as a consequence the business world has suffered another sad disappointment and business recovery has been further retarded," reported the *Commercial and Financial Chronicle*. The anxiety produced by the debts and the constant threat of their cancellation vastly outweighed the size of the debts. The amounts of money involved, although not unsubstantial, were not large enough to upset the American economy. Nevertheless, they posed a constant irritant to the well-being and confidence of bankers and people who depended on them. That the issue lingered on and on without resolution was probably worse than any economic reversal their cancellation or default would have caused. The debts also served as an albatross around the necks of the biggest New York bankers who had arranged and serviced the loans since the war. Many Americans lumped them with the South American loans of the 1920s that had gone bad since 1931 and held "international bankers" responsible for the financial plight of the nation. And such views were not limited to farmers on the plains; Francis Garvan, president of the Chemical Foundation in New York, blamed "international bankers," war loans, and subsequent loans to Europe to ease the financial turmoil of the 1920s for the Depression.[38]

The economy shuffled through June and July in the doldrums. Prices for stocks and bonds hit all-time lows in June. Then securities markets perked up in August, and business saw something of a rebound at the end of the summer. The summer was not kind to banks. After its tumultuous June, Chicago, the center of the 1932 crisis, muddled through the rest of the year without distracting drama: only ten more banks failed in Cook County. Another 65 banks failed throughout Illinois before the year was out; 52 of those were small state banks. July was a bad month for Iowa—although most months seemed to have been bad for Iowa banks—when 26 closed their doors, freezing $13.5 million in deposits. The Union Trust Company of Baltimore was subjected to a frightening run on August 18 with hundreds of customers besieging the bank's 18 branches. Bank officers assured their clients there was no cause for concern as the vaults held $20 million in cash. That night the trust company's directors asked the RFC for a $20 million loan. The Federal Reserve Bank lent a hand the next day rushing $5 million in new notes to the trust company's main office. The run died out the next day, Friday, and the trust company survived, though deposits continued to trickle away. The only spectacular failure of the season occurred in New Jersey, where the New Jersey National Bank and Trust Company foundered in Newark on June 11. Like so many other city banks that went under in the Depression, the New Jersey bank had expanded quickly in the late 1920s through mergers until by 1932 it held $13.9 million in deposits and was capitalized at $2.8 million, making it one of the larger institutions in the state, though far from the largest. The condition of the bank deteriorated rapidly in 1932, losing almost $1 million in deposits per month, until by June it held only $8 million. To make matters worse, it was saddled with $5.7 million in debts to other banks (including $381,000 to the RFC), and its portfolios were burdened by $13 million in dubious loans. The bank held large numbers of municipal bonds issued by Elizabeth and Newark, which was just then trying to sell more bonds, and finding no takers. The bank closed unexpectedly on a Saturday morning when a simple note appeared on the door of its main headquarters at Market and Broad Streets in the center of Newark's business district announcing that the bank's affairs had been handed over to federal examiners. A few days later a vice president of the bank's parent company, the Guaranty Company of Newark, asked federal examiners to take charge of that institution as well, as it had been discovered that the national bank's president, John J. Stamler, had illegally appropriated $200,000 worth of Guaranty Company stock to use as collateral for loans from his bank. A week later the Guaranty Company's president, Edward Shoen, killed himself by turning on a gas jet in his home and placing it and his head under a blanket.[39]

While RFC intervention in Illinois helped stave off financial collapse in the Midwest, the long deterioration of the economy had taxed the endurance of the mountain states to their limits. The disappearance of a sustaining market for mining, timber, and ranching had reduced many western regions to penury. Farming, livestock, wool, and copper prices all plunged after 1929 dragging down income in Arizona, which had fallen from $223 million in 1929 to a meager $43.2 million in 1932. Banking had suffered correspondingly as deposits in Arizona dropped from $93 million to $45 million. Arizona was served by 41 banks in June 1930 and only 26 by September 1932. Outstanding loans of a modest $36.6 million in June 1930 dwindled to a mere $20 million by September 1932. In 1931 loyal customers of the Bank of Douglas had livestock loans rejected, because the prospect of selling livestock for more than it cost to keep the animals alive dimmed. A grocery store in Douglas that had a running credit of $5,000 had it cut to $1,000. Two state banks and a small national bank failed in June 1932 freezing $4.6 million in deposits, more than 10 percent of the total in the state.[40]

With prices for agricultural commodities reaching new lows, Idaho had sunk into destitution by the summer of 1932. While banks in much of the country reduced the interest they paid on savings deposits, banks in Idaho and Montana stopped paying any at all. On August 9 the Boise City National Bank failed, freezing $2.4 million in deposits and provoking banks runs throughout southern Idaho, spilling into eastern Oregon. On August 31 the largest bank in Idaho, the First National Bank of Idaho in Boise, failed, taking nine affiliated banks with it. Together the banks held around $10 million in deposits. In two months 13 banks in Idaho failed, leaving only a single bank open in Boise and threatening to cause a general financial collapse in the mountain state. On September 3 the remaining banks in Idaho declared a withdrawal moratorium to head off a general bank failure while officials negotiated with RFC officials. Local bankers, businessmen, and state officials huddled with officers of the RFC to work out a rescue plan to save the remaining banks and, if possible, reopen the closed banks. While the talks dragged on, the town council in Twin Falls passed an ordinance allowing the mayor to declare a two-week bank holiday, closing all banks in town. The next day he did because local officials and businessmen were especially concerned about the condition of the largest remaining bank in town, the Twin Falls Bank and Trust Company. During the course of 1932, its loans had dwindled from $703,000 to $306,000; its investments from $381,000 to $292,000; and its deposits from $1,257,000 to $872,000; and the town's businessmen doubted the bank could survive. The Twin Falls National Bank had succumbed the previous December. With RFC loans eight Idaho banks were able to avoid receivership and reopen, unfreezing over $8.25 million in deposits. The Twin Falls Bank and Trust Company survived without help from the RFC. In 1932, 24 banks with $11.6 million in deposits failed in Idaho. Those numbers pale in comparison to the astounding numbers of banks that failed in Iowa and Illinois, freezing enormous amounts of money. But all banks in Idaho held only $40 million in deposits, so the frozen funds represented more than a quarter of all deposits in the state. Idaho was a success story for the RFC, but the fundamental problem that caused the collapse — economic stagnation in the mountain states— remained, and the most significant event to emerge from it was about to erupt.[41]

A week before voters went to the polls in November the crisis moved south. A minor tremor emitted from Nevada, which ultimately reverberated until it shook the nation, not financially, but politically. Governor Fred B. Balzar, faced with the imminent collapse of the largest banking chain in the state, ordered a statewide moratorium on banking, and closed all banks in the state for 12 days. Towns, such as Twin Falls, had declared such "holidays" before, but never had a governor shut down the banks of an entire state. He followed the precedent set in Germany, where all the banks in the country had been closed, but the situation in Germany had been vastly more dire than in Nevada. Nevertheless, the crisis in Nevada was bad enough and had been brewing since spring. The entire state had only 90,000 inhabitants and 41 banks, making it about the same size as Allentown, Pennsylvania. Unfortunately, the economy of Nevada was not so diversified as Allentown's. The state was entirely dependent on livestock raising and mining, two business sectors in serious doldrums by mid–1932. Prices for leather and meat on the hoof actually had risen midyear, because large numbers of ranchers and farmers had refused to sell their animals for the derisory prices offered at auctions. Unemployment in mining counties had reached 75 percent. Nevada was in serious financial straits.[42]

Banks, which served the state's mining companies and ranchers, were having difficulties collecting loans and feared extending further credit to such tottering clients. Like banks elsewhere, Nevada banks leached deposits, forcing weakened banks to dump securities to raise cash. Nevada banks suffered accelerated erosion of depositor confidence after a series of runs hit banks in California and Idaho in September and October. Nine banks in Idaho suspended operations in a few weeks. Correspondent banks in California, especially the Bank of America, had problems of their own and were ill-disposed to help out troubled banks in Idaho and Nevada. The RFC had extended a few million dollar in the spring to tide Nevada banks over, but only for six months. Most money in the state, including 65 percent of state government funds, were held in a chain of 12 banks owned by George Wingfield. Wingfield had posted the remaining assets of his banks as collateral for RFC loans in the summer, but when livestock prices failed to revive in the fall and Wingfield could wring no more money out of the RFC for his banks, he concluded he had to close. He informed Governor Balzar of his predicament on October 30. The governor immediately flew to Washington, D.C., for an urgent meeting with President Hoover and directors of the RFC. He tried to persuade them to release a $2 million loan to the Wingfield chain, but without success. The RFC directors told Balzar they would need to examine the entire Nevada banking system to authorize a loan, and that would take time. Thus the governor resolved to buy time: on the night of October 31, he telegraphed his lieutenant governor to proclaim an immediate bank holiday for 12 days.[43]

The 12-day moratorium gave the RFC enough time to review the situation in Nevada and proclaim it hopeless. The Wingfield banks were beyond rescue. Rather than allow the inevitable painful liquidation, Governor Balzar extended the holiday until mid–December. When the holiday ended on December 14, the Wingfield banks were declared insolvent and turned over to national banking authorities as receivers. Receivers ultimately judged that of $8.2 million in loans owned by the National Bank of Reno, $4,171,000 were doubtful and $2,193,000 were worthless. The First National Bank of Winnemucca was in similar straits: it held $600,000 in good loans; 1.2 million in doubtful loans; and $350,000 that were worthless. Nevada Senator Key Pittman was irate that the RFC and the federal government would allow the banking system of an entire state to fold. Because its funds were frozen in the Wingfield banks, the University of Nevada had to shut its doors, too. Pittman demanded that the RFC authorize loans to Nevada and that "the federal government should take a loss if necessary." His insistence did neither him nor his state any good. However, the import of the Wingfield collapse was not the calamity visited upon Winnemucca, but the precedent set by Governor Balzar of shutting down all banks in the state in a desperate effort to buy time.[44]

Bank difficulties worsened in November. The election results did not contribute to the problems even if rock-ribbed Republican bankers were no doubt deeply disappointed by the results. Before November was over, bank runs visited Illinois, Minnesota, and Iowa. Pennsylvania and Oklahoma both witnessed wide-scale bank failures that crippled some important banks. Trouble struck Oklahoma when banker H.T. Douglas was unable to come up with collateral worth $1.25 million demanded by eastern bank creditors to secure loans to keep his chain of 28 state and national banks afloat. When he failed to obtain a loan, he sacrificed six banks with combined deposits of more than $3.3 million, including the Shawnee National Bank that held almost $2 million. Two other small banks went down in the storm. Problems in Pittsburgh were somewhat larger. On November 12 the Diamond National Bank closed because its deposits had shrunk by $17 million in 18 months, leaving the bank with only $9.6 million. Saddled with $1.7 million in worthless loans, $8.75 million in doubtful loans, and only $3 million in paying loans, the board of directors viewed the situation as hopeless and voted to turn the bank's assets over to the comptroller of currency. Three days later, the Duquesne National Bank of Pittsburgh followed suit after heavy withdrawals. Its loan portfolio was similarly loaded with bad investments. The next day the Real Estate Savings and Trust of Pittsburgh closed its doors with deposits of $2.7 million after having dropped $900,000 since June. Even though neither of these banks had any outstanding RFC loans, RFC Chairman Atlee Pomerene promised the resources to make good their deposits and said they closed for strictly local reasons. Perhaps, but the RFC failed to save either Pittsburgh bank or any of those in Oklahoma. The pace of bank failures picked up nationwide: 65 in September, 97 in October, 95 in November, and 153 in December. The amount of money tied up in these failures was relatively modest compared to the astounding amounts witnessed earlier. And perhaps a bit of optimism was even warranted, as banks reopened at almost the same pace as they closed, freeing deposits locked up in temporarily suspended banks. While $257.9 million in deposits sat in banks that had suspended operations since June, $163.9 million was released in those newly reopened in the same period.[45]

By the end of a bad year, American banks were in poor shape. And yet it seemed that perhaps the worst of the Depression had already passed. Since the dark days of June, the pace of business had picked up a bit, and the overall condition of banks had stopped deteriorating at the rapid clip of late 1931 and early 1932. While banks made even fewer loans and held less in deposits in December 1932 than in June, the rate of diminution had markedly slowed. While banks offered $26 billion in loans, they had cut back by only $1,779 million in six months, the smallest six-month decrease since June 1930. Banks had eagerly bought the securities offered by the United States Treasury, so that total holdings of government securities grew, even while banks held fewer of other securities, such as railroad, utility, and municipal bonds. Even the rate at which currency left the banking system for tin cans slowed: $53 million fled banks in the last half of the year, leaving $4.67 billion outside of banks. However, excess reserves continued to mount in bank vaults as money languished unused. Colonel Leonard Ayers of the Cleveland Trust observed in early 1933 that large depositors—meaning treasurers of large corporations—moved large corporate accounts out of regional banks to safer havens in New York City. In order to release those funds to move to New York, regional banks had to liquidate assets. They had already been liquidating assets since 1931, and many interior banks were now left with only the hardest-to-sell assets. Continued demands for liquidity so that funds could be transferred around the country placed great strains on many interior banks. And those banks in New York that received new funds were less than happy to do so, for they, too, would have to keep the newly arriving funds as liquid as possible. This money had scant investment opportunities in any event.[46]

Economic gloom hung over the United States in December when Congress reconvened to conclude unfinished business. The spate of spending in the first half of 1932 occurred while tax revenues plummeted on all levels. The federal deficit had grown by $2.27 billion in one year, which was nearly half the federal budget for 1932-33. The government had to borrow $2.89 billion to keep going. Congressmen and President Hoover stared at the yawning budget gap with alarm, and all agreed that taxes would have to be raised and expenses cut. Taxes had already been raised once in 1932, but income taxes had been left alone. Secretary Mellon's hard-fought tax cuts were rescinded in 1930, and now President Hoover urged Congress to raise the rates higher: double for the highest brackets, but taxes were raised by 1,000 percent or more on the most modest taxpayers. Citizens with an income of $3,000 in 1932 had to pay $6 in income taxes; for 1933 they were told to pay $80. Hoover also asked the lame-duck Congress to reduce federal spending by $580 million, which they agreed to do. However, President-elect Roosevelt instructed Democratic leaders not to cooperate with President Hoover in reorganizing the executive branch, and to wait until

March 1933 to find any savings there, which they also agreed to do. Still, Hoover and Congress strove to reduce spending and increase revenues to narrow the widening budget chasm, but business opinion, wed to reigning economic orthodoxies about sound money and balanced budgets, continued to worry about ruined federal credit and out of control inflation. Agitation for induced inflation by various theorists only added fuel to the flames.[47]

Many proposals had been floated in Congress and in the popular press to inflate prices by increasing the money supply through various artifices. In fall of 1932, a concerted campaign was mounted to influence Congress and President-elect Roosevelt to adopt a "commodity dollar" that would stabilizes prices at some elevated level. This theory, suggesting a decrease of the gold content of the dollar until the average price of a basket of commodities reached levels seen in the mid–1920s, was propounded and pushed principally by Professors James Harvey Rogers, of Yale, and George F. Warren, of Cornell, both of whom had served as Roosevelt advisors during the 1932 election campaign. Warren was contacted by a group of midwestern businessmen who believed the debt problems of farmers and foreigners could be solved by inducing a cheap dollar to stimulate trade and ease repayment of the war debts. The businessmen organized themselves into a lobbying group, the Committee for the Nation, and set about proselytizing to any and all influential people who would listen.[48]

Arguments articulated by the committee were adopted by Father Coughlin and spread among his vast radio-listening audience. Committee members bombarded the Roosevelt election committees during the campaign with a hail of letters, pamphlets, and unsolicited advice, which continued to rain upon Roosevelt and his advisors after he won the balloting. Roosevelt declined to meet with members of the committee, but his advisors Raymond Moley and Rexford Tugwell did, and listened to their arguments without committing the incoming administration to any definite plan. And that was the problem: no one knew what the new administration would do because the administration members did not know either.[49]

Rumors swirled about what Roosevelt intended to do once he assumed the helm. There is no evidence that Roosevelt listened seriously to the ideas promoted by Warren, Rogers, and the Committee for the Nation until fall of 1933, after the economy failed to reignite that summer. But contacts between Roosevelt's advisors and "inflationists," some associated with the Committee for the Nation and others not, were well-known and much publicized. In fact, an "inflationist" claque within the Roosevelt camp had gathered around Harvard law professor Felix Frankfurter and lawyer Max Lowenthal. They urged policies to achieve inflation without acknowledging the real goal. This perturbed Adolf Berle, who opposed inflation and seriously objected to any dissimulation by calling it something else. Berle argued that inflation would help farmers and speculators and hurt everyone else. He advised Roosevelt, "Leaving aside the propriety of inflation, there is no excuse whatever for leaving the country in ignorance of what is being done. A policy of inflation might be undertaken consciously, as in 1870 or in Bryan's time; to undertake it secretly seems little short of folly." This sentiment was shared by advisor Walter Wheeler Stewart, an economist to business, who argued in early 1933 that the president-elect ought to articulate a policy and announce it. Rexford Tugwell and Raymond Moley disagreed, arguing that all options should be available to Roosevelt once he became president and none excluded beforehand. But even that was a policy of sorts that could have been announced and yet was not.[50]

Persistent rumors about Roosevelt's intentions to inflate the dollar through printing-press currency, reducing the gold content of the dollar, or going off the gold standard altogether agitated business opinion and dampened investment. The *Kiplinger Washington Newsletter* wrote on December 31, 1932, that Congress would take no action to inflate the money supply because of their inability to agree on what to do and that no one knew Roosevelt's stance toward inflation because the president-elect did not know it himself. Therefore, rumors of Roosevelt's intention to inflate the currency were just that, only rumors. Congressional Democrats were on no surer footing because they, too, lacked a plan on what to do. This deeply worried many Democrats who looked to the president-elect for guidance. Roosevelt's cabinet was in no better position to formulate a plan of action, for they, too, were disunited and lacked the necessary leadership that Roosevelt should have been providing. All of this fed the Washington rumor mill, as Washington newspaper correspondents cranked out "inspired dispatches" that reflected the thinking of high-ranking Democrats with access to Roosevelt. But the sharp divergence of the stories created highly conflicting versions of Roosevelt's intentions that fed the rumor mill with fresh speculations. All of this had a dampening impact upon business. The New York markets, especially, fell into doldrums as business postponed making any plans for the near future. Kiplinger's prognosis was for increased prolonged unemployment, slack consumer demand, and little business investment until the political landscape could be more clearly discerned by Roosevelt's actions.[51]

International banker James Warburg was among those increasingly worried by the deteriorating financial situation and Roosevelt's plan to address it.

> Bank failures increased alarmingly, and people began to hoard both currency and gold. As an executive of one of the big New York banks, I worried about what the future would bring. My associates in the bank felt it was impossible to plan an intelligent course of action without having some idea of what the policies of the new administration would be…. No one knew what policies Roosevelt would pursue as President. Hoover vainly tried to draw him out and enlist his cooperation during the interregnum. But the president-elect took the position that the crisis was not of his making and that the situation was deteriorating so rapidly that it was impossible to foresee what actions would be desirable or practicable when he took office.

Warburg eventually lunched with Raymond Moley for two hours in the new year to find out if Roosevelt would stick to his campaign promise of "sound money," or would initiate an inflationary monetary policy. Moley gave Warburg the strong impression that "no very definite ideas had as yet crystallized." He similarly met with Tugwell and Charles Taussig — who had served as an advisor during the campaign — for the same purpose and came away no better informed. In February 1933 Roosevelt finally met with Warburg and a group of interested people in New York and asked Warburg if he would work with Moley "on the banking and currency situation," which Warburg agreed to do. This may have inspired greater confidence about the future in Warburg, but it failed to make a deep impression among bankers and investors generally, who continued to harbor strong doubts.[52]

Even South Carolina Senator James Byrnes, a Roosevelt loyalist and confidante (to the extent that Roosevelt had any), took to the airways urging "the Democratic party" to hue to fiscally safe policies, a balanced budget, and reminded listeners that "Uncle Sam is not a Santa Claus, and the Treasury is not a Christmas tree…. It is not the duty of the government to support every man in the United States…. The next president will come into office with a definite program and for the accomplishment of that program will make a courageous fight." But words by Senator Byrnes were not enough to reassure jittery businessmen. Roosevelt maintained his silence. And Bernard Baruch, Democratic Party busybody, who perennially inserted himself into government affairs whether invited or not, took advantage of every opportunity to recommend "sound money and a balanced budget," hoping that Roosevelt would do likewise. He did not.[53]

CHAPTER FIVE

1933

As 1932 came to a close, conditions were bad and getting worse in most of the United States. By the end of 1932, the Depression had dragged on for 39 months, and conditions offered little hope of improvement in the near future. Except for a brief upturn in the summer of 1932, the economy had been on a continuous slide since August 1931 without respite. Fleeting interludes of optimism had not turned into recovery, and by December 1932 people were beginning to lose hope. Few predicted any improvements in the short run, and many people were running out of faith in the long run. Agrarian radicalism exercised greater appeal, not less, and the prairie rebellion was spreading. Votes for Socialist and Communist presidential candidates topped one million in 1932 versus barely over 300,000 in 1928. Communist William Z. Foster increased his vote from 21,181 in 1928 to 102,785 in 1932 — still only a fraction of the total, but nevertheless a five-fold increase.[1]

If few Americans turned to political radicals for solutions, ever more demanded vigorous action from their government. The efforts of Congress and the Hoover administration had delivered a brief respite and perhaps prevented conditions from turning even more rotten, but they had proved impotent to turn the economy around. More importantly, they had failed to provide the succor necessary for larger numbers of people falling into dire circumstances. People all across America demanded forceful measures, and if the federal government would not take the imperative steps, people demanded their state and local governments do so. And as 1932 ended and 1933 began, conditions turned ominously worse and cries for action grew more insistent.

As financial conditions had been poor in farm states the longest, demands for action grew the most urgent there first. The economic free fall in the United States had been worst in the Midwest since 1929, and the predicament there had worsened over time. During the course of 1932, bank clearings declined further in the Chicago Federal Reserve District — which included Illinois, Indiana, and Michigan — than in any other. By this measure, during 1932 business had contracted in these three states by 40 percent compared to 28 percent in the nation. Bank debits in the Chicago district in December 1932 had fallen 29 percent from the previous year. Building had practically stopped in Chicago and Detroit. Detroit, which issued building permits valued at $101 million in 1929 — when building activity had already slowed considerably — expected only $9 million worth of building in 1932. The slump in Chicago was even worse. The city that had issued building permits worth $364 million in 1926, issued permits worth only $4 million in 1932. By March 1933 rents in Chicago had fallen by half. The value of homes and apartments had been cut in half, and those of vacant lots had fallen 75 to 90 percent, when a buyer could be found at all. Often the unpaid taxes on land offered for sale were more than the land was worth, so it sat unsold, accumulating tax bills. Many landlords tore down empty buildings, betting they could make more money with a vacant lot, which could be rented out for parking. Chicago and Detroit both witnessed a surge of demolitions to create "tax-payer" parking lots because taxes were lighter on vacant land than on developed land. According to tax assessors, property value in Chicago had declined by half in 1932. Land that was worth $5 billion in 1928 fell another 20 percent by 1933, lowering the value to $2 billion. By 1933 the typical Chicago bungalow was worth less than the outstanding principal of its mortgage. The most expensive commercial property and luxury high-rise apartments plummeted the furthest in value. The highest priced property had the furthest to fall and did. The heated competition among stores, mostly chain stores, such as F.W. Woolworth, S.S. Kresge, and Walgreen Drug Store, had resulted in overbuilt retail space. Some store rents had declined by 90 percent. McCrory's, with 244 stores nationwide, filed for bankruptcy in January. Slack consumer demand caused stores to close and retail districts to empty. Sometimes landlords forgave unpaid rents just to keep a property occupied rather than vacant and attractive to vandals and other miscreants.[2]

By the end of December 1932, business for banks throughout the country remained sluggish as they found less and less demand for their services. Loans outstanding for all banks shrank to $26.1 billion; brokers' loans had dwindled to a mere $430 million, with banks outside of New York City putting up only $20 million of that money.

Table 9.1 — Bank Assets and Deposits, 1931–32 (in millions of dollars)

	Deposits	Loans	U.S. Securities	Other Securities	Total Assets
June 1931	51,769	35,235	6,662	13,320	55,267
Dec. 1931	45,925	31,395			50,046
June 1932	42,093	27,888	6,895	11,627	46,310
Dec. 1932	41,759	26,109			45,169

SOURCE: *Banking and Monetary Statistics*, 18.

With so little demand for loans, banks bought more government securities, which by December 1932 offered .08 percent interest. Money accumulated unwanted in bank vaults. Savings stashed in New York savings banks hit an all-time high of $5.3 billion in January 1933 when the banks announced they would cut interest on deposits to 3 percent. Most savings banks elsewhere already paid only 2 percent and some commercial banks were paying only 0.5 percent on time deposits. Banks in Boston asked the Post Office not to deposit any more money as they could not find any useful way to employ it. Excess reserves hit historic highs of $600 million, mostly stowed in banks in New York City. With mounds of uncalled-for cash sitting in banks, the number of bank failures mounted as the end of 1932 approached. In December 1932, 19 national and 134 state banks failed, freezing $83 million in deposits. Nearly half of those funds were immobilized in Illinois and Iowa. Over $54 million of it resided in accounts in the Midwest and Great Plains. National banks across the country had to submit statements of their condition to the comptroller of the currency as of December 31, 1932, and the condition of many of those banks was not good.[3]

Nationwide, weaker banks that had survived the financial gales of the previous years finally succumbed. The biannual inspection reports due on December 31 served as writs of execution for many fragile banks. Illinois and Iowa, already suffering, had not yet seen the end of their misery. The First National Bank of Herrin, Illinois — the last bank in town — failed to open on December 31, closed after examiners looked at its books. The State Savings and Loan of Quincy, Illinois, also closed on December 31, freezing more than one million dollars in its accounts. As recently as September, the bank had held $2.3 million in deposits, but, according to the bank president, steady and heavy withdrawals had depleted the bank's cash reserves. Davenport, Iowa, was left with only one bank on January 2 after two banks and a savings and loan closed on December 31. The South Central State Bank of Chicago closed on December 29. It had existed only since 1928 and never held more than $400,000 in deposits, but heavy withdrawals, which started in June 1931 and peaked again in the panic of June 1932, had drawn down its accounts until it contained only $80,000. Its directors thought it best to liquidate, so depositors were notified to come collect their funds. The Peoples Bank of Westboro, Iowa, closed December 27 when state agents, alarmed by the suicide of an officer of the bank, examined its books. The bank held only $43,000 in deposits, secured by $65,000 in resources.[4]

January 1933 proved to be one of the bleakest months for banks since catastrophic October 1931. Nationwide, 237 banks suspended operation, freezing $142.7 million in deposits. In the first five days of January 1933, three national and 25 state banks failed. The Wisconsin Bankshares Corporation, a bank holding company, announced at the end of the year that the deposits in all of its units had declined in the past year from $239 million to $200 million, and its outstanding loans had decreased from $170.5 million to $127 million. Like other prudent financial companies it had increased cash reserves and dumped corporate paper for government securities. On January 3 the Indiana State Bank and Trust Company of Warsaw, Indiana, failed to open, and deposits worth $1.4 million became frozen. A note in the bank's window said simply that it was closed on order of the directors. The Burnham Street State Bank of Milwaukee closed its doors on January 24, freezing all the funds of the town of West Allis. The same day the Northern National Bank and the Ashland National Bank closed, leaving Ashland, Wisconsin, without any banks. The Lake County State Bank in North Chicago closed on January 25 after being robbed for the second time in one year.[5]

Depressed business conditions often provided insufficient activity to keep banks open, even if they remained solvent. Banks all across America sat on excess reserves that could not be productively invested. Businesses were reluctant to borrow, and rates earned by banks on increasingly rare loans had by January 1933 dropped to almost nothing. Prime commercial paper paid only 1.38 percent, bankers' acceptances dropped in late January from 0.38 percent to 0.25, even the notorious brokers' loans earned only 0.5 percent by January, and government securities paid a mere 0.2 percent. New York Federal Reserve Governor George Harrison complained that New York and Chicago banks had to pay interest to other banks on $600 million in excess reserves that could not be profitably invested. Slow business took a further toll on banks all across the Midwest. The Roseland National Bank in Chicago closed after its deposits shrank from $1.25 million to $130,000 in two years. President Theophilus Schmid commented, "The drain on our deposits began when the Bain bank chain started to collapse. I am glad to get out of the banking business as there has been no profit in it for us in the last two years." The Hopkins Street State Bank in Milwaukee closed January 30 after its deposits shriveled from $660,000 to $96,000 in one year. The State Bank of Butler, Wisconsin, closed after the local railroad repair shop closed its doors, leaving insufficient money in town to justify a bank. The Warren State Bank in Warren, Ohio, also closed for lack of sufficient business to stay open. The Farmers Bank of Savannah, Ohio, and the Farmers' Banking Company of Wayne, Ohio, both closed on January 10 because the volume of business had dropped too low to keep their doors open.[6]

The spate of closings in December justifiably instilled anxiety in midwestern depositors.

A spate of runs on banks began soon after. The closing of the Ridgely Farmers State Bank of Springfield, where the former governor of Illinois, Louis Emmerson, was a director, provoked bank runs on the remaining three banks in Springfield — all of which survived — and on banks in nearby towns. One of those banks, the Third National Bank of Mt. Vernon, Illinois, closed on January 3, leaving the town with no bank. The Third National Bank was not a tiny rural bank at the crossroads: it still held $2.3 million in deposits when it closed its doors. Trouble mounted in nearby St. Louis, where the Hodiamont Bank closed due to slow collections on loans and heavy withdrawals. Like many other small, vulnerable banks, its depositors were local merchants and residents, and workers at nearby industrial plants. The Hodiamont held deposits of only $332,000 and belonged to neither the Federal Reserve System, nor the clearing house association. Its directors blamed "general business conditions"; it owned too many slow loans granted to local merchants, who could not collect from their customers. To make matters worse, the state bank examiner said the bank had experienced heavy withdrawals by depositors in order to pay taxes due in January. Heavy withdrawals — perhaps to pay taxes — visited many banks in just a few days: both banks in rural Walnut Grove, Missouri, closed on January 2.[7]

January proved to be a brutal month for Missouri overall. On January 6 the Hamilton State Bank in St. Louis closed because of heavy withdrawals provoked, according to its president, by the closure of the nearby Hodiamont Bank. The Hamilton State Bank resembled the Hodiamont in most ways: it was small, a member of neither the Federal Reserve System nor the clearing house association, and largely dependent upon local merchants and neighborhood residents who were having a tough time. Missouri was sailing in rough economic waters. Stoddard County was broke, had no more relief money, and had to close its home for the insane. The unfortunate residents of the home were taken to the county poor farm, where the staff protested that it was already too full and could not handle the insane, even if they came bound and shackled. The Rock Island Railroad announced it was suspending daytime passenger service between St. Louis and Kansas City, because it was losing money running it. The St. Louis–San Francisco Railroad defaulted on its interest payment on its RFC loan of $1.8 million. The troubled road was already in the hands of receivers, who could not make the line profitable under existing conditions. On January 7, William Remmert, a St. Louis real estate developer who had built numerous subdivisions and apartment buildings as recently as 1930, killed himself with carbon monoxide in his garage. When the National Lead Company announced on January 9 the imminent closure of its Missouri mines, the three banks in Desloge were immediately overrun with depositors demanding their money. They knew that the announced closing of the St. Louis Smelting and Refining Company works and three lead mines would throw 600 men out of work. Things were about to get worse.[8]

On January 11, the Park Savings and Trust Company of Saint Louis shut its doors. The small company had been losing deposits steadily since 1930, when it held $542,000. By December 1932, only $300,000 remained. The next day the Savings Trust Company followed the same route. In only two years its deposits had shrunk by half. Seven St. Louis banks failed on a single day, Monday, January 16, bringing the total number of bank closures in St. Louis to 18 since New Year's Day. Altogether, the closed banks held $16 million in frozen deposits. On Saturday, most St. Louis banks, this time including some of the larger banks downtown, experienced extremely heavy withdrawals. The University City Bank opened at 8 A.M. on January 14, but closed at 9:05 after continuous heavy demands for cash. The Scruggs, Vandervoort Bank — located in the back of the dry goods store of the same name, and the smallest bank in the downtown area, with $1.8 million in deposits— was still solvent when it closed at 1 P.M., and put up a notice announcing it would turn over its assets to the state finance commissioner, "owing to the general unrest in St. Louis." On Sunday night, five bank presidents reviewed the events of Saturday and concluding they would not survive another day of such withdrawals, decided not to open in the morning. On Monday, when seven banks closed— holding $7 million in deposits— the chairman of the St. Louis Chamber of Commerce asked citizens to be calm and not lose their heads. He assured the citizenry that all St. Louis banks were basically sound, but that it took time to convert assets into cash, so withdrawals could not always be met right away. A majority of banks in outlying regions of the city availed themselves of a provision allowing them to restrict withdrawals by demanding 30-days' notice for withdrawals of up to $100 and 60 days' notice for amounts greater than $100. The events of the week proved too vexing for the directors of the Shaw Bank and Trust Company, who posted a sign in their window on Wednesday morning announcing the bank was closed due to "heavy withdrawals and uncertain banking conditions in St. Louis." When the Pioneer Trust Company in Kansas City, Missouri, closed on January 25, it contained the deposits of two small Missouri banks, forcing them to close as well. Nine more Missouri banks closed in just two days, January 24 and 25, including the last bank in Walnut Grove, and three banks in New Cambria. Forty-five banks, with deposits of $24.15 million, shut their doors in Missouri during January. The excitement in Missouri cost the Fidelity National Bank— the largest bank in Kansas City— to surrender $36 million in deposits in the last five days of the month.[9]

By the end of January, 21 banks in Iowa, holding $3 million in deposits, had also failed. Another 19 banks in Nebraska and 11 more in Kansas failed, freezing $5.2 million in their accounts. All of the Great Plains states, except the Dakotas and Montana, had a rough start to the year: 109 banks holding $35.6 million in deposits had closed. Conditions were actually worse in the Great Plains states than in those of the Great Lakes Basin, where 59 banks with $28.9 million in deposits suspended operations in January. The greater catastrophe had visited Missouri and Iowa.[10]

Bank runs continued to plague institutions across the country. When the California National Bank of Sacramento— one of the oldest banks in the state— and its affiliate, the California Trust and Savings Bank, both closed on Saturday, January 21, a general run began on the remaining banks in Sacramento. Banks in San Francisco gathered armored cars and rushed $13 million in cash to the capital. The aid saved the other banks temporarily, but fearing a repeat on Monday, five more banks failed to open. The shuttered National Bank held $20 million in 9,000 commercial accounts, hampering the ability to conduct business in the city. It also held 36,000 savings accounts, leaving many citizens without access to cash, perhaps justifying the panicky response in the city.[11]

While some banks failures were dramatic, most banks that failed succumbed to the "slow run" of continuous withdrawals unbalanced by equal new deposits. Such persistent seepage of money from accounts caused lingering deaths. Money left the banks by two main escape routes: it was withdrawn by banks and corporations and sent to more secure facilities— usually in New York or Chicago— or it was withdrawn by local customers and placed for safekeeping in jars, drawers, and safe-deposit boxes. The greatest increase in currency hoarded outside of banks had occurred in late 1931, when $819 million fled banks throughout the country. During the course of 1932, hoards grew by another $199 million. One Pennsylvania businessman confessed to Pierre du Pont that his safe-deposit box contained $350,000 in currency and gold coins. But the rate of hoarding had slowed: in the last six months of the year only $53 million had left banks. During the same period inter-bank deposits grew by $316 million as banks liquidated assets and kept unused money on deposit in other banks. More noteworthy, such deposits in national banks had grown by $594 million, meaning money was migrating from state-chartered banks and trust companies to more secure national banks; $406 million found its way to banks in New York City. Excess reserves held by Federal Reserve Banks had grown by early December to $485 million. By the end of the year, district banks added another $69 million in excess reserves, and $446 million of those excess reserves were credited to banks in New York and Chicago. Big trust companies in New York that held $675 million for banks around the country in December 1931, held $878 million by the end of 1932.[12]

The flow of money from regional banks to larger banks in financial centers brought the end to some large regional banks in the new year. The East Tennessee National Bank, the largest bank in Knoxville and the third largest in Tennessee, closed its doors on January 20 after continuous heavy withdrawals. It held nearly $10 million in deposits on December 31— including $2 million belonging to the state of Tennessee — which then became frozen in the bank. The bank had already borrowed $8 million from the RFC and was not eligible to borrow more. Two more national banks in Tennessee, along with nine state-chartered banks, shut their doors in January, freezing over $13 million in deposits. Similarly, the Chelsea Second National Bank of Atlantic City closed its doors on Friday, January 27, after suffering "extraordinary and excessive withdrawals" that during the year drained half of its $11 million deposited in 22,000 accounts. The bank president estimated that by the end at least $1 million in cash —formerly deposits in accounts— resided in the bank's safe-deposit boxes. The following Monday the Atlantic City National Bank closed. It was the oldest bank in Atlantic City and, after having assumed the business of 14 other local banks, held the funds of 15,000 depositors. The bank closings in Atlantic City quickly sent ripples through southern New Jersey as other banks in the region suddenly closed as well in early February. The directors of the Peoples National Bank of Stamford, Connecticut, voted to dissolve their bank and turn its business over to another because of constant withdrawals. Both the Commercial Bank of Columbus, Nebraska, and the Washington State Bank of Port Angeles, Washington, gave up late in January after steady withdrawals emptied their vaults.[13]

Banks also ran into the kind of public disputes that caused Francis Karel's First America National Bank and Trust Company of Berwyn Heights, Illinois, to fail the previous summer. The First National Bank of Marmaroneck, New York, closed January 16 when the village reneged on an agreement to buy a bank building worth $275,000, which the bank had acquired when it agreed to take over the insolvent Marmaroneck Trust Company. After local taxpayers sued to stop the town from buying the building to use as a town hall, the agreement fell through. Additionally, many villagers were living on their savings, which drained $1.3 million from the First National Bank during the course of 1932. This left the bank with only $1.5 million in deposits, including $512,000 belonging to local governments, school districts, and utilities, but not enough to satisfy state reserve requirements. The bank had already borrowed $780,000 from the RFC the previous July, leaving it in fragile condition. When news of the First National Bank's closing hit the village, the Union Savings Bank, across the street, immediately suffered a run. People took their money out and deposited it in Post Office savings accounts despite a statement by the Savings and Loan Association of Westchester County that it stood behind the Union Savings Bank with its full resources of $135 million. Marmaroneck was just one of the hundreds of towns nationwide that had problems of their own. During the bitter month of January 1933, 242 banks, holding deposits of $134 million, failed nationwide.[14]

February looked like it would be little better as banks continued to close their doors—mostly in the Midwest where banks in Illinois, Missouri, and Nebraska especially succumbed. Throughout the country another 148 banks, holding $72.9 million in deposits, suspended operations in February. But the failed banks tended to be small, and much of the public excitement of January died down. The only large bank to fail was the Commercial National Bank in Washington, D.C., the fourth largest national bank in the District, with $11 million in deposits. The United Bank and Trust Company in Greensboro, North Carolina, closed with $2.3 million in deposits after continuous heavy withdrawals. The Middlesex Guarantee Title and Trust Company in New Brunswick, New Jersey, failed after heavy continuous withdrawals suddenly spiked on Friday and Saturday, February 11 and 12, when rumors became general that the institution, with deposits of $1.5 million, was in trouble. In fact, according to its directors, too many bonds and mortgages in their portfolio had defaulted for the bank to keep going. The Chester County Trust Company in Pennsylvania, of similar size, closed its tills the next day. However, after the first two weeks bank failures noticeably dropped off. When the Saint Joseph Loan and Trust Company in South Bend, Indiana, announced on February 18 it would suspend withdrawals for a period, other institutions in the city declared that they, too, would temporarily suspend or limit withdrawals. Those moves were followed by parallel announcements in nearby counties. In all likelihood, some small banks in Wisconsin and Illinois were saved from collapse by invoking the law that enabled them to shut their doors temporarily or by timely action by local officials in suspending banking in their community. Local government officials started more frequently to intercede to save banks.[15]

The wave of bank failures in January and early February provoked alarm in local public officials across the country, who determined to do what they could to arrest them. The Gibson City State Bank in Gibson, Illinois, closed on Thursday, December 29, leaving the First National the only bank in town. But when it, too, experienced heavy withdrawals on Saturday, Mayor Herman Krudup declared a city-wide bank holiday on January 3 for 30 days. After four banks in Wausau, Wisconsin, closed on January 1, Mayor Otto Muenchow declared a banking moratorium until March 1. The mayors of Rock Island, Moline, and East Moline, Illinois, all declared two-week bank holidays for their towns, closing six banks. The mayor of Muscatine, Iowa, declared a three-week business holiday ordering all businesses closed, including the town's banks. But as no municipal authority in Iowa — or anywhere else — had any legal basis to declare a general business holiday, officers of the Muscatine State Bank kept their bank open and suffered no consequences. The other two banks in Muscatine, the First National Bank and the Hershey State Bank, honored the holiday and remained closed. The mayor of Huntington, Indiana, likewise declared a business holiday for his town after the Huntington Trust and Savings Company failed on January 21, leaving two banks operating. Both honored the mayor's decree and promised to reopen when enough depositors had signed waivers of their right to withdraw their funds. When the mayor of Mount Carmel, Illinois, declared a two-week business holiday, almost 100 businesses honored the closure, with groceries and pharmacies operating on limited hours. The manager of the local J.C. Penny organized mass meetings to obtain depositors' signatures on petitions promising not to withdraw funds from the last bank in town. As a result, the American First Bank reopened on a limited basis: it cleared checks and accepted deposits, but allowed no withdrawals. Illinois State Auditor Oscar Nelson said state law did not recognize the legality of any "business holiday" and announced that his office would not honor any banking moratorium. Nevertheless, the same day the mayor of Galva, Illinois, announced a two-week holiday in his town. Mayors reacted to public anxiety over the banks, but not all bank officers shared that anxiety. Those that believed they could benefit from a local holiday honored the decrees, while bankers that saw no need to close frequently did not. Despite the questionable legality, local "holidays" gave officials a tool to calm local nerves and combat bank runs.[16]

Nevada was the first state to order statewide closings when the governor declared a holiday in November. Louisiana became the second when Governor Oscar Allen ordered all banks in the state to close on Saturday, February 4. He then issued an order allowing banks to reopen the following Monday after the RFC agreed to make a $20 million loan to the Hibernia Bank & Trust Company on the intervening Sunday. The Hibernia had been hit by a heavy run the week before after New York Congressman Hamilton Fish accused its president, Rudolph S. Hecht, of giving bad advice to the RFC directors in order to save his own bank. Fish maintained that the RFC had advanced money to the Union Indemnity Company of New Orleans only after Hecht had vouched for it and it subsequently went into receivership after repaying a loan to Hecht's Hibernia Bank. When Hecht denied being the source of the advice, Fish apologized, but the *Picayune-Times* had already reported the accusation and the damage had been done. Rumors quickly spread that Hecht's bank — the fourth largest in the state — was in trouble and state officials feared that the bank would be subjected to a run when it opened on Saturday morning, February 4. Thus, Governor Allen — acting on advice from Louisiana Senator Huey Long — groped for a reason to close all the banks in the state on Saturday. Grasping for the most dubious of fig leafs to cover his action, he declared the holiday was to honor the anniversary of breaking diplomatic relations with Germany in 1917. The RFC made the loan to the Hibernia on condition that it raise $4 million elsewhere and gain the cooperation of its depositors to not withdraw funds. Hecht assured RFC officials that he had telephoned the bank's biggest depositors and gained their promise not to withdraw funds. However, he was able to raise only $2 million in outside support to back the RFC loan. Even though the RFC had rigid rules regarding security and guarantees for loans, the loan to Hibernia was granted anyway.[17]

Wrestling with the problem of how to keep troubled banks operating, the Iowa legislature passed a law in January allowing the state superintendent of banks to take over and operate any state bank upon request of its directors. The law gave the superintendent discretion to either keep the bank going or to liquidate it, as he saw fit. Either way, the bank avoided an often drawn-out receivership. More importantly, the law allowed the superintendent to keep a bank operating on whatever "good" assets it still carried on its books, so that if half a bank's resources were still good, depositors still had access to half of their deposits. The law was invoked right away to take over operation of two banks in Ringgold County that had run out of cash. The superintendent took over the banks, kept their staff in place, and informed depositors they could access their savings on a limited basis as money became available. In the meantime, the banks accepted deposits with assurance that 100 percent of the new funds would be available upon demand. The superintendent said he would decide what to do with the bank after a "breathing spell." Within days, officers of the State Savings Bank of Creston, Iowa, asked the superintendent to take over their bank too.[18]

At the same time a bill was introduced in the legislature in Lincoln, Nebraska, to create a state bank with $25 million in capital and branches in all 93 counties. It would receive in deposit all government money and be authorized to issue mortgages to farmers, home-owners, and businesses. The following week the legislature passed a bill modeled after the Iowa law allowing the state superintendent of banks to operate failing banks with the assent of its depositors and creditors. The superintendent was authorized to keep insolvent banks out of receivership and to operate the banks on its "good" resources. Nebraska was not alone in taking note of what came to be called "the Iowa Plan." Proposals were placed before the United States Congress to adopt the Iowa Plan for national banks as an approach to ease the banking crisis and the economic mayhem it caused.[19]

In the wake of the "Iowa Plan," politicians in other states decided it was high time to initiate fundamental banking reforms and outlaw practices that were believed to have contributed to the banking crisis. A bill was proposed in the Maryland legislature forbidding directors, officers, or employees of banks from borrowing money from the institution. Additionally, it cut in half the amount allowed to one borrower to no more than 5 percent of a bank's capital and surplus. Nor could a bank accept its own stock as collateral for loans (a practice already illegal for national banks). A special committee in the New York state legislature recommended that the state form a $100 million fund to insure savings institutions. Under this plan all savings institutions in New York were called upon to place 3 percent of their assets with the fund, which would be controlled by a committee made up of its members. The committee recognized that real estate bonds held by savings insti-tutions constituted "a serious threat" because one-half of the $10 billion in bonds were in default.[20]

Not every state leader was so eager to hop onto the bandwagon. Minnesota Governor Floyd B. Olson refused to sign a law authorizing banking holidays, claiming the law was obviously unconstitutional. Furthermore, he declared a resolution passed by the state Senate requesting a moratorium on farm foreclosures carried no legal weight and was "an idle ges-ture," because not even the president of the United States, except under martial law, could suspend the collection of debts. He reminded legislators that although he had asked the Rural Credit Bureau to refrain from foreclosures in 1931, and the Minnesota Association of Mortgage Loan Companies had agreed to cooperate, that had been legal and within his powers. He maintained, however, that no governor had the right to declare a suspension of foreclosures, which would be rejected by any court.[21]

The Farm Crisis Peaks

Much of this frantic activity in state capitals was driven by turmoil organized by farm-ers, who angrily demanded attention as the crisis on America's farms came to a boil. Prices for farm commodities continued to fall in 1932, until they fetched only about half what they had on average in the early 1920s. Wheat sold for prices on the exchange that had not been seen for 362 years. Cotton fetched prices in New York so low that they had never been seen before: five cents per pound. America's farmers had seen their income decline by a third. They had earned almost $7.94 billion in 1922, but brought in only $5.25 billion in 1932. This collapse of farm income produced a parallel financial crisis in America's farming states that added to the feverish atmosphere spreading across the country. The plunge of farm income forced a rising wave of farm foreclosures, which farm-state politicians believed would swamp their constituencies. Legislators added to the rush of laws to save banks a related sheaf of proposals to save farms. However, the proposals in state legislatures designed to help farmers could also make precarious banks' conditions even worse by freezing loans and rendering county and municipal bonds worthless.[22]

By 1933, many Midwest farmers did not wait for the legislators to act and took matters into their own hands to stop farm foreclosures. The same regions that had witnessed violent strikes to keep produce off the markets during the previous summer, by January 1933 saw concerted and coordinated action to prevent tax and mortgage foreclosures of farms. In numerous Iowa counties, irate farmers forcibly halted tax and foreclosure sales of their neighbors' farms. A January foreclosure sale in Le Mars, Iowa, was held on the steps of the county courthouse, the typical location for sheriffs' sales in farm counties. Lawyer Herbert Martin, representing New York Life Insurance Company, which held the farmer's mortgage, bid $30,000 for Gus Johnson's 320-acre farm, which was mortgaged for $33,000. The bid by the mortgage owner, which did not even cover the amount of Johnson's debt, enraged the 700 to 1,000 farmers attending the sale, who surged up the courthouse steps and grabbed the lawyer, a local man well-known to all, and demanded that he bid the whole amount of the mortgage. When he tried to argue that he could not bid more than the amount authorized by his client in New York, the farmers dragged him bodily down the 18 stone steps of the courthouse. Sheriff R.E. Rippey, a physically slight man, tried to free the lawyer from the farmers' grasp but was slapped and abused in turn. Someone in the crowd produced a rope and threatened to put one end around lawyer Martin's neck and tie the other end to the bumper of a car and "take him for a ride." Another farmer asked Martin if he would send a telegram to his client in New York asking them to authorize payment of the full amount of the mortgage, because his "neck is in danger." New York Life obligingly telegraphed back authorization to bid the full amount. That satisfied the farmers and after the fracas ended, Martin was found back in the crowd talking to his neighbors.[23]

In fact, the $30,000 offered by New York Life for the 320-acre farm was perhaps generous. An average acre of Iowa farmland had been worth $119 in 1925 (down from $200 in 1920), but by 1930 had fallen to $94. If Gus Johnson's land were average, his 320-acre farm was worth only $28,200 — including his buildings — in 1930. By 1933, farmland in the United States had sunk in value another 38 percent, which would have made Johnson's farm worth no more than $17,443. Times were indeed tough for farmers, and they were difficult for "widows and orphans" of the insurance companies, too. Two days later, two more foreclosure sales occurred in Le Mars without incident. The Amundsen farm was sold to its mortgage holder, Prudential Life, for the full amount of the loan. Willie Wilson's farm likewise was sold to its mortgage holder, John Hancock Insurance, also for the full amount of his loan.[24]

While the subsequent more tranquil scene at Le Mars may have been the more typical, violent scenes nonetheless repeatedly took place in scattered counties in Iowa. A lawyer in Storm Lake, Iowa, telegraphed his insurance company client in New York: "These farmers are going to hang me if I can't raise our bid on this farm." Two days after a mob forced the sheriff to cancel the sale in Plymouth County, 700 farmers organized by the Iowa Farmers' Holiday Association halted the sale of a farm in Modale, Iowa. A week later, 400 farmers again turned out in Modale to stop the sale of Ernest Ganzhorn's 160-acre farm, on which he owed $4,237. The holder of the mortgage, U.S. representative from Nebraska Malcolm Baldrige (soon to be ex-representative), had attempted to negotiate a settlement with Ganzhorn without success. When his lawyer bid $3,000 on the farm, it provoked the same reaction met in Le Mars: farmers took over the courthouse portico and used it to make fiery speeches. The Harrison County sheriff called off the sale. A few days later 700 farmers in nearby Logan stopped a foreclosure sale on a $700 debt. In Forest City, Iowa, 600–700 farmers—again called together by the Farmers' Holiday Association—prevented a tax sale and persuaded all county officials to agree to give 20 percent of their pay to the county poor fund. In Appleton, Wisconsin, 300 farmers prevented the sale of a widow's farm after foreclosure was instituted by her own brother.[25]

Farmers also attempted to stymie foreclosure sales by offering no or derisory bids at auctions. In Cedar County, Nebraska, farmers at a foreclosure sale bid eight cents per hog and 50 cents per horse; a ton of corn fetched a dollar. When the sale was over, the buyers asked the farmer who was forced to sell if he would kindly watch over their hogs, horses, and corn for them. In Webster City, Iowa, farmers bid one dollar for farmer Huddleston's horses and 25 cents for his hogs. No one bid on his farm. Tax sales in Linn, Harrison, and Montgomery Counties, Iowa, were called off when farmers refused to bid anything. On January 11 a foreclosure sale was called off in Dakota City, Nebraska, when 500 farmers gathered and forbade anyone to make an offer on Thomas Sullivan's farm. No one bid. Just across the nearby Missouri River, in Union County, South Dakota, a similar event unfolded on the same day.[26]

In February the farm agitation crossed the Mississippi. On February 14, a crowd of farmers in Kankakee, Illinois, stopped a foreclosure sale and forced the agent of the Federal Joint Stock Land Bank of St. Louis to agree to their terms. The crowd of around 500 demanded and received a two-year moratorium on the mortgage, as well as a reduction in interest from 7 to 5 percent and a decrease of the principal from $6,000 to $5,000. The master of chancery and the attorney for the bank were taken to the sheriff's office where they held a phone conversation with their superiors in St. Louis, who okayed the adjustment. In Ithaca, Michigan, 900 to 1,200 farmers packed a farm auction and collectively bid $3.80 for everything owned by Roy Marzolf. Jersey cows went for 25 cents each, an auto for a dime, and a wagon for a nickel. The sheriff told the crowd their attempt to save Mazolf's farm and goods was noble but futile because he already had a sealed bid for $400 for everything. When the agitated farmers demanded to know who had submitted the bid, the sheriff revealed it was from a local auto dealer, who had the bad judgment to be present, and who voided his bid. But Peter Holman, an official from the United States Treasury Department and receiver of the bankrupt Ithaca National Bank that owned farmer Marzolf's mortgage, was also present. He was roughed up by the farmers, his glasses broken and face bruised and cut, and was forced to wait in the farmhouse while the bidding continued. When the farmers demanded that he accept the $3.80 to satisfy the mortgage, he replied he could not hand over the mortgage because it was in the bank. A band of farmers then accompanied Holman to the bank and waited while he retrieved the piece of paper from the vault. The sheriff did not intervene. Someone burned down the barns of a farm in Axe, Michigan, the night before its foreclosure sale, consigning to the flames all of the grain and animals inside. When a Canadian farmer bid $500 for the farm anyway, he was chased from the premises. The commotion spread west as well. In late February a riot broke out at a foreclosure sale in Utah. The Salt Lake City sheriff called off the sales after fighting broke out between sheriff's deputies and demonstrators. The deputies tried to break up the gathering with fire hoses, but after the demonstrators—led by the Communist Party candidate for governor, M.P. Bales—took the hoses away and turned them on the deputies, police resorted to tear gas to break up the crowd.[27]

Big, faraway insurance companies had acquired an unsavory reputation on the Great Plains. They experienced significant difficulty finding lawyers to handle their foreclosures, and sometimes could not find judges to hear them. When a judge in Madison County, Nebraska, announced his court would accept no more foreclosure cases, nor register sales on foreclosed property, other judges followed his example. Chicago banker Holman Pettibone observed that usually no one attended foreclosure sales except the holder of the mortgage in question, because no one who had money to invest wanted to put it into real estate.[28]

Although insurance companies played a high-profile part in the dramas staged on the prairies, they were actually only minor players in the farm-mortgage scene. The Department of Agriculture estimated the total value of farmland and buildings in the United States in 1933 at $30.8 billion, of which $8.5 billion was mortgaged. Banks owned farm mortgages worth about $1.4 billion, and insurance companies owned approximately another $1.9 billion, or 22 percent of farm mortgages. Just 14 companies, mostly headquartered in New York and New England, owned 82 percent of those mortgages, and by early 1933, many of those mortgages were seriously overdue. The small number of companies that owned large numbers of farm mortgages in just a few states gave them unsightly prominence when farm prices sagged ever lower and foreclosures mounted, casting the eastern insurance companies as villains in the foreclosure dramas. Mortgages worth $560 million existed on Nebraska farms alone. Mortgages worth $1.25 billion had been written for Iowa farms, and an additional $350 million worth were registered in South Dakota. However, insurance companies — whether headquartered in the East or not — owned only a fraction of those mortgages. All life insurance companies combined owned about $200 million in Iowa farm mortgages. Banks, various government agencies, and firms that specialized in farm mortgages owned more than half, and most of those were not located in New York or Boston, but in the Midwest.[29]

The Mutual Benefit Life Insurance Company of Newark had invested around $150 million, nearly 40 percent of its assets, in farm mortgages and by January 1932 had foreclosed on $14.25 million worth. Almost half the mortgages owned by another large insurance company were overdue by the summer of 1932. By June 1932 it had foreclosed on 1,300 farms, mostly taking outright possession of the farms themselves and either renting them to tenants or putting them under the care of professional farm managers. Insurance companies usually tried to work out an accommodation with the mortgagees, sometimes taking them on as tenants or managers, but it was clearly impossible to avoid a buildup of resentment among farmers against the eastern insurance companies that took possession of their farms. Farm mortgages written in the 1920s were generally more liberal than those written for city residences, which, ironically, made the situation worse for farmers in the 1930s. Farm mortgages required down payments of only 10 percent, while urban mortgages normally required up to half the cost of the house. And while house mortgages were usually for only five years, farm mortgages could last for 20 or 30 years. This posed a brutal problem for insurance companies that loaned money to farms that lost value over the years. Farmland that had been worth $50.5 billion in 1924 had lost one-third of its value by 1933. That same land had been assessed by the Department of Agriculture at $66.3 billion in 1920, when some mortgages were written. So fierce was the deflation in land prices during the Depression that farmland worth $47.8 billion in 1930 was assessed at only $30.8 billion just three years later. The life insurance companies, which promised money to the famous "widows and orphans," were obliged by their fiduciary responsibility to pay no more than market value for farms at foreclosure. This posed a particularly nettlesome problem that kindled intense anger among farmers: if a foreclosure sale did not raise enough money to pay off the debtor's obligation to the mortgage owner, the debtor was judged still liable for the balance, or "deficiency." But market prices were frequently less than the value of the mortgage, hence the infamous "deficiencies" still owed to the insurance companies by the unlucky foreclosed farmers.[30]

Faraway insurance giants were not the sole worry for midwestern farmers: local tax assessors posed a serious threat when taxes had to be paid in January. Linn County, Iowa, which included Cedar Rapids, posted the names of 5,705 tax delinquents in December 1932, every one of whom faced the prospect of a sheriff's sale in January if they could not come up with the amount due. Often the amounts were pathetically small: 98 cents, $1.51, $12.84. Almost all amounts due were less than $100, and the highest was only $698. When the auctions started on January 2 no bid was received despite a crowd of 125 before the courthouse steps—or perhaps because of it. The sheriff announced the postponement of the auction until some indefinite date.[31]

A reporter for the *Des Moines Register* who covered such events and talked to many farmers concluded that most of them disapproved of the tumult and thuggery, and large numbers expected conditions to improve once Franklin Roosevelt occupied the White House. Nevertheless, state politicians reacted to the wave of farm foreclosures and the attendant turmoil cresting on the Plains and in the Midwest. Iowa Governor Clyde Herring asked holders of mortgages to postpone foreclosures until the state legislature could act on pending "emergency legislation." The Iowa legislature passed a law allowing courts to grant continuance on mortgage foreclosures until March 1, 1935. The bill, which passed in the Senate 48 to 0 and 104 to 2 in the House, allowed courts to take custody of a property and set its rents, mortgage payments, and other related financial questions. The law, which surely would not have withstood challenge in court, would have had catastrophic impact on local banks that held mortgages. At the same time the Iowa legislature considered a bill to postpone tax seizures. Four bills pending in the Kansas legislature sought to relieve debtors: one proposed to abolish property taxes on owner-occupied dwellings; another sought to extend mortgages for an additional three-and-a-half years. Another would have doubled the redemption period for mortgages, and a fourth would have outlawed deficiency judgments in foreclosure suits. A law proposed in Oklahoma called for a two-year moratorium on foreclosures. The legislature in North Dakota suspended for three years the right of counties to seize farms in lieu of taxes.[32]

Once rolling, the anti-foreclosure ball gathered momentum and headed east. The Wisconsin legislature passed a law asking judges not to accept foreclosure cases. The Milwaukee County board of judges immediately agreed to a 30-day moratorium on foreclosure proceedings. Another law under consideration in Madison would have allowed judges to adjust the principal and interest of mortgages to favor debtors, as well as add three years to the mortgage redemption period. In mid–February, Wisconsin Governor Schmedeman signed the bills. He also approved a bill that allowed courts to establish "fair-value rents" on properties in foreclosure. Both houses in Indianapolis passed a bill in January postponing tax sales for one year. It then considered laws forbidding sheriffs' sales for one year, allowing back taxes to be paid over a period of five years, and two-year extensions on mortgages. The legislature in Michigan debated a bill to allow judges to extend the redemption period of mortgages, to allow a ten-year grace period on back taxes, and suspend farm foreclosures for a year. Michigan Governor Comstock signed a bill that whizzed through both houses in Lansing without opposition that postponed all tax sales of property for one year. The legislature in Springfield considered a five-year moratorium on farm foreclosures. The House in Little Rock passed a bill palpably hostile to mortgage owners: it demanded a two-year moratorium on foreclosure cases in courts, allowed the appointment of displaced owners as the receivers of property from which they had just been evicted, and outlawed deficiency judgments. Similar laws seeking relief for tax delinquents and debtors facing foreclosure were under consideration in California, Oregon, Washington, Idaho, Nevada, Texas, Georgia, Tennessee, North Carolina, and Ohio, though most of them contained less radical changes than those proposed in the Midwest and Great Plains states. All of these proposals would have made it nearly impossible for farmers to borrow money or states to fund their necessary programs with either loans or property taxes. A judge in Lansing pointed out that a tax-sale moratorium would halt all tax collections so no one would have to pay, even if able. It would also imperil $50 million in state bonds already sold, and end any ability to sell any more. He further pointed out that the law was probably not constitutional because it would renege on contracts to pay off state and municipal bonds. Mass public and private bankruptcy no doubt would have followed most of these midwestern proposals, but few in fact were ever implemented. Even in Nebraska, where 47 of 100 members of the legislature were themselves farmers, radical reform did not come to pass.[33]

In response to the appeal for forbearance by Iowa Governor Herring, executives of a consortium of northeastern insurance companies met to discuss what was obviously a problem for all of them. Afterward, the president of Prudential Life Insurance of Boston announced it would suspend foreclosures in Iowa. New York Life President Thomas Buckner declared shortly thereafter that it, too, they would follow suit. He took pains, however, to explain that mortgage holders were often forced into foreclosure by the claims of second-mortgage owners and that renewal of first mortgages became impossible if second-mortgage holders pressed their claims, even if most second mortgages were usually chattel mortgages on crops or animals. Company policy had been not to foreclose if a farmer paid the mortgage principal due, with taxes and interest being subject to negotiations. Equitable Life Assurance, which owned nearly $200 million worth of farm mortgages at the end of 1932, announced it would continue its policy of leniency toward farmers who had difficulty paying, but, while it would make arrangements with them on a case-by-case basis, it would not honor any blanket debt moratorium. Prudential Life, which owned 37,000 farm mortgages worth $210 million in the United States (10 percent of its portfolio), announced it would drop foreclosure claims against all of its delinquent U.S. and Canadian debtors. Frederick Ecker, president of Metropolitan Life, said his company did all it could not to foreclose on farm mortgages, but usually foreclosed if a farmer refused to discuss terms. A week later he announced that Metropolitan Life would extend to homeowners the same leniency shown toward farmers. Mutual Benefit Life Insurance of Newark, with $25 million in Iowa farm mortgages, and $150 million throughout the country, also agreed to Governor Herring's plea. Finally, John Hancock Insurance, headquartered in Boston and holding $175 million in farm mortgages, also agreed to temporarily suspend foreclosures in Iowa. The largest holder of farm mortgages, however, was not located in the East: Northwestern Mutual Life Insurance of Milwaukee owned farm mortgages worth $217 million and remained silent about the moratorium. Moreover, most farm mortgages were not owned by giant East-Coast insurance companies, but by small banks and even individuals located in the Midwest, which were having troubles enough of their own.[34]

Egged on by the farmers' response to foreclosure sales, the insurance companies' reaction to the outbreaks of violence, and the rush of legislation in statehouses, on February 5 Farmers' Holiday Association President Milo Reno called for a nationwide farmers' strike. Henry Lux, association head in Sidney, Nebraska, told 2,000 farmers, "If we don't get beneficial service from this legislature, 200,000 of us are coming to Lincoln and we'll tear that new state capital building to pieces." Despite the roaring cheers that greeted his threat, only 2,000 to 4,000 farmers actually descended upon the city on February 16. The column of singing and shouting men in overalls, and a few women, marched upon the Statehouse, where they met police armed with tear-gas bombs at the ready. At the Statehouse, the president of the Nebraska association presented a petition to the governor demanding prompt enactment of a law similar to the Iowa mortgage moratorium law.[35] A farmer from Tilden read a long list of demands from a relief conference, including an increased supply of federal greenbacks to repay all losses due to bank failures and farm debt in recent years, federal financing of all farm debts at 3 percent interest on long-term loans, a cessation of all mortgage foreclosures, and an immediate 25 to 50 percent reduction in governmental salaries. A spokesman for the farmers declared, "We are in revolt against the leadership of international bankers and other business men [whose] ... mad scramble for profits had reduced the masses to poverty." Governor Charles Bryan introduced the legislation the next day.[36]

Also on February 16, 5,000 farmers, including leaders of the staid Farm Bureau, met in Indianapolis to protest the failure of the legislature to enact "adequate tax relief." They called for a statewide meeting to plan for a tax strike, which was endorsed by Farm Bureau President William H. Settle. The farmers then marched to the Statehouse and presented a petition signed by 50,000 farmers to Governor Paul McNutt, demanding a transfer of the tax burden from real estate to a sales tax and higher income taxes. On the same day, the lower house in Idaho passed a bill for a two-year moratorium on mortgage payments, which also allowed district courts to grant a moratorium to those who could prove they could not pay.[37]

Tempers ran so high on the Great Plains that on January 16, state Senator W.E. Martin introduced a resolution in the North Dakota Senate proposing that the 39 states south and west of Pennsylvania secede from the United States, leaving the nine states of "the Financial East" to form a rump United States. The resolution proposed that the western states retain the stars on the blue field as their flag, leaving the red and white stripes to the east, which, Martin claimed, had enriched itself at the expense of the rest of the country. The resolution was introduced into the North Dakota House of Representatives the following day. The Senate did not put the resolution to a vote but did vote 28 to 20 to publish it. Some senators had the presence of mind to point out that it was clearly treasonous. But among others, feelings ran so hot that they proposed the new western United States have no trade, communications, relations, or treaties of any kind with "the Financial East." In the hot-tempered speeches delivered in Le Mars, Iowa, someone yelled, "We're going to draw a line at the Mississippi and have our own country west of it. Have a capital at Des Moines or somewhere; make our own laws, make our own money!"[38]

These sentiments were not confined to the West and Midwest, but were found every place farmers faced real distress. Nightriders were intimidating large landowners and mortgage holders in Arkansas to prevent farm foreclosures. The Farmers' Holiday movement had spread to Oklahoma by January, and 500 protesting farmers marched through the streets of tiny Okemah. When Professor Bruce R. Payne of the George Peabody College for Teachers, in Nashville, Tennessee, made three automobile tours of nearly 8,000 miles around the South in February and March, 1933, he encountered a litany of bitter complaints and alienation among southern farmers. He talked to farmers from Virginia to Tennessee to Florida who told him that politicians in Washington cared not a whit about farmers, only about banks, railroads, and the trusts. None expected any real relief from Washington. "The only hope of farmers is in some sort of revolution which will remove present political leaders, subservient to all other interests than agricultural interests, and elect in their stead political leaders sympathetic with farmers."[39]

Politicians scrambled as fast as they could to head off the foreclosure crisis as statehouses were besieged by indebted farmers seeking redress. On February 13, Governor Charles W. Bryan of Nebraska followed Iowa Governor Herring's example and announced an "emergency proclamation" calling for suspension of foreclosures until the legislature could pass a "respite or moratorium act." The governor appointed "reconciliation committees" to negotiate between mortgage holders and those who could not pay. Within two weeks the legislature had passed the measure that postponed all mortgage foreclosures for two years. The legislature in Albany considered a bill to stop all tax collections on property until assessors could adjust taxable value of property downward. The Utah Legislature passed a resolution asking President-elect Roosevelt to accept bimetallism, hoping to induce inflation to help debtors and farmers.[40]

Not to be outdone by state legislatures, when Congress reconvened in December 1932, congressmen proposed a wide array of bills that purported to solve problems that beset the United States. When Congress rushed through a bill authorizing the RFC to loan $90 million directly to farmers who agreed to cut output, President Hoover eagerly signed it. In February the Senate passed the Hull-Walcott Bill that authorized the RFC to loan $500 million to holders of mortgages if they agreed to stop foreclosures and waive all interest for two years. Tennessee Senator Cordell Hull had proposed it only for farm mortgages, but the banking committee added home mortgages as well. Minnesota Senator Shipstead offered a bill for federal assumption of all farm mortgages, funded by a massive bond offering, which was rejected. Arkansas Senator (and soon-to-be Majority Leader) Robinson submitted a bill that would have sheltered farmers from foreclosure while they reorganized their debts. Robinson had intended to submit the bill in the next congressional session, but was encouraged by none other than President Hoover to have the bill considered as an amendment to another bill then under consideration by the Judiciary Committee. South Carolina Senator Byrnes suggested that all farm debts should be adjusted downward with some federal assistance. In January the House Committee on Agriculture reported out a bill that ordered the Treasury to pay farmers the difference between "parity prices" (average commodity prices of the mid–1920s) and market prices for tobacco, cotton, hogs, and four other farm products. Indiana Congressman Sam Pettengill explained his vote against the bill to farmers back home by saying that the bill purported to shove the economy along by inflating the currency, but any money paid to farmers by the government would have been passed along to banks, where it then would have sat in vaults doing no one any good.[41]

Amidst all this hue and cry, Senator Glass's bank bill inched its way forward until it was finally passed on January 25 by the Senate in a 54 to 9 vote. However, Huey Long of Louisiana successfully filibustered the bill until the branch-banking provision was stripped away, denuding the bill of Senator Glass's principal palliative for American banking. The bill still had to be reconciled with Representative Steagall's bank bill that had passed the House the previous May. However, in the fevered atmosphere of early 1933, Congress had moved beyond such minor tinkering and was being urged to consider more drastic moves to address the national crisis. Representative James Buchanan of Texas proposed a bill to make the president — meaning Roosevelt, not Hoover — a "finance czar," with the power to reorganize the federal government and allocate money as he saw fit. While Minority Leader Bertrand Snell of New York denounced this proposal to create "an American Mussolini," it was endorsed by the *Detroit Free Press*. Walter Lippmann began a campaign urging Congress to vote Roosevelt "full powers," saying, "The situation requires strong medicine … this is the necessary thing to do."[42]

Legislators in Congress and in state after state threw caution to the wind because caution had failed to produce an economic recovery. Banks were already becoming the all-purpose scapegoat. Thomas MacMahon of the International Textile Workers' Union testified before Congress that most employers wanted to do good for their employees, "but the banks have got such a grip on them that they cannot call their souls their own. Several employers have told me that banks would only furnish money to meet payrolls on condition that wages were reduced." But the rise of populist-inspired legislation was disastrous for finance because it was intended to protect debtors at the expense of banks and insurance companies. Nothing could have been done to more effectively freeze credit in the United States than perhaps if such moves were made on the national level. Indeed, many congressmen had exactly such proposals in their vest pockets ready for consideration. Many such recommendations had already been considered, and a few, such as the Goldsborough Amendment and the first Bonus Bill, had already been enacted. In January, Idaho Senator William Borah had prepared his bill to impose monetary inflation on the United States through mandatory increases in Federal Reserve note circulation. This initiative greatly upset Federal Reserve Governor Eugene Meyer who worried that Congress would counter every move the Fed made to revive business activity. Treasury Secretary Mills told a gathering of the Federal Reserve Board that the proposed agriculture bill was "insane." Hoover stood as a sentinel to stop most unorthodox programs from being implemented should they get past the stewards in Congress: Senators Fess and Watson. Both of these conservative Republicans, however, were defeated in their bids for reelection in 1932 — as was Herbert Hoover — so the sentinels of economic orthodoxy would not be around after March 4, 1933, to deter any "experimentation."[43]

Speaker Garner had already succumbed to populist tenets. It remained to be seen how far he would go. Garner took the next step in January after an article by John T. Flynn appeared in *Harper's Magazine* charging that RFC loans were being channeled to a handful of large banks and corporations to bail out the politically well connected. Flynn repeated complaints about the enormous loans to "Charles Ninety-Million Dawes" and Amadeo P. Giannini, and beat the drum about RFC loans finding their way into the vaults of J.P. Morgan and Kuhn-Loeb. While none of these charges were new, frustration over the seeming impotency of the RFC and federal programs designed to counter the Depression had mounted, adding momentum to a call for hearings to investigate Flynn's charges. At the same time, ruined Chicago banker John Carroll told Congress that the RFC conspired with big Chicago banks to ruin small neighborhood banks so they would be easy prey once the Glass bank bill passed and branch banking was imposed upon the states. Nebraska Senator George Norris announced he was certain that charges of "secret loans" to enable corporations to pay dividends to stockholders or to repay loans to fat banks were true. Norris echoed Flynn's charges that "aid to the wealthiest class" was possible only because the RFC was "allowed to conduct its operations in secret." The chorus to release detailed information about both early and recent RFC loans grew louder and more persistent.[44]

Senator Couzens, no friend of the RFC and chair of a Senate committee that had been looking into RFC loan practices since the previous summer, recommended that the lists of RFC loans not be published. After reviewing the available documents behind closed doors, Couzens's committee concluded that the Dawes loan had been above board and the RFC loans all well placed and secured. Nevertheless, Congress voted to forego hearings and voted on January 6 to release particulars about RFC loans for the first five months of the agency's existence. The list was duly released before the end of the month despite the protests of both President Hoover and RFC Chairman Pomerene that such adverse publicity could only make things worse for the struggling companies that had received the loans.[45]

The soon-to-be Senate majority leader, Joseph T. Robinson, told Hoover that he would try to reverse the publicity decision, as he had promised the president the previous July, but was forced to concede that President-elect Roosevelt favored the publicity clause and, thus, Robinson could not gather the necessary support among Democrats to turn it back. Even South Carolina Senator James Byrnes, who voted for RFC publicity, became convinced that it was doing definite harm to the companies that borrowed from the RFC and, thus, defeating the purpose of the loans. By February he agreed with Henry Harriman, president of the United States Chamber of Commerce, that the publicity clause ought to be removed — but not until after the inauguration. RFC Chairman Pomerene was convinced that the renewed publicity released in early February was responsible for a cascade of new bank failures that quickly followed. In late January, he handed President Hoover a list of 62 banks with $70 million in deposits that he claimed had closed directly because of the recent RFC publicity. Hoover was certain that the publication of the earlier loans was ultimately responsible for the failure of more than 1,000 banks, holding deposits worth $200 million, in the weeks that followed. The Chester County Trust Company in Pennsylvania, for one, announced unequivocally that publication of RFC loans caused it to close on February 13. After publication of the company's RFC loan, heavy withdrawals commenced immediately. The Whaley-Eaton Service, which issued regular financial news and advice, reported in mid–February that gold was being withdrawn from banks on the lists. A vice president at the Chemical Bank and Trust Company had no doubt that RFC loan publicity led directly to the bank crisis of March.[46]

In fact, there is little evidence that publicity of RFC loans provoked any runs on any banks. Of 453 national banks that received RFC loans in 1932 that were subsequently publicized, only 29 failed. Of those failed banks, 11 experienced declines in deposits of more than 10 percent between their last filed reports to the comptroller of the currency and the date of their failures. Eight banks actually saw their deposits increase. In every case, the failed banks held extremely weak assets and were loaded down with bad or doubtful loans. With perhaps a few exceptions, it seems clear that the banks failed because of weak loans and not because of precipitous drops in deposits. Economist James Butkiewicz posits that, at worst, fear of bank runs caused by news of an RFC loan probably discouraged bank officers from seeking RFC loans when their banks would have benefited from them. Federal Reserve Governor George Seay in Richmond knew of banks in Virginia that hesitated to request RFC loans because of the publicity. Whether or not such reluctance actually led to any bank failures is a matter for idle speculation only. RFC loan publicity undoubtedly did not help any bank, yet probably hurt only a few. Despite many protests to the contrary at the time, there is little reason to believe it was responsible for the bank closings of January and February 1933.[47]

No doubt opponents of the publicity saw the lists as part of a concerted campaign against banks and big business generally, which it was, and greatly resented and abhorred the movement. John Flynn's article leaves no doubt about his ill will toward big banks and holding companies, and his push for publicity certainly was not intended to help them. Still, this particular effort to hamstring big business probably did little direct harm. It was not responsible for the bank failures of early 1933, but it did feed a growing progressive movement to handicap big business and supposedly favor small business. Late in February, Senator Norris introduced onto the Senate floor a large drawing of a spider, labeled "the spider web of Wall Street," purporting to illustrate how eight New York banks controlled America. Franklin Roosevelt played his own part in this effort. This ill-timed campaign did absolutely nothing to help small business and contributed to the stagnation of big business investment that was the principal cause of the Great Depression. So long as business investment remained stagnant all efforts to reverse the economic slump were in vain. This remained true up to 1941.[48]

The wave of bank failures that hit the country in December 1932 and January 1933 was not caused by adverse publicity, but by the continuing financial slump taking its toll on more weak banks. Large banks had proven susceptible to failure along with small banks. Big institutions in New York, Boston, Philadelphia, Pittsburgh, and Chicago had succumbed to the erosion produced by the Depression. But the biggest failures were yet to come, and the February failures in Detroit, brought on directly by the slump that dragged down the Motor City, proved the straw that broke the camel's back. When the financial crisis hit Detroit, national financial and political leaders were already scared and depressed by the waves of bank runs and failures of January and early February. Public officials at all levels were agitated and alarmed by the closures and feared public panic. Marching and rioting farmers added to the national sense of crisis, heightening the sense of urgency among the public, especially those with civic responsibilities. Thus, the reaction to the Detroit debacle was as much political as financial. And the political reactions across the country set in motion a flurry of financial transactions that provided the final push to topple the whole banking system of the United States. That foundering of 1933 provided the psychological stimulus necessary for a raft of congressional bills rushed through in the wake of the collapse that is still known as the New Deal.

Some people believed at the beginning of 1933 that the economic Depression was already at an end and that politics alone kept the economy inert. Charles Dawes looked forward to 1933 with gloom, believing it would be the hardest year of the Depression. But he also thought it would be the last, as all the bankruptcy proceedings and lawsuits over debts would be settled and big corporations would finally adjust to the new, lower price level. He also had confidence that "the masses" would see the end before the "intelligencia" and lead the nation back to prosperity through increased buying. Investment banker Alexander Sachs believed that the economy had finally — and painfully — readjusted to the new, lower price levels and that by January banks and companies were finally writing off or adjusting downward their debts. Sachs was convinced that companies and banks would stop worrying about liquidity and put their money into commodities, securities, and capital and consumer goods, "if political forces will permit it." Thomas Lamont largely agreed with Sachs's assessment of the situation. Indeed, by early February Eugene Meyer was coming around to this view and wrote an upbeat letter to President Hoover informing him that the locus where the Depression had in a sense started, Miami, was now out of it. The city had adjusted to the lower price levels, written off its debts, and started to hum again. Stores were full, sales were booming, empty apartments were filling up, and people seemed optimistic and chipper. The president of the First National Bank of Miami wrote Meyer, "If the whole country had adjusted themselves to present conditions as this place has, everything would be all right. There is no gloom." Only political uncertainty kept the country in gloom.[49]

Just as some were beginning to perceive light at the end of the tunnel, most of the country was as discouraged and frightened by the wave of bank failures of December and January, compounded by rioting in the countryside, as at any time in the last three years. While Congress clutched at straws, state legislatures entertained radical proposals to meet extreme circumstances. Politicians at all levels were willing to consider legislation that only the previous year would have had trouble attracting serious attention. Yet, politicians in the states had gotten the bit between their teeth and were ready to react with dispatch and firmness to the next crisis. The next crisis was about to erupt in Detroit.

CHAPTER SIX

Panic in Detroit

The banking collapse in Detroit led to a chain of events that produced profound changes within the United States. The aftermath loomed vastly larger than the seemingly trivial causes. The problems visiting Detroit were not greatly different from those seen in Chicago: banks carried too many delinquent mortgages for depreciated properties, which they could ill afford to liquidate. Businesses anxious to reduce debts used deposits to pay off loans, reducing both bank assets and deposits. Unemployed, or just anxious, depositors and businesses with less cash flow withdrew their savings from banks, which found it difficult to produce the cash on short notice. By late 1932 the Depression had put severe pressure on the economy and banks in many locales, none more so than in the Midwest. However, the troubles in Detroit were not so readily solved as those of Chicago. They overflowed the city and inundated the entire country. Prosaic headaches besetting head cashiers in neighborhood banks in Detroit improbably provoked epoch-making changes in the America economy, politics, and society. The mechanisms utilized in Chicago to resolve problems failed to salve the discomfort in Detroit because of especially quirky and prickly personalities who stood in positions to prevent a general collapse, and when asked to help, refused.

Detroit Before the Fall

Ironically, an earlier economic slump helped make Detroit the mighty metropolis it became. In the 19th century, Detroit grew as a center for manufacturing ships and railroad equipment. When railroad expansion went into temporary decline during the great bust of the 1890s, machine shops had to find other ways to occupy themselves, such as turning out bicycles and experimental motorized quadricycles. Fate, however, put four talented and lucky mechanics in Detroit in the 1890s: Henry Ford, Ransom E. Olds, and brothers Horace and John Dodge. Well-publicized competition among the tinkers attracted the curious and a few foolhardy, who dared invest money in the outlandish contraptions promoted by Ford, Olds, and the Dodge brothers. The persistence, imagination, and luck of these four men combined to turn Detroit into a center of automobile experimentation and development. Automobiles were made elsewhere in the United States: Warren, Ohio; South Bend and Aurora, Indiana; Kenosha, Wisconsin; and Buffalo, New York, to name just a few, but the quickly developing complexity of auto designs and the large number of subcontractors and specialty shops required to produce them drew auto specialists to Detroit in particular in the early 1900s. Ford's development of the simple and inexpensive ($850) Model T in 1908 revolutionized the auto industry by making a car for the common man that could sell in enormous numbers and required armies of workers to produce.[1]

The success of the auto industry attracted huge numbers of people to Detroit, whose population expanded from 285,704 in 1900 to 1,568,662 in 1930. The city grew and prospered until by 1929 it boasted 200,000 movie-theater seats and supposedly 10,000 speakeasies. Other towns in Michigan similarly prospered: Grand Rapids grew from 87,565 in 1900 to 168,592 in 1930; one Detroit suburb, Royal Oak, exploded from 468 to 22,904. Towns that hosted the biggest auto plants exploded in size: Flint boomed from 13,103 in 1900 to 156,492; Hamtramck grew from 3,559 in 1910 to 56,268; Highland Park hosted 427 people in 1900 and 52,959 in 1930.[2] Just as the auto industry expanded and contracted with the vicissitudes of the American economy, so the health of the auto industry mightily affected the rest of the United States. The American auto industry soon became the world's largest consumer of cotton, hardwood lumber, nickel, upholstery leather, plate glass, crude rubber, gasoline, and oil, and its fortunes affected the rest of the American economy. By the 1920s it also paid the highest wages. If the auto companies suffered so did many other businesses throughout the United States.[3]

After the depression of 1920-21, production took off. Except for the brief recession of 1924, the auto industry roared through much of the twenties. Production climbed every year through 1929. The industry that produced 2,227,000 vehicles in 1920 turned out 4,034,000 cars, trucks, and buses in 1923. The popularity of passenger cars expanded with each passing year: companies sold 1,906,000 in 1920 and 3,625,000 in 1923. Those numbers, fantastic in their own time, continued to climb: 3,784,000 passenger autos sold in 1926; 3,815,000 in 1928; reaching the astronomical figure of 4,587,000 cars in 1929. In addition, the industry produced 771,000 trucks in 1929. The auto industry fared so well that Ford introduced an unimaginable seven-dollar-per-day minimum wage to his 101,069 workers.[4]

The creativity and resourcefulness of the management team assembled at General Motors by Pierre S. du Pont and Alfred P. Sloan, and some serious fumbling by Henry Ford, allowed GM to overtake the Ford Motor Company as America's premier producer of cars and trucks in 1928. Ford, who had done so much to boost auto sales by mass producing the cheap Model T and had altered manufacturing by introducing the assembly line to the production of cars and trucks, set the Ford Motor Company, Detroit, and probably the American economy back by closing down his factories in May 1927. After producing his 15-millionth Model T, Ford decided to stop making the once-revolutionary car in favor of the up-to-date Model A. To convert his plants, he closed them for seven months and threw 60,000 men out of work in Wayne County alone. Another 40,000 men dependent upon orders from Ford Motor Company throughout the United States also went without work. With Ford manufacturing no passenger cars, production in the United States fell from 356,930 in May 1927 to 106,043 in December 1927 — a low for the 1920s. But Ford's loss was GM's gain, especially Chevrolet's, which competed directly with Ford in producing low-cost cars for the working family. Chevrolet sales in 1927 hit 940,277 — more than double the production of 1924 — and reached 1,118,993 vehicles in 1928. Chevrolet cars and trucks accounted for two-thirds of GM sales in 1928, and for a time GM was a nose ahead of Ford as America's largest producer of autos (even though Mr. Ford's new Model A outsold Chevrolet in 1929, 1.4 million to 1.26 million, and Ford briefly regained a slim lead in sales in 1930). With Ford back in production and Model As rolling out of Ford's River Rouge plant in December 1927, tens of thousands of auto workers were back at work. By fall 1928 almost 300,000 people found full-time employment in Detroit — an increase of more than 100,000 from just a year before. The auto industry was humming and so was Detroit and much of Michigan.[5]

And what was good for Chevrolet was good for Michigan. As auto sales piled up, Michigan's towns and factories attracted hundreds of thousands of workers, all of whom needed a place to live. In 1926 Detroit issued permits to construct buildings of all kinds worth $184 million. Even past its peak in 1929, Detroit issued building permits worth $100.5 million. This story was repeated on a smaller scale all over Michigan. Building peaked in Flint in 1927, when permits worth $22 million were issued, compared to $9.6 million in 1920. Pontiac, which issued permits worth $1.3 million in 1923, issued $13.3 million worth in 1928; Grand Rapids peaked early, in 1925, at $12.5 million in permits issued but still issued $8.2 million worth in 1929. Kalamazoo, which saw steady building from 1918 and did not experience the dramatic surge in construction seen elsewhere, nonetheless peaked in 1929 at $2.4 million (compared to $1.94 million issued in 1918). All this business and building was good for banks, which expanded enormously in Michigan during the 1920s.[6]

Banking laws in Michigan resembled those found in many midwestern states. Legislators sought to encourage local banking by allowing banks to operate only within a single municipality but permitted branch banking within city limits. Thus, in the 1920s, dozens of banks competed for business within Detroit city limits. Despite great competition among small neighborhood banks, Detroit was served by only two large national banks in 1929: the First National Bank of Detroit and the National Bank of Commerce. Between them they held $240 million in deposits and loaned $210 million to Detroiters in December 1929. The First National was about half again as big as the Bank of Commerce. After the First National merged with the state's largest state-chartered bank — the Peoples Wayne County Bank — it operated 194 branches within city limits. Michigan law also permitted companies to own stock in other companies, that is, it allowed holding companies. This allowed auto companies to buy important suppliers: GM, for example, bought the Klaxon Company that made horns. It also allowed holding companies to acquire banks. At the end of the 1920s, when the auto companies reached their peak roaring, Michigan became home to two of the largest bank holding companies in America: the Detroit Bankers Company and the Guardian Detroit Company.[7]

The Guardian Detroit Company was chartered in the spring of 1929 with the specific purpose of buying up banks and trust companies. The Detroit Bankers Corporation was founded for the same purpose in January 1930, just as the economy of the city and state began to slow. A third, smaller holding company, the Union Commerce Corporation, existed briefly but was taken over by the larger Guardian Detroit Company in March 1930, forming the Guardian Detroit Union Group — soon known simply as the Guardian Group. When the Guardian Detroit Company bought the Union Commerce Corporation, it acquired the second largest trust company in Detroit, the Union Trust Company, that held $32 million in deposits and had just built a spectacular 40-story art-deco skyscraper as its headquarters in downtown Detroit. The Union Trust Company became the Union Guardian Trust Company and its headquarters became the Guardian Building, which housed the Guardian Group's growing operations. Both the Guardian Group and the Detroit Bankers Corporation were many times larger than Caldwell and Company and both companies had close ties to the car industry. Each of the holding companies bought one of Detroit's national banks: the Guardian Group bought the National Bank of Commerce in December 1929, and the Detroit Bankers Company acquired the First National Bank of Detroit soon after.[8]

Both holding companies hoped to establish commercial banks large enough to keep most of the money generated by Detroit businesses inside Detroit, rather than see the money and business go to larger banks in Chicago and New York. The directors of the Detroit

Bankers Corporation planned to merge five banks and trust companies into the largest bank between New York and Chicago. The new bank would boast capital of $90 million, resources of $725 million, and 900,000 accounts. With such bulk, they hoped to attract the correspondent banking business of smaller banks in Michigan rather than see those funds channeled out of state, as was generally the case before 1929. When acquired by the Guardian Group, the Commerce Bank held deposits of about $91 million and carried on its books loans valued at $88 million. The First National held deposits of $148 million and loans of $112 million. Thus, in 1929, neither bank, although large, played in the same league as New York or Chicago giants. As the holding companies took over smaller banks around Michigan and attracted their correspondent deposits their resources grew — but not dramatically. By the end of 1930, the two banks held $240 million in deposits, and after a tumultuous 1931 that saw 110 small and medium-sized Michigan banks disappear, the two held $653 million. As the economy of the state and city slowed toward the end of 1932, and the condition of banking in Michigan grew more precarious — another 51 Michigan banks failed — the combined deposits in banks controlled by the two holding companies reached almost one billion dollars.[9]

The Guardian Group was assembled by a Detroit lawyer, Ernest Kanzler, who had previously directed Henry Ford's tractor business. Talented and a close friend of Henry's son, Edsel, Kanzler rose to the office of vice president of Ford Motor Company. But Kanzler clashed with the iron-willed Henry over the amount of money draining into the development of a revolutionary experimental engine, and Kanzler lost the contest. Despite the close family ties that bound Edsel and Ernest Kanzler — they had married sisters, Eleanor and Josephine Clay — Kanzler was sacked in 1926 by the increasingly autocratic and erratic Henry Ford. Work on the controversial engine quietly stopped soon after. After leaving the Ford Motor Company, Kanzler and a circle of friends, including Edsel Ford, formed the Guardian Detroit Company to cash in on the booming economy in Michigan. Edsel Ford was the Guardian Group's single largest shareholder and sat on the company's board of directors. The directors of the Guardian Group included a pantheon of auto industry and Detroit giants: Fred J. Fisher and Charles S. Mott, vice presidents of GM; William Fisher of Fisher Body Corporation; the architect Albert Kahn; Ralph Booth of Booth Publishing Company; Roy Chapin of Hudson Motor Car Company; Ransom Olds of the Reo Motor Car Company; and Edsel Ford, president of the Ford Motor Company.[10]

Ernest Kanzler, who sat as a director of the Guardian Group in 1929, was its elected chairman of the board in January 1932. President Robert O. Lord actually ran the company and supposedly kept an eye on the condition of the various banks acquired by the Guardian Group. At the end of 1929, the Guardian Group commanded a collection of banks, savings and loans, and trust companies that offered services all over Michigan: Saginaw, Grand Rapids, Kalamazoo, Battle Creek, Jackson, Port Huron, and many smaller towns throughout the peninsula. Little cash actually changed hands as the holding company swapped its stock for stock in the smaller banks, which became wholly owned entities of the Guardian Group, retained their own board of directors, and usually kept their old management and employees. When high-level personnel openings occurred within the banks around the state, the directors in Detroit had a large say in deciding how they were filled, but normally local directors could have their way and run their own operations. Oversight of the far-flung entities was loose.[11]

The Detroit Bankers Company went on a similar shopping spree, snapping up banks, trust companies, and savings and loans all over the state. The Detroit Bankers Company was organized, in the words of its second president, John Ballantyne, to eliminate "unnecessary wildcat competition" from banking in Detroit. In 1929, Detroit had 350 banks. Many busy commercial intersections had a bank on each corner, as did many not-so-busy intersections. When the Bankers Company started acquiring banks, it merged five Detroit banks that had formerly competed among themselves for customers and business. After the mergers, the Bankers Company controlled 250 branches within Detroit, and sometimes owned all four banks on all four corners of those busy, and less busy, intersections.[12]

Like their fellow bankers at the Guardian Group, the Detroit Bankers Company quickly expanded outside of Detroit. They invested heavily in the city's suburbs, picking up a string of banks belonging to the Peoples Wayne County Bank group: Peoples Wayne County Bank of Dearborn, of Detroit, of Hamtramck, of Highland Park, of River Rouge, and so on. In June 1930 they bought six banks in Hamtramck alone. Before their buying binge was finished the Detroit Bankers Company held the accounts of 900,000 Michiganders, worth $750 million. After the First National Bank of Detroit merged with the Peoples Wayne County Bank in December 1931, it had 194 branches and boasted the second highest number of branches of any bank in the United States outside of New York. All of these banks invested heavily in real-estate mortgages, holding mortgages on 60,000 houses in Detroit and its suburbs, with a book value of about $150 million.[13]

Mortgages typically allowed a ten-year term, though some were less; required a large cash down payment by the home buyer, often half the purchase price of the house; and generally offered only small amounts, about $2,500 to $2,800, payable quarterly. As in Chicago, banks in Detroit often loaned developers 100 percent of the cost of land for residential building. Most mortgages in Detroit and elsewhere were written by real estate salesmen in cooperation with building societies and local savings and loans. Both the Detroit Bankers Company and the Guardian Group bought mortgages from their member units, bundled them and resold them to their trust companies, which, in turn, sold them to their clients as investments. Because both companies sought to keep business within Michigan, both holding companies retained mortgages acquired from Michigan real estate brokers within their own network of banks and trust companies. The trust companies also held them as investments and counted on the steady payments of principal plus 5½ or 6 percent interest to pay dividends to the parent holding companies and pay off loans incurred by the units. Unfortunately, the mortgages held by units of both companies became troublesome as the economy slowed.[14]

Trouble

As Chairman E. Douglas Stair later put it, "The Detroit Bankers Corporation took over a great many area savings and loans, which exist to issue mortgages. At the time when we took them over, they were good mortgages."[15] Only later — and not so much later — they became bad mortgages. The auto industry felt the downturn of 1929 just as other industries did. Monthly passenger-vehicle production reached an all-time inter-war peak of 537,564 cars in April 1929. Truck production reached its inter-war pinnacle in June 1929 with 93,183 trucks rolling off assembly lines. But that summer the turnout turned down. By December auto production had slumped to 92,594 cars. Although business picked up in spring 1930, it failed to rev up and sputtered through 1930, producing a total of 2,784,745 cars. Even Ford's new low-cost Model A failed to revive sales. Unemployment in Michigan, which stood at 15,400 in May 1929, leapt up to 56,800 in September as sales slowed, and reached 212,500 in November as auto production stalled. When asked by Senate Counsel Ferdinand Pecora in 1934 when he knew the Depression had taken hold of Michigan, Ernest Kanzler responded, "I knew in October 1929 that we were going through something, and that impression magnified itself from month to month.... I think that things just got progressively worse from year to year and from week to week." When pressed by Pecora for a more specific date, Kanzler finally proffered, "the latter half of 1932." Kanzler could not have been paying much attention to his old pastime, because the auto industry was in dire straits by fall 1931, when car production dipped below 50,000 in November. By May 1932, production hit its annual peak at 184,285 cars and trucks. For the year, the totals reached paltry figures not seen since the war: 1,370,678 cars and trucks. It might have consoled Kanzler to know that auto production reached its nadir in October 1932 (48,702 vehicles), and then slowly revived — though the ride through the 1930s would be bumpy indeed.[16]

The auto industry, however, was fragile and the city of Detroit became completely hostage to its fortunes. As the lot of the industry worsened in 1930, the condition of Michigan's banks declined. The Guardian banks had borrowed massively from insurance companies and other banks to invest heavily in real estate mortgages in Michigan. Almost 72 percent of the assets of the Union Guardian Trust Company consisted of Michigan mortgages or mortgage bonds. As those mortgages defaulted, the Trust Company found itself saddled with houses and apartments it could not sell. Banks all over the United States experienced the same difficulties as real estate lost value and mortgage holders defaulted on their loans. To make matters worse for banks, their mortgage departments frequently had to race with local tax authorities, which seized houses for nonpayment of taxes at an accelerating rate in 1931, to get their hands on assets. One businessman whose companies held $500,000 in mortgages in Detroit reported in November 1931 that 70 percent were "in default, under foreclosure, or in the hands of the receivers." Furthermore, "There are thousands of vacant houses and apartments in Detroit. Tenants do not even have to pay rent if they will only stay in the houses and in one case the owner of about 300 houses even furnishes fuel so that the houses will not be unoccupied. One trust company has a list of hundreds of houses which it will sell with a very small down payment and the balance monthly."[17]

Despite souring economic conditions, both holding companies continued to acquire banks and trust companies throughout Michigan that were weak or going through tough times. In 1930 the Guardian Group acquired the National Bank of Inonia that, according to the chief national bank examiner for the district, Alfred P. Leyburn, was in very bad condition. In 1931 the Guardian Group acquired the Union Industrial Bank of Flint, which carried on its books a troubling number of defaulted loans. This made a good deal of sense if the directors believed the downturn were just fleeting. Detroit bankers assumed that the soft patch would soon end and business would recover. Even Examiner Leyburn assumed the trouble would be over soon and instructed the examiners who worked for him to evaluate bank assets liberally. But as a Texan business friend of Jesse Jones observed early in the Depression, when Jones suggested they buy some stocks while they were cheap, "Never rope a steer going down hill [*sic*]; he'll kill you every time."[18]

And the economy of Michigan was going downhill fast. Ford laid off nearly half of its work force by 1932. Half a million Michigan workers lacked jobs in January 1932. Another 250,000 joined the unemployment rolls by October. In May 1932, 80,000 unemployed massed in front of Detroit's City Hall demanding government action. In January 1932, moreover, Ford Motor Company ended the unrivaled seven-dollar-a-day minimum pay plan at its plants and cut wages to four dollars a day. The enormous Ford River Rouge plant that had paid more than $181.5 million in wages in 1929, paid $145 million in 1930, and only $76.7 million in 1931.[19]

The failing economy in Michigan hit banks throughout the state. Flint banks saw five to six million dollars drain out of its coffers in two months in 1930. Banks could not dump assets fast enough to raise cash to satisfy depositors, so Bethlehem Steel, American Rolling Mills, and Ford helped out by depositing large amounts of cash in the city's banks. Not all banks were so lucky. As the economy slowed in 1931 and 1932, 195 banks failed in Michigan, leaving many small towns with no banks at all. Throughout 1930 and 1931, the acquisitions by the bank holding companies seemed a blessing to the state. When smaller banks outside Detroit failed, or faltered badly, the two Detroit holding companies often came to the rescue. When the American State Bank of Redmond was about to close in March 1931, a consortium of ten banks that included members of both the Guardian Group and the Detroit Bankers agreed to take over the failing bank and all of its bad loans. In the deal they also acquired the American State Banks of Detroit and Highland Park, with portfolios of $10 million in worthless loans.[20]

A cascading crisis of failing banks hit the state in December 1931 when insurers refused to guarantee local government funds deposited in the Bay City Savings Bank. That meant town governments would have to find someplace else to deposit their money, which amounted to more than half of the $600,000 on deposit in the small bank. If the funds were withdrawn, the bank would immediately be forced to close. It closed. This had unfortunate consequences for the Detroit Bankers Company, which had bought a 20 percent stake in the little bank but did not come to its rescue. Word quickly spread that the holding company had allowed one of its own banks to fail, causing many to think the holding company was in trouble. The closing of the Bay City bank in December not only precipitated a run on the only other bank in town (which survived) but instigated runs on Detroit Bankers units in Lansing and Flint as well.[21]

Lansing experienced a particularly bad bank run in December 1931 that wiped out the American State Bank of Lansing, one of the three largest banks in the capital, and endangered the City National Bank, which lost a serious percent of its deposits. When it appeared that it, too, would topple, the Guardian Group took it over and guaranteed all of its deposits. Although that stopped the run in Lansing and rescued the residents' savings, 1932 proved to be an especially bad year for the city. In December 1931 local banks cleared $8.2 million in checks, while the following December they cleared only $2 million. Banks in Lansing cleared $145.4 million during all of 1931, and only $62 million for all of 1932. The volume of business in Michigan's capital nearly collapsed putting unwelcome pressure on the Guardian Group.[22]

Both holding companies acquired a lot of very dubious assets when they bought banks and savings and loans as the Depression deepened. In the course of 1931, the Detroit Bankers Company diverted $23 million to shoring up the capital positions of their weaker units, making up lost deposits, helping to write off bad loans, and paying off debts owed to out-of-state banks. During the year, units of the Detroit Bankers Company wrote off $49 million in bad loans. When the Detroit Bankers Company acquired the string of Peoples Wayne County Banks, they inherited huge numbers of overdue mortgages. An internal audit of the bank found mortgages that had not paid a dime since 1927! There were not many of those, but there were far too many that had stopped paying anything in 1930 and 1931. The

First National Bank of Detroit had filed foreclosures on $8 million worth of mortgages by May 1932, and a bank examiner reported that all of the bank's mortgages were "more or less in trouble" as property values continued to plummet. In February 1931 examiners judged the bank had $16 million in slow assets and $2 million in hopeless loans. By May 1932 that had turned into $70 million in slow assets, $54 million of doubtful assets, and $49 million in lost loans. The Detroit Bankers had bought themselves an awful lot of trouble. Although the examiner's report listed $70 million in slow loans, Examiner Leyburn assured the comptroller of the currency he was being lenient and the real figure was closer to $90 million. By November 1932 units of the Detroit Bankers owned about $50 million in bad loans and had to write off $11 million as hopeless.[23]

If the Depression had bottomed out in June 1932, as many informed people believed it would, the two holding companies would have found themselves in a very advantageous position. Both holding companies could have taken pride in the crucial assistance they had provided to Michigan banks, depositors, towns, and businesses when that service was most needed. And they would have reaped the benefits as well once the Michigan economy boomed again. The economy, however, did not bottom out in the summer of 1932, and both companies faced serious quandaries as business failed to revive and more units began to totter. If the money-losing units paid no dividends, the holding companies received no income, which they needed to service loans they had taken from New York and Chicago banks — especially Bankers Trust in New York — to acquire the banks in the first place. By June 1932, the Guardian Group owed $14.5 million to New York and Chicago banks, which incurred annual interest of $850,000. The Detroit Bankers owed the Guaranty Trust Company in New York $7.2 million borrowed to purchase Michigan banks. Thus, the holding companies had to keep their units not just solvent, but profitable, or go under themselves. The Guardian Group scrambled to stay afloat in 1931. Edsel Ford loaned the Guardian Group $1 million in December 1930 and then $5 million to shore up its books. He also loaned the Group $5 million worth of municipal bonds as collateral for a loan from Bankers Trust of New York. Shareholders loaned the company progressively larger amounts of money to back loans from out-of-state banks. By the end of 1932, Guardian directors (including Ford) had loaned the various units $27 million in cash and collateral to cover loans by out-of-state banks.[24]

The auto companies did what they could to shore up the creaking system of banks. The Ford Motor Company made loans to Guardian units and increased its deposits to boost bank reserves. In December 1932 the company loaned the Guardian Group an additional $3.5 million to cover dubious assets held by member units. By January 1933, Edsel deposited an additional $12 million of Ford's money in the Guardian National Bank of Commerce alone, bringing the Ford account in that bank to more than $25 million. Ford then had about $32.5 million deposited in various Guardian units around the state. Henry and Clara Ford also had $5 million of their personal funds deposited in the bank. When the Detroit Bankers Company bought the Peoples Wayne County Banks it also acquired $18 million of Ford money deposited in the various banks. Both GM and Chrysler also had millions of dollars deposited in the Guardian National Bank of Commerce. GM, too, helped the Detroit Bankers Company, even if not on the same scale as Ford aided the Guardian Group: in early 1932, for example, GM deposited $1 million in the First National Bank of Pontiac to increase its badly depleted reserves.[25]

By mid–1932, banks in Michigan were in serious trouble because of slack business conditions and widespread unemployment. The volume of business conducted in Detroit plummeted throughout the year. In 1931 Detroit banks cleared $6.2 billion in checks; in 1932 they cleared $3.2 billion to pay for the city's business. The Detroit Bankers Company, especially, had far too many branches active in a city with slack demand for them. By fall 1932, the company was closing one or two banks per week. By February 1933, the First National Bank of Detroit had closed 30 branches and reduced its payroll by $1 million. Chairman Stair of the Bankers Company joined Examiner Leyburn in lamenting that the holding company had expanded too fast and acquired too many units while the economy unraveled. He hoped to streamline operations and make them more efficient, but time was not on his side. Leyburn was scathing in his assessment of the company, later calling it "a monkey house." The Guardian Banks similarly reduced their staff and cut overhead. In 1932 the Union Guardian Trust Company cut its operating expenses by 30 percent.[26]

By January 1933 all banks in Detroit and the flagship operations of both holding companies—the Guardian National Bank of Commerce and the First National Bank of Detroit—tottered on the edge of insolvency. National bank examiner Leyburn was pessimistic about the fortunes of both big banks. In December he found the First National Bank carried on its books $78 million in slow loans, $84 million in doubtful loans, and $6 million in uncollectible loans—and that was after writing off $50 million in bad loans! The December examination of the Guardian National Bank of Commerce revealed that its condition had deteriorated since the previous summer. It still held $110 million in deposits, but also held $25.4 million in slow loans, $18.7 million in doubtful loans, and $456,942 in defaulted mortgage bonds. By February, estimations of dubious loans held by the Guardian National Bank of Commerce had grown to $49 million, and worthless loans had mounted to $8.6 million. The bank did still carry $79.6 million in good loans, however. After examining units of the Guardian Group, Leyburn told Ernest Kanzler, Robert Lord, and Union Guardian Trust Company President Clifford Longley that the Trust Company "was the worst I'd ever seen ... [and] hopelessly insolvent." The trust companies' deposits had plummeted from $38.2 million to $31.4 million between September and December 1932.[27]

Both companies had borrowed to their limits from out-of-state banks, principally in New York and Chicago. When homeowners began to default on their mortgages in large numbers, the bankers knew it would not be long before the larger banks in Detroit also went under. Prodded by Father Coughlin's ranting against "banksters," people in Michigan — and elsewhere — began drawing larger amounts of money from their accounts. Coughlin broadcast corrosive accusations of bankers' malfeasance on Sunday afternoons, and banks noted exceptionally heavy withdrawals on Monday mornings. Douglas Stair noted, "Over a period of two years I should say at least a million and a half dollars a week of deposits were oozing out through the unfortunate publicity of the radio priest there." When large depositors started transferring funds from Detroit banks to New York banks, Detroit bankers knew the end was near unless some financial guardian angel intervened. They looked to the Reconstruction Finance Corporation to save the situation.[28]

From Turmoil to Crisis

The Reconstruction Finance Corporation was established in January 1932 as a lender of last resort to a limited number of corporations with cash-flow difficulties. The RFC loans were intended to help struggling banks, insurance companies, and railroads through temporary hard times. The law was carefully written so that the RFC would assist only those companies that needed a temporary boost, but were otherwise sound concerns that could manage on their own. It was not intended as charity for corporations. Companies seeking loans were fully responsible for the money they borrowed and had to post adequate security for it. Thus, it was purposely limited in what it could do to help companies swimming in rough waters. It was not designed to save stockholders' investments but to prop up the entire financial system by strengthening its weakest links. The RFC was created to help companies such as the Union Guardian Trust Company so that Detroit, Michigan, the auto industry, and the entire Midwest could be spared the turmoil that would be caused by the Trust Company's collapse and the subsequent chain reaction that it might unleash. The Guardian Group presented the RFC with its biggest challenge to date and tested the limits of intervention by the Hoover administration. As events unfolded, Washington's reaction to the troubles in Detroit demonstrated the feebleness of the system put into place in 1932 and its limited ability to solve the problems which confronted it.

In May 1932 the troubled Union Guardian Trust Company had applied for and received a loan from the RFC for $4.25 million. It quickly exhausted that money, and by June the Trust Company was back seeking $15 million more from the RFC. Over the Fourth of July holiday of 1932, officers of the Guardian banks approached a director of the RFC, Jesse Jones, with news of growing difficulties in Detroit. The Trust Company in particular was in deep trouble. Edsel Ford had already personally guaranteed a large loan to the Trust Company by a group of Chicago banks. When, shortly thereafter, Michigan bank examiners questioned the value of securities held as assets by the Trust Company, Edsel responded by loaning the bank another $3.5 million. On July 5 the RFC approved a six-month loan of $8.7 million to tie the bank over while the Fords worked out a rescue plan. The RFC judged the assets pledged to secure the loan very weak, and, indeed, their value and the condition of the Trust Company continued to deteriorate with the economy.[29]

In September, Guardian Group banks received another RFC loan for around $3 million. Nevertheless, in October Guardian officers were back seeking more. Despite assistance from the RFC, the condition of the banks deteriorated, and by January 1933 the Guardian Group asked that the earlier six-month loans, now due, be extended. As their request for an extension was being considered, an insurance company pressed the Union Guardian Trust Company for payment for nonperforming mortgages, which the beleaguered trust company could not make. Chairman Ernest Kanzler talked the situation over with federal bank examiner Alfred Leyburn, who called the Trust Company "hopelessly insolvent." Nevertheless, Leyburn agreed that with proper guarantees from the directors—especially the Fords—the RFC might grant another loan.[30]

After presenting a typically upbeat picture of the company at the annual Guardian Group shareholders' meeting on January 24, 1933, Ernest Kanzler boarded a train for Washington, D.C., where on the 26th he applied for another RFC loan. This time he asked for an extension of the previous $15 million Guardian Group loan and an additional $50 million to cover various Guardian units, pledging $88 million worth of collateral as security. The RFC board of governors sent Chief Examiner John K. McKee to Detroit the next day to go over the books to determine the condition of the banks and the worthiness of the collateral. For a week McKee and a crew of 12 men pored over the assets of the Guardian units around Michigan. They found that the Guardian banks held $55.7 million in cash in their vaults, $44.8 million in municipal and corporate bonds, $34 million in United States government securities, $66.6 million in real estate mortgages, and $133 million in commercial loans. All of this was balanced by $276.6 million in deposits. However, much of the Group's assets were already pledged to cover previous loans from the RFC and from banks in Chicago and New York. Furthermore, the face value of the commercial loans and mortgages was far from their liquidation value, the standard used for collateral by the RFC. On February 6 McKee reported back to RFC headquarters that the available assets of the Group were worth around $20 million. He, thus, proposed a loan for that amount. This was far below the amount Kanzler was seeking, so Guardian directors immediately set about searching for additional security for the loan.[31]

Kanzler approached Walter Chrysler and Alfred Sloan to discuss the possibility of help from Chrysler and GM, but won no commitments. Leyburn and McKee suggested to Kanzler that the loan application might meet more favorable consideration if, instead of the Guardian Group applying for a loan for numerous units, it were submitted by a single entity. The examiners proposed that all available Guardian assets be transferred to a new mortgage-holding company that would then submit the loan application to the RFC. Thus, Wolverine Mortgage was chartered to hold assets and request the loan, and on February 6 another application was made by Wolverine to the RFC for $43.2 million. The Guardian Group pledged additional bonds as collateral, various Guardian directors pledged more security, and Edsel Ford promised Kanzler that the Ford Motor Company would subordinate $7.5 million deposited in the Union Guardian Trust Company, effectively removing it from the books as liabilities. McKee and his crew again set to work assessing the value of the collateral and this time found it worth $37.7 million. When all the pledged security was added up, Wolverine was still short about $6 million. To make matters worse, Kanzler and Union Guardian Trust Company President Clifford Longley were having trouble finding anyone to subscribe to the necessary $5 million capital to set up the new company. Henry Ford would not allow the Ford Motor Company to put any money into it, and Edsel was close to tapped out. He offered no money to help set up the operation.[32]

Kanzler, Edsel Ford, Longley, and Leyburn all traveled to Washington, D.C., on February 6 with hopes of selling the new loan application to the RFC with appropriate political backing. When Treasury Secretary Ogden Mills asked Edsel about subordinating the $7.5 million of Ford money in the Union Guardian Trust Company, he gave a noncommittal reply — presumably because he had already discussed it with his father, who either had expressed reservations or already said no. In any event, Kanzler and Longley told government officials they did not want to ask any more of Edsel Ford, who "had done enough" in the past three years for the Guardian Group. Nevertheless, government officials seemed to believe that the Fords held the fate of the Guardian Group in their hands. Chief Bank Examiner Leyburn later testified that RFC and Treasury officials involved in the negotiations implicitly asked, "Why should we bail out Mr. Ford?" Despite imputing bad faith on the part of government officers, Leyburn, himself, characterized Henry Ford as "unpredictable." RFC Chairman Atlee Pomerene, who also happened to be a director of the (unrelated) Guardian Trust Company of Cleveland, said Ford had already withdrawn $2 million from that bank, and doubted that he could be counted upon to assist. RFC President Charles Miller suggested that President Hoover personally invite Henry Ford to the White House and ask his support for the Michigan banks. Longley, who, aside from being president of the Union Guardian Trust Company also happened to be Henry Ford's personal lawyer, agreed to telephone Henry Ford immediately with the suggestion that he come to Washington. When he returned to the meeting he reported, "Mr. Ford's answer was that no matter who called him down to Washington the answer would be 'no.'" Knowing that the Wolverine Company did not have enough collateral for the full loan, Undersecretary of the

Treasury Arthur A. Ballantine and Pomerene then suggested that Kanzler and Longley approach Michigan Republican Senator James Couzens to support the loan. Kanzler and Longley, however, told the government officials they wanted Couzens kept entirely out of the discussions. The RFC officials felt between a rock and a hard place in handling the Guardian loan. They feared the political and financial reactions if they granted the loan, and the responses if they refused it. Shifting responsibility for the decision elsewhere, such as to the White House, would greatly ease their anxiety.[33]

President Hoover had been kept apprised of the unpleasantness developing in Detroit since mid–January. On February 8 he convened a meeting at the White House, gathering Arthur Ballantine, Secretary of Commerce (and Hudson Motor Company executive) Roy D. Chapin, and Charles Miller to discuss the storm then brewing in Detroit. Hoover talked to Henry Ford on the phone about the situation and secured his agreement to subordinate the $7.5 million previously pledged by Edsel. But when Clifford Longley — back in Michigan — talked to Henry Ford about the money, Ford refused to subordinate the funds. Longley immediately called Washington and informed President Hoover of Ford's answer. Hoover then decided to ask Michigan's Republican senior senator, James Couzens — a wealthy man in his own right — to help. Couzens was the last man to whom the president should have turned. Kanzler and Longley had specifically avoided involving him in any of the Washington, D.C., negotiations even though asking congressmen to endorse RFC loans had become routine. The senator had once been a business partner of Henry Ford, and had carried on a running feud with Detroit's business elite since before the war. Couzens had lately taken to echoing Father Coughlin's denunciations of "banksters" on the Senate floor, and was not likely to look upon a rescue operation with great sympathy. Though uninvolved, Couzens had already heard about the RFC loan application from RFC director Jesse Jones while discussing a Michigan railroad's request for a loan.[34]

Because of his background, the Republican senior senator from Michigan nursed antipathy for many people and institutions, including Henry Ford, Herbert Hoover, the Treasury Department, banks, and utilities, making his cooperation extremely unlikely. All of his life Couzens exhibited a rigidly righteous temperament, which sometimes worked to his advantage and advancement, but also won him legions of detractors. Like Ford, he hated to compromise and possessed no diplomatic skills or tact. When Couzens became president of the Bank of Detroit, he refused to join the Detroit Clearing House Association, inaugurating less than friendly relations with most Detroit bankers. Senator Couzens's running feuds with Treasury Secretary Andrew Mellon, with their history of accusations, counter-accusations, and mutual investigations, ensured Couzens's enduring hostility toward the Treasury Department. Moreover, Couzens, who never passed up an opportunity to make enemies, had gratuitously made one of future commerce secretary Roy Chapin in 1912 when Couzens publicly challenged a claim by Chapin's Hudson Motor Car Company that its staff included "the foremost engineer in the industry."[35]

The Meeting at the White House

On Thursday, February 9, Michigan Senator Arthur Vandenberg received a note in the Senate Chamber informing him that two bankers from Detroit wished to confer with him about some urgent business. The two bankers, Clifford Longley and executive vice president of the Guardian Group James Walsh, requested the senator's assistance in securing a loan from the RFC to help the tottering Wolverine Company. The two also paid a call on Senator Couzens hoping against hope to enlist his support for the RFC loan. Both senators had to be called off the floor of the Senate, where Couzens was defending his proposal to open Army camps to unemployed youths and, thus, in little mood to hear special pleading from "banksters." When the two Detroit bankers made their pitch for support for the RFC loan, Couzens brusquely cut them off and told them exactly what he thought about supplicant bankers. He lectured them about the impropriety of the Dawes loan and the public benefits derived from allowing poorly run banks to fail.[36]

Later that day both senators received calls from the White House requesting their assistance that evening to discuss the RFC loan with the president. Couzens assumed that now President Hoover was going to make a personal appeal to him to support the loan. Like most progressives, Couzens resented big banks making huge demands upon the resources of the RFC, as exemplified by the Dawes loan. He especially resented big banks making big demands for public assistance when so many unemployed workers wandered the streets seeking help from any quarter. That day in Michigan, schools closed because local governments did not have the money to clear snowdrifts from the roads. Twenty children were treated in local hospitals for frostbite. Five citizens died in Detroit in the -13° weather as the mayor and municipal council debated what else to cut from the city budget. Senator Couzens went to the White House prepared to let everybody know just what he thought about special privileges for the rich.[37]

At the White House that evening the two Michigan senators met for two hours with President Hoover, Secretary of the Treasury Ogden Mills, Undersecretary Ballantine, RFC President Miller, and Secretary of Commerce Chapin. In the Lincoln Room, Miller and Mills explained to the Michigan senators that the Guardian Group offered insufficient collateral to qualify for any RFC loan big enough to save the Trust Company. Miller made a long disquisition on the history of the loan, explaining why it had to be rejected. Believing his exposition was an apology to the Michigan senators for the RFC's helplessness, he explained that there was no legal basis for approving the loan. Not having talked to Longley and Walsh, who were on their way back to Detroit, Miller expected Couzens to plead for approval, rather than bluster against the loan. When Vandenberg and Hoover both urged the RFC officials to accept the proffered Guardian collateral at face value, Couzens burst out that he would "shout against it from the housetops and on the floor of the Senate," if the law were not followed to the letter and the loan were granted with insufficient security. Intimidated by the irascible Couzens, Vandenberg faded into the background while Couzens argued with Hoover and his staff. Couzens said if the Fords and their bank had gotten into trouble, the Fords, who had plenty of resources, should get themselves out of trouble. Instead of beseeching Couzens to support the loan, Hoover suggested that the former mayor of Detroit should put up $2 million of his personal fortune to help bail out the Guardian banks. Despite pleas from the president that the savings of more than one million Michiganders were at stake, Couzens refused to consider helping the banks. Hoover told the Michigan senator, "If 800,000 small bank depositors in my home town [San Francisco] could be saved by lending three percent of my fortune, even if I lost, I would certainly do it." Couzens, convinced that the RFC loan to the Guardian Group would not only be illegal, but "immoral," refused to be moved.[38]

The next day, February 10, Hoover dispatched Secretary Chapin and Undersecretary Ballantine to Detroit to see what could be done. Couzens talked to Jesse Jones several times during the next few days making clear his view that the RFC could not loan any money to banks not clearly solvent — as stated in the RFC charter. Trying another tack, Hoover asked GM President Alfred P. Sloan and Walter Chrysler on the phone if they would back the Trust Company's deposits until Tuesday morning (Monday, February 13, was a holiday — Lincoln's Birthday). Hoover, Mills, Sloan, Chrysler, and Miller met at the White House on Friday morning, February 10, to see if any way could be found to save the situation in Detroit. Sloan and Chrysler agreed to back additional Guardian deposits if Ford agreed to subordinate his deposits at the Guardian banks. All at the meeting feared that closing the Union Guardian Trust Company would precipitate a run in Detroit that would overwhelm local banks and provoke a severe crisis throughout Michigan, which would surely have national repercussions. Firemen, police, and teachers were already owed back pay by the city, contributing to a gloomy and tense atmosphere in shivering Detroit. Mayor Frank Murphy was proposing to lay off another 162 policemen. A strike by 6,000 workers had shut down Briggs Manufacturing, which supplied auto bodies to Ford. One man was shot, three stabbed, and four beaten so badly they required hospitalization in a confrontation between strikers and workers trying to get into the Briggs plant. The Briggs strike idled 50,000 Ford workers at the giant River Rouge plant, which in turn idled 100,000 more workers dependent upon parts fabricated at River Rouge. Another 3,000 workers walked out of the Hudson Motor Company in a dispute about wages, hours, and unionization, idling another 2,500 workers. With car production grinding to a halt, Sloan and Chrysler asked if the RFC would at least loan money to the city to pay back wages. But they all agreed that such a loan, even if approved, was unlikely to help the banks in the short run, and no one close to the situation could be found to promise any additional deposits in Guardian banks.[39]

The Meeting in Detroit

When Ballantine and Chapin arrived in Detroit on Saturday morning they went directly to the Guardian Group headquarters and met with Guardian and federal officials already on the scene. They assured Longley and Lord that the federal government was eager to help if possible. Examiners McKee and Leyburn explained the situation at the Guardian Group in some detail to the two men from Washington, who soon conceded that it had only about $5 million of assets not already pledged to cover previous loans. Chapin and Ballantine spent the day talking to local businessmen trying to arrange a rescue package using local resources and generally found them willing to help. On the phone, Hoover told Ballantine that General Motors, Chrysler, and Hudson's Department Store would subordinate their deposits with Guardian units, freeing them as security for an RFC loan, if Ford agreed to do the same. Both Chrysler and GM were in positions to help the banks if they so chose. GM, GMAC (GM's consumer-credit arm), and Cadillac had $7,043,440 deposited in the Guardian National Bank of Commerce, the Chrysler Corporation had $2,775,187 on deposit, and Hudson's had another $3,347,748. This additional $13.1 million pledge appeared to give the Guardian Group a good deal of breathing room. As of Saturday night, Ballantine evidently still believed Ford was willing to subordinate Ford Motor Company deposits in the Guardian banks, so the immediate situation seemed salvageable. Everything depended on the cooperation of Henry Ford.[40]

A collection of mighty American financiers and industrialists assembled in Detroit on Saturday, February 10, to see if a rescue plan could be drawn up for the Guardian Group. Melvin Traylor, president of the First National Bank of Chicago, and Abner Stillwell, vice president of Continental Illinois National Bank — the largest bank in Illinois — joined officers of the Guaranty Trust Company, Bankers Trust, and Central Hanover Bank from New York to confer with financial officers of Chrysler and General Motors. When Walter Chrysler returned to Detroit from Washington, D.C., he too joined the talks in the Guardian's flamboyant art-deco headquarters. All day and night the men talked with Chapin, Ballantine, and officers of the Guardian Group trying to arrive at a solution to the complicated puzzle, which seemed possible if Henry Ford cooperated.[41]

Unfortunately, the situation in Detroit was even more complicated than the industrialists and financiers believed, because the Guardian banks were not the only institutions in Michigan in deep trouble. On Saturday, February 11, Examiner Leyburn met with Wilson W. Mills, president of Detroit's largest bank, the First National Bank, at the Detroit Club to alert him about the Guardian predicament and ask if his bank could help out. He hoped that Mills would see the obvious advantage in preventing a colossal financial breakdown in Michigan. This was a most peculiar request for Leyburn to make of Mills because both men were well aware that the First National Bank was not only in no condition to lend a hand to any Guardian bank, it was tottering on the edge of collapse itself. Only 11 days before, Mills had written to Leyburn inquiring how his bank might obtain a loan like the one the Dawes Bank had received. That could only mean the First National Bank needed a very large loan, indeed. Mills became "rather peeved" for not having been informed of the disastrous state of affairs sooner, and informed Leyburn that the First National could offer only minimal help. Mills did not discuss the trouble at the First National with Leyburn, but immediately presumed the unwholesome consequences for his own bank if a major Detroit bank failed. Right away Mills started an application for an RFC loan to his own bank, asking $100 million — only $10 million more than Dawes had received.[42]

On Monday, February 13, Senator Couzens mused to the senators, reporters, and others gathered to observe the "Pecora hearings" that, perhaps, the RFC should be allowed to go out of business. He, for one, could not justify RFC loans to banks and railroads while so many towns and counties were denied aid to keep essential public functions viable. That same morning, stories circulated that the senator had told a news reporter that weak banks in America should be allowed to fail so that strong banks could take over — a view not inconsistent with that of Andrew Mellon. When told of Couzens's comments, Ford responded, "For once in his life, Jim Couzens is right!" After a few hours of sleep, the bankers and government officials gathered again in the Guardian Building on Sunday. They kept in touch with Washington, D.C., and Ballantine informed Hoover about their lack of progress. Hoover personally telephoned Ford in an effort to gain his cooperation, without success. He then asked Chapin and Ballantine to go see Ford.[43]

Chapin and Ballantine resolved to try to budge Ford one last time. They called on Henry Ford at his office in Dearborn on Monday, Lincoln's Birthday, where he persistently refused to cooperate in any rescue plan. He said he had misunderstood the situation several weeks ago when he had said he would consider subordinating his money on deposit in the Guardian National Bank of Commerce, and, in any event, he had changed his mind. Moreover, he told the men from Washington, if the Union Guardian Trust Company failed to open the next morning he would withdraw all $25 million of Ford Motor Company money from the First National Bank as well. Even without Ford's cooperation, it might still have been possible to save the Guardian banks, but with this new threat from Henry Ford, the situation in Detroit suddenly became hopeless. The First National Bank was in almost as bad shape as the Guardian Trust, and was far larger. If Ford withdrew his deposits, the First

National would surely collapse and could bring down all the banks in Michigan with it. Despite the entreaties of Chapin and Ballantine, Ford would not be moved. They tried to convince Ford that his refusal to help would lead to a general collapse of banking in Michigan with disastrous consequences not just for business, but for the people. Such a calamity also would surely not be confined to Michigan, but would spread like a fire out of control. Ford accused them of threatening him and railed, "I am not likely to leave my money in a bank in order to prevent Jim Couzens from spouting on the floor of the Senate." He continued that he did not believe the federal government would allow the banks to fail and it was not up to him to save them. He went on to hint that dark forces were behind all of this, revealing shades of paranoia. Ford claimed that the same forces that were behind the strike at the Briggs plant were responsible for the plan to have Ford put his money at risk to bail out Detroit, the government, and Senator Couzens. When Chapin tried to reason with Ford, as an "auto man," that a general collapse would ruin not only Ford's competitors, but the Ford Motor Company as well, Ford replied, "All right, then let us have it that way; let the crash come." Ford insisted he "felt young" and would start again from scratch. He mused that perhaps a complete economic collapse might not be such a bad thing for the people of the United States, in fact it might be a very good thing to go through such an experience. Chapin and Ballantine finally decided that Ford was beyond reason and would be of no help.[44]

After Ballantine and Chapin left, Ford received a visit from Wilson Mills, of the First National Bank of Detroit, who joined him for lunch. It was impossible to hide that Mills came as a supplicant pleading with Ford to subordinate his deposits in the Guardian banks and not to withdraw Ford money from the First National. Ford refused: "No, no, there is no reason why I should. There is no reason why the government should make me the goat. And there isn't any reason why I should tie up several million to keep Senator Couzens from shouting from the housetops. And there isn't any reason why I, the largest individual taxpayer in the country, should bail the government out of its loans to banks." Ford repeated his argument about federal assistance to Mills, "I think it is up to the government to save these institutions by making them loans. They saved the Dawes bank." Mills joined the others at the Guardian building around six o'clock and reported that he could not budge Ford. That night, Wilson Mills called Jesse Jones in Washington, promising to open the First National Bank in the morning if Jones would promise to approve a $100 million loan. Jones knew then that the end of the line had finally come. The stubborn refusal of two very stubborn men, Ford and Couzens — once partners — to cooperate with anyone had doomed any rescue plan.[45]

With Ford unhelpful and the assets of the Guardian banks demonstrably too weak or already pledged to cover earlier loans, the out-of-town bankers met separately with Chapin and Ballantine to discuss their limited options. The men's thinking had come to encompass the First National Bank as well, and its precarious situation had become common knowledge among the grandees gathered to ponder Detroit's fate. After examining the First National's books, Melvin Traylor pronounced the bank "hopeless." They all agreed that if the Guardian Trust opened on Tuesday morning it would quickly run out of funds to meet the anticipated heavy withdrawals and would be forced to close. If that happened, the closure of the First National Bank of Detroit would follow within hours, if not minutes. The funds of most of the remaining banks in Michigan would be frozen in the Detroit banks, forcing a general closure of banks in the state. Such an event would precipitate crises in Toledo and Cleveland, and so on. The only question was how far the ripples from this plummeting rock would spread? Banks nationwide would start to withdraw their money on deposit in New York in order to meet local demands, so New York was not likely to remain high and dry. Traylor of Chicago found it hard to believe that Mr. Ford understood how this crisis would affect the auto industry. Ballantine called Ford's private secretary, Ernest Liebold, one more time to see if the giant of Ford Motors could not be persuaded to save his own industry. He could not.[46]

While the industrial and financial grandees conferred in Detroit on Monday, February 13, Couzens and Vandenberg met again with the president, Ogden Mills, Jesse Jones, and Atlee Pomerene to see if anything further could be done in Washington. Pomerene told the president that a collapse in Detroit would provoke a flight of gold from the country and currency from banks, leaving the RFC no choice but to back the Union Guardian Trust Company despite opposition from Couzens. Hoover agreed that everything possible should be done to save the situation. A grand gathering of officialdom — RFC leaders, Federal Reserve governors and directors, Governor Eugene Meyer, the Michigan senators, and Treasury officials— was convened at the RFC headquarters. After reviewing the situation they all agreed that Ford held the key to saving the situation. If he withdrew his funds from the Detroit banks, havoc would follow, with unpredictable results. New York Fed Governor George Harrison and acting comptroller of the currency Francis Awalt argued against a bank holiday in Michigan, but agreed it would be preferable to allowing Henry Ford to withdraw all of his money from Michigan's banks. When Ballantine informed them over the phone from Detroit that Ford had again threatened to withdraw all Ford money from all Detroit banks, Couzens agreed to make one last phone call to try to convince Henry Ford to cooperate. Couzens adopted an uncharacteristically reasonable, even friendly, manner with Ford, to no avail. The cause was hopeless. After talking to Ford, Clifford Longley called Couzens at his home in Washington, D.C., to report on events in Detroit. Couzens suggested to Longley that he telephone Ford again and tell him that Couzens had agreed to put up half the necessary money to save the banks, if Ford would put up the other half. Ford irritably rebuffed Longley when he telephoned with the offer. For his part, Awalt ordered the First National Bank not to open in the morning.[47]

The out-of-town men in Detroit, the officials in Washington, and the officers of the Guardian agreed: time was running out and the only way that Michigan could avoid a debacle was to close all the banks for a few days until a rescue could be worked out. They asked Governor William A. Comstock to come down from Lansing to discuss the crisis. The governor arrived around midnight and was briefed on the situation by Kanzler and Ballantine. He agreed that a holiday would be necessary but that he would need the legislature to pass enabling legislation and that the request for the holiday had to come from some responsible organizations. He asked Eugene Stevens, of the Chicago Federal Reserve Bank, if the Federal Reserve could request the holiday, but Stevens objected that such an action lay outside the purview of the Federal Reserve System. Nevertheless, he strongly approved of the holiday proposal because he was certain if all banks did not close, then the big corporations would withdraw their deposits from the big Detroit banks on Tuesday morning and transfer them out of state. Even small Michigan banks would withdraw what they could — law demanded they keep half their reserves in-state —forcing the big banks in Detroit to close their doors. Robert Lord, chairman of the Detroit Clearing House Association (and Guardian Group president), suggested that the clearing house could formally request the holiday. Since most of its members were present, they held a meeting in an adjacent room and soon presented the governor with a petition. The governor wrote out his proclamation.

> Whereas, in view of the acute financial emergency now existing in the City of Detroit and throughout the state of Michigan, I deem it necessary in the public interest, and for the preservation of the public peace, health and safety ... at the request of the Michigan Bankers Association, and the Detroit Clearing House, and after consultation with banking authorities, both local and national, with representatives of the United States Treasury Department, the Banking Department of the State of Michigan, the Federal Reserve Bank, the RFC, and with the US Secretary of Commerce, I hereby proclaim ... [a moratorium] closing banks, trust companies and all other financial institutions within the state of Michigan, from February 14 to 21 inclusive. signed 1:32 A.M.[48]

Governor Comstock had been in constant touch with legislative leaders in Lansing, who drew up an enabling law. Around three A.M. their work was done, and the governor released an announcement to the press proclaiming a bank holiday for the next eight days.[49]

The governor stepped outside the building to talk to the growing crowd of journalists who had caught wind around midnight that something extraordinary was brewing in the Guardian Building. He briefly outlined the difficulties that centered on the Union Guardian Trust Company and explained, "The crisis was caused by the inability to realize immediately upon the assets of the institution to meet threatened withdrawals. For the protection of smaller depositors in our institutions and to prevent the withdrawal of large sums from the State of Michigan it was deemed wise to declare a banking holiday for a period sufficiently long to allow the situation to be cleared up." He advised the reporters that the holiday was a "request" and not mandatory; however, it would be "unwise," he said, for banks to ignore the holiday under the circumstances, for banks that remained open would surely be subjected to runs by nervous depositors. The Detroit Clearing House Association voted to honor the holiday. Banks in the Upper Peninsula, within the Minneapolis Federal Reserve District, elected to remain open. The moratorium was set to end on Washington's Birthday, and by then, the governor and bankers agreed, a national moratorium would be necessary. They were off by two weeks.[50]

A Holiday in Michigan

The people of Michigan, Detroiters especially, reacted with perhaps pardonable surprise to the news on Tuesday morning. All the negotiations and hand wringing about Detroit banks had taken place behind firmly shut doors. The press and public were not invited to discuss these delicate matters, so when the news was released on Tuesday morning that all banks in Michigan were closed, the public was shocked and unprepared. Even Detroit Mayor Frank Murphey knew almost nothing about the brewing crisis and the bank holiday struck him "like a bolt out of the blue." Five hundred and fifty institutions holding $1.5 billion were shuttered. Jacob Seibert of the *Commercial and Financial Chronicle* tried to put the best face on the problem: "It appears to have been handled with consummate skill and that it seems possible to say that the worst of the trouble now lies behind." President-elect Roosevelt issued a similar upbeat statement agreeing that "the worst of the trouble now lies behind, with good reasons for thinking there will be an early return to the normal." The legislature in Lansing rushed through two resolutions to give the governor's actions the semblance of legality, without actually bestowing it. One bill ordered all banks and trust companies in the state to close, and the other gave the governor the authority to close banks in the event of an emergency. But the truth was, like the moratoria declared elsewhere by mayors and governors alike, it never would have survived a court challenge. No mayor, county or state judge, governor, or state legislature had the legal authority to close national banks, which answered exclusively to the United States comptroller of the currency. Nor did the comptroller have any statutory right to close solvent banks. Governor Comstock had frankly admitted in the first instance that he could not force banks— national or state — to close, and he hoped they would cooperate.[51]

Not every bank got word of the moratorium in time, so some opened up for business as usual on Tuesday morning. When bankers from Alpena and Monroe, Michigan, telephoned Governor Comstock asking why they could not conduct business as normal, as they were in perfectly good shape, the governor admitted that if banks wanted to operate despite the proclamation they were free to do so. All banks in Monroe elected to remain open. Upper Peninsula banks carried on business as usual. But the majority of banks cooperated with the governor's request. The Detroit stock market also remained closed, but was under no obligation to do so. The Clearing House Association of Kalamazoo, which consisted of the presidents of the remaining four Kalamazoo banks, met on Tuesday morning when they heard the news and voted to cooperate with the governor. They issued a statement to the press that all the banks were sound, and they would work out a plan to honor and clear checks during the eight-day closure.[52]

Detroiters were caught surprised and without cash. When they heard about the bank holiday on Tuesday morning, like everybody else, the judges in Detroit's courthouse pooled their resources and discovered they had $1.50 between them. One judge's wife, who collected change in a sugar bowl, announced that he could have one dollar per day to spend, and no more. One man reportedly desperate for gasoline paid the filling station with a gold cufflink. Shoeshiners complained of a marked drop-off in business because customers did not want to spend their scarce change. Waitresses complained of receiving no tips, and people became angry when stores refused to accept $20 bills, because they did not want to give up their precious change. A&P grocery stores announced they would accept checks from their regular customers and hold them until the end of the holiday.[53]

To meet the situation, the Detroit Clearing House Association announced they would implement a plan to allow Detroiters access to $25 million in cash on Thursday. The Federal Reserve Bank in Chicago used 15 detectives to transfer $20 million in gold from its vaults to the branch in Detroit. The head of the Secret Service dispatched 350 agents to Michigan to prevent rumor mongering. In the first five weeks of 1933, the Federal Reserve increased currency in circulation by more than $200 million. In the week following the governor's proclamation, it added another $149 million. The Federal Reserve poured $65 million in cash into Detroit, making it available to banks for limited withdrawals after Thursday, February 16. Big, out-of-state banks, mostly in Chicago and New York, used the Federal Reserve System to transfer large amounts of cash to Detroit. The big auto companies all maintained accounts in other cities, especially New York and Chicago, that they drew upon to pay their employees in Michigan. The Detroit banks made these infusions of cash available to companies immediately, segregating new deposits from old. Thus, Michigan banks, with acquiescence of the governor and banking authorities, implemented a plan granting companies access to fresh infusions of cash held separate from prior deposits, before the legislature had actually gone through the formality of passing a law allowing it.[54]

Big companies shifted as best they could to keep operations going. Chrysler took out a full-page advertisement in the *Detroit Free Press* on February 15 promising to cash employees' checks, and opened temporary offices around Michigan, which served as company banks where employees could cash checks. Like Chrysler, General Motors promised to open 11 cash offices to allow its 65,000 employees to cash checks. GM, which held $173 million in cash and government securities in banks around the United States—mostly in New York—declared it would pay its 36,255 workers in Flint in cash with money trucked in from out of state. Hudson's Department Store also promised to pay its 6,000 employees in cash. Small companies sent trusted employees to New York or Chicago to fill suitcases with cash to bring back to Detroit to meet their needs. Banks in nearby Toledo divulged that withdrawals were heavier than normal for midweek, but their condition had improved remarkably since 1931 and they held plenty of cash. They also announced they would accept checks written on Michigan bank accounts but hold them until the end of the holiday. Telegraph companies in Michigan were swamped with people lining up to send telegrams requesting money from out-of-state relatives. To meet the heavy demand for money, Western Union also had to ship cash in from New York and Chicago.[55]

Despite the serious situation, Detroiters took their predicament in stride and with at least some good humor. Milk dealers in Detroit announced they would continue delivery regardless of ability to pay. To reassure the cashless population, the city printed $42 million in scrip to serve as cash until the banks could reopen, should it be needed. The city of Kalamazoo also announced that it would print scrip and use it to keep the city functioning during the moratorium. The Armour Meat Company, which had five packing houses in Michigan, trucked in money from other states to pay their workers. Other companies resorted to paying their employees with scrip. Detroit courts postponed imposing fines for minor infractions until after the holiday. Utility companies likewise postponed collecting bills until after the banks reopened.[56]

Even before he issued his holiday decree, Governor Comstock agreed with Michigan bankers and state politicians about the urgency of a law to allow depositors to gain access to a portion of their accounts. Michigan law allowed no such favors, yet the governor announced on the morning of February 15 that by the next day customers could withdraw 5 percent of their accounts from solvent banks. Such a bill was indeed introduced on February 15, although it immediately became bogged down in committee. While legislators in Lansing argued about how best to modify the law to accommodate the situation, the governor signed another decree of dubious legality granting depositors access to 5 percent of their accounts. As promised, on Thursday, February 16, Michiganders were allowed to retrieve 5 percent of their funds from their accounts. Everyone was surprised when few did so and the anticipated long lines failed to appear. Detroit was amazingly quiet. Detroit Savings Bank President W.L. Dunham said he was "somewhat surprised" by the calm that prevailed in the city. Another described it as "like a normal Saturday." Michiganders were eligible to withdraw up to $75 million, but took out only $30 million on Thursday. Detroiters could have withdrawn $26 million, but took only $4.6 million. Detroiters also had on deposit $32 million in Post Office savings accounts, which remained open and freely available throughout the bank holiday. The Post Office brought in an extra $5 million in cash the day after the holiday began, but did not need it as deposits outpaced withdrawals. In the two days immediately after the declaration of the bank holiday, only 200 new Post Office accounts were opened. In response to the light demand for cash, President Dunham announced that Detroit Savings Bank depositors would not be limited to 5 percent of their accounts, but could withdraw all the money they wanted. Even that policy—effectively exempting the savings bank from the holiday—produced no unusual crowds at the bank for the rest of the week.[57]

The holiday atmosphere could not last forever. While department stores in Detroit revealed that sales were about normal — that is, not very good — wholesalers reported that sales were very slow. The bank situation impeded efforts to arrange credit for customers who normally paid cash. Big companies, such as the Michigan Central Railroad and Consumers Power Company, with access to cash from other sources, could manage for a while, but others could not. A Detroit butcher and meat wholesaler, Jack Cinnamon, announced on Friday that he would open his company's safe and cash customers' checks until his $16,000 was exhausted, which happened by the end of the day. The city of Detroit faced severe troubles. It had managed to pay 3,200 of its employees in cash on Thursday after the holiday was declared, but without access to more than 5 percent of its funds, the city soon ran out of money. Detroit already owed teachers, police, and firemen back pay. State troopers withdrew sacks of cash from the First National Bank and drove it to Lansing so state employees could cash their paychecks.[58]

The governor's decree bought the Detroit banks one week to arrange an RFC loan or some other arrangement to bring solvent banking back to the Motor City. By the end of the week, little had been accomplished to restore banking to the city. When other city banks opened limited access to accounts, the Union Guardian Trust Company remained shuttered. While the governor released vague statements about the ills that beset the city's banks, Detroiters surmised that banks in the Guardian Group were suspect. Only the Guardian National Bank of Commerce had long lines of customers seeking money, and the tranquil experience of other banks suggests that Guardian customers were withdrawing money not because they needed it for daily expenses but out of fear for its security. Nevertheless, the bank had $5.2 million in cash available for withdrawal, yet only $1.2 million was demanded on Thursday. The bank doled out $600,000 on Friday and another $620,000 on Saturday and Monday, so the amounts diminished with each day regardless of the sum available. Banks throughout the state with correspondent accounts with Detroit banks were subject to the same 5-percent rule as all other account holders and did not have free access to their reserves. Even solvent and liquid banks in the state had to impose limits on withdrawals because the limits imposed by the Detroit Clearing House Association forced them to.[59]

The *Detroit Free Press* reported on February 15 that negotiations to save the banks had broken apart on the shoals of enmity between Couzens and Ford. This version of events was then broadcast nationwide by Walter Lippmann in his column reprinted in 115 papers. It further related that Ford had agreed to freeze his accounts in the Guardian banks only if others did as well and that he had rebuffed a personal plea for cooperation from President Hoover. But Douglas Stair's *Detroit Free Press* reserved its most pointed criticism for Senator Couzens: "If it had not been for Senator Couzens's protests the loan would have been granted." It reported the RFC wanted to grant the loan and President Hoover begged Couzens not to block it, but the mulish senator refused to budge. When the chairman of the GM Finance Committee later recapitulated the events leading to the Michigan crisis, he laid blame at the feet of both Henry Ford and Senator Couzens. Governor Comstock pointed accusingly at Henry Ford, publicly claiming if he had cooperated the RFC would have granted the loan to the Union Guardian Trust Company. Comstock added fuel to the fire by saying that intense rivalry between the auto companies had contributed to the crisis. The next day he retracted that comment, saying he "had misunderstood the facts." For his part, Ford said he had no comment, "yet."[60]

The day after Governor Comstock declared the holiday in Michigan, Senator Vandenberg went to see President Hoover at the White House to discuss the situation. Vandenberg tried to assuage Hoover's ill temper toward Senator Couzens, evidently without much effect. But more importantly he wanted to push an idea to have the comptroller of the currency sign an order allowing the application of state laws to national banks. This would at least give a fig leaf of legality to the governor's decree closing all national banks in Michigan, which were untouched by state law. It would have the additional benefit of allowing restricted withdrawal plans, such as those in effect in Missouri, to apply to national banks as well as state banks in all states. Vandenberg suggested that a joint resolution passed by Congress would allow the comptroller to issue such a ruling. Hoover had already discussed with Federal Reserve officers and Secretary Mills the idea of legislation allowing national banks to operate on a restricted basis, and all agreed in view of Senator Glass's opposition that such a bill was not likely to pass anytime soon, and if approved would immediately ignite runs on national banks all over the country. However, Vandenberg's suggestion would achieve the same end with less national excitement. Hoover approved the idea and discussed it with Secretary Mills, who also thought it a good compromise. When Federal Reserve officers expressed their approval it acquired the political weight necessary to gain the backing of Senate Democratic leader Robinson and Speaker Garner, who both promised to support the proposal. When Vandenberg suggested to Senator Couzens that the two Michigan senators jointly propose the bill, the senior Michigan senator was cool to the idea. Senator Couzens was soon swayed by the powerful head of political steam building behind the bill and then agreed to support it. But he thought it a bad idea for two senators from the same state to propose it, and suggested, instead, that the senior senator sponsor the bill alone. Even though Senator Vandenberg had been shepherding the idea on Capitol Hill, he agreed to defer to Couzens, and thus, the "Couzens Resolution" was put before the Senate Banking Committee by February 20. Senator Glass thought the idea ill-advised, but agreed not to actively oppose it. His was the only dissenting voice when the committee voted that day to support the resolution. With the backing of Speaker Garner and Representative Henry Steagall, the law allowing national banks to operate under the same rules as state banks sped through the House and reached the president's desk on February 25. President Hoover immediately signed it into law.[61]

When the holiday declared by Governor Comstock lapsed on February 22, no rescue plan had been agreed upon that would allow the Detroit banks to reopen. The situation was as grave as ever. So the governor asked the legislature to renew the holiday for another week, and they did. The Detroit Clearing House Association issued a congratulatory proclamation commending the governor for his wisdom and decisiveness. The governor urged the legislature to adopt an Iowa Plan for Michigan that would allow bank customers access to the "good portion" of their deposits and 100 percent of any new deposits, which would be kept segregated from the old. A legislator proposed that the state run its own bank to hold the reserves of Michigan's banks. The governor and Detroit bankers issued optimistic statements about the prospects for imminent RFC loans, but the bank restrictions were starting to bind. Despite the announcement by the governor that any bank in Michigan could release as much money as it wanted to, few did. Flint banks had been closed all along, but now declared they would allow 5 percent withdrawals; Bay City banks were fully open and operating; Port Huron banks were captive to the decision of the Detroit Clearing House Association. Banks in Kalamazoo announced they would not allow any more withdrawals. By the end of the week, account holders had withdrawn $14.24 million, still only about half of the total amount allowed by law. Even the Guardian National Bank of Commerce still held almost 40 percent of the amount eligible for withdrawal.[62]

By the end of the week, Detroiters in immigrant neighborhoods started to run out of cash and went to their local banks for more, only to be told that they were limited to 5 percent of their deposits until the end of the holiday. For many of these modest people, this was a paltry sum and not enough to get by on. For the first time since the beginning of the holiday, banks in immigrant quarters saw large crowds of people trying to get money. The city had exhausted its ability to raise funds. As Michigan's congressmen scrambled, harangued, and pleaded with the RFC for loans to Detroit, Michigan counties, and the beleaguered state government, bond payments came due. The city of Detroit defaulted on its obligations and could pay its employees only in scrip.[63]

Plans for new banks to replace the Guardian banks and the First National Bank stumbled over the inability of Michigan bankers to raise sufficient funds in New York and Chicago—a prerequisite for RFC aid. Henry Ford suddenly announced he would buy the banks and run them himself, a proposal that met bemused disbelief among both bankers and government officials and went nowhere. Efforts to reach an agreement to unfreeze the Detroit accounts—and therefore the rest of Michigan's as well—stumbled over the many roadblocks in the path. As if the titanic egos of Henry Ford and James Couzens were not enough impediment to agreement, the depositors faced the interests of the RFC, New York bankers, Secretary Mills, the *Detroit Free Press*, acting Comptroller Awalt, Governor Comstock, and the entire Michigan legislature. Before any plan could be successfully negotiated, the financial pandemic had spread beyond the borders of Michigan and infected the rest of the country. The problem was now much bigger than Michigan, and the solution presumably was to be found on the national, and not the state level.[64]

CHAPTER SEVEN

The Spreading Panic

As Detroit teetered on the brink of financial catastrophe—unknown to its populace or anyone else outside a small circle of business leaders and government officials—the same financial problems that beset Michigan were causing widespread distress elsewhere. Ubiquitous discussion of the banking crisis in newspapers and trade publications convinced some Americans that the country suffered from a pathological banking system that verged on collapse. This anxiety piled on top of mounting reports of rioting farmers and something that looked like revolt spreading up and down the Mississippi Valley. Businessmen, politicians, and leading citizens across the country voiced louder demands that something be done to save the situation. Many people had given up hope that salvation would come from Washington, D.C., or assumed that banking was primarily a state responsibility anyway. Either way, frustrated state legislators and governors increasingly looked to their own resources to save themselves.

The crisis in Michigan initiated a wave of fear, which swept over American officialdom from coast to coast. The public remained mostly calm. As in Detroit, depositors did not rush to their banks to withdraw their funds out of fear whipped up by the press, which mostly urged calm. The most anxious and excited men in Michigan were found in the Guardian Building, fretting over the fate of their banks and fearing a public panic that never arrived. Emanuel Goldenweiser of the Federal Reserve Board observed on February 21, "Personally, I am inclined to think that conditions are not as bad as these big bankers think. Most of the people are not aware of the seriousness of the situation and, therefore, may be able to cross the chasm on a thin plank without being affected by vertigo the way the bankers are who are looking into the depth below." Fear of the public easily spread from bankers to politicians. In a single week, legislatures in 16 states passed emergency banking laws that allowed the governor or state bank superintendent extraordinary powers to close banks, or granted banks the discretion to limit withdrawals. On February 21 the legislatures in New York and New Jersey passed laws allowing banks to restrict withdrawals with permission of the state bank superintendent. Bank Superintendent Broderick assured the legislature in Albany that New York needed such a bill. The president of the largest remaining financial institution in Atlantic City, the Guarantee Trust Company, used the law the very day it was signed by Governor Harry Moore to limit withdrawals from the 25,000 accounts in his company, which had been quickly draining in the past month. The governor denied rumors that he was about to declare a bank moratorium in New Jersey, asserting that the new law had been passed to avoid such extreme measures. Banking historian Cyril James believed these reactions were a form of hysteria sweeping across the land and ultimately a disaster for banking in the United States.[1]

Governor Paul McNutt of Indiana signed a new law on February 24 giving the state

Banking Department extraordinary powers to limit withdrawals from banks and to operate banks while in receivership. The next day the governor of Missouri signed a new law authorizing him to close any bank that suffered ruinous withdrawals. The House in Columbus took 29 minutes on February 27 to consider and pass two bills drafted over the weekend granting the state banking department extraordinary powers to close or regulate banks in Ohio and allowing banks to limit withdrawals to 5 percent of accounts for 60 days. There was one dissenting vote. The Ohio Senate took only seven minutes to pass the bills "practically unanimously." Legislators in Delaware and West Virginia passed similar laws on the same day, with the law in West Virginia passing unanimously.[2]

On February 28, the legislature in Kansas passed a law making it easier for insolvent banks to avoid receivership and remain operating. On March 1 the legislature in Idaho passed a law allowing the governor to close banks and delay foreclosures up to 90 days. The next day he did just that for 15 days, after the mayors of Coeur d'Alene, Moscow, and Lewiston all declared bank holidays in their towns. Also on the first, Governor Floyd B. Olson of Minnesota, who had previously shown himself resistant to political stampedes, signed a law allowing the State Banking Commissioner to limit withdrawals in state banks for up to 15 days. The largest bank holding company in the United States, the Northwest Bancorporation, which owned 127 banks in eight states from Washington to Nebraska and was based in Minneapolis, immediately issued a statement saying that all of its banks were sound and would not be limiting withdrawals. Not to be outdone, the First National Bank of Saint Paul — the second largest bank in the state — put out a statement that the bank would remain open even if the governor called for a bank moratorium. The next day the piqued state legislature passed a bill in record time allowing the state bank commissioner to seize banks and operate them under his own rules for up to 60 days in the event the governor declared a state of emergency. First National Bank President Louis W. Hill assured depositors he would make their deposits available regardless of what the governor might do. On March 2 the state assembly in Raleigh voted to grant "dictatorial powers" to the state bank commissioner to take charge of banks in North Carolina, and the upper house in Little Rock passed an undoubtedly unconstitutional law suspending all debts, public and private, in Arkansas for 90 days.[3]

Duly armed with laws, governors and bank superintendents across the country began to restrict withdrawals or shut down banking in their states starting with Maryland on Saturday, February 25. Withdrawals from Baltimore banks escalated after the Title Guarantee and Trust Company of Baltimore closed on Monday, February 20. When withdrawals from city banks mounted to $7 million in the following days, Governor Albert Ritchie met on Thursday night with nervous Baltimore bankers who urged him to declare a holiday for Friday morning. He demurred, wanting to see if the situation would calm down on Friday. Instead withdrawals amounted to $6 million on Friday. Members of the Baltimore Clearing House Association met with Ritchie in an emergency meeting on Friday evening when the governor agreed to declare a three-day bank holiday for the state starting the next morning. "Small depositors" had withdrawn from Baltimore city banks $13 million (out of $500 million in the city and $889 million in the state) in a single week. The drain had been limited to city banks and did not extend even to Baltimore County institutions. While unusual, the amount was not enormous and should have been manageable for sound banks. However, when the third largest institution in the state, the Union Trust Company, requested another $4.1 million loan from the RFC, Governor Ritchie declared a holiday that closed all 205 financial institutions in Maryland. The governor announced the heavy withdrawals "unjustified" and urged Marylanders to put their money back into their banks where it would be safe. The announcement on February 16 that banks in the Baltimore Clearing House Association would drop interest rates to 0.5 percent might have influenced large depositors to place their money elsewhere. Regardless, Governor Ritchie hoped three days would be enough for the legislature in Annapolis to finish work on new banking legislation allowing an "Iowa plan" for Maryland. He extended the holiday one day at a time for the next week.[4]

Indiana — next to Michigan — acted next on Sunday, February 26, when Governor Paul McNutt signed another law allowing banks to limit withdrawals to 5 percent. Banks in Indianapolis did just that on Monday morning after a Sunday-night poll of Clearing House Association members. The single remaining bank in Kokomo, the Union Bank and Trust Company, quickly decided to follow the lead of the Indianapolis banks and limited withdrawals on Monday morning. By Tuesday banks in 20 other Indiana towns followed the lead of Indianapolis, and as national banks were now allowed to conform to state laws on such matters, national banks restricted withdrawals along with state banks. By Wednesday, about one-half of the banks in the state had announced their intention to restrict withdrawals. When the Ball brothers, of Ball Jar fame, promised to personally guarantee all bank deposits in Muncie, all banks in that town allowed unlimited access to depositors' money. Banks in Madison and Evansville, across the Ohio River from Kentucky, did as they pleased: those in Madison remained open as normal, while banks in Evansville allowed companies access to their accounts as usual and restricted only savings accounts. The two newly opened banks in Hammond, which had been without a bank for 14 months, did not want to close and remained fully open until normal closing time at noon, Saturday.[5]

The Michigan holiday actually had remarkably little impact on neighboring Ohio until Michigan Governor Comstock extended the holiday on February 22. Until then, only a few Ohio banks had seen slightly elevated withdrawals, but nothing that could not be handled. However, starting on Monday, February 27, some Ohio banks started to experience large withdrawals provoking the clearing house associations in Akron, Dayton, and Lima to limit withdrawals without clear legal authority to do so. The bills passed by the legislature in Columbus that morning and signed by the governor that night removed any legal hurdles. On Tuesday, the clearing house associations of Cincinnati, Cleveland, and Columbus, all voted to follow the trend, bringing the number of affected banks to 200. Limitations by banks in cities forced those in small towns to follow suit because they could not retrieve their own deposits held in larger commercial banks in the cities. By Thursday, March 2, 500 Ohio banks had limited withdrawals, and some ran out of space in their vaults to store all the cash they had received that week, which by law had to be kept segregated from money already posted to accounts. Toledo was the last city in Ohio with all banks completely open. The Federal Reserve Bank of Cleveland experienced the heaviest demands for its discounting services since 1920 as district banks borrowed $77 million in the week starting February 27. In the first four days of March, banks borrowed another $40 million. District banks additionally sold $141 million in acceptances and government securities to the Fed and drew down their reserves in the last two weeks of February, all in a scramble for cash "as member banks anticipated large individual cash withdrawals."[6]

Pennsylvania Governor Gifford Pinchot signed a resolution passed unanimously by both houses in Harrisburg just before midnight, February 27, allowing banks to limit withdrawals if approved by the state bank commissioner. The governor announced there would be no bank moratorium in the state, and few banks applied to limit withdrawals before

March 1, when some banks in Philadelphia began to impose limitations. Governor Moore made a parallel anodyne announcement as more banks in New Jersey — mostly in Hoboken — decided to limit withdrawals. Governor C. Douglas Buck of Delaware released a statement saying there was no banking problem in his state and all banks were sound. He also announced new banking legislation allowing restrictions on withdrawals. Comptroller of the Currency Awalt announced that according to the recently passed "Couzens law," national banks were free to follow state laws that applied to state banks, if they chose, but were under no obligation to restrict withdrawals or close for holidays. By the end of February, the only Kentucky banks to limit withdrawals in response to the restrictions imposed in Ohio were found in Covington, across the river from Cincinnati. But then, on Wednesday, March 1, the storm broke.[7]

On Tuesday the legislature in Alabama granted Governor George Miller power to shut down all banks in the state. On Wednesday he did — for ten days. When the three largest banks in Mobile declined to close, the governor admitted that the closure was advised and not mandatory. Governor Ruby Laffoon of Kentucky had no such power either, but he did have the authority to designate the date of "Thanksgiving." In 1933, Thanksgiving arrived in Kentucky on March 1, and Kentuckians were so lucky as to celebrate for the rest of the week. The governor said the holiday was forced upon Kentucky by neighboring states that had curtailed bank activities, compelling companies to look to banks in Kentucky for accessible money. When many bankers looked askance at the proclamation and chose to ignore it, the governor explained that the holiday was not mandatory. Banks in Louisville elected to shut down, but those in Covington already limiting withdrawals just continued to do so. Two banks in Covington remained open as normal. Other banks in Kentucky also chose to remain open but limited withdrawals to 5 percent. Across the Ohio River in Indiana about one-half of all banks were then restricting withdrawals. In Tennessee Governor McAllister declared a holiday until March 6 after "heavy withdrawals from Tennessee banks by out-of-state firms seeking to pay out-of-state obligations with Tennessee deposits." Banks in Chattanooga decided to ignore the holiday while banks in Memphis chose to go along; some banks in Knoxville announced they would remain open with limited withdrawals. When asked his opinion, the state attorney general agreed that the closing was only a "request" made by the governor, and not mandatory. Thomas Preston, president of the Hamilton National Bank — the largest bank in Knoxville — and former president of the ABA, said his bank would remain open, confident that it could meet all obligations because it was 85 percent liquid. More banks in Arkansas elected to limit withdrawals to 5 percent, as did the three largest banks in East St. Louis, Illinois. In Louisiana, Governor Oscar Allen declared a three-day holiday.[8]

On March 2, Governor Clarence Martin of Washington state declared a three-day bank holiday. The just-passed Bank Stabilization Act allowed insolvent banks to open and operate under restrictions, as allowed by the Iowa Plan. The state supervisor of banking later reported that in two days his department examined the condition of all 163 state-chartered financial institutions in Washington State, and "as a result of our careful analysis of each individual situation, 105 banks were licensed for unrestricted opening and 58 placed under restriction." Perhaps the governor believed that his professional corps of bank examiners could actually analyze the condition of 163 banks in two days, when the last routine examination of the Bank of United States in New York had taken three months and an emergency audit ordered by Superintendent Joseph Broderick in December 1930 had taken three weeks, but it seems unlikely. When the comptroller of the currency turned 100 accountants loose on the National Bank of Kentucky in November 1930, six weeks later they were still going over its books. Perhaps the citizens of Washington believed it when announced, but more likely those who wanted to believe it believed it. The purpose of the holidays and the "examinations" was not to restore the health of sick banks but to restore the confidence of supposedly shaken depositors. Such steps were not financially prudent acts but political bromides intended to soothe the presumably jangled nerves of the citizenry, or more likely of anxious bankers and government officials.[9]

Bankers, the governor, and state officials in California had been monitoring national events nervously all week. On Thursday, California Governor James Rolph flew from Sacramento to San Francisco to confer with Jared Sullivan, president of the Crocker National Bank and president of the California Bankers Association, and other leading bankers, including officers from the Bank of America and the First National Bank of Los Angeles. On Thursday night, Governor Rolph declared a state holiday for three days, starting on Friday morning, March 3. The state attorney general said it was a legal holiday that closed all public offices — including courts, schools, and libraries — and asserted that banks would be expected to honor it. Superintendent Edward Rainey refused to say whether the holiday was mandatory, but publicly asked all banks to cooperate even if the telegrams he dispatched to state banks left little doubt that the holiday was obligatory. Rolph said the holiday would give the legislature in Sacramento time to pass a bill allowing the state superintendent of banking to limit withdrawals or suspend banking altogether in time of emergency. The move had become necessary, he added, because the holidays already declared in 15 states provoked out-of-state banks and businesses to withdraw funds from California banks. Superintendent Rainey went further, blaming the holiday on "weak-kneed persons" who withdrew money from California banks. As always, such mandatory orders could not be enforced against national banks, some of which decided to ignore the holiday. The state treasurer assured Californians that the banks were fundamentally sound and had lots of cash available, but the holiday was necessary to "protect depositors from their own fears." He added that withdrawals had been unusually heavy lately because of a whispering campaign organized by communists. "We have all been conscious of a definite destructive influence from communists who are endeavoring to spread destruction and hysteria. Many bank failures in the past have been traced directly to the insidious propaganda from this source."[10]

Humorist Will Rogers wrote:

> 'Twas a lovely morning sun shining bright ... the birds were singing. Why? Because they couldn't read the papers. The papers said the bank clerks had worked so hard lately that they should have a holiday, so we are all on a holiday. Let's take it on the chin and grin. The Rogers having laid in no supplies against such an emergency will be living on horse meat as that's our sole product. I love horses and I only ask don't let me know which one we are eating today. I hear they have called a moratorium on inaugurations.[11]

In reaction to the moratorium in California, a wave of state-mandated bank holidays rolled across the West as neighboring states responded with closings of their own. Oregon, caught between California and Washington, closed its banks on Friday. Utah, Arizona, New Mexico, and Idaho followed suit. Governor Balzar of Nevada, already beset with enough banking headaches, said the remaining banks in Nevada were all sound, but the closure in California left his state no choice but to close all banks to protect their remaining deposits. He extended the holiday until the following week. Governors Murray of Oklahoma and Miriam Ferguson of Texas made the same protest. Governor "Ma" Ferguson held a late-night conference with leading bankers and Texas state officials who all concurred that the holiday was necessary until the legislature passed a law — then under consideration — allowing withdrawal restrictions. But not all banks heeded the governor's decree and some remained open with limited withdrawals. Three banks in Austin remained open, but imposed a $15 limit on withdrawals. Wisconsin, Mississippi, Georgia, Kansas, and Oklahoma, all joined the holiday movement before the day was over.[12]

Arizona Governor Benjamin Moeur was awakened at 4 A.M. by a banker friend, Walter Bimson, who pounded on his door and told him of the California closing. Every bank in Arizona kept money in correspondent banks in California, and all that money was now frozen. The sleepy governor told Bimson to come see him at the Capitol at 9 A.M., but Bimson replied the unfolding crisis would not wait that long. Then the governor told Bimson that he had no authority to close any banks, to which Bimson responded, "Nor did other governors, but that hadn't stopped them." Still insufficiently alarmed, the governor said he would consult the attorney general in the morning. Despite pleas from Bimson to call him immediately, Governor Moeur refused and told Bimson he would see him the following morning at the Capitol. Not to be deterred Bimson called Attorney General John L. Gust himself at 6 A.M. and arranged to meet him at Bimson's bank right away. Together they wrote out a proclamation closing all financial institutions in the state until March 6. When the governor arrived at his office at 8 A.M., they presented the proclamation for his signature and he signed. Even though the legislature of Arizona voted a resolution approving the governor's actions, the president of the First National Bank of Nogales defiantly announced his bank would stay open. So did J.S. Douglas, president of the Douglas National Bank in Douglas — and father of congressman and future budget director under President Roosevelt, Lew Douglas. In response, the legislature voted Governor Moeur the power to declare martial law and seize banks if he believed it necessary.[13]

Other western bankers resented the cascade of orders from jumpy governors. Oscar Newton Beasley of the Beverly Hills National Bank said he stayed open because "no one consulted me about whether I wanted to close the bank. And since my bank didn't need a holiday while its customers did need its services, I decided to keep it open. The first I knew about the holiday was when I read about it in the papers in the morning." N.S. Gandy, president of the Santa Monica National Bank, called the holiday "ridiculous" and kept his bank open as well. Business leaders in Los Angeles lined up to express their support for the moratorium and optimism about the outcome, and shrugged off the holiday as a minor inconvenience. The source of the problem lay entirely outside of California, and Los Angeles had witnessed no bank run at all. Bankers in Santa Ana approved of the holiday and the proposed banking legislation even while declaring banks in Orange County strong. They said that even if they were allowed to limit withdrawals, few Orange County banks would do so. When the holiday spread to Wisconsin on March 3 the National Bank of Milwaukee refused to shut its doors and cashed checks for its customers as usual. The exasperated governor of Oklahoma ordered the National Guard to close the First National Bank of Enid, which of course he had no legal right to do. The "Couzens law" authorized national banks to conform their practices to those of state banks, but did not mandate they do so.[14]

After consultation with leading bankers and clearing house associations in Georgia, Governor Eugene Talmadge declared that banks in Georgia were sound, but the banking moratorium in neighboring states forced Georgia to close its banks until Tuesday to prevent funds from fleeing the state. This was the same argument used in Texas and most of the West. However, the governor did not reach this decision until midmorning on Friday, when banks throughout the state had already opened for business. They were instructed to shut at 11 A.M. The order was immediately endorsed by the Atlanta Clearing House Association, the mayor, and Clark Howell, editor of the *Atlanta Constitution*. Banks around the state — including national banks — evidently obeyed, although banks in Savannah stayed open until 2 P.M., Friday. By the end of Friday, North Carolina and Virginia joined the ranks of states limiting withdrawals, although few banks did so in Virginia. After consulting with the governor of the Federal Reserve Bank of Richmond, George Seay, Virginia Governor John Pollard announced a holiday was not needed in Virginia as banks were fundamentally sound. Seay had taken a telephone poll of banks all over the state and found little anxiety provoked by the heavy withdrawals in Baltimore or the holiday in Maryland.[15]

After the bank holiday was imposed in Maryland, some banks in Washington, D.C., experienced unusual withdrawals from demand deposits. Even though local banks and savings associations reported no large withdrawals from savings accounts in the District of Columbia, a small national bank and nine savings institutions announced on Thursday they would require 60 days notice for savings withdrawals starting immediately. On Friday, two more small banks announced limitations on withdrawals, but all the main banks carried on as normal. Some city residents grew apprehensive after two large District institutions, the Continental Trust Company and the Commercial National Bank, slipped into receivership on February 28, while banks in neighboring Maryland were closed, but depositors in the nation's capital remained calm. Nevertheless, a bill was rushed through both houses of Congress the next day allowing the comptroller of the currency wide latitude in dealing with any banking emergency in the District. The District's corporate counsel broadcast a radio appeal for Washingtonians to have faith in their banks.[16]

Reaction to the holidays was mixed: 500 of Ohio's 800 banks limited withdrawals, while the number choosing the option in Pennsylvania had grown to only 40. One bank in Cincinnati — the First National Bank — had no limits on withdrawals and reported receiving several large deposits from corporations. Other banks in Ohio reported that after an excited Tuesday, when restrictions started to be implemented, crowds disappeared and everything appeared to be normal. The Cincinnati Clearing House Association pronounced that the restrictions were put into place to avoid panic, and there was no panic, therefore the action was a success! Some Ohio banks relaxed their restrictions and began to allow larger withdrawals, which few clients took advantage of. Many banks announced they would allow companies to withdraw enough money to meet payrolls even if the withdrawals exceeded the 5 percent limit. Some large companies arranged to ship cash in from other states to meet payrolls. On Friday, March 3, banks in Cincinnati received more deposits than withdrawals, and when some banks started easing restrictions, the Clearing House Association began discussing returning to normal operations. Cash was piling up in their vaults and banks wanted to accept and clear local checks.[17]

Marylanders "were more amused than alarmed," by the banking moratorium. Change was hard to come by, and many businesses were unable to pay their employees in cash as they did normally on Fridays. Some employers gave their workers checks, which they were unable to either cash or deposit. Many stores extended credit to regular customers. Stores reported somewhat lighter traffic than normal for a Saturday, and one store owner in Montgomery County worried about leaving so much cash in his store overnight, but he did not want to take it home, either.[18]

The response in California to the holiday was also mixed. A University of Southern California faculty meeting voted approval of the state holiday and expressed their confidence in the banking system even as the Los Angeles and San Francisco Clearing House Associations printed scrip to be put into circulation if need be. The Lions Club of Chico passed a resolution condemning the state holiday. Stores and businesses in Los Angeles reported sales and transactions more or less as usual. Grocers offered limited credit to good customers, yet two big grocery chains refused to accept checks. Horse racing carried on without interruption in Santa Ana, where stores reported business "about normal." Stores in nearby Orange reported the same. The Navy announced it had enough cash to pay its personnel in San Pedro, which it did on Friday, March 3, infusing $500,000 into circulation in California.[19]

The situation was watched closely by financial leaders and state officials in Illinois and New York. Illinois Governor Henry Horner announced after discussing the situation with Federal Reserve and state officials, Loop bankers, and representatives of the Illinois State Bankers Association, that he had decided not to declare a holiday. Some towns in Illinois had already declared bank holidays—all banks in East St. Louis allowed only restricted withdrawals—but the big Chicago banks saw no need for it. They had plenty of cash and liquidity, and the Chicago Federal Reserve was well provisioned to help should it be required. It had already paid out $75 million in direct response to the moratorium in Michigan after Chicago became a major source of cash for Detroiters. The First National Bank sent out $555,000 per day, five times more than normal. Although correspondent banks steadily withdrew funds from the big Loop banks, Chicago's bankers judged the situation manageable. In the last week of February, demand deposits in Chicago banks fell more than $100 million and correspondent banks demanded another $100 million. By closing time Friday, March 3, Chicago banks had paid out $350 million; most of that was issued to banks with correspondent accounts in Chicago. Depositors withdrew $20 million from the First National Bank alone and area correspondent banks withdrew another $15 million. In the first three days of March, another $50 million left the bank, accounting for almost one-half of all cash withdrawn from Chicago banks in those three days. In turn, Chicago banks withdrew $60 million from New York banks.[20]

Alarmed by the events, excitable Melvin Traylor concluded that a national moratorium would be necessary to stop the flight of money from banks. Other Chicago bankers disagreed. On Thursday evening, March 2, area bankers met with Federal Reserve directors and Illinois Governor Horner, who came up from Springfield to discuss the situation. The bankers talked until three o'clock Friday morning and decided a moratorium was not needed. The banks needed to weather the depleting storm until noon Saturday, March 4, when most were confident that Roosevelt's inauguration would calm the troubled waters. Governor Horner issued a public statement saying Chicago banks were strong and no holiday would be called in Illinois. But Friday was a bad day: withdrawals from Illinois banks were extremely heavy. In a single week $350 million had left Chicago banks. And shortly after noon, the New York Federal Reserve asked to sell the Chicago Federal Reserve another $150 million in commercial paper, reducing available cash in Chicago to $90 million. Normally that would be plenty of cash to tide the city over for a few days, but the last few days had been far from normal, and Chicago bankers did not expect the next 24 hours to be any different.[21]

Chicago bankers, including the Chicago Federal Reserve's James McDougal, had clashed with the New York board of governors just weeks before, in January, when Chicago banks revolted against the easy-money policy adopted by the Federal Reserve Board in Washington. The Chicago banks refused to buy proffered government bonds that yielded less than 0.1

percent interest per annum. Chicago banks preferred to keep their cash, which by January 1933 equaled 55 percent of deposits. Bonds that paid less than 0.25 percent did not earn enough to pay the clerks who registered them in the banks' books. When the Federal Reserve Bank of New York urgently requested to borrow another $150 million from the Chicago Federal Reserve Bank on Friday, the Chicago bankers balked. A loan of that size under the circumstances in Illinois was out of the question. Edward E. Brown of the First National Bank suggested to an assembly of Chicago bankers that they immediately present the Chicago Federal Reserve Bank with $150 million in Federal Reserve notes and demand they be redeemed in gold. This would deplete the reserves of the Chicago Federal Reserve Bank so badly that they would be unable to ship any more cash to New York. Charles Dawes thought it a very bad idea. Most other bankers agreed, especially those indebted to the Federal Reserve Bank, but Traylor backed Brown and ordered armored cars assembled to deliver $75 million in Federal Reserve notes to the Federal Reserve Bank of Chicago. Federal Reserve Governor McDougal was outraged by the demand and talked Brown and Traylor out of it; however, in return, he promised to send no more money to New York.[22]

Most Chicago bankers wanted to avoid a moratorium, but believed sending their available money to New York would make a bank holiday in Illinois unavoidable. Governor Horner was also reluctant to close the banks, but remained on the phone to Washington on Friday night to keep closely informed of events. After heavy withdrawals from banks throughout Illinois, many banks began limiting withdrawals to 5 percent of accounts. No Loop bank invoked this rule, but numerous banks in outlying Chicago neighborhoods did. At 4 P.M. Chicago's leading bankers gathered at the Clearing House Association offices, located inside the Federal Reserve Building at Jackson and LaSalle Streets. They remained in continuous discussions about the deteriorating situation and stayed in constant touch with Washington and New York bankers, who were likewise on the phone to Washington. By 9:15 P.M. the directors of the Chicago Federal Reserve Bank voted to send a recommendation for a national bank holiday to the Federal Reserve Board. The directors in New York had already done so. Everyone wanted someone else to act. By March, Federal Reserve Governor Eugene Meyer's nerves were frayed, and Treasury Secretary Ogden Mills—ex-officio member of the board—took greater command of board actions to meet the crisis. Mills stayed in close contact with Federal Reserve officials and helped guide the discussions. Yet, the Federal Reserve Board had abdicated the leading role in addressing the growing crisis because they saw their responsibility as maintaining the proper supply of currency to feed commerce. As the Federal Reserve Board in Washington and the Fed governors in New York judged the currency supply adequate, they believed others should take the lead in addressing the troubles then overwhelming the nation's shaky banking system.[23]

American bankers were not alone in their anxiety, foreign central bankers were also becoming increasingly nervous about the stability of the dollar and even short-term prospects for convertibility. Legitimately concerned about the United States remaining on the gold standard, the Bank of England was rushing to convert dollars into gold. In February foreign central banks had $178.3 million in gold in New York vaults earmarked for their accounts, removing them from United States gold stocks, even though the gold physically stayed in New York. In late February and early March, the Bank of England instructed traders in Paris to exchange pounds for francs, which they then traded for dollars in Paris, which were in turn exchanged for gold in New York. In one week foreign banks—principally the Bank of England—deposited $200 million in cash in the Federal Reserve Bank of New York and earmarked a corresponding amount of gold for shipment to England.[24]

Americans nervous about President-elect Roosevelt's intentions put equal pressure on the Federal Reserve's gold supply. In the last week of February, the gold window at the New York Federal Reserve Bank paid out $100 million in gold and gold certificates. They released the same amount in the first two days of March. Americans were as anxious to dump dollars of doubtful value for gold as foreigners—chiefly British—were. While the gold drain of the first two days of March was remarkable, the total outflow of gold was not unprecedented. Larger amounts had fled in October 1931 and June 1932, but not so quickly. Indeed, U.S. gold stocks had hit an historic low in 1932, but afterward gold flowed back into Fed vaults. The same had happened after the unprecedented outflow of fall 1931, and there was little reason to believe that March 1933 would be any different. In fact, gold continued to flow out of the United States for the rest of 1933 before the tide reversed in 1934. Regardless, Federal Reserve bankers could be excused for reacting with alarm to the sudden flight of gold.[25]

Crowds at the recently opened RKO Roxy Theater on Seventh Avenue or at the equally new Radio City Music Hall, who watched King Kong run amok in New York City, were unaware that real trouble of a different kind threatened the Empire State. Banks and big businesses around the country were drawing money from New York accounts to handle transactions throughout the United States. A&P in Kentucky announced that it would pay its vendors with checks drawn upon accounts at the Chase National Bank or the National City Bank. Even though the *Boston Globe* headed an article, "New York Banks Easily Meet Demand for Liquid Funds" on March 2, New York banks doubled their rates for loans to banks from 1 to 2 percent. They also borrowed $183 million from the Federal Reserve Bank to meet heavy demands for money from depositors—mostly correspondent banks—around the country. The Bowery Savings Bank, with 402,000 customers and $543 million in deposits, was inundated by customers on March 2, some evidently wanting to withdraw money and others wanting to deposit. Bank President Henry Bruère announced that the bank added 755 new accounts and $672,200 during the day. Nevertheless, Bowery officers were spooked and wanted to invoke the 60-day waiting period for withdrawals. They urged all savings banks in New York City to do the same, which the other banks were reluctant to do. When Federal Reserve Board members and staff heard about the proposal in New York, they feared it would start runs on commercial banks in the city.[26]

By March 1, the Federal Reserve Bank of New York needed cash, so it sold $75 million in United States bonds to the Chicago Federal Reserve and raised another $30 million by selling trade acceptances. In fact, the gold reserves of the New York Federal Reserve Bank had dropped below the legal minimum, even though it still had enough securities in its vaults to cover the notes it had issued. Members of the New York Federal Reserve Bank met far into the night discussing the perilous situation. New York Governor Herbert Lehman had already canceled his trip to Washington to attend the inauguration in order to keep close tabs on the deteriorating situation in New York City. On Friday night he met with Fed directors and leading New York bankers in an all-night meeting to discuss the best course to follow. As in Illinois, all hoped to avert a holiday in New York. New York Federal Reserve Governor George Harrison told Lehman the New York gold supply had dropped to 24 percent of note issuance, 16 percent below legal minimum, and recommended that the governor declare a bank holiday in New York. Although the Fed would be the primary beneficiary of a bank holiday, Harrison still maintained the bank had no responsibility for the situation that plagued it, and refused to officially request a holiday. In any event, a holiday declared for the state of New York was not certain to stop that drain because the state had no authority to close the gold-trading desk at the Federal Reserve Bank. Harrison also advised Treasury Secretary Mills that the United States could stop convertibility as one way to stanch the outflow of gold, but he added a national bank holiday declared by the president would be preferable. As in Chicago, authorities in New York hoped someone else would act. They looked to Washington, D.C.[27]

Governors around the country also looked to Washington, D.C., for a resolution of the banking problem. Governor Lafoon extended "Thanksgiving" in Kentucky until March 11, saying that that would give the federal government time to devise a plan to address the national problem. Like most newspapers around the states, the *Louisville Courier-Journal* reported optimistically that President Hoover and President-elect Roosevelt were huddled together with their advisors late at night working on a solution for the crisis. In fact, after Michigan Governor Comstock extended the bank holiday, President Hoover approached the Federal Reserve Board on February 22 to ask their advice on what to do. The board declined to make any recommendations officially, but board member Adolph Miller and ex-officio member Treasury Secretary Mills both recommended privately to Hoover that he enlist the cooperation of President-elect Roosevelt and invoke the section of the Trading with the Enemy Act of 1917 that allowed the president to clamp controls on the movement of funds into and out of banks, and suspend the export of gold. Hoover had discussed with Attorney General William Mitchell using the act in February 1932, when he feared the United States might be forced off the gold standard, and was advised that the act had probably lapsed with the signing of the peace treaty in 1919 and was no longer in force. Hoover brought the act up again during the bank scare in Chicago in June, still hoping it might prove useful. In late February 1933, Hoover again asked the attorney general for his opinion. Mitchell again expressed his doubts about the propriety of using the act and suggested consulting with congressional leaders. Leading senators were unsure if the law would pertain during peacetime. Senators La Follette and Reed were uncertain; conferring with Bernard Baruch — chairman of the War Industries Board in 1917, who doubted the law could be invoked in peacetime — clarified nothing. Most presidential advisors agreed that the law might be used to stop gold trading, but because of such uncertainty congressional support should be obtained first. Attorney General Mitchell proved the most skittish and argued forcefully with the Federal Reserve Board that President Hoover could be impeached if he did not first attain unanimous approval from Congress to invoke the act. The support of Democratic leaders could only be had if first approved by President-elect Roosevelt. In view of past events, it hardly seemed probable that the president-elect would go along with the suggested use of the law.[28]

Searching for another solution, Hoover decided that a temporary federal guarantee of deposits might calm the populace enough to get the banks through the inauguration. This would obviously require an act of Congress and, therefore, the approval of Roosevelt, which was not likely to be forthcoming. Nevertheless, Hoover wrote the Federal Reserve Board again on Tuesday, February 28, asking its opinion. The board met from 8:30 P.M. to 1:30 in the morning discussing the question. A majority believed a federal guarantee would have to cover all deposits or none. If the government guaranteed only half the deposits, then the other half would quickly be withdrawn from banks. This was an unlikely prospect, but it reflected the anxiety then current among members of the Federal Reserve Board and bankers generally. Mills thought a temporary federal guarantee might work. But it would have to be enacted quickly to have any effect, and the board did not reply to Hoover until the next day, Thursday, March 2, when it informed him the board did not support the proposal.[29]

Some thought that a nationwide application of the "Iowa Plan"— separating bank funds into solvent and insolvent portions, and giving depositors free or perhaps limited access to the "good" funds in banks— would stop the spreading panic. Michigan Senator Vandenberg first plugged for the application of such a plan for Michigan. When he discussed the plan with Michigan bankers they were, as usual, divided on the question: Detroit bankers, who wanted to start entirely new banks in their city, generally opposed it, while bankers from outside Detroit tended to favor the idea. Senator Couzens backed the Detroit bankers' proposal. Then Vandenberg pushed the Iowa Plan in Washington for banks nationwide. Governor Comstock saw the Iowa Plan as the simplest and quickest way to give Michiganders access to their frozen accounts, so he dispatched former governor Groesbeck to Washington, D.C., to lobby for it. In a meeting with Vandenberg, Comptroller Awalt, and Secretary Mills, Awalt and Mills assured Groesbeck that any such proposal was contrary to current federal law. And no one believed that Congress could change the law quickly or easily. Nevertheless, President Hoover promised Groesbeck he would ask Congress to change federal law to allow an "Iowa Plan" for national banks. The likelihood of such action before Saturday, March 4, was remote, to say the least. Regardless, Mills and Meyer believed such legislation would be helpful and asked Federal Reserve General Counsel Walter Wyatt and Comptroller Awalt to draft it, which they did in mid–February. They sent the draft to Mills, who approved and forwarded it to President Hoover. Hoover also approved the proposal but refused to send it to Congress without promises of Democratic support. Senators Glass and Robinson agreed that chances of congressional action before March 4 were unlikely. A national "Iowa Plan" was not to be under President Hoover.[30]

On Thursday, March 2, Adolph Miller again urged Hoover to use the Trading with the Enemy Act to calm the spreading financial tumult. Mills and Meyer supported such a move and had been assured by Walter Wyatt that the act allowed the president to request the Federal Reserve to embargo gold sales. Wyatt should have known — he wrote the clause inserted as an amendment to the act in 1918. Furthermore, Wyatt had discussed with Secretary Mills the possibility of using the act during the Chicago bank crisis in June 1932, and assured Mills the act was alive and well, and applicable. Wyatt was certain the act was still enforceable: it had been invoked in an alien custodian case in 1922, and the Federal Circuit Court for New York had ruled the law still applicable. That ruling was upheld by the Supreme Court. Attorney General Mitchell was skeptical and asked, with only 36 more hours in office, "Why not let things ride and leave it to the new administration?" When Wyatt insisted the act provided "sufficient color of authority to justify issuing an executive order," Attorney General Mitchell advised the president that he could use the act to shut down the banks, but its legality remained uncertain. The act never mentioned banks and conveyed no specific authority to close them, but it did allow the president to prohibit the hoarding of currency: how could he do that other than by closing banks? Because of the vagueness of the act, Mitchell counseled coordination with the incoming administration before using it. In view of the circumstances, Mills and Miller also advised coordinating any action with the incoming Democrats. Mills wanted to use the act, but only with assurances that Congress would endorse it in a special session.[31]

Hoover thought that if the Federal Reserve Board officially requested the president to use the act, not to close the banks but to stop gold sales and limit withdrawals from banks, then Roosevelt might be persuaded to go along. To help gain Roosevelt's cooperation, Hoover wrote the board again on Thursday, March 2, asking for an official request. The Federal Reserve Board met again that night to discuss the possibility of a national banking holiday using the Trading with the Enemy Act and, advised by Wyatt and prodded by Mills, voted unanimously to recommend that Hoover declare a nationwide bank holiday from Friday, March 3, until Tuesday, March 7. But they did not communicate this until Friday morning, March 3, when Eugene Meyer talked to Hoover, too late for action that day. They also declined to make an official request for the moratorium because they did not see such a request as within the purview of the Federal Reserve Board. The board sent word to Roosevelt's designated secretary of the Treasury, William Woodin, entreating him to gain the president-elect's approval for a national moratorium. On a midnight phone call from New York, Woodin informed the board that Roosevelt would not recommend such a course of action, but suggested that Hoover use his authority to declare a bank holiday until noon, March 4, after which President Roosevelt would assume responsibility. When Woodin confirmed to Mills over the phone that the president-elect would not support a holiday declared by Hoover, Mills told Woodin, "All of us have got to get together and go down the line. This is war!" But Woodin would not be swayed. Mills tried to call President Hoover at 2 A.M., Friday morning, to urge him to declare a bank holiday, but was told Hoover had retired for the night. Then the board decided to retire as well and meet again in the morning.[32]

In an effort to gain Roosevelt's cooperation, Hoover met with Democratic Senators Glass and Robinson at the White House on Friday, hoping they would agree to temporary federal deposit guarantees or to using the 1917 act, and, in either event, persuade Roosevelt to acquiesce. They said nothing to raise Hoover's expectations of success. Nevertheless, the next day Democratic senator from Oklahoma, Thomas Gore, submitted a bill that would authorize federal guarantee of all deposits. Senator Robinson promised to push for the bill as soon as President Roosevelt convened the special congressional session.[33]

While President Hoover wrestled with his limited options on Thursday, March 2, Secretary Mills asked Senator Byrnes to meet him at the Treasury to discuss the country's deteriorating banking situation. During the meeting, Mills telephoned Winthrop Aldrich, president of the Chase National Bank in New York, and asked him to come back to Washington to consult on the situation. Aldrich, who had just left Washington, where he had been testifying before a Senate committee, and was preparing for a trip to Bermuda, tried to put Mills off, but Mills insisted that if Aldrich did not help, his own bank in New York would not survive if all the others failed. Byrnes, who knew Mills as a cautious man not given to dramatics, was stunned by his statements. Aldrich agreed to return to Washington that night.[34]

Roosevelt and his Brain Trust entourage also left New York and headed by train for Washington, D.C., on Thursday evening, March 2. They were all immensely busy from the moment they arrived at the Mayflower Hotel. William Woodin immediately met with Hoover administration and Federal Reserve officials to see what could be done to save the situation. By then, Federal Reserve Counsel Walter Wyatt, Treasury Counsel John Harlan, and Attorney General Mitchell had prepared a draft proclamation for the president to sign declaring a national bank holiday. They also wrote draft legislation for Congress authorizing the holiday that could be submitted that night for consideration if Congress agreed to help. Woodin and Roosevelt-advisor Raymond Moley then met with Ogden Mills and Comptroller Awalt at the Treasury to discuss a possible bank holiday without resolution.[35]

When President-elect and Mrs. Roosevelt visited the White House on Friday afternoon for the customary social call by the incoming president, the White House usher whispered to the president-elect that the president, Governor Meyer, and Secretary Mills would like a word with him in private. Roosevelt asked that Moley be called to the White House immediately. The men had a fruitless discussion about the validity of the Trading with the Enemy Act and whether it should be used to close the banks. Both Mills and Hoover argued that the act should be used to control foreign exchange and domestic withdrawals of gold. Only Meyer argued for a complete shutdown of banks. While insisting that he had legal advice the act was still in force and could, indeed, be used to close all the banks, Roosevelt refused to be drawn into any decision to use the act, insisting the decision was for Hoover alone to make. As he left, Roosevelt told Hoover, "I shall be waiting in my hotel, Mr. President, to learn what you decide." When Hoover called Roosevelt that night at the Mayflower Hotel to ask his views, Roosevelt replied that he was just then meeting with Senator Glass, who opposed a national moratorium, as did he, and the matter should be left up to the governors.[36]

The Federal Reserve Board met again Friday night, March 3 at 9:15, mulled various options and decided that Board Governor Eugene Meyer should talk to the President and urge upon him a nationwide banking moratorium. The Federal Reserve Board stayed in continuous session all day Friday and into the night. They were joined intermittently by incoming Treasury Secretary Woodin and Budget Director Lew Douglas, Undersecretary of the Treasury Arthur Ballantine and Attorney General Mitchell. The board finally resolved there was no real alternative to declaring a national holiday to save the country's banks and decided that Governor Meyer should try one more time to convince President Hoover to declare a national bank moratorium. When Meyer telephoned the president around 11:30 at night to urge him to sign the executive order closing all the banks, he told Hoover of the board's actions and Roosevelt's response. Hoover replied that he preferred to invoke the Trading with the Enemy Act to limit withdrawals and suspend convertibility of dollars into gold until the inauguration, rather than shut down the entire banking system. But when pressed by Meyer and warned of the deteriorating situation around the country, Hoover agreed to request a national moratorium for Saturday and Monday if Roosevelt would go along, which the president-elect had already refused to do. Meyer reminded Hoover he was still president, not Roosevelt, and he should sign it. When Hoover still refused, Meyer told him, "You're fiddling while Rome burns," to which Hoover responded peevishly and cryptically, "I have been fiddled at enough and I can do some fiddling myself." He resented being pressured on his last night in the White House and refused to act.[37]

When pleading on the phone produced no results, the Federal Reserve Board then discussed sending a formal request for a national bank moratorium to the White House. Mills and Mitchell both opposed the idea as being futile at this late hour and after the president had already made his views clear. Adolph Miller pointed out that the board had not responded to Hoover's letter received on Thursday asking its views on a holiday, and suggested the board should make a formal reply now. Thus, the board drafted a letter after midnight under Governor Meyer's signature declaring, "The Federal Reserve Board feels that it cannot too strongly urge that the situation has reached a point where immediate action is necessary to prevent a banking collapse." As Congress would not meet on Saturday, only an executive order by the president, invoking the Trading with the Enemy Act, could produce a national bank holiday. The letter containing the draft order drawn up on Thursday by Wyatt, Mills, Mitchell, and others, and copies of draft resolutions voted by the Federal Reserve Bank directors in New York and Chicago requesting a national bank holiday was hand carried by Meyer's secretary, F.L. Fahy, to the White House.[38]

President Hoover anticipated such a letter, however, and took steps not to receive it.

Completely fed up with his inability to gain the cooperation of the incoming administration, Hoover had probably resolved to leave the entire mess to President Roosevelt. In any event, he left instructions with the Secret Service agent on night duty, James Stringfellow, that under no circumstances was he to be disturbed to receive any communications from anyone. Stringfellow had worked at the White House for 12 years, and in that time the standing orders had been to awaken the president for any urgent communication. In those 12 years, only once had any president ever given instructions not to be disturbed, and that was Herbert Hoover on the night of March 3, 1933. In view of the president's order, Stringfellow called Secretary Mills, who knew what the letter contained and told the agent not to disturb the president. Greatly perturbed, Stringfellow then called Hoover's secretary, Laurence Richey, who was evidently ignorant of Hoover's instructions and warily advised the agent to awaken the president and deliver the letter. The next morning Stringfellow "caught hell" from Mrs. Hoover for delivering the very letter the president did not want to receive. Governor Meyer caught hell too the next day when he received an irate letter from still–President Hoover scolding him for sending the letter. He asserted that the governors of New York and Illinois had decided to declare holidays in their states upon the recommendation of the Federal Reserve Board, obviating the need for a national holiday or an executive order. "In view of the above I am at a loss to understand why such a communication should have been sent to me in the last few hours of this administration, which I believe must now admit was neither justified nor necessary." Hoover wanted no responsibility for the holiday.[39]

Bankers and officials in Chicago and New York looked to Washington for action all day Friday and anxiously awaited word of developments. Tired of waiting any longer, New York Fed Governor Harrison tried to talk to President Hoover late Friday night, but called too late and was told Hoover had gone to bed. Harrison did talk to Secretary Mills on the phone and learned that Hoover, following the advice of his attorney general, would not declare a holiday without President-elect Roosevelt's assent, which he had not gained. With presidential action obviously not forthcoming, Federal Reserve Board Governor Meyer agreed to waive the minimum gold deposit requirements in New York to back the bank's Federal Reserve notes. In truth, the New York bank had sufficient government securities and commercial paper to back all of its notes, so the waiver of gold-reserve requirements ought to have relieved the pressure on notes issued by the New York Federal Reserve Bank posed by the drain of gold. However, there was no way of knowing what the British would do in the morning. In view of President Hoover's inaction, the board decided they had to rely on governors in states with Federal Reserve Banks, such as Horner of Illinois and Lehman of New York, to declare bank holidays in order to shut the Federal Reserve district banks and stop the flight of currency and gold. Yet, the Federal Reserve Board did not believe it had the statutory authority either to close the Federal Reserve Banks or to request such a closure from state governors. Despite their reticence, Fed governors discussed the situation on the phone with numerous state governors who had yet to declare bank holidays, urging them to do so. New York Governor Lehman would not declare a holiday without an official request from someone. The New York City Clearing House Association advised Governor Lehman to declare a holiday to stop the drain of gold from the Federal Reserve Bank, but as New York banks were perfectly sound, they asserted it made little sense for the Clearing House Association to make a formal request. They thought the Federal Reserve Bank should make the application, which Harrison was reluctant to do because he did not think it the responsibility of the Fed, nor did he think that such a declaration by a state governor would be legally binding on the Federal Reserve. Harrison was probably right on the latter score, but showed a remarkable lack of courage and resolve on the former. Chicago Fed Chairman Eugene Stevens faced the same dilemma. He favored closing the banks and advised Illinois Governor Horner that he should declare a holiday, yet the Chicago Bank likewise refused to make any official request. No one involved in the confusing discussions on Friday night could agree about who had the authority to close the gold-trading desk in New York, but most agreed that they would honor a request by President Hoover to do so. But Hoover did not want to sign anything without a formal request and absolute assurance of support from Congress and the incoming administration. Because such assurances were out of the question, Hoover just went to bed, removing himself from the picture.[40]

Finally, at the insistence of Superintendent Broderick, the New York City Clearing House Association formally requested a bank holiday because of a "continued and increasing withdrawal of currency and gold from the banks of the country." They wanted to make it clear that the financial problem did not originate from Manhattan banks, which was largely true. When Lehman persisted and asked Harrison's advice about what to do, Harrison agreed that a state bank holiday should be declared — but Harrison still refused to request it in writing. However, when Harrison learned from Board Governor Meyer in Washington that both Roosevelt and Hoover had retired for the night and no holiday would be declared by Hoover for Saturday, Harrison and the New York Fed directors put the question to a vote and agreed to formally advise Governor Lehman to close the banks in New York. The New York Fed's governors also agreed that a national holiday was needed and passed a resolution to that effect to the board in Washington.[41]

Governor Lehman signed the decree ordering a two-day holiday and told the press, "The Clearing House Association, with the advice and recommendation of the Federal Reserve Bank of New York, has asked me to proclaim a banking holiday lasting until the close of business Monday, March 6," in order to avert "hysteria." Like other governors, he complained that restrictions in other states forced his hand in New York. The *New York Times* even added that Governor Lehman signed the decree after learning that Governor Horner had already closed the banks in Illinois, which is not likely.[42]

When Governor Lehman closed the banks, the exchanges decided they had little choice but to close as well. Word of the closures did not reach brokers and other exchange employees before they arrived at Wall Street to find the New York Stock Exchange shuttered. Saturday morning, the New York Federal Reserve Bank announced that since the beginning of February, deposits in New York Federal Reserve member banks had declined by $800 million, or 12 percent; $400 million of that money had left in the last week of February. Although this was true, it also insinuated that deposits fleeing commercial banks in the state provoked the holiday, which was not true. The Fed also announced that since the beginning of February, $200 million in gold had left their vaults. Another $116 million left in the first two days of March. The New York Clearing House Association released the preposterous statement: "The unthinking attempt of the public to convert over 40 billions of dollars from deposits into currency at one time is, on its face, impossible." They stated furthermore that New York banks could meet demands for every dollar on deposit, but they decided to close "to enable the proper authorities to consider and adopt remedies to meet the situation, not for New York primarily, but of the nation as a whole." Even after the fact, authorities in New York still sought to dodge responsibility for the bank holiday in New York.[43]

At three o'clock on Saturday morning, word arrived in Chicago that Governor Lehman had signed a decree for a two-day bank holiday in New York and that the Federal Reserve Bank of New York was closed. Chicago bankers, still meeting at the Federal Reserve Building, immediately roused Governor Horner from his sleep at the Congress Hotel and urged him to join them. Relieved, Horner agreed to sign a decree for a three-day holiday for Illinois, which he did at 3:30 in the morning, Chicago time. Withdrawals would be restricted for an additional seven days afterward. Horner announced that he decreed a bank holiday "at the request of the Chicago Clearing House banks and the Illinois Bankers Association and with the approval of the Federal Reserve Bank of Chicago ... after a day of unprecedented withdrawals." He added, "It had also been expected that the National government might take some general action, but no word in that regard has been received by me. The picture has materially changed since yesterday."[44]

When the Federal Reserve Board, still meeting at 4 A.M. on Saturday, got word of the Illinois and New York holidays it discussed closing the Federal Reserve Bank, and decided all Federal Reserve district banks should honor local holidays and shut down operations as well — passing the buck downward to the district level. Fed personnel had difficulty rousing some of the Federal Reserve district governors, and, once accomplished, the many governors reached their staffs only with more difficulty. Governor Meyer did not want board staff in Washington, D.C., to contact state governors lest such overtures be construed as the Federal Reserve Board's request that state governors declare holidays. Nevertheless, Meyer discussed the possibility of a national holiday with the governors of Iowa and Ohio after midnight. For some reason, Meyer believed it would be acceptable for district Fed governors to make such requests, demonstrating a sad lack of leadership and courage.[45]

With banks closed in America's financial centers of New York City and Chicago, states that had seen no reason to close their banks now saw one. Iowa's governor, Clyde Herring, in Washington for the inauguration, like many other state governors, had kept in close phone contact with Iowa Lieutenant Governor Nelson G. Kraschel, who, in turn, kept in constant touch with the Iowa superintendent of banking. All stayed in phone contact with officials in Illinois. When Kraschel told Herring about Governor Horner's action, Herring called Chicago Fed Chairman Stevens to ask his advice. Stevens recommended closing all Iowa banks, as did Fred Figg, president of the Iowa Bankers' Association. Herring authorized the lieutenant governor to issue the order. Although Iowa had an "Iowa Plan" for its banks, it had no law authorizing limited withdrawals, so Kraschel signed an order closing all 835 banks in Iowa "indefinitely" as of Saturday morning, because of the closings in Illinois and New York, "to protect depositors." Not all bankers went along with the "mandatory" closing. President Roy Maxfield of the First National Bank of Council Bluffs retorted that his bank answered to the comptroller of the currency and not state officials, and would remain open until ordered to close by the comptroller. National banks in Dubuque and Mason City issued similar statements and kept their tills open for business. All national banks in Iowa owned by the intractable Northwest Bancorporation were ordered by headquarters in Minneapolis to remain open.[46]

Minnesota Governor Olson had been en route to the inauguration in Washington, D.C., when he received word of the holidays in New York and Illinois. He authorized Lieutenant Governor K.K. Solberg to issue a proclamation closing Minnesota banks temporarily, yet indefinitely, starting on Saturday morning. He then turned around and headed back to Minnesota. Olson declared that the closure of the Federal Reserve Bank in Minneapolis on Saturday forced all banks in the state to close as well, while Federal Reserve Bank of Minneapolis Governor W.B. Geery announced that the Federal Reserve Bank had closed to honor Governor Olson's proclamation of a state bank holiday. The Minneapolis–St. Paul Clearing House Association went along with the closure yet announced member banks would issue scrip and remain open to honor withdrawals and accept deposits in scrip. New deposits of cash would be 100 percent available immediately.[47]

Governors all across New England, who had remained aloof from the holiday movement until Friday night, closed their banks for Saturday and Monday. In view of the judgment of the state superintendent of banking that he had no authority to close solvent banks, all closings in Connecticut were voluntary. The clearing house associations of New Haven and Hartford voted to keep their banks open but limit withdrawals. With Massachusetts Governor Joseph Ely in Washington for the inauguration, acting Governor Caspar Bacon met all night with leading Boston bankers, Federal Reserve directors, and officers of the Clearing House Association at the Federal Reserve Bank on Pearl Street. They kept in close touch with Governor Ely by phone, and a tight cordon of police held curious newsmen at bay until dawn, when a single banking department official left the building, refusing to divulge anything. He returned a while later with a five-gallon can of hot coffee and disappeared back inside. The meeting broke up at 8:30 in the morning, and an announcement finally was released stating that the Federal Reserve Bank, all financial institutions in the state, and the stock exchange would be closed for two days effective immediately. The legislature would be asked to pass an emergency banking act authorizing the action by Monday evening. Police quickly deployed around Boston banks to ensure civil tranquility.[48]

Philadelphia Federal Reserve Governor George Norris was awakened at 3:45 A.M. by a phone call from Secretary Mills, informing him that New York and Illinois had just declared a bank holiday. Norris immediately realized what this would portend for banks in Philadelphia and decided that banks had to close in Pennsylvania as well. Knowing that Governor Pinchot was in Washington for the inauguration, Norris decided to contact the state's lieutenant governor to ask him to close the banks, but he did not know who the lieutenant governor was! Nor did anybody else who he felt he could call at 4 A.M. He knew some reporters who probably knew, but Norris decided not to arouse their suspicions by such unusual and obviously urgent probing. Undeterred, Norris called Joseph Wayne of the Philadelphia National Bank to organize a meeting of all the most important bankers in Philadelphia as soon as possible. Wayne suggested calling the state attorney general, William Schnader, which Norris did. However, Schnader was not convinced the matter was important enough to roust the governor from his bed in Washington. Counsel to the Philadelphia Federal Reserve Bank, John Sinclair, warned Attorney General Schnader that wire transfers could empty all the big banks in Philadelphia in one hour if they opened at 9 A.M. When convinced, Schnader's phone calls to the house on Rhode Island Avenue in Washington, D.C., where the governor was staying, went unanswered.[49]

Many of the city's bankers gathered at 7 A.M. at the Philadelphia National Bank on Chestnut Street to determine what to do. The assembled bankers quickly agreed that banks "outside Philadelphia" would demand cash as soon as banks opened on Saturday morning, subjecting Philadelphia banks to unbearable strain. They decided Governor Pinchot had to be found and convinced to close the banks in Pennsylvania at least until Monday. A quaint story made it into the newspapers that Pinchot could not be roused from his sleep in Washington at 5 A.M. when Federal Reserve staff went round to the house and pounded on the door, so the services of the Washington, D.C., Fire Department were enlisted and they rousted Governor Pinchot from his bed. Federal Reserve Counsel Walter Wyatt (and the board's Assistant Secretary E.M. McClelland)—the "Federal Reserve staff" who failed to awaken the governor—assured Norris that the fire department was never summoned; a servant responded to his pounding on the door and windows of the house and indeed awakened the governor. Like every other governor, Pinchot did not want to close the banks. He had released a public statement just days before assuring the citizenry that the banks were sound and Pennsylvania would have no bank holiday. Norris insisted to Pinchot that a moratorium for Pennsylvania was "absolutely necessary." Thus warned, Pinchot wanted to put out a statement that he was closing the banks upon the advice of the governor of the Federal Reserve Bank of Philadelphia, George Norris. Like everybody else, Norris wanted his name left out, but to get Pinchot to agree to the moratorium he agreed to accept responsibility for the holiday. Pinchot then dictated a statement over the phone to a stenographer at the Philadelphia National Bank, closing all the banks until Tuesday, upon the request of the Federal Reserve Bank. Once the decree was typed up, Attorney General Schnader signed Pinchot's name to it at 8:30 and released it immediately to the press. The Philadelphia Clearing House Association questioned the legality of the move — which the attorney general refused to corroborate — but vowed to cooperate nonetheless.[50]

In Pittsburgh, former Treasury Secretary Mellon's brother, Richard, chose to keep his banks and trust companies operating as normal. They offered an illustration of what other banks feared on the bleak Saturday had they not closed: 10,000 customers crushed into Pittsburgh's largest (and Pennsylvania's second largest) bank, the Mellon National Bank. Dick Mellon climbed a step ladder in the bank and told the crowd, "Please don't be apprehensive. We have just obtained all the cash you could possibly need or use, so withdraw any amount you want." He added that he was glad of the opportunity to meet so many of his customers. Fortunately for the Mellon banks, many of their clients were actually there to transfer funds from other banks, even if only from the Mellon-owned Union Trust Company to the Mellon National Bank! Both institutions and all the banks owned by the Mellon holding company, the Mellbank Corporation, survived the day and subsequent travails. Nevertheless, spooked by the public tumult, the Pittsburgh Clearing House Association announced on Sunday that all banks in the city would be honoring the holiday on Monday.[51]

Afraid that he would be unable to get telegrams to all banks in Pennsylvania in time to avert openings at 9 A.M., Norris sent the cashier of the Federal Reserve Bank to the downtown office of Western Union to warn them to prepare to send out 1,000 telegrams. Norris then ordered telegrams sent to all 70 national banks in his district in eastern Pennsylvania informing them of the closure while President Wayne of the Philadelphia National Bank did the same for the 467 state banks that had accounts at his bank. Many Pennsylvania banks had already opened for the day before they received word and opted to close once they received the news. But not all banks heeded the advice to close and, like the Mellon Bank, continued to carry on as normal. No bank in Harrisburg bothered to close. Norris also called his counterpart in Boston, R.A. Young, to inform him that the Federal Reserve Bank in Philadelphia was closed, only to be told that the bank in Boston itself was already closed. Such was not the case with the Federal Reserve Banks in Cleveland and Dallas. However, when the Dallas bank received a telegram from a bank in Pittsburgh requesting $10 million in cash, and informing them that a plane was on its way to pick it up, the Fed governor in Dallas decided it was time to close.[52]

With New York banks closed, New Jersey officials thought it prudent to close their banks as well. Virginia Governor Pollard met with Federal Reserve officers in Richmond, who advised him that with the Federal Reserve Bank in New York closed, they would have to close as well, and, considering that most major Virginia banks kept large amounts of cash deposited in now-inaccessible New York banks, Virginia banks were in a vulnerable position. Besides, banks were closed in all neighboring states and Washington, D.C., so prudence dictated that Virginia banks should follow suit. Pollard saw the reason of this argument and signed the decree on Saturday, closing Virginia banks on Monday and Tuesday.[53]

Around 10:30 on Friday night, Missouri Governor Guy Park received a phone call from the head of the Kansas City Clearing House Association with news that Kansas was about to declare a holiday. Kansas City, Missouri, banks had weathered heavy withdrawals all day, and on Friday evening its clearing house association voted to limit withdrawals to 5 percent, effective Saturday morning. With the largest banks in Kansas City limiting withdrawals, Governor Park recognized that the contagion could not be contained to the western portion of the state. He talked to St. Louis Clearing House Association officers and bankers in Chicago on Friday night, trying to decide how to respond. Despite a 25 percent decline in deposits in two years, members of the association were divided about whether a holiday was needed. When he received reports that both New York and Illinois were considering declaring bank holidays, he tried to talk to Governor Lehman in New York but failed to reach him. Instead, he looked to the St. Louis Federal Reserve Bank attorney for guidance. At 1 A.M., the attorney assured him that banking opinion in Missouri was "unanimous" that banks in the state needed "a breathing spell." When the head of the St. Louis Clearing House Association backed up the Federal Reserve attorney, and Governor Park was assured that both New York and Illinois were about to close their banks, he resolved to declare a holiday for Missouri. Shortly after 1 A.M. the governor issued a "request" that banks close for two days. He emphasized that the closure was voluntary but assumed that any bank that believed it needed to close would do so. In the meantime, he discussed with leaders in the state Senate legislation empowering the governor to issue emergency decrees to restrict banking. The bills were submitted for urgent consideration on Saturday. While most banks in the state honored the governor's request to close, not all did: banks in Columbia, Hannibal, and a number of other towns elected to carry on as usual.[54]

Colorado Governor Edward Johnson, like many other governors, had repeatedly asserted that Colorado banks were strong and there was no need for a bank moratorium in his state. However the holiday in Kansas City changed things. A late-night meeting between the governor, members of the Denver Clearing House Association, and Denver Federal Reserve Bank staff produced a reluctant consensus all around that Colorado should close its banks so long as those in Chicago and New York were closed. Harold Kountze, president of the clearing house association, protested that Denver banks were well stocked with cash and under no strain, but would defer to the advice of the local Federal Reserve Bank, which in view of events elsewhere, recommended a holiday. At 9:50 in the morning, the governor declared a four-day legal holiday, which the clearing house association accepted grudgingly.[55]

By noon, Saturday, March 4, every state in the union except Delaware availed itself of whatever laws it had on the books to restrict or close banks in order to stop heavy withdrawals that started, or were feared to start, in the wake of the Michigan holiday. Wyoming, Florida, and South Carolina gave their institutions authority to close or limit withdrawals if they chose to. South Dakota banks were also closed "indefinitely" while those in North Dakota were closed "temporarily." The governor of North Dakota additionally declared "all indebtedness" in the state temporarily suspended, which had no obvious meaning, but was obviously illegal. Officials in 27 states ordered their banks closed; all others imposed or authorized restrictions on withdrawals. By noon, Saturday, March 4, the only jurisdictions in the United States with all banks open and operating normally were Delaware and the 15 counties in the Upper Peninsula of Michigan, which remained exempt from Governor Comstock's decree. Banks in the territory of Alaska were all open and operating. With the Federal Reserve Banks closed, and all deposits in New York, Philadelphia, and Baltimore banks inaccessible, Governor Buck of Delaware decided before Saturday ended that his state, too, should join the general trend, and he declared a one-day bank holiday for Monday. Left to decide for themselves, Federal Reserve Banks in Cleveland, Richmond, Kansas City, and San Francisco chose to remain open on Saturday.[56]

Why had the banking situation come to this? The holiday movement was not a response to a rising crescendo of bank runs or failures. January had been a brutal month for banks, and February had been pretty rough, but not so bad as the previous December. Closings had notably slowed and runs diminished even before the holiday movement began: 242 banks failed in January; 154 in February; and 24 in the first four days of March. The banks shuttered in the first few days of March collectively held $3.3 million in deposits, or less than 5 percent of the deposits ($72.9 million) held by banks that failed in February, and half again less than the failures of January ($142.7 million.) The first four days of March predicted that the month would be coming in like a lamb compared to those just past and positively tranquil compared to the more tumultuous months of years past. Another 42 banks failed during the holiday and presumably would have failed anyway. Before the month was through, another 39 banks with deposits of $25 million would close. In any event, we know that governors and their Federal Reserve advisors were not responding to the bank failures of early March, or even failures of February. They were responding to shifting funds, fleeing gold, and each other's anxiety about what *might* happen.[57]

Bankers, governors, and government officials at the time claimed to be putting a stop to hoarding, but, in fact, "hoarding" as commonly understood, was not the problem. After the declaration of the Michigan holiday, large companies and banks throughout the United States began shifting funds away from the principal banking centers, especially New York City, to banks in smaller interior towns and cities. At first, funds were withdrawn in cash from big banks and physically shipped to Michigan to replace money frozen in accounts there. All Michigan banks held only $1.5 billion, or about 3.5 percent of the nation's deposits. Not all of that money belonged to large corporations or out-of-state banks, but even if it had, it was not impossible to shift $1.5 billion from other states— principally Illinois and New York— to allow Michigan companies, such as Ford, to continue operations. As the holiday movement gained momentum, company and bank managers— like some politicians and depositors— became nervous and started shifting funds from financial centers to regional cities to ensure access to cash close by in the event that jumpy politicians in some distant state decided to freeze bank deposits. The Armour Meat Company transferred $10 million from banks in New York, Chicago, and Cleveland to the Stockyards National Bank in Dallas on March 3 to ensure money to buy and feed cattle. New York could supply Texas and Michigan and perhaps a dozen other states with cash to keep going for a week— maybe two— but it could not provide cash for every state. Even the banking titans at J.P. Morgan— Thomas Lamont, Russell Leffingwell, and Parker Gilbert— realized the seriousness of the situation and urged Fed Governor Harrison, Governor Meyer, and Secretary Mills to intervene in what had become a real crisis.[58]

This shifting of funds from big banks in Cleveland, Philadelphia, Seattle, and such cities made big-city bankers nervous, which made governors and bank superintendents nervous. Many depositors became nervous as well, however there seem to have been few genuine bank runs leading up to the holiday. Some jumpy officials of the day and historians since have claimed the holiday was the culmination of a rising crescendo of bank runs. It was not so. The Howard Savings Institution in Newark, New Jersey, was one of the few banks actually subjected to a run on March 2; however, like other "runs" in those few days, it is not likely that the crowds gathered in order to withdraw their savings from a bank that had lost their confidence. Rather, they believed the governor was about to declare a holiday and cut off access to money in their bank. Large crowds gathered in front of New Jersey's largest mutual savings bank (and one of the largest banks in the state) on March 1—"interest day"—in order to post interest to their savings accounts right away in case the governor closed the bank. The imposing crowd attracted larger crowds who nervously continued to discuss the crowds that night. The next day the bank was subjected to a run by 3,000 depositors. Despite pleas by local clergy, politicians, and the bank management, another 1,800 people withdrew $3.8 million on Friday, March 3. Like most sound institutions subjected to runs, the bank was supported by other local banks and the Federal Reserve Bank of New York, paid out all money demanded, and suffered no long-term damage. Large crowds also showed up at the Hamilton Bank in Knoxville, but when the bank president announced the bank would not close for the holiday and everybody was welcome to as much money as they wanted, the crowd melted away.[59]

Rather than being withdrawn by passbook holders standing in long lines, most money left banks as wire transfers through district Federal Reserve Banks from large banks to smaller banks. Just as deposits left banks in small towns for larger towns in the course of 1931 and 1932—seeking the greater security offered by big banks—and then left regional centers, such as Louisville, for safer havens such as Chicago, so in February 1933 deposits left Chicago and New York and returned to regional banks. New York banks released $100 million through wire transfers on March 2 alone. Much of this fleeing money was withdrawn by small or regional banks, bringing their cash home in case it might be needed very suddenly, probably to quench a bank run. The First National Bank of St. Paul and its corporate clients recalled about $6 million from other banks. The First National Bank of Denver and its clients recalled more than $5 million from banks in San Francisco, Los Angeles, Chicago, and Cleveland. Other banks in Denver did the same, as did some Denver companies. From a list of 124 large depositors with demand accounts with the First National Bank of Denver before and after the bank holiday, it is difficult to generalize about the movement of monies, but Colorado-based companies more often moved money to Denver while national companies tended to move money away from Denver. While there were exceptions to those trends, business accounts at the end of the holiday contained $852,000 more than before the holiday. Deposits of the 11 largest individual account holders dropped by $136,700. Whether this was due to hoarding is impossible to say, but these accounts fell by only 18 percent, which does not approach even close to "emptying the vaults" as feared by Fed bankers and others.[60]

No doubt some money leaving banks all over the nation belonged not to companies or other banks, but to individuals. That was certainly the case in Denver. People across the country with large and small accounts no doubt pulled money out of banks to keep in cookie jars and pillow cases. California Senator Hiram Johnson wrote his son in late February, "I have a growing fear of the banks. Among a few people whom I run into ... I find some very quietly taking their accounts out of banks with which they have dealt, and I think this has become common all over the country with the result as we have seen in Michigan and Maryland, a result which may communicate itself to other states as well."

But in February and March 1933, the banking panic that drained over a billion dollars from big-city banks was not led by small savers hoping to protect their life's savings from collapsing banks. It was provoked — as noted by Tennessee Governor McAllister — by other bankers and big businessmen trying to secure access to some very large sums of cash in the very realistic expectation that they would need that cash and if left in the financial centers it would be unavailable. Unlike in earlier panics, however, the monies were shifted to protect them from political storms, not economic catastrophe.[61]

The persistent notion that the bank holidays capped a "rising crescendo of runs on banks" and their subsequent failures was probably produced by the gloomy atmosphere of February in the aftermath of dreadful runs of January. But those runs had petered out even by early February, leaving bankers and officials nervous and more panicky than depositors. The swiftly shifting corporate and bank funds moved by wire transfers had only a secondary relation to the runs and panics of January. The panicky reaction of bankers to the shifting funds was the financial response to the business response to the political response to the public response, which is the way history really works: "one damn thing after another."

So this is what happened: During the course of 1932, as banks around the nation shed securities held as assets in order to raise cash, the lion's share of those securities were sold in New York markets. The proceeds of those sales then remained in New York banks as deposits from out-of-state banks. By the end of 1932, banks all over the country remained extraordinarily liquid, with an astounding percent of their deposits kept in cash. Federal Reserve Banks held $417 million in excess reserves in February 1933. Unused cash deposited in correspondent accounts mounted to 11.5 percent of all deposits — a record since the formation of the Federal Reserve Bank. New York banks held about $1.66 billion of these deposits on February 1, 1933 — almost half of such deposits in the United States — and $300 million more than required by law. In the week after the declaration of the Michigan holiday, money held by New York member banks for other banks declined by $480 million. In the following week they fell another $278 million as banks around the United States called money home. A week after the Michigan holiday, demand deposits in Chicago member banks fell a mere $4 million, and money owed to other banks slipped $28 million. In the last week of February, banks withdrew another $73 million from Chicago member banks, leaving $168 million of other banks' reserves still on deposit. Other deposits dropped $132 million. In the last week of February, New York City member-bank demand deposits fell $397 million. New York City banks still held $900 million of other banks' money, nearly $5 billion in demand deposits, and $776 million in time deposits. Large amounts of money clearly left New York City and Chicago in just two weeks: both cities' banks lost between 12 and 14 percent of their deposits, but banks in both cities were strong and liquid enough to withstand such drains, and did. The money flowed back in the weeks following the national bank holiday.[62]

In fact, this phenomenon struck Federal Reserve–member banks in most financial centers. Smaller banks called home money placed on deposit in member banks in cities all over the United States. Debits at all banks for the week ending March 1 were $8.16 billion, an advance of an astounding 56 percent over the prior week and somewhat more than the same week in 1932. Banks especially took money out of banks: correspondent accounts at member banks fell by $746 million in the last week of February and the first days of March. The ebb of funds was remarkable in every Federal Reserve district except Minneapolis and Dallas, where the amounts of reserves kept on deposit were not large to begin with. A lot of money left banks, but most debits were soon entered as credits at some other bank. Nevertheless, demand deposits in member banks fell $1.3 billion during February, and time deposits declined $360 million, meaning $1.66 billion left the banking system entirely. The Federal Reserve discounted and bought $1.67 billion in bills in February and March 1933 — almost exactly the same amount as withdrawn from the banking system. Although the bank had routinely dealt in such amounts in 1928 and 1929, it had not done so since the Depression set in. In the week ending March 4, the Fed infused the financial system with $1.344 billion through discounting or purchases of government securities and commercial bills. Nearly $600 million of that amount remained within the various Reserve Banks as excess reserves. Nevertheless, its actions in February and March showed the bank could still step in when it needed to, and did. George Norris claimed that in one month, one-third of the money in circulation was pulled out of banks. There is no way to know how much of that money was withdrawn by small savers who shoved it under their beds versus large corporations, such as Kroger supermarkets or Brown and Williamson Tobacco, which kept currency out of their banks and in their vaults in early March in order to pay employees in cash. There were certainly many thousands of corporations that temporarily resorted to cash in order to continue operations.[63]

This shifting of funds was in nervous anticipation of bank holidays in banking centers, expectations by bankers of imminent bank runs by customers of small banks, and banks and big companies moving funds from small banks close to operations to larger, and presumably more secure, banks in regional financial centers. With those funds leaving, smaller banks had to retrieve cash on deposit in places such as Philadelphia and Cleveland, as well as New York City and Chicago. Large amounts of money shifted from bank to bank, and state to state, in response to all of these circumstances, with different banks moving funds for different reasons. For a variety of reasons, large sums of money shifted around the country seeking refuge from some imagined imminent storm. The high-profile part played by Federal Reserve district governors, who advised state governors and bank superintendents to declare bank holidays, suggests that nervousness among the most elite bankers and businessmen was instrumental in causing the wave of bank holidays and restrictions. Yet, in most cases, these supposedly well-informed people maintained that "the problem" lay outside their state. There was no problem in Texas, Iowa, Alabama, or Indiana. "The problem" emanated from elsewhere.

While bankers and officials fretted about potential problems that may not have been truly threatening, a problem for the nation really was brewing in New York: an alarming amount of gold was leaving or being earmarked in the New York Federal Reserve Bank for foreign vaults.[64] This outflow of gold posed a real problem for the nation's monetary and banking system, with potentially graver consequences than the shutdown in Michigan. On March 1, the New York Federal Reserve Bank held $711 million in gold. By March 4 this had dwindled to $381 million, and foreign firms and governments still held $600 million on deposit in New York banks. The Fed did not have enough gold in its vaults to cover those deposits should their owners develop bad nerves and demand their funds in gold, which was their legal right. If the British and perhaps the French and other European financial powers continued to demand gold for dollars, the United States would be forced off the gold standard. Fed Governor Meyer had already waived the 40 percent legal minimum of gold necessary to back currency notes issued by the New York Federal Reserve Bank, so the New York Fed did not have to start recalling notes in circulation. Plenty of gold, commercial paper, and government securities remained in Federal Reserve vaults in other districts to cover notes then in circulation nationally, so the nation's money supply was not in danger.

But if the British presented the New York Federal Reserve Bank with large stacks of Federal Reserve notes on Saturday morning and demanded gold that the Fed could not deliver, the United States would be *forced* off the gold standard, rather than leaving it voluntarily. In the Federal Reserve Board discussions of this predicament, Emanuel Goldenweiser argued that being forced off the gold standard by a shortage of gold would be preferable to voluntarily leaving the standard, which would crush foreign confidence in the dollar. While Governor Meyer agreed with Goldenweiser, Adolph Miller scoffed and urged President Hoover — on the phone — to formally request the board to close the gold-trading desk. In urging the closing New York banks, the Federal Reserve governors reacted against future expectations of actions by European central bankers, who acted on their own worries about the future value of the dollar under President Roosevelt.[65]

If Roosevelt indeed intended to devalue the dollar, as persistent rumors maintained and his stubborn silence on the question seemed to confirm, foreign holders of dollars would have been wise to convert as many of them as possible to gold before he took office at noon on Saturday, March 4. There was a real flight from the dollar by foreign central banks. Some Americans joined this flight by withdrawing gold and gold certificates from banks for the same reason after persistent reports that Roosevelt intended to either devalue the dollar or take the United States off the gold standard. Between New Year's Day and March 4, Americans took $320 million in gold and gold certificates out of American banks. One Chicago man reportedly withdrew $500,000 in gold from the Federal Reserve Bank in early March, and others around the country did the same out of fear for the dollar and not for their banks. After March 4, 1933, President Roosevelt both devalued the dollar and took the country off the gold standard. There was more to fear than fear itself.[66]

CHAPTER EIGHT

The Crisis in the White House

President Hoover waited for word from President-elect Roosevelt before formulating a presidential response to the unfolding banking crisis. Even though all the country's banks might close in a matter of days, Hoover was convinced there was nothing he could do without the concurrence of the president-elect. Because he believed his power to do anything effective—such as closing the banks—was not clearly defined in the law, he presumed he would need the cooperation of the Democratic-controlled House of Representatives, still under the gavel of Vice President–elect Garner, and the uncooperative Senate, still under the sway of a coalition of Democrats and progressive Republicans. He rightly assumed such cooperation would not have been forthcoming from either house without the explicit approval of Roosevelt. In Hoover's mind, everything depended upon Roosevelt. Given the enthusiasm for Roosevelt among congressmen and the breakdown of cooperation between the Capitol and the White House, it is hard to conclude Hoover was mistaken.

Many people were waiting for Roosevelt. Since the November balloting, people had been waiting for the president-elect to clarify his positions on many things, especially the state of the budget, the currency, and the war debts. They waited for Roosevelt to name a cabinet. They waited for Roosevelt to announce his program. And by late February, they waited for Roosevelt to pronounce his views on the banking situation. But Roosevelt remained silent. President Hoover tried to convince the president-elect to clarify his program before he took the helm and coordinate it with that of the still-in-office president in order to achieve more effective results in the short run. But President-elect Roosevelt refused. Hoover's failure to gain Roosevelt's cooperation on urgent matters in the fall of 1932 inflamed relations on both sides, but it especially soured Hoover's attitude toward Roosevelt. The bitter clash between the two men over the war-debts question made it impossible for Hoover to gain Roosevelt's collaboration to confront the even more urgent bank crisis that subsequently erupted in the United States.

Just before the 1932 balloting and confident about the outcome, the former chairman of the Democratic National Executive Committee, Jouett Shouse, wrote to Roosevelt (who had Shouse ousted from his party position) offering some unsolicited advice: "Every word that you utter, every position that you take, every act that you countenance should be weighed with the gravest care, not for its effect on the election but for its effect upon the American people. You are charged with the responsibility of the American presidency as definitely now as you will be after next March fourth. I am certain such responsibility makes an appeal both to your patriotism and to your judgement." Roosevelt ignored this counsel from the former DNC executive and weighed every word that he uttered—or perhaps more importantly did not utter—not for the benefit it might deliver to the people, government, or economy in the short run, but for the political gain to be derived after March 4.[1]

Shortly after the American voters chose Roosevelt as president, Hoover faced the daunting question of what to do about foreign war debts owed to the United States. The one-year debt moratorium had expired in June 1932, and the next scheduled payments by Britain and France were due on December 15. Hoover had already received a note from the British and French asking for a postponement of the payment in order to reach a final agreement on a new schedule for repayment of the loans. In December 1931 Hoover had asked Congress for a new debts commission to negotiate such a schedule but had been rebuffed. Congress agreed to the one-year repayment moratorium, but balked at any new schedule, which they assumed would lead to a reduction in payments, if not cancellation. So negotiations about a new payment schedule never took place. In November 1932 the British and French announced their refusal to accept the pre-moratorium payment schedule and demanded further postponement and new negotiations. Hoover believed that his lame-duck administration could not negotiate a repayment schedule favorable to U.S. interests; thus, it behooved him to involve President-elect Roosevelt in the discussions or gain his endorsement of a negotiating strategy. Furthermore, because any new agreement would require congressional sanction, it made sense to involve congressional leaders early in the process, and such involvement could be attained only with a nod from the president-elect. More importantly, any new agreement would be implemented by the Roosevelt administration, and not Hoover's; hence, Hoover foresaw the necessity of involving the president-elect in choosing a commission and gaining the cooperation of Congress. Both Treasury Secretary Ogden Mills and New York Federal Reserve Governor George Harrison shared Hoover's view that Roosevelt's involvement would be necessary for fruitful negotiations with our erstwhile allies.[2]

Shortly after the election, Hoover sent a long telegram to Governor Roosevelt suggesting that the U.S. government agree to readjust the terms of the loans. Roosevelt believed that reopening negotiations with the European debtors would stir up Congress and the American populace, and recoiled from being associated with such a proposal. He certainly did not want to begin his first days in office entangled in such an unpopular and intractable dilemma. Neither Roosevelt, nor his principal economic advisors, Adolf Berle, Rexford Tugwell, and Raymond Moley, approved of debt cancellation, which, according to Moley, was the prevailing East Coast "opinion" and the prevailing wisdom at Columbia University where he taught political science. Roosevelt and Moley met with Hoover and Secretary Mills at the White House on November 22 when Hoover proposed that a debt commission, made up of experts appointed by the president and acceptable to a Democratic Congress, be constituted to negotiate some settlement short of cancellation. Hoover and Mills both believed that they had gained Roosevelt's agreement to a new commission and that Roosevelt had agreed to convince congressional Democrats of the wisdom of the plan. When Hoover asked for a joint public statement in favor of such a commission, Roosevelt suggested issuing separate statements after Hoover met with congressional leaders. When Hoover met congressional leaders the next day, he was astonished that the Democrats had had no word from the president-elect on the war-debt question and that they uniformly opposed any new debt commission. When Roosevelt released his public statement on the question it said questions about the war debts should be handled through normal diplomatic channels and not through any presidential commission. Mills and Hoover were both furious that Roosevelt publicly rejected Hoover's proposal that, they believed, he had agreed to in the White House meeting, and had evidently sabotaged the commission among congressional Democrats. Roosevelt had additionally refused to inform Hoover of his position before the president released his public statement, humiliating Hoover and his administration.[3]

French diplomats did not believe that any new talks with Hoover's lame-duck admin-istration would be worthwhile and had no intention of meeting their $19 million obligation due on December 15. Indeed, on December 14 French Deputies overthrew the government of Edouard Herriot when a resolution of support for French payment of the war debt was voted down in the Chamber of Deputies. Despite formal legal advice from the Ministry of Finance that France's legal obligation to pay was in no way altered by the vote in the Cham-ber, France defaulted on its debt and never paid another *centime*. France was joined in default that December by Poland, Greece, Hungary, Austria, Belgium, and Estonia. The British made their $95 million payment on time while insisting it was a good-will payment and not obligatory, subject to renewed negotiations.[4]

Hoover then resolved to fold talks about the war debts into the (presumably) upcoming World Economic Conference and sent the president-elect another long telegram in a renewed effort to gain his cooperation in establishing an agenda for talks that would take place under Roosevelt's watch and not Hoover's. Roosevelt responded to Hoover's telegram with a telegram of his own, declining to take part in any discussions about the agenda. Roosevelt saw no urgency in the problems facing the United States and the European debtors and, hence, saw no reason to expedite discussions. Certainly Roosevelt's phlegmatic response to the problem once he took office suggests he did not imbue the problem with any particular importance, but he never made that position clear to Hoover or anyone else before March 4. Roosevelt may have been right. Perhaps the question really was not so urgent and had no great impact on the course of the American economy. However, that was not the advice he received from advisors connected to international finance, who believed the upcoming conference to be very important and urged preparations for it.[5]

Throughout these exchanges between Hoover and Roosevelt, the president-elect insisted that while Hoover was still president, he could do as he liked and did not need Roosevelt's cooperation. This was certainly not true in view of Hoover's need for congres-sional cooperation that could only be gained with a nod from the president-elect to the Democratic leadership. Of course, Hoover did not really require congressional approval to undertake a wide variety of tasks, such as appointing a commission to discuss the war debts or plan an agenda for the upcoming World Economic Conference. But Hoover rightly rec-ognized that any discussions between his administration and foreign governments would be an exercise in futility, which was also recognized by foreign leaders who clearly stated so. There was little the lame-duck administration could achieve without the cooperation of the incoming Democrats, and Roosevelt was dead set against cooperating. Democrats were engaged in a lively debate at the time about the merits of close cooperation between Democrats and Republicans to face the economic crisis from a stronger basis. The Al Smith wing of the Democratic Party, supported by Columbia University President Nicholas Murray Butler, argued for a nonpartisan "national government" along the lines of the British National Government that brought together Labour, Liberals, and Conservatives within one cabinet. Indeed, once president, Roosevelt developed a solid record of appointing pro-gressive Republicans to positions within his administration. Nevertheless, he would have nothing to do with Hoover and his administration.[6]

Roosevelt had his own rather radical ideas about how to handle the transition and urgent matters that needed attention during the interregnum. Far from approving a "national government," he had suggested to Brain-Truster Adolf Berle as early as June 1932 that if the Democratic victory in November were overwhelming, President Hoover ought to see it as a repudiation of his presidency and make way immediately for a Roosevelt

administration without waiting for March 1933. He suggested to Berle, evidently in all seriousness, that Hoover should fire Secretary of State Henry Stimson, appoint Roosevelt as
secretary of state, have Vice President Curtis resign and then Hoover should himself resign
so that Roosevelt could become president right away. Like cooperating with Hoover on debt
negotiations, this stratagem would have been perfectly constitutional, if rather more
unorthodox and even less likely. Berle noted, "He indicated that he thought there might
even be some possibility of this happening, though he did not consider it probable."[7]

While he squabbled with Hoover, Roosevelt received earnest supplications from New
York Democrats involved in finance, and especially international finance, to do something
about the urgent war debts problem. Many on Wall Street— regardless of party affiliation,
and despite mythology, plenty of Democrats worked in high finance— believed the amount
repaid to American creditors or whether they were paid at all was eclipsed in importance
by the cloud of uncertainty the lingering question cast over international finance. Oliver
Sprague tried to convince important bankers and Treasury officials that Britain's war debts
should be massively reduced. His arguments were generally received sympathetically, but
all agreed that political realities would not allow it. Despite entreaties from Wall Street,
Roosevelt waited until February to begin doing anything about the upcoming international
economic conference and started by asking Tugwell to gather some data and materials for
the meeting. Roosevelt thought it a good idea to gather Republican progressives, all far
from New York and antagonists of Wall Street, to form a small team to prepare for the
international talks. He asked California senator and arch-isolationist Hiram Johnson, who
harbored an obsessive loathing for international bankers, to lead the group consisting of
New Mexico Senator Bronson Cutting, Wisconsin Senator Robert La Follette, and Chicago
lawyer Harold Ickes. All declined the honor, though Ickes indicated that he would be
delighted to be secretary of the interior. After some dithering, Roosevelt ultimately handed
preparations for the conference over to Bernard Baruch, who effectively excluded anyone
else from discussions, meaning there were no discussions and no preparations for the conference.[8]

President Hoover greatly resented Governor Roosevelt's refusal to cooperate. When
Roosevelt invited— through Harvard Law professor Felix Frankfurter— Secretary of State
Stimson to come to New York to continue talks, Hoover told Stimson if Roosevelt wanted
to cooperate he could come to Washington or send responsible delegates to talk about the
economic conference, but he had no intention of having further talks with Roosevelt about
talking. By Christmas, Hoover no longer trusted Roosevelt, and when Roosevelt called the
White House on January 4 to suggest a Roosevelt visit to the White House, Hoover refused
to take the call until he had a stenographer on another line. After agreeing to the meeting,
Hoover joked with his secretary, Theodore Joslin, that Roosevelt would now probably tell
the press that Hoover had called Roosevelt to invite him to the White House. Hoover then
gave Stimson permission to discuss discussions with Roosevelt, which Stimson did on January 9, 1933. Roosevelt suggested to Stimson that he had no faith in commissions and
believed the debt question would best be solved by himself personally because he was convinced that only he could convince Congress to pass the necessarily distasteful legislation
ratifying any new agreement. To that end Roosevelt wanted to open discussions right away
with British representatives. Stimson agreed to this, as did Hoover.[9]

After Roosevelt met with the French ambassador, Paul Claudel, on January 11, 1933,
at Roosevelt's Manhattan town house to discuss the war-debt question, he agreed to stop
by the White House on his way south to convalesce in Warm Springs, Georgia. The January

20 White House meeting between Hoover, Mills, and Stimson on one side, and Roosevelt and Raymond Moley on the other, produced little, but heightened animosity. Hoover had agreed to the White House meeting only because Stimson had assured him it might achieve something. They did at least agree that Roosevelt should openly meet with British representatives to discuss the debt question. Hoover and his advisors believed it very important to have these meetings covered by the press so that the public would know that the issue was moving forward. Nevertheless, Roosevelt and Moley insisted they would not initiate any talks leading to the World Economic Conference in London. The outgoing and incoming administrations could not agree on negotiating strategies, so the Hoover appointees could not provide the British with an advance agenda for talks.[10]

Hoover's and Stimson's distrust of Roosevelt was reciprocated by Moley and the president-elect. Moley told California Senator Hiram Johnson, "The cooperation which had been requested in our foreign relations by Hoover from Roosevelt was simply a well-baited trap by which Roosevelt was to be left holding the bag, exactly as Hoover and those he represented, desired." Moley saw Stimson as a pro–British mouthpiece of Wall Street, while Stimson developed a loathing for Moley as a result of their dealings in December and January. Both Moley and Tugwell believed there was a Republican–Wall Street plot to set the Roosevelt administration upon a road to war debt cancellation, which would infuriate Congress and the American people, who resolutely opposed any such move. Once Congress was alienated and voters antagonized, the Democratic legislative program would be impossible to pass and a Republican return to power set in motion.[11]

Adolf Berle believed Roosevelt's obstinacy might have grown out of Hoover's earlier refusal to cooperate with Governor Roosevelt's efforts to coordinate New York public water-power development along the St. Lawrence River with federal authorities negotiating a river-way treaty with Canada. Discussions about creating the St. Lawrence Seaway had already dragged on for years by the time Hoover became president. At the same time many New Yorkers had caught a fever of enthusiasm for various plans to produce hydroelectric power from public plants on the St. Lawrence River. However, diverting water from the river to generate electricity required the cooperation of Ontario, Canada, and the United States government. Governor Roosevelt had failed to interest President Hoover in his plans and greatly resented his noncooperation in forwarding New York's project. After a series of letters over several years, Roosevelt made one last effort to enlist Hoover's help in July 1932, as the election campaign was gearing up. Hoover refused to help. That exchange of letters on the subject was the last communication between the two men before Hoover's telegram of November 12. It is possible that Hoover's antipathy for publicly generated and distributed electricity induced him to drag his feet on helping New York, provoking the resentment of the New York governor, but it is impossible to say how much this spat between the president and the governor kindled Roosevelt's later obstinacy. No doubt, it aggravated already complicated relations between the two antagonists.[12]

Raymond Moley explains that Roosevelt's refusal to cooperate stemmed from the dramatically differing views of the president and the president-elect on the sources of the Depression. Hoover believed it was caused by international economic difficulties, while Roosevelt believed it arose from domestic conditions. If economic conditions within the United States caused the Depression, then international discussions about the best way to end it would do little good. Thus Roosevelt insisted on separate talks about debts and international cooperation to boost trade and encourage credit. Roosevelt believed they had nothing to do with each other, and the latter talks would be of little importance in any event.

If the solution to America's economic problems were to be found within our borders, talks about trade and international credit were hardly urgent. And because he did not favor further reductions in the amounts owed to the United States by the Europeans, there was not much to talk about. Roosevelt assigned little importance to talks about either war debts or economic cooperation, but he never communicated this lack of concern to Hoover or members of the outgoing administration. Instead, he raised phony and insincere objections on matters of procedure and protocol that baffled and frustrated Hoover and his staff. Relations between Hoover and Roosevelt and their respective advisors were already cool by November. As the end of Hoover's days in the White House approached, their rapport was close to freezing and both men assigned low motives to the others' words and actions.[13]

A close friend of Charles Dawes's observed, "I believe that Franklin Roosevelt will live to rue the day when he declined to cooperate with Mr. Hoover in his efforts to do something about the [war] debt situation, but I think I can see on the other side that Mr. Hoover has not handled his approach to Roosevelt with very much skill ... but even at that I think Roosevelt has probably declined because he hasn't any plan to suggest and doesn't know what it is all about." This judgment was probably close to the mark except regarding Roosevelt's capacity for regret. Events suggested that Roosevelt had little interest in the question and no plan. In his dealings with the incoming Brain Trusters, Herbert Feis was struck by their divisions over important and pressing foreign economic policy matters, and how President-elect Roosevelt "seemed to be teetering between these divergent groups of supporters."[14]

The importance of these exchanges between Roosevelt and Hoover surpassed the gravity of the war debt question. Although many people, especially those involved in high finance, were intensely interested in its resolution, and the lingering unhealed sore did indeed depress many in need of cheering up, the bitter feelings between the president and the president-elect ultimately proved disastrous for efforts to coordinate actions to save the tottering banks. When Roosevelt's cooperation was needed most urgently, Hoover failed to gain it.

The Bank Crisis

The reaction across the United States to the banking crisis in Michigan posed a problem for all Americans, many of whom believed the crisis demanded a federal response. As money gushed out of big-city banks because of very justifiable fears that accounts were about to be frozen in state after state, a torrent of gold simultaneously poured out of Federal Reserve vaults. Foreign central banks removed $200 million in gold from Federal Reserve vaults in a single week. With pressure so great for cash in the country, the Fed could not afford to lose much more gold, because the amount in Federal Reserve vaults directly determined how many Federal Reserve notes could circulate. In February 1933 monetary circulation had reached $6.54 billion — an increase of $1 billion in a single month and an historic zenith — of which $3.4 billion were Federal Reserve notes — also an historic high. The demand for cash reached such unprecedented amounts that the Bureau of Engraving and Printing had to hire 587 temporary workers to ensure the notes were printed quickly. Any failure by the Fed to make money available would lead to unknown, but frightening consequences, and the diminishing stocks of gold imperiled the money supply. Closed banks in Chicago and San Francisco could not demand gold, but open banks in London, Paris, Zurich, and Amsterdam could. The only way to stop gold from leaving American shores was to close the Federal Reserve Bank, and no state governor could do that. It was not even clear how the president could.[15]

After Governor Comstock closed the banks in Michigan, but before the closings began to spread to neighboring states, President Hoover became alarmed at what lay ahead for the country. He saw no way out of the predicament of the banking crisis other than swaying the national temper away from anxiety to optimism. This, of course, had been his tactic from 1929 to late 1931 and it had not proven effective. Federal injections of money through loans to fragile corporations and municipalities had not delivered many tangible improvements either. The country was in a worse state than ever, and Hoover believed that was the case because the national mood had darkened since summer 1932. Indeed, anger and anxiety had increased since then and the pressing question was why had that happened? Hoover believed actions, words, inactions, and inappropriate silence by Democrats, progressive Republicans, and the president-elect were principally to blame for the deteriorating condition. Thus, Hoover decided that only President-elect Roosevelt held the key to restoring national hopefulness and confidence, which would turn the economy around and ease the relentless pressure on banks.

On February 17, 1933, President Hoover wrote a letter to President-elect Roosevelt upon the latter's return from an extended fishing trip in Florida.

My Dear Mr. President Elect,
   A Most critical situation has arisen in the country of which I feel it is my duty to advise you confidentially....
   The major difficulty is the state of the public mind, for there is a steadily degenerating confidence in the future which has reached the height of general alarm. I am convinced that an early statement by you upon two or three policies of your Administration would serve greatly to restore confidence and cause a resumption of the march of recovery.
   The large part which fear and apprehension play in the situation can well be demonstrated by repeated experience of the last few years and the tremendous lift which has come at times by the removal of fear can easily be demonstrated. [*The only thing we have to fear is fear itself!*]
   One of the major elements in the broad problem of recovery is the re-expansion of credit so critically and abruptly deflated by the shocks form Europe during the last half of 1931. The visible results were public fear, hoarding, bank failures, withdrawal of gold, flight of capital, falling prices, increased unemployment....
   The facts about this last interruption [in the economic recovery of the summer and fall of 1932] are simple and they are pertinent to the action needed. With the election there came the natural and inevitable hesitation all along the economic line pending the demonstration of the policies of the new administration. But a number of very discouraging things have happened on top of this natural hesitation. The breakdown in balancing the budget by the House of Representatives; the proposals for the inflation of the currency and the widespread discussion of it; the publication of RFC loans and the bank runs, hoarding and bank failures from this cause; increase in unemployment due to imports from depreciated currency countries; failure of the Congress to enact banking, bankruptcy and other vital legislation; unwillingness of Congress to face reduction of unnecessary expenditures; proposals to abrogate constitutional responsibility by The Congress with all the chatter about dictatorship, and other discouraging effect upon the public mind. They have now culminated to a state of alarm which is rapidly reaching the dimensions of a crisis. Hoarding has risen to a new high level; the bank structure is weakened as witness Detroit and increased failures in other localities. There are evidences of flight of capital and foreign withdrawals of gold. In other words we are confronted with precisely the same phenomena we experienced late in 1931 and again in spring of 1932....

I therefore return to my suggestion at the beginning as to the desirability of clarifying the public mind on certain essentials which will give renewed confidence. It is obvious that as you will shortly be in a position to make whatever policies you wish effective, you are the only one who can give these assurances ... [which will turn the tide] ... if there could be prompt assurance that there will be no tampering or inflation of the currency; that the budget will be unquestionably balanced even if further taxation is necessary; that the government credit will be maintained by refusal to exhaust it in issue of securities. The course you have adopted in inquiring into the problems of world stability are already known and helpful. It would be further help if the leaders were advised to cease publication of RFC business.[16]

There can be little doubt that Hoover was not displaying his best judgment in sending this tactless letter to his rival, the president-elect, urging him to adopt particular enumerated policies in advance of the inauguration and publicly promising to keep his word. It was not a diplomatic letter for one rival to send to another, despite the good intentions of the president. But Hoover's reasoning was sound on at least one level: public consternation over Roosevelt's stubborn silence about his intentions was adding to the financial crisis. Banks and businesses were beginning to pull cash out of banks, and foreign central banks were beginning to pull gold out of the United States. It is entirely possible that reassuring statements by the president-elect about his policies at this early stage would have made a difference. Hoover wrote and sent this letter just after the declaration of the banking holiday in Michigan and before large sums of money had started to shift around the country in worried anticipation of the next crisis looming. State legislatures were just then debating various emergency measures, and banks in Indiana and Ohio had not yet limited withdrawals. The bank-closing wave had not yet formed and reassuring words and gestures from Hoover and Roosevelt might have stopped it from swelling. They may also have made little difference; however, ten days passed as the banking crisis built and Hoover received no reply.[17]

While waiting for a reply form the president-elect, Hoover received a visit from Pennsylvania Republican Senator David Reed, who assured the president that leading Democrats would cooperate if he decided to suspend the convertibility of the dollar into gold. Hoover replied to the senator in a memo that suggested that the flight of gold was not the main problem but only a symptom of the real problem, which was the silence of the president-elect on his monetary and fiscal intentions. People feared Roosevelt would undertake foolish experiments and subject the nation to disastrous policies. George Creel, a public information officer under President Wilson, wrote an article in *Colliers Magazine* claiming Roosevelt intended to institute a "four-year plan" for the American economy, in imitation of Stalin's "five-year plan" being implemented in the Soviet Union. Hoover wrote to the senator, "They run a grave danger of precipitating a complete financial debacle. And if it is precipitated, the responsibility lies squarely with them for they have had ample warning—unless, of course, such a debacle is part of the 'new deal.'" Hoover made no effort to mask the depth of his bitterness toward Roosevelt and revealed his dark suspicions about his motives.[18]

Hoover's skepticism about Roosevelt's intentions was shared by Democratic Virginia Senator Carter Glass. Roosevelt believed having Woodrow Wilson's last secretary of the Treasury in his cabinet would lend reassurance to the nation that its finances were in experienced, sober, and reliable hands. Roosevelt first asked the stately and much respected Virginian to become his secretary of the Treasury in a hurried interview in Washington on January 9 as Roosevelt was passing through the capital on his way to Warm Springs, Georgia. Glass, however, would not be rushed and asked for time to consider the proposal. Roosevelt asked Raymond Moley to coax Glass into the cabinet, which he tried to do over the next several weeks. Glass consistently postponed making a commitment in part because he was genuinely worried about his wife's poor health and feared his own fragile health would not permit him to undergo the rigors the office would impose. But he also harbored doubts about Roosevelt's commitment to balanced budgets and "sound money." Glass had not been a Roosevelt enthusiast at the Chicago Convention, and his wariness was not appeased by the evasive bromides Roosevelt had dispensed during the campaign and since November in response to Republican accusations that he intended to devalue the currency. Rumors of Roosevelt's designs reached Glass around the same time the president-elect denounced the proposed national excise tax that Glass, Garner, and the Democratic leadership had promised Hoover and other Republicans they would support — with the understanding that Roosevelt also favored it. After all, it would be implemented under his watch. This reversal disturbed Glass, as it had disturbed Garner, and it deepened Glass's doubts about Roosevelt's trustworthiness and commitment to balancing the budget.[19]

When Moley, who harbored great respect and affection for the old Virginian, tried to coax Glass on board, Glass told him he wanted a crystal clear statement from Roosevelt about inflation. He also wanted to be free to pick his own subordinates, indicating he specifically wanted Russell Leffingwell, of Morgan and Company, as his undersecretary, the position Leffingwell held under Glass in the Wilson administration. When told of Glass's demands Roosevelt erupted that he would have no "Morgan men" in his administration and that he would not reject an idea simply because it had been labeled "inflationist." Unconvinced of Roosevelt's commitment to balanced budgets and the gold standard, Glass asked for more time to think over the offer. Roosevelt gave him 24 hours, which was all the time Glass needed to decline the offer. Roosevelt was not a man used to taking "no" for an answer. Moreover, when both Bernard Baruch and Woodrow Wilson's physician and close advisor, Cary Grayson, heard of Glass's refusal, they urged Roosevelt to persuade Glass to accept the proffered post. Hence, Roosevelt again insisted Glass join his cabinet and refused to be denied. South Carolina Senator James Byrnes agreed to try to convince his Virginia colleague to take the post. Glass asked for more time to reconsider, and Roosevelt reluctantly conceded.[20]

Glass boarded Roosevelt's train as it headed north from Florida in early February, and the Virginian interviewed the president-elect about his views and intentions. Roosevelt reacted badly to the interrogation but continued to insist that Glass accept the post. Glass still found Roosevelt's answers evasive and contrived, and again said "no." Roosevelt insisted he could not accept "no" for an answer. In that case, Glass responded, he would require more time to consider his future. Three days later, Glass telephoned Roosevelt and turned him down definitively. The senator released a public statement to that effect on February 20, stating he declined the post entirely out of concern for his health, the Senate, and his Virginia constituents, and not at all because of any disagreements with the president-elect over policy. This last qualification was another small dissimulation proffered by Glass out of consideration of public reaction if the full truth were known. News of Glass's acceptance would have immediately reassured many who looked to the Virginia senator as the main defender of "sound money" and conservative fiscal policies, just as his refusal would have the opposite effect. In fact, Glass assumed he would not agree with Roosevelt on policy and personnel, and by late February Glass joined the ranks of those who believed the rising tide of bank withdrawals and fleeing gold was caused primarily by national ill ease about Roosevelt's intentions.[21]

As the crisis atmosphere in the country deepened at the end of February, a growing chorus demanded the president-elect make a statement about his intentions. Twenty prominent economists — mostly aligned with the Democratic Party and including Benjamin Anderson, Edwin Kemmerer, Broadus Mitchell, and Bernhard Ostrolenk — wrote an open letter to the president-elect in January urging him to publicly support a list of policies, most of which were consistent with the Democratic platform of 1932. Roosevelt made no public reply. The *New York Times* urged the president-elect to make a public statement of his intentions, as did the Roosevelt-friendly syndicated columnist Arthur Krock. Democratic Chicago banker Melvin Traylor assured a Senate committee that it would help immensely to restore calm if the president-elect made a clear statement that he did not intend to devalue the dollar. The Federal Reserve Advisory Council likewise urged Roosevelt to announce his intentions and received no reply. Senator Byrnes of South Carolina, who acted as Roosevelt's liaison with Senate Democrats, wrote to the president-elect, "The newspapers of South Carolina desire to publish on March 4th a special edition devoted to an effort to inspire confidence in the people as to the future. I think we can agree that the conditions of which we today complain are seriously aggravated by the lack of confidence and that any effort by the President to restore confidence is to be commended. They would appreciate from you a few words as to the wisdom of their course." South Carolina newspapers received no word from Roosevelt.[22]

Rumors, fed by Committee for the Nation circulars and a persistent trickle of articles and newsletters proffering "insider" advice, persisted that Roosevelt intended to take the United States off the gold standard and inflate the currency. When the president of International Harvester, Alexander Legge, was prodded by a Senate committee to comment on President-elect Roosevelt's views on the proposed national sales tax, he responded he could not, because, despite much coverage by the national press on the question, he did not know what Roosevelt's views were. "I have read the statements [in the press] but they cannot all be true, because they are conflicting." Chairman Smoot interjected that the president-elect had first said he favored a manufacturers' excise tax, and then said he opposed it. No one, even Roosevelt's advisors, could say for certain what his attitude toward the proposed tax was.[23]

New York Federal Reserve Governor George Harrison sought a meeting with the president-elect in February to discuss monetary issues that faced the nation, but he could gain access only to recently designated secretary of the Treasury, William Woodin, and Raymond Moley. Roosevelt refused to talk to him, fearing adverse reaction to "conspicuous comment." One might conclude that Roosevelt derived some sort of political advantage from not dealing with President Hoover, but given the national circumstances it is difficult to understand why the president-elect refused to be seen talking to the head of the New York Federal Reserve Bank. While Roosevelt declined to meet with George Harrison, he communicated to Jesse Jones that he wished to be consulted before any deal was brokered between the Detroit banks and the RFC. As Secretary Mills and the RFC were still trying to put together a rescue plan for the Detroit banks, Mills heeded the summons and took the train to New York City to find out what Roosevelt had in mind. Once there he did not meet with Roosevelt, as he had expected, but with William Woodin. Having been summoned to New York, Mills was told by Woodin that the president-elect would be glad to be kept informed of events and that the RFC should decide on its own what to do and accept the responsibility. This was a very odd message to be summoned to New York to receive. What was the point, if not to hint to Mills that no decision should be made until the new administration was in place? No decision was made and no rescue was arranged for the Detroit banks before the inauguration.[24]

James Rand, president of the typewriter manufacturing company Remington-Rand and president of the Committee for the Nation, had also been trying to arrange an appointment with President-elect Roosevelt for months, without success. He hoped to convince him to lower the gold content of the dollar, thus devaluing it in order to raise prices. He did manage to schedule an appointment to have lunch with Roosevelt advisor Rexford Tugwell in New York City in late February in order to discuss his committee's proposal about the dollar and a temporary guarantee of bank deposits. At the lunch, Tugwell indiscreetly told Rand that Roosevelt and his Brains Trust "were fully aware of the bank situation and that it would undoubtedly collapse within a few days which would place the responsibility in the lap of President Hoover." He went on to say that as soon as Roosevelt was inaugurated, the administration would embargo gold, suspend gold payments, and reinflate the currency. Greatly surprised, Rand called the White House and told Hoover's secretary, Ted Joslin, about his conversation with Tugwell. When Hoover read Joslin's notes on his conversation with Rand, he exploded. He assigned low motives to Tugwell and assumed that Roosevelt's plan to allow the nation's banks to collapse and ascribe full blame for the crisis to Hoover explained why Hoover had not received a reply from the president-elect to his letter of February 18: Roosevelt was just biding his time waiting for the implosion which was visibly building everyday.[25]

Despite his anger, Hoover wrote a short and more tactful letter to Roosevelt on February 28, by which time the banking crisis was demonstrably unfolding. He wrote, "I am confident that a declaration even now on the line I suggested at that time [18 February] would contribute greatly to restore confidence and would save losses and hardships to millions of people." Roosevelt responded the following day with two letters. The first he claimed he wrote a week before, but that his secretary had not sent it because she was under the impression that it was just a draft. The other was an apology and explanation about the first letter and a note that Roosevelt concurred with Hoover that a special session of Congress needed to be called right away after the inauguration. Raymond Moley asserts that both letters from Roosevelt, the first dated February 19 and the covering note dated March 1, were, in fact, dictated by Roosevelt to his stenographer on the same day: March 1. In his first letter, Roosevelt doubted that "mere statements" by anyone would do any good because "the real trouble is that on present values very few financial [institutions] anywhere in the country are actually able to pay off their deposits in full, and the knowledge of that is widely held — Bankers with the narrower viewpoint have urged me to make a statement but even they seriously doubt it would have a definite effect." This explanation is hard to take seriously. Banks exist on the premise that some depositors will always leave some of their money in accounts for banks to loan. If all depositors demanded all of their money, not a single bank in the United States would survive. Roosevelt's statement was analogous to that of the New York Clearing House Association, claiming Americans were trying to withdraw $40 billion from banks, which was an absurd assertion.[26]

Roosevelt categorically refused to make any public comment about the spreading panic on the dubious premise that such a statement would do no good. This contention was counter to all advice that Roosevelt was then receiving. When many clamored to meet with the very busy president-elect to offer unsolicited advice, Roosevelt did solicit the counsel of Morgan partners Russell Leffingwell and Thomas Lamont. On February 27, Lamont talked to Roosevelt on the phone and followed up with a letter:

I enclose a memorandum of the points which I made to you over the telephone just after lunch today. I do not wish to be alarmist: in fact, I am perhaps usually inclined to be too much the other way. But when I came back this morning from the South, on a hurry call, I found the situation far more critical than I had dreamed. I believe in all seriousness the emergency could not be greater. That is my opinion and that of my partners, including cool-headed Russell Leffingwell and Parker Gilbert, former Treasury officials, who have discussed the problem within the past forty-eight hours with Mr. Woodin and Secretary Mills, with Governor Harrison and Governor Meyer. The things to be done to save the situation are not complex, but they are vital. And it is your say-so alone that will save the country from disaster. Every hour in the next few days counts.

The president-elect ignored Lamont's advice.[27]

On Thursday, March 2, Roosevelt and his entourage arrived in Washington, D.C., from New York for the inauguration. The governor of California announced the bank holiday in his state that evening. Federal Reserve Director Adolph Miller went to the Mayflower Hotel to discuss the bank crisis with the president-elect, but could not gain access to him. He did reach him on the phone and tried to explain the seriousness of the situation, but to no avail. That night Secretary Mills asked Senator Byrnes to urge Roosevelt to join Hoover in a joint statement to the country reassuring the people that the banks were basically sound and advising them to remain calm and to have confidence in their government. When Byrnes met that night with Roosevelt, Cordell Hull and others at the Mayflower Hotel, Roosevelt told Byrnes emphatically that he would not join Hoover in any statement, he would not associate himself with any statement by Hoover, and he would wait until after the inauguration to say anything about the situation. When Byrnes told Mills of Roosevelt's refusal, Mills beseeched Byrnes to try again, which Byrnes declined to do. He suggested instead that Mills coordinate whatever plan the Hoover administration proposed with Roosevelt's designated Secretary of the Treasury William Woodin. The *Santa Ana Register* in California took note that the president-elect had nothing to say about the spreading bank holidays. The next day, Friday, witnessed a crescendo of bank moratoria across the land.[28]

Hoover tried again to gain the cooperation of Roosevelt in meeting the developing situation. He asked Senators Joseph Robinson (soon to be majority leader) and Carter Glass to the White House ostensibly to brief them on developments and urge them to pass the Glass-Steagall Act right away as a confidence-restoring measure. He also asked if they could not reason with the president-elect to issue a public statement approving the use of the Trading with the Enemy Act to close the banks. They assured the president that they had discussed the question with Roosevelt and that he adamantly refused to issue any statement so long as he had no legal responsibility for the situation. However, both senators agreed that Hoover should not invoke the act without the cooperation of Roosevelt.[29]

When Roosevelt and Raymond Moley met with Hoover, Meyer, and Mills, at the White House on Friday afternoon, the day before the inauguration, Roosevelt refused to be drawn into the crisis, maintaining it was the responsibility of President Hoover to do what he thought best. Another White House council was arranged for Friday afternoon, gathering Moley, Hoover, Mills, and Meyer. Meyer again advised a national bank moratorium, Hoover still preferred limits on foreign exchange withdrawals, while Moley refused to commit to any action and wanted to discuss the question further with Roosevelt.[30]

Hoover interrupted a meeting with his advisors at the White House to call Roosevelt on the telephone at eleven o'clock that night, March 3, to try one last time to gain his cooperation. He urged Roosevelt to issue a statement saying he approved of invoking the Trading with the Enemy Act to close banks until after the inauguration. Senator Glass was in the room when the president-elect took the call and refused to agree to anything. After a brief exchange with Hoover on the phone, Roosevelt turned to Glass and told him,

> "The Federal Reserve Board telephoned the White House this afternoon with a request that a proclamation be issued tomorrow morning, closing all banks before they could open."
>
> "What did Mr. Hoover say to this request?"
>
> "He told me he told the Federal Reserve Board he did not think such a step was necessary. Thinks most of the banks that are still open are solvent. I told him, as you heard me say, that you thought the same way."
>
> Glass grunted.
>
> "This is the second time the Federal Reserve Board has made the same request within three days."
>
> "Yes, I know."
>
> "The previous time I sent Woodin to Mills to tell him I would not give my approval to such a proclamation."
>
> "I see. What are you planning to do?" asked Glass.
>
> "Planning to close them, of course," answered Roosevelt.[31]

Glass countered that he did not believe the president had the authority to do any such thing and that Attorney General William Mitchell had issued an opinion that the Trading with the Enemy Act did not confer such powers on the president. Roosevelt responded that he had been advised otherwise. Glass was dismayed to hear the president-elect's plans. Glass repeated his assertions that the act did not apply to the circumstances and argued further that it would never survive a challenge in court. Even if the act were applicable, no act of Congress could give any president the authority to close solvent banks, especially those chartered by the states. The Constitution did not allow it. Roosevelt responded, "Nevertheless, I am going to issue such a proclamation." Glass left the hotel that night with grave foreboding about the future of the United States.[32]

Roosevelt was not going to make any statement about his intentions and was not interested in cooperating or coordinating with the Hoover administration to calm the rising panic. Newspaper editors were under the mistaken impression that President-elect Roosevelt was working closely with President Hoover to solve the banking crisis. On Friday morning, March 3, the *Boston Globe* ran the headline, "Roosevelt Tackles Job, Confers on Bank Situation." It continued in the same vein on Saturday morning, the day of Roosevelt's inauguration, "Roosevelt Takes Helm on Eve of Inauguration — Confers with Hoover and Financial Experts on Banking Situation." As late as Sunday, March 5, the *St. Louis Post-Dispatch* reported that Hoover and Roosevelt had discussed a plan to guarantee 50 percent of all deposits. The *Richmond Times-Dispatch* reported on its front page that President Hoover and the president-elect had discussed the financial situation for an hour and ten minutes on Friday, which invigorated Washington with renewed confidence. The newspaper advised that the president-elect had the situation well in hand and conferred with Secretaries-designate William Woodin and Cordell Hull, Senator Glass, RFC Director Jesse Jones, and advisor Raymond Moley. Moley and Woodin, furthermore, were consulting closely with members of the Federal Reserve Board and Secretary Mills. Arkansas Senator Robinson announced after a meeting between Roosevelt and Democratic congressional leaders, "A definite statement on the banking situation and other matters will be forthcoming in the near future." All these discussions led nowhere and produced neither decisions nor actions to calm the crisis, nor were they intended to. Only the financial newsletter, Whaley-Eaton Service, reported on March 3 that Hoover and Roosevelt were not cooperating and there was no plan for federal action. It also predicted that the new president would *not* nationalize the bank holiday and would probably guarantee all deposits. On Saturday morning, before his inauguration, Roosevelt announced about the financial situation and his discussions: "There is nothing I can say."[33]

While most newspapers put an upbeat face on the behind-closed-door stalling in Washington, the *Chicago Tribune* took a darker view. It complained that although Democratic and business leaders had urged Roosevelt to issue a statement about what he intended to do, either jointly with Hoover or alone, he had refused. The paper editorialized, "New Dealers" are "wholly content with Mr. Roosevelt's policy of hands off right up to the moment he takes the oath ... with an eye to the main chance of making political capital.... As they view the situation, the economic conditions of the country, which has slumped violently in the last fortnight, will have reached its lowest depths as the Republican regime comes to an end at noon Saturday." Of course, that is exactly what happened.[34]

What were the intentions of the president-elect? No one knew and no one knows. What we do know is that Roosevelt's ideas on economics and monetary issues were relatively orthodox, yet not dogmatic. He wanted to achieve stable prices but was as uneasy about inflation as any banker. He was more willing to experiment than Hoover had been, though Hoover was willing to implement innovative programs, such as the Farm Board and the RFC, if he were convinced they would help the economy. His attitude toward gold differed little from that of Hoover: he preferred to stick to the gold standard but would depart from it if convinced it were necessary. Adolf Berle judged that Roosevelt would have preferred to remain on the gold standard but that he had no deep commitment to it. Owen Young, chairman of General Electric and deputy chairman of the New York Federal Reserve Bank, discussed the gold standard with Governor Roosevelt the previous June and advised him that leaving it would not produce calamitous results. The first evidence that Roosevelt toyed with the idea of departing from the gold standard appeared in early January 1933 when Roosevelt was thinking seriously about what to do about Britain, the depreciated pound, imperial preference (Commonwealth countries had agreed in 1932 to discriminate in favor of each others' imports), war debts, tariffs, and stagnating trade. In discussing these issues with trusted advisors, including Vincent Astor, Tugwell, and Moley, he revealed that he believed the inflated value of the dollar compared to the pound was a grand hindrance in all matters and that lowering the gold content of the dollar, or divorcing the dollar from gold entirely, would make tackling these issues easier. He also thought — not without reason — the British who were unencumbered by the gold standard were conspiring to keep the dollar overvalued.[35]

Thus, during the first week of January, the president-elect began making inquiries about the Trading with the Enemy Act and its current validity. He preferred using the act because it would allow the United States to depart from the gold standard quickly without first enduring a long congressional debate with uncertain outcome. When Tugwell discussed the act with several people at the Treasury Department, he learned that Hoover had already reviewed it with Treasury officials but had not decided to use it. By February 27 Roosevelt had contacted Democratic Senators Key Pittman and James Byrnes to discuss congressional support for using the act to suspend trading in gold, and they responded favorably. It is likely that Roosevelt resolved to embargo gold sales and exports after the wave of bank holidays had already gathered momentum but before Governor Lehman decided to close New York banks on Saturday morning, March 4. The first intimation of any decision to close the banks was given to Carter Glass on Friday night, March 3. All we know is that Roosevelt had developed a keen interest in the Trading with the Enemy Act by early February even before the Michigan crisis exploded. And like Federal Reserve Chairman Meyer and Governor Harrison, his concern was for the U.S. gold stock and not for the banks themselves.[36]

After the Michigan crisis broke, every New York banker with entree to the president-elect seems to have tried to contact him in order to persuade him to do something to help the faltering banks. Winthrop Aldrich and Charles McCain of the Chase National Bank, Owen Young of the New York Federal Reserve Bank, and others urged Roosevelt to save the banks. According to Tugwell, on February 17, "[Roosevelt] took it all smiling and could see no reason why he should save these bankers; it was more important, he said to us, to save the folks. I was proud of him." Roosevelt rejected suggestions to guarantee deposits, and at least listened to arguments to use the Post Office to distribute scrip, should it be required, and to have a liquidating corporation assume control of insolvent banks. There was not yet any suggestion of a federal bank holiday. Roosevelt was known to prefer that all banks operate under the same set of rules — presumably as national banks — and evidently had flexible views about the role of the Federal Reserve Bank. We cannot know when he decided to declare a national holiday, nor what such a holiday was supposed to accomplish. He had instructed William Woodin to do nothing in concert with the Hoover administration and wait until after the inauguration to take any action. Unlike President Hoover, once in the White House, President Roosevelt took command and made a decision.[37]

Hoover's fecklessness in February and March in responding to the unfolding banking and monetary crises was not atypical of presidents before the Roosevelt presidency. President Roosevelt would not have behaved so timidly, waiting for someone else's approval before taking decisive action, even if that action were of dubious legality. Americans have become accustomed to brash presidential initiatives in the teeth of congressional opposition, because that was a style and method brought to the White House by Franklin D. Roosevelt, and practiced beforehand by only the most forceful presidents: (Roosevelt's hero) Andrew Jackson, Abraham Lincoln, Teddy Roosevelt, and Woodrow Wilson. Such methods would have outraged Hoover, and, in fact, did when practiced by Roosevelt as president. Hoover did not approve and, thus, would hardly have acted so during his own tenure. It was in neither his character, nor his philosophy of presidential power, to act brashly and boldly in defiance of Congress and, perhaps, the law. Roosevelt had advised Tugwell, "You'll have to learn that public life takes a lot of sweat, but it doesn't need to worry you. You won't always be right, but you mustn't suffer from being wrong." The real problem may have been that Roosevelt did not worry enough.[38]

On the day after the Detroit banks closed, February 15, an unemployed bricklayer, Giuseppe Zangara, consumed with stomach problems and hatred for the rich and powerful, fired several shots at President-elect Roosevelt as he sat in an open car in a Miami park. He missed Roosevelt but gravely injured several bystanders and Chicago Mayor Anton Cermak, who had approached Roosevelt in his car to say a few words. Raymond Moley, who was present, was astounded at Roosevelt's coolness and absolute control throughout the event and afterward as his car rushed the wounded Cermak to a hospital.[39] Moley later recalled,

> Roosevelt's nerve had held absolutely throughout the evening [while they waited word from the hospital on Cermak's condition]. But the real test in such cases comes afterward, when the crowd, to whom nothing but courage can be shown, are gone. The time for the let down among his intimates was at hand. All of us were prepared, sympathetically, understandingly, for any reaction that might come from Roosevelt now that the tension was over and he was alone among us. For anything, that is, except what happened.

There was nothing, not so much as the twitching of a muscle, the mopping of a brow, or even the hint of a false gaiety— to indicate that it wasn't any other evening in any other place. Roosevelt was simply himself, easy, confident, poised, to all appearances unmoved.[40]

Moley relates that Roosevelt's reaction was similar five days later when he received Hoover's letter of February 28, handed to him by a Secret Service agent while attending an evening of fun and skits at New York's Astor Hotel, telling him — in Moley's words— that,

> the banking crisis was getting out of hand. We had expected that to happen.... The only question in our minds had been how long the credit structure and the human beings on whose confidence it rested could stand the strain.
>
> But the letter from Hoover announcing the breaking point had come somehow made the awful picture take on life for the first time, and nothing I had imagined eased the shock of that reality. I looked up at Roosevelt, expecting, certainly, to see a shadow of the grim news on his face or manner. And there was nothing— nothing but laughter and applause for the play actors, pleasant bantering with those who sat at table with him, and the gay, unhurried autographing of programs for half a hundred fellow guests at the dinner's end.
>
> I thought then, "well, this can't go on. The kickback's got to come when he leaves the crowd. This is just for show. We'll see what happens when he's alone with us."
>
> But when we got back to the 65th Street house — Roosevelt and three or four of us— there was still no sign. The letter from Hoover was passed around and then discussed. Capital was fleeing the country. Hoarding was reaching unbearably high levels. The dollar was wobbling on the foreign exchange as gold poured out. The bony hand of death was stretched out over the banks and insurance companies.
>
> And Roosevelt was, to all appearances, unmoved.
>
> It was not until I left the Roosevelt house at two o'clock that Sunday morning that the curious parallel occurred to me. Here were two sequences of stimulus and reaction — Roosevelt alone with his friends after the attempt on his life and ... after hearing the news that the banking system was mortally stricken. And the response had been alike![41]

Moley then went on to question the effect upon Roosevelt of Hoover blaming the crisis on fear of Roosevelt's possible policies and suggesting a statement by Roosevelt endorsing a conservative response to the economic crisis— similar to Hoover's and that promised by Roosevelt during the 1932 election campaign. He mused that Roosevelt reacted to Hoover's imperiousness more than the news, but Moley later discounted that motive as an explanation for Roosevelt's phlegmatic reaction to both the letter and the assassination attempt.[42]

Roosevelt had a strangely detached reaction to pressing problems: what inspired dread and anxiety in others aroused no concern in Roosevelt. On the train chartered to take Roosevelt and his associates from New York to the inauguration in Washington, D.C., Henry Wallace fretted to Rex Tugwell that considering the national dilemma, Roosevelt's cheerfulness seemed "so preposterous as to approach irresponsibility." Indiana Democratic Representative Louis Ludlow recalled in the summer of 1933, "All of last winter I was worried almost sick because it seemed to me the president elect was drifting, drifting without a program and without taking any steps to prepare one. My lugubriousness almost overwhelmed me one evening last February when Representative Greenwood and I spent an evening in the president-elect's room at the Mayflower Hotel.... There was not even a semblance of a furrow of care on his handsome face. He was jovial, happy, apparently without a worry in the world. My heart was in my boots as we left his presence and I said to Greenwood, gloomily 'I wonder if that man realizes what we are up against.'" Many people who knew Roosevelt commented on his nonchalance and good cheer in the face of danger and crisis. Hiram Johnson of California commented, "The new president is perfectly serene, and entirely confident of his ability, not only to handle all the terrible domestic conditions, but every foreign controversy as well. The Lord gave him a remarkable disposition. I don't think he has any nervous system. If he has, there is no evidence that it disturbs under any circumstances at any time his serenity." Moley became convinced this was no act put on for the benefit of observers: it was who Franklin Roosevelt really was. He did not see danger where others did. He failed to become concerned about issues that greatly troubled everyone else. He really was sanguine and that prevented him from taking seriously weighty problems he really should have considered very cautiously and with deep reflection. He dismissed such trivia with the wave of his hand. And that is how he reacted to the bank crisis of 1933. It failed to arouse his concern. He would confront it when he had to, which was not until the afternoon of March 4. And he knew what he would do: he would close all the banks in America, without a "furrow of care" on his brow, or a drop of sweat forming on his face out of concern for the probable consequences.[43]

CHAPTER NINE

President Roosevelt Takes the Helm

Franklin Delano Roosevelt was sworn in by Chief Justice Charles Evans Hughes on the Capitol steps at noon on March 4, before a crowd of 100,000. Afterward, he gave a brief inaugural address that was probably unique among inaugural speeches for its attacks upon the business class of America. After announcing to the assembled thousands that he was going to speak only "the whole truth, frankly and boldly," and paraphrasing President Hoover, "that the only thing we have to fear is fear itself," he told the people that America was witnessing terrible times because the

rulers of the exchange of mankind's goods have failed through their own stubbornness and their own incompetence, have admitted their failure, and have abdicated. Practices of the unscrupulous money changers stand indicted in the court of public opinion, rejected by the hearts and minds of men.

True they have tried, but their efforts have been cast in the pattern of an outworn tradition. Faced by the failure of credit they have proposed only the lending of more money. Stripped of the lure of profit by which to induce our people to follow their false leadership, they have resorted to exhortations, pleading tearfully for restored confidence. They know only the rules of a generation of self seekers. They have no vision, and where there is no vision, the people perish.

The money changers have fled from their high seats in the temple of our civilization. We may now restore the temple to the ancient truths. The measure of the restoration lies in the extent to which we apply social values more noble than mere monetary profit.... And there must be an end to a conduct in banking and business which too often has given to a sacred trust the likeness of callous and selfish wrong doing. Small wonder that confidence languishes, for it thrives only on honesty, on honor, on the sacredness of obligations, on faithful protection, on unselfish performance; without them it cannot live.[1]

Roosevelt went on to say that we must put people back to work, and recommended sending "those best fitted for the land" back to it. He insisted on the importance of "strict supervision of all banking and credits and investments, so that there will be an end to speculation with other people's money; and there must be provision for an adequate but sound currency." He offered no concrete proposals about what he intended to do. He did say, "I shall ask Congress for broad executive power to wage a war against the emergency, as great as the power that would be given to me if we were in fact invaded by a foreign foe."[2]

This was a peculiar address for a president to give at an inauguration. Just who were the "money changers" and what did he propose to do about them? In a speech devoid of specifics, Americans were left to guess what this meant, just as they had been guessing about Roosevelt's intentions since the previous summer. Were we at war? Against whom? California Republican progressive Hiram Johnson was thrilled by Roosevelt's denunciation of "the money changers." Delaware Republican Senator Hastings commented, "Everyone agrees with what the president said; the weakness of the speech was that he offered no remedy." The Senate's most insistent proponent of inflation by pumping billions of dollars worth of silver into the monetary system, Montana's Burton Wheeler, said he did not know what the president meant by "adequate but sound currency.... What the people want is stable money." *The Boston Globe* announced, "Roosevelt Tells Plans to Meet The Emergency, Proposes 'Adequate But Sound Currency' He would Curb 'High Finance.'" Just what plan the *Globe* found in the inaugural address is hard to say, but they accurately detected Roosevelt's tilt against business. The Republican-friendly *New York Herald Tribune* editorialized: "We think there must be general agreement that the new executive of the nation speaks with courage and confidence, like a true leader, who realizes the difficulties before him and faces them unafraid.... President Roosevelt has started well." The *Chicago Tribune* took note of his call to return people to the land, but also noted he said nothing about inflation, which presumably signified he still did not rule it out. It also noted his attack upon "the exchanges" and, in light of recent revelations, approved of his proposal to put them under "strict supervision." Arthur Krock, the special correspondent for the *New York Times*, much respected, reprinted, and heeded around the country, also noted that Roosevelt's strenuous call to action was devoid of specific recommendations.[3]

The reactions of business leaders to Roosevelt's oration were almost as peculiar as the speech, and offer an important insight into the reaction of businessmen, generally, to looming government. The *St. Louis Post-Dispatch* announced, "Business Leaders Commend Speech of New President." Myron Taylor, president of U.S. Steel, said of the address, "President Roosevelt's inaugural address and its definite promises impress me profoundly. I hasten to re-enlist to fight the depression to the end. American industry and all classes will continue their fullest support of the nation and its chief executive." Walter S. Gifford, president of AT&T, beamed, Roosevelt can "start the country again afresh and overwhelmingly united in its war against the Depression." Frederic Williamson of the cash-strapped New York Central Railroad said, "In my opinion the president's inaugural address is a very strong document. I like it for its brevity and force. I feel that its directness presages immediate and forceful action." Money-changer-in-chief Frank Sisson, president of the ABA and a vice president of Morgan's Guaranty Trust Company, offered, "I regard the message as a very courageous and inspiring appeal to the American people for their cooperation and confidence. It is reassuring in its general expression and particularly in its reference to the need for a sound and adequate currency. His suggestion for a high degree of discipline in American private and public life must win universal approval." Former Commerce Secretary Roy Chapin, back at his desk at Hudson Motors commented, "The new administration has promised affirmative action in this emergency. It is certainly our duty to support every constructive move that it makes." Alfred Cohen, president of the Peoples Bank and Trust Company in Cincinnati, called the speech "a splendid enheartening message." W. Howard Cox, president of the Union Central Life Insurance Company in Cincinnati, said he was "very much impressed ... it was very encouraging." These were strange reactions from men threatened by the president with obscure menace, but not unusual for those without any real defense from overwhelming power. Most businessmen put on a brave face and whistled as they walked quickly past the graveyard that might be beckoning. As business depends on optimism about the future, many looked for the most favorable interpretation of Roosevelt's otherwise threatening speech. Ohio attorney Robert Goldman viewed it clearsightedly; it was "a fighting speech ... I did not agree with everything President Roosevelt said, but it is plain that he means business and proposes to get to action."[4]

Congress met that same afternoon and Vice President Garner handed the House gavel over to the new Speaker, Henry Rainey, and Vice President Charles Curtis gave the Senate's gavel to Garner soon after. New members were sworn in and Roosevelt's cabinet confirmed. The confirmation would have taken only a few minutes of brief formality if not for Senator Couzens's insistent questions about Treasury Secretary–designate William Woodin's business holdings. Had he resigned from his corporate boards? Sold his stock? Did he retain his connections to railroads? Senators from all ranks — progressive Republican Borah, conservative Democrat Glass, and Republican Reed — sprang to his defense, and he was soon confirmed.[5]

Secretary of the Treasury William Woodin had been hard at work since his arrival in Washington, D.C., on Thursday. He had been in almost constant conference with members of the Federal Reserve Board and Hoover's Treasury staff discussing ways to address the crisis. After he took over at Treasury, he asked Ogden Mills and acting Comptroller of the Currency Francis Awalt to stay in Washington and help out in an unofficial capacity to see the country through its banking difficulties. Both agreed to volunteer their services — in stark contrast to Roosevelt's response when asked to help before he assumed the presidency. A great many people drifted into the Treasury Building over the next several days and contributed to the decisions made there, among them Parker Gilbert of J.P. Morgan and Company and various bankers from New York, Chicago, Boston, and Philadelphia. Mills explained to Woodin what steps had been taken already, going over memos and proposed legislation that had been prepared with the assistance of Federal Reserve staff. Mills, Awalt, Undersecretary Arthur Ballantine, Federal Reserve economist Emanuel Goldenweiser, and others met with Woodin to help decide how to proceed. They all agreed that a national bank moratorium would be needed and reopening the banks would be more difficult than closing them. On Saturday, March 4, the staffs of the two administrations met to draw up plans for the closings and reopenings, and met more or less continuously until early Tuesday morning when a definite plan was on paper.[6]

The ad hoc group in the Treasury Building first turned their attention to closing the banks by nationalizing the bank holidays and restrictions already declared in the states. They gave a copy of the executive order prepared for Hoover by Walter Wyatt and Secretary to the Federal Reserve Board Chester Morrill to Woodin, who took it to the White House. The proclamation was worked over by the new attorney general, Homer Cummings; Woodin; and President Roosevelt, and by midnight Sunday had been typed up and was ready for the president's signature. The order signed by Roosevelt explained that the country suffered from "unwarranted withdrawals" and speculative foreign demands upon the nation's gold supply, endangering the bank deposits of all, thus justifying the bank closures. It invoked the Trading with the Enemy Act, without calling it that, and asserted the president's right to close all banks in its name. The proclamation also allowed the secretary of the Treasury to grant exemptions to the closures to allow banks to perform their usual functions, to authorize clearing house associations to issue scrip, and to permit banks to receive new deposits so long as they were neither mingled with old deposits nor invested in any new assets except United States securities.[7]

After the executive order had been communicated to the White House, but before it was issued on Sunday night, the group at Treasury turned their attention to reopening the banks. A plan previously sketched out by Mills, Awalt, and Goldenweiser for President Hoover had, of course, not been used under Hoover, but Awalt resurrected it when meeting with Woodin. Awalt estimated that out of nearly 6,000 national banks, 2,200 were sound and could be reopened as soon as possible. The officials designated such banks "Class A" banks, which should be opened first. "Class B" banks would require some help to stay open. Some banks would require increased capital, and if private sources could not be arranged, they suggested the range of RFC activities should be widened to include buying stock in troubled companies. Thus, as they drew up what would become the Emergency Banking Act, they inserted a section (Title III) allowing the RFC to buy preferred stock in rickety banks. They all agreed some banks would be beyond redemption; these they designated "Class C." For insolvent banks the officials advised a modified "Iowa Plan," which would allow the comptroller of the currency to appoint a conservator who could run the bank, merge it with another, or liquidate it, as the conservator considered most appropriate. This approach was intended to avoid the hardship imposed on so many towns and depositors when insolvent banks were simply shuttered and handed over to receivers for liquidation. Thus, a section was inserted into the bill (Title II) creating federal conservators to assume control of national banks unlicensed to reopen. The officials hoped these changes in national banking law, hashed out in conferences from Sunday through early Wednesday morning, would not only bring the holiday to a happy ending, but also end the bank crisis that had plagued the country since 1930.[8]

Throughout the almost continuous conferences in the Treasury Building, the former Hoover administration officials, Mills, Ballantine, and Awalt, worked from plans previously drawn up for President Hoover. The ideas formalized in the emergency act had been mulled over for considerable time by bankers and government officials in 1932 or early 1933. Awalt had suggested federal conservators take over faltering banks the year before and, aided by Walter Wyatt, had drafted a law to allow it in 1932. When ideas for the RFC were mulled over in early 1932, a New Jersey banker and former congressman, Franklin W. Fort, had urged Hoover that the RFC be allowed to acquire stock in banks as a means to strengthen their capital base. Hoover did not like the idea at the time, but by summer a new crop of bankers, including George Harrison and Owen Young of the Federal Reserve Bank of New York, were boosting the concept and Hoover listened. By 1933 acting Comptroller Awalt and Eugene Meyer had accepted the idea and again urged it upon Hoover, who talked it over seriously with Melvin Traylor. When Traylor accepted it enthusiastically, Hoover asked Walter Wyatt to draft appropriate legislation. However, when the Democrat Traylor broached the plan with Carter Glass, the Virginian, who still championed a liquidation corporation, expressed only antipathy toward it, which meant it would have little chance in Congress. The idea was revived by Awalt and Mills, who had also come around by March, and Wyatt's draft was incorporated into the bill emerging in the Treasury Building.[9]

The new administrators brought to Washington by Roosevelt—Woodin, Raymond Moley, and Columbia University law professor Adolf Berle—were mostly on their own and without a plan. When Moley joined Woodin and the others at the Treasury Building the night before the inauguration, he had no instructions from Roosevelt about what to do. Since his belated appointment as secretary of the Treasury, Woodin had met twice with the president-elect for a few hours at his homes in Hyde Park and Manhattan, and again while riding the train together from New York to the inauguration. Nevertheless, upon arrival in Washington, Woodin had no idea that Roosevelt intended to use the Trading with the Enemy Act to close the banks. He wanted Moley at the Treasury Building because Woodin did not know what Roosevelt wanted and was under the mistaken impression that Moley did. On Friday night they focused most of their attention on talking with the state governors and Federal Reserve bankers of New York and Illinois, trying to persuade them to close the banks. Saturday and early Sunday were taken up with the presidential proclamation closing the banks, and the days following with how to reopen them. As the men at Treasury devised their plans, which took shape as the Emergency Banking Act, Moley and Arthur Ballantine (another classmate of Roosevelt at Harvard) kept in touch with Roosevelt, who considered the proposals as they were formulated and dispatched across the street to the White House.[10]

While deliberating, Woodin, Mills, Awalt, and others discussed plans to issue scrip, but Meyer and Federal Reserve staff vigorously opposed any such proposals. The Federal Reserve, after all, had been created to avoid just such contrivances, and resorting to scrip would have both bypassed the Fed and been an admission of abject failure of the Federal Reserve Bank to fulfill its role. Scrip proposals were trotted out in the states and cities, but were generally discouraged by officials in Washington, D.C. Nevertheless, the president's order authorized the secretary of the Treasury to allow clearing house associations to issue scrip should it prove necessary after March 10. Federal Reserve officials insisted they had sufficient reserves to back new issues of currency, which could be infused into the system through member banks even while the holiday was in effect. Despite assurances of sufficient backing, many involved believed it best to have a contingency plan, just in case gold stocks dropped lower than anticipated. Thus, a section was inserted into the emerging banking bill (Title IV) to broaden the base of assets backing Federal Reserve notes. By the Glass-Steagall Act of February 1932, notes were backed by bankers' acceptances and commercial paper, which were running in rather short supply by March 1933; gold, which had proven fickle by its inclination to flee at the first whiff of danger; and government securities, of which there were plenty and soon to be more. The advisors in Treasury then included a clause into the emerging Emergency Banking Act that allowed the Fed to issue notes based on 100 percent of most assets in its portfolio that qualified as security for loans, and 90 percent of the value of all other assets.[11]

While the staff of the two administrations labored in the Treasury Building, Roosevelt and the White House staff remained mum about their intentions. Roosevelt had told Garner and Rainey he wanted no last-minute banking legislation passed by the outgoing Congress and the new one should await his proposals, which would be coming soon. After a Sunday meeting with financial and business leaders, Secretary Woodin told the press that the government was not contemplating leaving the gold standard. Despite this disavowal, because the new administration was so tight-lipped about what they were contemplating, the press filled in the gap with rumors and speculation. Because Secretary of State Cordell Hull had been included in discussions on how to handle the bank holiday, the *St. Louis Post-Dispatch* reported on Sunday the administration probably was considering some sort of gold embargo, which Woodin quickly denied. When Roosevelt told 25 state governors gathered at the White House on Monday that he would prefer a unified banking system in the United States, with all banks following the same set of national rules, speculation flourished about plans to corral all the banks in the country under the supervision of the comptroller of the currency and into the Federal Reserve System. However, he released no public statement on what his proposals might be to meet the emergency, stoking the rumor mill afresh. The national press speculated about the possibility of a federal guarantee of bank deposits, which many still wrongly assumed Roosevelt favored. Rumors about inflationist plans persisted, as did guesses about leaving the gold standard, or at least an embargo on gold exports. Bookies in London were reported to be entertaining wagers about the United States leaving the gold standard and giving odds of five to one.[12]

The team laboring in the Treasury Building was, indeed, very worried about the flight of gold, and the ability of the dollar to withstand any sudden rush to gold as a hedge against inflation. Most bankers were wed to the gold standard, and separating the dollar from gold would not contribute to reinforcing confidence in the financial system among those responsible for large pools of capital. But many others were convinced that gold somehow lay at the center of the nation's financial headaches. The group in the Treasury Building agreed that the sale of gold to foreigners or Americans had to be banned at least temporarily. Who knew what would happen to the country's gold stock after the holiday ended? If the government could establish a monopoly on gold, the amount in its possession would swell and the monetary shocks delivered by foreign raiding of American supplies would be permanently ended. Thus, as the men crafted the Emergency Banking Act, Title I allowed the secretary of the Treasury to establish a federal monopoly on gold by demanding all private gold holdings — except those allowed by license — be relinquished to the government or Federal Reserve Bank. With government and Fed reserves replenished from private holdings, there would be no shortage of gold available to back circulating notes.[13]

A majority of the advisors meeting in the Treasury Building agreed that some form of deposit guarantee would be necessary. Despite a flood of telegrams and letters to the new president and Democratic congressmen pleading for a temporary federal guarantee, and much public discussion of such a program as the surest way to restore public faith in banking, a deposit guarantee clause was not inserted into the Emergency Banking Act because Democratic leaders knew Roosevelt would not accept it. He said so privately to anyone who talked to him about it and publicly at his first press conference on Wednesday, March 8. Yet, there was wide public approval for just such a step. The Indiana Senate voted to send an urgent memorial to president Roosevelt asking for immediate federal bank deposit guarantees. Four hundred bankers meeting in Lansing sent a memorial to the president pleading for federal guarantee of bank deposits, as did the leaders of eight major farm organizations, including the National Grange. The Queens Clearing House Association and the Long Island Bankers Association urged the same upon New York Representative John J. O'Connor. Influential Seattle banker Andrew Price — no visionary or progressive — advised Senator Glass now was the time to develop a federal guarantee program. Kentucky bankers and railroad union workers beseeched Representative Fred Vinson at a minimum to guarantee deposits.[14]

Even more radical suggestions poured into Carter Glass's office, mostly originating from sober and experienced people. Former Congressman Phillips called for federal banks that would offer guarantees for all deposits and accept mortgages as collateral for federal loans to distressed banks around the country. A former chief bank examiner and 20-year bank vice president from St. Louis urged a national "Iowa Plan." A machine company president from New Orleans suggested the federal government take over all loans in the country and use them to back a new currency. A bank vice president in Virginia urged national bank examiners be given nearly dictatorial powers over the banks they supervised. A bank commissioner in Arkansas suggested now was the time to abolish the two-tier system of banks and force all banks into the national system. He was joined by Thomas Cochran, a partner in J.P. Morgan and Company, who wrote to John Raskob, "If we could get a unified banking system out of this catastrophe it may be that the catastrophe would have paid." Du Pont economist Edmund Lincoln also advised Pierre du Pont the federal government should use the national emergency to impose a unified banking system. When Representative O'Connor gave a speech demanding the federal government take over operation of all banks in the United States he received a flood of congratulatory letters and telegrams. Many Americans seemed ready for radical solutions.[15]

Perhaps most remarkably, the bankers and officials pondering the crisis in the Treasury Building proposed many quite radical proposals to save the banking system. Melvin Traylor was among the most alarmed, seemingly certain that the sky was about to fall unless deposits were guaranteed and all banks assumed into the national bank system. Almost all present presumed the banking system would immediately collapse under assault by depositors demanding instant withdrawal of all their monies. Traylor, perhaps traumatized by what he had seen last June as his First National Bank of Chicago was besieged by nervous customers, led the charge for drastic action and argued that the bank holiday might have to last for 60 or 90 days. George W. Davison of Central Hanover Bank and Trust Company of New York remained calmer yet still agreed that some form of deposit guarantee and short-term scrip would undoubtedly be necessary. Emanuel Goldenweiser pushed for a "gold bullion standard" as used by France and England, before it departed the gold standard entirely in 1931. That standard would allow dollars to be exchanged only for gold bars worth around $8,000 apiece, effectively barring most holders of dollars from demanding gold. He further urged that the government be given the authority to requisition private holdings of gold if it needed to increase its hoard of gold. When Adolph Miller of the Federal Reserve Board was impertinent enough to snap at Davison that the New York Clearing House should have implemented a scrip plan last week, Davison retorted that the Federal Reserve Board should have embargoed gold last week. When all agreed that President Roosevelt should be given a free hand to manage the crisis, only Mills was astute enough to point out that meant giving *themselves* a free hand, as *they* were the staff working out the president's response. This attempt to pass the buck never left the room.[16]

The gentlemen in the Treasury Building reprised scenes already played out all over the United States during the previous week: big bankers and Federal Reserve and government officials with responsibility for overseeing the financial networks pushed hard for government intervention to meet the crisis. Men who possessed the most experience and knowledge to end the crisis demanded drastic action to stop hoarders from draining bank vaults dry. This, of course, presumed "hoarders" were the problem. They imagined mobs of hysterical passbook holders screaming for their money, queuing up at bank doors, and quaked at the thought of what lay ahead when the banks reopened. The mandarins in the Treasury Building were not alone. James Warburg expressed his dire concerns to Raymond Moley about a "secondary reaction" that might wreck state banks when the holiday ended. It is difficult to take their concerns seriously, no matter how sincerely held, because hoarders were not the problem. Correspondent banks and large corporations with multi-state operations fearing *bank holidays* were the problem. When the holidays ended their fears would disappear and so would "the problem."[17]

At 1 A.M. on Monday, President Roosevelt signed Executive Proclamation Number 2039 ordering all banks in the United States closed until Friday morning and embargoing the export or sale of gold.[18]

Holiday Living

Americans started the first week of the New Deal administration just as they had ended the last week of the Hoover administration, without normal banking services. Most Americans had already had at least a little time to get used to the idea of life without banks — at least temporarily — and accepted the news calmly. All over the country people talked quietly about the situation and, exhorted to remain calm by newspapers of all political persuasion, went about their business stoically. Stores opened as usual on Monday morning, but saw few customers. Confusion and embarrassment visited travelers caught in hotels, restaurants, and train stations without cash. Most businesses reacted philosophically and accepted checks or IOUs from regular customers and familiar out-of-towners. The public mood was generally upbeat. People expressed confidence in the new president and believed that he was doing the right thing given the dire circumstances. The *Rocky Mountain News* spoke for many when it editorialized that the "President had no choice." Of course, few people really knew what was going on or recognized that the president actually had many choices, but he chose to close the banks.[19]

Will Rogers, no doubt, reflected the thinking of many Americans — Republicans included — when he submitted this to run on Monday morning:

> America hasn't been so happy in three years as they [*sic*] are today. No money, no banks, no work, no nothing, but they know they got a man in there who is wise to Congress, wise to our big bankers, and wise to our so-called big men. The whole country is with him even if what he does is wrong. They are with him, just so he does something. If he burned down the Capitol we would cheer and say, "Well, we at least got a fire started, anyhow." We have had our years of "don't rock the boat." Go on and sink it if you want to, we just as well be swimming as like we are.[20]

From the start confusion reigned among bankers and state officials about what the new rules allowed. After stating that Post Office savings accounts would be closed along with all the banks that actually held the Post Office's money, Secretary Woodin reversed himself and assured Americans that all Post Office accounts would be accessible during the holiday. Similarly, the public was initially told that trust accounts would be closed like all others, but the next day Woodin told the press that trust accounts and safe-deposit boxes would be accessible. In addition, banks could make money available to groceries, pharmacies, and other concerns necessary for the public well-being. Banks could also accept deposits and make those monies available during the holiday if kept segregated from old deposits. Many state bankers were unsure if the president's order simply extended the state holiday with the same rules, or if new federal rules now governed state banks. When confused Michigan bankers and public asked for clarification, the state bank commissioner assured them banks could operate during the national holiday just as they had during the state holiday: the 5 percent rule still applied. The commissioner also assured the public that trust departments of banks would remain open, as before, and trust accounts remained fully accessible during the renewed holiday. Throughout much of the country, banks used the discretion granted to them by Secretary Woodin to remain open and conduct a limited business. In fact, on Tuesday, March 7, banks were open and operating on a limited basis in 16 states. On Wednesday banks in Oregon, Oklahoma, and the Dakotas were open and doing a limited business. Banks in Wyoming continued to follow the 5 percent rule. The Nebraska bank commissioner allowed all 420 state banks to open and conduct finite business.[21]

Reactions varied from state to state. At closing time on Saturday, most banks in Indiana had elected to restrict withdrawals, but all banks were still open and Governor McNutt saw no reason to order them closed just because the banks in Chicago had closed. However, when the president declared a national moratorium, the governor followed Roosevelt's order to the letter and ordered all Hoosier banks closed for the duration. Even Post Office savings windows were shuttered. Governor George White took a parallel stand in neighboring Ohio, where all banks were ordered shuttered on Monday to honor the federal holiday declared by the president. Ohio banks were allowed to reopen under the 5 percent rule on Tuesday morning. Banks opened and operated on a limited basis in the Carolinas throughout the holiday. When the state holidays expired on Monday in Massachusetts, Illinois, and Kansas, many banks reopened; some allowed customers limited access to their accounts, and others remained closed. When bankers sought direction from state bank authorities in all three states, officials contacted Washington for clarification and were instructed to close the banks, which they did. Banks in Kentucky were advised that the "Thanksgiving" rules applied on Monday; all banks in Louisville remained closed until noon and then opened for limited business for the rest of the day.[22]

On Monday night New York Governor Lehman met with a group of savings bank presidents to discuss the holiday and informed them he would extend the state holiday through Thursday, keeping the savings banks closed. On Tuesday morning he met with commercial bank presidents and agreed that banks should be allowed to conduct limited business to furnish necessary cash to allow businesses to operate. This led to a good deal of confusion about what banks were allowed to do in New York State. On Wednesday, banks in New York City released $10 million to clients who argued it was urgently needed and to employers who needed cash to pay their workers. Both National City Bank and Chase National Bank let the city draw cash to pay its workers, and most banks accepted deposits and made change for stores. New Yorkers seemed to go about their business normally, spending money in stores, which, bankers noted, demonstrated just how much money was already circulating outside of banks before the holiday was declared. So many banks in New York City seemed to be open and operating normally that some bankers beseeched the governor to explain what was going on. Instead of issuing any new clarification, he released an edict calling for all New Yorkers to lend their full support to President Roosevelt and cooperate fully with federal rules.[23]

Similar confusion reigned in California where banks in San Francisco were permitted by state authorities to cash checks, make change, and receive deposits. Some San Francisco banks allowed clients to cash paychecks received since the previous Thursday, but checks drawn on other banks were not accepted for deposit. The same rules did not apply in Los Angeles, for murky reasons, though on Tuesday morning some banks in Southern California opened to receive cash deposits, make change, and carry on other limited activities. When the Los Angeles Clearing House Association sought clarification from state and federal authorities they were told to adhere to Secretary Woodin's guidelines, which remained hazy. When other banks around the country seemed to be operating on a more liberal basis, the Los Angeles bankers announced on Thursday they would allow employers access to $20 for every worker on their payrolls. They also noted that California fruit, nut, and vegetable growers had reported that shipments east continued normally because New York banks permitted wholesale buyers and shippers access to their accounts to conduct business as usual. Everyone was getting paid, so why, Los Angeles businessmen wanted to know, could not business and government in Los Angeles have access to their accounts as usual so they could get back to normal business?[24]

Bankers in Denver were similarly annoyed by the holiday. They had closed reluctantly when ordered to by Governor Ed Johnson on Saturday, and the clearing house association proposed to reopen banks on Wednesday using scrip or even locally minted silver coins. The governor approved the proposal so long as it gained the assent of officials in Washington, D.C., which it did not. The First National Bank of Colorado Springs printed scrip to distribute to depositors, but when they lined up for two blocks to accept it, bank officers had to explain that the Treasury Department refused to authorize its release. For the rest of the week, Colorado bankers besieged their representatives in Congress and Treasury officials with requests for permission to reopen, to no avail. Bankers agreed to remain closed until the Colorado legislature passed emergency bank legislation allowing banks to restrict withdrawals, which the House passed within minutes of its introduction and the Senate passed minutes later without debate. After the governor signed the law on Wednesday, March 8, Colorado bankers wanted to know why they could not reopen on a limited basis. Even before the governor signed the bill, Denver banks operated to the full extent allowed by a liberal interpretation of Secretary Woodin's guidelines.[25]

In fact, confusion reigned among officials in Washington who were supposedly in charge of the situation. No one was sure what the rules were. President Roosevelt and Secretary Woodin wanted trust departments to remain open and operating as usual with complete access to funds held there for clients. But Eugene Meyer vigorously opposed the idea, which delayed its acceptance into regulations by several hours. Roosevelt wanted banks to be able to release money "for relief," but the officials responsible for writing such a rule — Arthur Ballantine and Walter Wyatt — found it so vague they objected that they could not formulate a regulation to allow it. They eventually released Order Number Ten, which effectively permitted banks to release cash at their discretion so long as it was not for the purpose of hoarding.[26]

Faced with confusion and urgent calls from state governors and bank officials, Secretary Woodin issued regulations on Monday, March 6, and again on Tuesday, attempting to define more acutely what banks were allowed to do. The secretary released 13 news releases to clarify the rules governing banks during the emergency. Based on the secretary's advice, the Federal Reserve issued its own circular on Tuesday to member banks. This helped because member banks had more and regular contact with their district Federal Reserve officers and routinely relied on their counsel. Federal Reserve regulations dispersed on Tuesday went far to clear up much of the confusion that had the Chase National Bank opening and closing repeatedly on Tuesday and Wednesday. By Wednesday afternoon — only one day before the holiday was set to expire — the rules were evidently generally understood and followed at least by member banks. State banks that were not members of the Federal Reserve were still free to operate on whatever guidelines state bank supervisors issued. In most cities with clearing house associations, bankers met to discuss the rules, looked to the district Federal Reserve Bank for guidance, and decided locally how to operate. This is what happened in Philadelphia, yet each bank was left to decide who was allowed access to their money and how much. After receiving telegrams from the state superintendent of banking authorizing banks to release 5 percent of accounts and 100 percent of new deposits, the Cincinnati Clearing House Association decided to reopen banks on Tuesday afternoon. Ohio banks reverted to the 5 percent rules for the rest of the week and reported no large crowds or demands for money.[27]

There were undoubtedly banks that had never bothered to follow any holiday guidelines at all. State banks, members of neither the Federal Reserve System nor a clearing house association, were under less pressure to cooperate. Efforts to enforce the rules would necessarily have involved the courts — something no one was eager to do. One such bank belonged to Budget Director Lew Douglas's father in Douglas, Arizona. J.S. Douglas, president of the Douglas National Bank, had refused to close when ordered to by Governor Moeur on March 2, and was not going to close his bank even if ordered to by the president of the United States himself. When the governor heard that Douglas was continuing to operate his bank despite President Roosevelt's edict, he threatened Douglas that he would send the national guard to close it. When Douglas told him, "go ahead," he sent national bank examiner Les Bailey instead, who ordered the bank closed and put a sign on the door saying so. As soon as Bailey left, the head cashier took down the sign and reopened the doors. The bank was closed for only a few minutes. Douglas's other bank, the Bank of Bisbee, also refused to close when Governor Moeur decreed a holiday and continued to operate during the national holiday. J.S. Douglas later moved to Canada and renounced his citizenship to protest the trampling of American traditions by the New Deal administration. His son, Lewis, did not move to Canada, but he resigned the administration in a huff in August 1934 in protest of FDR's fiscal policies and became a forceful and vocal opponent of the New Deal.[28]

Stores, banks, the Federal Reserve, transit companies, and shoppers all displayed nervousness early in the holiday about scarcity of cash. On the first day of the holiday, stores on Chicago's busy State Street refused large bills proffered by customers, because they did not dare part with smaller bills out of fear of running out. Stores in New York City, Richmond, and St. Louis announced they would accept checks from customers with good credit. Many chain stores were bound by rules that forbade them to accept checks or to extend credit, so they had little choice but to continue operating on a cash-only basis. A grocery chain in Michigan refused to give change to customers, but gave back only store scrip, good for future purchases. A 16-year-old boy in Elgin, Illinois, who had saved 17,357 pennies toward his college education was besieged by merchants looking for coins on the first day of the closings when word got out about his treasure. Bus and trolley tokens widely circulated as coins. The *Louisville Courier-Journal* and the *Louisville Times* both announced on Tuesday they would pay their employees on Wednesday with scrip, which would circulate just like cash. The newspapers had cut deals with their advertisers to accept the scrip that the papers in turn would accept from the businesses as payment for future advertisements in the papers.[29]

On Sunday, March 5, the Federal Reserve Bank of Chicago announced it would open on Monday to accept cash deposits and make change. On Monday, after President Roosevelt had decreed the nationwide bank holiday, 34 windows of Chicago's National Bank of the Republic remained open all day dispensing change and paying cash for gold. Once banks announced they would allow companies access to their funds in order to pay workers, as St. Louis banks did on Tuesday, March 7, much anxiety over scarce cash dissipated. Stores such as A&P and Walgreens had initially been anxious about their ability to pay their workers, but were soon so flush with cash they had no difficulty paying them directly from the tills.[30]

In fact plenty of cash remained outside of banks and circulated freely during the holiday. The nation was awash in stories about people leaving IOUs for beleaguered shoeshine boys, waitresses, and taxi drivers, yet stores in New York, Chicago, Los Angeles, Boston, Indianapolis, and St. Louis all reported business back to normal by Tuesday and shoppers with plenty of cash. Stores were initially nervous about making change for large bills because they were afraid they would run out of small bills and change, but no store reported real distress because of lack of change. And by Wednesday, banks all over America were open and freely making change for large bills. Banks in San Francisco were reportedly crowded with storekeepers making deposits and people fetching money for necessities. When a wrestling promoter in New York announced as a publicity stunt his venue would accept goods in lieu of cash for entrance to a match, the *New York Daily News* convinced boxing promoters to announce they, too, would accept goods worth 50 cents for admission to the Golden Gloves fight at Madison Square Garden. But this, too, was just a gimmick. Jimmy Johnston, in charge of the box office retorted, "If they have no dough —cash money — they stay outside. If they got any food, let them lug it home where it belongs.... Say, can you imagine what a guy would look like trying to swap a bucks worth of cabbage for ring-side seats?" This stunt was reported seriously by William Manchester in a magazine article about the bank holiday as late as 1960 and repeated by Raymond Moley in his 1966 memoirs because it made good copy. Tales of barter, of people using eggs and potatoes as cash, of a woman in Indiana who agreed to pay eight chickens for a Victrola, or a barber who cut the hair of a farmer and his four sons in exchange for a two-week supply of eggs and bacon, and the like were picked up by the press and passed around the country. However, whether true or not, they little characterized the national condition during the bank holiday. Perhaps it was true that a millionaire had to borrow a dime from his butler, a baby in Dallas swallowed a family's only dime, business was lousy for bookmakers in St. Louis and bootleggers in Denver, and the Methodist Hospital in Indianapolis accepted cows, hogs, chickens, and even strawberry plants as payment for medical bills. But these things occurred mostly in the first day or two because people, such as Herbert Hoover and Governor Pinchot, were caught unaware and without cash. Most importantly these things occurred and were reported because people were initially nervous about parting with cash when surprised by the holiday.[31]

Almost all problems faced by communities actually occurred in the first few days of the holiday and were provoked by uncertainty rather than dire circumstances. The experience of a Massachusetts lawyer well replicates the nation's dilemma: "When the banks closed a week ago Saturday I had a dollar and a quarter for over the weekend. However with credit we managed to fare very well. As far as I can learn there has been very little real hardship around here."[32] When the holiday in Michigan dragged on, rumors started to circulate that grocery stores were about to run out of food and money to restock. Executives of Kroger and A&P announced they had plenty of food and complete access to their bank accounts: business would carry on as usual. Grocery executives in other cities, such as St. Louis and Louisville, made similar announcements. Wholesale and retail food dealers in Chicago said the city had a ten-day supply, enough to see the city through the holiday, though they expected prices to rise. Processors and dealers could not pay dairies for milk, but agreements were quickly made to pay when the holiday ended. Milk production and supply remained normal in Chicago throughout the holiday. Business continued routinely at Chicago's produce market, where sellers accepted checks from regular customers and agreed to hold them until the holiday ended. Trading continued at the Indianapolis stockyards on a cash basis until dealers arranged credit with buyers and sellers. In Chicago, on the other hand, trading broke down when meatpackers struck deals directly with suppliers, bypassing stockyard dealers, who shut down the market in protest on Monday. Wholesale prices immediately shot up and the market reopened. Dealers, brokers, and farmers came to similar arrangements in Iowa in order to keep the livestock markets open and food flowing. Farmers agreed to accept and hold checks, but murmured that they could not do so for long. Prices for hogs immediately spiked, encouraging further cooperation by farmers. The Louisville stockyards remained open on a cash basis, but many farmers could not pay the railroads cash to bring animals to market, so there was little business. On the other hand, tobacco auctions were suspended in Louisville as were horse auctions in Mount Sterling.[33]

The bank holiday also presented opportunities. Hollywood executives announced that due to the holiday, they could not pay their employees, and movie production would probably shut down in the next few days. However, this was in fact a ploy by the studios to force a 50 percent pay cut on their unionized workers. The ploy worked, the workers accepted the cut, and the studios kept on cranking out movies. However, the West Coast premiere of King Kong was postponed until after the holiday out of fear that it would play to empty seats.[34]

When banks allowed limited withdrawals during the holiday, as already seen in Detroit before March 4, few people actually availed themselves of the opportunity to take money out. In most locales, even before the holiday ended, banks reported heavier than normal deposits, and only light withdrawals. On the first day of the bank holiday in Chicago, withdrawals at the Post Office savings windows outpaced deposits two to one for the first time in its 24-year history. The windows in Chicago's Federal Building normally closed at 1:00 P.M. on Saturday, but on this day the Post Office remained open until 10:00 P.M. to allow people access to their accounts. When Post Office officials became nervous they consulted with Federal Reserve officers, who promised to make available enough cash to meet demands for all $80 million in postal accounts, should it prove necessary. It did not. The Saturday rush was produced by initial jitters and did not recur. Events followed similar courses in Indianapolis, Detroit, and Denver: an initial scurry to the Post Office for cash and money orders was followed by quiet or more deposits than withdrawals.[35]

There proved to be no shortage of money during the holiday. Federal Reserve officers who strenuously opposed any national scrip succeeded in definitely killing such plans by Tuesday, yet in his first press conference on Wednesday, March 8, President Roosevelt maintained the option of issuing scrip was still being considered. By then it was clear that the Fed could make available as much cash as necessary to see the country through the bank holiday. Most of the major clearing house associations and many states and municipalities discussed issuing scrip, but most such plans were abandoned when the Federal Reserve objected. In order for the Federal Reserve Bank to flush the country with an extra $635 million in new notes, the district Federal Reserve Banks had to remain open during the holiday to dole out cash to banks, which then released it into public hands on a case-by-case basis. Thus, Federal Reserve Banks, which had voted to close on March 4, announced on Tuesday they would reopen for business to make money available to all member banks that cooperated with the holiday. Cash would be made available to any bank that could explain and justify its need. The Fed was very busy during the holiday ensuring banks had sufficient cash. Money in circulation expanded to its largest amount in American history to that date: $7.54 billion by Wednesday, March 8. The Fed had pumped an additional $733 million into circulation just since Saturday, March 4. During the holiday the Fed loaned $574 million to member banks; $567 million of that amount had been loaned by Wednesday. In all, the Federal Reserve made an unprecedented $3.66 billion available to member banks during the holiday. And for the first time in its history, the St. Louis branch loaned money to the New York branch. The Fed also released cash directly to companies that had accounts with the bank. When Smith Corona Typewriter Company in Syracuse, New York, complained to the Federal Reserve Bank in New York that the Chase National Bank refused to release funds to pay workers outside of New York City, the Federal Reserve Bank transferred the funds to the Syracuse Trust Company, which then released the payroll.[36]

Federal Reserve banks remained open not just to ensure district member banks were well supplied with cash, they also kept their teller windows open to receive gold and gold certificates from the public. The Fed did not really need to increase its holdings of gold to back the extra notes pumped into the system, but the process of acquiring the gold had been set into motion and now had to play out. Having been mightily spooked by the flight of gold, New York Fed Governor George Harrison had been the most insistent upon including the gold-surrender section in the Emergency Banking Act. In order to scare up as much gold as possible from the public hesitant about parting with their precious caches, the Fed announced on Wednesday they had ordered lists prepared of people who had withdrawn quantities of gold from the Federal Reserve Banks in the past few months and had not yet turned the gold back over to the Fed or other banks. The board assured the press they would be given lists of names to publish of those so unpatriotic as to not relinquish their gold immediately. This tack served its purpose and gold came rushing into banks and the Fed in the next few days: $200 million in gold was turned over to Federal Reserve Banks on Friday alone. One man surrendered over $2 million in gold to the Federal Reserve Bank in St. Louis "as his patriotic duty." An armored car had to be dispatched to fetch the gold, which weighed more than three tons. Fed officials explained that gold pouring in now obviated the need for scrip as Fed vaults contained plenty of gold to back as much money as might be needed. The Federal Reserve Bank of Philadelphia warned that it would assist banks through the holiday by keeping them well stocked with cash only so long as banks cooperated in rounding up gold and gold certificates. Fed Chairman Meyer's 30-day suspension of the requirement for gold backing of Federal Reserve notes was not renewed after the holiday ended, and the threatened lists of gold hoarders never appeared. After all private gold hoards were swept up into federal custody, the Treasury was so loaded down with bullion that it had to build a special repository at Fort Knox to store it all.[37]

Did the United States really remain on the gold standard if dollars could not be exchanged for gold? Although Secretary Woodin insisted the United States had not departed the gold standard, it was hard to see how the country remained committed to the standard if dollars were not convertible. A meeting of New York bankers agreed on Monday the United States was "technically" off the gold standard, at least until Friday. President Roosevelt brought up the gold standard himself at his first press conference on Wednesday, and remained evasive about whether the nation still adhered to it by jesting that "no one knows what the gold standard or gold basis really is." While the president joked about it, some did worry in private about the implications of the government's stance on gold. R.P. Babcock, president of the Long Island Bankers Association, telegraphed New York Representative John J. O'Connor, urging the maintenance of the gold standard. The house economist at DuPont, Edmund Lincoln, wrote a confidential memo to Pierre du Pont warning that the new administration might impose policies that encourage inflation and advising that the gold standard ought not to be violated. But public demands for the retention of the gold standard were hard to find.[38]

That a handful of men huddled inside the Treasury Building should conclude such a revolutionary overthrow of centuries-old thinking and practice should have been not just shocking, but inconceivable. But more shocking yet, was the public reaction when announced: silent compliance. That the general population would either take little notice of this provision or show nodding acceptance is not too surprising. After all, populists had been thundering against the tyranny of gold for decades and had not all European countries renounced gold as recently as 1914 and the majority again since 1931? But after months of conservative fretting over "sound money," where was the hue and cry against not just leaving the gold standard, but over criminalizing the ownership of gold? It certainly did not issue from the *American Bankers Association*, which printed the word "gold" only once in its April *Journal* issue — and that only in passing in a platitudinous article attempting to dismiss any qualms about inflation. After pages devoted to "sound money" and inflation in the March issue of the *ABAJ*, gold appeared not at all in the May issue after it had become moot. Former Republican Representative from Pennsylvania Thomas Phillips surrendered his cache of gold coins without a murmur.[39]

Some of the nation's most important economists were skeptical about the importance of the gold standard, especially as it influenced prices. In a memo prepared for Eugene Meyer, Federal Reserve economist Emanuel Goldenweiser professed himself agnostic about any relation between the gold content of the dollar and commodity prices. Chief economist for the Chase National Bank, Benjamin Anderson, agreed with Goldenweiser and saw no link between the price of gold and commodity prices, but still thought cutting the gold content of the dollar or departing the gold standard entirely bad ideas because gold — like Nicholas Biddle's bank — imposed credit discipline on banks. To fiddle with gold invited overexpansion of credit with mischievous results. The Committee for the Nation, which had been agitating for lower gold content in the dollar since the previous October, fervently believed in such a link and expressed great satisfaction at the president's action, even if it were not so radical as the committee recommended. The National Industrial Conference Board also believed that prices were linked to gold, and applauded the president's move as an important step to raising prices and restoring prosperity.[40]

News that the Fed would freely print new notes and flood the country with another billion dollars was received with glee by much of the population, including merchants, manufacturers, and many bankers. Amadeo Giannini of the Bank of America approved of the increase in the money supply, saying it would boost commodity and securities prices, and restore confidence in banks. When knowledge of the increase became general, people flocked to stores all across the country on a national buying spree even before banks were fully operating. As early as Wednesday, March 8, bankers and businessmen in York, Pennsylvania, reported a pervasive cheerful mood, and stores once again thronged with shoppers after ordinary depositors were allowed access to portions of their accounts. Department stores on State Street in Chicago were packed with shoppers again on Saturday, March 11, and the Loop was crowded with people in a festive mood. Stores in San Francisco also saw large crowds. Lew Hahn, president of the National Dry Goods Association in New York, predicted when the holiday ended a wave of buying would wash over retail stores as not seen since 1929. Others agreed: steel executives predicted a surge in orders, and one plant in Cleveland announced it would start rehiring laid-off men as soon as the holiday ended. Business groups in Ohio echoed that optimism and predicted an immanent turnaround in fortunes. The Indiana Furnishers and Clothing Association likewise issued an upbeat announcement of an impending boom in sales. Officials of the New York Stock Exchange also foresaw a surge in business and eagerly awaited the reopening of the exchanges. Louisville residents interviewed at random on the city's streets all expressed optimism about the near future. All of this rampant optimism preceded President Roosevelt's Sunday-night "fireside chat" of March 12 that supposedly revived America's spirits.[41]

On Sunday, March 5, President Roosevelt issued an executive proclamation summoning Congress to a special session at noon on Thursday, March 9 — the day the bank holiday was set to expire at midnight — "to receive such communication as may be made by the Executive." Roosevelt remained tight-lipped or evasive about what such communication might contain, so rumors continued to abound. The press reported a two-hour cabinet meeting on Tuesday, but had no word on what was discussed or if anything had been decided. Congressional leaders were no better informed, yet promised to act speedily on anything sent to the Hill by the White House. Stories spread that Roosevelt had called for cuts in the budget from $150 to $200 million, but no one knew for sure. Hoover had pocket vetoed the last veterans' appropriation, and papers speculated that Roosevelt would ask Congress to pass it again, or let the veto stand. The contents of the Emergency Banking Act could only be guessed at; nevertheless, stories continued to circulate that Roosevelt wanted a unified banking system. Some Democratic leaders guessed that he would demand immediate passage of the Glass and Steagall bank bills. People still believed he would ask for federal deposit guarantees or for a large boost in the money supply. Others believed Roosevelt would exercise some kind of personal control over all banks for the immediate future.[42]

No one knew what laws the president might ask Congress to pass or what the body might do when it met. The nation had been nervous and jumpy since the attempt on President-elect Roosevelt's life on February 15. The nation's newspapers had been full of stories about Japanese aggression in China, and steady Chinese defeats were reported with dismay. Worse news came when the Reichstag in Berlin burned down on the night of February 27. The just-installed Nazi regime of Adolf Hitler blamed German Communists and started a wholesale purge of Communists and other foes across Germany. Every day brought fresh tales of rampaging stormtroopers and the toll of dead and arrested mounted. Amid this chaos and the gloom of the banking crisis, some Americans called for a dictatorship in the United States. Most people who called for giving Roosevelt "extraordinary powers" spoke of dictatorial powers metaphorically, or at least few really demanded an American Mussolini or Hitler. Speculating on what lay ahead, the *Indianapolis News* suggested a "temporary imbalance of power between the executive and legislature may be necessary to meet the situation." The *Chicago Tribune* reported that Washington was rife with rumors during the inauguration weekend and FDR would resort to "dictatorship if necessary." The editors believed he might assume such powers to implement whatever plan he had to send people back to the land, and reported that leaders of both parties agreed that Roosevelt should be given "dictatorial powers" to reorganize the government to save money and improve efficiency. Walter Lippmann called almost daily for dictatorial powers for Roosevelt to deal with the bank crisis, and his appeal found wide backing from the press. Like other proposals, Lippmann's was consistent with the Constitution, and he never envisioned FDR becoming an American Mussolini. When the Emergency Banking Act passed Congress the *Detroit Free Press* ran a picture of FDR with a crown on his head along with the bold headline, "Roosevelt made Dictator Over All Banks in Nation," which is hard to call an exaggeration given the control he usurped over banks. The paper ran an editorial approving of such bold action and also discussed granting Governor Comstock "dictatorial powers" to take command of Michigan banks as Roosevelt had done with national banks.[43]

Such calls for a form of dictatorship were not limited to newspapers and columnists. They emanated from every corner of America. Will Durant proposed that Congress should give Roosevelt extraordinary powers to meet the bank crisis and defeat the Depression. South Carolina cotton planter and governor of the Richmond Federal Reserve Bank, David Coker, wrote to South Carolina Senator James Byrnes:

> My opinion is that the President should have conferred on him very promptly practically unlimited dictatorial powers so that for the period of the emergency he can control practically the entire business, financial and social structures of the country. The people will support such a measure now, but may not do so if a venal opposition is allowed to consolidate

itself. I believe we should have at once an organization with the powers of the War Indus-tries Board which will dictate production, consumption and, if necessary, prices on all manufactured and farm commodities, and that the quicker such an organization is set up the better. I fear that a large proportion of the banks will not be reopened, except in a lim-ited way, and the financial uneasiness may continue when it is found that deposits in many banks will not be available for some time. Under a dictatorship such a situation can be handled, pending the reorganization of industry and agriculture, so that supply and demand may balance and prices be restored to a point where business can function more normally. It seems to me a publicity bureau headed by David Lawrence or some other well-equipped and patriotic publicist, should be set up at once with branches in each state.[44]

Not everyone joined the chorus. Idaho Senator William Borah, an old Bull Moose pro-gressive, became angry at all the chatter about dictatorship and publicly denounced it as hysteria. Just before his departure from the White House, Hoover warned that the govern-ment must "adhere rigidly to the constitution." Thomas Lamont cautioned Roosevelt against the temptation to "resort to the extra-constitutional expedients which have been resorted to in some parts of continental Europe."[45]

At noon on Thursday, March 9, both houses of Congress met in special session to receive and consider the Emergency Banking Act of 1933. The special message from President Roosevelt asked Congress to pass the act, but a much edited draft of the bill had been rushed to the Government Printing Office only at three o'clock that morning, so copies of the bill were not yet available. To meet the situation House Banking Committee Chair Henry Stea-gall read aloud to House members from the only available copy of the bill, a draft given to him with penciled-in changes and sections crossed out, which his committee had just con-sidered and approved. The visitors' gallery was packed. Eleanor Roosevelt sat in the front with her knitting. Debate was limited to 40 minutes, but before it had elapsed members were shouting "vote! vote!" The bill passed overwhelmingly in a voice vote, or "unani-mously," according to news accounts. The members of the House then marched over to the Senate to watch the debate and vote that took place there.[46]

Proceedings went about as smoothly in the Senate, which had no copy at all of the bill. Senator Glass initially explained the provisions of the bill to the Banking Committee. Although Glass had been personally involved in drafting the bill — and very dubious about its constitutionality and several of its provisions — he had Walter Wyatt dictate a summary of the bill's provisions to his secretary in Glass's Senate office. Glass discussed the bill with the committee until Wyatt rushed in with his summary, when Glass had Wyatt take over the discussion. Huey Long made such a nuisance of himself that eventually Glass refused to give him the floor. Glass and the committee had several different much-edited versions of the bill to work with, but not the version passed by the House. The committee voted the bill to the floor of the Senate without having seen a final copy of it. Senator Glass then repeated his performance for the assembled Senate. After voting in the House, Represen-tative Steagall made his copy available to the Senate for reading and debate. Before the vote was taken, however, freshly printed copies came into the chamber and were distributed to the senators. Huey Long tried to submit an amendment empowering the president to enroll all state banks into the Federal Reserve System so they could reopen at the same time as member banks. Long thundered, national banks "already have loaded the poor state banks down with foreign bonds and German Marks. You have made the word of Charles E. Mitchell as law and now it is only banks like his that you propose to reopen." This was too much for Senator Glass who rose to defend the bill, despite his reservations. Glass, who had always resented state banks that refused to join the Federal Reserve System, was indignant at the idea that the system would be forced to provide its services to banks that had not qualified for them and contributed nothing to make the system work. He ridiculed Long's proposal. In arguing for the bill, he said he, too, found numerous provisions of the bill offensive, especially the one that allowed member banks to present "cats and dogs" at the Fed's discount windows as collateral for loans, and then that collateral could be used to back Federal Reserve notes! That provoked some debate and comment among the senators until Glass explained he was speaking metaphorically and, of course, "cats and dogs" would not be acceptable as collateral. Michigan Senator Vandenberg was deeply disappointed that no provision had been included for emergency guarantees for deposits, and tried to submit an amendment providing for such guarantees. His amendment was voted down; nevertheless, Vandenberg declared that while he normally would never support such a bill, he would under present circumstances and voted for it. Most of the seven senators who voted against the bill were progressives who believed it did not go far enough in immediately overhauling the entire banking system. Only one senator, Porter Dale, Republican from Vermont, voted against the act because it went too far.[47]

President Roosevelt signed the Emergency Banking Act into law one hour and 15 minutes later in the Oval Office full of reporters, flashbulbs popping. Photos showed a wide grin on the president's face, who was laughing because Mrs. Roosevelt's excited terrier, Meggy, would not stop barking. The act demanded that banks reopen only with a license granted by the Treasury, which the staff could not possibly grant by Friday morning. Fed officials estimated they would need until Monday morning, March 13, to review examiners' reports and bank applications in order to issue licenses just for "Class A" banks. Because the bank holiday was set to expire at midnight — only three and a half hours after the act became law — the president signed an executive order at 10:10 — dated Friday, March 10 — extending the moratorium and the embargo on gold exports indefinitely. He did this to allow the plan for reopening banks as outlined in the Emergency Banking Act to operate, whether needed or not. The Federal Reserve Board was more concerned about continuing the embargo on gold, which had been the board's chief concern all along. President Roosevelt had sounded out Governor Meyer about the question on Thursday morning, and Meyer assured the president that continued curbs on gold transactions were still needed.[48]

Banks in many locales around America had announced they were ready to reopen on Friday morning before the president decreed otherwise. The Federal Reserve Bank of Cleveland trumpeted that all banks were ready to reopen and awaiting word from the comptroller of the currency to honor payrolls on Friday morning. Chicago clearing-house bankers informed Fed staff on Wednesday they were all set to reopen on Friday morning and were awaiting word from Secretary Woodin to do so. Bankers in San Francisco, Los Angeles, Orange County, Denver, Kansas City, St. Louis, Indianapolis, Louisville, Cincinnati, Philadelphia, and New York were also just waiting for the telegrams to arrive from Washington, D.C., to reopen on Friday morning. Instead, they received telegrams instructing them to remain closed. Banks in Denver and surrounding counties that remained shuttered on Friday decided to go ahead and release cash for payrolls on Saturday. Denver bankers had been chafing all week to reopen and were "keenly disappointed" when told to remain closed on Friday. Even Joseph E. Olson, the managing director of the Denver branch of the Federal Reserve Bank, thought area banks ought to be allowed to reopen on Friday. The Federal Reserve Bank of San Francisco had already provisioned city banks with millions of dollars to meet payrolls on Friday, so banks went ahead and released cash as planned, making $1 million available to the city to pay its workers, and agreed to cash customers' checks for up to $50. The Los Angeles Clearing House Association likewise voted to make funds available to employers and agreed to cash paychecks up to $15. Banks in Orange County followed their lead. Banks in Cincinnati had arranged to meet city payrolls on Friday and went ahead and released the funds. The Philadelphia and Denver Clearing House Associations were prepared to clear checks again on Friday, and both went back into discussions after they received word of Roosevelt's new order. The New York clearing house Association was already back in business clearing checks for members in anticipation of a Friday-morning opening. When they received word they were not to open, clearing house leaders huddled with their lawyers for two hours late at night exploring their options. They saw little real alternative to cooperating with the president. The Cleveland Federal Reserve Bank had already authorized check clearings in Ohio to begin on Friday, so state clearing house associations went ahead and cleared checks as planned.[49]

On Friday morning bankers in many cities improvised as best they could to meet the unexpected development. The chief bank examiner in Kansas City, Irwin Wright, complained to Denver banker Harry Kountze that confusion reigned in Kansas City and that he got his information about what was going on not from Washington, D.C., but from local newspapers. New York and Chicago bankers judged they would not need scrip and shelved plans to issue it. Most banks in New York were open on a limited basis and making cash available to employers to pay their workers on Friday afternoon. Business appeared to be normal in New York as banks accepted deposits and cashed checks at their discretion. The same was true in Chicago, where Loop banks freely cashed employees' paychecks issued on Friday, as well as in towns throughout Illinois where banks were open and cashing checks. The Philadelphia National Bank had made sure it had enough cash on hand to meet the Pennsylvania Railroad payroll on Friday, and when workers showed up with paychecks on Friday and Saturday, the bank paid out $1 million in cash to honor them. The bank had made the same provision for the city Board of Education, and when teachers queued at tellers' windows all over Philadelphia, banks paid out another $1 million to cash them. Banking appeared to be returning to normal even after the president extended the holiday "indefinitely." On the other hand, cities such as Seattle, Nashville, and Knoxville, which had counted on reopening banks on Friday, decided on Thursday night to go ahead and issue scrip that had just been put aside as unneeded. Banks in those cities opened on Friday morning and freely handed out scrip to those who would accept it instead of cash. Bank employees in Denver handed out leaflets on the sidewalks in front of their closed banks on Friday morning explaining the situation to customers as extra police patrolled the financial district.[50]

Carter Glass fumed when he learned that President Roosevelt had used the Emergency Banking Act to extend the holiday indefinitely. He groused that he had been assured that banks would reopen on Friday morning, and had he known that Roosevelt would not reopen them, he would not have voted for it. But as he usually did, Glass calmed down and came around to endorsing the president's action. The chair of the Senate Banking Committee, Duncan Fletcher, had already announced to the public that banks would begin to reopen on Friday morning and had to retract his words. Other congressmen were similarly caught unaware and very upset by the edict. Both Democratic senators from Colorado, Alva Adams and Edward Costigan — one of the "sons of the wild jackass" who voted against the bill because it was too timid — were unhappy about the extension, but continued to express confidence in the new president. Another "wild jackass," Hiram Johnson, related that the renewed moratorium provoked "an undercurrent of dissatisfaction and resentment in the Congress."[51]

By midweek, before the Emergency Banking Act was passed, confidence was returning to most locales in the United States. On Friday evening the *Santa Ana Register* reported, "Confidence in the banking situation in Santa Ana appeared to have crystallized yesterday and today as a definite move by depositors in opening new demand accounts was noted by bank officials." Crowds lining up at banks and Post Offices in Orange County deposited more money than they withdrew. However, instead of reopening and going back to business as normal — or, in some states, such as Michigan, with some restrictions still in place — banks were told to wait for a license issued by state or Treasury officials, all theoretically blessed by the president and the secretary of the Treasury. Bankers, businessmen, and the public were eager to get back to normal, but instead were instructed to await a government imprimatur to ensure banks were stable enough to reopen. Even a director of the Federal Reserve Bank of Dallas, J.H. Frost, was puzzled and frustrated by the delay. He wrote to Fed Governor Meyer on Friday seeking clarification and urged Meyer to prod Secretary Woodin to open banks on Saturday. Americans were not informed until Sunday night, when President Roosevelt broadcast his first "fireside chat," that the purpose of these inspections was "to restore confidence." No one outside of the Treasury Building, the White House, or several Federal Reserve offices had heard a word about these inspections and accompanying licenses that were supposedly crucial to restoring confidence until word was spread by newspapers on Thursday evening and Friday morning. When people awoke on Friday morning many expected to go to their bank to deposit or cash checks they had been hoarding all week; instead they were told to wait until next week so that confidence in their banks could be restored by a grand charade of "examinations."[52]

Treasury, Federal Reserve, and state bank supervisory staff had the weekend to conduct their examinations, which consisted of reviewing the latest reports on file for every bank in America. Fed Governor George Seay described conditions at the district bank in Richmond as staff and regional bankers scrambled to license banks to reopen: "The auditorium is full, the directors' room has been full, our discount room is full, and the lobby pretty well occupied, and most all office desks have bankers conferring — we are trying our best to avoid physical breakdown of the officers." The Illinois state bank commissioner called in 30 accountants to help his staff pore over state examiners' reports of 600 banks. As in state capitals across America, Indiana State Bank Commissioner Luther Symons and his employees worked throughout the weekend to review reports and applications to reopen. Officials in Missouri were able to review reports of only 450 out of 723 state banks by Monday morning.[53]

Walter Wyatt mused to Arthur Ballantine much later, "What would it have done to public confidence if we had published the formula finally adopted for determining which were sound banks and that were to be permitted to reopen?" Federal Reserve Bank of Philadelphia Governor George Norris knew it would be impossible to review examination reports of 800 banks over the weekend, so he sat down with the president of the Philadelphia National Bank, Joseph Wayne, and the two compiled a list of banks they both believed were sound and passed the list, along with applications for a license to reopen, to the Treasury Department with a recommendation that the banks be granted licenses. Even aided by this shortcut, Norris, Wayne, other Philadelphia bankers, Fed staff, and employees of the Pennsylvania Department of Banking still spent a nerve-wracking weekend in the Federal Reserve Bank reviewing examination reports. Walter Wyatt and other officials at the Federal Reserve had hardly slept all week and were not in prime condition to stay up all weekend reviewing bank examiners' reports. Wyatt had already professed to the board that his staff was "so shot to pieces from over work that he had to have help." The experience was too much for the chief examiner of the Federal Reserve Bank, Ernest Hill, who suffered a nervous break-down and took the next year off to recover. Norris, who had left the bank building for only brief periods over the past week, sought relief from the ordeal in sedatives prescribed by his doctor. Arthur Ballantine was convinced that the week's ordeal pushed William Woodin to an early death in 1934.[54]

It made sense that banks in central reserve cities would have to be open in order for smaller dependent banks to have access to their correspondent accounts. This was the logic behind opening banks in Federal Reserve cities first: they held the most correspondent accounts. However, that should not have precluded banks in non-reserve cities, such as Indianapolis or even Kokomo, from also reopening. The big banks in Chicago, Philadelphia, and New York were ready and willing to serve the smaller banks on Friday morning but were not allowed to. They were not even allowed to on the following Monday morning when reserve-city banks opened their doors. Secretary Woodin, President Roosevelt, and congressmen were barraged by telegrams all weekend from irate state bankers and their political representatives— including Maryland Governor Albert Ritchie, New York Governor Lehman, and Senator Arthur Vandenberg — protesting the cumbersome and discriminatory arrangements. Despite much shouting and finger waving in the Senate on Friday, the anxious and tired men in the Treasury Building had put a process into place and it had to proceed, whether needed or not.[55]

Despite the limitations imposed by Washington, D.C., many banks appeared to be back in business on Friday morning as they opened their tills to allow employers to pay their workers. Perhaps affairs appeared normal in New York and Chicago banks on Friday, but conditions were far from normal in Detroit. All the car companies felt secure enough to announce they would pay their workers fully in cash — over $1 million — but Detroit bankers remained nervous and uncertain about the future. John McKee met with the bankers to explain the rules that allowed banks to reopen. Still, no one knew if any bank in Detroit would reopen on Tuesday and, if so, on what basis. Robert Lord of the Guardian Group remained optimistic that the Guardian National Bank of Commerce would be allowed to reopen on a limited basis, operating on its good assets. Wilson Mills of the First National Bank told the press his bank was applying for a license and hoped to reopen as soon as pos-sible. Both banks held substantial amounts of city and state money in accounts, as well as huge correspondent and Post Office savings accounts, and all wanted access to their funds. But it was not to be. On Sunday night the boards of both banks met and unhappily delivered their banks over to federal conservators who would decide how best to dispose of the crip-pled giants. Most guessed they would be liquidated and replaced by newly chartered banks, which is what eventually happened. When the federal conservators assumed control, their first acts were to fire all the officers of both banks. No bank fully opened in Michigan on Monday. Michigan bankers begged the comptroller of the currency to treat correspondent accounts in Michigan banks as trust accounts and allow other banks access to their funds. He refused and 300 banks in Michigan remained closed because their funds remained frozen in larger banks. One bank in Grand Rapids held $20 million in accounts for smaller banks, all of which remained locked up and frozen after the holiday expired.[56]

Banks in the 12 Federal Reserve cities began to reopen on Monday, March 13. Of course, many banks were never really completely closed, but something approaching normal bank-ing returned to some locales. Authorities withheld licenses to more banks in Chicago and St. Louis than in other Federal Reserve cities: 23 banks remained shuttered in Chicago, as did 11 in St. Louis (holding 10 percent of the city's $336 million in deposits). When banks did reopen on Monday, they were generally mobbed by customers trying to cash checks, make deposits, surrender gold, or open new accounts. Because many businesses had issued paychecks to employees for the first time and more checks were written than ever before, many people stood in long lines to cash or deposit their checks. Despite the rush to cash paychecks, deposits outpaced withdrawals almost everywhere. That was the case in Kansas City, where business resumed calmly on Monday morning, the commodity markets once again functioned normally, and deposits outpaced withdrawals. All the big banks in the Loop reopened, as did 29 smaller Chicago banks, having been given a clean bill of health by state and federal examiners and making available 97 percent of the banking resources of Chicago. Every bank in San Francisco reopened and all were packed with cheerful customers, who also shared their good cheer with local stores. All banks in Boston were permitted to reopen on Monday morning, although access to accounts in savings banks in Boston remained restricted. Customers withdrawing cash from their accounts had to sign "anti-hoarding certificates" testifying they were not taking the money out to hoard it. Despite Treasury rules mandating the certificates nationwide, some Illinois banks required them only for people withdrawing $500 or more.[57]

On Tuesday morning, the turn for member-banks in cities with clearing house associations arrived, and thousands of national and state banks reopened in all 48 states. Banks in non–Federal Reserve cities, such as Indianapolis, Detroit, Los Angeles, and more than 100 major towns, reopened. Indiana Governor McNutt ordered state banks subject to the same 5 percent rule that had governed them when they closed. National banks in Indiana opened fully, but state banks were not allowed to honor checks for more than $10 without a good reason. As the critical condition of banks in Michigan had instigated the national shutdown, it was little surprise that as banks reopened in all other states, most remained closed in Michigan. Only four banks opened in Detroit: three savings banks and the Commonwealth-Commercial State Bank. The open banks were thronged by customers seeking to cash checks, open accounts, deposit money, turn over gold, and transact normal banking business. Only the Commonwealth-Commercial State Bank was fully open allowing unrestricted access to all accounts, and the bank's president announced that deposits outran withdrawals two to one. Banks also reopened on Tuesday in Kalamazoo, Grand Rapids, Battle Creek, and other Michigan towns. In a few banks customers had full access to their money, so long as they signed the affidavit swearing they were not withdrawing money for hoarding. Michigan was hardly alone. Of 1,875 banks in the St. Louis Federal Reserve District, only 52 were fully open on Tuesday.[58]

By Wednesday, restrictions were lifted on all banks licensed by state and federal examiners. "Class B" banks in Indiana were allowed to open on their good assets subject to restrictions. The two remaining banks in Howard County were both fully operational and packed with cheerful customers, who, as elsewhere, generally deposited money rather than withdrew it. Clerks in Kokomo's only bank had to work late registering new accounts and keeping up with the heavy flow of business, but were reportedly happy to do it. Banks in 200 Illinois towns reopened, restoring normal banking services, and the Chicago Stock Exchange and the Board of Trade resumed operations. All 127 credit unions in Illinois were allowed to reopen. By Wednesday, 742 banks in the San Francisco Federal Reserve District were operating, leaving only about 30 banks shuttered. George Norris of the Federal Reserve Bank of Philadelphia repeatedly called the Federal Reserve and Treasury in Washington, urging them to telegraph approval to reopen all the banks that he had recommended were sound. Norris had a stack of telegrams ready to go to bank presidents in Pennsylvania and southern New Jersey, authorizing them to open on Wednesday morning. He promised a carton of cigarettes to his friend John Kiely, permanent secretary to the secretary of the Treasury, if he would send telegrams to open the rest of the banks on his list. Norris impatiently placed calls to the Treasury and waited until 1 A.M., but got no response. When he could raise only a night porter at the Federal Reserve Board, he knew the game was up and decided to go home to bed. One hundred and forty-one banks remained without permission to reopen in his district.[59]

By Thursday, March 16, the federal holiday was over, federal and state bank examiners had licensed a majority of banks to reopen, and the system was inching back to normal. As banks gradually reopened across the country, most locales reported deposits outpaced withdrawals nearly two to one. When all branches of the Bank of America reopened, deposits outran withdrawals by $1.2 million in two days. Amadeo Giannini reported the reopenings had proceeded smoothly and calmly, as was generally the case in California. But all was not well: 1,400 national banks in the entire country — holding $1.94 billion in deposits — and 3,150 state banks had yet to reopen. In all 12 Federal Reserve districts, 1,778 member banks were refused licenses to reopen as of March 17. Of the 141 banks in the Philadelphia Federal Reserve District that did not receive licenses, 36 never did reopen. Only seven national banks were placed into the hands of conservators and six given over to receivers during the holiday, but many more unlicensed banks were to follow in the months ahead. While more than $16 billion in national banks became available to depositors by Wednesday, March 15, a lot of money remained locked up in unlicensed banks. The monies deposited within those shuttered banks — about $4.36 billion — remained frozen and mostly inaccessible until examiners, conservators, or receivers determined the fate of each bank separately.[60]

State banks were reopened according to various state rules. By mid–April state officials had reopened 7,400 banks nationwide, but that still left 3,150 state-regulated banks closed or operating on a restricted basis. Out of 916 banks in New York state, 798 were open and fully operating, including every savings bank. Banking Supervisor Joseph Broderick was pleased to report that only six state-chartered, non-member commercial banks remained unlicensed. In Washington State 105 out of 163 state banks reopened by March 16. After the legislature in Olympia passed the Bank Stabilization Act, providing Washington with an "Iowa Plan," the remaining 58 were allowed to reopen partially on their good assets. Nine banks disappeared through mergers yet lived on as branches of other banks. About 100 banks in the Minneapolis Federal Reserve District did not reopen, but a majority of them were allowed to offer limited services based on their good assets so that small towns on the northern prairies of Montana and the Dakotas would not be entirely bereft of services and access to at least portions of clients' accounts. Only 19 state banks fully reopened in Pennsylvania, where state examiners took the rest of the week to license banks to reopen. The state banking secretary estimated all 981 banks in Pennsylvania would be fully operating by Saturday. Banks in South Carolina did not get off quite so easily. When the federal holiday lapsed, the governor extended the state holiday until Saturday, March 18. Even though the Bank of Hartsville was licensed by the Federal Reserve Bank of Richmond to reopen, state regulators kept it and all other banks operating under restrictions for the rest of the week. State conservators took over 21 of 110 state banks in South Carolina during the holiday. Only six of those 21 banks reopened by the end of the year. Like many states, South Carolina was prodded by the bank holiday to rewrite its banking laws, giving the new office of the Board of Bank Control greater powers to oversee bank management within the state, and requiring for the first time minimum cash reserves for state banks.[61]

The banking holiday was over and President Roosevelt, Congress, and the country turned their attention to other matters. Most immediately, the president wanted Congress to cut the federal budget and they obliged. President Roosevelt had ignored calls for more radical action to take on the troubled banks and had been satisfied with the federalization of the moratorium and the plan to keep the weakest banks shuttered for the time being. He did not want his presidency to start off with a wave of bank runs and failures, so he took the action he believed was required to avoid that. But his immediate aims were very immediate indeed. The Glass and Steagall bank-reform bills languished in committees and were readily available as panaceas, but President Roosevelt was content for the time being with the Emergency Banking Act. President Hoover had dejectedly asked Democratic congressmen if the bills could not be reconciled and rushed through both houses in the last few days of his administration, and was told they could not without a nod from President-elect Roosevelt. The new president could have given the nod once in office and taken credit for overhauling the banks as his first act. He did not. Instead he chose the strange and confusing theatrics of the holiday. The great drama did real damage to the economy in the short run, probably saved few banks, and provided a single thrust to the flywheel of the economy that restarted the engine he had helped to stall. The engine did chug back to life in 1933, but whatever new vigor reanimated American business that summer proved fleeting, and the doldrums returned in the fall.

CHAPTER TEN

Recovery and Reform

Franklin Delano Roosevelt entered the presidency with the audacious and obtrusive federal bank holiday. That hesitant Herbert Hoover was no longer in the White House could not be more obvious. The holiday was only the first of Roosevelt's bold acts that constituted "the first hundred days" of reforms. Encouraged by the swiftness with which Congress obligingly dispatched the Emergency Banking Act, Roosevelt kept Congress in session even though the declared purpose of the emergency session had been fulfilled. He asked Congress to quickly address a number of pressing issues related to the Depression, and a stream of legislation gushed from the White House to Capitol Hill for urgent consideration: budget cuts, farm subsidies, support for farm and home mortgages, federal assumption of relief for the unemployed, development of the Tennessee River Valley, emergency relief employment in reforestation projects, federally sanctioned cartelization of American industry, reform of the securities markets, and thorough bank reform. While this reform legislation was being churned out by the White House and Congress, the economy responded by reigniting. The long slump that had started in 1929 and steepened frighteningly in the summer of 1931 had at last hit bottom and the economy rebounded. The long deflation had stopped and prices, especially of commodities, started to mount. While the cause of this "reinflation," as Roosevelt called rising prices, was almost certainly linked to the devaluation of the dollar, the longer term rise in prices and its impact on the economy is harder to pin down. That the economy began a long and slow recovery is indisputable, but whether the stream of reform legislation played any part in fostering it is less certain.[1]

On Sunday, March 12, President Roosevelt broadcast the first of his "fireside chats" over national radio. Roosevelt had finally decided that a few words from the president about the soundness of banks would restore the confidence of depositors sufficiently to save the banking system. Raymond Moley wrote of the first "fireside chat," "The response to this appeal has been common knowledge in the generation since." Arthur Schlesinger called his radio address "the climax of a week of resurgent hope." Historians since have echoed Moley's claim that this speech restored confidence among panicky Americans and thus saved the banking system. Roosevelt had insisted to Hoover and others in February and March that a few words from him about the banking crisis would make no difference. How strange that when he could have made a difference he said nothing. When it was all over and confidence was already on the rebound throughout the nation, Roosevelt is credited with saving everything by his speech. History is indeed odd.[2]

The Sunday night chat was devoted, not surprisingly, to the bank crisis and the process of reopening banks, to start the following morning, and intended to reassure the public that all was well. He said,

What happened then during the last few days in February and the first few days of March? Because of undermined confidence on the part of the public there was a general rush by a large portion of our population to turn bank deposits into currency or gold. A rush so great the soundest banks could not get enough currency to meet the demand. The reason for this was that on the spur of the moment it was impossible to sell perfectly sound assets of a bank and convert them into cash except at panic prices far below their real value. By the afternoon of March 3 [sic] barely a bank was open in the country to do business. Proclamations closing them in whole or in part had been issued by governors in almost all the states. It was then that I issued the proclamation providing for the nation wide bank holiday. And this was the first step in the government's reconstruction of the nation's financial and economic fabric.

Near the end of his talk he said Americans felt insecure about their banks because "dishonest or incompetent" bankers had been allowed to speculate with other peoples' money again, undermining confidence in "the vast majority of our banks" run by ethical businessmen. This presented a plausible explanation for the collapse of hundreds of small banks and perhaps even a few of the large commercial banks that failed to survive the onslaught of runs that hit them after the summer of 1930. However, the wave of holidays declared by governors was not provoked by public loss of confidence in banks; it was unleashed by corporations and correspondent banks withdrawing funds in anticipation of further government-mandated holidays.[3]

President Roosevelt certainly had a lot of company who also believed that hoarding and bank runs caused the banking crisis. Fears that businesses and correspondent banks would drain the big Detroit banks once their condition became known were certainly justified. Governor Ritchie's response to the money draining from banks in Baltimore was probably also reasonable. We do not know what Governor Rolph knew about the weak condition of the Bank of America that may have prodded him to declare the holiday in California. Perhaps he knew enough to frighten him into closing banks in California, which started a contagion of holidays across the West. However, except perhaps for Maryland — which is not really clear either — none of this was provoked by hoarders; all of it was prompted by fears about the reaction of correspondent banks and large corporate depositors. Nevertheless, the fears of small depositors frequently ended up in official explanations for state holidays. The big banks in New York and Chicago ultimately jumped on the bandwagon, not out of fear of money fleeing to the interior of the country, but from fear of gold flowing overseas. After a drumbeat of stories in newspapers vilifying "hoarders," congressmen were besieged by urgent demands for "anti-hoarding" legislation to criminalize hoarding and to punish transgressors with heavy fines or jail time. The only voice against this storm that I found was Pierre du Pont's, and he argued against it only in private letters.[4]

No doubt a lot of cash left banks in the last week of February and the first few days of March 1933. If the auto companies in Detroit had $1 million in cash on hand to pay their workers on Friday, March 10, that money had to have come from somewhere. Brown and Williamson Tobacco was one of many companies that had cash on hand to pay its 3,000 workers in Kentucky. We have seen how employers dispatched trusted agents to Cleveland, New York, and Chicago to fetch suitcases of currency in order to pay workers during the Michigan holiday. With workers being paid in cash all over the United States on March 10, a lot of money was obviously not in bank vaults. During February, and no doubt mostly during the last week, demand deposits of member banks fell by more than $1.3 billion. Time deposits shrank by $360 million. Banks scraped together this cash partly by selling or discounting commercial paper and other investments to Federal Reserve Banks. Many banks, especially in the larger cities, had made lots of cash available to companies specifically to pay their employees, as allowed by Secretary Woodin's instructions. As already noted, large sums of money fled banks in the first few days of March, not because employers feared bank failures, but because they feared bank closures by nervous governors. In New Jersey those fears had spread to the average citizenry, who had good reason to worry the governor might close the banks. If these large withdrawals constituted "hoarding," then there was a good deal of hoarding occurring just before the inauguration, but it is an irregular use of the word. And this "hoarding" failed to mirror events described by President Roosevelt in his fireside chat.[5]

Many banks had been pushed to the edge of the precipice in late 1932 and early 1933 by a number of hostile forces working against their interests that mostly sprouted from the same root: uncertainty about the future. Businesses reduced loans out of fears of future demand and prices; hoarders kept money out of banks from fear of future bank failures. Banks authorized loans reluctantly out of fear of future insolvency by debtors, and banks sold assets by dumping them on unwilling markets in order to face the uncertain future with the greatest possible liquidity. Businesses hoarded cash in safes to have it available in case of bank failures, producing the "slow run" that so many bankers complained was killing banks. Deflation worsened as banks dumped an ever mounting supply of assets onto markets with slack demand: prices for securities and mortgages fell month after month, and the value of assets still on the books either fell or slid into that fearful category, "doubtful," that is, of unknown value. Doubtful loans made skeptical bank examiners even more suspicious about the health of fragile banks. So long as prices for goods fell, assets of banks continued to diminish, pushing many to the edge of solvency.

Bankers who released credit only slowly were not paranoid, for loans and securities owned by banks continued to go sour in 1933. National banks wrote off $231.4 million in bad loans between June 1932 and June 1933, bringing the total for national banks alone between the summers of 1929 and 1933 to $781.6 million (see Table 11.3, p. 229). It is perhaps surprising that given the horrendous economic conditions, write-offs accounted for only 11.7 percent of the reduction of national-bank loans from 1929 to 1933. Compounding banks' difficulties, between June 1929 and June 1933, 16 percent of non–United States government bonds held by national banks had defaulted. From June 1929 to June 1933, national banks wrote off another $619 million in worthless securities for a total write-off of $1.4 billion in securities and loans since June 1929. Losses for state-chartered institutions have never been calculated, but when estimated, the losses to the country's banks through default on loans and securities from June 1929 to June 1933 mounted to $3.7 billion. That is, bank investments held in June 1929 had dropped by around 7.8 percent because of defaults. The decline in bank investments due to the drying up of credit was much larger: 23.7 percent. As bad as defaults were, the retreat of credit caused by both hesitancy on the part of bankers to lend and slack demand by business was worse.[6]

Did the holiday break the fearsome downward cycle for banks, prices, and the economy? There is no way to know for sure, but it probably helped. The *Commercial and Financial Chronicle* and many newspapers noted the renewed optimism and enthusiasm that gripped the country as banks reopened. While shopping had decidedly picked up on the Friday and Saturday before banks reopened, stores all over the country were mobbed with customers on Monday and Tuesday. Atlanta, Denver, Dallas, and San Francisco all reported department stores and retail districts swarming with shoppers flush with cash. Sears noted a sharp increase in the number of people applying for credit accounts. Furniture stores in California also reported renewed interest in installment buying. The Louisville Retail Merchants' Association claimed on Monday — before any banks reopened in Kentucky — that the retail sales outlook was the best it had been in three years, and the Louisville Automobile Dealers' Association beamed, "An increase in business is inevitable." Newspapers nationwide reported stores buying double the normal space for advertisements. Advertising in general was up in newspapers all over the country. Audiences flowed back into movie theaters. The whole country seemed to have regained confidence even before the banks reopened, but it remained to be seen how long it would last.[7]

This gush of optimism did not spring from Roosevelt's fireside chat, which undoubtedly reinforced the trend, but built upon an earlier swell of renewed confidence that had been mounting slowly in anticipation of the new administration. Even though no one knew what the new president and his colleagues would do, Americans generally expected conditions to improve with a fresh face and a new approach in the White House. A railroad freight agent in Iowa in touch with large numbers of businessmen reported just before the inauguration that most people he talked to expected the economy to improve in the fall. Some thought it might take a turn for the better that spring. An Iowa insurance agent also familiar with the opinions of large numbers of businessmen said that people believed Roosevelt would clean up the war-debts mess and then East Coast capitalists would once again begin investing. Despite the eruption of violence among farmers, Iowa farmers generally believed that prices would rise and conditions improve in 1933. Similar sentiments were reportedly widespread in Colorado, where opinion leaders in business and politics looked forward to Roosevelt's inauguration with renewed confidence in the future. Reports from Los Angeles just before the inauguration echoed this outlook despite the bank holiday just imposed by Governor Rolph. After the inauguration, reports of renewed confidence in the future continued to be broadcast in the press, both before and after FDR's declaration of a national bank holiday. Roosevelt's fireside chat reflected the spirit that was already widespread across the country, boosting optimism that was already growing and had been for some time.[8]

Despite this renewed buoyancy, the impact of the bank closings on business had in fact been calamitous. So many banks were already closed or operating at a reduced level that check clearing the week before the inauguration dwindled to paltry levels.[9] Business nearly ground to a halt because banks failed to provide the exchange and financing services upon which business depended. Banks offer credit, and while Chase National and big banks in the Loop may have cashed paychecks during the holiday, they did not act as credit intermediaries for business. New York banks kept fruits and vegetables flowing from California to the rest of the country, but otherwise credit operations necessary to the conduct of business and government were dead. Business was on hold in the entire nation while the banks were closed. Spurgeon Bell of the Bureau of Research at Ohio State University had warned Ohio Senator Robert Bulkley that the bank closings invading Ohio from Michigan in late February were having a catastrophic economic impact on Ohio. "The process now adopted of freezing bank deposits is highly destructive ... [and pushing] the depression to still further depths." At the end of February, refurbishing work had stopped at a clothing plant in Kokomo, Indiana, recently acquired by the Reliant Corporation that planned to expand its operations. It had ordered new sewing machines and could not install them until the building was ready to receive them. Workers preparing the building were willing to keep working and accept promises of payment in the near future if the company could not pay them immediately because of the bank holiday. But the company could not pay for materials or transporting them, so the workers had no work. And with a March 15 opening date, it could not be sure to pay the 200 new workers it expected to hire. Everything was on hold for the duration of the state-mandated holiday. When the federal holiday kicked in, the freeze only deepened.[10]

Kokomo was not unique. A banker in Herington, Kansas, telegraphed Carter Glass, "all business at standstill [stop] public confidence gone [stop]." Conditions remained uncertain so long as thousands of "Class C" banks remained closed. James Rand of Remington-Rand wrote to Rex Tugwell, "I have nothing but praise for the leadership of the President and I merely suggest that perhaps the Secretary of the Treasury has overlooked the negative effect of the drastic shrinkage in the deposit circulating medium heretofore used in the transaction of 90 percent of the business in this country. Several large industrials [*sic*] who have placed sizable orders in the expectation of expansion of credit and currency, have recently canceled all orders and are now planning to shut down completely." He went on to argue that closed "Class C" banks contained $10 billion and that removing that much money from usage would cause a "catastrophic" contraction of the money supply and "violent deflation" that would push the country only deeper into depression. The enthusiastically pro–Roosevelt publisher of the *Philadelphia Record*, J. David Stern, echoed the argument that by keeping "Class C" banks closed and freezing their deposits: "You [FDR] have out–Hoovered Hoover in accelerating deflation and bringing on a complete economic collapse." Henry Harriman of the U.S. Chamber of Commerce came to the same conclusion. The trade magazine *Steel* reported, "With bank holidays and restrictions tending to paralyze trade, steel demand was approaching a stand still last week."[11]

In fact pig-iron production dipped during the holiday due to the inability of small furnaces to finance purchases of basic materials, iron and coal. Auto manufacturing provided practically the only demand that kept steel mills open and producing in February, even on a paltry level, and auto sales plummeted during the holiday. Buick announced on March 10 it would shut down its plant in Flint for want of demand. Chevrolet stopped shipments of new cars because lots were full and closed some plants until demand picked up again. There may have been as many as 350,000 unemployed in Detroit alone in March. The shutdown of auto production rumbled through the entire economy of the Midwest. Lack of orders closed both steel and auto plants in March; no new orders for steel were received during the holiday. Prior orders kept the industry limping along at 15 percent of capacity. Normally, orders received by steel plants picked up in February and March and kept mills rolling in the summer. Those orders failed to arrive in 1933. When the banks in Cleveland and Akron closed, so did the tire plants in northern Ohio, for want of rubber. When the big tire plants shutdown operations so did scores of smaller businesses that served them. The Federal Reserve Board's own assessment of March was dire: "The course of business in the latter part of February and the first half of March was influenced by the development of a crisis in banking, culminating in the proclamation of March 6 of a national banking holiday by the President of the United States." Factory output remained unchanged from January to February and declined considerably in March, when in past years it rose. Building construction orders for the first quarter of 1933 were down from the last quarter of 1932. Railroad traffic, which normally increased in February and March, slowed considerably in March 1933 from an already low level in February. The Pennsylvania Railroad handled 10,000 fewer freight cars that week than during the same week the year before. Nationwide, freight-car loads dropped a full 10 percent during the week of the bank holiday, and cars full of merchandise and commodities stood motionless and unloaded in rail yards because shippers could not pay to have the goods delivered.[12]

Federal Reserve economists reported in districts, as they did in Boston, "During March the general business activity in New England reflected the financial situation which existed throughout the country, and there was a decrease of the rate of activity from the levels of January and February." Thirty thousand jewelry workers in Massachusetts found themselves without access to gold and unable to fabricate jewelry. Much business had been slowed or stopped since the year before waiting to see what the near future held. Orders for manufactured goods that had perked up some in January and February were canceled in March. Coal production had increased considerably in January and February, when normally it declined, until the last week of February and the bank holiday when mining was sharply cut back. And while business waited in late February and early March, the economy slid to its lowest performance of the Depression. March 1933 marks the low point of the Depression, after which things got only better. During the week before the inauguration almost no new loans were approved by banks, which dumped $434 million in assets in order to raise cash. The bank holiday aggravated an already bad situation, prompting the layoff of still more workers, as employers of all kinds — even public — laid off yet more employees. Joblessness reached a new record: 12.7 million men and women without work. Already low prices for finished goods fell even lower as wholesale purchasing almost completely stopped.[13]

Money frozen in unlicensed banks held back business for months in communities across the United States. By mid–April, 12,817 banks containing $31 billion in deposits were granted licenses by the Treasury Department to reopen, but that still left 4,194 banks containing $3.98 billion unlicensed and shuttered. Deposits in those banks remained largely frozen and unavailable to depositors. This severely hampered the ability of businesses, customers, and farmers to carry on and contribute to economic recovery. From the Armstrong Cork Company in Lancaster, Pennsylvania, the Kalamazoo Vegetable Parchment Company, and the McGill Manufacturing Company in Valparaiso, Indiana, to the Omaha Flour Mills Company in Nebraska, businesses tried to carry on at a minimal level without access to their bank accounts. Small companies in small towns in particular found it very difficult to pay their bills and to collect payments from customers. An appliance manufacturer in Philadelphia reported it had full access to its bank, but that was not true of its distributors throughout Pennsylvania, who resorted to paying for machines with cash — if they could get it. In South Bend, Indiana, home to Studebaker and Bendix Radio, banks with only $6 million in deposits remained licensed, open, and operating in July 1933. In October 1932 South Bend banks contained deposits of $14.6 million.[14]

Many bankers and businessmen complained bitterly as the economy improved in the summer of 1933 that they could not benefit because their banks remained unlicensed and accounts frozen. Bankers argued that bank examiners had changed their criteria for evaluating bonds: bonds that had been accepted at face value in 1932 were depreciated in the summer of 1933 by examiners who had adopted the standard used by the RFC to evaluate loan collateral. Federal conservators called in good loans made by unlicensed banks, placing great hardships on otherwise sound businesses. A rubber plant and a steel-rope factory in Williamsport, Pennsylvania, were forced to close because they could not renew loans at unlicensed banks. By fall, the Roosevelt administration decided that deposits languishing in unlicensed banks were a drag on the recovery so it authorized a Deposit Liquidation Board to be administered by the RFC. Late in 1933, the board began to disburse loans to closed banks, but by then the economy was already sliding back into depression.[15]

The economic life of the country during the bank holiday replicated the national experience of the Great Depression, only to a more extreme degree. Consumers continued to shop and spend on small items—while perhaps skimping on restaurant meals, taxis, shoeshines, and other easily postponed services—but put off big purchases. During the Depression decade they put off large purchases, such as cars and houses, while continuing to buy hats and shoes. During the holiday, businesses operated on a constricted level; workers with jobs continued to report to work and carry on to some degree. During the Depression—as during the holiday—businesses postponed big expenditures and investment was put off for the future. In the 1930s power companies built few generators; phone companies hung little wire; railroads did not replace old locomotives, bridges, or track. While continuing to spin yarn for blankets and sweaters, spinning mills bought little new machinery. This was the Depression: people kept shopping at a reduced level, while business investment ground to a halt.

The bank holiday was a disaster that has lived on as a great victory—a financial Dunkirk—in American memory. It was portrayed at the time as a grand success by the press and public, used to putting the best face on a bad situation. Instead of criticizing the new president, which would have done no good at all, Herbert Hoover urged all Americans to lend him their "whole-hearted support." No one that I have been able to find criticized the federal holiday as a bad idea. Americans from the Essex County, New Jersey, Bar Association to the Hour of Pleasure Federated Colored Club of Sioux City telegraphed the new president their hearty congratulations on his bank policy. In Philadelphia, Paul Thompson of the Corn Exchange National Bank, Walter Hardt of the Integrity Trust Company, and Howard Loeb of the Tradesmen National Bank and Trust Company all praised President Roosevelt and his bold action. Thompson told the press, "We need a boss ... and I hope Congress gives Mr. Roosevelt all the power he asks." That sentiment was echoed by Loeb. Melvin Traylor and Amadeo Giannini joined the chorus, and the very personification of international banking, James Warburg, praised Roosevelt's handling of the bank crisis even in retrospect after he became a leading critic of President Roosevelt. Even John D. Rockefeller, Sr., said during the holiday it was the duty of every American, whether Democrat or Republican, to stand by the president; he was certain the banking system was sound and everything would turn out alright when the holiday ended. Cyril James, professor of finance at the University of Pennsylvania, praised FDR's actions in the crisis as "statesmanlike." Only Indiana Republican Senator Arthur Robinson called the Emergency Banking Act, ill-considered and "half-baked." Senator Glass and the *Indianapolis News* questioned its constitutionality but supported its intent. Regardless of the nearly universal support the holiday received in its day, it was a rash act ineptly carried out.[16]

People accepted President Roosevelt's proclamation because they believed its purpose was to allow Congress enough time to pass bank legislation that would in some way address the larger bank crisis; just as state governors across the country closed banks or restricted access to them in order to allow state legislatures time to pass laws to fix the problem—whatever it was. So the American people expected the president to ask for dramatic and fundamental changes in the nation's banking laws, such as a federal guarantee of deposits or the imposition of a unified banking system under the Federal Reserve Bank. They got nothing of the kind. At his Wednesday press conference, President Roosevelt told reporters Congress did not have enough time to consider real reform in just a few days, so they would be asked to pass a bill to allow the president to handle the crisis until comprehensive reform could be considered. Of course, real reform had been awaiting action in both houses of Congress for more than half a year: the Glass bank-reform bill and the Steagall bill both promised real reform and awaited action. Carter Glass's bill had finally passed the Senate in January and awaited action in the House. The Steagall bill promised federal guarantee of bank deposits, and Majority Leader Henry Rainey and Representative Steagall both assured the press a federal guarantee could be enacted right away. President Hoover had anxiously inquired of congressmen about any prospects of action on the bills as the banking crisis mounted in February and March, only to be told that nothing could happen without the support of the president-elect. With the president-elect inaugurated, what was preventing a vote? Both stalled bills eventually would be reconciled and passed in June as the Glass-Steagall Act of 1933, but in March President Roosevelt had not yet made up his mind that he supported the reforms in the bills. As late as March 3, President-elect Roosevelt answered Speaker Garner, who was trying to persuade him to publicly support federal deposit guarantees, "It won't work Jack. The weak banks will pull down the strong." Garner retorted that FDR would have to back it sooner or later, which is not only what happened, but Roosevelt took full credit for the program once enacted. Wanting to see some sweeping bank legislation come out of Congress, President Roosevelt finally embraced the Glass-Steagall Act of 1933 that set the fundamental laws governing banking in the United States until undone by yet more bank reforms after 1976. FDR has been accorded full credit for the Glass-Steagall Act, which he accepted hesitantly and without enthusiasm.[17]

Instead, in March America got the Emergency Banking Act that legalized retroactively what the president had already done, which he claimed was already legal by virtue of the Trading with the Enemy Act. It provided a cumbersome, time-consuming, and unnecessary process for reopening banks after a charade of inspections. It also allowed the RFC to buy stock in banks, which Jesse Jones claimed, "prevented the failure of our whole credit system." Eventually, the RFC bought $1.17 billion in preferred stock in 6,104 American banks, but he admitted banks were so reluctant to sell stock to the RFC—giving it a say in their affairs—that many bankers had to be browbeaten into accepting the RFC as a partner. The contribution of the RFC to strengthening the capital of many thousands of banks no doubt saved some and helped many more. Thomas Lamont had recommended to President-elect Roosevelt that the RFC simply deposit funds in troubled banks, relieving the banks of the burden of finding good collateral for RFC loans. Banks' best assets could then be used for other purposes to further strengthen banks. With deposits buttressed by the RFC, banks would not be forced to sell assets on depressed markets. Lamont's suggestion was ignored (and so was Lamont until his advice was needed in 1939 when a different sort of crisis loomed).[18]

Title One of the Emergency Banking Act that established a federal monopoly on the holding of gold achieved an important goal in the long run: it allowed the Treasury (really, President Roosevelt) to manipulate the value of the dollar without fear of domestic raids on Federal Reserve gold stocks. Raids by foreign holders of dollars remained a different problem. Nevertheless, the administration had the tools available to alter the value of the dollar, and thus to push up prices—which is what it did, ending the devastating deflation of 1929-33. In the short run, all the president really needed to do, however, was close the gold-trading window of the New York Federal Reserve Bank, which the holiday managed to do.

Efforts to open the Federal Reserve's discount window to non-members were again pressed after the end of the holiday. Joseph Robinson introduced a bill on March 13 that would allow all banks to borrow from the Fed on the same terms. Carter Glass, as usual, led the opposition to this proposal, but congressional disappointment in the feckless operations of the Federal Reserve had grown and a majority no longer looked upon the Fed with the same reverence as Senator Glass. After some tinkering by the Banking and Currency

Committee to meet some of the Fed's objections, the bill was passed the following week. Representative Steagall shepherded a similar bill through the House, which passed after perfunctory debate. The version signed by the president on March 24 gave Federal Reserve district banks a good deal of discretion in granting loans to non-member banks. In fact, the district banks proved reluctant to authorize discounts to non-member banks: by November they had loaned only $560,000 under the program.[19]

Before the banks reopened, Roosevelt asked Congress to slash the federal budget by $500 million. The National Economy Act cut veterans' benefits and reduced federal salaries, including those of post-office workers, by 15 percent. The president believed the economy measures were good for the country, but he was aware that reducing government outlays would also reduce the amount of money in circulation with a deflationary result. He wanted to counter such deflationary programs with some inflationary counterprograms, a position he made explicit in his press conference of April 7. Members of the Roosevelt administration largely agreed that some inflation would be a good thing, but if it got out of hand it would create chaos, so they proceeded cautiously. Commerce Secretary Daniel Roper was sympathetic to the arguments of Cornell economist George Warren and his supporters in the Committee for the Nation who argued for deliberate inflation. So was Henry Morganthau, Jr., who was a friend to both Warren and Roosevelt, and who FDR installed as head of the Farm Credit Administration. Other influential economists and financial leaders, such as Frank Vanderlip, Irving Fisher, and Thomas Lamont, also urged the administration to promote inflation. While most within FDR's inner circle agreed that restoring 1926 prices would be helpful to righting the economy, they disagreed about how to do it.[20]

Some on Wall Street believed that reducing the gold content of the dollar, as advocated by the Committee for the Nation, would indeed push prices higher. Russell Leffingwell convinced Walter Lippmann to write a column urging just that, which Lippmann not only did, he let Leffingwell edit it before running it in 115 American newspapers. The day after Lippmann's column urging the devaluation of the dollar, President Roosevelt issued an executive order demanding all private hoards of gold be handed over to the Treasury. Two weeks later he issued Executive Order 6111 embargoing the export of gold except by permission of the Treasury. The United States was effectively off the gold standard, and the value of the dollar in foreign markets immediately started to slip. By year's end it had lost 35 percent of its value. This devaluation of the dollar was codified by the Gold Exchange Act of 1934, which once again made the dollar convertible into gold, but only for export. Instead of receiving 25.8 grams of gold per dollar, after January 1934 foreign holders of dollars who demanded gold — meaning foreign central banks— received only 15.24 grams. This had no dramatic impact on exports, which grew slowly until they had almost recovered to pre-crash levels in 1940.[21]

Carter Glass was mortified by the president's move to set aside the gold standard and inflate the value of the dollar. However, he should not have been very surprised. He made a vigorous defense of "the sound dollar" in the Senate, but he was now in a lonely minority of congressmen devoted to the gold standard. The experiences of the last several months had shaken the faith of many in the sanctity of "sound money." Many Americans had come to believe that money left to shift for itself was likely to falter and to ill serve the country.[22]

The purpose of cutting the gold content of the dollar was overtly inflationary, yet some economists at the time doubted it would have any effect upon prices. Indeed, commodity prices began to rise before the dollar was devalued and even while the bank holiday was still in place. As people's fears of shortages became acute during the moratorium, prices began to rise. Inflation had begun while banks and most exchanges were closed, and the prices of securities and commodities for future delivery remained unknown. Cash sales of commodities for immediate delivery at the Board of Trade in Chicago saw prices rise all across the board. At first this rise was in anticipation of scarcity and, like the rampant anxiety over coins and small bills, was in reaction to expected shortages rather than real scarcity. In Chicago's livestock market, prices for hogs and steers shot up with the news of the bank holiday, drawing such a horde of swine to the Chicago stockyards they could hardly be handled. In Kansas City the sudden spike in prices for meat on the hoof attracted a flood of pigs, cattle, and lambs to inundate the stockyards, and business boomed again even while the banks were still closed. Not surprisingly, this sudden rush of animals forced prices back down again, but never so low as seen before the holiday. Eleven markets tracked by the Chicago Livestock Exchange reported similar trends. As commerce restarted after the bank holidays, prices continued to rise until livestock flowed back into the markets and prices fell again, but they never reached the lows seen before the holidays. The Federal Reserve noted that when commodity exchanges reopened prices rose considerably from February levels. Afterward prices "declined somewhat," but the bottom of the deep trough of the Depression had already been fathomed and left behind. Prices paid for beef and pork equaled those of early 1932, a considerable rebound, and in some cases surpassed them.[23]

Other commodity prices followed the same path as livestock. With the markets closed brokers, buyers, and sellers grew increasingly anxious. Almost all predicted that when trading resumed prices would shoot up. Cocoa traders foresaw a sharp jump in prices when the exchange reopened, so did cotton traders. Brokers in the Boston wool market expected prices to advance 15 to 20 percent when the market reopened. Stocks of wool in New England's mills had dropped to almost nothing and would need replenishment as soon as the banks and markets reopened. Mill owners had tried to buy wool futures while the market was closed, but brokers had refused to sell, not because trading was suspended, but because they believed wool would fetch higher prices if they held out longer. The same held true for cotton, wheat, rubber, zinc, copper, lead, and other commodities: when markets reopened, prices were bid up all across the board. When cotton sales resumed on March 9, prices rose by 10 percent in Georgia, Oklahoma, and Texas. Wheat rose not only on the exchange in Chicago, it advanced two cents in Winnipeg — untouched by the bank closures — in anticipation of greater demand. Most commodities shared a common ordeal: prices spiked sharply and then declined a bit; in some cases prices floated back down to February levels by the end of the week. But in almost all cases the price floor had been reached. Deflation was over. In many cases, such as cotton, wheat, and rubber, prices rebounded by the end of the month and continued to climb into the spring.[24]

When securities exchanges reopened, they experienced the same spark of enthusiasm and jump in prices. Securities markets saw the same sharp jump as seen in commodities markets: prices initially spiked higher as sales increased in volume. Prices then relaxed by the end of the month and volume decreased, so the markets resumed something resembling normal operations of late 1932 — which was pretty far from the norm of the late 1920s, yet a considerable improvement over the past winter. By the end of April, stock prices had risen by about 42 percent over the depths of February. Even bank stocks had recovered about 20 percent of their value. On March 15 the U.S. government had to disburse $59 million in interest on Treasury bonds and roll over a debt of nearly $700 million. This necessity to raise and pay such huge sums had greatly worried Thomas Lamont in late February as the bank crisis mounted, and meeting this obligation was one of his principal concerns communicated to President-elect Roosevelt. Fulfilling this obligation briefly reinvigorated the bond market and diverted money that might have otherwise found its way back into corporate securities. From a low for the century of 35.9 (100 = index average 1935–1939) registered in June 1932, stock prices edged up to 61.5 in September 1932, only to slump again through the winter to 45.6 in March 1933. From that low, securities prices climbed to 85 by July, an index last seen just before the British stopped selling gold in September 1931. By summer 1933 securities markets were lively once again.[25]

Economic activity noticeably picked up in the summer of 1933 as prices rose. Sales in department stores, variety stores, and mail-order houses all increased from the historic lows of March and returned to levels last seen before the trough of June 1932. Mail-order sales actually reached new heights by Christmas 1933. The surge in prices for farm commodities led farmers once again to order new automobiles— usually low-cost Fords and Chevrolets. Thus, auto production picked up in spring and summer to levels last seen in spring 1931. The jump in demand for autos provoked a swell in orders for steel, which also swung back into action with smoke once again billowing from smelters and rolling mills and workers swinging lunch boxes on their way back to work. The great deflation of the Great Depression was over, and with it economic recovery could proceed. With the post-holiday convalescence the U.S. economy found itself about in the same position it had been in late 1931. The horrible decline of that winter and the stubborn slide throughout 1932 had been overcome; however, the conditions of 1931 were still bad enough and left the country with a great deal of recovery yet to be achieved.[26]

In April 1933, DuPont economist, Edmund Lincoln, advised Pierre du Pont that prices and the economy would both surge in coming months as business dumped dollars in exchange for commodities and goods in anticipation of general inflation. Businesses would compete to build inventories of necessary supplies while they were cheap before the price increases to come. But he also advised the surge in activity would be temporary and once it ran its course would peter out. This is very close to what happened. The economy surged in late spring and summer 1933 and then slumped in the fall. Chase National Bank economist Benjamin Anderson — a vocal critic of inflation and the abandonment of the gold standard — called the hike in commodity prices a "flight from the dollar." An economic report produced for internal use at U.S. Steel in 1938 reviewed the path of the recovery after March 1933: the short-lived "boom of 1933" was produced by the inflationary policy of the Roosevelt administration, a resurgence of confidence, and speculative hopes. Short-term confidence was stimulated by the spurt of government legislation of 1933, which caused the stock market to rally, and followed by rises in commodity and wholesale prices. Wages declined until June 1933, when large volumes of orders, placed in anticipation of rising wages and prices mandated by the National Industrial Recovery Act, pushed both wages and prices higher. During the summer of 1933 wages rose 15 percent while wholesale prices rose 7 percent. The collapse began in August; as inventory stocks mounted, factories cut back production and let go workers only recently rehired.[27]

In the previous three years America had seen other moments of confidence in the near future that had turned to disappointment soon enough. The stock market had rallied before, just as bond prices had risen and output seemed to recover, only to fizzle. The economic upturn after March 1933 was stronger and more prolonged than any of the previous abortive recoveries since the fall of 1929. The slackening of yet another "recovery" in late 1933 underscores the fleeting benefits of political ploys such as the national bank holiday. One can conclude that the holiday paid real dividends, despite the real economic price that had to be paid. The president reaped political rewards for his bold actions that continue to echo to this day. It is fair to say that the mood of the country did improve after the holiday was declared — no doubt in part due to public gratitude for action at last — as life carried on despite the holiday, and again when it was all over. The spirit of the populace improved even though employment picked up only a bit, and Milo Reno, a leader of protests by farmers, continued to attract crowds in the plains. The noticeable national psychological shift perhaps explains the end of falling commodity prices. The holiday bought the president and the New Deal administration time and support to implement the "100 Days" program of reforms; however, by late summer time was running out.[28]

Close observers of Washington and markets began to develop doubts after the initial flush of legislation and the rising markets. One Wall Street advisor hailed the first wave of laws enacted in March, but when Democrats revived farm schemes that failed to gain support in the 1920s, he began to worry. Many commodity traders and representatives of agricultural interests expressed alarm and dismay at proposals emanating from Henry Wallace's Department of Agriculture. The Agricultural Adjustment Act of 1933 (AAA), which paid farmers to curtail production, was passed on May 12, after spring planting had already started for 1933, so farmers resorted to plowing under crops— principally cotton — already sown. This and photographs of farmers slaughtering six million young piglets provided powerful propaganda to opponents and skeptics of the bill for years to come. Raymond Moley, Rex Tugwell, and Broadus Mitchell later agreed the purpose of the bill was not really to reduce farm production or even raise commodity prices, but to undercut Milo Reno and militant agrarian populists who had seemingly mesmerized discontented midwestern farmers. Roosevelt was unconcerned about the details of the bill, so long as Congress passed something that would assuage farm-state politicians.[29]

The AAA was one of many reform measures rammed through Congress in the 100 days of the special congressional session. From March to June, a blizzard of legislation whipped through Congress after limited debate and in many cases no hearings. Alcoholic drinks were again legalized (and taxed) after the repeal of the Nineteenth Amendment. The Civilian Conservation Corp was created to put 500,000 youths to work in reforestation and soil conservation programs. Congress created the Tennessee Valley Authority to produce government-controlled electricity, fertilizer, and other products in an experiment in government economic control near to the hearts of socialists and many progressives. It also provoked a bitter backlash by supporters of free markets and private enterprise that ensured the experiment was not applied to the entire nation, which was the intention of its principal sponsor, Senator George Norris of Nebraska. The Federal Securities Act passed late in May mandated public disclosure of minimal corporate information from any corporation seeking to raise capital through a new stock issue. The Home Owners Refinancing Act authorized $2.2 billion in government-insured bonds to purchase mortgages from banks. This provided welcome relief to banks looking to shed mortgages on a market that previously had received them coldly.[30]

The most momentous legislation for banks, however, was the long-anticipated (in some quarters dreaded) Banking Act of 1933, better known as the Glass-Steagall Act, which was taken up again by both houses of Congress in mid–May. Glass's Senate bill sought more reporting on the condition of banks; to forbid member banks from speculating in securities, commodities, or real estate; to impose branch banking on the states; to forbid interest on demand deposits; to bar loans to banks officers; and to separate investment banking from commercial banking. Glass also wanted to forbid the use of stocks as collateral for loans because, like many others, he blamed brokers' loans for the banking crisis and even the Depression. But this provision, like his plan for a national liquidation corporation to take over suspended banks and a mandate for branch banking, proved too controversial for ultimate inclusion. Glass, who blamed the 1928-29 securities-market bubble on brokers' loans, sought to do more than separate securities sales from banking, he wanted to put an end to all brokers' loans. Thomas Lamont warned that this would be catastrophic for American business and Treasury Secretary Woodin harbored similar fears about restrictions the bill placed on bank underwriting of security issues. Nevertheless, a sufficient head of steam had developed behind the move to separate securities sales from commercial banking among the public, politicians, businessmen, and even bankers that by the spring of 1933 it was a foregone conclusion. The heart of Representative Steagall's bill remained the federal guarantee of deposits up to $2,500.[31]

Congress held no hearings, which kept bankers' disagreements over the shape of reform from influencing the debate and the final outcome. Senator Glass, seeing some sort of deposit guarantee as inevitable, acquiesced to a measure in the Senate bill protecting deposits in member banks only. The House version proposed guarantees for all banks, including non-members, which upset Glass's push to corral more banks within the Federal Reserve System. But congressional opinion of the Federal Reserve had been souring for more than a year and reached a new low with the bank holiday. During the House debate on the details of the guarantee program, Texas Representative Wright Patman successfully attached an amendment to eliminate any role for the Federal Reserve in naming the board of directors of the Federal Deposit Insurance Corporation (FDIC). Any effort by Glass to enhance the power of the Fed was doomed, especially as most Americans believed it was controlled by Wall Street.[32]

Michigan Senator Arthur Vandenberg, who had been a banker in Grand Rapids, had become a leading champion of federal deposit guarantees and submitted a bill to achieve it the day after Congress passed the Emergency Banking Act. Senator Glass saw to it that it was relegated to his committee where it could be neutered. Yet, Glass clearly perceived which way the wind was blowing and agreed to incorporate a provision for federal deposit guarantees into the bill. But Vice President Garner was now president of the Senate, a believer in the guarantees, and determined to see them enacted without any strings attached to the Fed. He conspired with Vandenberg to have a more expansive guarantees provision attached to the Senate bank bill by amendment on the floor, rather than allow them to be hobbled in Glass's committee. Glass faced the inevitable and accepted the floor amendment, hoping to ensure a rigorous review process for membership in the federal insurance program. Somewhat mollified by a provision of the bill that mandated that non-member banks protected by federal deposit insurance had to join the Federal Reserve System by July 1935, Senator Glass actually spoke in favor of deposit insurance and argued that eliminating interest on demand deposits—then averaging between 0.76 and 1.23 percent—would enable banks to pay for it.[33]

The bill passed the House 262 to 19 and the Senate by a voice vote on June 16. A conference bill still had to reconcile the provisions for deposit guarantees. And it still required President Roosevelt's signature, which was far from assured as he still opposed federal deposit guarantees. After having expressed strong reservations off the record about such guarantees at his first press conference, Roosevelt told his cabinet that he believed both the Glass and Steagall bills extremely flawed, but he especially opposed federal guarantees. And he told Glass, Steagall, Secretary Woodin, the new governor of the Federal Reserve Board,

Eugene Black, and others in the Oval Office, that if the bill arrived on his desk with federal deposit guarantees he would veto it. Members of the Federal Reserve were equally dismayed at the provision and commiserated with Secretary Woodin about all the problems it was likely to unleash upon banking. Together with Woodin and James Warburg, they orchestrated a campaign to deluge the president with telegrams urging him to veto the bill. However, Vice President–elect Garner was right when he had told Roosevelt on March 3 that he "would have to accept it sooner or later." When Congress agreed to delay the guarantee until January 1, 1934, and enforce strict standards for coverage, Roosevelt relented and signed the bill.[34]

Despite some grumbling from bankers and securities dealers, the separation of investment banking and securities dealing from commercial banking operations went rather smoothly. When Winthrop Aldrich announced in March that the Chase National Bank was going to separate itself from its securities-selling affiliate, the Chase Securities Corporation, other banks soon followed. Initially, spokesmen for the besmirched National City Bank had no comment on Aldrich's announcement, but it took only a few days for them to announce that the National City Bank would also divorce its securities-selling affiliate, the National City Company. Former president of the National City Bank, Frank Vanderlip, had announced in favor of separation in November 1932, by which time some banks had already shed their unprofitable securities affiliates. The quick and evidently painless separation of the Chase National and National City Banks' securities operations from their respective banks made the divorce of security affiliates more easily accepted by remaining skeptical bankers who dreaded chaos. And after the bad publicity drummed up by congressional hearings and a torrent of newspaper articles about worthless South American bonds and utilities stock sold by bank affiliates to hapless depositors, disentangling banks from their ungainly securities-selling tar babies struck many bankers as good advice.[35]

There was a better reason to extricate banks from securities underwriting: by 1933 the affiliates made no money. Underwriting securities had been a profitless venture since 1930, and a real money-losing proposition since summer 1932 when security underwriting and sales were absolutely becalmed. In 1929 American corporations issued $7.76 billion in new stocks, compared to $23 million issued in 1932. By the first quarter of 1933, new corporate stock issues amounted to $6 million; new corporate bond issues totaled $20 million. Even new municipal and state bond issues had dwindled to $63 million, as most entities had given up trying to raise money on credit. The Chase Securities Corporation paid no dividends in 1932 or 1933, and the Chase National Corporation had to set aside $120 million in reserves to cover losses. Divorce made a virtue of necessity, and cursed and condemned bankers jumped at the opportunity to demonstrate their virtue. What better *auto de fe* than to renounce securities underwriting and sales?[36]

The situation was more complex for private banks such as Kuhn, Loeb and J.P. Morgan and Company, which had accepted deposits for decades but also had long served as securities underwriters. Both initially remained mute about their intentions, though some in banking circles saw Aldrich's proposal as the beginning of his campaign to have Chase replace J.P. Morgan and Company at the top of the New York banking pyramid. Secretary of Commerce Roper urged the president to ban the underwriting of securities by private banks as well. In the end, all deposit-accepting institutions were banned from underwriting securities, and J.P. Morgan and Company created Morgan Stanley to continue Morgan's traditional underwriting, while the parent firm carried on as a private bank. By 1933, there was little obvious need for a private bank to accept deposits in New York if it could not offer the unique underwriting services previously supplied by J.P. Morgan. The future of J.P. Morgan looked cloudy.[37]

After bankers joined the race to separate from security sales, the Glass-Steagall Act of 1933 outlawed the entangling of directorships of bank and security-sales operations. No banker, henceforth, could sit on a board or serve as an officer of a company offering to sell securities. Although many at the time blamed banking woes on stock-selling affiliates of banks, there seems to be little evidence for the accusation. Economic historian Eugene Nelson White's research strongly suggests that banks with securities affiliates fared better and survived more frequently than those without. Most of the largest banks in finance centers operated affiliates in 1930, much as the Chase National Bank or National City Bank did, and very few failed before affiliation was banned by the Glass-Steagall Act of 1933. We have discussed a few such banks that did fail — the Bank of Tennessee, the Bank of United States, the Federal National Bank of Boston, the Guardian National Bank of Commerce, and the First National Bank of Detroit — but only the Bank of Tennessee was clearly brought down by bad investments of its parent-affiliate, Caldwell and Company. In the other cases, bank loans to securities-selling affiliates contributed to the frailty of the faltering institutions, but it would be impossible to say they provided the straw that broke the camel's back.[38]

Public pressure for some kind of reform bill had been reinforced by the Senate hearings on "Stock Exchange Practices," which had greatly enlarged its dragnet under Chief Counsel Ferdinand Pecora to include practices of bankers. The hearings started in January 1932 and would continue until May 1934, filling 27 volumes of testimony in an extended effort to dig up dirt on brokers, bankers, and others caught up in the financial maelstrom that was Depression-era America. Pecora and the investigating senators devoted a good deal of the hearings to delving into insider loans and various sweetheart deals, especially the "preferred list" of J.P. Morgan clients who were offered preferred prices for new offerings. But thousands of pages of testimony and long indignant rants never substantiated that these insider privileges had contributed to banking difficulties since 1929. Pecora paraded a four-page list of America's biggest companies that suffered from Morgan partners sitting on their boards of directors. Such insider mischief certainly proved obnoxious to the public, politicians, and many bankers, but outlawing them in the Glass-Steagall Act did nothing to save banking. Bank directors were henceforth forbidden to sit on the boards of corporations that received bank loans. This was a radical departure from practice and represented the victory of one school of thought about conflict of interest. It was badly received by banking and corporate interests, and it cannot be credited with improving the subsequent operations of banks or corporations in the United States.[39]

When Senator Glass had the poor judgment to defend Jack Morgan from incessant attacks and repetitive interrogation by the committee, he received a stream of vitriolic hate mail from the public and a rebuke from the *New York Times*'s Arthur Krock. Public reaction was not uniformly hostile to Morgan and Glass: The *Corvallis Gazette-Times* in Oregon editorialized, "The Roman Holiday in Washington is becoming more and more hilarious as the savages dance around the bonfire which scorches the flesh of J.P. Morgan and Co.... And yet the howling dervishes in congress, the yellow press, the demagogs, and the public agitators scream at the top of their voices for Morgan blood." Letters to Glass ran about two-to-one against Morgan and Glass. When Senator Glass protested that the hearings were degenerating into a "circus" that required lemonade and peanuts, a Ringling Brothers Circus publicist obliged and created a sensation for press photographers by bringing a circus midget, Lya Graf, to hop onto Jack Morgan's lap.[40]

Never had bankers' stock sunk so low and public opprobrium grown so harsh as in mid–1933. Bankers had rarely attracted much public admiration since the formation of banks in the early days of the Republic; however, public condemnation of bankers for mis-deeds, as well as typical and sound bank management, had grown more insistent since the bitter debates over the fate and funding of the RFC in the summer of 1932. By March 1933 public disdain for bankers had become widespread and common. Jokes about bankers had grown so harsh the ABA considered steps that bankers could take to counter them. Senate hearings probing banker recklessness and malfeasance had stoked public distrust and anger that was compounded by well-publicized felonious behavior by bankers, such as Joseph Harriman of the Harriman Bank in New York City. He was arrested by federal authorities in March 1933 for embezzling, and his bank taken over by conservators after he was accused of taking loans for $1.4 million in other peoples' names and using the money to gamble on the stock market. There was not much unusual about a letter to the editor of the *St. Louis Post-Dispatch* that blamed the bank holiday on banker attachment to the gold standard, and even found them responsible for unemployment: "The big banker is responsible for the stringency and therefore is responsible for conditions of the present day." Will Rogers contributed, "Every American international banker ought to have printed on his office door, 'Alive today by the grace of a nation that has a sense of humor.'"[41]

The progressive senators who dominated the hearings were singularly uninterested in discovering the causes for the nation's distress or weaknesses in the operations of banks or stock exchanges that might have contributed to the nation's economic problems. They were looking for people to hang and for witches to burn. They caught several. Pecora believed it fell into the purview of the committee to investigate the income taxes of big bankers, such as Jack Morgan, Albert Wiggin, Charles Mitchell, and Richard Whitney, lately the president of the New York Stock Exchange. When it transpired that the latter two—no seri-ous dirt could be found on Morgan—might have dodged income taxes or engaged in fraud or larceny, Mitchell and Whitney were prosecuted. Mitchell was found innocent, but Whit-ney went to Sing Sing Prison for grand larceny. Wiggin was shown to have borrowed money from his bank, Chase National, to speculate in its stock, selling it short in anticipation that its value would fall—a practice that turned out to be legal but highly distasteful. No charges were brought against Wiggin, but he was vilified in the press, dumped from the Chase National board of directors, and ostracized by the new Chase chairman, Winthrop Aldrich.[42]

As Congress debated bank reform, Michigan Representative John Dingell from Detroit and Senator Couzens petitioned that the congressional hearings on financial matters be broadened to include the Michigan fiasco of February, certain they would uncover dark and nefarious doings by predatory swindlers. Senator Couzens had a personal interest in the hearings because much of the blame for the catastrophe had been unfairly laid at his doorstep. In June, Michigan Judge Harry Keidan had opened a grand jury inquiry into the matter that ultimately concluded—unjustly—that Couzens was more responsible than any-one else for the collapse. To make matters worse, a banker from the Guardian Group insin-uated that Mrs. Couzens had made a "smart money" withdrawal from the Union Guardian Trust Company just before the bank closed. Couzens was understandably outraged and determined to clear his and his wife's names.[43]

The Detroit crisis became the subject of Pecora's committee hearings in December 1933 and extended into the following February. As in the preceding inquiries into J.P. Mor-gan's activities and the sale of foreign bonds by New York banks, the committee was less interested in getting to the bottom of the problem than in finding people to blame. For example, it was revealed that numerous Guardian banks had loaned $4.5 million to directors and officers of the banks, some of whom posted Guardian bank stock as collateral. This practice was legal so long as the stock was not from the same bank authorizing the loan, but still raised eyebrows. Michigan bank examiners certainly objected to the practice, as did Senator Couzens, who claimed when he was a banker he had never authorized loans to bank officers. After devoting much attention to the matter no one suggested it caused any bank to fail. The committee was not even interested in finding out if the loans were repaid.[44]

Eventually, after federal auditors sifted through the wreckage of the Guardian records, 33 Guardian officers were indicted for illegal banking practices. Only one, Herbert Wilkin of Flint, was found guilty and sent to prison for signing a year-end bank statement that misrepresented the condition of the bank. To show the Flint bank was solvent, an overnight loan of $600,000 had supposedly been wired from a Detroit bank. It never arrived, yet Wilkin claimed the $600,000 as cash in the vault on the report. Wilkin paid the price for the habit of shunting money around between Guardian banks for bookkeeping purposes, which was legal, but as Guardian officers grudgingly admitted, not good banking practice. His actual offense that made him the target of relentless interrogation may have been something entirely different. Wilkin was the Guardian banker who implied that Senator Couzens's wife had withdrawn money from the Union Guardian Trust Company on an inside tip of trouble brewing.[45]

The hearings may have been successful in casting many players in the Detroit drama in dim light, but they failed to restore Senator Couzens's reputation. He earned the enmity of just about every banker in Michigan and alienated most state Republicans. Bankers resented that Couzens's hearings heaped scorn on bankers, whose reputations among Americans had already sunk miserably low, and helped cement the view that they created problems not only for themselves, but for all Americans. Couzens was described as "the most hated man in Detroit" even though his son, Frank, became mayor. After endorsing Roosevelt for reelection in 1936, he lost his bid for renomination to his Senate seat and retired from politics. He died before the polling in November.[46]

While unlicensed banks were slowly reopening and the economy came back to life in May 1933, the House Ways and Means Committee favorably reported out a bill to institute national economic planning: the National Industrial Recovery Act. While this proposal for economic coordination of prices, standards, wages, and hours had widespread support among industrialists—Walter Teagle of Standard Oil, Alfred Sloan of GM, Gerard Swope of General Electric (who originated the idea), and Pierre S. du Pont, among others—it also introduced tremendous uncertainty into every corner of the economy because no one knew how it was going to work, or whether it would work. In the end it did not work very well, but in the short run while the bill was being debated and passed, and the National Recovery Administration was being set up in the summer of 1933, businesses scrambled to place orders for supplies before the unknown arrived. When the "codes" accepted by industries started to come into force in the fall, business activity noticeably slowed. Most industries agreed to advance wages higher than prices had moved, meaning most businesses were going to lose money in the short run. Additionally, thousands of companies had pledged to hire more workers in anticipation of increased production to come—that never came. While many businessmen remained skeptical about boosting wages and employment before production and sales had rebounded, all saw it as preferable to a bill being pushed by Alabama Senator Hugo Black to impose a 30-hour work week on all companies with interstate sales. By December, many companies covered by NRA codes had to begin shedding workers again to cut costs. As unemployment lines grew again, companies kept wages up but cut hours in an effort to control costs. Auto production starkly revealed the trends: factory output mounted in the summer to 207,597 passenger cars in June—a figure last seen in spring 1931. By November output had fallen back to 42,365—the second lowest figure of the Depression years. Auto manufacturing employment that had risen to an index of 61.5 in September, dipped to 56.4 in November. Payrolls that had climbed to an index of 52.5 in August, slumped to 37.3 in November as hours were sharply cut back.[47]

High unemployment and slack business continued to bedevil the United States until 1942 and banks continued to suffer, but never to the same extent as witnessed in winter 1932-33. The best efforts by Congress and the New Deal administration in 1933 to restart the economy met with mixed results. The fate of America's banks was directly linked to the economy, and vice versa; neither could prosper if the other ailed. The economy expands only when credit expands, which requires banks. If the government could prod the economy back to life, the banks should follow. But was the reverse also true? If banks were revived by government aid and legal reform, would the economy then respond accordingly? Reforms instituted by Congress and the New Deal administration were intended to help banks. It is far from clear that aside from the creation of the FDIC, the Glass-Steagall Act of 1933 really did much to restore the system to health. The bank crisis was over, but the bank-system reforms of the 100 days contributed less to that end than the suspension of the gold standard by President Roosevelt. Departing the gold standard did more to ease the economic slide than any act of Congress and provided the relief that banks needed desperately to face the rough waters that still lay ahead.

The Banks and the
Depression After the Holiday

Monetary inflation helped to stop the free fall of prices, which helped to reanimate the economy and saved the banks. Despite this reprieve, banks continued to need and to receive a great deal of attention and aid in 1933 and the years that followed. After the holiday, the comptroller of the currency and state banking supervisors retained control of thousands of unlicensed banks for many months, and in some cases, years, pending reorganization or liquidation. The RFC stock acquisition program funneled enormous sums into the capital bases of banks, helping to shore up many thousands of state and national banks. The federal guarantee of bank deposits by the Federal Deposit Insurance Corporation (FDIC), which came into force on January 1, 1934, may have helped restore confidence in banks, helping to nurture them back to health, but Americans still kept large sums of money in private stashes and Post Office savings accounts continued to grow. At least the insurance program probably saved the financial system from several severe shocks, which might have had a depressing impact upon other banks and the economy. These measures certainly helped some individual banks and saved many tens (perhaps hundreds) of thousands of depositors the anguish suffered by millions from 1930 to early 1933 who lost money or had accounts frozen in failed banks.

It is unlikely, however, that the Glass-Steagall Act helped save many banks or contributed anything to end the waves of collapsing banks. At least the Glass-Steagall Act was obtrusive evidence that Congress was taking charge of the situation and doing something that supposedly safeguarded the public interest. As Congress acted, the waves of collapsing banks ended, offering *post hoc, ergo propter hoc* confirmation that congressional intervention helped save the day. All of this served useful political ends even if the economic impact of congressional intervention was less consequential. The calm banking sector delivered a welcome psychological boost to the American populace that was a necessary precondition for sparking business back to life. If the economy failed to reanimate after 1933, the fault evidently did not lie with the weak banking sector.

The damage inflicted upon banks by the Depression was sobering. Between January 1930 and March 1933, 5,522 banks, holding deposits of nearly $3.5 billion, disappeared. Some of them were swallowed by other banks without adverse effect upon customers, but most fell into federal or state receivership. Despite vigorous government intervention and an improved economic atmosphere, 1933 still proved to be a vexing year for banks. The toll taken on banks by administrative fiat in 1933 was almost as bad as the harm previously wrecked by the downwardly spiraling economy. When measured in frozen deposits, it was worse. State and federal administrators chose not to license 4,507 banks after the bank holiday, freezing deposits worth $4.1 billion. Fully $640 million more was removed from the economy by governmental fiat than by bank failures. No doubt, the assets of those unlicensed banks had deteriorated badly during the economic tumult that preceded the holiday; still, the banks had survived until closed by the licensing process. In spite of improvements in the economy and stronger markets for banks to sell their assets, they continued to fail, even if in reduced numbers from the horrendous toll seen as recently as January. Despite the precaution of granting licenses only to strong banks, 39 licensed banks failed anyway before the end of March 1933. The ranks of licensed banks that shut their tills declined as the year progressed: 36 in April, 18 in May, 15 in June, and so on. By the end of the year, 221 banks deemed licensable in March failed regardless. Together they held $152.5 million in deposits—only $10 million more than held by the banks that had failed in January 1933 alone, which, although a bad month, was far from the worst. So, even if $152.5 million was a lot of money to be frozen in 1933, it was a tolerable amount compared to the horrendous sums caught in earlier bank catastrophes.[1]

After March 15, 1,105 solvent banks were placed into the hands of federal conservators, tasked with reorganizing or merging them. Some conservators judged the banks too far gone and asked that they be placed into receivership for liquidation. With more than 1,000 banks on his hands after March 1933, the comptroller did not have enough qualified personnel to operate them, so in many cases the old management was left in charge if recommended by a federal examiner familiar with the bank and its operations. The old management carried on but answered to a new boss, the comptroller of the currency. After January 1, 1934, banks insured by the FDIC that fell into terminal trouble were taken over by that agency, which then appointed its own conservators and receivers with the same purpose.[2]

Despite much fretting by bankers, the FDIC system worked fairly well and bankrupted neither the government nor member banks. As a bank insurance program, the FDIC was quite successful. In its first year of operation, 1934, it paid almost $2 million to depositors of only nine failed banks. Half of that amount was paid to depositors of a single bank, the Bank of America Trust Company of Pittsburgh. The sums paid out grew to $13.5 million in 1935, when 26 insured banks failed. Two banks in Pennsylvania again accounted for $9 million in losses. In 1936 losses mounted to $27.5 million when 69 insured banks failed. Three banks in Ann Arbor that failed on the same day, February 15, accounted for almost half of all losses: $12.2 million. More than half the suspensions occurred in states that were depressingly familiar with bank failures: Missouri, Indiana, and North Dakota. However, if its primary purpose was to coax hoarders into putting money bank into banks, it was not a grand success: the amount of currency outside of banks increased as the Depression lingered.[3]

After four years of slow improvements the Depression worsened in 1937, and bank failures and attendant losses mounted: 77 banks with $33.13 million in deposits failed in 1937. FDIC payouts almost doubled in 1938 when 74 banks with $62 million in insured deposits failed. However, half of that amount was contained in just two banks in Camden, New Jersey. The failure of the Camden Safe Deposit and Trust Company, with $22.6 million in deposits, ranked in seriousness with that of the Federal National Bank of Boston or the Bank of Kentucky. This pattern—large bank failures requiring very large pay outs by the FDIC—continued for the remainder of the Depression years. While small banks still collapsed, the nation also witnessed the kind of spectacular failures that bankers, government officials, and the public found so alarming in 1930–33. Despite the crashing of some huge banks, both the insurance and the banking systems continued to function without interruption. Failures in 1939 accounted for losses of $160.8 million. Again, 17 New Jersey banks sank with the lion's share of the losses. The Trust Company of New Jersey in Jersey City went under with $48.8 million in deposits putting it in league with the Bank of United States or the Bank of Pittsburgh, N.A.—the two largest failures in American history until the founderings in Detroit. The New Jersey Title and Trust in Jersey City and the Hudson Trust Company in Union City between them took down $46 million in deposits. Losses in 1940—when the Depression was winding down—amounted to a still substantial $143.8 million. The failure of the Integrity Trust Company in Philadelphia, one of the city's largest institutions in 1930 with deposits of $60.8 million, accounted for losses of $29.4 million. That paled in comparison to the $48.3 million held by the First Trust and Deposit Company of Syracuse or the First Citizens Bank and Trust Company of Utica that held $34.3 million when they failed in 1940. Three banks out of 43 failures accounted for more than two-thirds of all losses in 1940. Even in 1941, when the Depression was quickly abating, 15 failed banks held $29.6 million in insured deposits. Two-thirds of that resided in three failed banks in New York State. Thus, the FDIC did not stop big banks from foundering. So long as the economy remained weak, banks continued to fail.[4]

The suspensions of these large banks and trust companies in the post–Glass-Steagall era differed from earlier failures in that most of the large casualties were taken over by the FDIC and continued to operate in a national "Iowa Plan." The deposits within them were not frozen and the bank failures did not contribute to the economic woes of the towns and cities that depended on the failed institutions. FDIC-appointed conservators assumed control of 27 out of 69 failed banks in 1936, including all three failed institutions in Ann Arbor. Nevertheless, three banks with deposits of more than $4 million in New York, Connecticut, and Ohio were allowed to close. All depositors were paid off and the FDIC was able to recoup its losses by liquidating the banks' assets. The FDIC assumed control of most of the big banks that failed in New Jersey in the late 1930s—the New Jersey Title Guarantee and Trust Company that failed in 1939 with $21.7 million in deposits was allowed to close— saving the Garden State a good deal of anguish.[5]

While the number of failed banks in the remaining years of the Depression paled by comparison to the legions of dead banks found in the early 1930s, or even the 1920s, the amounts of money involved in the banking flops remained large. The creation of the FDIC benefited the general economic well-being of the country when it assumed the management of failed banks and preserved the deposits of bank clients. The banking system, many locales, and the economy generally avoided the shocks that came from the collapse of banks. Some of those failed banks in New Jersey and New York in particular were quite large, and the shock waves emanating from their fall could have been very destabilizing. Or the shock could have been merely local, as in the case of the Bank of United States; there is no way to know. In any event, it seems reasonable to conclude that the FDIC muffled severe blows that otherwise would have been fully absorbed by the economy, whether locally or nationally.

Comptroller of the Currency J.F.T. O'Connor, appointed by President Roosevelt, reported that the successful operation of the FDIC restored customer confidence in banks and stopped runs. This is unlikely as runs had faded away long before the bank insurance became operative on January 1, 1934. Additionally, there was no rush by savers to move their life savings to insured banks. Almost half of all time deposits—savings—continued to reside in uninsured banks after the creation of the FDIC. Federal deposit insurance was available only to banks that belonged to the Federal Reserve System, and most savings banks did not. In January 1934, when the temporary insurance program took effect, Americans kept almost $9.5 billion deposited in 576 mutual savings banks, out of a total of $21.7 billion in all time-deposit accounts. Only 66 mutual savings banks belonged to the FDIC system, a number that declined over the years rather than increased. By the end of 1940, only 53 mutual savings banks belonged to the system, and 498, with $8.8 billion in deposits, remained outside. That is, in June 1934, 37.8 percent of time deposits were entrusted to uninsured banks; by December 1940 that figure remained as high as 31.9 percent. By and large, savings did not migrate to insured banks as feared by opponents of the federal guarantee program. Once again, bankers' fears were greater than those of depositors and were unjustified.[6]

Table 11.1: Bank Deposits, Reserves, and Currency Outside of Banks, 1929–1941 (in millions of dollars)

	Assets	Deposits	Reserves	Currency Outside Banks
June 1929	58,899	53,963	3,191	3,639
Dec. 1929	58,848	55,146	3,178	3,557
June 1930	58,556	54,703	3,227	3,369
Dec. 1930	56,602	52,937	3,316	3,605
June 1931	55,267	51,769	3,307	3,651
Dec. 1931	50,046	45,925	3,131	4,470
June 1932	46,310	42,093	2,829	4,616
Dec. 1932	45,169	41,752	3,198	4,669
June 1933	40,305	38,089	2,995	4,761
Dec. 1933	40,606	38,588	3,463	4,782
June 1934	42,552	41,875	4,676	4,659
Dec. 1934	43,422	44,599	4,946	4,655
June 1935	44,347	45,492	5,985	4,783
Dec. 1935	45,697	48,656	6,699	4,917
June 1936	48,412	50,998	6,448	5,222
Dec. 1936	49,445	53,323	7,791	5,516
June 1937	49,565	52,890	7,973	5,489
Dec. 1937	48,427	52,186	8,128	5,638
June 1938	47,212	51,961	9,181	5,417
Dec. 1938	48,831	53,835	9,970	5,775
June 1939	49,616	55,990	11,352	6,005
Dec. 1939	50,885	58,342	13,079	6,401
June 1940	51,336	60,582	15,204	6,699
Dec. 1940	54,170	65,022	15,828	7,325
June 1941	57,946	67,172	14,798	8,204
Dec. 1941	61,101	70,791	14,194	9,615

SOURCES: *Banking and Monetary Statistics*, 18, 34–5; Friedman and Schwartz, 739–40.

The FDIC may have restored the confidence of some depositors in the security provided by banks. However, "lack of confidence" in banks was not the principal problem plaguing banks: a becalmed economy and slack business was. And so long as the economy remained in a slump, banks would continue to have problems and fail. Even with the FDIC working effectively, many Americans continued to keep their savings stashed away in hiding places. More currency remained outside of banks after the holiday ($4.76 billion in June 1933) than in December 1932 ($4.70 billion). In the weeks that followed the reopening of the banks in March 1933, cash and gold flowed from banks into the Federal Reserve System.

By the end of March, $1.19 billion in cash and $600 million in gold had returned to the Fed, greatly reducing the amount of currency in circulation. But this money did not leave the public's hoard because of restored confidence. The gold was retrieved by force of law, and the currency, which served a real purpose in early March when companies and the public needed cash in a bankless world, had served its useful purpose and was no longer needed by corporations that had withdrawn it from banks. And despite the soothing actions of the FDIC, money held outside of banks continued to mount as the 1930s ground on (see Table 11.1): from $4.78 billion in June 1935 to $9.6 billion in December 1941, when the Depression was rapidly coming to a close. The grandfather of a friend of mine who lived in Bunkie, Louisiana, kept all of his savings in a freezer in his basement until he died in the 1970s. The grandmother of another friend, who lived in southern Illinois, into the 1980s hid money all over her house and never in a bank. The confidence of many people never was restored, yet banks in their towns continued to carry on anyway. The FDIC made a valuable contribution to the United States, but it did not save the banking system. The end of economic deterioration and plummeting prices did.[7]

The Reconstruction Finance Corporation was the other federal agency that provided relief to banks that helped stem the waves of failures of the early 1930s. Even though Jesse Jones initially opposed it, by the end of June 1933, the RFC had made use of the provision of the Emergency Banking Act that allowed it to purchase preferred stock in banks to invest $43 million in unlicensed banks so they could reopen fortified with new capital. Two new banks opened in Detroit with the assistance of the RFC and the auto companies— GM owned half of the stock in the new National Bank of Detroit. The "Ford bank" ostentatiously refused to sell any stock to the RFC (see below). Rudolph Hecht's Hibernia Bank and Trust Company in New Orleans that had received a $20 million RFC loan in February fell victim to the licensing process and went into liquidation. It was replaced by the Hibernia National Bank, buttressed by $1.5 million in stock sold to the RFC and minus half of its deposits. The troubled Union Trust Company of Baltimore was also refused a license to reopen when other banks in the city opened their doors on March 14. The RFC offered to loan the staggering institution another $5.2 million if it would recharter as a national bank and sell the RFC $2 million in new stock. Negotiations dragged on until December when the bank finally reopened as a rechartered state institution, a member of the Federal Reserve System, and (soon to be) protected by the FDIC.[8]

RFC Chairman Jesse Jones strong-armed bankers into selling preferred stock to the RFC even if their banks did not need to issue new stock. When Jones convinced the New York Clearing House Association to cooperate, Irving Trust, Central Hanover, and Bankers Trust — all in strong positions in 1933 — each sold $5 million worth of stock to the RFC just so that Jones and other bankers could proclaim that even strong banks sold stock to the RFC. This lifted an onus from those banks that really needed the infusion of capital the RFC purchases provided, such as the Union Trust Company of Cleveland, which sold $10 million in stock to the RFC and took a $35 million loan in order to reopen. Some of the largest banks in the country benefited from this program: the First National Bank of Chicago, the Continental Illinois, National City Bank of New York, and Chase National Bank all sold large blocks of stock to the RFC. National City and Continental Illinois each sold the RFC $50 million in stock, and in both cases, large write-offs of worthless assets ($120 million and $73 million, respectively) made the sales beneficial to the banks. Even Chase National sold the RFC $30 million in stock, and First National of Chicago and Manufacturers Trust Company of New York each sold the RFC $25 million in stock. A write-off of $79 million in Chase National assets at the end of 1933 (followed by $48 million more in 1934) justified the sale for the New York bank. By May 1934, the RFC had purchased more than $1.1 billion in preferred stock from 6,500 of the country's banks. Of the nation's largest banks, only the First National Bank of Boston eluded Jesse Jones's ever-expanding portfolio. By the time the RFC stopped buying bank stock in 1936, it had invested $1.3 billion in 6,800 banks, or 40 percent of the country's banks. The RFC owned one-third of the capital stock of the nation's banks.[9]

Jesse Jones was even less enthusiastic about the loan program pushed onto him by President Roosevelt to allow weak banks to enroll in the FDIC by the January 1, 1934, deadline. At Roosevelt's insistence, the RFC granted loans to hundreds of unlicensed banks so that they could reopen and qualify for insurance. Between June and October the RFC loaned such banks $300 million so they could obtain licenses. Despite help from the RFC, 1,905 banks, holding $1.2 billion in deposits, remained unlicensed and shuttered at the end of 1933. Another 1,105 banks, with $1.87 billion in deposits, had been placed in receivership and faced liquidation. To avoid dumping billions of dollars worth of assets belonging to the unlicensed banks onto unwilling markets, the comptroller instructed federal receivers to hold assets for as long as it took to reap a reasonable compensation for them. That meant it could take many years to wind up the affairs of banks in federal hands, which had frequently been the case even before 1930, but became a more extended affair after 1933. By June 1934, 623 banks still remained unlicensed, yet not in receivership, freezing around $350 million within them. The RFC loaned many of these banks money to pay off depositors. By 1938, the RFC had loaned $1.275 billion to 2,700 banks in the hands of receivers— $84 million was loaned to relieve depositors of the First National Bank of Detroit alone. Thus, 700,000 small depositors were allowed to withdraw money from the big Detroit banks if they wanted to. Jesse Jones drew up rules that forced big accounts, such as Ford, to wait.[10]

Jones retained the same banker's attitude of the previous RFC heads and proceeded cautiously in considering each loan. Under Jones, the RFC was just as reluctant to grant loans to closed banks as it had been during the Hoover administration. The days were over when banks could carry bonds and loans on their books at face value so long as they were not actually in default. The harsher standards of the RFC were widely applied after the Holiday. Years afterward, a vice president of the First National Bank of Denver complained, "Then the bank examiners came in and they were a bunch of rough customers under Roosevelt in those days. They threw their weight around, and they didn't care whether they were honest or not. They made you charge off loans right and left on a basis of that particular point that day. They would write it off." Jones also attracted the same kind of populist ire that had dogged Charles Dawes and Atlee Pomerene when Oklahoma Senator Elmer Thomas took aim at the RFC under Jones and accused it of doing too little to help the closed banks that served millions of small farmers. Roosevelt wanted to head off such attacks and defuse the rural agitation that continued to simmer on the plains. To meet this criticism and get around Jones, Roosevelt created the Deposit Liquidation Corporation, which closely resembled the Liquidation Corporation that Carter Glass had pushed unsuccessfully in 1932 and early 1933. The body actually worked through the RFC, using some of its employees, but also worked around it by using more lenient criteria for evaluating collateral and offering lower interest rates. Before the corporation went out of business in 1936, it loaned over $800 million to hundreds of closed banks, allowing them to pay off their depositors long before all the banks' assets were sold off.[11]

As the RFC and FDIC became more important to stabilizing the banking system, the Federal Reserve Bank became less so, although the advance of the former two did not cause the retreat of the latter. The Federal Reserve became less important and influential because its primary purpose — to provide liquidity to the system — had become irrelevant in a system awash in liquidity. As business demanded less credit and banks were displaced by various federal mortgage-buying agencies, banks had billions of dollars to loan and no borrowers. The federal government had long been the most important creditor in the United States, but by mid–1933 that was truer than ever. As the 1930s dragged on, the amounts banks loaned to businesses barely budged. At the end of the decade, December 1940, loans amounted to $23.75 billion, even though deposits (not counting interbank deposits) had rebounded from $38.1 billion in June 1933 to $65 billion. A Michigan banker complained in the winter of 1933 that a newly chartered bank in Pontiac — to replace those that had collapsed — had attracted $2 million in deposits in only a few months but had made only $70,000 in loans.[12]

Regardless of the creation of the RFC, the FDIC, and other federal agencies to help troubled banks, ad hoc intervention by government and big business that had been used since the 19th century continued to be employed effectively. The auto companies, RFC, and big New York banks cooperated to create new banks to serve Detroit, while the affairs of the First National Bank and the Guardian banks were being sorted out. Backed by GM, Chrysler, and the RFC, the National Bank of Detroit opened for business on March 24, 1933. Alfred Sloan was persuaded to have GM put up nearly half of the stock for the bank with the RFC subscribing to the other half. Walter Chrysler agreed to buy only $500,000 worth, which was half a million dollars more than the Detroit public could be convinced to buy. Sloan and Chrysler both sat on the board of directors of the new bank. By the end of the year, the bank had attracted 90,000 customers and $190 million in deposits. Ford put only $3 million into the stock of Detroit's other new bank, the Manufacturers National Bank, that held deposits worth nearly $56 million by the end of the year. The Fords declined to share their bank with the RFC, although they, too, tried to offer shares to a very reticent public, who declined to become involved. Henry and Edsel Ford likewise sat on the board of the new bank that opened in the summer of 1933, with Edsel serving as chairman until he died in May 1943. In spring 1945, GM sold its shares in the National Bank of Detroit and got out of the banking business. In 1947, the RFC also sold its shares at a profit.[13]

The Banking System 1934–1941

Throughout the remainder of the Depression, banks failed to significantly increase commercial loans — the principal means by which the money supply expands. Banks reduced their risk by lending more money to the federal government and less money to businesses. Commercial loans constituted a smaller percentage of bank portfolios in the 1930s than in previous decades, so that precarious business loans did not necessarily jeopardize a bank's existence. Bank loans continued to decrease in 1934 by more than one billion dollars, mostly because worthless loans were written off and others were sold to federal entities, such as the Federal Farm Mortgage Corporation, created to buy loans.

Loans, which amounted to $22.24 billion in June 1933, did not grow as the economy slowly recovered. They shrank further. By the end of the year, all banks carried business loans worth $22 billion. As indicated in Table 11.2, the amounts continued to dwindle. Business loans amounted to only $21.36 billion at the end of 1936, supposedly a boom year when loans were being offered in New York City at 1.74 percent. Low rates were insufficient inducement for business to borrow. Short-term borrowing by business—the original purpose of American banks—fared no better. While $1.5 billion worth of bankers' acceptances and commercial paper were routinely held by banks in a typical month of the 1920s, the amount slipped to $792 million in January 1933. A year later, the tally stood at $879 million, and a year after that at $687 million. At the end of the recovery year of 1936, the figure had slumped to $588 million. Before 1942, it rarely rose higher, and often dipped lower.[14]

Banks continued to suffer losses on loans and securities as the Depression lingered. In 1934 national banks (see Table 11.3, statistics are not available for state banks) wrote off a massive $379 million in bad loans and $242 million in worthless bonds; 3.7 percent of their investments and 5.6 percent of their non-federal assets. It is difficult to see how banks survived in these conditions. In 1935 national banks wrote off another $188 million in bad loans and added further losses of $136.74 million from worthless bonds—almost 7 percent of non-federal securities owned by national banks. While losses on bad loans and bonds diminished as the Depression continued, they remained stubbornly high: $166 million for national banks alone in 1940. As national banks added more and more federal securities to their portfolios, the percent of investments written off diminished with each passing year, falling below 1 percent in 1938.[15]

Table 11.2: Bank Assets in Millions, June 1933–1941

	Assets	Loans	Commercial Paper*	Federal Securities	Other Securities
1933	40,305	22,243	760	8,199	9,863
1934	42,552	21,246	686	11,278	9,968
1935	44,347	20,213	502	14,258	9,876
1936	48,412	20,636	485	17,323	10,453
1937	49,565	22,410	649	16,954	10,201
1938	47,212	20,982	489	16,727	9,503
1939	49,616	21,320	426	18,746	9,553
1940	51,336	22,340	429	19,666	9,330
1941	57,946	25,311	512	23,521	9,114

SOURCE: *Banking and Monetary Statistics*, 18.
*includes bankers' acceptances

According to the comptroller of the currency, national banks carried $223 million in worthless loans in early 1934, or 2.9 percent of the total loan portfolio; $324 million, or 4.2 percent, were doubtful; 27 percent were slow. Thus, one-third of all loans in national banks were problematic, even after the bank crisis had passed and the economy was on the mend. Figures for non-member insured banks were similar: 6.7 percent of loans were worthless, 1.3 percent were doubtful, and 32.6 percent were slow; 40.6 percent of loans were problematic. And national banks were presumably the strongest banks in the country. It seems little wonder that in 1933 national banks lost $230 million. Despite the calming of the banking crisis, the Glass-Steagall Act of 1933, the creation of the FDIC, and the intervention of the RFC, national banks still lost $300 million in 1934. In 1935 they registered a net profit of $70 million—one wonders how.[16]

**Table 11.3: Losses Incurred
by Banks, 1930–1940 (in millions)**

	Losses On Loans National Banks	Losses On Bonds National Banks	Losses On Loans All Banks	Losses On Bonds All Banks
1930	103.8	61.4	283.5	160.7
1931	186.9	119.3	501.0	311.7
1932	259.5	201.8	705.6	517.7
1933	231.4	236.6	645.0	579.8
1934	379.3	241.8	1,052.5	550.7
1935	188.2	136.7	517.5	383.2
1936	154.6	93.3	412.7	241.5
1937	111.0	94.1	282.4	246.9
1938	66.2	103.0	165.8	268.9
1939	67.0	109.0	166.3	287.6
1940	58.2	107.9	140.7	265.9

SOURCE: *Annual Report of the Comptroller of the Currency* (1930) 74, (1931) 76, (1932) 68, (1933) 79, (1934) 89, (1938) 98, 113 (1940) 142, (1941) 153; *Banking and Monetary Statistics*, 21.[17]

In view of the large numbers of worthless or doubtful loans carried by banks, it is little wonder that banks saw commercial loans as risky. In the worst years of the slump, 1931–33, rates on commercial bonds rose steadily, even as deflation made dollars more expensive. Bonds graded Aaa by Moody's in January 1931 paid on average 4.42 percent. Rates rose to 5.32 by the end of the year. Railroads had to pay on average 8.48 percent. By June 1932 — the nadir of the Depression until March 1933 — commercial bond rates hit 5.41 percent. Shakier corporations with Baa ratings had to pay on average 11.52 percent; railroads had to pay 9.14 percent. Afterward, rates on high-grade corporate bonds eased, sliding to 4.35 percent by January 1934, and below 4 percent by June. Even as rates slid, corporate indebtedness remained low.[18]

Banks seemed to be in business after 1933 to provide credit to the government and handle checks of business clients. If the money on deposit in banks earned only meager interest from federal bonds, almost all banks had imposed service fees on demand deposit accounts, which provided banks with at least enough income to pay employees. Banks made less profit on government securities, but they were less risky. Securities issued by the federal government made up 10 percent of bank assets of commercial banks in 1929. By June 1933, they comprised 24.6 percent of bank assets. And that reflects conditions created by policies put into place by the Hoover administration; changes effected by the New Deal administration had yet to show results. By June 1936, federal securities made up 39.6 percent of bank assets. That figure remained about steady until war preparations consumed an even larger share of the resources of the financial system.[19]

The federal government soaked up much of the credit offered by banks — it owed banks $8.2 billion in June 1933 and $21 billion in December 1940 — however, much of the new deposits fattening banks lay dormant and unused as excess reserves. The last time American banks had exhausted their reserves at the Federal Reserve banks and relied on the central bank as a white knight to save the system had been not March 1933, but February 1932, when member banks had to borrow $3 million from the Fed to meet their legal reserve requirements. From then on, member banks kept excess reserves at their district banks. Even in March 1933, member banks had $249 million more on deposit at the Reserve banks than legally required — 112.8 percent of requirements. Excess reserves dipped to $129 million on March 8 (and the Bank discounted $1.4 billion in bills), and yet they steadily mounted in the weeks and months that followed. Excess reserves kept piling up in Fed vaults as deposits in member banks returned but borrowers did not: $859 million by December; $1.8 billion a year later; and $2.84 billion by the end of 1935. Except for a decline during the "Roosevelt Depression" of 1937-38, the languishing money just kept mounting: by the end of 1940 Fed banks held $6.5 billion in excess reserves with nothing to do. The becalmed money did not even earn interest for member banks. And with so much money lying unused, the Federal Reserve Board remained powerless to influence the banking system through the only tools available to it: open market operations, adjusting reserve requirements, or changing discount rates. The Federal Reserve banks discounted 7.76 times more bills in February 1933 ($582 million) than in all of 1936 ($75 million). The Federal Reserve Bank of Chicago accepted $83,000 in discounts for the entire state of Iowa in fall 1933. Carter Glass worried needlessly about "cats and dogs" wanting in at the Fed discount window.[20]

The banking system in the United States survived the Depression, even if, by and large, its services were little used by business. The system had not really been brought to its knees by the Depression, even in March 1933. Banks overly invested in troubled local markets— usually small banks— had been decimated by the economic slump, while large banks with diversified portfolios almost all survived. From June 1929 to June 1933, 10,590 banks disappeared from the landscape. By December 1941, another 320 would fail, but 652 new banks would open: in June 1941 there were more banks with more deposits (and fewer loans) than in June 1933. Some once-strong banks, such as the Dawes Bank and the First National Bank of Detroit, had been brought low by bad economic conditions. They were not ineptly managed; they were overly burdened by too many slow or worthless loans, offered and taken in good faith in better times. Even the strongest banks in America, such as the Guaranty Trust Company of New York and the Chase National Bank, suffered enormous losses due to the Depression, but they survived. One of the weakest links in the banking system, bank holding companies, survived the Depression despite an adverse economic and political climate. Some, such as the Northwest Bancorporation, eventually prospered, even if they paid no dividend from 1933 to 1939.[21]

Despite the hardships of the post–1933 Depression years, America's banks generally survived. Business for banks was quiet even as the nation girded for war, but they muddled through. The numbers of banks had been thinned considerably since 1929, when the country was served by 25,113 banks of all kinds. By June 1941 the ranks had fallen to 14,855 banks. The reduction had been particularly severe in the thinly populated West: South Dakota had 396 banks in 1929 and 162 in 1941; North Dakota, 433 and 160; Idaho, 137 and 50; Iowa, 1,286 and 644; Oregon, 235 and 73; Arizona, 46 and 12; and so on. By 1941, there were notably fewer "pawnshops on the prairies." The smallest banks with the fewest clients had been pitilessly weeded out, leaving larger banks with more clients and better chances of survival. With the FDIC to muffle the reverberations when banks fell — especially big trust companies in the mid–Atlantic states— banks contributed little to the continuing economic problems of the country. This was in stark contrast to the early years of the Depression when bank failures helped drive deflation by freezing deposits and spurred depositors to withdraw funds, principally in late 1931. If banks did little in the latter 1930s to push the country toward recovery, at least they did not hold the country back.

Conclusion

The bank holidays that unfolded across the United States after the crisis in Michigan became public knowledge were the product not of a panicky public, but of nervous bankers, Federal Reserve staff and state officials. President Roosevelt echoed their excuses when he blamed the crisis on an overly jumpy public. Like the governors, Roosevelt claimed that he closed the banks to protect them and the public that relied on them. It is difficult to know exactly what Roosevelt was thinking when he decided to close the banks as he left no written record of his thoughts, besides the flimsy boilerplate that ended up in his fireside chat. As the banks were already mostly closed as of noon March 4 — though as we have seen, many banks were still open and operating more or less as usual — what purpose did federalizing the holiday serve? The usual argument, and certainly the one repeated and believed at the time, was that a national holiday made it easier to reopen the banks once closed. Complaints by bankers at the time, however, suggest there is little substance to this assertion. Most banks were ready, willing, and able to reopen by at least mid-week after FDR's inauguration. Banks in most states probably could have reopened on Monday, March 7, and would have had they been permitted to.

While massive withdrawals posed a problem for some banks in March 1933, they were not "runs" as the word is usually understood. Banks had faced runs, "slow runs," and continuous heavy withdrawals since 1930, sometimes, perhaps even a majority of times, because depositors feared for the safety of their deposits. However, that was generally not the case in February and March 1933 when deposits were shifted from bank to bank by nervous businessmen and other bankers for reasons that had little to do with confidence in any particular bank. The banking system had seen this before in 1931 when regional banks called their excess deposits home when they became nervous about local conditions, which forced large correspondent institutions in New York and Chicago to liquidate assets. The extreme volatility in 1931 convinced bankers everywhere of the wisdom of maintaining large pools of excess reserves. Besides, investments other than federal securities, which paid practically nothing, were beginning to look too precarious for bank books anyway, so maintaining mounds of currency in vaults, rather than commercial loans and bonds, seemed like a good idea.

As business slackened, commercial banks — often national banks and members of the Federal Reserve System — sought alternative investments for their deposits. Bankers had to find other uses for money that previously would have been loaned to businesses or used to buy trade acceptances. Often banks used that money to buy government bonds or ended up doing nothing at all with it. But as interest paid on government bonds declined to almost nothing, money could no longer be gainfully employed and banks found it difficult to make a profit. If they could maintain a fairly stable deposit base and avoid any major shocks, with occasional help from the RFC, Federal Reserve banks, correspondent banks, or fellow members of the local clearing house association, they could muddle through. After spring 1933, most that remained open for business did. The RFC bought millions of shares of stock, strengthening the capital base of banks and increasing liquidity. Once the FDIC became operative in January 1934, with depositor confidence supposedly strengthened, muddling through should have been easier. However, as the amount of money that remained outside banks only increased after 1934 and savings failed to migrate to insured institutions, it is hard to conclude that the FDIC instilled much confidence in banks. At worst, it did no harm; at best, its management of wobbly banks saved local businesses and depositors from the shocks that usually accompanied bank failures.

Hoarding had indeed posed a problem for banks in late 1930 and again in late 1931, forcing many to liquidate billions of dollars worth of assets in order to meet demands for cash. As Friedman and Schwartz point out, this caused a tightening of credit when the country needed more credit and not less. Hoarding also worried Federal Reserve officials — and Governor Meyer in particular — because it negated open market operations to increase the money supply. If the Fed pumped cash into the system and it went directly under mattresses (or sat in vaults), the Fed was increasing the money supply and depleting "free gold" for no good reason. From December 1929 to March 1933 the amount of cash kept outside of banks increased by almost $2 billion, while in the same period money held in deposits shrank by $19 billion. Because of the deposit multiplier working in reverse, meeting demands for cash would have accounted for almost three quarters of that decline. In the judgment of Emanuel Goldenweiser, the rest of the decline was probably caused by a flight from debt by borrowers. The Federal Reserve judged that inordinate withdrawals killed 572 banks (out of 5,191 suspensions) from January 1929 to March 1933. "Silent runs" of constant heavy withdrawals contributed to the death of another 1,934 banks, containing $1.62 billion in deposits. Over $2 billion in deposits were frozen in such banks by the spring of 1933. Weak assets led to the demise of another 1,274 banks and contributed to the fall of 1,934 more (the same banks noted above).[1]

Bankers and officials during the Depression were obsessed by bank runs, hoarding, and "lack of confidence" as powerful agents sinking banks deeper and deeper into crisis. Of course, the three ills were related: lack of confidence led to bank runs, which produced hoarding. Bank runs scared bankers into increasing liquidity and keeping more cash on hand that was then not available as credit. If only confidence could be restored by, say, federal deposit insurance or a fireside chat, then the problem would be solved. As seen in Chicago and Pittsburgh, however, money often left one bank and migrated to another, rather than ending up in sugar bowls. Lack of confidence in banks provoked only a few runs in February 1933 and maybe none at all in March 1933. After a spate of runs in Illinois, California, Missouri, New Jersey, and New York State in December 1932 and January 1933, the fever died down. I found only one run in February — in New Brunswick, New Jersey. The only identifiable runs in March were in Newark, New York City, Pittsburgh, and Knoxville, and they were probably provoked by rumors of an impending bank holiday and not lack of confidence in banks. The money flying out of banks in late February and early March did not leave in runs at all, but most often by wire transfer, and was not impelled by lack of confidence in banks, but out of fear of bank holidays. Thus, repeated claims of "restored confidence" were greatly overstated, both before the March crisis and since. Confidence was not restored for many mattress stuffers after the crisis, and it made little difference to the banking system because "hoarding" was only one part of the problem and not "the problem." The greater problem in early 1933 was confidence in the dollar.

Banks remained reluctant to grant loans until the very end of the Depression and continued to carry huge volumes of government securities as assets long after the March 1933 crisis passed. Their eagerness to place money in the hands of borrowers remained curbed until the economy recovered in the 1940s. Commercial loans carried by member banks in June 1937, when the recovery had been under way for four years (and banks loans were at their post–1933 peak and about to plummet again), remained $919 million below the level of December 1932. With bank failures down, bank runs a distant memory, and the whole system buttressed by the FDIC, RFC loans, and numerous federal agencies to assume the riskiest loans to farmers and householders, bank loans still remained hard to come by. Bankers' attitudes toward large cash reserves, easily liquidated government securities, and even short-term loans remained unchanged, and bank loans did not regain the level of December 1932 until December 1941. Bank reserves kept on hand at Federal Reserve Banks or as cash in the vault only grew larger as the 1930s advanced and did not dwindle after the March panic. Bank credit in depressed Canada — with no lack of confidence in the small number of large banks serving all provinces and no history of bank runs — remained just as tight as in the United States.[2]

The RFC loan in 1932 to the Dawes Bank turned out to be a disaster. Perhaps it delayed the foundering of the bank, but it created such a public stink and soured so many peoples' attitudes toward the RFC, banks, and the Hoover administration's efforts to save the situation, the price paid was surely too high. Both Henry Ford and James Couzens — two men positioned to have averted the Detroit banking crisis — were obsessed with the Dawes loan. Dawes had requested an absurd loan possibly with the hope and belief that it would be rejected, so his bank could fold and he could retire from banking. Instead, RFC officials approved the unprecedented loan, with disastrous political consequences. Skeptical progressives and populists viewed any loans to large banks as special favors granted to the least deserving, but the Dawes loan in particular stank of rank favoritism granted by the federal government to politically well connected friends in finance. It turned Senator Couzens, Speaker Garner, and many other powerful people against the RFC when their help was needed most.

What would have happened had Michigan Governor Comstock not declared a bank holiday? At the worst, Henry Ford would have carried out his promise to withdraw all of his money from Detroit's largest banks, and absent help from the Fed, they would have been forced to close, freezing hundreds of millions of dollars of Michigan money in correspondent accounts. Banks all over Michigan would have had to temporarily close, and Michiganders would have been denied access to their money for an unknown period of time until bankers and authorities could straighten out the mess. This is pretty much what happened anyway, except it happened to the United States rather than just Michigan.

The Michigan bank holiday started an avalanche of holidays that rolled across the country. That cascade of holidays provoked a run on the dollar by nervous Europeans that scared Federal Reserve bankers into demanding a national shutdown. FDR obliged. When President Roosevelt stopped convertibility of the dollar, foreign purchases of United States gold stopped as it was no longer for sale. After the March bank holiday, President Roosevelt induced price inflation as had been demanded by populists since the deepening of the farm crisis in the mid–1920s. With prices inflating, bank assets stopped losing value so banks stopped selling assets at a loss. When the market value of assets started to resemble the face value, it became easier for banks to balance their books and keep their doors open. Through the licensing process the federal government closed many of those bank doors that might have stayed open in order to save President Roosevelt the potential embarrassment of presiding over yet another wave of bank failures. To head off those failures, fragile banks were closed by fiat, freezing billions of dollars in inaccessible accounts.[3]

What should President Hoover have done when faced with the cascade of state bank holidays? As President-elect Roosevelt never tired of pointing out to President Hoover, the president did not need the permission or even cooperation of the president-elect in order to sign an executive order. An executive order closing the banks or suspending gold exports would have been received with greater sympathy by the public, and especially the Democrat-controlled Congress, had it been issued by Hoover with Roosevelt's cooperation. When it became clear, however, that such cooperation was not forthcoming, nothing prevented Hoover from signing such an order without the assent of either Congress or the president-elect. Because the real problem during the first week of March 1933 was the flight of gold from American vaults, Hoover did not need public or congressional support to halt gold trading, which was the real and unambiguous purpose of the Trading with the Enemy Act in any event. He needed only the support of the Federal Reserve Board, which would have been forthcoming, and of a few key congressmen, such as Carter Glass who had been calling for the suspension of gold trading for six months before March. However, as noted, such boldness was neither in Hoover's conception of the presidency nor his character.[4]

If the wave of state holidays, capped by the federal holiday, was an overreaction, what would have been the right reaction? In hindsight, it is easy to say that the Federal Reserve Board should have taken command and assured nervous state governors that plenty of cash would be available to supply correspondent banks cut off from their normal supply in Detroit and Baltimore. In fact, the Federal Reserve Banks of Chicago and New York did engage in open market operations to infuse the system with $1.5 billion, which is what the Fed was created to do. Fed officials at the regional level acted responsibly by staying on the phone or in late-night meetings with bankers and governors throughout the crisis. However, on both the district and national level, Fed officials insisted they were not and ought not to be in charge. This reflected a view of the Federal Reserve Bank in an era when the potential of power and sway of the Fed was feared rather than hoped for. If the Fed was supposed to be a super–clearing house, it could have — and in hindsight should have — taken the lead in the crisis as soon as it was recognized, after Governor Ritchie declared a holiday in Maryland.

As we have seen, clearinghouse association members usually gathered quickly in the face of local financial excitement and assumed responsibility and command. Since 1929 they had acted quickly and decisively in Houston, Boston, Chicago, New York, Philadelphia, Toledo, and other cities beset by closures and panics. Why did not the Fed act as the super–clearing house association that it was supposed to be? Because, out of fear of centralized billions of dollars, nobody wanted it to, especially the men who ran the Federal Reserve Board. It took decades for the Federal Reserve Bank to take a commanding lead and only after the Federal Reserve Bank of New York was forcibly displaced by the board in Washington, D.C., which was, in turn, subordinated to the federal government by New Deal legislation intended to curb "Wall Street." Just as such brazen command was not in Hoover's conception of the presidency, nor was it in Eugene Meyer's idea of the Federal Reserve Board. Indeed, during the worst of the crisis, Meyer abdicated leadership to Treasury Secretary Mills and Fed economist Emmanuel Goldenweiser because Meyer's nerves were frayed.[5]

Was the holiday necessary to restore confidence in the banks to stop hoarding and thus restore banks to health? No. Many people never trusted banks again and always kept large amounts of cash hidden in cupboards long after the effective functioning of the FDIC made such actions uncalled for. Bank runs haunted bankers who maintained high levels of liquidity in response, contributing to tight credit. Bankers anxious about runs kept a close eye on their reserves, but such anxiety does not explain the billions of excess dollars that steadily mounted in bank and Fed vaults up to 1942.[6] A falloff of business activity and loans to sustain it does. Business demanded few loans and they asked for almost no trade acceptances or commercial paper, as trade had slackened to paltry proportions. In October 1929 all banks offered $42.2 billion in loans; by June 1933 that figure had ebbed to $22.2 billion, a drop-off even greater than the decline in deposits. Even bonds—the usual investment of excess cash—paid so little as to be unattractive to bankers looking for income-generating assets. What would bankers have done with the extra money that came out of the publics' tin cans?

The most important measure taken by President Roosevelt was the embargo on gold sales. This move effectively removed anxiety over Federal Reserve gold holdings from Fed officials' thinking about setting proper interest rates. The Fed raised interest rates at least three times (May and July 1928, and October 1931) in reaction to gold leaving American banks for foreign vaults. Raising rates was intended to keep the gold in American accounts and available to back Federal Reserve notes. Raising rates unquestionably hurt the American economy by tightening credit when it should have been loosened. When Chairman Meyer waived the rule demanding 40 percent gold backing for Federal Reserve Bank notes on Friday night, March 3, fears of foreign raids upon American gold reserves weakening the dollar should have been eliminated. The subsequent flood of gold into Treasury coffers after the enactment of the Emergency Banking Act gave the Federal Reserve access to enough gold to back a mountain of notes to enlarge the money supply and credit in the United States much beyond what could reasonably be used in 1933.[7]

Leaving the gold standard, which the United States effectively did after two presidential orders (March 25 and April 5, 1933), probably had little direct effect on prices or the money supply. The real advantage of leaving the gold standard was to remove it as a factor in setting interest rates: from March 1933 the Federal Reserve could set rates to stimulate or dampen the American economy free of worries about foreign raids on gold supplies in New York. If the vaults in New York had been emptied of gold in March 1933—a real possibility— then the United States would have been effectively *forced* off the gold standard. President Roosevelt took the United States off the gold standard for all practical purposes on March 6 anyway. It was certainly better to suspend the gold standard voluntarily than to be forced off of it by raids by foreign bankers. The Emergency Banking Act confirmed that move, which was confirmed yet again in the Gold Contract Act of 1933 and the 1934 Gold Devaluation Act.

The Glass-Steagall Act of 1932 had already given the Fed great flexibility in expanding money in circulation, and after the Emergency Banking Act allowed Federal Reserve notes to be based on "cats and dogs," it could print even more. Perhaps an expanded money supply did not provoke the surge in prices of 1933, but at least a want of Federal Reserve notes—or a *fear* of scarcity—did not depress prices after the spring of 1933. President Roosevelt then devalued the dollar by lowering its gold content (not convertible domestically), thus allowing prices to rise further. Deflation was at an end and banks, especially rural banks, could fend for themselves because their clients could more readily repay loans. Farmers especially were better positioned to recoup their expenses and, thus, repay loans to banks. Property prices hit bottom, which did not in itself help banks recoup real-estate loans. Only a recovered economy that provided more employment would help debtors repay mortgages more easily, and after March 1933 the economy did recover somewhat and did provide more employment. Nevertheless, banks continued to write off billions of dollars in bad loans for the next several years.

Did the holidays not save the banks? They did not. The nationalization of the holidays served no useful purpose. The supposed purpose of the holidays on both the state and national levels was the same as the earliest holidays declared in small towns in Illinois and Oklahoma: to stop or prevent bank runs. After most state legislatures passed laws allowing banks to restrict withdrawals, banks had effective means at their disposal to prevent runs in those states. The "Couzens Law" made those tools available to national banks in February 1933. When President Roosevelt closed the banks in Indiana he did not stop runs as withdrawal restrictions had already accomplished that — even assuming there actually were any runs to stop. But did not the holidays "restore confidence in the banks"? Despite constant repetition since 1933, there is little evidence that they did and some that they did not. Money did not flee banks in February and March because people distrusted banks, it fled because people — mostly corporate finance officers and bankers—feared what state governors were about to do, and then did: close the banks.

Certainly the closure lasted too long and the charade of licensing was unnecessary. In state after state, bankers itched to reopen, and impatient citizens wanted to know when their banks would reopen and, like the bankers in Los Angeles, wondered what was taking so long. Bankers and examiners reviewing examination reports from the previous December or June did nothing to restore banks to health. If examiners wanted to close shaky banks they could do so at any time, as they did to Jesse Binga's bank in Chicago. Banks were ready to reopen and their clients waited impatiently on Friday, March 10, when they were originally scheduled to reopen by FDR's March 6 proclamation. The closures that lingered on into the next week fulfilled a single function: they satisfied the procedures mandated by a handful of tired, jumpy, and overworked government officials in the Treasury Building. The licensing process was a *Grand Guignol* staged to restore confidence that did not need restoring. The process further kept billions of dollars frozen in accounts desperately needed by businesses and citizens to carry on. The licensing process that lingered into 1934 acted as a drag on the economy that needed all the help it could get.

Milton Friedman and Anna Schwartz argued forcefully in 1963 that the bank crisis contributed mightily to the depth and length of the Great Depression. MIT economist Peter Temin doubted it in 1976 and a debate has ensued ever since. Temin asserts that the depressed economy pushed banks into crisis rather than the other way round. When I started this work, I was inclined to agree more with Temin than with Friedman and Schwartz, even while recognizing the merit of their argument. It seemed reasonable to conclude that bankers' anxiety to lend made it more difficult for businesses to operate and kept commerce and industry sluggish. However, Friedman and Schwartz's thesis rests on simple arithmetic: as currency left banks the deposit multiplier worked in reverse from 1930 through 1932, causing bank loans to diminish. This restriction of credit aggravated the Depression. Even if we can point to individual banks or groups of banks that were sunk by collapsing industrial demand, such as the banks in Pennsylvania's coal country or in Missouri's lead-mining district, the larger explanation of restricted credit carries enormous weight. Certainly the bank crisis contributed to the Depression and no doubt the bank panic of 1933 caused the economy to reach it lowest point of the Great Depression in March 1933. But as noted, the panic of March 1933 was less a problem of weak banks than frightened bankers and politicians. Herbert Hoover's hesitancy and Franklin Roosevelt's obstinacy both helped to turn the 1933 crisis into a panic, which could have and should have been avoided.[8]

Chapter Notes

Abbreviations

Publications

ABAJ—*American Bankers Association Journal*
ISCNB— Comptroller of the Currency, *Individual Statements of Conditions of National Banks at the Close of Business, December 31* (1929–1934)
SEP— United States Senate, *Hearings Before the Committee on Banking and Currency*, 73rd Cong., May 23, 1933 — January 1934, *on Stock Exchange Practices*.

Papers

AAB Adolf A. Berle Papers
AP Andrew Price Papers
AWB Alben W. Barkley Papers
CG Carter Glass Papers
CGD Charles G. Dawes Papers
CWT Charles W. Taussig Papers
DRC David R. Coker Papers
EAG Emanuel A. Goldenweiser Papers
EAR Edward A. Rumely Papers
EM Eugene Meyer Papers
ES Edward Stettinius, Jr. Papers
FDRF Franklin Delano Roosevelt Family Papers
FDRG Franklin Delano Roosevelt Governorship Papers
FDRO Franklin Delano Roosevelt Papers, Official File
FDRP Franklin Delano Roosevelt Papers, Personal File
FJC Frank J. Cannon Papers
FMV Frederick M. Vinson Papers
FNBD First National Bank of Denver Papers
HBW Herman B Wells Papers
HFB Harry F. Byrd, Sr. Papers
HDP Holman D. Pettibone Papers
HM Henry Morganthau, Jr., Papers
IP Irénée du Pont Papers
JC James Couzens Papers
JES James E. Stevens Papers
JFB James F. Byrnes Papers
JJO John J. O'Connor Papers
JJR John J. Raskob Papers
JPB James P. Buchanan Papers
JS Jouett Shouse Papers
LL Louis Ludlow Papers
MER Mark E. Reed Papers
OM Ogden Mills Papers
PCHA Philadelphia Clearing House Association Papers
PSP Pierre S. du Pont Papers
RGT Rexford G. Tugwell Papers
RM Raymond Moley Papers
SM Sterling Morton Papers
TWL Thomas W. Lamont Papers
UW Urey Woodson Papers

WLW Wendell L. Willkie Papers
WW Walter Wyatt Papers

Introduction

1. *Indianapolis News*, eve. ed., 6 March 1933; *Detroit Free Press*, 7 March 1933; *St. Louis Post-Dispatch*, 8 March 1933; bank slip from Takoma Park Bank to Walter Wyatt, 28 February 1933, WW box 61.

2. Alan Brinkley, *The End of Reform: New Deal Liberalism in Recession and War* (New York: Vintage, 1996) contains a good discussion of the tension between recovery and reform initiatives within the Roosevelt administration; Arthur M. Schlesinger, Jr., *The Age of Roosevelt*, vol. 2, *The Coming of the New Deal* (Boston: Houghton Mifflin, 1958) remains the best discussion of the "hundred days."

3. Elmus Wicker, "Roosevelt's 1933 Monetary Experiment," *Journal of American History* 57, no. 4 (1971): 864–79. On the link between the Depression and the gold standard, see Barry Eichengreen, *Golden Fetters: The Gold Standard and the Great Depression, 1919–1939* (New York: Oxford University Press, 1995).

4. Speech of Sen. Arthur Vandenberg at Advertising Fed. of America convention, Grand Rapids, 26 June 1933, Speeches and Writings, WLW box 2; P.S. du Pont to J. Leib, 1 September 1933, PSP box 1281.

5. Susan Estabrook Kennedy, *The Banking Crisis of 1933* (Lexington: University of Kentucky Press, 1973).

6. David M. Kennedy, *Freedom from Fear: The American People in Depression and War, 1929–1945* (New York: Oxford University Press, 1999), 132; Jonathan Alter, *The Defining Moment: FDR's Hundred Days and the Triumph of Hope* (New York: Simon & Schuster, 2006).

7. Milton Friedman and Anna Jacobson Schwartz, *A Monetary History of The United States, 1867–1960* (Princeton: Princeton University Press, 1993), 324–32, 398; Barrie A. Wigmore, "Was the Bank Holiday of 1933 Caused by a Run on the Dollar?" *Journal of Economic History* 47, no. 3 (1987): 739–55; Elmus Wicker, *The Banking Panics of the Great Depression* (Cambridge, UK: Cambridge University Press, 1996).

Chapter One

1. Eugene Nelson White, *The Regulation and Reform of the American Banking System, 1900–1929* (Princeton, NJ: Princeton University Press, 1983), 76–7, 82–6; Robert H. Wiebe, *Businessmen and Reform: A Study of the Pro-*

gressive Movement (Chicago: Ivan R. Dee, 1989), 62–4, 68; Robert F. Bruner and Sean D. Carr, *The Panic of 1907: Lessons Learned from the Market's Perfect Storm* (Hoboken, NJ: John Wiley & Sons, 2007), 13–5.

2. White, *Regulation and Reform*, 97–9; Rixey Smith and Norman Beasley, *Carter Glass: A Biography* (New York: Longmans, Green, 1939), 113–14, 120–24.

3. United States Department of Commerce, Bureau of the Census, *Historical Statistics of the United States: Colonial Times to 1957* (Washington, DC: GPO, 1960), 711.

4. Allan H. Meltzer, *A History of the Federal Reserve*, vol. 1, *1913–1951* (Chicago: University of Chicago Press, 2003), 90–103; *Historical Statistics*, 116. Prices rose from 68.1 (1926 = 100) in 1914 to 117.5 in 1917, and then to 154.4 in 1920. Russell Leffingwell to Carter Glass, 1 April 1929; Glass to Leffingwell, 5 April 1929, CG box 283; Meltzer, *Federal Reserve*, 1:93–103; Federal Reserve Board, *Banking and Monetary Statistics, 1914–1941* (Washington, DC: Federal Reserve System, 1943), 439, 450.

5. David Cannadine, *Mellon: An American Life* (New York: Alfred Knopf, 2006), 278–84, 287–92; *Historical Statistics*, 224.

6. Allan Nevins and Frank Ernest Hill, *Ford: Expansion and Challenge, 1915–1933* (New York: Charles Scribner's Sons, 1957), 200–16, 255–57, 279–99, 687; United States Department of Commerce, Bureau of the Census, *Statistical Abstract of the United States* (Washington, DC: GPO, 1932), 358, hereafter cited as *U.S. Statistical Abstract*. In 1928 Ford shut down his original plant in Highland Park and moved production of all of his Michigan vehicles to the River Rouge plant, but all 1,870,000 Fords were not made in Michigan in 1929.

7. *Historical Statistics*, 362, 458–59.

8. *Historical Statistics*, 379; "Mortgage Shop Talk," address by Holman Pettibone before Chicago Mortgage Bankers' Assn., 18 March 1931; Carl Perry, Research and Stat. Div. of Federal Reserve Board, to Louis K. Boysen, First Union Trust and Savings Bank, Chicago, 1 October 1931, HDP box 1.

9. Marquis James, *The Metropolitan Life: A Study in Business Growth* (New York: Viking Press, 1947), 251, 256; William Rankin Ward, *Down the Years: A History of the Mutual Benefit Life Insurance Company, 1845 to 1932* (Newark, NJ: Mutual Benefit Life Insurance Company, 1932), 176.

10. *Commercial and Financial Chronicle* (20 October 1928), 2148; (28 January 1933), 555–61; Federal Reserve Board, *Annual Report*, 1928 (Washington, DC: GPO, 1929) 3–5, hereafter cited as *Annual Report of the Federal Reserve Board*, with appropriate year; *Historical Statistics*, 379–80.

11. Emanuel Goldenweiser's papers vividly illustrate the discord and bewilderment often expressed on the Federal Reserve Board; see memo about discussion at Federal Reserve Board, 2 May 1929; talk with Gov. Owen Young, 3 June 1929; Meeting of Open Market Comm., 24 Sept 1929; Talk to the Board on 22 October 1929, EAG box 1; memo from W. Randolph Burgess to George Harrison, 29 December 1930, EAG box 2. Milton Friedman and Anna Jacobson Schwartz's severe criticism of the Federal Reserve system's performance in the 1920s in *A Monetary History of The United States, 1867–1960*, has proven to be widely influential.

12. *U.S. Statistical Abstract* (1930): 647–49; Robert Conot, *American Odyssey* (New York: William Morrow, 1974), 202; Benjamin J. Klebaner, *American Commercial Banking: A History* (Boston: Twayne, 1990), 121.

13. *Banking and Monetary Statistics*, 286–90.

14. Fred A. Shannon, *The Farmer's Last Frontier: Agriculture, 1860–1897* (White Plains, NY: M.E. Sharpe, 1973), 183–84, 188–90, 222–26; Samuel P. Hays, *The Response to Industrialism, 1885–1914* (Chicago: University of Chicago Press, 1957), 28–32.

15. Commission for Study of the Banking Structure, "Banking Developments in New York State, 1923–1934" (New York State Bankers Assn., 1935), 8, AP box 1; Eugene Nelson White, "Before the Glass-Steagall Act: An Analysis of the Investment Banking Activities of National Banks," *Explorations in Economic History* 23, no. 1 (January 1986): 36–7, 42.

16. National Industrial Conference Board, *The Availability of Bank Credit* (New York:, 1932), 10–11. "The 100 Per Cent Reserve Proposal," n.d., [by Goldenweiser], EAG box 1, discusses credit trends of the 1920s.

17. Klebaner, *Commercial Banking*, 35; *Annual Report of the Federal Reserve Board* (1926), 150; (1928), 119. Oddly, the annual report stopped reporting holdings of corporate stocks by member banks after 1928. The holdings of corporate stock by banks would include $147 million in Federal Reserve Bank stock paid in by member banks; *Annual Report of the Federal Reserve Board* (1928), 65.

18. Klebaner, *Commercial Banking*, 123–24; Goldenweiser "talk to the [Fed. Res.] Board," 22 Oct 1929, EAG box 1.

19. Klebaner, *Commercial Banking*, 122–24; John D. Hicks, *The Republican Ascendancy, 1921–1933* (New York: Harper & Row, 1963), 227; John Kenneth Galbraith, *The Great Crash* (Boston: Houghton Mifflin, 1988), 35–7; Smith and Beasley, *Carter Glass*, 95–7; *Annual Report of the Federal Reserve Board* (1930), 126.

20. *Banking and Monetary Statistics*, 494; *Annual Report of the Federal Reserve Board* (1929), 6–7; Federal Reserve Bank of New York, *Monthly Review of Credit and Business Conditions* (1 November 1929); talk with Gov. Young, 3 June 1929, EAG box 1.

21. *Commercial and Financial Chronicle* (6 October 1928), 1843; (27 October 1928), 2305–06; (17 November 1928), 2765.

22. *Commercial and Financial Chronicle* (6 October 1928), 1845; (20 October 1928), 2147; (7 October 1933), 2514–15; *Banking and Monetary Statistics*, 441; White, *Regulation and Reform*, 123; Charles Hamlin to Walter Lichtenstein, 19 May 1932, EM box 33; Goldenweiser "talk to the [Fed. Res.] Board," 22 October 1929, EAG box 1; Galbraith, *Great Crash*, 46–51.

23. Meltzer, *Federal Reserve*, 1:245–52; James L. Butkiewicz, "Eugene Meyer and the Great Contraction," August 22, 2006, www.lerner.udel.edu/economics/WorkingPapers/2005/UDWP2005-01.pdf, 11–13, 16–17.

24. Federal Reserve Bank of New York, *Monthly Review of Credit and Business Conditions* (1 November 1929), 1; *Annual Report of the Federal Reserve Board* (1929), 10; *Commercial and Financial Chronicle* (8 November 1930), 2981; *U.S. Statistical Abstract* (1932), 359; Klebaner, *Commercial Banking*, 124. For a good blow-by-blow narration of the Crash, see Barrie A. Wigmore, *The Crash and Its Aftermath: A History of Securities Markets in the United States, 1929–1933* (Westport, CT: Greenwood Press, 1985), 3–87, especially 6–26; for a muckraker's view (who was there and invested at the time), see Matthew Josephson, *The Money Lord: The Great Finance Capitalists, 1925–1950* (New York: Waybright and Talley, 1972), 80–105. The role of the Crash in propagating the Depression is unclear, and economists differ on the question. Christina Romer has a

thoughtful discussion of the question in "The Great Crash and the Onset of the Great Depression," *Quarterly Journal of Economics* 105, no. 3 (August 1990): 597–624.

25. Federal Reserve Bank of New York, *Monthly Review of Credit and Business Conditions* (1 November 1929), 1; *Annual Report of the Federal Reserve Board* (1930), 130, 167; Wigmore, *Crash*, 6–26; *Banking and Monetary Statistics*, 83.

26. *Annual Report of the Federal Reserve Board* (1930), 130, 167.

27. The fascinating tale of Caldwell and Company is ably told by John Berry McFerrin in *Caldwell and Company: A Southern Financial Empire* (Nashville: Vanderbilt University Press, 1969), originally published by the University of North Carolina Press in 1939.

28. *St. Louis Post-Dispatch*, 7, 13–20 November 1930; *Louisville Courier-Journal*, 7, 14–18 November 1930; *Commercial and Financial Chronicle* (15 November 1930), 3151; (22 November 1930), 3310–11; (29 November 1930), 3473.

29. McFerrin, *Caldwell*, 186–87; *St. Louis Post-Dispatch*, 18, 19 November 1930; *Commercial and Financial Chronicle* (22 November 1930), 3310.

30. McFerrin, *Caldwell*, 186–87; *St. Louis Post-Dispatch*, 20 November 1930; *Commercial and Financial Chronicle* (22 November 1930), 3310; (29 November 1930), 3473–74; (27 December 1930) 4150; *ABAJ* (July 1931): 15; *Annual Report of the Comptroller of the Currency* (1931), 243.

31. "The Growth of the Bank of United States," by Levy Bros., 10 May 1929; "Bank of United States," pamphlet, JJR file 141; *New York Times*, 12 December 1930; M.R. Werner, *Little Napoleons and Dummy Directors: Being the Narrative of the Bank of United States* (New York: Harper & Brothers, 1933), 2–8; Paul Trescott, "The Failure of the Bank of United States, 1930: A Rejoinder to Anthony Patrick O'Brien," *Journal of Money, Credit and Banking* 24, no. 3 (1992): 389, 391; Wicker, *Banking Panics*, 37.

32. Saul Singer, Pres. Bankus Corp. to stockholders, 1 April 1930; Bernard Marcus to stockholders, 7 April 1930; Bank of United States pamphlet, May 29, 1930, JJR file 141; Werner, *Little Napoleons*, 97–102, 105; Trescott, "Failure of the Bank of United States," 391.

33. Joseph L. Lucia, "The Failure of the Bank of United States: A Reappraisal," *Explorations in Economic History* 22, no. 4 (1985): 405; Wicker, *Banking Panics*, 37; Werner, *Little Napoleons*, 134.

34. *New York Times*, 11 December 1930.

35. *New York Times*, 11, 12 December 1930; Wicker, *Banking Panics*, 37; Friedman and Schwartz, *Monetary History*, 309–10.

36. *New York Times*, 12 December 1930; Trescott, "Failure of the Bank of United States,"387.

37. *Philadelphia Evening Bulletin*, 22 December 1930; *Philadelphia Inquirer*, 23, 24 December 1930.

38. *Philadelphia Inquirer*, 23, 24 December 1930.

39. *Annual Report of the Federal Reserve Board* (1933), 72–74; *Banking and Monetary Statistics*, 371, 413; Friedman and Schwartz, *Monetary History*, 340–43; see Wicker, *Banking Panics*, 49, 52–55.

40. *Federal Reserve Bulletin* (February 1931), 113; *Annual Report of the Comptroller of the Currency* (1931), 1034, 1036; *Farm Real Estate Situation, 1930–31*, USDA circular no. 209 (December 1931), 1–2, 17; Robert E. Wait, Arkansas Bankers Assn. to Herman Wells, 2 December 1931, HBW box 17. Arkansas and North Carolina (93), along with Missouri (104) and Illinois (126), reported the most bank failures in 1930 and also suffered

the most severe declines in value of farmland (both 23 percent.) However, Virginia and Minnesota suffered the second worst depreciation in farmland values (17 percent) and suffered relatively mild bank failures (20 and 22, respectively.) Gary Richardson, "Bank Distress During the Great Contraction, 1929 to 1933, New Data From the Archives of the Board of Governors," *National Bureau of Economic Research Working Paper*, no. 12590 (2006): 12, notes the large number of banks forced temporarily into difficult straits in the fall of 1930 by weak correspondent banks. Forty percent of all bank suspensions in 1930 were temporary. That figure fell in subsequent years.

41. For the survival of the fittest argument, see the statement by ABA President Harry Haas in *ABAJ* (November 1932): 53; Daniel R. Fusfeld, *The Economic Thought of Franklin D. Roosevelt and the Origins of the New Deal* (New York: Columbia University Press, 1954), 183–87; C. David Tompkins, *Senator Arthur H. Vandenberg: The Evolution of a Modern Republican, 1884–1945* (n.p.: Michigan State University Press, 1970), 85. On the other hand, the Federal Reserve Bank estimated that 153 banks failed in 1930 due to defalcation and mismanagement, or 11 percent of failures. See Richardson, "New Data, " 42. *Commercial and Financial Chronicle* (13 December 1930), 3812; Fusfeld, *Economic Thought*, 183–89; "A Message to the Legislature for the Protection of Thrift Accounts in Commercial Banks, 24 March 1931," in Samuel Rosenman, ed., *The Public Papers and Addresses of Franklin D. Roosevelt*, vol. 1, *The Genesis of the New Deal, 1928–1932* (New York: Random House, 1938), 535–37.

43. Peter Atherton, Glenview, KY, to Jouett Shouse, 27 December 1930; Shouse to Atherton, 30 December 1930, CG box 267; *Boston Globe* (11 December 1930), 25; (12 December 1930), 40; (13 December 1930), 17; *St. Louis Post-Dispatch*, 7–20 November 1930; *Atlanta Constitution* (13 November 1930), 1, 7; *Annual Report of the Federal Reserve Board* (1933), 163; *Denver Post*, 10, 11 December 1930. I found no mention of the Bank of United States collapse in either the *Philadelphia Evening Bulletin* or the *San Francisco Chronicle*, 11, 12 December 1930. As noted by many financial observers of the era, mutual savings banks actually gained deposits as commercial banks lost them. See, for example, *ABAJ* (July 1931): 5, and *Annual Report of the Comptroller of the Currency* (1931), 114; mutual savings banks time deposits rose from $9.2 billion (June 1930) to $10 billion (June 1931), *Banking and Monetary Statistics*, 34. Friedman and Schwartz are the leading proponents of the argument that money bleeding from banks due to lack of public confidence worsened the Depression.

44. *Banking and Monetary Statistics*, 18, 34; Advisory Council Meeting on May 18 [*sic*]," 15 May 1931; "Notes on Credit Policy in 1932," 7 January 1932, EAG box 1.

45. *ABAJ* (July 1931): 5; (August 1931): 103; *U.S. Statistical Abstract* (1932), 358–59; (1935), 277; *Indianapolis News*, 2 December 1930; *Denver Post*, 10 December 1930; *San Francisco Chronicle*, 11, 12 December 1930; *Annual Report of the Federal Reserve Bank of New York* (1931), 5; Advisory Council Meeting on May 18" [*sic*], May 15, 1931, EAG box 1. Bank debit numbers are reported monthly in the *Federal Reserve Bulletin*. Bank deposit figures exclude deposits held for other banks. Milton Friedman and Anna Schwartz argued in their seminal book *A Monetary History of the United States, 1867–1960* (301–05, 342–46, 351–52) that the hoarding process that started after the collapse of Caldwell and Company and the Bank of United States in fall 1930 forced banks to

liquidate assets. To pay out cash, banks had to dip into reserves and call in loans, which acted as a negative multiplier on bank deposits: in order to pay off recalled loans, companies signed over deposits to banks, effectively removing both loans (assets) and deposits (liabilities) from banks' ledgers. When currency outside of banks grew by $236 million from June 30 to December 31, 1930, banks were forced to liquidate a large amount of assets to replenish reserves of currency in their own vaults, correspondent banks, and the Federal Reserve banks. Because the deposit multiplier (that makes it possible for banks to loan and reloan deposits worth the inverse of cash reserves set aside to meet day-to-day demands for cash) worked in reverse in 1930 — destroying bank money rather than creating it — banks had to liquidate assets worth $1.71 billion to replace funds withdrawn by nervous depositors. Reserves in mid–1930 for Federal Reserve member banks were around 13.8 percent, meaning a $1,000 deposit could multiply into future deposits of $7,246 (7.246 is the inverse of 0.138.) If the multiplier works in reverse, which it did in 1930, banks would have had to surrender deposits worth $1.71 billion to pay out $236 million in cash. In fact, deposits actually fell $1.74 billion in late 1930, which is 102 percent of the expected amount. Friedman and Schwartz's explanation that blamed currency hoarding for the dramatic decline in bank lending and deposits fits the crisis of late 1930 perfectly.

46. "Advisory Council Meeting on May 18" [sic], 15 May 1931, EAG box 1; *Federal Reserve Bulletin* (January 1932), 78; (March 1932), 196–99; (April 1932), 270; *Annual Report of the Federal Reserve Bank of New York* (1931), 5; *Commercial and Financial Chronicle* (12 December 1931), 3884; *U.S. Statistical Abstract* (1932), 359.

47. *Federal Reserve Bulletin* (1932), 78; *Annual Report of the Federal Reserve Board* (1931), 18, 20; (1932), 120; (1933), 206; National Industrial Conference Board, *The Banking Situation in the United States* (New York, 1932), 131–33; *ABAJ* (July 1931): 37. English economist John Maynard Keynes invented the term "liquidity trap" to describe the condition when money languished unused in vaults.

48. Friedman and Schwartz assert the second bank crisis of the Great Depression started in March 1931, but say little about it and nothing about its cause, *Monetary History*, 313–14. Aurel Schubert, *The Credit-Anstalt Crisis of 1931* (New York: Cambridge University Press, 1991), 19–31, provides a good discussion of economists' assessment of the importance of the Austrian crisis. *Credit-Anstalt* is often spelled *Kreditanstalt*, the spelling used in Germany, and not Austria. Walter Spahr, "Money without Gold," *ABAJ* (December 1931): 281; Alexander Dana Noyes, *ABAJ* (February 1932): 499; William Starr Myers and Walter H. Newton, *The Hoover Administration: A Documented Narrative* (New York: Charles Scribner's Sons, 1936), 100–01; Charles P. Kindleberger, *The World in Depression, 1929–1939* (Berkeley: University of California Press, 1973), 129–31, 148–51, 160; *Commercial and Financial Chronicle* (16 May 1931), 3637; (20 June 1931), 4465–67. Herbert Feis, an economic advisor in the State Department in 1931, gives a clue about American reaction to the collapse of the Credit-Anstalt in his memoir, *1933: Characters in Crisis* (Boston: Little, Brown, 1966), 5, where he relates discussing "*late in 1931* ... the report just received [that] the Kredit Anstalt, the great Austrian bank, had just collapsed," when the collapse occurred in May. For a good overview of economic thinking about the international dimension of the Depression, see Barry Eichengreen, "Did International Economic Forces Cause the Great Depression?" *Contemporary Policy Issues* 6, no. 2 (1988): 90–114. Peter Temin has few doubts about the importance of the European financial debacle on converting the severe Depression of 1930 and early 1931 into the catastrophe that we know. See Peter Temin, "The Great Depression," *National Bureau of Economic Research Working Paper*, no. 62 (1994): 17–20. James Hamilton agrees that international money flows aggravated the Depression in 1931 in "Role of the International Gold Standard in Propagating the Great Depression," *National Bureau of Economic Research Working Paper*, no. 62 (1994): 67–89. Economists in 1931 were just as puzzled and contentious about the deteriorating economy in 1931. See William J. Barber, *From New Era to New Deal: Herbert Hoover, the Economists, and American Economic Policy, 1921–1933* (New York: Cambridge University Press, 1985), 115–24. Barry Eichengreen's *Golden Fetters: The Gold Standard and the Great Depression, 1919–1939* comes as close as any work to putting an end to much debate about the Great Depression with his authoritative discussion of the disastrous impact of efforts to maintain the international gold standard despite the massive damage done to currencies and economies.

49. Federal Reserve Bank of Cleveland, *Monthly Business Review* (1 August 1931), 1–5, 7; *Annual Report of the Federal Reserve Board* (1931), 199–200, 205–15; *Banking and Monetary Statistics*, 466, 475, 481, 489; debits from monthly *Federal Reserve Bulletin* (1931–32).

50. *Annual Report of the Federal Reserve Bank of New York* (1931), 8–9.

51. *Federal Reserve Bulletin* (December 1931), 664

52. *Banking and Monetary Statistics*, 412, 441, 445, 457, 464, 466. Friedman and Schwartz in *Monetary History*, 315–18, assert that Fed actions to calm the waters were insufficient, and in fact hurt American banks in the interior scrambling to come up with cash. In view of the results, I am inclined to agree with them.

53. *Annual Report of the Federal Reserve Board* (1933), 4–5; *Annual Report of the Federal Reserve Bank of New York* (1931), 6; *ABAJ* (March 1932): vii, 557; Myers and Newton, *Hoover Administration*, 120–21, 159. Debits are culled from monthly *Federal Reserve Bulletin*.

54. *Annual Report of the Comptroller of the Currency* (1931), 128; *Annual Report of the Federal Reserve Board* (1931), 88, 161, 206, 212–13; *Banking and Monetary Statistics*, 34. Bank-clearing data are drawn from issues of the *Commercial and Financial Chronicle*. Bank debits are from the *Federal Reserve Bulletin*. Again following Milton Friedman and Anna Schwartz, from June to December 1931, depositors withdrew $819 million in currency from banks, forcing banks to liquidate assets worth nearly $5 billion. Banks held 16.5 percent of deposits in reserve — more than double their legal requirements — in 1931, so to come up with cash they had to surrender deposits worth the inverse of 0.165, which is 6.06, times $819 million, which equals $4,963 million. Deposits actually fell $5,221 million in late 1931, which is 105 percent of the expected amount.

55. *Chicago Tribune*, 6–12 June 1931; *ISCNB* (1930): 30–31; Frank Cyril James, *The Growth of Chicago Banks*, vol. 2, *The Modern Age, 1897–1938* (New York: Harper & Brothers, 1938), 1001–5.

56. *Annual Report of the Federal Reserve Board* (1931), 191–92, 202–05; *Commercial and Financial Chronicle* (11 April 1931), 2707; (9 May 1931), 3457; (3 October 1931), 2209–10. On Toledo, see Timothy Messer-Kruse, *Banksters, Bosses, and Smart Money: A Social History of the Great Toledo Bank Crash of 1931* (Columbus: Ohio State University Press, 2004).

57. All bank-clearing statistics from *Commercial and Financial Chronicle*; *Annual Report of the Federal Reserve Board* (1931), 204–05; Thomas K. McCraw, *American Business, 1920–2000: How It Worked* (Wheeling, IL: Harlan Davidson, 2000), 40–42.

58. McCraw, *American Business*, 42–54, discusses the case of Proctor and Gamble in Cincinnati during the 1930s; Federal Reserve Bank of Cleveland, *Monthly Business Review* (1 August 1931), 1, 4, points out that retail and consumer industries in the Cleveland district provided the only good news.

59. *Commercial and Financial Chronicle* (17 October 1931), 2556; *Annual Report of the Federal Reserve Board* (1932), 114; *Federal Reserve Bulletin* (January 1932), 78; (April 1932), 270. *Banking and Monetary Statistics*, 235, reports debits for New York City in 1931 were (in millions): January, $24,556; July, $21,007; November, $14,464. Bank clearings are from *Commercial and Financial Chronicle*.

60. *New York Times* (6 November 1931), 46; (1 March 1933), 17; *Commercial and Financial Chronicle* (3 October 1931), 2196.

61. *ISCNB* (1929), 80–1, (1931) 70–1; *New York Times*, 27 December 1931; *Boston Globe*, 16 December 1931; *Commercial and Financial Chronicle* (17 October 1931), 2556.

62. *New York Times*, 27 December 1931; *Commercial and Financial Chronicle* (13 June 1931), 4352, (19 December 1931), 4104–05.

63. *Federal Reserve Bulletin* (February 1932), 134; *Annual Report of the Comptroller of the Currency* (1931), 241–53. The comptroller stopped recording the reasons for a banks falling into receivership after 31 October 1931. He reported that banks often failed because of both poor or dishonest management and poor local conditions, but after August 1930 the number that failed because of poor economic conditions alone increased markedly.

Chapter Two

1. Myers and Newton, *Hoover Administration*, 23–28; Herbert Hoover, *The Memoirs of Herbert Hoover*, vol. 3, *The Great Depression, 1929–1941* (New York: Macmillan, 1951–52), 21–8; Barber, *From New Era*, 80–1.

2. Herbert Hoover, *The Memoirs of Herbert Hoover*, vol. 2, *The Cabinet and the Presidency* (New York: Macmillan, 1951–52), 115–17; Myers and Newton, *Hoover Administration*, 445; David Burner, *Herbert Hoover: A Public Life* (New York: Alfred Knopf, 1979), 256–57; Tompkins, *Vandenberg*, 49–55, 60–64; Stephen Skowronek, *The Politics Presidents Make: Leadership from John Adams to Bill Clinton* (Cambridge, MA: Belknap Press, 1997), 264–74.

3. Hoover, *Memoirs*, 2:303–05; Gaylord Warren, *Herbert Hoover and the Great Depression* (New York: Oxford University Press, 1959), 72–5, 92.

4. Theodore G. Joslin, *Hoover Off the Record* (New York: Doubleday, 1939), 69–71; Charles Michelson, *The Ghost Talks* (New York: G.P. Putnam's Sons, 1944), 17–19, 29–32; Burner, *Herbert Hoover*, 254–55; Harry Barnard, *Independent Man: The Life of James Couzens* (New York: Charles Scribner's Sons, 1958), 143; Myers and Newton, *Hoover Administration*, 32; Warren, *Herbert Hoover*, 56–61; Tompkins, *Vandenberg*, 49–50; Hicks, *Republican Ascendancy*, 216–17.

5. Claude Bowers, *New York World*, to Jouett Shouse, 12 June 1930, 6 October 1930; Shouse to Bowers, 16 June 1930, JS box 2; Radio address by Raskob 27 October 1930, "A Democratic business view of the tariff," PSP box 1281; Robert Harriss, Esq., NYC to Raskob, 24 October 1930, JJR box 144; *Cincinnati Times-Star*, 18 November 1930; Michelson, *Ghost*, 22–25; *Commercial and Financial Chronicle* (4 October 1930), 2105, 2123–26, reprints Hoover's ABA speech (11 October 1930), 2278; (8 November 1930), 2953; (15 November 1930), 3093; Hoover, *Memoirs*, 3:58; "Press Statement, June 15, 1930. Announcement of Intention to Sign Tariff Bill, The Reasons for Approval," in William Starr Myers, ed., *The State Papers and Other Public Writings of Herbert Hoover*, 2 vols. (Garden City, NY: Doubleday, Doran, 1934), 1:314–18; Michael John Romano, "The Emergence of John Nance Garner as a Figure in American National Politics, 1924–1941," (Ph.D. Diss., St. John's University, New York, 1974), 92–98, 101–02, 110–11; Hicks, *Republican Ascendancy*, 237–39; Charles P. Kindleberger in *The World in Depression, 1929–1939*, suggests the Smoot-Hawley Tariff had greater political than economic impact, 131–34. Douglas A. Irwin in "The Smoot-Hawley Tariff: A Quantitative Assessment," *Review of Economics and Statistics* 80, no. 2 (May 1998): 326–34, similarly concludes that the tariff had negligible impact on either imports or on the U.S. economy. Warren, *Herbert Hoover*, 84–97, offers shrill commentary on the Republican drive for the tariff, but notes Hoover's passivity. Despite his overt hostility to the tariff, Warren echoes the argument that the tariff did not cause the Depression but made it worse.

6. James Cox, Publisher of *Dayton Daily News*, to Jouett Shouse, 24 September 1930; Shouse to Cox, 25 September 1930; Claude Bowers to Shouse, 6 October 1930; press release, "The Collapse of an Administration," address by Claude Bowers over CBS radio network, 23 October 1930; Shouse to Daniel Roper, Washington, DC, 15 November 1930, JS box 2; *St. Louis Post-Dispatch*, 7 November 1930; Hoover, *Memoir*, 3:100–01; Hicks, *Republican Ascendancy*, 239–40.

7. Carter Glass to Norman Finninger, NYC, 7 January 1928; Glass to Robert Maddox, First National Bank of Atlanta, 20 January 1930, CG box 252; Smith and Beasley, *Carter Glass*, 286, 289, 297–301; Hoover, *Memoirs*, 3:57; Myers and Newton, *Hoover Administration*, 33; Helen M. Burns, *The American Banking Community and New Deal Reforms, 1933–1935* (Westport CT: Greenwood Press, 1974), 7–8; Sue C. Patrick, *Reform of the Federal Reserve System in the Early 1930s: The Politics of Money and Banking* (New York: Garland Publishing, 1993), 42–4. Carter Glass served as secretary of the Treasury under Wilson after the resignation of William McAdoo. He was appointed to the Senate for Virginia in 1919 and reelected to the position in 1924.

8. United States Senate, *Hearings Before a Subcommittee of the Committee on Finance* (71st Cong., January 19–February 25, 1931) *Operation of the National and Federal Reserve Banking System*; Smith and Beasley, *Carter Glass*, 304–05.

9. Address by Comptroller of the Currency John W. Pole to ABA Convention, San Francisco, 2 October 1929; Statement of John W. Pole, before the Banking and Currency Comm. House of Representatives, 25 February 1930, CG box 266; *Annual Report of the Comptroller of the Currency* (1931), 1; Burns, *American Banking Community*, 10–12.

10. Thomas Patten, General Counsel to ABA to Glass, 2 December 1926; ABA pamphlet, "The Debate on the McFadden Bill" (November 1926), CG box 248; Glass to Paul Warburg, 13 September 1926, CG box 249;

Rudolph S. Hecht, "The Situation that Confronts Banking," Economic Policy Commission of ABA (New York, 1931), 7–9, 18–19, 22, AP box 1; Howard H. Preston, *Multiple Banking, with Special Reference to Conditions in the State of Washington* (Seattle: Washington Mutual Savings Bank, 1931), 3; *Commercial and Financial Chronicle* (4 October 1930), 2122–23.

11. Skowronek, *Politics*, 275–80. Robert La Follette, Jr., of Wisconsin sat as a Progressive, rather than a Republican.

12. *Annual Report of the Federal Reserve Board* (1931), 159, 163.

13. Magnus Alexander, "Preface" in *The Banking Situation in the United States* (New York: National Industrial Conference Board, 1932), v.; G.A. Middleton, Middleton Cotton Co., Charleston, SC, to Glass, 23 December 1932, CG box 285; Brownlow Jackson, Pres. State Trust Co. of Hendersonville, NC, to Glass, 23 April 1932; Benjamin M. Anderson, Jr., "The Goldsborough Bill and the Government Security Purchases of the Federal Reserve Banks," *Chase Economic Bulletin* (16 May 1932), CG box 290/291; Helen M. Burns in *The American Banking Community and New Deal Reforms, 1933–1935*, 20, repeats this assertion about tight-fisted bankers; *ABAJ* (December 1931): 403; (January 1932): 447–48; (February 1932): 500.

14. *Annual Report of the Federal Reserve Bank of New York* (1931), 7; Butkiewicz, "Eugene Meyer," 33–48; Arthur Vandenberg to Eugene Meyer, 19 September 1931; Meyer to Vandenberg, 21 September 1931; Vandenberg to Meyer, 26 September 1931, EM box 42; William Pearson, Ashland, KY, to Rep. Fred Vinson, 13 June 1932, FMV box 24.

15. *ABAJ* (January 1932): 465–66, 469; (June 1932): 474–75. Ben S. Bernanke in "Nonmonetary Effects of the Financial Crisis in the Propagation of the Great Depression," *American Economic Review* 73, no. 3 (June 1983): 257–76, argues that the Depression produced a vicious cycle of contracting credit and, hence, money supply. The more the money supply declined the more credit restricted, causing the money supply to contract further. Charles W. Calomiris and Joseph R. Mason in "Consequences of Bank Distress during the Great Depression," *American Economic Review* 93, no. 3 (June 2003): 937–47, argue that supply of credit, indeed, affected overall economic activity on the state and county level. Why that should be true, rather than vice versa, they fail to explain. Peter Temin in "The Great Depression," 16–7, argues that by early 1931 businesses expected further deflation and, thus, refused to borrow money knowing they would have to pay it back when prices for goods would be even lower. That is, expectation of deflation discouraged borrowers.

16. National Industrial Conference Board, *The Availability of Bank Credit* (New York, 1932), 29–32, 39–40, 60, 69, 72–4, 92, 97–9, 111, 120–22. The survey concluded that between 20 and 25 percent of firms denied loans in 1931–32 that would have been provided credit prior to 1930 (pp. 114, 123.) and that the grievances against bankers were largely not justified (pp. 123–24.)

17. *ABAJ* (July 1931): 37 ;(September 1931): 125; (December 1931): 403; C.L. Corcoran, V.P. Central United National Bank, Cleveland to Sen. Robert Bulkley, 7 September 1932, CG box 299; *Annual Report of the Federal Reserve Board* (1932), 148.

18. *Annual Report of the Federal Reserve Board* (1933), 4–5; *Annual Report of the Federal Reserve Bank of New York* (1931), 6; *ABAJ* (March 1932): vii, 557; Myers and Newton, *Hoover Administration*, 120–21, 159. Debits are culled from monthly *Federal Reserve Bulletin*.

19. *Annual Report of the Comptroller of the Currency* (1931), 128; *Annual Report of the Federal Reserve Board* (1931), 87–88, 161, 206, 212–13, provides the industrial production index where 100 = 1923–25 adjusted average; *Banking and Monetary Statistics*, 34. Bank-clearing data are drawn from the *Commercial and Financial Chronicle* (February 1931 to January 1932). Bank debits in the New York Federal Reserve District alone plunged from $41.715 billion in March 1930 to $23.192 billion in November, see *Federal Reserve Bulletin* (February 1931–January 1932).

20. Hoover, *Memoirs*, 3:82–88; Myers, *State Papers*, 2: 4–7; Myers and Newton, *Hoover Administration*, 118; James, *Chicago Banks*, 2:1026; James Stuart Olson, *Herbert Hoover and the Reconstruction Finance Corporation, 1931–1933* (Ames: Iowa State University Press, 1977), 24–26.

21. Hoover, *Memoirs*, 3:85–91; Olson, *Herbert Hoover*, 26–7.

22. Clinch Heyward Belser, "Banking in South Carolina, 1910–1940" (M.A. thesis, University of South Carolina, 1940), 56–7; *Federal Reserve Bulletin* (December 1931), 664; bank clearings are from *Commercial and Financial Chronicle* (8 October 1932), 2447; (5 November 1932), 3310; (10 December 1932), 3987; (8 July 1933), 269; (5 August 1933), 994; (9 September 1933), 1892. Throughout the 1920s bank clearings typically dropped during the summer and picked up in the fall, but the drop and recovery in October 1931 were particularly notable. *ABAJ* (Oct 1931): 191; (November 1931): 345; Hoover, *Memoirs*, 3:96; Olson, *Herbert Hoover*, 27–8.

23. Testimony of Wilson Mills, Chairman of the Board, Peoples Wayne County Bank, in *SEP* (12): 5485; Mills to Hoover, 17 October 1931, exhibit in *SEP* (12), 5565; Mills to Vandenberg, 15 December 1931, *SEP* (12), 5571; *Commercial and Financial Chronicle* (17 October 1931), 2546–8; *The Hoosier Banker* (Indianapolis: Indiana Bankers Association, January 1932), 12; Belser, "Banking," 54, 57–60.

24. *U.S. Statistical Abstract* (1935), 240, 277; *New York Times* (2 November 1931), 36; *Boston Globe*, 18 December 1931; Frank Cannon to William E. Borah, 4 January 1932, FJC box 2; Wicker, B*anking Panics*, 98; Olson, *Herbert Hoover*, 30.

25. Vandenberg to Mills, 15 October 1931, exhibit in *SEP* (12), 5562; Mills to Vandenberg, 16 October 1931, *SEP* (12), 5563: Mills to Hoover, 27 October 1931, *SEP* (12), 5565; Mills to Vandenberg, 10 December 1931, *SEP* (12), 5569.

26. *ABAJ* (February 1932): v; Olson, *Herbert Hoover*, 29–32; James, *Chicago Banks*, 2:1026n; Belser, "Banking,"56.

27. Mills to Henry Robinson, San Francisco Federal Reserve Bank, 14 November 1931, exhibit in *SEP* (12): 5512; *New York Times*, 2, 15 January 1932; *Chicago Tribune*, 26 January 1932; Hoover, *Memoirs*, 3:94–5; Myers and Newton, *Hoover Administration*, 149.

28. George Anderson, Washington correspondent for the *ABAJ* (December 1931): 403; *New York Times*, 5, 6 February 1932.

29. *Annual Report of the Comptroller of the Currency* (1933), 210; Hoover, *Memoirs*, 3:30–31, 108; Cannadine, *Mellon*, 439–45. One influential economist who agreed with Mellon was Benjamin Anderson of the Chase National Bank. See *Chase Economic Bulletin* (12 June 1931).

30. Bascom N. Timmons, *Garner of Texas: A Personal History* (New York: Harper Brothers, 1948), 20–25.

31. Romano, "Emergence of John Nance Garner," 24, 31–37, 40–52; Cannadine, *Mellon*, 286–88, 315–18.

32. Cannadine, *Mellon*, 317–18, 345–48, 381; Barnard, *Independent Man*, 161–67.

33. Barnard, *Independent Man*, 14–37, 63–4.

34. Ibid., 3–8, 99–100, 117–121.

35. Ibid., 130–36.

36. Byrnes to Joe Robinson, 4 November 1931, JFB box 54.

37. James F. Byrnes, *All in One Lifetime* (New York: Harper & Brothers, 1958), 61.

38. *Chicago Tribune*, 9, 23 December 1931; Byrnes, *Lifetime*, 61; Timmons, *Garner*, 137–38.

39. Jouett Shouse, "Minute Men of the Democratic National Committee," 1 March 1932, PSP box 1281; Vandenberg to Mills, 15 October 1931, exhibit in *SEP* (12): 5562; Arthur Mann, *La Guardia: A Fighter Against His Times, 1882–1933* (Philadelphia: Lippincott, 1959), 302; *Chicago Tribune*, 12 January 1932; Hiram Johnson, *The Diary Letters of Hiram Johnson*, vol. 5, *1929–1933* (New York: Garland, 1983), 23 January 1932.

40. *Baltimore Evening Sun*, 15 January 1932; *Chicago Tribune*, 22 December 1931; 2, 13, 17 January 1932; *New York Times*, 8, 15, 16 January 1932; Florida State Savings Building and Loan Assn. to Glass, 4 February 1932, CG box 285; *ABAJ* (December 1931): 403; (February 1932): v., 489–90, 528; Chamber of Commerce of the USA, Banking Committee Report on Banking Legislation, May 1932, CG box 304.

41. Myers and Newton, *Hoover Administration*, 149; Hoover, *Memoirs*, 3:108; Bascom N. Timmons, *Jesse H. Jones: The Man and the Statesman* (New York: Henry Holt, 1956), 162–64; Olson, *Herbert Hoover*, 39–41.

42. Bascom N. Timmons, *Portrait of an American: Charles G. Dawes* (New York: Henry Holt, 1953), 27–37.

43. Dawes had served no active part in running the "Dawes Bank" since 1924 and did not even sit on its board. His participation in the bank amounted in 1932 to owning 52 shares with a book value of $5,200 and a market value of $2,444. Nevertheless, upon his return to Chicago in June 1932 he was elected chairman of the board of the Central Republic Bank and Trust Company. Dawes Brothers, Inc., owned hundred-thousand dollars in the bank's stock. See Timmons, *Dawes*, 316.

44. James, *Chicago Banks*, 2:1193–95.

45. *ABAJ* (April 1932): 619; Olson, *Herbert Hoover*, 40–43.

46. *Federal Reserve Bulletin* (December 1931), 664; (January 1932), 74; (February 1932), 133; (March 1932), 190; (April 1932), 279; (May 1932), 338; *ABAJ* (March 1932): 557; (July 1932): 7; Timmons, *Dawes*, 313–14; Olson, *Herbert Hoover*, 49–50.

47. Hoover, *Memoirs*, 3:108; Cannadine, *Mellon*, 449–53.

48. Myers and Newton, *Hoover Administration*, 167–68; Burns, *American Banking Community*, 19; Olson, *Herbert Hoover*, 49.

49. *ABAJ* (April 1932): 621.

50. Press Release of Sen. Wagner, 25 January 1932, JJO box 13; Sen. Phillips Lee Goldsborough, MD, to Glass, 5 January 1932; "The Goldsborough Bill and the Government Security Purchases of the Federal Reserve banks" by Benjamin M. Anderson, Jr., in *The Chase Economic Bulletin* (16 May 1932); Sen. Thomas Gore, OK, to Glass, 17 May 1932; "The Hopeless Folly of Inflating Commodity Prices," by E.C. Harwood, MIT, (1932), CG box 290/291; *Chicago Tribune*, 12 January, 16 April 1932; *New York Times*, 15 January 1932; Smith and Beasley, *Carter Glass*, 350–51; Patrick, *Reform*, 83–6.

51. CG box 290/291 is devoted to Glass's January 1932 bill; *ABAJ* (February 1932): 498, 532; Smith and Beasley, *Carter Glass*, 305–06; Burns, *American Banking Community*, 17; Patrick, *Reform*, 90–2.

52. P.S. du Pont to Sen. John Townsend, 19 May 1932, PSP box 1281; Smith and Beasley, *Carter Glass*, 306; Patrick, *Reform*, 92–6.

53. *ABAJ* (April 1932): 621; pamphlet, Econ. Policy Commission of the ABA, "The Guaranty of Bank Deposits" (New York, May, 1933), HBW box 17; Patrick, *Reform*, 88–90.

54. CG boxes 285 and 290/291 are full of letters both supporting and opposing the deposit guarantee proposal. FMV box 22 also holds dozens of letter for and against deposit guarantee. For big business, see Charles H. Sabin, Chairman of Guaranty Trust Co. of NY, to Sen Robert Wagner, NY, 25 May 1932; P.S. du Pont to Seward Prosser, Bankers Trust Co. NY, 28 March 1932; P.S. du Pont to Sen. John Townsend, 19 May 1932, PSP box 1281; Tompkins, *Vandenberg*, 87; Burns, *American Banking Community*, 18; Jesse H. Jones and Edward Angly, *Fifty Billion Dollars: My Thirteen Years with the RFC (1932–1945)* (New York: Macmillan, 1951), 45.

55. Kentucky Rep. Fred Vinson received scores of letters both opposing and favoring the two bank bills. See, for example, Henry Stephens, Jr., First National Bank, Prestonburg, KY, to Vinson, 5 February 1932; telegram from Harry G. Smith, secy, KY Bankers Assn., Louisville, to Vinson, 12 March 1932, FMV box 22; Glass received hundreds of communications, both pro and con, see, for example, State Savings and Building and Loan Assn., St. Petersburg, Fla., to Glass, 4 February 1932, CG box 285; telegram from F.M. McWhirter, Pres. and L.A. Andrew, V.P. of Am. Bankers Assn. State Div. to Glass, 25 April 1932; Walter Lichtenstein, secy., Federal Advisory Council of Federal Reserve, Chicago, to Glass, 30 March 1932, CG 290/291; Allan M. Pope, Pres. of Investment Bankers Assn. of America, New York, to Glass, 17 May 1932, CG box 296; Chamber of Commerce of the USA, Banking Committee Report on Banking Legislation, May 1932, CG box 304; Charles H. Sabin, Chairman of Guaranty Trust Co. of New York to P.S. du Pont, 2 May 1932; Sabin to Sen. Robert Wagner, 25 May 1932, PSP box 1281; Bennet Bean, Commercial Union Insurance Co., NY, to Sen. Alben Barkley, 1 July 1932, AWB box 8; Jones and Angly, *Fifty Billion Dollars*, 45.

56. Patrick, *Reform*, 71–7; Hoover *Memoirs*, 3:115–18; *Annual Report of the Federal Reserve Board* (1932) 16–19, 148; outstanding commercial paper and banker's acceptances would drop to $81 million, and $710 million before the year was done. Friedman and Schwarz, 398–406, argue the Federal Reserve Bank was not so worried about the gold problem as the White House and Treasury were, but recognized the theoretical potential for a problem, so went along with the proposal to back Federal Reserve notes with government securities as well.

57. Hoover, *Memoirs*, 3:116–18.

58. *ABAJ* (March 1932): v., 556; *Annual Report of the Federal Reserve Board* (1933), 19, 100; Meltzer, *Federal Reserve*, 1: 481n136, 356–57; Butkiewicz, "Eugene Meyer," 36–9, 46; Russell Leffingwell to Eugene Meyer, 9 January 1932, EM box 32.

59. Robert K. Straus to FDR, 29 April 1932, RGT box 25. "Notes on Credit Policy in 1932" [by Goldenweiser] 7 January 1932, EAG box 1; *Federal Reserve Bulletin* (February 1932), 134; (March 1932), 199; *Federal Reserve Annual Report* (1933), 207; *New York Times*, 4 January 1932; *Commercial and Financial Chronicle* (5 November 1932), 3310; (10 December 1932), 3987.

60. *Federal Reserve Bulletin* (March 1932), 198; (May

1932), 341; (July 1932), 469; (September 1932), 617; *U.S. Statistical Abstract* (1932), 359; (1941), 418.

Chapter Three

1. Hoover, *Memoirs*, 3:159.

2. Russel Leffingwell to Carter Glass, 3 May 1932, CG box 283; Kemmerer to Glass, 12 February 1932, CG box 285; CG box 285 contains dozens of letters from bankers and businessmen urging bank reform as a means to restore confidence in banks especially, but in the overall economy as well. Raskob to Sen. Pat Harrison, MS, 27 May 1932, JJR file 144; Bennet Bean, Commercial Union Ins. Co., NY, to Alban Barkley, 1 July 1932, AWB box 108; *Testimony Before House Ways and Means Committee Hearings*, NYC, 2 May 1932, RM box 107; Benjamin M. Anderson, Jr., "The Goldsborough Bill and the Government Security Purchases of the Federal Reserve Banks," *Chase Economic Bulletin* (May 1932); *Chicago Tribune*, 12 January 1932; *New York Times*, 6 January 1932; *ABAJ* (April 1932): viii; (May 1932): v, vii; Johnson, *Diary Letters*, 5:6 March 1932. Bank-clearings are drawn from the *Commercial and Financial Chronicle*.

3. *Commercial and Financial Chronicle* (16 April 1932), 2773; Testimony of Father Coughlin before House Ways and Means Committee on Veterans' Bonus Bill, 12 April 1932; N. Brophy, Union Trust Co., St. Petersburg, Fla. to Sen. Glass, 9 May 1932, CG box 296.

4. Olson, *Herbert Hoover*, 50–51; Jones and Angly, *Fifty Billion Dollars*, 105–10; *ABAJ* (February 1932): v, vii; (March 1932) vii, 561.

5. William Battle to Harry F. Byrd, 18 Feb 1932, HFB box 111; typescript memo on RFC-railroad controversy, n.d., JC box 140; Robert K. Straus to FDR, 29 April 1932, RGT box 25, recounts Straus's conversation with the unnamed ICC commissioner; Olson, *Herbert Hoover*, 51–2; Jones and Angly, *Fifty Billion Dollars*, 121–24; Barnard, *Independent Man*, 238–39; Timmons, *Jones*, 209–13. The RFC made three loans to the Missouri-Pacific: $1.5 million on 12 February, $2.8 million on 23 February, and $12.8 million on 26 March, see *Commercial and Financial Chronicle* (4 February 1933), 772; *Chicago Tribune*, 22 April 1932. Dawes, who approved the first loans, contested only the last. In fact, neither Morgan nor Kuhn-Loeb owned the bigger loans. They had underwritten the Missouri-Pacific bonds, just as they underwrote hundreds of millions of dollars of other railroad bonds, which they then sold as investments to savings banks, insurance companies ("widows and orphans"), and the like. Morgan had arranged a $40 million loan to the Missouri-Pacific in 1930, but that was not the loan repaid by the RFC in 1932. The Missouri-Pacific in fact defaulted on its Morgan loan in 1935, and its stock, pledged as collateral, was sold at auction for a pittance, costing Morgan and Guaranty Trust $18 million. See Ron Chernow, *The House of Morgan: An American Banking Dynasty and the Rise of Modern Finance* (New York: Atlantic Monthly Press, 1990), 325, 413–14. See John T. Flynn, "Inside the RFC: An Adventure in Secrecy," *Harper's Magazine*, January 1933, 161–69, for a hostile account of the RFC railroad loans.

6. O.M. Nelson, Pres. U.S. Sugar Co., New Haven, to Hoover, 8 February 1932, CG box 285; *New York Times*, 5 February 1932; *Chicago Tribune*, 12 January 1932; *ABAJ* (April 1932): 666; Olson, *Herbert Hoover*, 53.

7. *Annual Report of the Federal Reserve Board* (1932),

118, 121; Jones and Angly, *Fifty Billion Dollars*, 519–20; Olson, *Herbert Hoover*, 60; Eugene Meyer to Walter Lippmann, 23 April 1932, EM box 33; Eugene Meyer to Paul Shoup, 7 March 1932; Shoup to Meyer, 21 March 1932, EM box 41; United States Senate, *Hearings Before the Committee on Banking and Currency* (73rd Cong., May 23, 1933–January 1934) *On Stock Exchange Practices* (10): 4643, 4724–26, 4740; (12): 5796, 5834–40.

8. *New York Times*, 15 January 1932.

9. *Chicago Tribune*, 22 April 1932; Timmons, *Jones*, 168–9; Olson, *Herbert Hoover*, 53–8, 61; Jones and Angly, *Fifty Billion Dollars*, 517–20.

10. "Testimony of John Janney, Ch. of Bd. of Am. Soc. of Practical Economists, before Ways and Means Committee Hearings, NYC," 2 May 1932, RM box 107; "Testimony of Father Coughlin before House Ways and Means Comm. on Bonus Bill," 12 April 1932; "Statement by Robert Harriss, cotton trader, before Ways and Means Comm.," 14 April 1932, JJR file 144; Charles Coughlin to Edward A. Rumely, 4 November 1932, EAR box 38; *Chicago Tribune*, 12 April 1932; Alan Brinkley, *Voices of Protest: Huey Long, Father Coughlin and the Great Depression* (New York: Vintage, 1983), 103.

11. *Chicago Tribune*, 5 May, 3, 16 June, 17 July 1932; Burner, *Herbert Hoover*, 309–12; Donald A. Ritchie, *Electing FDR: The New Deal Campaign of 1932* (Lawrence: University of Kansas Press, 2007), 116–20. Hoover became greatly embittered about agit-prop surrounding the eviction of the Bonus Marchers. See Hoover, *Memoirs*, 3:225–32.

12. Hoover, *Memoirs*, 3:132–42; *Chicago Tribune*, 21 March, 3 April 1932; Mann, *La Guardia*, 303–4; Timmons, *Garner*, 141–50; Romano, "Emergence of John Nance Garner," 123–35, 155; Jordan, A. Schwarz, *The Interregnum of Despair: Hoover, Congress, and the Depression* (Urbana: University of Illinois Press, 1970), 119–24.

13. Romano, "Emergence of John Nance Garner," 159–63, 167–78; Timmons, *Garner*, 153–57.

14. *Chicago Tribune*, 20, 29 May 1932; Romano, "Emergence of John Nance Garner," 136–38.

15. Walter Lippmann to Eugene Meyer, 22 April 1932; Meyer to Lippmann, 23 April 1932, EM box 33; Paul Shoup to Eugene Meyer, 2 July 1932, EM box 41.

16. *Commercial and Financial Chronicle* (21 May 1932), 3773; *Chicago Tribune*, 29 May 1932; Hoover, *Memoirs*, 3:146–47; Romano, "Emergence of John Nance Garner," 137–41.

17. "The 'Forgotten Man' Speech," in Rosenman, *Public Papers and Addresses*, 1: 624–27; memo, no author [probably Robert K. Straus to FDR], n.d., RGT box 25, frankly discusses the merits of the RFC in view of the speech; *Chicago Tribune* 14 April 1932; William McAdoo to Alben Barkley, 23 March 1931, AWB box 60, calls for taking the party out of the hands of "Tammany" (i.e. Al Smith) and giving it to progressives; Shouse-FDR correspondence of 1932 contained in JS box 3, testifies to the coolness of their relations; FDR to Harry Byrd, Sr., 21 March 1932, FDRF, box 23, is more blunt; *New York Evening Journal*, 17 May 1932, discusses the break between FDR and Smith; Olson, *Herbert Hoover*, 53; James MacGregor Burns, *Roosevelt: The Lion and the Fox* (New York: Harcourt, Brace, 1956), 130–34; Ritchie, *Electing FDR*, 86–7.

18. I. du Pont to Senator Townsend, 25 March 1932, IP box 103; telegram Paul Warburg to Raskob, n.d. [April 1932], JJR file 144; B. Baruch to Edward O'Neal, Pres. American Farm Bureau, 14 April 1932, reprinted in *Commercial and Financial Chronicle* (23 April 1932),

3024, and testimony of Dawes, 3032, speech by Anderson (19 November 1932), 3417; *Chicago Tribune*, 22 April 1932.

19. News release Wilmington, Delaware, Chamber of Commerce, 30 March 1932, IP box 103; A.P. Sloan to P.S. du Pont, 2 May 1932; W. Albert Haddock, Chairman of General Contractors Assn. Delaware to P.S. du Pont, 12 May 1932, PSP box 1173; Harry Hayes, Managing Dir. New York State Highway Chapter of Associated General Contractors of America, Albany, New York, to O'Connor, 19 March 1932, JJO box 13; Raskob to Sen. Pat Harrison, 27 May 1932, JJR file 144.

20. Walter B. Kester, Chicago Mortgage Bankers Assn., to P.P. Pullen, 3 April 1933; Hugh Michels to Kenneth Brown, Chicago Title and Trust Co., 14 February 1931; Kenneth Brown to Holman Pettibone, V.P., Chicago Title and Trust Co., 23 February, 16 March 1931; H.C. Eigelberner, Chicago Title and Trust Co., to Pettibone, Pres., 10 May 1932, HDP box 1; Homer Hoyt, *One Hundred Years of Land Values in Chicago* (Chicago: University of Chicago Press, 1933), 266–70.

21. Federal Reserve Bank of Chicago, *Business Conditions* (30 July 1932), 1, 4–6; *Chicago Daily News*, 7 July 1932; *Chicago Evening American*, 7 July 1932; Annual Statement of Whitestone Co., 1932, JES box 7.

22. James, *Chicago Banks*, 2:1029; Ferdinand Pecora, *Wall Street Under Oath: The Story of Our Modern Money Changers* (New York: Simon and Schuster, 1939), 226–27, 231–32.

23. *Chicago Tribune*, 17, 23, 26 June 1932.

24. *Commercial and Financial Chronicle* (7 January 1933), 184; (14 January 1933), 198.

25. Hoover, *Memoirs*, 3:251–52.

26. *Annual Report of the Comptroller of the Currency* (1933), 217, 285; James, *Chicago Banks*, 2: 1028, 1225; *ISCNB* (1929), 32–3; (1931), 30–1; *Chicago Defender*, 16 July 1932.

27. *Chicago Tribune*, 20 January, 14 May 1920, 6 July 1931. Stedman had also run on the Socialist ticket against Chicago Mayor Big Bill Thompson in 1915, but Stedman was prosecuted by Thompson's sworn enemy, State's Attorney Swanson, so no political vendetta was likely involved. See Lloyd Wendt and Herman Kogan, *Big Bill of Chicago* (Indianapolis: Bobbs-Merrill, 1953), 99.

28. *Chicago Tribune*, 2 November 1931.

29. *Chicago Tribune*, 6 March, 2 November 1931, 3 June 1933; *Chicago Defender*, 16, 23 July 1932; St. Clair Drake and Horace R. Clayton, *Black Metropolis* (New York: Harcourt Brace, 1945), 467.

30. *Chicago Tribune*, 6 March, 6 July, 2 November 1931; 28 June 1932; 17 February, 22 June 1933; Marcus Nadler and Jules I. Bogen, *The Banking Crisis: The End of an Epoch* (New York: Dodd, Mead, 1933), 23. In December 1931 the comptroller of the currency instructed federal bank examiners to accept bonds at face value as bank assets unless they were actually in default; see: *SEP* (10): 4639.

31. *Chicago Tribune*, 14, 28, March, 2, 26, 27 April, 4 November 1933; 12 March 1935; 13 March 1936; 8 June 1938; 18 April 1941.

32. *Chicago Tribune*, 16, 18, 20, 23–25, 28 June 1932; *Commercial and Financial Chronicle* (22 August 1931), 1237.

33. *Chicago Tribune*, 16, 18, 20, 23–25, 28 June 1932.

34. *Commercial and Financial Chronicle* (4 June 1932), 4086–87; (25 March 1933), 2012; Conrad Black, *Franklin Delano Roosevelt: Champion of Freedom* (New York: Public Affairs, 2003), 226.

35. *Indianapolis News*, 12 December 1930; State of Washington, *Annual Report of the Supervisor of Banking* (Olympia, 1932), 22.

36. *Annual Report of the Comptroller of the Currency* (1931), 37, 86–96, 105; Charles W. Calomiris and Joseph R. Mason, "Contagion and Bank Failure During the Great Depression: The June 1932 Chicago Banking Panic," *American Economic Review* 87, no. 5 (December 1997): 878–80. Statistics gathered by the Federal Reserve Bank and analyzed by Gary Richardson in "Quarterly Data on the Categories and Causes of Bank Distress During the Great Depression," *National Bureau of Economic Research Working Paper*, no. 12715 (2006), 41, 43, reveal that 130 American banks closed their tills in 1930 because of defalcation or mismanagement, which are not quite the same thing. Another 24 banks suspended operations temporarily and then reopened. In 1931, 142 banks closed forever and another 17 suspended business for a time. Out of 1,345 banks that failed in 1930 and 2,298 that failed in 1931, between 7 and 10 percent did so because of dishonesty or incompetence, or both. These figures would have looked much too low to State's Attorney Swanson.

37. John R. Averne, Hamden, CT to Dawes, 24 June 1932, CGD box 248. On Biddle's trial, see Bray Hammond, *Banks and Politics in America from the Revolution to the Civil War* (Princeton: Princeton University Press, 1985), 518–26.

38. *Chicago Tribune* 24, 25 June 1932; James, *Chicago Banks*, 2:1032–36.

39. Jones and Angly, *Fifty Billion Dollars*, 73; Henri Couteron, Equitable Life Assurance Soc'y of U.S., Chicago, to Charles Dawes, 24 June 1932, CGD box 248, *Commercial and Financial Chronicle* (2 July 1932) 70–71.

40. Robert K. Straus to FDR, 29 April 1932, RGT box 25, discussed rumors about the Dawes Bank; *Chicago Tribune*, 17 June 1932; Timmons, *Dawes*, 313–16; Timmons, *Jones*, 169; Olson, *Herbert Hoover*, 58. The Dawes Bank RFC application is found in the Eugene Meyer Papers, box 140, and gives the condition of the bank as of 27 June 1932.

41. *Chicago Tribune*, 26 June 1932; *Commercial and Financial Chronicle* (2 July 1932), 70.

42. Jones and Angly, *Fifty Billion Dollars*, 73; Timmons, *Dawes*, 317–19; Hoover, *Memoirs*, 3:170; memo [Eugene Meyer] 27 June 1932, EM box 140. From the information contained in the RFC application it is not obvious why Dawes believed his bank doomed. In 1932 it held $8.5 million in dubious loans, $3 million of worthless loans, and $5 million of depreciated bonds in its portfolio. It had limited cash reserves and surplus ($15.7 million), but it also had many good assets it could pledge for loans from the Federal Reserve Bank ($47 million in government and other securities.) The RFC accepted $90 million worth of collateral, so the bank seemed sound enough, even if it had lost about 25 percent of its deposits in six months. Condition as of 31 December 1931 is given in the *Annual Report of the Federal Reserve Board* (1931), 247.

43. Jones and Angly, *Fifty Billion Dollars*, 74–75; Hoover, *Memoirs*, 3:170, claims Traylor called him about the Dawes Bank and the urgency of an RFC loan on Saturday, 25 June 1932, after which Hoover called Jones in Chicago telling him to look into it. Jones, 75, states that Traylor asked him to call Hoover on Sunday afternoon after the meeting at the Dawes Bank. Also, the $90 million loan amount to "cover all deposits" in the Dawes Bank has become etched in history. However, the RFC application dated 27 June 1932 claims the bank had $127,686,000 in deposits, EM box 140.

44. Memo [Eugene Meyer] 27 June 1932, EM box 140; *Commercial and Financial Chronicle* (2 July 1932), 3–4; Timmons, *Dawes*, 318–20; James, *Chicago Banks*, 2:1037–39; Jones and Angly, *Fifty Billion Dollars*, 76–9; Hoover, *Memoirs*, 3:170.

45. Memo by M.G. Bogue, General Counsel of RFC, 27 June 1932; memo [Meyer] 27 June 1932, EM box 140; Dawes to G.R. Cooksey, RFC, 3 March 1933, CGD box 257; *Bank and Quotation Record* (5 August 1932), 111; James, *Chicago Banks*, 2:1040; Timmons, *Dawes*, 321.

46. Timmons, *Dawes*, 321–22; *Commercial and Financial Chronicle* (January 14, 1933), 198. CGD box 248 contains dozens of letters from around the United States attacking Dawes for the 1932 loan.

47. *Commercial and Financial Chronicle* (2 July 1932), 71; (9 July 1932), 167–68, sings the praises of the Federal Reserve Bank's handling of the Chicago crisis, but from the numbers presented for the week and month for the Chicago district or for Illinois in the *Federal Reserve Board Annual Report* (1932), it's difficult to tell there was a crisis. Discounting and open market operations were both at near historical lows in June 1932. Calomiris and Mason conclude in, "Chicago Banking Panic," 864–65, 880–82, that banks that failed during the panic were all weak banks that would have failed soon even without the panic.

48. Hoover, *Memoirs*, 3:170; *Chicago Tribune*, 27 June 1932; James, *Chicago Banks*, 2:1031–33; Ritchie, *Electing FDR*, 89–90; note from Democratic National Committee files, 17 September 1931; M.H. McIntyre to "Louie" [Howe], 1 November 1931, FDRP 220; Memorandum on Communist Rumor Campaign against financial institutions and the proposed campaign against insurance companies compiled by the American Vigilant Intelligence Federation, 14 May 1932, CGD box 248; Wendt and Kogan, "*Big Bill*," 234, 268.

49. Romano, "Emergence of John Nance Garner," 182–90; Timmons, *Garner*, 159–67; Ritchie, *Electing FDR*, 105–09; notes of Henry Morganthau, Jr., on Democratic Party convention delegate count, 11 June 1932, HM box 460.

50. *Chicago Tribune*, 30 June 1932.

51. George Anderson in *ABAJ* (December 1931): 403; (February 1932): 490, 498; Carter Glass in (March 1932): 556; (May 1932): vii; editorial (July 1932), 4, and article by Edmund Platt, Vice Gov. of Federal Reserve Bank and V.P. of Marine Midland Bank, Thomas Preston, past Pres. of ABA and Pres. of Hamilton National Bank of Chattanooga, editorial and guest editorial by Mark Sullivan, in (September 1932), 14–15, 19, 28, 67. One banker who denied that any of the reforms suggested by Glass would have prevented the Crash or the Depression was Charles Sabin, chairman of the Guaranty Trust Co., New York, in a letter to New York Sen. Robert Wagner, [May 1932] PSP box 1281. The Democratic Party platform is discussed in *ABAJ* (July 1932): 22.

52. *Commercial and Financial Chronicle* (2 July 1932), 1–2.

53. See "Radio Address on Public Utility Regulation, 23 April 1930," "Campaign Address, Syracuse, 22 October 1932," and "Campaign Address, Albany, 24 October 1930" in Rosenman, *Public Papers and Addresses*, 1: 238–46, 419–26, 426–32.

54. "Governor Accepts the Nomination," in Rosenman, *Public Papers and Addresses*, 1: 649–50, 653, 659; the presidents of Guaranty Trust and Chase National Banks were among those on Wall Street who supported federal supervision of securities markets; see Charles S. McCain, chairman Chase National Bank, and William

C. Potter, Pres. of Guaranty Trust Co. of New York to Carter Glass, 29 April 1932, PSP box 1281.

Chapter Four

1. *Chicago Tribune*, 17 July 1932.

2. Hoover, *Memoirs*, 3:112–15; William Martin, governor of Federal Reserve Bank of St. Louis, in *ABAJ* (July 1932): 16, 23; (September 1932), 51; *New York Times*, 6 February, 28 August 1932; *Chicago Tribune*, 26 January, 16 June 1932.

3. See Edmund Platt, Vice Gov. of Federal Reserve Bank and V.P. of Marine Midland Bank, New York and Thomas Preston, past Pres. of ABA and Pres. of Hamilton National Bank, Chattanooga, in favor of the Glass bill in *ABAJ* (August 1932): 13–15; Felix M. McWhirter, Pres. of Peoples State Bank of Indianapolis, and Pres. of State Bank Div. of ABA, opposed to the Glass bill in *ABAJ* (July 1932): 11; editorial, *ABAJ* (September 1932): 28; (November 1932): 41.

4. Hoover, *Memoirs*, 3:168; Olson, *Herbert Hoover*, 73–4.

5. *Chicago Tribune*, 26, 28 June, 17 July 1932; *ABAJ* (August 1932): 8, 22, 24; James Stuart Olson, *Saving Capitalism: The Reconstruction Finance Corporation and the New Deal, 1933–1940* (Princeton, NJ: Princeton University Press, 1988), 60, 70–3.

6. George E. Anderson in *ABAJ* (July 1932): 14; Olson, *Saving Capitalism*, 73–7, 89; *Orange Daily News*, 4 March 1933. Even the Fed was frustrated by the slow pace of disbursements for public works; see "Statement on Inflation" [Goldenweiser], n.d., EAG box 1.

7. Olson, *Saving Capitalism*, 80–81.

8. *Commercial and Financial Chronicle* (3 December 1932), 3796; *ABAJ* (September 1932): 7; Olson, *Saving Capitalism*, 82–6. By March 1933 the RFC had loaned: Ill., $44.7 million; Mich., $13.8 million; New York, $13.2 million; Ohio, $12.5 million; Wisc., $11.9 million. Hoover carried Penn. with 1,454,000 votes to 1,296,000 for Roosevelt, *Historical Statistics*, 686–87.

9. Olson, *Saving Capitalism*, 72; La Guardia quoted in Olson, 75.

10. *Chicago Tribune*, 17 July 1932; Romano, "Emergence of John Nance Garner," 142–44; Garner quoted in Lawrence Sullivan, *Prelude to Panic: The Story of the Bank Holiday* (Washington, DC: Statesman Press, 1936), 16.

11. *Commercial and Financial Chronicle* (23 July 1932), 544; Romano, "Emergence of John Nance Garner," 144–46; Olson, *Saving Capitalism*, 72. FDR advisor Raymond Moley later claimed that Garner wanted the list detailing RFC loans published in order to embarrass banks in Uvalde, Texas, that competed with his own two banks, which had no RFC loans. This hardly seems likely as only those loans granted after Hoover signed the bill on July 21 were to be publicized. See Raymond Moley, *The First New Deal* (New York: Harcourt, Brace & World, 1966), 133. *Commercial and Financial Chronicle* (4 February 1933), 763–72, reprints the full list of RFC loans from February to July 1932, and no bank in Uvalde, Texas, is listed. However, the Commercial National Bank of Uvalde does appear on the list of loans authorized in August, *Commercial and Financial Chronicle* (22 October 1932), 2770, so it is possible that Garner had advance knowledge of the application.

12. *Chicago Tribune*, 8 August 1932; *Chase Economic Bulletin* (17 November 1932), 5–7; *ABAJ* (July 1932): 14; (December 1932): 16, cites a study of the bond market

conducted by the *New York Herald Tribune*; Sullivan, *Prelude*, 19; Berle to Frankfurter, 6 August 1932; Frankfurter to Berle, 8 August 1932, AAB box 15; Berle to FDR, 2 August 1932, AAB box 16; Vincent Astor to FDR, 19 August 1932, FDRF, box 23.

13. *Chicago Tribune*, 1 November 1932; *Commercial and Financial Chronicle* (1 October 1932), 2207–09; (15 October 1932), 2646–50; (5 November 1932), 3145–59; *Kiplinger Newsletter*, 8 October 1932; Alexander Sachs to Eugene Meyer, 7 February 1933, EM box 40; *ABAJ* (August 1932): 5–9, 24, 59; (September 1932): 5–8, 37, 51–53; (December 1932): 7; *Federal Reserve Bulletin* (September 1932), 617; (November 1932), 725; (January 1933), 54; (March 1933), 205; *Annual Report of the Federal Reserve Board* (1932), 2–5, 165–82; *U.S. Statistical Abstract* (1940), 418, in October 1928 auto companies churned out 338,883 passenger cars; Vincent Curcio, *Chrysler: The Life and Times of an Automotive Genius* (New York: Oxford University Press, 2000), 487–95; Johnson, *Diary Letters*, 5:6 December 1931.

14. *Commercial and Financial Chronicle* (9 July 1932), 188; (19 November 1932), 3466; (4 February 1933), 762, 773; *Annual Report of the Federal Reserve Board* (1932), 165–66; Wigmore, *Crash*, 337–39.

15. *Historical Statistics*, 379–80; *Commercial and Financial Chronicle* (5 November 1932), 3397; (25 February 1933), 1368; *ABAJ* (August 1932): 19; *Denver Post*, 17 January 1933; *Baltimore Sun*, 18 February 1933; Paul Shoup, Pres. S. Pac. RR., to Eugene Meyer, 2 July 1932, EM box 41; Wigmore, *Crash*, 337, 339–41.

16. *Commercial and Financial Chronicle* (7 January 1933), 186; Mayor John Murphy, Somerville, MA, to FDR, 19 March 1933, FDRO 230.

17. *Annual Report of the Federal Reserve Board* (1932), 138–42, 65; *ABAJ* (July 1932): 4, 7–9; (August 1932): 5.

18. *Banking and Monetary Statistics*, 18, 34.

19. *Annual Report of the Comptroller of the Currency* (1931), 76; (1932), 68; *Banking and Monetary Statistics*, 18, 21. In June 1930, 1931, and 1932 state institutions owned 63 percent of all bank loans and 61–62 percent of all bank-owned securities. If assets of state-chartered banks defaulted at the same rate as those of national banks — and they probably defaulted at a higher rate — then default rates would have been 1.58 and 1.63 times higher for loans and securities, respectively.

20. *New York Times*, 10 January 1932; *Denver Post*, 11 December 1930; *Philadelphia Evening Bulletin*, 11 December 1930; *ABAJ* (September 1932): 37; *U.S. Statistical Abstract* (1932), 589; (1936), 558–59.

21. Farmers' and Taxpayers League, Columbia, to SC Senate, 10 February 1933, DRC box 13; Joseph S. Cullinan to Raskob, 18 April 1932, IP box 103; Rumely to C.T. Revere, NYC, 9 December 1932, EAR box 39; *ABAJ* (March 1932): 604; (August 1932): 19; Olin S. Pugh, *Difficult Decades of Banking: A Comparative Survey of Banking Developments in South Carolina and the U.S., 1920–1940* (Columbia: University of South Carolina Bureau of Business and Economic Research, 1964), 6; *Historical Statistics*, 123–24.

22. Rumely to C.T. Revere, NYC, 9 December 1932, EAR box 39; G.W. de Lamatre, Omaha, to Charles Dawes, 26 October 1932, CGD box 249; Theodore Saloutos and John D. Hicks, *Twentieth-Century Populism: Agricultural Discontent in the Middle West, 1900–1939* (Lincoln: University of Nebraska Press, 1951), 435–43; Brinkley, *Voices of Protest*, 42–43; Charlotte Hubbard Prescott, "An Iowa Foreclosure," *The Nation*, 22 February 1933, 1989.

23. "A.H.B.," President of Agricultural Bond and Credit Corp, Chicago, to board of directors, 25 August 1932, EAR box 38; *New York Times*, 28 August 1932.

24. Mary Heaton Vorse, "Rebellion in the Corn Belt," *Harper's Magazine*, December 1932, 1–9.

25. Saloutos and Hicks, *Populism*, 443–47.

26. Francis Gloyd Awalt, "Recollections of the Banking Crisis in 1933," *Business History Review* 43, no. 3 (1969): editor's introduction, 347; *Commercial and Financial Chronicle* (8 October 1932), 2447; (5 November 1932), 3310; (10 December 1932), 3987; *Banking and Monetary Statistics*, 235.

27. Hoover, *Memoirs*, 3:218–347; "The Failures of the Preceding Administration, address at Columbus, Ohio, 20 August 1932," in Rosenman, *Public Papers and Addresses*, 1:669–84.

28. *ABAJ* (October 1932): 10; Black, *Roosevelt*, 31; Moley, *New Deal*, 388; Raymond Moley, *After Seven Years* (New York: Harper & Row, 1939), 59n., 72; Joslin, Hoover, 332–33; Hoover, *Memoirs*, 3:178–81; Byrnes, *Lifetime*, 71; Feis, *1933*, 35.

29. Alexander Jamison, Esq, Wilmington to Irénée du Pont, 11 July 1932, IP box 103.

30. Cullinan to Magnus Alexander, 29 August 1932, EAR box 38; Thomas Phillips, Jr., to Shouse, 29 October 1932, JS box 3; I. du Pont to E.C. Stokes, Trenton, 29 September 1932, IP box 103; P.S. du Pont to Joseph Lieb, 23 September 1932; note from "Geesey" to P.S. du Pont, 15 March [1933], PSP box 1281; P.S. du Pont to Mabel B. McClure, Enid, OK, 20 December 1935, PSP box 1282.

31. Moley to Tugwell, 22 January 1965, RGT box 15; Rexford G. Tugwell, "The Principle of Planning and the Institution of Laissez Faire," *Papers and Proceedings of the American Economic Association*, December 1931; R.K. Strauss and R.G. Tugwell, "Money and the Financial Complex," typescript, n.d. [summer 1932], RM box 107; Arthur M. Schlesinger, Jr., *The Age of Roosevelt*, vol. 1, *Crisis of the Old Order* (Boston: Houghton Mifflin, 1957), 193–98, 399–402.

32. "Address at Oglethorpe University, May 22, 1932," and "Campaign Address on Progressive Government at the Commonwealth Club, September 23, 1932," in Rosenman, *Public Papers and Addresses*, 1:641–42, 644–46, 742–56; Feis, *1933*, 9. Events of 1933–35 revealed that business distrust was justified, but misplaced. Under the National Industrial Recovery Act of 1933, the federal government encouraged economic planning by businessmen, themselves, which proved just as maladroit as any planning conceivable by Rex Tugwell and friends. But that subject must await a different book.

33. *New York Herald Tribune*, 20 September 1932; *New York Times*, 23 September 1932; *Chicago Tribune*, 2 November 1932; *ABAJ* (August 1932): 29; Hoover, *Memoirs*, 3:284–86; Smith and Beasley, *Carter Glass*, 314–20.

34. Memos by Berle, 17 October, 7 November 1932, AAB box 15; Berle to Moley, 10 November 1932, AAB box 16. In October FDR huddled with Moley, Tugwell, Hugh Johnson, Va. Rep. Shirley, William Woodin, Samuel Rosenman, and Basil O'Connor about how to answer Hoover's Des Moines speech. A statement by FDR on the gold standard was actually removed from an upcoming speech, and a speech by Glass took its place.

35. *ABAJ* (August 1932): 29; Dr. William Bennet Munro address to ABA convention, *ABAJ* (November 1932): 28; William Rodman Fay in *Commercial and Financial Chronicle* (26 November 1932), 3583; Joslin diary, 31 July 1932, cited in Timothy Walch and Dwight M. Miller, eds., *Herbert Hoover and Franklin D. Roosevelt: A Documentary History* (Westport, CT.: Green-

wood Press, 1998), 52, hereafter cited as *Hoover and Roosevelt*.

36. *Chicago Tribune*, 1 November 1932.

37. *Commercial and Financial Chronicle* (October 29, 1932), 2865; Jesse Ricks, New York, to Urey Woodson, Kentucky, 28 October 1932, UW box 2; Edward Rumely to J.-G. Stein, NYC, 5 November 1932, EAR box 38.

38. *Commercial and Financial Chronicle* (19 November 1932), 3393, 3395, 3414, 3417; (November 26, 1932), 3561; *ABAJ* (August 1932): 5; (September 1932), 7, 28; (October 1932), 20, 30–31; "Summary" n.d. [March 1933], no author [probably Meyer], EM box 28; Francis Garvan, The Chemical Foundation, NYC to Dawes, 7 June 1932, CGD box 248.

39. *New York Times*, 12, 17, 23 June 1932; James, *Chicago Banks*, 2:1041n; *Commercial and Financial Chronicle* (27 August 1932), 1435; Elliott T. Cooper, *A Documentary History of the Union Trust Company of Maryland* (Baltimore: Union Trust Company, 1970), 127; *Federal Reserve Bulletin* (July 1932), 467; (August 1932), 552; (September 1932), 614; (October 1932), 672; (November 1932), 722; (December 1932), 784; (January 1933), 45; (March 1933), 200; *Annual Report of the Comptroller of the Currency* (1932), 218, 285; *Banking and Monetary Statistics*, 481. Union Trust Company deposits that had been $60.4 million in December 1930, dwindled to $45.3 million by December 1932. By May 1933 they would drop to $34.9 million.

40. Pam Hait, *The Arizona Bank: Arizona's Story* (n.p.: Arizona Bank, 1987), 80–82; *Annual Report of the Comptroller of the Currency* (1930), 622, 708; (1932), 355, 514, 544, 546. Large mining companies, such as Phelps-Dodge, would have taken loans in large financial centers, not from Arizona banks. Arizona had only one bank capitalized at $1 million, the Valley Bank and Trust Co. of Phoenix, which held nearly 40 percent of all deposits in Arizona in 1930, *Annual Report of the Federal Reserve Board* (1930), 307.

41. *New York Times*, 1 September 1932; *Los Angeles Times*, 8 October 1932; *Commercial and Financial Chronicle* (1 October 1932), 2283; *ABAJ* (September 1932): 13; *Annual Report of the Comptroller of the Currency* (1932), 90; (1933), 213; *Annual Report of the Federal Reserve Board* (1931), 254; (1932) 307; *Federal Reserve Bulletin* (September 1932), 614; (March 1933), 200; Olson, *Saving Capitalism*, 94.

42. James S. Olson, "Rehearsal for Disaster: Hoover, the R.F.C., and the Banking Crisis in Nevada, 1932–1933," *Western Historical Quarterly* 6, no. 2 (1975): 150–51; *Federal Reserve Bulletin* (August 1932), 482.

43. Olson, "Rehearsal," 151–56.

44. Olson, "Rehearsal," 156–58; *Annual Report of the Comptroller of the Currency* (1933), 296–97. Elmus Wicker asserts the significance of the Nevada episode is found in the complete absence of the Federal Reserve Bank from the crisis. It had abdicated its role to the RFC, which refused to step in. See Wicker, *Banking Panics*, 115.

45. *Commercial and Financial Chronicle* (19 November 1932), 3396; *Bank and Quotation Record* (5 August 1932), 117; *Federal Reserve Bulletin* (August 1932), 552; (September 1932), 614; (October 1932), 672; (November 1932), 722; (December 1932), 784; (January 1933), 45; *Annual Report of the Comptroller of the Currency* (1932), 221, 292–93, 296–97.

46. *Banking and Monetary Statistics*, 18, 74; loans are for all banks; call-date holdings of securities are for member banks only. Ayers views on the bank crisis are in *Commercial and Financial Chronicle* (18 March 1933), 1781–82.

47. William P. Helms in *ABAJ* (December 1932): 38; Sullivan, *Prelude*, 55–57; *Historical Statistics*, 711, 716; "summary" n.d. [March 1933], no author [probably Meyer], EM box 28; *New York Times*, 30 December 1933.

48. George F. Warren, "Stabilization of the Measure of Value," mimeograph of American Farm Bureau Fed., Chicago, 6 December 1932, EAR box 39; Edward Rumely to Vincent Bendix, 25, 30 August 1932; Rumely to Roy Howard, Scripps-Howard Newspapers, NYC, 3 October 1932; Rumely to Frank Vanderlip, NYC, 1 October 1932, EAR box 38.

49. Charles Coughlin to Rumely, 4 November 1932; Rumely to Coughlin, 8 November 1932, EAR box 38; Father Coughlin transcripts, "Gold-Master or Servant?" (30 October 1932) and "Revaluation," (6 November 1932) Detroit: Radio League of the Little Flower, CG box 299; Max W. Schwerdt, Brookline, MA to FDR, forwarded to Moley, 29 July 1932; Robert M. Harriss, cotton trader, NYC, to Moley, 17 October 1932, Robert Owen to Moley, 15 December 1932; radio address by Robert Owen, 21 December 1932, RM box 107; Rumely to FDR, Warm Springs, GA, 29 November 1932, EAR box 38; Rumely to FDR, 3 December 1932; Rexford Tugwell to Rumely, 6 December 1932; Rumely to Tugwell, 22 December 1932, EAR box 39.

50. Berle to Moley, Tugwell, Samuel Rosenman, and Charles Taussig, 10 August 1932; Berle to FDR, 10 August 1932, AAB box 15; Tugwell, *Diary*, 77–8.

51. *Kiplinger Washington Newsletter*, December 31, 1932, EAR box 39.

52. James Warburg, *The Long Road Home: The Autobiography of a Maverick* (New York: Doubleday, 1964), 105–07.

53. Radio address of Sen. James Byrnes, 28 January 1933, DRC box 13; *New York Times*, 13 February 1933.

Chapter Five

1. *Historical Statistics*, 682. Socialist candidate Norman Thomas attracted 881,951 of those votes in 1932.

2. Thomas J. Anketell, Detroit, to Jouett Shouse, 30 November 1931, CG box 267; Robert M. Fogelson, *Downtown: Its Rise and Fall, 1880–1950* (New Haven: Yale University Press, 2001), 224; *Hoosier Banker* (March 1932), 15–16; Hoyt, *Land Values*, 272–75; *Denver Post*, 16 January 1933; *Commercial and Financial Chronicle* (7 January 1933), 112–13.

3. *Commercial and Financial Chronicle* (11 February 1933), 936, 939; *Banking and Monetary Statistics*, 18, 494; Federal Reserve Bank of New York, *Monthly Review of Credit and Business Conditions* (1 February 1933), 9–10; (1 March 1933) 21–2; *Federal Reserve Bulletin* (January 1933), 45. Loans outstanding would sink even lower: they hit bottom at $20.2 billion in June 1935 and would not rise above $22 billion until the end of 1940.

4. *St. Louis Post-Dispatch* (1 Jan 1933), 4; *Commercial and Financial Chronicle* (7 January 1933), 86–8; (14 January 1933), 264, 281–82.

5. *Commercial and Financial Chronicle* (7 January 1933), 86; (21 January 1933), 444; (28 January 1933), 608–10; (4 February 1933), 786; (11 February 1933), 965; *Federal Reserve Bulletin* (February 1933), 105.

6. *Banking and Monetary Statistics*, 457, 460; Charles Hamlin Diary, 4 January 1933, Library of Congress; *Commercial and Financial Chronicle* (14 January 1933), 281; (21 January 1933), 444; (4 February 1933), 786.

7. *St. Louis Post-Dispatch* (3 January 1933), 6; (6 Jan-

uary 1933), 3; *Commercial and Financial Chronicle* (7 January 1933), 86–8; (14 January 1933), 264, 281–82.

8. *St. Louis Post-Dispatch*, 4, 5, 7, 8, 9, 11 January 1933.

9. *St. Louis Post-Dispatch*, 16, 18 January 1933; *Commercial and Financial Chronicle* (21 January 1933), 438–39, 443; (28 January 1933), 610; (25 February 1933), 1325; *Federal Reserve Bulletin* (February 1933), 105; Olson, *Saving Capitalism*, 1988), 27. Banks in St. Louis may have been "basically sound," but resources in trust companies had fallen by 30 percent and deposits by 42 percent in two years (December 1930 to December 1932). Eight of 24 trust companies had also disappeared in the meantime. See *Commercial and Financial Chronicle* (25 February 1933), 1267.

10. *Federal Reserve Bulletin* (February 1933), 105.

11. *Commercial and Financial Chronicle* (21 January 1933), 443–44; (28 January 1933), 611; *ISCNB* (1932), 182–3; *Federal Reserve Bulletin* (February 1933), 105.

12. T.W. Phillips, Pres. Phillips Gas and Oil, Butler, PA, to P. du Pont, 14 March 1933, PSP box 1176; *Commercial and Financial Chronicle* (25 February 1933), 1313–18; *Banking and Monetary Statistics*, 19, 21, 177, 387, 397–98.

13. *Commercial and Financial Chronicle* (7 January 1933), 86; (21 January 1933), 443; (28 January 1933), 608; (4 February 1933), 787–88; (11 February 1933), 964; (18 February 1933), 1152; *New York Times*, 28, 31 January, 5 February 1933.

14. *Commercial and Financial Chronicle* (21 January 1933), 440; *Annual Report of the Comptroller of the Currency* (1933), 662.

15. *Annual Report of the Comptroller of the Currency* (1933), 223–24; *Federal Reserve Bulletin* (March 1933), 201; Mary Alexine Beatty, *Bank Failures in the District of Columbia in the Twentieth Century* (Washington, DC: Catholic University of America Press, 1949), 50; *ISCNB* (1932) 20–21; *Commercial and Financial Chronicle* (11 February 1933), 966; (18 February 1933), 1152; (25 February 1933), 1309–12. The run on the Middlesex Guarantee Title and Trust Company in New Brunswick was the only bank run I found in February 1933. The *Commercial and Financial Chronicle* said numerous banks failed after "heavy withdrawals," which might have meant runs, but the *Chronicle* did not usually hesitate to call a run a run.

16. *St. Louis Post-Dispatch*, 3 January 1933; *Commercial and Financial Chronicle* (7 January 1933), 87; (21 January 1933), 419, 443; (28 January 1933), 609; (11 February 1933), 937, 965.

17. *Commercial and Financial Chronicle* (11 February 1933), 966; T. Harry Williams, *Huey Long* (New York: Alfred Knopf, 1970), 614–16.

18. *Commercial and Financial Chronicle* (28 January 1933), 593; (4 February 1933), 786.

19. *Des Moines Register*, 21 January 1933; *Commercial and Financial Chronicle* (21 January 1933), 419.

20. *Commercial and Financial Chronicle* (7 January 1933), 57; (11 February 1933), 935. The $10 billion claimed by the committee was chimerical, as the Federal Reserve estimated that no more than $3.5 billion was outstanding in 1931. See Carl Perry, Research and Stat. Div., of Federal Reserve Board, to Louis K. Boysen, First Union Trust and Savings Bank, Chicago, 1 October 1931, HDP box 1.

21. *Commercial and Financial Chronicle* (11 February 1933), 937.

22. *Commercial and Financial Chronicle* (21 January), 377, 383.

23. Prescott, "Iowa Foreclosure," 198–99; *Des Moines Register*, 5 January 1933; *St. Louis Post-Dispatch*, 4 January 1933; *Financial and Commercial Chronicle* (21 January 1933), 435; (28 January 1933), 691.

24. *St. Louis Post-Dispatch* (6 January 1933), c14; *Historical Statistics*, 278; *U.S. Statistical Abstract* (1936), 563.

25. *Commercial and Financial Chronicle* (21 January 1933), 435; (28 January 1933), 604.

26. *Cedar Rapids Gazette*, 2 January 1933; *Des Moines Register*, 11 January 1933; *St. Louis Post-Dispatch* (3 January 1933), 7; Prescott, "Iowa Foreclosure," 198–99; *Financial and Commercial Chronicle* (21 January 1933), 434–35; (28 January 1933), 604.

27. *Commercial and Financial Chronicle* (18 February 1933), 1144; *Detroit Free Press*, 9 February 1933; *Cincinnati Enquirer*, 24 February 1933; *Cincinnati Times-Star*, 4 March 1933.

28. *Commercial and Financial Chronicle* (28 January 1933), 604; H. Pettibone, "Real Estate Credit," address before Ill. Assn. of Real Estate Boards, 20 January 1933, HDP box 1.

29. *Historical Statistics*, 286; *Commercial and Financial Chronicle* (28 January 1933), 604.

30. *Historical Statistics* 278; Ward, *Down the Years*, 175–76; *Commercial and Financial Chronicle* (4 February 1933), 784; A. Cloyd Gill in *ABAJ* (June 1932): 757–58, which does not identify "one insurance company." For mutual insurance companies, such as Mutual Benefit Life that owned $150 million worth of farm mortgages in January 1933, the policy holders literally owned the company, which had no stockholders aside from "widows and orphans."

31. *Cedar Rapids Gazette*, 24 December 1932, 2 January 1933.

32. *Des Moines Register*, 5 March 1933; *Commercial and Financial Chronicle* (21 January 1933), 434; (28 January 1933), 603, 691; (February 18, 1933), 1145.

33. *Detroit Free Press*, 10, 11 February 1933; *Commercial and Financial Chronicle* (28 January 1933), 603–04, 691; (11 February 1933), 953; (18 February 1933), 1145.

34. *Commercial and Financial Chronicle* (28 January 1933), 604; (4 February 1933), 783–84; (11 February 1933), 950; A. Cloyd Gill in *ABAJ* (June 1932): 757.

35. *Commercial and Financial Chronicle* (11 February 1933), 956; (18 February 1933), 1144.

36. *Commercial and Financial Chronicle* (18 February 1933), 1144.

37. Ibid.

38. *Commercial and Financial Chronicle* (28 January 1933), 533.

39. *Denver Post*, 22 January 1933; Bruce R. Payne, Nashville, to Sen. Richard Russell, 25 March 1933, DRC box 14.

40. Radio speech by Frank Vanderlip, 26 December 1932, published by Home Mortgage Advisory Board [advising the RFC], "A Message of Hope to Homeowners," JJO box 14; M.H. Welling, Sec. of State of Utah to FDR, 25 January 1933, transmitting House Concurrent Memorial No. 1, RM box 107; *Commercial and Financial Chronicle* (18 February 1933), 1144; *Los Angeles Times*, 3 March 1933.

41. House Joint Resolution 529 [authorizing RFC loans to farmers], 23 December 1932; Report of Agricultural Committee on H.R. 13991, 3 January 1933, JJO box 14; radio address by Sen. Byrnes, 28 January 1933, DRC box 13; *Elkhart* (Indiana) *Truth*, 16 January 1933; *St. Louis Post-Dispatch*, 1 March 1933; *Commercial and Financial Chronicle* (28 January 1933), 604; (11 February 1933), 949, 956.

42. *Commercial and Financial Chronicle* (28 January 1933), 532; *Detroit Free Press*, 10 February 1933; *Cincinnati Enquirer*, 24 February 1933.

43. *St. Louis Post-Dispatch*, 3, 19 January 1933; Charles Hamlin Diary, 4 January 1933.

44. John T. Flynn, "Inside the RFC: An Adventure in Secrecy," *Harper's Magazine*, January 1933, 161–69; *St. Louis Post-Dispatch*, 1 January 1933; *Commercial and Financial Chronicle* (14 January 1933), 198.

45. *St. Louis Post-Dispatch*, 6 January 1933; *ABAJ* (November 1932): 7; *Commercial and Financial Chronicle* (21 January 1933), 432; Hoover, *Memoirs*, 3:198.

46. Byrnes to Moley, 13 February 1933, JFB box 54; Frank K. Houston, 1st V.P., Chemical Bank and Trust Co., NYC, to O'Connor, 25 April 1933, JJO box 16; Hoover, *Memoirs*, 3:198–99; Joslin, *Hoover*, 351–53; Whaley-Eaton Service newsletter, 18 February 1933; *Commercial and Financial Chronicle* (18 February 1933), 1152.

47. James L. Butkiewicz, "The Reconstruction Finance Corporation, the Gold Standard, and the Banking Panic of 1933," *Southern Economic Journal* 66, no. 2 (October 1999): 273–76; George Seay, FRB Richmond to Meyer, 27 February 1933, EM box 77. Eugene Meyer was also convinced that RFC publicity provoked runs and the collapse of "thousands of banks;" see "summary," EM box 28; J. Miller, Richmond, to Glass, 27 February 1933, CG box 271; Thomas Sheahan, Hagerstown, MD, to FDR, 28 February 1933, FDRO 230. Bank data is drawn from the *Commercial and Financial Chronicle* (27 August 1932), 1423–24; (22 October 1932), 2767–70; (19 November 1932), 3462–64; (31 December 1932), 4483–85, 4490; *Annual Report of the Comptroller of the Currency* (1933), 293–301; *ISCNB* (1931) and (1932).

48. Flynn, "Inside the RFC," 161–69; *Baltimore Sun*, 23 February 1933.

49. Dawes to James Harbord, NYC, 29 December 1932, CGD box 250; Alexander Sachs to Eugene Meyer, 7 February 1933, EM box 40; Meyer to Hoover, 6 February 1933, EM box 77; T. Lamont to C. Dawes, 5 January 1933, TWL box 91.

Chapter Six

1. Conot, *American*, 127–31.

2. *U.S. Statistical Abstract* (1932): 34–9. Hamtramck was also distinguished in 1930 by its population which was 92.6 percent foreign-born or first-generation American, the highest proportion in the nation. John T. Flynn, "Michigan Magic: The Detroit Banking Scandal," *Harper's Magazine*, December 1933, 2; Conot, *American*, 147.

3. United States Senate, *Hearings before the Committee on Banking and Currency* (73rd Congress), *on Stock Exchange Practices*, pt. 9 (19 December 1933–4 January 1934), [*SEP* (9)] 4210.

4. Alfred P. Sloan, Jr., *My Years with General Motors* (New York: Doubleday, 1990), appendix; Nevins and Hill, *Expansion*, 529, 588n.; *U.S. Statistical Abstract* (1932), 359.

5. Conot, *American*, 248; Sloan, *My Years*, 162–63, appendix; Nevins and Hill, *Expansion*, 431, 452–57; Allan Nevins and Frank Ernest Hill, *Ford: Decline and Rebirth, 1933–1962* (New York: Charles Scribner's Sons, 1962), 3–4; *Commercial and Financial Chronicle* (6 October 1928), 1879.

6. *Commercial and Financial Chronicle* (21 January 1933), 558.

7. Sloan, *My Years*, 24.

8. Letter to stockholders of Peoples Wayne Co. Bank, First National Bank of Detroit and Security Trust Co., Bank of Michigan, and Peninsular State Bank, 5 October 1929, JC box 141; *SEP* (9): 4204–5, 4211, 4406; (10): 4619; (11): 5058; *Bank and Quotation Record* (7 March 1930), 105; Pecora, *Wall Street*, 235–36.

9. Letter to stockholders of Peoples Wayne Co. Bank, First National Bank of Detroit and Security Trust Co., Bank of Michigan, and Peninsular State Bank, 5 October 1929, JC box 141; Comptroller of the Currency, *Individual Statements of Condition of National Banks at the Close of Business December 31, 1929* (U.S. GPO, 1930), 86–7; (1931), 80–1; (1932), 76–7; (1933), 70–72; *Annual Report of the Federal Reserve Board* (1931), 192; (1932), 157.

10. *SEP* (9): 4210; Robert Lacey, *Ford: The Men and the Machine* (Boston: Little Brown, 1986), 294–97.

11. *SEP* (9): 4203, 4211–13, 4543–44; (10): 4589, 4598.

12. *SEP* (11): 5064–65, 5078.

13. *Commercial and Financial Chronicle* (28 November 1931), 3577; *SEP* (11): 5082–84, 5233, 5330, 5395; Pecora, *Wall Street*, 235–36. Before the merger the Peoples Wayne County Bank held $368 million (31 September) in deposits and the First National Bank of Detroit held $163 million, or $531 million combined. After the merger the First National held only $484 million in deposits. See *Bank and Quotation Record* (6 November 1931), 113; (5 February 1932), 113.

14. Examiner's Report of First National Bank of Detroit, November 1932, JC box 141; *SEP* (10): 4554, (11): 5295–5327, (12): 5488, 5499.

15. *SEP* (11): 5399.

16. *U.S. Statistical Abstract* (1932), 359. Auto production usually peaked in spring or summer and declined in winter, usually hitting a low in December or January. The slump in November and December 1929 was exceptional and the pickup the following spring was sluggish. Conot, *American*, 259; *SEP* (10): 4590, 4595; *U.S. Statistical Abstract* (1941), 418.

17. Typescript [by Couzens?] about bank crisis in folder, "Bank Closings, 1932–34," p. 10, JC box 140; Thomas Jackson Anketell, Detroit, to Jouett Shouse, 30 November 1931, CG box 267.

18. *SEP* (10): 4619; Jones and Angly, *Fifty Billion Dollars*, 57–8.

19. Nevins and Hill, *Expansion*, 587–88; Barnard, *Independent Man*, 204.

20. Folder, "American State Bank," especially letter to stockholders of the American State Bank, 16 March 1931, JC box 140; *SEP* (11): 5399–5400, 5485–86. Wilson Mills testified the American State Banks loans were worth $50 million (p. 5485). The *Annual Report of the Federal Reserve Board* (1930) reports them worth $39 million as of December 1930 (p. 301.)

21. *SEP* (9): 4215; (10): 5010–11; (12): 5568–71.

22. *Commercial and Financial Chronicle* (7 January 1933), 112–13; *SEP* (9): 4546–47.

23. Thomas Lamont to W.R. Hearst, n.d. [13 March 1933], TWL box 98; typescript [by Couzens?] about bank crisis in folder, "Bank Closings, 1932–34," p.10, JC box 140; Typescript, "First National Bank," 16 August 1933, JC box 141; *SEP* (9): 4214; (11): 5167–83, 5188, 5388, 5394–95, 5413, 5410, 5440, 5451; (12): 5771, 5764.

24. *SEP* (9): 4218, 4494–95; (10): 4619, 4663–64; (11): 5102–03.

25. Typescript, "Guardian National Bank of Commerce," with list of deposits as of 11 February 1933, JC

box 144; *SEP* (9): 4218, 4504; (10): 4636–38, 4696; Jones and Angly, *Fifty Billion Dollars*, 61.

26. *Commercial and Financial Chronicle* (January 7, 1933), 112–13; *SEP* (9): 4556; (10): 4815; (11): 5401, 5413–14, 5451; (12): 5763, 5769.

27. Typescript, "First National Bank," 16 August 1933; typescript by Alfred Leyburn, JC box 141; *Bank and Quotation Record* (9 December 1932), 113; (10 February 1933), 113.

28. George Levey, Financial Services Co., Detroit, to Couzens, 27 March 1933, JC box 140; *SEP* (11): 5407; Jones and Angly, *Fifty Billion Dollars*, 58–9.

29. "Confidential memorandum to [RFC] Pres. Miller," n.d. [penciled in 9 July], JC box 141; United States Senate, *Hearings Before the Committee on Banking and Currency* (73rd Cong., May 23, 1933—January 1934) *on Stock Exchange Practices* [*SEP*] (10): 4807–10; Barnard, *Independent Man*, 216; Jones and Angly, *Fifty Billion Dollars*, 58.

30. Typescript memo by Alfred Leyburn, n.d., JC box 141; *SEP* (10): 4624, 4811–13.

31. "Confidential memorandum to [RFC] President Miller," n.d.; typescript memo by Alfred Leyburn, n.d., JC box 141; *SEP* (9): 4554; (10): 4722–26. Barrie Wigmore points out that national bank examiners accepted assets at face value—the standard directed by the comptroller—for determining the solvency of banks. That standard was not used by the RFC, thus banks judged solvent by the comptroller, could be judged insolvent by the RFC, and refused loans. See Wigmore, *Crash*, 440–43.

32. *SEP* (9): 4554, 4578; (10): 4627, 4691–93, 4728.

33. Couzens, "Michigan Banking Situation" n.d.; typescript narrative of Detroit bank crisis by Alfred Leyburn, n.d., JC box 141; Leyburn to Couzens, 28 September 1933, JC box 140; *SEP* (9): 4563; (10): 4627, 4693–94.

34. Couzens, "Michigan Banking Situation," n.d., JC box 141; *SEP* (10): 4627; (12): 5793; Joslin, *Hoover*, 354; Barnard, *Independent Man*, 206, quoting *Congressional Record* (11 July 1932), 222. Jones claims that Hoover talked to Henry Ford on the phone on February 9, and when asked to subordinate money, Ford replied, "it's done." (Jones and Angly, *Fifty Billion Dollars*, 60.) In his memoirs Hoover claims to have talked to Ford, who agreed to subordinate the money, but provides no dates or details. He implies it was before his meeting with Couzens at the White House. See Herbert Hoover, *Memoirs*, 3:207. Edsel Ford testified in Senate hearings that he gave no definite reply to Secretary Mills, when he asked Edsel to subordinate the money on February 8 (*SEP* (10): 4694). Couzens's biographer, Harry Barnard, believes that Henry Ford had reneged on Edsel's pledge before Edsel met with either Mills or Hoover on February 8. Quoting a memorandum written at the time by Charles Miller (that I did not find in the Couzens papers), he doubts that Hoover ever talked to Ford about the subordination. See Barnard, *Independent Man*, 219–22. However, in Couzens's own narration of events, "Michigan Banking Situation," Ford's lawyer, Clifford Longley, told Couzens on February 9 that Henry Ford had agreed to subordinate the funds, and Couzens continued to believe the Ford deposits committed as security until February 13. See also testimony of Couzens before Judge Keidan Grand Jury, 17 August 1933, JC box 141. Ford biographer, Robert Lacey, states that no one knows what Edsel and Henry discussed about the Guardian situation, but he believes that Couzens's ranting about the "Ford bank" probably jolted Henry into

mulish refusal to help the banks. That chronology supports Jones, Hoover, and Couzens who claim that as of February 9, Ford was still cooperating to save the banks. See Lacey, *Ford*, 330–36. Nevins similarly ascribes Couzens's negative attitude toward helping the banks and toward Ford to explain Ford's refusal to assist. See Nevins and Hill, *Decline*, 13. But Nevins supplies neither a chronology, nor a source for his supposition, which I assume is Barnard's biography of Couzens. Couzens made elaborate statements after the fact that no enmity existed between him and Henry Ford. See Couzens to George Levey, Detroit, 16 February 1933; Couzens to Don Carrigan, Esq. Port Huron, 23 February 1933, Couzens to Walter Lippmann, 6 March 1933, JC box 140; "Michigan Banking Situation" n.d., JC box 141. I think Barnard is probably right, Jones confused, and Hoover misremembered.

35. Cannadine, *Mellon*, 345–48; Jones and Angly, *Fifty Billion Dollars*, 56; Barnard, *Independent Man*, 84. Barnard's account is rather more sympathetic to Couzens's account of his fight with Mellon, see Barnard, *Independent Man*, 158–67. As Henry Ford notoriously drove talented engineers and designers away from his company, Couzens's complaint against Chapin almost assuredly lacked merit. See Nevins and Hill, *Expansion*, 440.

36. Couzens, "Michigan Banking Situation," n.d., JC box 141; *New York Times*, 10 February 1933; *Detroit Free Press*, 14 February 1933; Tompkins, *Vandenberg*, 76; Barnard, *Independent Man*, 222–24.

37. *Detroit Free Press*, 10 February 1933; Barnard, *Independent Man*, 245–25.

38. Not surprisingly, the versions of this meeting offered by participants differ in detail, but agree on substance. Mss narrative of 9 February 1933 White House meeting [by Couzens?], n.d., JC box 140; "Michigan Banking Events," n.d., and "Michigan Banking Situation," n.d., JC box 141; Hoover, *Memoirs*, 3: 206; Ballantine, "Banks Closed," 135; Tompkins, *Vandenberg*, 76–7; Barnard, *Independent Man*, 225–27.

39. Ballantine, "Banks Closed," 135; General Motors Corp., memo from Donaldson Brown, Chairman of Finance Comm., to Finance Comm., re: Detroit banking situation, 27 March 1933, ES box 1; Sullivan, *Prelude*, 85; Barnard, *Independent Man*, 224–27; *SEP* (12): 5795; *Commercial and Financial Chronicle* (11 February 1933), 916–17; *Detroit Free Press*, 8 February 1933.

40. "Guardian National Bank of Commerce," typescript list of deposits as of 11 February 1933, JC box 144; *SEP* (12): 5793–95; Jones and Angly, *Fifty Billion Dollars*, 61; Ballantine, "Banks Closed," 136.

41. *SEP* (11): 4732, 5797; Jones and Angly, *Fifty Billion Dollars*, 63.

42. Photostat of examiner's report of First National Bank of Detroit, 5 June 1932; memo by Leyburn [month obscured] 10, 1933; Wilson Mills to Alfred Leyburn, 31 January 1933, JC box 142; *SEP* (10): 4735; (12): 5567, 5769–70.

43. *Detroit News*, 13 February 1933; *SEP* (10): 4735; (12): 5795; Jones and Angly, *Fifty Billion Dollars*, 58–9, 63–4. Jones asserts that Couzens told a reporter from the *Detroit Free Press* that weak banks should be allowed to fail, but I found no such statement in the *Detroit Free Press* in any February 1933 edition.

44. Awalt, "Recollections," 350–54; Jones and Angly, *Fifty Billion Dollars*, 62; Ballantine, "Banks Closed," 136; Nevins and Hill, *Decline*, 14. The *Detroit Free Press* reported on 8 February 1933 that communists had fomented the Briggs strike.

45. *SEP* (12): 5511, 5797; Jones and Angly, *Fifty Billion Dollars*, 63. Jones joined Hoover and many Detroiters in finding Couzens as much to blame as Ford.

46. Awalt, "Recollections,"354–55; Jones and Angly, *Fifty Billion Dollars*, 64; memo from Donaldson Brown, Chairman of GMC Finance Comm., re: Detroit banking situation, 27 March 1933, ES box 1. In the *SEP* and relevant memoirs, there was no discussion of the First National Bank until Ford threatened to withdraw his funds. Awalt, McKee, Leyburn, and perhaps Jones were certainly well aware of its tottering state, but in all the excitement about the much smaller Guardian Trust, it does not seem to have attracted much notice.

47. Mss narrative of 9 February 1933 White House meeting and subsequent events, n.d., 4, JC box 140; Couzens testimony before Judge Keidan Grand Jury, 17 August 1933, JC box 141; Donaldson Brown memo, 27 March 1933, ES box 1; Awalt, "Recollections," 354–57; Tompkins, *Vandenberg*, 78; Barnard, *Independent Man*, 232–33; Jones and Angly, *Fifty Billion Dollars*, 61–2.

48. *Kalamazoo Gazette* (14 February 1933), 1.

49. *Commercial and Financial Chronicle* (18 February 1933), 1149; *SEP* (10): 4628; (12): 5798–5800, 5811–15; Jones and Angly, *Fifty Billion Dollars*, 65.

50. *Detroit News*, 14 February 1933; *Kalamazoo Gazette*, 14 February 1933.

51. Sidney Fine, *Frank Murphy: The Detroit Years* (Ann Arbor: University of Michigan Press, 1975), 374; *Detroit Free Press*, 15 February 1933; *Kalamazoo Gazette*, 14, 15 February 1933; *Commercial and Financial Chronicle* (18 February 1933), 1063.

52. *Detroit News*, 15 February 1933; *Commercial and Financial Chronicle* (18 February 1933), 1150; *Kalamazoo Gazette*, 14 February 1933.

53. *Detroit News*, 15 February 1933; *Detroit Free Press*, 15, 16 February 1933; *Commercial and Financial Chronicle* (18 February 1933), 1151.

54. *Detroit Free Press*, 15 February 1933; *New York Times*, 15 February 1933; *Commercial and Financial Chronicle* (18 February 1933), 1064, 1150; Jones and Angly, *Fifty Billion Dollars*, 67.

55. *Detroit News*, 15, 16 February 1933; *Detroit Free Press*, 15, 16, 17 February 1933; *Kalamazoo Gazette*, 14 February 1933; *New York Times*, 15 February 1933; *Commercial and Financial Chronicle* (18 February 1933), 1064, 1066, 1151.

56. *Detroit News*, 15, 16 February 1933; *Detroit Free Press*, 16, 17 February 1933; *Kalamazoo Gazette*, 14, 15 February 1933; *Commercial and Financial Chronicle* (18 February 1933), 1150–51.

57. *Detroit News*, 16, 17, 18 February 1933; *Detroit Free Press*, 15, 16, 17, 22 February 1933; *Commercial and Financial Chronicle* (18 February 1933), 1151.

58. *Detroit News*, 16, 18 February 1933; *Detroit Free Press*, 17 February 1933.

59. *Detroit News*, 16, 17, 18, 21 February 1933; *Detroit Free Press*, 17 February 1933.

60. *Detroit Free Press*, 15 February 1933; Walter Lippmann in *New York Herald Tribune*, 21 February 1933; *Kokomo Tribune*, 15 February 1933; Couzens to Lippmann, 6 March 1933; Lippmann to Couzens, 8 March 1933, JC box 140; Donaldson Brown memo, 27 March 1933, ES box 1; *Commercial and Financial Chronicle* (18 February 1933), 1150–51; Tompkins, *Vandenberg*, 81.

61. Telegram Nieschlag and Co., New York, to Glass, 27 February 1933, CG box 271; *Detroit News*, 25, 26 February 1933; *Detroit Free Press*, 21, 25 February 1933; Tompkins, *Vandenberg*, 78–9; Sullivan, *Prelude*, 88–9.

62. *Detroit News*, 22, 23, 24, 25 February 1933; *Detroit Free Press*, 21, 22, 24 February 1933.

63. *Detroit News*, 23, 24, 27, 28 February 1933.

64. *Detroit News* 27, 28, 29 February 1933.

Chapter Seven

1. Goldenweiser, "February 21, 1933," EAG box 1; *New York Times*, 22, 25 February 1933; Whaley-Eaton Service, 18 February 1933; James, *Chicago Banks*, 2:1056–57.

2. *Commercial and Financial Chronicle* (4 March 1933), 1481–87; *Cincinnati Enquirer*, 28 February 1933; *Cincinnati Times-Star*, 28 February 1933.

3. Louis W. Hill, Pres. FNB of St. Paul, MN to John Evans, Pres. FNB Denver, 3 March 1933, FNBD box 5; *Commercial and Financial Chronicle* (4 March 1933), 1481–87; *New York Times*, 1 March 1933; *St. Louis Post-Dispatch*, 3 March 1933; reprint from *Fortune Magazine* (December 1932) in JJR file 144.

4. *New York Times*, 22, 25 February 1933; *Baltimore Sun*, 16, 25 February 1933; *Washington Post*, 26 February 1933; *St. Louis Post-Dispatch*, 25 February 1933; *Commercial and Financial Chronicle* (4 March 1933), 1484; Cooper, *Union Trust Company*, 130; according to *Bank and Quotation Record* (10 February 1933), 112, Title Guarantee and Trust Company of Baltimore was a relatively minor bank in Baltimore, with deposits (December 1932) of about $4.9 million. There were 12 bigger banks in the city.

5. *Boston Globe*, 28 February, 1 March 1933; *Indianapolis News*, 27, 28 February 1933; *Kokomo Tribune*, 27 February, 1 March 1933; *Washington Post*, 5 March 1933.

6. Federal Reserve Bank of Cleveland, *Monthly Business Review* (1 April 1933), 1–2; *Commercial and Financial Chronicle* (4 March 1933), 1482–85; *Rocky Mountain News*, 27 February 1933; *Cincinnati Enquirer*, 28 February 1933; *Cincinnati Times-Star*, 28 February 1933. The Cleveland Federal Reserve District includes western Pennsylvania and eastern Kentucky.

7. *Commercial and Financial Chronicle* (4 March 1933), 1483–85; *New York Times*, 25 February, 1 March 1933; *Boston Globe*, 28 February, 1 March 1933.

8. *Commercial and Financial Chronicle* (4 March 1933), 1484–85; *Cincinnati Enquirer*, 28 February 1933; *Louisville Courier-Journal*, 1 March 1933; *St. Louis Post-Dispatch*, 1 March 1933; *Indianapolis News*, 1 March 1933; *Chicago Tribune*, 1, 2 March 1933; *New York Times*, 1, 2 March 1933.

9. State of Washington, *Annual Report of the Supervisor of Banking 1933* (Olympia, WA, 1933), 3; Atherton to Shouse, 27 December 1930, CG box 267; *Santa Ana Register*, 3 March 1933.

10. *Orange Daily News*, 2 March 1933; *San Francisco Chronicle*, 2 March 1933; *Santa Ana Register*, 2 March 1933; *Los Angeles Times*, 3 March 1933; telegram from Agnew, FRB San Francisco, to W. Wyatt, 3 March 1933, WW box 24.

11. *Los Angeles Times*, 3 March 1933.

12. *New York Times*, 2, 3, 4 March 1933; *Commercial and Financial Chronicle* (4 March 1933), 1482, 1487.

13. Hait, *Arizona Bank*, 86–8.

14. *Santa Ana Register*, 2 March 1933; *Los Angeles Times* 3, 4 March 1933; *Boston Globe*, eve. ed., 4 March 1933.

15. George Seay, FRB Richmond, to Eugene Meyer, 27 February 1933, EM box 77; *Boston Globe*, 3 March

1933; *Richmond Times-Dispatch*, 4 March 1933; *Atlanta Constitution*, 4 March 1933.

16. *Washington Post*, 28 February, 2–4 March 1933; Beatty, *Bank Failures*, 81.

17. *Cincinnati Times-Star*, 28 February, 1–3 March 1933.

18. *Washington Post*, 26 February 1933.

19. *Orange Daily News*, 2, 3 March 1933; *Santa Ana Register*, 3 March 1933; *Los Angeles Times*, 4 March 1933.

20. *Chicago Tribune*, 5 March 1933; James, *Chicago Banks*, 2:1053–54, 1059–61.

21. *Chicago Tribune*, 4 March 1933; James, *Chicago Banks*, 2:1060–62.

22. *Commercial and Financial Chronicle* (7 January 1933), 3; James, *Chicago Banks*, 2:1062–64. I don't know what time Traylor and Brown backed down from their threat to demand Fed gold, but the threat was invoked by Chicago Chairman Eugene Stevens as late as midnight and used by Governor Meyer in his argument to persuade President Hoover to order a national moratorium that night. See below.

23. Walter Wyatt, "notes on conversation, August 1, 1944, with Goldenweiser, re: bank holiday," WW box 61; Charles Hamlin Diary, 3 March 1933; *Chicago Tribune*, 4 March 1933; *Boston Globe*, 2 March 1933; Meltzer, *Federal Reserve*, 1:377–81; James, *Chicago Banks*, 2:1064; Wicker, *Banking Panics*, 154–58.

24. *New York Times*, 4 March 1933; *Annual Report of the Federal Reserve Board* (1933), 138; Meltzer, *Federal Reserve*, 1:386n135. Meltzer cites the Harrison papers to support his contention that the Bank of England was buying dollars in Paris. Barrie Wigmore asserts in "Was the Bank Holiday of 1933 Caused by a Run on the Dollar?" *Journal of Economic History* 47, no. 3 (1987): 742, that the Bank of England was selling dollars in Paris in early March 1933.

25. *Annual Report of the Federal Reserve Board* (1933), 8–12, 138–39; *Banking and Monetary Statistics*, 537; Nadler and Bogen, *Banking Crisis*, 155.

26. *Louisville Courier-Journal*, 2 March 1933; *Chicago Tribune*, 4 March 1933; *New York Times* (3 March 1933), 25; Goldenweiser notes, "Board Meeting Mar 2, 1933, 10 pm," EAG box 7; The *Chicago Tribune* reported a run on the Bowery Savings Bank, which was not mentioned in the *New York Times*. Indeed, the *Times* ran an upbeat story on the savings bank, claiming it had signed up hundreds of new clients rather than experienced a run.

27. Goldenweiser notes, "Meeting of Fed. Res. Bd., 10 pm, 3 March to 4 am, 4 March [1933]," EAG box 7; *New York Times*, 2, 3, 4 March 1933; Meltzer, *Federal Reserve*, 1:386–87.

28. *Louisville Courier-Journal*, 3 March 1933; Walter Wyatt to Arthur Ballantine, 1 August 1944, WW box 61; Goldenweiser notes, "Board Meeting Mar 2, 1933, 10 pm," EAG box 7; Hoover, *Memoirs*, 3:210; Myers and Newton, *Hoover Administration*, 363–64; United States Senate, *Hearings Before the Committee on Finance* (72nd Cong., February 13–28, 1933) *Investigation of Economic Problems*, 32. Mitchell's fears of Hoover's possible impeachment in retrospect appear absurdly overblown.

29. Walter Wyatt's notes, "conference in Gov. Meyer's Ofc. Tues. night, February 28, 1933, WW box 61; Hoover, *Memoirs*, 3:210–12; Myers and Newton, *Hoover Administration*, 358–64; Meltzer, *Federal Reserve*, 1:384–85. Hoover's efforts to coax or cajole Roosevelt into cooperating are discussed in greater detail in Chapter Eight.

30. Walter Wyatt to Arthur Ballantine, 1 August 1944, WW box 61; "February 21, 1933," Meeting of Fed. Res. Advisory Council, notes by Goldenweiser, EAG box 1;

Commercial and Financial Chronicle (18 February 1933) 1150; Olson, *Saving Capitalism*, 111; Tompkins, *Vandenberg*, 79–81. Ultimately, the U.S. did get something close to an "Iowa Plan" in 1934 when the FDIC gained the power to operate insolvent banks, discussed in the Epilogue.

31. Hamlin Diary, 2 March 1933; memo: Trading with the Enemy Act, n.d., no author [Wyatt], WW box 24; notes of Walter Wyatt, 2 March 1933, WW box 61; Goldenweiser notes, "Board Meeting, March 2, 1933, 10 pm," EAG box 7.

32. Hamlin Diary, 2 March 1933; memo, "FLF" [Fahy, secy to Meyer], 3 March 1933, EM box 77; Goldenweiser notes, "Board Meeting, March 2, 1933, 10 pm," EAG box 7; Hoover, *Memoirs*, 3:210, 212; Myers and Newton, *Hoover Administration*, 364–65; Moley, *New Deal*, 157; Meltzer, *Federal Reserve*, 1:383–85, 389; Awalt, "Recollections," 357–58; Olson, *Saving Capitalism*, 107.

33. *Richmond Times-Dispatch*, 4 March 1933; *Denver Post*, 4 March 1933; Hoover, *Memoirs*, 3:212–13; Myers and Newton, *Hoover Administration*, 363–65.

34. Byrnes, *Lifetime*, 70–71.

35. Hamlin Diary, 2, 3 March 1933; Moley, *New Deal*, 145–46.

36. Moley, *New Deal*, 148–49; Myers and Newton, *Hoover Administration*, 365–66. Hoover did not even mention the meeting in his memoirs. The Hoover–Roosevelt battle over the crisis is discussed at greater length in Chapter Eight.

37. Hamlin Diary, 2, 3 March 1933; Moley, *New Deal*, 147–48n, Wyatt to Moley, 16 March 1966.

38. Hamlin Diary, 4 March 1933; Meyer to Hoover, 3 March 1933; Executive Order "L-23"; resolution voted by the Federal Reserve Bank of Chicago, 3 March 1933; resolution voted by the Federal Reserve Bank of New York, 3 March 1933, EM box 28.

39. Hamlin Diary, 4 March 1933; memo by F.L. Fahy, 4 March 1933; memo [by Fahy?] 7 April 1933; Hoover to Meyer, 4 March 1933, EM box 28.

40. Hamlin Diary, 3 March 1933; Goldenweiser notes, "Board Meeting, March 2, 1933, 10 pm," and "Meeting of Fed Res Bd, 10 pm, 3 March to 4 am, 4 March [1933]," EAG box 7; Awalt, "Recollections," 358–60; Olson, *Saving Capitalism*, 110; Meltzer, *Federal Reserve*, 1:381, 387nn137, 138.

41. Hamlin Diary, 3 March 1933; Meyer to Hoover, 3 mar. 1933, EM box 28, contains copies of the formal requests from the directors in New York and Chicago. *Philadelphia Evening Bulletin*, 4 March 1933; Meltzer, *Federal Reserve*, 1:387–88.

42. *New York Times*, 4 March 1933; *Boston Globe*, eve. ed., 4 March 1933; *Philadelphia Evening Bulletin*, 4 March 1933. Walter Wyatt to Arthur Ballantine, 1 Aug 1944, WW box 61, claims a deal had been struck for the governors in Illinois and New York to declare holidays in their states simultaneously. If such a deal had been struck, which seems unlikely, it was not kept. Wyatt repeated the claim in a letter to Raymond Moley written in 1966, see Moley, *New Deal*, 127. Different sources report the decrees of the two governors at different hours, but it is rarely clear what time standard was being reported at the time. Charles Hamlin recorded in his diary (4 March 1933) that the Federal Reserve Board in Washington received word that Governor Lehman was set to sign a proclamation at 3:10 a.m., and Governor Horner signed at 3:20 a.m. Hamlin was presumably referring to Washington, D.C., time.

43. "Statement for the press," Fed. Res. Board, 2 March 1933, EAG box 7; *Boston Globe*, eve. ed., 4 March 1933; *Philadelphia Evening Bulletin*, 4 March 1933.

44. *Chicago Tribune*, 4 March 1933; James, *Chicago Banks*, 2:1065–6.

45. *Chicago Tribune*, 5 March 1933; *Annual Report of the Federal Reserve Board* (1933), 10; Meltzer, *Federal Reserve*, 1:386n134, 387–88; Moley, *New Deal*, 127–28 and 147n, letter from Walter Wyatt; Hamlin Diary, 4 March 1933. In 1933 New York and Washington were not in the same time zone.

46. *Des Moines Register*, 4, 5, 8 March 1933. The superintendent of banking operated 121 of the closed banks under the law passed only weeks before.

47. *Philadelphia Evening Bulletin*, 4 March 1933; *Des Moines Register* (6 March 1933), 10.

48. *Boston Globe*, eve. ed., 4 March 1933.

49. George W. Norris, *Ended Episodes* (Philadelphia: John Winston, 1937), 225–27; *Philadelphia Evening Bulletin*, 4 March 1933.

50. Norris, *Episodes*, 228–30; *Philadelphia Evening Bulletin*, 4 March 1933; Awalt, "Recollections,"360, repeats the apocryphal story about the D.C. Fire Department having to wake the governor. Goldenweiser affirms it is not true in "Meeting of Fed. Res. Bd., 10 pm, 3 March to 4 am, 4 March [1933]," EAG box 7.

51. Cannadine, *Mellon*, 467–68; *St. Louis Post-Dispatch*, 5 March 1933. The "run" on the Mellon bank is oddly similar to the "run" on the Bowery Savings Bank of March 2; in both cases management claimed afterward that clients were really there to deposit money and not withdraw it.

52. Norris, *Episodes*, 229–31; *Philadelphia Evening Bulletin*, 4 March 1933; *Commercial and Financial Chronicle* (11 March 1933), 1673; Meltzer, *Federal Reserve*, 1:388n139. Meltzer does not identify the "bank in Pittsburgh," which was, most likely, the Mellon National Bank.

53. *Richmond Times-Dispatch*, 5 March 1933.

54. *St. Louis Post-Dispatch*, 4, 5 March 1933.

55. Telegram from Gov. Johnson of Colorado, 4 March 1933; telegram from Denver Clearing House Assn., 4 March 1933, FNBD box 21; *Rocky Mountain News*, 3, 5 March 1933; *Denver Post*, 4 March 1933.

56. *Boston Globe*, 4 March 1933; *Philadelphia Evening Bulletin*, 4 March 1933; *Richmond Times Dispatch*, 5 March 1933; *St. Louis Post-Dispatch*, 5 March 1933; *Chicago Tribune*, 5 March 1933; *New York Times*, 5 March 1933; Olson, *Saving Capitalism*, 110; Moley, *New Deal*, 161n, Wyatt to Moley, 16 March 1966.

57. *Federal Reserve Bulletin* (February 1933), 105; (March 1933), 201; *Annual Report of the Federal Reserve Board* (1933), 223.

58. McKinney, FRB Dallas, to Washington, 8 March 1933, National Archives, Record Group 92, #470, box 2158; Thomas W. Lamont to FDR, and attached memorandum on the banking crisis, 27 February 1933, FDRP 70; Benjamin Anderson in *Chase Economic Bulletin* (May 6 1933), 4.

59. Press release of Federal Reserve Board, 28 March 1933, DRC box 14; *Annual Report of the Federal Reserve Board* (1933), 5–6; James, *Chicago Banks*, 2:1055; *New York Times* (2 March 1933), 25; *Commercial and Financial Chronicle* (4 March 1933), 1486; (11 March 1933), 1689.

60. Goldenweiser notes, "Meeting of Fed. Res. Bd., 10 pm, 3 March to 4 am, 4 March [1933]," EAG box 7; Statement of Condition of First National Bank of Denver, 24 March 1933; Statement of Condition of First National Bank of St. Paul, 15 March 1933; memos of First National Bank of Denver, 14 March 1933, and n.d. [March 1933]; memo from Development Dept. to John Evans, 15 March 1933, FNBD box 21.

61. Memo from Development Dept. to John Evans, Pres. First National Bank of Denver, 15 March 1933, FNBD box 21; Johnson, *Diary Letters*, 5:26 February 1933, p. 7; Benjamin Anderson in *Chase Economic Bulletin*, (9 May 1933), 4.

62. Benjamin Anderson, "Some Fallacies Underlying the Demand for Inflation," *Chase Economic Bulletin* (9 May 1933); *Annual Report of the Federal Reserve Board* (1933), 166; Federal Reserve Bank of New York, *Monthly Review of Credit and Business Conditions* (1 March 1933), 1; *New York Times* (2 March 1933), 25; *Commercial and Financial Chronicle* (25 February 1933), 1281; (4 March 1933), 1455; *Banking and Monetary Statistics*, 19, 81.

63. *Banking and Monetary Statistics*, 376; *Annual Report of the Federal Reserve Board* (1933), 93; press release Federal Reserve Board, 2 March 1933, EAG box 7; press release Federal Reserve Board, 28 March 1933, DRC box 14; *Commercial and Financial Chronicle* (4 February 1933), 800; (25 February 1933), 1336; (4 March 1933), 1503; *Philadelphia Inquirer*, 10 March 1933; *Louisville Courier-Journal*, 11 March 1933; James, *Chicago Banks*, 2:1055; Norris, *Episodes*, 222. Thomas Lamont of J.P. Morgan, advised George Harrison and Eugene Meyer the moratorium movement had to be stopped before it inflicted real damage on the economy. Lamont suggested aggressive moves by the RFC and the U.S. Treasury could calm the situation. See memo with attached recommendations, Lamont to FDR, 27 February 1933, FDRP 70.

64. In fact, gold never left New York vaults; it was simply "ear marked" property of the Bank of England within the vaults, where it remained. See Meltzer, *Federal Reserve*, 1:381.

65. Goldenweiser notes, "Meeting of Fed. Res. Bd., 10 pm, 3 March to 4 am 4 March [1933]," EAG box 7; Ballantine, "Banks Closed," 133–35, 137–38; *Annual Report of the Federal Reserve Board* (1933), 8–9. Wigmore in "Bank Holiday," 745, reports that $380 million in gold was being held in the Federal Reserve Bank of New York for the U.S. Treasury, out of total holdings in New York of $761 million. Wigmore argues that the alarm among Federal Reserve governors, especially Harrison of New York, provoked the national bank moratorium. Thus, the stock of Federal Reserve gold, and not the condition of the country's banks, provoked the shutdown (749–50, 754). This supports Wicker's assertion that the Federal Reserve Board failed to provide leadership as the crisis mounted from mid–February, and left the initiative to Fed district governors and state governors, and ultimately President Roosevelt, who stepped into the breech (134–38, 148–49.) Thomas Lamont's 27 February 1933 letter and memo to FDR, FDRP 70, does not mention gold flight, but expressed great alarm about the inevitable consequence for New York banks of a nationwide bank moratorium. As of February 27 the gold flight had not yet started and was not anticipated by Lamont.

66. *Annual Report of the Federal Reserve Board* (1933), 15, 26, 138–39; *Louisville Courier-Journal*, 7 March 1933; Whaley-Eaton Service, 18 February 1933, reported that FDR would either abandon the gold standard or adopt bimetallism; on March 3 it reported that the U.S. would almost certainly depart the gold standard under FDR. Strangely, the amount of gold leaving banks and the Federal Reserve System — especially for foreign accounts— was dwarfed by the tons that left in late 1931 or even mid–1932, making the reaction of 1933 all the more outlandish. Emanuel Goldenweiser reports that the Guaranty Trust Co. of New York made one of the rare efforts

to defend the dollar by buying $110 million of them in Paris on March 3 with money (francs) borrowed from the bank of France. See "Meeting of Fed. Res. Bd., 10 pm, 3 March to 4 am, 4 March [1933]," EAG box 7.

Chapter Eight

1. Shouse to FDR, n.d. [November 1932], JS box 3. Michelson, *Ghost*, 3–10, offers a lively and unflattering account of FDR's role in evicting Shouse from the party Executive Committee.

2. *Documents Diplomatiques Français, 1932–1939, Ire Série (1932–1935)* vol. 2, *(15 novembre 1932–17 mars 1933)* (Paris: Imprimèrie Nationale, 1966), 190–201, 226; Hoover, *Memoirs*, 3:178–79; Moley, *Seven Years*, 141–42; Feis, *1933*, 40–1; Meltzer, *Federal Reserve*, 1:382.

3. Hoover, *Memoirs*, 3:178–83; Moley, *Seven Years*, 68–78; Frank Freidel, *Franklin D. Roosevelt: Launching the New Deal* (Boston: Little, Brown, 1973), 18–30, dwells extensively on this episode. Myers and Newton, *Hoover Administration*, 282–88; Moley, *New Deal*, 23–35; Feis, *1933*, 36–7. See Rosenman, *Public Papers and Addresses*, 1:867.

4. Ambassador Paul Claudel to For. Min. Edouard Herriot, 10 December 1932, in *Documents Diplomatiques*, Ire Série, 2:226; Herriot to Claudel, 14 December 1932, and Germain-Martin, Fin. Min. to Herriot, 14 December 1932, p. 248; Herriot to Claudel, 15 Dec 1932, p. 250; *Commercial and Financial Chronicle* (17 December 1932), 4073. France was clearly able to pay the installment due of $19,261,432, but chose not to. While Poland apologized for its inability to pay the $3,302,980 due, Hungary defaulted on a payment of $40,729 and Estonia on $266,370, signaling a refusal, rather than an inability to pay.

5. Telegram Hoover to FDR, 17 December 1932; FDR to Hoover, 19 December 1932, in Walch and Miller, *Hoover and Roosevelt*, 80–84. British Ambassador Ronald Lindsay told Stimson that he had not pursued any further discussions with Stimson about the debt issue because he thought any discussions with the outgoing administration would necessarily have to be reopened with the new administration. See Stimson memo, 19 January 1933, in Walch and Miller, *Hoover and Roosevelt*, 109–10. René Leon to Moley, 20 December 1932; Moley to FDR, 20 December 1932; F. Altschul, Lazard Frère & Co., NY, to Moley, 20 December 1932, FDRP 743; "Four Causes of the Depression" by Bernard Baruch, n.d. [January 1933]; FDR to Moley, 18 January 1933, RM box 107.

6. Berle to Moley, 14 November 1932, AAB box 16. Hoover and most Republicans were incensed that one of the first acts of Roosevelt's Republican secretary of the interior, Harold Ickes, was to rename "Hoover Dam," "Boulder Dam."

7. Memo by Berle, 7 November 1932, AAB box 15.

8. "Confidential notes," 5 August 1932, EAG box 1; F. Altschul, Lazard Frère & Co, New York to Moley, 20 December 1932; René Leon to Moley, 20 December 1932; Moley to FDR, 20 December 1932, FDRP 743; Berle to Moley, 14 November 1932, AAB box 16; Tugwell to Moley, 12 January 1965; Moley to Tugwell, 22 January 1965, RGT box 15; Johnson, *Diary Letters*, 5:12 February 1933; Moley, *New Deal*, 93–4; Moley, *Seven Years*, 71. On Johnson, La Follette, and Cutting, see Ray Tucker and Frederick R. Barkley, *Sons of the Wild Jackass* (Seattle: University of Washington Press, 1970), 96–122, 148–70, 196–220. "Standard Trade and Securities" (vol. 66, 26 December 1932) 13, AAB box 16, [thus, seen by Berle]

well summarizes Wall Street arguments to settle the debt question. Munds, Winslow & Potter, NYSE, "Commodities and Inter-Governmental Debts" (23 November 1932), EAR box 39, makes the Wall Street argument for outright cancellation.

9. Hoover to Stimson, 4 January 1933; Stimson memo, 9 January 1933; Hoover to Stimson, 15 January 1933, in Walch and Miller, *Hoover and Roosevelt*, 100–104.

10. Claudel to Premier Paul-Boncour, 11 January 1933, *Documents Diplomatiques (Ire Série)* 2:14–20; Stimson Diary, January 20, 1933; White House Statement, January 20, 1933; Hoover Memorandum, January 20, 1933, in Walch and Miller, *Hoover and Roosevelt*, 114–23; Moley, *New Deal*, 51–4; Tugwell, *Diary*, 64–5.

11. Stimson Diary, 20 January 1933, White House Statement, 20 January 1933, Stimson Memorandum, 20 January 1933, and Hoover Memorandum, 20 January 1933, in Miller and Walch, *Hoover and Roosevelt*, 114–23; "Statement, January 20, 1933, on Conference with President-elect Roosevelt," in Myers, *State Papers*, 2:581–82; Johnson, *Diary Letters*, 5:12 February 1933, 3; Moley to Tugwell, 22 January 1965, RGT box 15; Tugwell, *Diary*, 26, 65.

12. Memo by Berle, 7 November 1932, AAB box 15. On the St. Lawrence Waterway talks, see Rosenman, *Public Papers and Addresses*, 1:159–206, esp. "introductory note," 159–66, FDR to Hoover, 9 July 1932, and reply, 10 July 1932, 203–06; Hoover, *Memoirs*, 2:122–3, 234–6.

13. Moley, *Seven Years*, 84–90; Frank Freidel, "Hoover and FDR: Reminiscent Reflections," in Lee Nash, ed., *Understanding Herbert Hoover: Ten Perspectives* (Stanford: Hoover Institution Press, 1987), 138–39. When the International Economic Conference did occur in London in summer 1933, Roosevelt sent a squabbling delegation with neither clear instructions nor leadership. It accomplished nothing. See Schlesinger, *Age of Roosevelt*, 2:200–32; Moley, *New Deal*, 420–96; Warburg, *Long Road Home*, 126–38.

14. James Harbard to Charles Dawes, 23 December 1932, CGD box 250; Feis, *1933*, 13.

15. Norris, *Episodes*, 223; *Annual Report of the Federal Reserve Board* (1933), 142; *Commercial and Financial Chronicle* (11 March 1933), 2009.

16. Myers and Newton, *Hoover Administration*, 338–40, also reprinted in Walch and Miller, *Hoover and Roosevelt*, 130–32; *Annual Report of the Federal Reserve Board* (1933), 142.

17. *Banking and Monetary Statistics*, 536–37. While gold was being bought by foreign central banks at an enormous rate in February and March 1933 ($278 million), it was not unprecedented. More gold fled the U.S. in September and October 1931 ($386 million) and May and June 1932 ($401 million).

18. *Santa Ana Register*, 3 March 1933; Myers and Newton, *Hoover Administration*, 340–41.

19. Byrnes, *Lifetime*, 66–67; Smith and Beasley, *Carter Glass*, 309, 314, 326–27; Moley, *Seven Years*, 118–19; Moley, *New Deal*, 80–2. William J. Barber, *Design Within Disorder: Franklin D. Roosevelt, the Economists, and the Shaping of American Economic Policy, 1933–1945* (New York: Cambridge University Press, 1996), 14–8, 21–2, discusses numerous "inflationists," such as Professors Irving Fisher, George Warren, and Frank Pearson, who hovered around FDR's campaign probably without much influence.

20. Smith and Beasley, *Carter Glass*, 328, 333–35; Byrnes, *Lifetime*, 67; Moley, *New Deal*, 50, 80–2; *St.*

Louis Post-Dispatch, 17 January 1933; Glass to FDR, 7 February 1933, FDRP 687. According to the Stimson Diary (15 January 1933) cited by Walch and Miller, *Hoover and Roosevelt*, 107, Roosevelt told Stimson that before he discussed the war debt question with British Ambassador Lindsay, he turned to none other than Russell Leffingwell for advice. Roosevelt also stayed in touch with Morgan partner Thomas W. Lamont on financial questions, see for example Thomas Lamont to FDR, 27 February 1933, FDRP 70.

21. Glass to FDR, 7 February 1933, FDRP 687; Smith and Beasley, *Carter Glass*, 336–37; Moley, *New Deal*, 83–4; *Cincinnati Enquirer*, 20 February 1933.

22. Byrnes to FDR, 13 February 1933, JFB box 54; *Commercial and Financial Chronicle* (7 January 1933), 71; *New York Times*, 19 February, 1, 2 March 1933; Myers and Newton, *Hoover Administration*, 340–42.

23. United States Senate, *Hearings Before the Committee on Finance* (72nd Cong., February 13–28, 1933) *Investigation of Economic Problems*, 565; "Interim Reports and Immediate Recommendations of the Committee for the Nation," (February 1933), EAR box 39, which contains reams of Committee for the Nation publicity from November 1932 to March 1933, all calling for a devalued dollar; Whaley-Eaton Service, Washington D.C., 18 February 1933; Alvin T. Simonds and John G. Thompson, "Looking Ahead" (Fitchburg, Mass., 23 February 1933), DRC box 13; Moley, *New Deal*, 134–35. It is impossible to say why Roosevelt changed his mind — if he did — on the national sales tax. A memo from Berle to FDR (2 December 1932, AAB box 16) suggests that Roosevelt turned down the sales tax to satisfy Rep. La Guardia and the progressive faction in the House, but the memo is obscure and open to interpretation.

24. Meltzer, *Federal Reserve*, 1:385n; Freidel, *Launching the New Deal*, 183–84; Wigmore, *Crash*, 443–44. Wigmore suggests that Woodin more than hinted to Mills that no rescue package be approved before March 4, but there is no record of what Woodin said to Mills.

25. Joslin, *Hoover*, 364; Hoover, *Memoirs* 3:214–15; Myers and Newton, *Hoover Administration*, 356; Walch and Miller, *Hoover and Roosevelt*, 133–34.

26. Walch and Miller, *Hoover and Roosevelt*, 134; Moley, *New Deal*, 144–45.

27. Freidel, *Launching the New Deal*, 183, 187; Thomas W. Lamont to FDR, 27 February 1933, FDRP 70. In January Stimson recounted to Tugwell and Moley a conversation Roosevelt had with Leffingwell; see Tugwell, *Diary*, 67.

28. Hamlin Diary, 3 March 1933; Byrnes, *Lifetime*, 71; *Santa Ana Register*, 2 March 1933.

29. Hoover, *Memoirs*, 3:212–13.

30. Hamlin Diary, 3 March 1933; Myers and Newton, *Hoover Administration*, 365–66; Moley, *New Deal*, 146–48n., Wyatt to Moley, 16 March 1966, and 148–49; Awalt, "Recollections," 359; Meltzer, *Federal Reserve*, 1:385–87.

31. Smith and Beasley, *Carter Glass*, 340–41. I cannot determine when Roosevelt decided to use the Trading with the Enemy Act to close the banks. Tugwell reports he had discussed it extensively with Roosevelt before leaving New York for Washington, but provides no dates for those discussions. See Rexford Tugwell, *Roosevelt's Revolution: The First Year — A Personal Perspective* (New York: Macmillan, 1977), 22–23.

32. Hoover, *Memoirs*, 3:213; Smith and Beasley, *Carter Glass*, 339–42. This exchange was reported in the biography of Glass by Glass's secretary, Rixey Smith. I have explored Carter Glass's papers looking for some confir-

mation of this exchange with Roosevelt, but, not surprisingly, found nothing. Smith, himself, left no papers and the "Rixey Smith" folder within the Glass papers reveals nothing useful.

33. Whaley-Eaton Service, 3 March 1933; *Boston Globe*, 3, 4 March 1933; *Richmond Times-Dispatch*, 4 March 1933; *Philadelphia Evening Bulletin*, 4 March 1933; *St. Louis Post-Dispatch*, 5 March 1933.

34. *Chicago Tribune*, 2 March 1933.

35. Memos by Berle, 17 October and 7 November 1932, AAB box 15; Tugwell, *Diary*, 50–51.

36. Tugwell, *Diary*, 60, 76–7.

37. Tugwell, *Diary*, 82–3; "summary" [by Eugene Meyer?] n.d., EM box 28; Arthur Krock in *New York Times*, 2 March 1933.

38. Burner, *Herbert Hoover*, 339–41; Tugwell quoted in Schlesinger, *Age of Roosevelt*, 2:531. See also Stephen Skowronek, *Politics*, 260–85; Freidel, "Hoover and FDR: Reminiscent Reflections," 127–31.

39. Moley, *New Deal*, 65–8.

40. Moley, *Seven Years*, 464–65.

41. Ibid., 140–41. President Hoover instructed the Secret Service agent to hand the letter to FDR personally, suggesting the level of mistrust in which Hoover then held FDR. See Agent John M. West to W.H. Moran, Secret Service Chief, WDC, 27 February 1933, OM box 11.

42. Moley, *Seven Years*, 141–42.

43. *Shelbyville* (Indiana) *Democrat*, 16 September 1933; Tugwell, *Roosevelt's Revolution*, 21; Johnson, *Diary Letters*, 5:19 February 1933, 4–5. Frank Freidel's judgment, in *Launching the New Deal*, 195, is that faced with divided counsel on all sides, just as Hoover was, Roosevelt chose the path of least resistance, which was to do nothing.

Chapter Nine

1. "Inaugural Address," in Rosenman, ed., *Public Papers and Addresses*, 2:11–12.

2. Ibid., 13–16.

3. Johnson, *Diary Letters*, 5:5 March 1933; *St. Louis Post-Dispatch*, 5 March 1933; *Boston Globe*, eve. ed., 4 March 1933; *Chicago Tribune*, 5 March 1933; *New York Times*, 5 March 1933; Gary Dean Best in *Pride, Prejudice, and Politics: Roosevelt Versus Recovery, 1933–1938* (New York: Praeger Publishers, 1991), 24–6, discusses the deviant nature of Roosevelt's speech. Barrie A. Wigmore called it "vitriolic anti-business sentiments that were mellowed by his wonderful voice," in *The Crash and Its Aftermath*, 423.

4. *St. Louis Post-Dispatch*, 5 March 1933; *Chicago Tribune*, 5 March 1933; *Cincinnati Times-Star*, 6 March 1933; *Detroit Free Press*, 7 March 1933. I found only a single telegram rebuking Roosevelt, criticizing his attack upon "money changers"; see Loren Wood, Pres., First National Bank of Bound Brook, NJ, to FDR, 6 March 1933, FDRO 230.

5. *St. Louis Post-Dispatch*, 5 March 1933.

6. Moley, *New Deal*, 151–53, 160–62, 166–76; Awalt, "Recollections," 360–63; Ballantine, "Banks Closed," 138–39; Walter Wyatt notes, 5 March 1933, WW box 61; A. Berle, Memorandum of Treasury Conference, AAB box 17.

7. Moley, *New Deal*, 147, 156n, 156–61; Rosenman, *Public Papers and Addresse*, 2:24–26, 28. Adolf Berle's papers, box 17, contains extensive notes on the discussions within the Treasury Building on Sunday and Monday, March 5 and 6, which are reproduced in George

McJimsey, ed., *Documentary History of the Franklin D. Roosevelt Presidency*, vol. 3, *The Bank Holiday and the Emergency Banking Act, March 1933* (n.p.: University Publications of America, 2001), 78–98. A vigorous debate erupted after the *Chicago Tribune*, 7 March 1933, reported that the Executive Order signed by FDR had been drafted for Hoover, who only awaited FDR's approval to sign it. The debate among participants about the responsibility for the order remained lively well into the 1960s. Walter Wyatt claimed the executive order signed by FDR was almost exactly the same as the one prepared for Hoover by Attorney General Mitchell, Wyatt, and Morrill. FDR claims in his state papers that the draft was prepared by Secretary Woodin, Attorney General Cummings, "the outgoing officials of the Treasury Department, and myself." FDR also reports that he had consulted with Attorney General designate Thomas Walsh before his untimely death on March 2, and was assured the Trading with the Enemy Act was still in force and germane. Tugwell reports that FDR was mistaken about that and Cummings, appointed at the last minute after Walsh's sudden demise, had no time to prepare anything. See Tugwell, *Roosevelt's Revolution*, 21–2. A copy of a draft by Wyatt exists in the Berle Papers, box 16, and varies from the order reprinted in Rosenman, *Public Papers and Addresses*, 2:24–6. However, Wyatt prepared numerous versions, and one ("L-23") dated March 3 found in EM box 28 is very similar to the final order signed by FDR.

8. Goldenweiser notes, "Sat. March 4, 1933," EAG box 7; *Annual Report of the Federal Reserve Board* (1933), 13; Moley, *New Deal*, 166–68; Awalt, "Recollections," 362–66.

9. Awalt, "Recollections," 364–65n; Olson, *Saving Capitalism*, 38–9.

10. Moley, *New Deal*, 151–52; Ballantine, "Banks Closed," 138–39; Tugwell, *Roosevelt's Revolution*, 21, 23; *Cincinnati Enquirer*, 23, 26 February 1933; oral history of Arthur A. Ballantine, Jr., Colorado Historical Society. The debate over the provenance of the Executive Order was relived in disagreements about the principal authorship of the Emergency Banking Act. According to Awalt, Ogden Mills was the principal author, Awalt, "Recollections," 360–62. Wyatt told Moley that Mills approached him to draw up legislation to permit federal conservators in February 1933, Moley, *New Deal*, 168. An annotated copy of the proposed bill dated March 2, 1933, is found in the Berle Papers, box 16.

11. Moley, *New Deal*, 166–68; *Annual Report of the Federal Reserve Board* (1933), 12; Wyatt, "notes on conversation August 1, 1944 with Goldenweiser re bank holiday"; handwritten notes by Wyatt, 5 March 1933, WW box 61; Goldenweiser notes, "Monday night, March 6, 1933," EAG box 7.

12. Jonathan Bourne, Jr., to Frank J. Cannon, 8 March 1933, FJC box 1; Whaley-Eaton Service, 7 March 1933, FNBD box 5; "Address before the Governors' Conference at White House, March 6, 1933," Rosenman, *Public Papers and Addresses*, 2:19; *Indianapolis News*, eve. ed., 4 March 1933; *Boston Globe*, eve. ed., 4 March 1933; *St. Louis Post-Dispatch*, 5 March 1933; *Detroit Free Press*, 5 March 1933; *Chicago Tribune*, 5 March 1933; *New York Times*, 5 March 1933.

13. Wyatt to Ballantine, 1 August 1944, WW box 61; Goldenweiser notes, "March 5, 1933, conference called by Pres.," EAG box 7; *Annual Report of the Federal Reserve Board* (1933), 9.

14. Memorandum of Treasury Committee, AAB box 17; telegram, First National Bank Herington, KS, to Glass, 4 March 1933; telegram, Thomas H. Cullinan, Phil. to Glass, 4 Mar 1933; telegram, Andrew Price, Pres. National Bank of Commerce, Seattle, to Glass, 5 March 1933; telegram, Wayles R. Harrison, V.P. American National Bank & T.C., Danville, VA, to Glass, 6 March 1933; telegram, Frank Nicks, V.P. First National Bank, St. Louis, to FDR, 4 March 1933, CG box 271, which contains about 75 such telegrams from around the country. Box 22 of Kentucky Representative Fred Vinson's papers also brims with such pleas from February and March 1933, although they tend to demand more radical solutions than those sent to Glass. See telegram, Louisa Rotary Club, KY, to Vinson, 7 March 1933; A.G. Howard, Pres. Brotherhood of Railroad Trainmen, Ashland, KY, to Vinson, 8 March 1933; telegram, First Natl Bank of Prestonburg, KY, to Vinson, 7 March 1933. Telegram R.P. Babcock, Pres. L.I. Bankers' Assoc. to J. O'Connor, 6 March 1933; telegram, Queens Clearing House Assoc. to J. O'Connor, 7 March 1933, JJO box 13; telegram, W.D. Haas, Jr., Grand Master of Louisiana Masons, Bunkie, LA, to FDR, 4 March 1933, FDRO 230; *Detroit Free Press*, 6 March 1933; *Indianapolis News*, 4 March 1933; *St. Louis Post-Dispatch*, 9 March 1933; Rosenman, *Public Papers and Addresses*, 2:37.

15. "Phillips Gives Views on Ending Business Slump," *Butler* (Pennsylvania) *Eagle*, 4 March 1933; telegram, J. Edgar Monroe, Pres. Boland Machine Co., New Orleans, to Glass, 4 March 1933; telegram, R.G. Dickinson, bank commissioner, AR, to Glass, 6 March 1933, CG box 271; Stephen Mayorick to O'Connor, 7 March 1933, JJO box 13; memo from E.E. Lincoln to P. du Pont, 8 March 1933, PSP box 1173.

16. Memorandum of Treasury Conference, AAB box 17; Goldenweiser notes, "March 5 1933 conference called by Pres.," EAG box 7.

17. Moley to FDR, 13 March 1933, FDRO 230. In 1944 Walter Wyatt recalled to Arthur Ballantine, "by [March 3] the public was in such a panic and currency was being pulled out of banks and gold out of the federal reserve so rapidly that a complete suspension was inevitable." Wyatt's perception of the situation at the time and in retrospect was fanciful. In his review of Charles Michaelson's *The Ghost Talks*, in the *New York Herald Tribune*, 23 August 1944, Arthur Ballantine asserts that bank runs "had reached a climax" by March 3. I searched American newspapers of 27 February to 4 March 1933 and found only the "runs" on the Bowery Savings Bank and the Hamilton National Bank of March 2, and the Howard Savings Institution in Newark and the Mellon bank on March 4

18. Rosenman, *Public Papers and Addresses*, 2: 24–6.

19. *Boston Globe*, 6 March 1933; *Chicago Tribune*, 5, 6 1933; *Des Moines Register*, 5, 6, 7 March 1933; *Detroit Free Press*, 7 March 1933; *Indianapolis News*, 7 March 1933; *Kokomo Tribune*, 6 March 1933; *New York Herald Tribune*, 5 March 1933; *New York Times*, 5, 6 March 1933; *Richmond Times-Dispatch*, 6 March 1933; *Rocky Mountain News*, 5, 6, 7 March 1933; *St. Louis Post-Dispatch*, 7 March 1933.

20. *Louisville Courier-Journal*, 6 March 1933.

21. *Detroit Free Press*, 6, 7, 8 March 1933; *Commercial and Financial Chronicle* (11 March 1933), 1672–74.

22. *Indianapolis News*, eve. ed., 4 March 1933; *Cincinnati Times-Star*, 6 March 1933; *Kokomo Tribune*, 6 March 1933; *Louisville Courier-Journal*, 7 March 1933; *Detroit Free Press*, 7, 8 March 1933; *Commercial and Financial Chronicle* (11 March 1933), 1673.

23. *Commercial and Financial Chronicle* (11 March 1933), 1668–70.

24. *San Francisco Chronicle*, 8, 10 March 1933; *Orange Daily News*, 9, 10 March 1933; *Los Angeles Times*, 8, 9, 10, March 1933; *Santa Ana Register*, 10 March 1933; *Commercial and Financial Chronicle* (11 March 1933), 1671.

25. Denver Clearing House Assn. to Woodin, 5 March 1933; telegram from Federal Reserve Bank, Kansas City, to all banks, 7 March 1933; telegrams from First National Bank of Denver [to correspondent banks] 8, 9 March 1933; telegram from FNB Denver to Woodin, 10 March 1933, FNBD box 5; telegram Denver Clearing House Assn. 4 March 1933; telegram from Gov. Ed Johnson [to all banks] 4 March 1933; memo about telephone conversation between Mr. Evans [Pres FNB Denver] and Mr. Barnett, of Treasury Dept. in Washington D.C., 9:45 a.m. Wed. March 8, 1933; memo of conversation between "HK" [Harry Kountze] and Irwin Wright, chief bank examiner [in K.C.], 8:15 am 10 March 1933; memo, 10 March 1933, FNBD box 21; pamphlet, Marshall Sprague, "First Century at the First National Bank of Colorado Springs" (Colorado Springs: FNBCS, 1973) Colorado Historical Society; *Rocky Mountain News*, 5–10 March 1933; *Denver Post*, 7, 10 March 1933.

26. Handwritten notes of Walter Wyatt, 6 March 1933, WW box 61.

27. *Commercial and Financial Chronicle* (11 March 1933), 1667–70; *Cincinnati Times-Star*, 7–9 March 1933; *Detroit Free Press*, 8 March 1933; *New York Times*, 9 March 1933; *Philadelphia Inquirer*, 8 March 1933; WW box 61 contains a complete set of Treasury Dept. advisories released on Monday, 6 March 1933; Federal Reserve Bank, Kansas City to all banks, 6 and 7 March 1933, FNBD box 5.

28. Hait, *Arizona Bank*, 88–91; Schlesinger, *Age of Roosevelt*, 2:289–92, and vol. 3, *The Politics of Upheaval* (Boston: Houghton Mifflin, 1960), 515–17.

29. *Denver Post*, 3 March 1933; *Chicago Tribune*, 5, 7 March 1933; *New York Times*, 5 March 1933; *Richmond Times-Dispatch*, 6 March 1933; *Detroit Free Press*, 5 March 1933; *St. Louis Post-Dispatch*, 7, 8 March 1933; *Louisville Courier-Journal*, 7 March 1933.

30. *Chicago Tribune*, 5, 7 March 1933; *New York Times*, 5 March 1933; *St. Louis Post-Dispatch*, 7, 8 March 1933.

31. *Chicago Tribune*, 5, 8, 12 March 1933; *Los Angeles Times*, 7 March 1933; *New York Times*, 5 March 1933; *Des Moines Register*, 5 March 1933; *Boston Globe*, 6 March 1933; *Indianapolis News*, 1, 6, 9 March 1933; *Rocky Mountain News*, 5, 7 March 1933; *St. Louis Post-Dispatch*, 8 March 1933; *San Francisco Chronicle*, 8 March 1933; Moley, *New Deal*, 163–64, repeats the William Manchester story in *Holiday*, February 1960.

32. William C. Drohan, Esq., Brockton, Mass., to O'Connor, 13 March 1933, JJO box 14.

33. *Kokomo Tribune*, 28 February 1933; *Louisville Courier-Journal*, 3, 7, 8 March 1933; *Chicago Tribune*, 5, 6, 7 March 1933; *Des Moines Register*, 5, 6, 8 March 1933.

34. *Detroit Free Press*, 7 March 1933; *St. Louis Post-Dispatch*, 5, 7 March 1933; *Los Angeles Times*, 8, 9, 16 March 1933.

35. *Chicago Tribune*, 4, 8, 14 March 1933; *Indianapolis News*, eve. ed., 7, 8, 9 March 1933; *Detroit Free Press*, 7 March 1933; *Rocky Mountain News*, 8 March 1933.

36. Denver Clearing House Assn. to Woodin, 5 March 1933; Federal Reserve Bank of Kansas City to all banks, 7 March 1933; telegram from First National Bank of Denver [to correspondent banks], 8 March 1933, FNBD box 5; memo: telephone conversation between Mr. Evans [Pres FNB Denver] and Mr. Barnett, Treasury

Dept., 8 March 1933, FNBD box 21; telegram from H.W. Davies, Smith Corona Typewriters, to A. Phelan, Federal Reserve Bank of New York, 10 March 1933, WW box 24; *Philadelphia Inquirer*, 10 March 1933; *St. Louis Post-Dispatch*, 10 March 1933; Rosenman, *Public Papers and Addresses*, 2:32; *Annual Report of the Federal Reserve Bank* (1933), 77, 89.

37. *Philadelphia Inquirer*, 8 March 1933; *Detroit Free Press*, 8, 9 March 1933; *Chicago Tribune*, 9 March 1933; *St. Louis Post-Dispatch*, 11 March 1933; Wyatt to Ballantine, 1 August 1944, WW box 61.

38. Rosenman, *Public Papers and Addresses*, 2:34–5; Telegram, R. Babcock, Pres. L.I. Bankers' Assoc., and Nat'l Assoc. of Finance Cos. to J. O'Connor, 6 March 1933, JJO box 13; memo, E.E. Lincoln to P. du Pont, 8 March 1933, PSP box 1173. I found no public protests of the ban on ownership of gold in March 1933; *St. Louis Post-Dispatch*, 5 March 1933; *Louisville Courier-Journal*, 6 March 1933; *Detroit Free Press*, 6 March 1933.

39. "Congress" by Frank Kent, "The New Administration," by Mark Sullivan, "As of March 4th," "Inflationism," "Barter and Scrip," and "What Is Inflation?" in *ABAJ* (March 1933): 11–19, 32–6, 61–2, 66–68, 72; "The Word Inflation" (April 1933): 36–7; (May 1933) passim; T.W. Phillips, Butler, PA, to P.S. du Pont, 14 March 1933, PSP box 1173; circular of Comm. for Nation, 3 April 1933, EAR box 39.

40. Memo, E. Goldenweiser to Eugene Meyer, 13 April 1933, RM box 107; Benjamin Anderson, "The Gold Standard and the Administration's General Economic Programme," *Chase Economic Bulletin* (6 May 1933); Anderson, "Some Fallacies Underlying the Demand for Inflation," *Chase Economic Bulletin* (9 May 1933); National Industrial Conference Board, Memo no. 5, "The Gold Standard: Recent Developments and Present Status," 5 May 1933, CWT box 22.

41. *Louisville Courier-Journal*, 7 March 1933; *Detroit Free Press*, 9 March 1933; *Indianapolis News*, 7, 9 March 1933; *San Francisco Chronicle*, 10, 11 March 1933; *Los Angeles Times*, 11 March 1933; *Chicago Tribune*, 12 March 1933; *Philadelphia Inquirer*, 9 March 1933. Los Angeles, which suffered a devastating earthquake on March 11, was a big exception to the general shopping spree which overtook the country.

42. Whaley-Eaton Service, 3, 7 March 1933; *Detroit Free Press*, 8–10 March 1933; *St. Louis Post-Dispatch*, 7, 8 March 1933; *Rocky Mountain News*, 8 March 1933.

43. *Cincinnati Enquirer*, 24 February 1933; *Indianapolis News*, eve. ed., 4 March 1933; *Chicago Tribune*, 5 March 1933; *Detroit Free Press*, 7, 10 March 1933.

44. *Cincinnati Times-Star*, 6 March 1933; Coker to Byrnes, 13 March 1933, DRC box 24.

45. *Cincinnati Enquirer*, 28 February 1933; *St. Louis Post-Dispatch*, 8 March 1933; Lamont memo attached to Lamont to FDR, 27 February 1933, FDRP 70.

46. Moley, *New Deal*, 175–77; *New York Times*, 10 March 1933.

47. *New York Times*, 10 March 1933; *St. Louis Post-Dispatch*, 10 March 1933; Moley, *New Deal*, 175–77; handwritten notes of Wyatt, 9 March 1933, WW box 61. WW box 61 also contains a draft of the Emergency Banking Bill much edited by Glass, the summary of the bill with handwritten annotations, as well as final copies of H.R. 1491 and S1, the Emergency Banking Act. Events described in Wyatt's 1933 notes and in his 1966 letter to Moley vary slightly. I did not find Wyatt's letters to Moley among Wyatt's papers at the University of Virginia.

48. *New York Times*, 10 March 1933; Rosenman, *Pub-*

lic Papers and Addresses, 2: 54–6; Eugene Meyer to FDR, 9 March 1933, EM box 40.

49. Telegram from First National Bank of Denver, 8, 9 March 1933; telegram from FNB Denver to W. Woodin, 10 March 1933, FNBD box 5; memo [of FNB Denver Pres. Evans], 10 March 1933, FNBD box 21; *Indianapolis News*, 9 March 1933; *New York Times*, 9, 10 March 1933; *St. Louis Post-Dispatch*, 9, 10 March 1933; *Rocky Mountain News*, 9, 10, 11 March 1933; *Orange Daily News*, 9, 10 March 1933; *Denver Post*, eve. ed., 10 March 1933; *Santa Ana Register*, 10 March 1933; *Richmond Times-Dispatch*, 10 March 1933; *Cincinnati Times-Star*, 10, 11 March 1933; *San Francisco Chronicle*, 10, 11 March 1933; *Philadelphia Inquirer*, 11 March 1933; *Louisville Courier-Journal*, 11 March 1933; *Chicago Tribune*, 12 March 1933; James, *Chicago Banks*, 2:1076.

50. Exec Order of Gov. of Colo, Ed C. Johnson, 9 March 1933; memo of conversation between "HK" [Harry Kountze] and Irwin Wright, chief bank examiner [in K.C.], 8:15 am, 10 March 1933; memo of First National Bank of Denver, 10 March 1933, FNBD box 21; *Indianapolis News*, 9 March 1933; *Chicago Tribune*, 9 March 1933; *Philadelphia Inquirer*, 10 March 1933; *New York Times*, 9 March 1933; *San Francisco Chronicle*, 10 March 1933.

51. *Orange Daily News*, 9, 10 March 1933; *Denver Post*, eve. ed., 10 March 1933; *New York Times*, 10 March 1933; Smith and Beasley, *Carter Glass*, 345; Johnson, *Diary Letters*, 5: 12 March 1933, 3.

52. *Indianapolis News*, 8–10 March 1933; *Chicago Tribune*, 9 March 1933; *New York Times*, 9 March 1933; *St. Louis Post-Dispatch*, 9, 10 March 1933; *Santa Ana Register*, 10 March 1933; telegram from J.H. Frost, Frost National Bank, San Antonio, to Meyer, 10 March 1933, EM box 77.

53. *St. Louis Post-Dispatch*, 10 March 1933; *Indianapolis News*, 11 March 1933; *Chicago Tribune*, 12 March 1933; George Seay to Coker, 20 March 1933, DRC box 13.

54. Wyatt to Ballantine, 1 August 1944, WW box 61; Norris, *Episodes*, 225, 232–33; handwritten notes of W. Wyatt, March 9 1933; Arthur Ballantine, draft, "The Ghost and the Banks," WW box 61. Woodin resigned as secretary of the Treasury on 5 July 1933 due to ill health; see Woodin to FDR, 5 July 1933, FDRP.

55. *Indianapolis News*, 10 March 1933; *St. Louis Post-Dispatch*, 11 March 1933; *Chicago Tribune*, 11, 12 March 1933; telegram from First National Bank Denver to Secy W. Woodin, 10 March 1933, FNBD box 5; Gov. Ritchie to FDR, 9 March 1933, with resolution of Md. Senate, FDRO 229; telegram Gov. Lehman to Meyer, 9 March 1933, EM box 77. Box 77 contains many such telegrams from banks to Meyer.

56. *Detroit Free Press*, 10, 11, 13, 15 March 1933.

57. WW box 61 contains a complete list of all banks licensed to reopen on March 13, and those banks not licensed. *St. Louis Post-Dispatch*, 13 March 1933; *Chicago Tribune*, 14 March 1933; *Los Angeles Times*, 15 March 1933; James, *Chicago Banks*, 2:1086–87; telegram Roy Roberts, *Kansas City Star*, to Steve Early, 13 March 1933, FDRO 230; *Commercial and Financial Chronicle* (18 March 1933), 1829.

58. *Detroit Free Press*, 15 March 1933; *New York Times*, 15 March 1933; *Los Angeles Times*, 15 March 1933.

59. *Kokomo Tribune*, 15, 16 March 1933; *Commercial and Financial Chronicle* (18 March 1933), 1829–32; Norris, *Episodes*, 216, 234–35.

60. Telegram A.P. Giannini to Jesse Jones, 14 March 1933; Giannini to M.H. McIntyre, secy to FDR, 15

March 1933, FDRO 230; *Los Angeles Times*, 15, 16 March 1933; *New York Times*, 16 March 1933; *Annual Report of the Comptroller of the Currency* (1933), 2–3, 90; *Annual Report of the Federal Reserve Board* (1933), 22; Norris, *Episodes*, 216. The amount of money frozen in unlicensed banks at the end of the third week of March has never been determined. In 1935 Walter Wyatt stated that 4,194 banks, holding $3.98 billion in deposits, remained unlicensed as of April 12. Between March 17 and April 12, 327 banks holding $383 million in deposits were allowed to reopen. See "Banking Suspensions, 1892–1935," 56, 61, WW box 62. For other estimates see *Annual Report of the Federal Reserve Board* (1933), 223; *Federal Reserve Bulletin* (October 1933), 594–5; Kennedy, *Banking Crisis*, 201; Nadler and Bogen, *Banking Crisis*, 177; C.D. Bremer, *American Bank Failures* (New York: Columbia University Press, 1935), 12, 40–1.

61. *New York Times*, 16 March 1933; State of Washington, *Annual Report of the Supervisor of Banking* (1933), 3, 6; *Annual Report of the State Banking Department of South Carolina* (1934) [covers 1 October 1932 to 30 June 1934] 3, 10; *Annual Report of the Comptroller of the Currency* (1933), 109; Belser, "Banking," 13, 53–4, 59, 64; *Commercial and Financial Chronicle* (4 February 1933), 769; (18 March 1933), 1831–2.

Chapter Ten

1. *The Coming of the New Deal*, the second volume of Arthur Schlesinger, Jr.'s, *The Age of Roosevelt*, remains the best and most comprehensive history of Roosevelt's first two years in office. On the importance of initiating a "new policy regime," see Peter Temin and Barrie Wigmore, "The End of One Big Deflation, 1933," *Explorations in Economic History* 27, no. 4 (October 1990): 483–502.

2. Moley, *New Deal*, 196; Schlesinger, *Age of Roosevelt*, 2:13. Amos Kiewe, *FDR's First Fireside Chat: Public Confidence and the Banking Crisis* (College Station: Texas A&M Press, 2007) embodies the received wisdom about FDR's chat and its importance in history. Reliance on the "chat," as the bromide that fixed all extends to economists, see for example Sangkyun Park, "Bank Failure Contagion in Historical Perspective," *Research Paper of the Federal Reserve Bank of New York*, no. 9103 (February 1991): 16–8.

3. Rosenman, *Public Papers and Addresses*, 2:61–5.

4. *Los Angeles Times*, 3 March 1933; *New York Times*, 4 March 1933; *Chicago Tribune*, 5 March 1933; "Phillips Gives Views on Ending Business Slump," *Butler* (Pennsylvania) *Eagle*, 4 March 1933; telegram First National Bank of Prestonburg, KY, to Fred Vinson, 7 March 1933; telegram W.F. Steele, Pres. Security Bank and Trust and J.N. Kehoe, Pres., Bank of Maryville, KY, to Vinson, 8 March 1933, FMV box 22; telegram Nieschlag and Co., Wall St., to Glass, 27 February 1933; telegram, R.E. Fort, Nashville, to Glass, 2 March 1933, CG box 271; P. du Pont to T.W. Phillips, 8 March 1933; P. du Pont to S.D. Townsend, Atlantic City, 13 March 1933, PSP box 1173. The Bank of America had taken $64.9 million in loans from the RFC from February to July 1932 and repaid all but about $7 million (*Commercial and Financial Chronicle* [4 February 1933], 764); yet, in 1933 was evidently in poor enough condition that Treasury did not want to license it to reopen on 13 March; see Johnson, *Diary Letters*, 5:14 March 1933.

5. *Indianapolis News*, 11 March 1933; *Louisville Courier-Journal*, 11 March 1933; Federal Reserve press

release, 28 March 1933, DRC box 14. Banks also reduced loans by $539 million in February.

6. *Annual Report of the Comptroller of the Currency* (1930), 74; (1931), 76; (1932), 68; (1933), 79. Losses in loans and bonds are for national banks only, see chapter 4, n.4. The *Annual Report of the Federal Deposit Insurance Corporation* (1934), 212, reports that 6 percent of assets held by insured non-member banks were worthless in June 1934.

7. *Detroit Free Press*, 14, 15 March 1933; *Los Angeles Times*, 16 March 1933; *Louisville Courier-Journal*, 15 March 1933; *Commercial and Financial Chronicle* (18 March 1933), 1755; (25 March 1933), 2003–07.

8. *Rocky Mountain News*, 3 March 1933 (FDR won 55 percent of the vote in Colorado); *Los Angeles Times*, 3, 4 March 1933; *Des Moines Register*, 4, 5 March 1933; *Richmond Times-Dispatch*, 5 March 1933; *Detroit Free Press*, 7 March 1933; *Philadelphia Inquirer*, 9 March 1933.

9. Check clearings were so low in some districts ($1 million in Dallas, $9 million in both San Francisco and Philadelphia) that the system was obviously not fully functioning. In other districts (Cleveland, Chicago, and New York) banks cleared checks as usual. See *Commercial and Financial Chronicle* (11 March 1933), 1692.

10. Spurgeon Bell to Sen. Bulkley, 28 February 1933, cc to FDR, FDRO 230; *Kokomo Tribune*, 28 February 1933.

11. Telegram, First National Bank of Herington, KS, to Glass, 4 March 1933, CG box 271; Rand to Tugwell, 14 March 1933, RGT box 22; J. David Stern to FDR, 22 March 1933, FDRO 230; *Steel* quoted in *Chicago Tribune*, 6 March 1933; statement of Henry Harriman before N.I.R.A. Hearings before the Committee on Ways and Means, House of Representatives, 20 May 1933. Stern's devotion to FDR is discussed in Jones and Angly, *Fifty Billion Dollars*, 231.

12. C.F. Marshall, Marshall & Co., Cotton for the Rubber Industry, Akron, to D. Coker, 22 March 1933, DRC box 13; press release of Federal Reserve Board, 28 March 1933, DRC box 14; Fine, *Frank Murphy*, 376; *St. Louis Post-Dispatch*, 7 March 1933; *Indianapolis News*, 8 March 1933; *Chicago Tribune*, 9 March 1933; *Los Angeles Times*, 10, 11, 16 March 1933; *Philadelphia Inquirer*, 9 March 1933; *Commercial and Financial Chronicle* (25 March 1933), 1962; Federal Reserve Bank of Atlanta, *Monthly Review* (31 March 1933), 1; Federal Reserve Bank of Cleveland, *Monthly Business Review* (1 April 1933), 1–5; Federal Reserve Bank of Chicago, *Business Conditions* (31 March 1933), 4–5.

13. Telegram Federal Reserve Bank of Boston to Federal Reserve Board, 8 March 1933, N.A. Record Group 82, #470, box 2158; Federal Reserve Bank of Boston, *Monthly Review* (1 May 1933), 1; Federal Reserve Bank of Cleveland, *Monthly Business Review* (1 April 1933), 1, 3–4; see also Federal Reserve Bank of Atlanta, *Monthly Review* (31 March 1933), 1–2; Federal Reserve Bank of Chicago, *Business Conditions* (31 March 1933), 1; Federal Reserve Bank of Kansas City, *Monthly Review* (1 April 1933), 1; *St. Louis Post-Dispatch*, 10 March 1933; "Business Conditions" in *Annual Report of the Federal Reserve Board* (1933), 240–51, shows March 1933 as the nadir for employment and payrolls for most industries and for wholesale prices. It competes with summer 1932 for the low point for most indices of production. As noted, the *Federal Reserve Bulletin* never reported bank debits for March 1933, yet, oddly, neither February nor April 1933 are the lowest reported months for bank debits in the U.S. That distinction was held by November 1932, when debits nationwide fell to $22.53 billion (vs. $24.13 billion in February 1933).

14. H.W. Prentis, Armstrong Cork Co., Lancaster, PA, to J.H. Rand, July 18, 1933; James H. McGill, McGill Manufacturing Co., Valparaiso, IN, to J.H. Rand, 20 July 1933; R.A. Hayward, Kalamazoo Vegetable Parchment Co., to J.H. Rand, 20 July 1933; W.J. Coad, Omaha Flour Mills Co., NE, to J.H. Rand, 20 July 1933; N.H. Gellert, Natl Public Utilities Corp., Phil. to J.H. Rand, 21 July 1933; Rep. Sam Pettengill to J.H. Rand, 21 July 1933, EAR box 39.

15. Charles Haas, Farmers' and Wabash Natl Bank, IN, to J.H. Rand, 19 July 1933; George Graf, Pres. Chamber of Comm., Williamsport, PA, to Harold Beach, 11 August 1933; Harold Brown, V.P. Lycoming Trust Co., Williamsport, PA, to Harold Beach, Williamsport, 14 August 1933, EAR box 39; *Federal Reserve Bulletin* (December 1937), 1208; Cyril B. Upham and Edwin Lamke, *Closed and Distressed Banks: A Study in Public Administration* (Washington, DC: Brookings Institution, 1934), 166–72. As noted in the previous chapter, a good deal of confusion remains about how much money was available or frozen because of the holiday. The amount frozen on 15 March 1933 will never be known, but even how much was available and frozen as of April 12 remains confusing. See *Annual Report of the Federal Reserve Board* (1933), 23; Upham and Lamke, *Closed*, Appendix C; "Banking Suspensions, 1892–1935," 1, 56–61, WW box 62.

16. *Indianapolis News*, 6, 10 March 1933; *St. Louis Post-Dispatch*, 8, 11 March 1933; *New York Times*, 10 March 1933; *Philadelphia Inquirer*, 10, 12 March 1933; telegram Essex Co., N.J., Bar Assn. to FDR, 7 March 1933; telegram, Hour of Pleasure Federated Colored Club of Sioux City, IA, to FDR, 14 March 1933; telegram A.P. Giannini to Jesse Jones, 14 March 1933, FDRO 230; Traylor to FDR, 20 March 1933, FDRP 220; James P. Warburg, *The Money Muddle* (New York: Alfred Knopf, 1934), 90–93. I have found no historian or economist who has characterized the bank holiday as a failure. Peter Temin wrote, "The bank holiday was a failure of economic policy," but does not elaborate on the statement, in "The Great Depression," *National Bureau of Economic Research Working Paper*, no. 62, (1994), 24.

17. *Detroit Free Press*, 4, 6, 11 March 1933; *St. Louis Post-Dispatch*, 7 March 1933; *New York Times*, 10 March 1933; Rosenman, *Public Papers and Addresses*, 2:32–33; Byrnes, *Lifetime*, 215; Tompkins, *Vandenberg*, 85.

18. Jones and Angly, *Fifty Billion Dollars*, 25; memo attached to Lamont to FDR, 27 February 1933, FDRP 70. The impact of the RFC stock purchasing program is discussed in the Epilogue.

19. Patrick, *Reform*, 145–46.

20. FDR to Col. House, 5 April 1933, cited in Burns, *American Banking*, 77–8; Secy. of Commerce D. Roper to J.H. Rand, 20 March 1933; Melvin Traylor, First Nat'l Bank of Chicago, to E.A. Rumely, 20 March 1933; Rumely to Vanderlip, 22 March 1933, EAR box 39; T. Lamont to FDR, 19 April 1933, FDRP 143; Memo by Berle, 24 April 1933, AAB box 15; telegram Irving Fisher to Glass, 24 April 1933, CG box 298; "Tenth Press Conference, April 7, 1933," "Thirteenth Press Conference," "Executive Order No. 6111, April 20, 1933," Rosenman, *Public Papers and Addresses*, 2:119–21, 137–41, 141–43; Moley, *New Deal*, 252; Wicker, "Monetary Experiment," 874.

21. *Annual Report of the Federal Reserve Board* (1933), 12, 29; Benjamin Anderson, "The gold standard and the administration's general economic programme," *Chase Economic Bulletin* (May 1933); Wicker, "Monetary Experiment," 864–79; Chernow, *House of Morgan*, 357–58; *Historical Statistics*, 540, 546.

22. CG box 298 contains about 200 telegrams congratulating Sen. Glass for his orthodoxy. Some praise him simply for sticking to his word when he campaigned for sound money in 1932.

23. *Chicago Tribune*, 5 March 1933; *St. Louis Post-Dispatch*, 8 March 1933; *Detroit Free Press*, 9 March 1933; *Indianapolis News*, 6, 7, 8, 9 March 1933; *Des Moines Register*, 8 March 1933; *Rocky Mountain News*, 8, 9 March 1933; *Philadelphia Inquirer*, 9 March 1933; press release of Fed. Res. Board, 28 March 1933, DRC box 14; Federal Reserve Bank of Chicago, *Business Conditions* (31 March 1933), 3, notes that prices for lamb and sheep remained low. One hundred pounds of beef on average cost $6.40 wholesale in February 1932 and still only $5.35 in March 1933. But it had rebounded from $4.85 in February 1933. In March 1933 U.S. meat exports faced severe restrictions in Britain and Germany that had not existed a year before, which would have depressed prices on U.S. markets. E. Goldenweiser was among those skeptical about any connection between prices and the cost of gold; see memo from Goldenweiser to Meyer, 13 April 1933, RM box 107; as was Edmond E. Lincoln, see telegram to Sen. Glass, 24 April 1933, CG box 298.

24. Circular from S.T. Hubbard, Jr., commodity broker, New York, n.d. [Mar, 1933], DRC box 14; Federal Reserve Bank of New York, *Monthly Review of Credit and Business Conditions* (1 May 1933), 39; *Louisville Courier-Journal*, 7 March 1933; *Philadelphia Inquirer*, 10 March 1933; *Richmond Times-Dispatch*, 9 March 1933; *Commercial and Financial Chronicle* (18 March 1933), 1756.

25. *Banking and Monetary Statistics*, 481; Federal Reserve Bank of New York, *Monthly Review of Credit and Business Conditions* (1 April 1933), 28–9; (1 May 1933), 36; *Commercial and Financial Chronicle* (18 March 1933), 1756; Wigmore, *Crash*, 456.

26. *U.S. Statistical Abstract* (1934), 762; (1940), 418; *Annual Report of the Federal Reserve Board* (1933), 241–42, 245–49, 252–53; Temin and Wigmore, "Big Deflation," 495–99. Peter Temin argues that Roosevelt's "reflationary" program was the most important policy measure to propel the United States out of the Depression; see *Lessons from the Great Depression* (Cambridge, MA: MIT Press, 1989), 96–100. Temin also argues that the only way to stop the deflation was through devaluation by abandoning the gold standard; see "Transmission of the Great Depression," *Journal of Economic Perspectives.* 7, no. 2 (1993): 91–2. Ben Bernanke and Harold James also argue for the importance for recovery of leaving the gold standard in "The Gold Standard, Deflation, and Financial Crisis in the Great Depression: An International Comparison," in Bernanke, *Essays on the Great Depression* (Princeton: Princeton University Press, 2000).

27. Memo by "E.E.L." [Lincoln], "Some A,B,C's of Monetary Inflation," 25 April 1933, PSP box 1281; Benjamin Anderson, "The gold standard and the administration's general economic programme," *Chase Economic Bulletin* (May 1933), 8; Special Economic Research Section of U.S. Steel, "An Analysis of the Business Recession of 1937–1938" (n.d.), ES box 67.

28. Louis Ludlow, "New Leadership Tonic to Nation," *Indianapolis Star*, 26 March 1933, is typical fare of the era; Serrell to P.S. du Pont, 23 March 1933, PSP box 1173; press release of Federal Reserve Board, 28 March 1933, DRC box 14.

29. Pipkin to Liggon, 20 March 1933; D.H. Williams to Coker, 21 March 1933; memorandum: Emergency Agricultural Adjustment Act, J.W. Garrow, Chairman of Economics Committee of American Cotton Shippers Assoc., 20 Mar 1933, DRC box 13; "'The New Deal' and Its Economic Implications," Munds, Winslow, & Potter, NY, 14 April 1933, DRC box 14; Moley to Tugwell, 5 April 1965; Tugwell to Moley, 15 April 1965, RGT box 15; Schlesinger, *Age of Roosevelt*, 2:40–44; Broadus Mitchell, *Depression Decade: From New Era through New Deal, 1929–1941* (New York: Rinehart, 1947), 179–80, 189–91.

30. See Schlesinger, *Age of Roosevelt*, 2:1–353.

31. Synopsis of the Glass Banking Bill, S 1631, 11 May 1933, CG box 275/276; Thomas Lamont to Steve Howe, 27 March 1933, FDRP 70; Charles H. Sabin, Chairman of Guaranty Trust Co. of New York to Sen. Robert Wagner, New York, 25 May 1932; Charles S. McCain, Chairman Chase National Bank, and William C. Potter, Pres. of Guaranty Trust Co. of New York to Sen. Glass, 29 April 1932, PSP box 1281; Patrick, *Reform*, 169, 177.

32. Burns, *New Deal Reforms*, 181; Patrick, *Reform*, 171–72.

33. *ABAJ* (April 1933): 23–5; Patrick, *Reform*, 173–74; Tompkins, *Vandenberg*, 83–93; Burns, *New Deal Reforms*, 128. For an intelligent discussion of the Glass-Steagall Act of 1933, see Burns, passim. The bill is reprinted in Herman E. Krooss and Paul A. Samuelson, *Documentary History of Banking and Currency in the United States*, vol. 4 (New York: Chelsea House, 1969), 2725–69.

34. Burns, *New Deal Reforms*, 80–1; Jones and Angly, *Fifty Billion Dollars*, 45–6; Patrick, *Reform*, 173–75; Tompkins, *Vandenberg*, 83–93; Rosenman, *Public Papers and Addresses*, 2:37–38; Harold L. Ickes, *Secret Diary of Harold L. Ickes*, vol. 1 (New York: Simon and Schuster, 1953), 41.

35. "Banking Week," Bureau of National Affairs, 11 November 1932, AAB box 16; *Commercial and Financial Chronicle* (11 March 1933), 1603; Joseph Wayne announced Phil NB would not divorce itself from Philadelphia National Co., its securities affiliate. *Philadelphia Inquirer*, 10 March 1933; Burns, *New Deal Reforms*, 84–5.

36. *Commercial and Financial Chronicle* (28 October 1933), 3073; *Historical Statistics*, 658. Corporate bonds were somewhat more active: $620 million in 1932.

37. *Detroit Free Press*, 10 March 1933; *New York American*, 10 March 1933; memo by Thomas Lamont, 11 March 1933, TWL box 80; Roper to FDR, 28 March 1933, FDRO 230; Chernow, *House of Morgan*, 374–91.

38. White, "Before the Glass-Steagall Act," 40–52. George J. Bentson, *The Separation of Commercial and Investment Banking: The Glass-Steagall Act Revisited and Reconsidered* (New York: Oxford University Press, 1990), passim, dwells at length upon the thin or irrelevant evidence of danger posed to the banking system by securities-dealing affiliates.

39. United States Senate, *Hearings before the Committee on Banking and Currency* (73rd Cong. May 23–25, 1933) *on Stock Exchange Practices* 1: 3–98; Patrick, *Reform*, 170.

40. *SEP* (1): 29–33; *New York Times*, 22 February, 28 May 1933; *Corvallis Gazette-Times*, 1 June 1933; Chernow, *House of Morgan*, 359–69. CG box 295 contains about 300 letters condemning Glass's defense of Morgan, many in very hateful terms; CG box 258 contains about 500 more. Jouett Shouse, 27 May 1933, sent one of the approximately 400 letters of praise in CG box 273.

41. "What New Practical Measures for Increasing Good Will Toward Banks?" *ABAJ* (April 1933): 72; *St. Louis Post-Dispatch*, 4 March 1933; *Louisville Courier-Journal*, 9 March 1933; *Detroit Free Press*, 15 March 1933; Pecora, *Wall Street*, 152–61.

42. *New York Times*, 23 June, 28 October, 1 November 1933; *Commercial and Financial Chronicle* (4 November 1933), 3231–35; Chernow, *House of Morgan*, 421–29.

43. Rep. John Dingell (MI) to J. O'Connor, 22 May 1933, JJO box 14; mss. "Who Killed Cock Robin?" [defense of Couzens] n.d.; "transcript" [of Keidan hearings] n.d., JC box 140; Barnard, *Independent Man*, 275–90.

44. Testimony of Guardian Group Vice President Bert K. Patterson, formerly federal bank examiner (1918 to 1924) and chief examiner of the Federal Reserve Bank in Minneapolis (1924 to 1929), *SEP* (9): 4488–95; memo "Detroit Banking Situation," John S. Pratt, DOJ, to Asst. Atty. Genl. Keenan, 22 March 1934, JC box 141, which asserts that few prosecutable offenses had occurred, and many of the censured practices were legal. Even Ferdinand Pecora, no friend of banks and bankers, found that the practice of banks loaning money against their own holding-company stock as collateral was legal, but somehow shady. See Pecora, *Wall Street*, 245.

45. Memo "Detroit Banking Situation," John S. Pratt, DOJ, to Asst. Atty Genl Keenan, 22 March 1934, JC box 141, outlines Wilkin's feud with Couzens. Lacey, *Ford*, 330–32. See Wilkin's fatal testimony: *SEP* (10): 5008–12. Wilkin told the Pecora Committee that in 1931, when he was president of a Guardian bank in Flint, he had been assured on the phone that $600,000 had been wired from a Detroit bank to his bank on December 31 to improve its balance sheet for the year-end report to the comptroller of the currency. That Guardian banks shuffled money around for a few days twice a year for the purpose of enhancing balance statements infuriated Judge Pecora and several senators on the Banking Committee, but it was a legal and common practice within the industry. Pecora's grilling of bank president Robert Lord about the practice filled nearly 200 pages before Lord finally admitted it was probably not a good practice, see *SEP* (9):4220–4400;

46. Barnard, *Independent Man*, 314.

47. Report of Ways and Means Comm. on proposed bill, National Industrial Recovery Bill, 23 May 1933; HR 5755 N.I.R.A., 23 May 1933, JJO box 15; I. du Pont to Sen. Townsend, 24 May 1933, S 1712, N.I.R.A., 23 May 1933, IP box 103; Mark Reed to Robert LeRoux, Wash., D.C., 22 June 1933, MER box 5; NRA press release #10, 23 June 1933, #20, 28 June 1933 [on wages and employment], ES box 25; Speech by Pres. Kobak of Advertising Fed. of America, June 26, 1933, Grand Rapids, Speeches and Writings, WLW box 2; "Black Bill" file in JJO box 13; *Chicago Tribune*, 16, 19 July 1933; T.M. Merchant, Pres., Victor Monaghan Co., Greenville, SC, to David Coker, 4, 6 September 1933; B.W. Montgomery, Treas. Pacolet Manufacturing Co., Pacolet, SC, to David Coker, 12 September 1933, DRC box 14; P.S. du Pont to Joseph Lieb, South Bend, IN, 7 September 1933, PSP box 1281; telegram St. Louis Cham. of Commerce to FDR, 12 September 1933, ES box 29; *St. Louis Post-Dispatch*, 15 October 1933; Commerce Department, *U.S. Statistical Abstract* (1932), 359; (1940), 418; *Annual Report of the Federal Reserve Board* (1933), 249.

Epilogue

1. *Annual Report of the Federal Reserve Board* (1933), 223; Bremer, *Bank Failures*, 40.

2. Upham and Lamke, *Closed*, 53–6.

3. Federal Deposit Insurance Corporation, *FDIC: Historical Statistics on Banking, 1934–1992, A Statistical History of the United States Banking Industry* (Washington, DC: FDIC, 1993), 564–67.

4. *FDIC*, 570–75, 578.

5. *FDIC*, 566–67; Upham and Lamke, *Closed*, 56–8.

6. *Annual Report of the Comptroller of the Currency* (1933), 87; *Annual Report of the Federal Reserve Board* (1933), 163, 166; *Banking and Monetary Statistics*, 17, 35.

7. *Banking and Monetary Statistics*, 34–5; Federal Reserve Bank of New York, *Monthly Review of Credit and Business Conditions* (1 April 1933), 26.

8. Walter Wyatt to Arthur Ballentine, 1 August 1944, WW box 61; Wigmore, *Crash*, 451; *ISCNB* (1933), 50–1, 61; *SEP* (10): 4217; *Annual Report of the Federal Reserve Board* (1932), 300; *Commercial and Financial Chronicle* (22 April 1933), 2734–35; (23 December 1933), 4474; Cooper, *Union Trust Company*, 131. For a general discussion of the RFC and the restructuring of banks during the New Deal, see James Stuart Olson, *Saving Capitalism: The Reconstruction Finance Corporation and the New Deal, 1933–1940*.

9. Wigmore, *Crash*, 468–70; Jones and Angly, *Fifty Billion Dollars*, 35–7; Olson, *Saving Capitalism*, 80–2.

10. *Annual Report of the Comptroller of the Currency* (1933), 663; Upham and Lamke, *Closed*, 24, 47; James F.T. O'Connor, *The Banking Crisis and Recovery Under the Roosevelt Administration* (Chicago: Callaghan, 1938), 59; Jones and Angly, *Fifty Billion Dollars*, 55.

11. Oral History of Charles Baer (Colorado Historical Society), 16–17; Olson, *Saving Capitalism*, 72–6.

12. *Banking and Monetary Statistics*, 18; C.J. Huddleston to Couzens, 2 December 1933, JC box 144.

13. Jones and Angly, *Fifty Billion Dollars*, 68–69; *ISCNB* (1933), 61; memo from Donaldson Brown, Chairman of GM Finance Comm., re: Detroit banking situation, 27 March 1933, ES box 1.

14. *Banking and Monetary Statistics*, 18, 464–7.

15. *Annual Report of the Comptroller of the Currency* (1938), 98, 113; (1940), 152; (1941), 153; *Banking and Monetary Statistics*, 21.

16. Federal Deposit Insurance Corporation, *Annual Report of the Federal Deposit Insurance Corporation* (1934) (Washington, DC: FDIC, 1935), 43–45, 212; Treasury Dept. chart "Active National Banks, Net Addition to Profits, 1912–1935," JC box 141.

17. Losses for all banks are extrapolated from losses to national banks. The comptroller of the currency reported losses for national banks but not for state banks. No agency has gathered figures for state banks; *Banking and Monetary Statistics* reports the total amounts of loans and bonds held by national and state banks. It is probably safe to assume that bonds held by state banks defaulted at about the same rate as those held by national banks, so I have estimated the total of defaulted state-held bonds simply by multiplying the default rate for national banks (0.89 percent in 1930 and so on) by the percent of total bonds held by state banks. Default rates for loans were probably higher for state banks than for national banks, but not knowing how much higher, I have estimated state-bank losses by using the same rate as for national banks, producing a conservative estimate of total losses.

18. *Banking and Monetary Statistics*, 470–71.

19. Commission for Study of the Banking Structure, "Banking Developments in New York State, 1923–1934," (New York State Bankers Assn., 1935) 71, AP box 1; *Banking and Monetary Statistics*, 19.

20. *Banking and Monetary Statistics*, 376–77, 387; C.J. Huddleston to Sen. Couzens, 2 December 1933, JC box 144.

21. George Richard Slade, *Banking in the Great Northern Territory* (Afton, MN: Afton Historical Society, 2005), 1; James, *Metropolitan Life*, 275, 281, 285–93.

Conclusion

1. Memo from E. Goldenweiser to Eugene Meyer, 13 April 1933, RM box 106; "notes" [about collapse of credit in 1931] by Goldenweiser, n.d.; Advisory Council Meeting on May 18" [*sic*] May 15, 1931, EAG box 1; Richardson, "Quarterly Data," 47–8.

2. *Banking and Monetary Statistics*, 18, 74, 76–7; Bernanke, "Nonmonetary," 266.

3. Goldenweiser, "Notes on trip to New York, March 12–13," 16 March 1931, EAG box 1; James L. Butkiewicz, "The Impact of Lender of Last Resort during the Great Depression: The Case of the Reconstruction Finance Corporation," *Explorations in Economic History* 32, no. 3 (1995): 202–204, concludes that falling farm prices was the strongest predictor of bank failures.

4. During the debate on the Emergency Banking Act, Glass said, "I am coming to have less and less respect for a gold reserve, which can not be used when it is needed to relieve the country.... I have been urging [the Federal Reserve Board] for six months to make the suspension and they did it just three or four days ago." *New York Times*, 10 March 1933.

5. "Notes on conversation August 1, 1944 with Goldenweiser re bank holiday," WW box 61. This is not the place to discuss changes in the Federal Reserve that occurred after the spring of 1933. For that readers should consult Allan Meltzer, *A History of the Federal Reserve*, vol. 1, *1913–1951*.

6. *Commercial and Financial Chronicle* (11 June 1932), 4270; *Annual Report of the Federal Reserve Board* (1932), 161, 163; *Banking and Monetary Statistics*, 17, 348–50. Excess bank reserves held by the Fed grew from $1.5 billion in late 1929 to $12.4 billion in December 1941.

7. Rosenman, *Public Papers and Addresses*, 2:111–16. The Gold Contract Act of 1933 voided clauses in bonds that promised to pay in gold if demanded by the bond holder; the 1934 Devaluation Act established the value of the dollar at a lower amount of gold and laid out a process for acquiring and selling gold. Both of these acts were intended to clear up grey areas in the law left by previous acts. Eichengreen, *Golden Fetters*, 21, states, "The advantage ... [of going off the gold standard] was that it freed up monetary and fiscal policies. No longer was it necessary to restrict domestic credit to defend convertibility."

8. Friedman and Schwartz. *Monetary History*; Peter Temin, *Did Monetary Forces Cause the Great Depression?* (New York: W.W. Norton, 1976), *Lessons from the Great Depression* (Cambridge, MA: MIT Press, 1989), and "The Great Depression," *National Bureau of Economic Research Working Paper*, no. 62 (1994). "Simple arithmetic" proved my weak point when I wrote the original version of this work, *Drifting Toward Mayhem* (2009). A simple miscalculation of the amout of currency that fled U.S. banks in late 1930 caused me to reject the Friedman-Schwartz thesis as applied to 1930. I got the figure right for 1931, however, where I judged their thesis highly applicable. This time I got the number right for both years, causing me to reverse my conclusions about the applicability of the Freidman-Schwartz thesis to the first four years of the Depression.

Bibliography

Manuscript Sources

Baer, Charles. Oral History. Colorado Historical Society.

Ballantine, Arthur A., Jr. Oral History. Colorado Historical Society.

Barkley, Alben W. Papers. Special Collections Library. University of Kentucky.

Berle, Adolf A. Papers. Franklin Delano Roosevelt Presidential Library.

Buchanan, James P. Papers. Center for American History. University of Texas, Austin.

Byrd, Harry F., Sr. Papers. Special Collections Library. University of Virginia.

Byrnes, James F. Papers. Special Collections. Clemson University Libraries. Clemson University.

Cannon, Frank J. Papers. Colorado Historical Society.

Coker, David R. Papers. South Caroliniana Library. University of South Carolina.

Couzens, James. Papers. Manuscripts Division. Library of Congress.

Dawes, Charles G. Papers. Special Collections Library. Northwestern University.

du Pont, Irénée. Papers. Hagley Museum and Library. Wilmington, Delaware.

du Pont, Pierre S. Papers. Hagley Museum and Library. Wilmington, Delaware.

Federal Reserve Papers (Record Group 82). National Archives, College Park.

First National Bank of Denver Papers. Colorado Historical Society.

Glass, Carter. Papers. Special Collections Library. University of Virginia.

Goldenweiser, Emanuel A. Papers. Manuscripts Division. Library of Congress.

Hamlin, Charles. Papers. Manuscripts Division. Library of Congress.

Lamont, Thomas W. Papers. Baker Library Historical Collections. Harvard Business School.

Ludlow, Louis. Papers. Lilly Library. Indiana University.

Meyer, Eugene. Papers. Manuscripts Division. Library of Congress.

Mills, Ogden. Papers. Manuscripts Division. Library of Congress.

Moley, Raymond. Papers. Hoover Institution Archives. Stanford University.

Morganthau, Henry, Jr. Papers. Franklin Delano Roosevelt Presidential Library.

Morton, Sterling. Papers. Chicago Historical Society.

O'Connor, John J. Papers. Lilly Library. Indiana University.

Pettibone, Holman D. Papers. Chicago Historical Society.

Philadelphia Clearing House Association. Papers. Historical Society of Pennsylvania.

Price, Andrew. Papers. Special Collections. Allen Library. University of Washington.

Raskob, John J. Papers. Hagley Museum and Library. Wilmington, Delaware.

Reed, Mark E. Papers. Special Collections. Allen Library. University of Washington.

Roosevelt, Franklin Delano. Papers. Franklin Delano Roosevelt Presidential Library.

Rumely, Edward A. Papers. Lilly Library. Indiana University.

Shouse, Jouett. Papers. Special Collections Library. University of Kentucky.

Stettinius, Edward, Jr. Papers. Special Collections Library. University of Virginia.

Stevens, James E. Papers. Chicago Historical Society.

Taussig, Charles W. Papers. Franklin Delano Roosevelt Presidential Library.

Tugwell, Rexford G. Papers. Franklin Delano Roosevelt Presidential Library.

Vinson, Frederick M. Papers. Special Collections Library. University of Kentucky.

Wells, Herman B Papers. Indiana University Archives.

Willkie, Wendell L. Papers. Lilly Library. Indiana University.

Woodson, Urey. Papers. Special Collections Library. University of Kentucky.

Wyatt, Walter. Papers. Special Collections Library. University of Virginia.

Newspapers and Periodicals

American Bank Association Journal (1929–1933)
Atlanta Constitution (1930, 1933)
Baltimore Evening Sun (1932)
Baltimore Sun (1933)
Bank and Quotation Record (1929–1933)
Boston Globe (1930–1933)
Cedar Rapids Gazette (1932–1933)
Chicago Defender (1932)
Chicago Evening American (1932)
Chicago Tribune (1920–1933)
Cincinnati Enquirer (1930, 1933)
Cincinnati Times-Star (1933)
Commercial and Financial Chronicle (1914–1933)
Denver Post (1930, 1933)
Des Moines Register (1933)
Detroit Free Press (1933)
Detroit News (1933)
Hoosier Banker (1930–1933)
Indianapolis News (1930, 1933)
Kalamazoo Gazette (1933)
Kokomo Tribune (1920–1933)
Los Angeles Times (1933)
Louisville Courier-Journal (1930, 1933)
New York Times (1930–1933)
Orange Daily News (1933)
Philadelphia Evening Bulletin (1930, 1933)
Philadelphia Inquirer (1930, 1933)
Richmond Times-Dispatch (1933)
Rocky Mountain News (1933)
St. Louis Post-Dispatch (1930–1933)
San Francisco Chronicle (1930, 1933)
Santa Ana Register (1933)
Washington Post (1933)

Government Documents and Reports

Auditor of Public Accounts. *Annual Report of Mutual Building and Loan Homestead Assns, State of Illinois.* 1931–1934.
_____. *Statement Showing Total Resources and Liabilities of Illinois State Banks at the Close of Business, Dec. 31.* 1929–1932.
Comptroller of the Currency. *Annual Report of the Comptroller of the Currency.* Washington, DC: GPO, 1919–1941.
_____. *Individual Statements of Conditions of National Banks at the Close of Business, December 31.* 1929–1934.
Federal Deposit Insurance Corporation. *Annual Report of the Federal Deposit Insurance Corporation* (1934). Washington, DC: FDIC, 1935.
_____. *Report of Operations.* Washington, DC: FDIC, 1934.
Federal Reserve Bank of Atlanta. *Monthly Review.* Atlanta: Federal Reserve Bank, monthly, 1930–1933.

Federal Reserve Bank of Boston. *Monthly Review.* Boston: Federal Reserve Bank, monthly, 1931–1933.
Federal Reserve Bank of Chicago. *Annual Report of the Federal Reserve Bank of Chicago.* Chicago: Federal Reserve Bank, 1932–1933.
_____. *Business Conditions.* Chicago: Federal Reserve Bank, monthly, 1930–1933.
Federal Reserve Bank of Cleveland. *Monthly Business Review.* Cleveland: Federal Reserve Bank, monthly, 1931–1933.
Federal Reserve Bank of Kansas City. *Monthly Review.* Kansas City: Federal Reserve Bank, monthly, 1933.
Federal Reserve Bank of Minneapolis. *Monthly Review of Agricultural and Business Conditions.* Minneapolis: Federal Reserve Bank, monthly, 1926–1933.
Federal Reserve Bank of New York. *Annual Report of the Federal Reserve Bank of New York.* New York: Federal Reserve Bank, 1931–1933.
_____. *Monthly Review of Credit and Business Conditions.* New York: Federal Reserve Bank, monthly, 1921–1933.
Federal Reserve Bank of Philadelphia. *Annual Report of the Federal Reserve Bank of Philadelphia.* Philadelphia: Federal Reserve Bank, 1933.
Federal Reserve Board. *Annual Report of the Federal Reserve Board.* Washington, DC: GPO, 1926–1933.
_____. *Federal Reserve Bulletin.* Washington, DC: GPO, monthly, 1930–1933.
Ministère des Affaires Etranges. *Documents Diplomatiques Français, 1932–1939, 1re Série (1932–1935).* Vol. 2, (15 novembre 1932–17 mars 1933). Paris: Imprimèrie Nationale, 1966.
State Bank Examiner of South Carolina. *Annual Report.* Columbia, 1928, 1930–1932.
State Banking Department of South Carolina. *Annual Report.* Columbia, 1932–1934.
State of Indiana Department of Banking. *Annual Report.* Indianapolis, 1921–1933.
State of Washington. *Annual Report of the Supervisor of Banking.* Olympia, 1924–1933.
Study Commission for Indiana Financial Institutions. *Report.* Indianapolis, 1932.
United States Department of Commerce, Bureau of the Census. *United States Census of Agriculture: 1935.* Vol. 3. Washington, DC: GPO.
United States Senate. *Hearings Before a Subcommittee of the Committee on Finance.* 71st Cong., Jan. 19–Feb. 25, 1931. *Operation of the National and Federal Reserve Banking System.*
_____. *Hearings Before the Committee on Banking and Currency.* 73rd Cong., May 23, 1933–January 1934. *On Stock Exchange Practices.*
_____. *Hearings Before the Committee on Finance.* 72nd Cong., Feb. 13–28, 1933. *Investigation of Economic Problems.*

Memoirs and Contemporary Works

Barkley, Alben W. *That Reminds Me.* Garden City, NY: Doubleday, 1954.

Byrnes, James F. *All in One Lifetime.* New York: Harper & Brothers, 1958.

Feis, Herbert. *1933: Characters in Crisis.* Boston: Little, Brown, 1966.

Hoover, Herbert. *The Memoirs of Herbert Hoover,* 3 vols. New York: Macmillan, 1951–52.

Ickes, Harold L. *Secret Diary of Harold L. Ickes.* 3 vols. New York: Simon & Schuster, 1953–54.

Johnson, Hiram. *The Diary Letters of Hiram Johnson.* Vol. 5, *1929–1933.* New York: Garland, 1983.

Jones, Jesse H., and Edward Angly. *Fifty Billion Dollars: My Thirteen Years with the RFC (1932–1945).* New York: Macmillan, 1951.

Joslin, Theodore G. *Hoover Off the Record.* New York: Doubleday, 1939.

Louchheim, Katie, ed. *The Making of the New Deal: The Insiders Speak.* Cambridge, MA: Harvard University Press, 1982.

Michelson, Charles. *The Ghost Talks.* New York: G.P. Putnam's Sons, 1944.

Moley, Raymond. *After Seven Years.* New York: Harper & Row, 1939.

_____. *The First New Deal.* New York: Harcourt, Brace & World, 1966.

Myers, William Starr, ed. *The State Papers and Other Public Writings of Herbert Hoover.* 2 vols. Garden City, NY: Doubleday, Doran, 1934.

_____, and Walter H. Newton. *The Hoover Administration: A Documented Narrative.* New York: Charles Scribner's Sons, 1936.

Nadler, Marcus, and Jules I. Bogen. *The Banking Crisis: The End of an Epoch.* New York: Dodd, Mead, 1933.

National Industrial Conference Board. *The Availability of Bank Credit.* New York, 1932.

_____. *The Banking Situation in the United States.* New York, 1932.

Norris, George W. *Ended Episodes.* Philadelphia: John Winston, 1937.

O'Connor, James F.T. *The Banking Crisis and Recovery under the Roosevelt Administration.* Chicago: Callaghan, 1938.

Pecora, Ferdinand. *Wall Street Under Oath: The Story of Our Modern Money Changers.* New York: Simon & Schuster, 1939.

Preston, Howard H. *Multiple Banking, with Special Reference to Conditions in the State of Washington.* Seattle: Washington Mutual Savings Bank, 1931.

Rosenman, Samuel, ed. *The Public Papers and Addresses of Franklin D. Roosevelt.* 5 vols. New York: Random House, 1938.

Sloan, Alfred P., Jr. *My Years with General Motors.* New York: Doubleday, 1990.

Stuart, William H. *The Twenty Incredible Years.* Chicago: M.A. Donohue, 1935.

Sullivan, Lawrence. *Prelude to Panic: The Story of the Bank Holiday.* Washington, DC: Statesman Press, 1936.

Tucker, Ray and Frederick R. Barkley. *The Sons of the Wild Jackass.* Reprint. Seattle: Washington University Press, 1970.

Tugwell, Rexford G. *The Brains Trust.* New York: Viking Press, 1968.

_____. *The Diary of Rexford G. Tugwell: The New Deal, 1932–1935.* Edited by Michael Vincent Namorato. Westport, CT: Greenwood Press, 1992.

_____. *Roosevelt's Revolution: The First Year, A Personal Perspective.* New York: Macmillan, 1977.

Upham, Cyril B., and Edwin Lamke. *Closed and Distressed Banks: A Study in Public Administration.* Washington, DC: Brookings Institution, 1934.

Warburg, James P. *The Long Road Home: The Autobiography of a Maverick.* New York: Doubleday, 1964.

_____. *The Money Muddle.* New York: Alfred Knopf, 1934.

Werner, Morris R. *Little Napoleons and Dummy Directors: Being the Narrative of the Bank of United States.* New York: Harper & Brothers, 1933.

Secondary Sources

Alter, Jonathan. *The Defining Moment: FDR's Hundred Days and the Triumph of Hope.* New York: Simon & Schuster, 2006.

Barber, William J. *Design Within Disorder: Franklin D. Roosevelt, the Economists, and the Shaping of American Economic Policy, 1933–1945.* New York: Cambridge University Press, 1996.

_____. *From New Era to New Deal: Herbert Hoover, the Economists, and American Economic Policy, 1921–1933.* New York: Cambridge University Press, 1985.

Barnard, Harry. *Independent Man: The Life of James Couzens.* New York: Charles Scribner's Sons, 1958.

Beatty, Mary Alexine. *Bank Failures in the District of Columbia in the Twentieth Century.* Washington, DC: Catholic University of America Press, 1949.

Belser, Clinch Heyward. "Banking in South Carolina, 1910–1940." M.A. thesis, Economics, University of South Carolina, 1940.

Bentson, George J. *The Separation of Commercial and Investment Banking: The Glass-Steagall Act Revisited and Reconsidered.* New York: Oxford University Press, 1990.

Bernanke, Ben S. *Essays on the Great Depression.* Princeton, NJ: Princeton University Press, 2000.

Bernstein, Michael A. *The Great Depression: Delayed Recovery and Economic Change in America, 1929–1939.* New York: Cambridge University Press, 1987.

Best, Gary Dean. *Pride, Prejudice, and Politics: Roosevelt versus Recovery, 1933–1938.* New York: Praeger Publishers, 1991.

Black, Conrad. *Franklin Delano Roosevelt: Champion of Freedom.* New York: Public Affairs, 2003.

Bremer, C.D. *American Bank Failures.* New York: Columbia University Press, 1935.

Brinkley, Alan. *The End of Reform: New Deal Liberalism in Recession and War.* New York: Vintage, 1996.

_____. *Voices of Protest: Huey Long, Father Coughlin and the Great Depression.* New York: Vintage, 1983.

Bruner, Robert F., and Sean D. Carr. *The Panic of 1907: Lessons Learned from the Market's Perfect Storm.* Hoboken, NJ: John Wiley & Sons, 2007.

Burner, David. *Herbert Hoover: A Public Life.* New York: Alfred Knopf, 1979.

Burns, Helen M. *The American Banking Community and New Deal Reforms, 1933–1935.* Westport CT: Greenwood Press, 1974.

Burns, James MacGregor. *Roosevelt: The Lion and the Fox.* New York: Harcourt, Brace, 1956.

Cannadine, David. *Mellon: An American Life.* New York: Alfred Knopf, 2006.

Chastenet, Jacques. *Histoire de la Troisième République.* Vol. 6, *Déclin de la Troisième, 1931–1938.* Paris: Hachette, 1962.

Chernow, Ron. *The House of Morgan: An American Banking Dynasty and the Rise of Modern Finance.* New York: Atlantic Monthly Press, 1990.

Clough, Shepard B. *A Century of American Life Insurance: A History of the Mutual Life Insurance Company of New York, 1843–1943.* New York: Columbia University Press, 1946.

Conot, Robert. *American Odyssey.* New York: William Morrow, 1974.

Cooper, Elliott T. *A Documentary History of the Union Trust Company of Maryland.* Baltimore: Union Trust Company, 1970.

Curico, Vincent. *Chrysler: The Life and Times of an Automotive Genius.* New York: Oxford University Press, 2000.

Drake, St. Clair, and Horace R. Clayton. *Black Metropolis.* New York: Harcourt Brace, 1945.

Dublin, Louis I. *A Family of Thirty Million: The Story of the Metropolitan Life Insurance Company.* New York: Metropolitan Life Insurance Company, 1943.

Eichengreen, Barry. *Golden Fetters: The Gold Standard and the Great Depression, 1919–1939.* New York: Oxford University Press, 1995.

Fine, Sidney. *Frank Murphy: The Detroit Years.* Ann Arbor: University of Michigan Press, 1975.

Fogelson, Robert M. *Downtown: Its Rise and Fall, 1880–1950.* New Haven, CT: Yale University Press, 2001.

Freidel, Frank. *Franklin D. Roosevelt: Launching the New Deal.* Boston: Little, Brown, 1973.

Friedman, Milton. *Money Mischief: Episodes in Monetary History.* New York: Harcourt Brace Jovanovich, 1992.

_____, and Anna Jacobson Schwartz. *A Monetary History of the United States, 1867–1960.* Princeton, NJ: Princeton University Press, 1993.

Fusfeld, Daniel R. *The Economic Thought of Franklin D. Roosevelt and the Origins of the New Deal.* New York: Columbia University Press, 1954.

Galbraith, John Kenneth. *The Great Crash.* Boston: Houghton Mifflin, 1988.

Hait, Pam. *The Arizona Bank: Arizona's Story.* N.p.: Arizona Bank, 1987.

Hawley, Ellis W., ed. *Herbert Hoover as Secretary of Commerce: Studies in New Era Thought and Practice.* Iowa City: University of Iowa Press, 1981.

Hays, Samuel P. *The Response to Industrialism, 1885–1914.* Chicago: University of Chicago Press, 1957.

Hicks, John D. *The Republican Ascendancy, 1921–1933.* New York: Harper & Row, 1963.

Hoffman, Susan. *Politics and Banking: Ideas, Public Policy, and the Creation of Financial Institutions.* Baltimore: Johns Hopkins University Press, 2001.

Hoyt, Homer. *One Hundred Years of Land Values in Chicago.* Chicago: University of Chicago Press: 1933.

James, Frank Cyril. *The Growth of Chicago Banks.* 2 vols., *The Formative Years, 1816–1896,* and *The Modern Age, 1897–1938.* New York: Harper & Brothers, 1938.

James, Marquis. *The Metropolitan Life: A Study in Business Growth.* New York: Viking Press, 1947.

_____. *Mr. Garner of Texas.* Indianapolis: Bobbs-Merrill, 1939.

Josephson, Matthew. *The Money Lords: The Great Finance Capitalists, 1925–1950.* New York: Waybright and Talley, 1972.

Kennedy, David M. *Freedom from Fear: The American People in Depression and War, 1929–1945.* New York: Oxford University Press, 1999.

Kennedy, Susan Estabrook. *The Banking Crisis of 1933.* Lexington: University of Kentucky Press, 1973.

Kiewe, Amos. *FDR's First Fireside Chat: Public Confidence and the Banking Crisis.* College Station: Texas A&M Press, 2007.

Kindleberger, Charles P. *The World in Depression, 1929–1939.* Berkeley: University of California Press, 1973.

Klebaner, Benjamin J. *American Commercial Banking: A History*. Boston: Twayne, 1990.

Lacey, Robert. *Ford: The Men and the Machine*. Boston: Little Brown, 1986.

Leuchtenburg, William E. *Franklin D. Roosevelt and the New Deal, 1932–1940*. New York: Harper & Row, 1963.

Mann, Arthur. *La Guardia: A Fighter Against His Times, 1882–1933*. Philadelphia: Lippincott, 1959.

McCraw, Thomas K. *American Business, 1920–2000: How It Worked*. Wheeling, IL: Harlan Davidson, 2000.

McFerrin, John Berry. *Caldwell and Company: A Southern Financial Empire*. Nashville, TN: Vanderbilt University Press, 1969.

Meltzer, Allan H. *A History of the Federal Reserve*. Vol. 1, *1913–1951*. Chicago: University of Chicago Press, 2003.

Messer-Kruse, Timothy. *Banksters, Bosses, and Smart Money: A Social History of the Great Toledo Bank Crash of 1931*. Columbus: Ohio State University Press, 2004.

Mitchell, Broadus. *Depression Decade: From New Era through New Deal, 1929–1941*. New York: Rinehart, 1947.

Nash, Lee, ed. *Understanding Herbert Hoover: Ten Perspectives*. Stanford, CA: Hoover Institution Press, 1987.

Nevins, Allan, and Frank Ernest Hill. *Ford: Decline and Rebirth, 1933–1962*. New York: Charles Scribner's Sons, 1962.

_____. *Ford: Expansion and Challenge, 1915–1933*. New York: Charles Scribner's Sons, 1957.

Olson, James Stuart. *Herbert Hoover and the Reconstruction Finance Corporation, 1931–1933*. Ames: Iowa State University Press, 1977.

_____. *Saving Capitalism: The Reconstruction Finance Corporation and the New Deal, 1933–1940*. Princeton, NJ: Princeton University Press, 1988.

Patrick, Sue C. *Reform of the Federal Reserve System in the Early 1930s: The Politics of Money and Banking*. New York: Garland Publishing, 1993.

Pugh, Olin S. *Difficult Decades of Banking: A Comparative Survey of Banking Developments in South Carolina and the United States, 1920–1940*. Columbia: Bureau of Business and Economic Research, School of Business Administration, University of South Carolina, 1964.

Ritchie, Donald A. *Electing FDR: The New Deal Campaign of 1932*. Lawrence: University of Kansas Press, 2007.

Romano, Michael John. "The Emergence of John Nance Garner as a Figure in American National Politics, 1924–1941." Ph.D. Diss., St. John's University, New York, 1974.

Rowlands, David Thomas. "Two Decades of Building and Loan Associations in Pennsylvania." Ph.D. Diss., University of Pennsylvania, Philadelphia, 1940.

Saloutos, Theodore, and John D. Hicks. *Twentieth-Century Populism: Agricultural Discontent in the Middle West, 1900–1939*. Lincoln: University of Nebraska Press, 1951.

Schlesinger, Arthur M., Jr. *The Age of Roosevelt*. 3 vols. Boston: Houghton Mifflin, 1957–60.

Schubert, Aurel. *The Credit-Anstalt Crisis of 1931*. New York: Cambridge University Press, 1991.

Schwarz, Jordan A. *The Interregnum of Despair: Hoover, Congress, and the Depression*. Urbana: University of Illinois Press, 1970.

Shannon, Fred A. *The Farmer's Last Frontier: Agriculture, 1860–1897*. White Plains, NY: M.E. Sharpe, 1973.

Skowronek, Stephen. *The Politics Presidents Make: Leadership from John Adams to Bill Clinton*. Cambridge, MA: Belknap Press, 1997.

Slade, George Richard. *Banking in the Great Northern Territory*. Afton, MN: Afton Historical Society, 2005.

Smith, Rixey, and Norman Beasley. *Carter Glass: A Biography*. New York: Longmans, Green, 1939.

Temin, Peter. *Did Monetary Forces Cause the Great Depression?* New York: W.W. Norton, 1976.

_____. *Lessons from the Great Depression*. Cambridge, MA: MIT Press, 1989.

Timmons, Bascom N. *Garner of Texas: A Personal History*. New York: Harper Brothers, 1948.

_____. *Jesse H. Jones: The Man and the Statesman*. New York: Henry Holt, 1956.

_____. *Portrait of an American: Charles G. Dawes*. New York: Henry Holt, 1953.

Tompkins, C. David. *Senator Arthur H. Vandenberg: The Evolution of a Modern Republican, 1884–1945*. N.p.: Michigan State University Press, 1970.

Walch, Timothy, and Dwight M. Miller, eds. *Herbert Hoover and Franklin D. Roosevelt: A Documentary History*. Westport, CT: Greenwood Press, 1998.

Ward, William Rankin. *Down the Years: A History of the Mutual Benefit Life Insurance Company, 1845 to 1932*. Newark, NJ: Mutual Benefit Life Insurance Company, 1932.

Warren, Harris Gaylord. *Herbert Hoover and the Great Depression*. New York: Oxford University Press, 1959.

Wendt, Lloyd, and Herman Kogan. *Big Bill of Chicago*. Indianapolis: Bobbs-Merrill, 1953.

White, Eugene Nelson. *The Regulation and Reform of the American Banking System, 1900–1929*. Princeton, NJ: Princeton University Press, 1983.

Wicker, Elmus. *The Banking Panics of the Great Depression*. Cambridge, UK: Cambridge University Press, 1996.

Wiebe, Robert H. *Businessmen and Reform: A Study of the Progressive Movement.* Chicago: Ivan R. Dee, 1989.

Wigmore, Barrie A. *The Crash and Its Aftermath: A History of Securities Markets in the United States, 1929–1933.* Westport, CT: Greenwood Press, 1985.

Williams, T. Harry. *Huey Long.* New York: Alfred Knopf, 1970.

Articles

Awalt, Francis Gloyd. "Recollections of the Banking Crisis in 1933." *Business History Review* 43, no. 3 (Autumn 1969): 347–71.

Ballantine, Arthur A. "When All the Banks Closed." *Harvard Business Review* 26, no. 2 (1948): 129–43.

Bernanke, Ben S. "Money, Gold, and the Great Depression." Remarks by Governor Ben S. Bernanke at the H. Parker Willis Lecture in Economic Policy, Washington and Lee University (2 March 2004). *www.federalreserve.gov/boarddocs/speeches/2004/200403022.*

_____."Nonmonetary Effects of the Financial Crisis in the Propagation of the Great Depression." *American Economic Review* 73, no. 3 (June 1983): 257–76.

Butkiewicz, James L. "Eugene Meyer and the Great Contraction." Paper, August 22, 2006. www.lerner.udel.edu/economics/WorkingPapers/2005/UDWP2005-01.pdf.

_____. "The Impact of Lender of Last Resort during the Great Depression: The Case of the Reconstruction Finance Corporation." *Explorations in Economic History* 32, no. 3 (1995): 197–216.

_____. "The Reconstruction Finance Corporation, the Gold Standard, and the Banking Panic of 1933." *Southern Economic Journal* 66, no. 2 (October 1999): 271–293.

Calomiris, Charles W. "Financial Factors in the Great Depression." *Journal of Economic Perspectives* 7, no. 2 (1993): 61–85.

Calomiris, Charles W., and Joseph R. Mason. "Causes of U.S. Bank Distress during the Depression." *National Bureau of Economic Research Working Paper*, no. 7919 (2000).

_____. "Consequences of Bank Distress during the Great Depression." *American Economic Review* 93, no. 3 (June 2003): 937–47.

_____. "Contagion and Bank Failure during the Great Depression: The June 1932 Chicago Banking Panic." *American Economic Review* 87, no. 5 (December 1997): 863–83.

_____. "Fundamentals, Panics, and Bank Distress during the Depression." *American Economic Review* 93, no. 5 (December 2003): 1615–47.

Carlson, Mark, and Chris James Mitchner. "Branch Banking as a Devise for Discipline: Competition and Bank Survivorship During the Great Depression." *National Bureau of Economic Research Working Paper*, no. 12938 (2007).

Eichengreen, Barry. "Did International Economic Forces Cause the Great Depression?" *Contemporary Policy Issues* 6, no. 2 (April 1988): 90–114.

_____. "The Origins and Nature of the Great Slump Revisited." *Economic History Review* 45, no. 2 (May 1992): 213–39.

Flynn, John T. "Inside the RFC: An Adventure in Secrecy." *Harpers Magazine,* January 1933, 161–69.

_____. "Michigan Magic: The Detroit Banking Scandal." *Harper's Magazine,* December 1933.

Friedman, Milton, and Anna J. Schwartz. "The Failure of the Bank of United States: A Reappraisal; A Reply." *Explorations in Economic History* 23, no. 2 (April 1986): 199–204.

Hamilton, David E. "The Causes of the Banking Panic of 1930: Another View." *Journal of Southern History* 51, no. 4 (November 1985): 581–608.

Hamilton, James D. "Role of the International Gold Standard in Propagating the Great Depression." *Contemporary Policy Issues* 6, no. 2 (April 1988): 67–89.

Irwin, Douglas A. "The Smoot-Hawley Tariff: A Quantitative Assessment." *Review of Economics and Statistics* 80, no. 2 (May 1998): 326–34.

Lucia, Joseph L. "The Failure of the Bank of United States: A Reappraisal." *Explorations in Economic History* 22, no. 4 (October 1985): 402–16.

O'Brien, Anthony Patrick. "The Failure of the Bank of United States: A Defense of Joseph Lucia: Note." *Journal of Money, Credit and Banking* 24, no. 3 (August 1992): 374–84.

Olson, James S. "Rehearsal for Disaster: Hoover, the R.F.C., and the Banking Crisis in Nevada, 1932–1933." *Western Historical Quarterly* 6, no. 2 (1975): 149–61.

Park, Sangkyun. "Bank Failure Contagion in Historical Perspective." Research Paper of the Federal Reserve Bank of New York, no. 9103 (February 1991).

Prescott, Charlotte Hubbard. "An Iowa Foreclosure." *The Nation,* 22 February 1933.

Richardson, Gary. "Bank Distress During the Great Contraction, 1929 to 1933, New Data From the Archives of the Board of Governors." *National Bureau of Economic Research Working Paper*, no. 12590 (2006).

_____. "Bank Distress During the Great Depression: The Illiquidity-Insolvency Debate Revisited." *National Bureau of Economic Research Working Paper*, no. 12717 (2006).

_____. "Quarterly Data on the Categories and Causes of Bank Distress during the Great Depression." *National Bureau of Economic Research Working Paper*, no. 12715 (2006).

Romer, Christina D. "The Great Crash and the Onset of the Great Depression." *Quarterly Journal of Economics* 105, no. 3 (August 1990): 597–624.

_____. "The Nation in Depression." *Journal of Economic Perspectives* 7, no. 2 (1993): 19–39.

Temin, Peter. "The Great Depression." *National Bureau of Economic Research Working Paper*, no. 62 (1994).

_____. "Transmission of the Great Depression." *Journal of Economic Perspectives* 7, no. 2 (1993): 87–102.

_____, and Barrie Wigmore. "The End of One Big Deflation, 1933." *Explorations in Economic History* 27, no. 4 (October 1990): 483–502.

Trescott, Paul. "The Failure of the Bank of United States, 1930: A Rejoinder to Anthony Patrick O'Brien." *Journal of Money, Credit and Banking* 24, no. 3 (August 1992) 384–99.

Vorse, Mary Heaton. "Rebellion in the Corn Belt." *Harper's Magazine*, December 1932.

White, Eugene Nelson. "Before the Glass-Steagall Act: An Analysis of the Investment Banking Activities of National Banks." *Explorations in Economic History* 23, no. 1 (January 1986): 33–55.

_____. "The Merger Movement in Banking, 1919–1933." *Journal of Economic History* 45, no. 2 (June 1985): 285–91.

_____. "A Reinterpretation of the Banking Crisis of 1930." *Journal of Economic History* 44, no. 1 (March 1984): 119–38.

Wicker, Elmus. "Roosevelt's 1933 Monetary Experiment." *Journal of American History* 57, no. 4 (March 1971): 864–79.

_____. "What Caused the Great Depression 1929–1937? A Survey of Recent Literature." Conference paper, August 1989.

_____, and James M. Boughton. "The Behavior of the Currency-Deposit Ratio during the Great Depression." *Journal of Money, Credit, and Banking* 4, no. 11 (November 1979): 405–18.

Wigmore, Barrie A. "Was the Bank Holiday of 1933 Caused by a Run on the Dollar?" *Journal of Economic History* 47, no. 3 (1987): 739–55.

Reference Works

Federal Deposit Insurance Corporation. *FDIC, Historical Statistics on Banking, 1934–1992: A Statistical History of the United States Banking Industry.* Washington, DC: FDIC, 1993.

Federal Reserve Board. *Banking and Monetary Statistics, 1914–1941.* Washington, DC: Federal Reserve System, 1943.

Krooss, Herman E., and Paul A. Samuelson. *Documentary History of Banking and Currency in the United States.* New York: Chelsea House, 1969.

McJimsey, George, ed., *Documentary History of the Franklin D. Roosevelt Presidency.* Vol. 3, *The Bank Holiday and the Emergency Banking Act, March 1933.* N.p.: University Publications of America, 2001.

United States Congress. *Biographical Directory of the United States Congress, 1774–1989.* Washington, DC: Government Printing Office, 1989.

United States Department of Commerce, Bureau of the Census. *Historical Statistics of the United States: Colonial Times to 1957.* Washington, DC: GPO, 1960.

_____. *Statistical Abstract of the United States, 1919–1948.* Washington, DC: GPO.

Index

273

DATE DUE

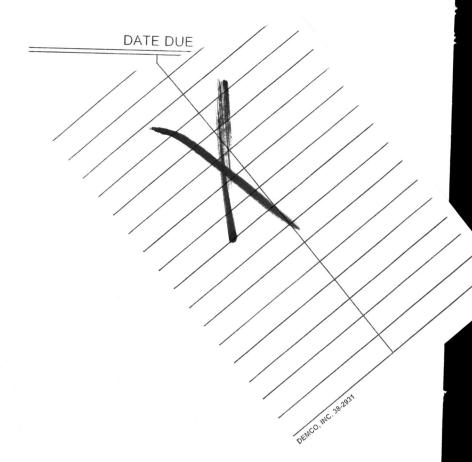

DEMCO, INC. 38-2931